GRADE 9 | VOLUME TWO

myPerspectives®

ENGLISH LANGUAGE ARTS

SAVVAS
LEARNING COMPANY

Savvas Learning Company LLC, 15 East Midland Avenue, Paramus, NJ 07652

Cover image "Birds on Wire" is a combination of illustrations from various artists, and credited to; Rodica Bruma/123RF, Laschi Adrian/123RF, and Peony/Fotolia.

Attributions of third party content appear on page R77, which constitutes an extension of this copyright page.

ISBN-13: 978-1-41-837116-6
ISBN-10: 1-41-837116-5

5 2022

Welcome!

*my*Perspectives™ *English Language Arts* is a student-centered learning environment where you will analyze text, cite evidence, and respond critically about your learning. You will take ownership of your learning through goal-setting, reflection, independent text selection, and activities that allow you to collaborate with your peers.

Each unit of study includes selections of different genres—including multimedia—all related to a relevant and meaningful Essential Question. As you read, you will engage in activities that inspire thoughtful discussion and debate with your peers allowing you to formulate, and defend, your own perspectives.

*my*Perspectives *ELA* offers a variety of ways to interact directly with the text. You can annotate by writing in your print consumable, or you can annotate in your digital Student Edition. In addition, exciting technology allows you to access multimedia directly from your mobile device and communicate using an online discussion board!

We hope you enjoy using *my*Perspectives *ELA* as you develop the skills required to be successful throughout college and career.

Authors' Perspectives

*my*Perspectives is informed by a team of respected experts whose experiences working with students and study of instructional best practices have positively impacted education. From the evolving role of the teacher to how students learn in a digital age, our authors bring new ideas, innovations, and strategies that transform teaching and learning in today's competitive and interconnected world.

"The teaching of English needs to focus on engaging a new generation of learners. How do we get them excited about reading and writing? How do we help them to envision themselves as readers and writers? And, how can we make the teaching of English more culturally, socially, and technologically relevant? Throughout the curriculum, we've created spaces that enhance youth voice and participation and that connect the teaching of literature and writing to technological transformations of the digital age."

Ernest Morrell, Ph.D.

is the Macy professor of English Education at Teachers College, Columbia University, a class of 2014 Fellow of the American Educational Research Association, and the Past-President of the National Council of Teachers of English (NCTE). He is also the Director of Teachers College's Institute for Urban and Minority Education (IUME). He is an award-winning author and in his spare time he coaches youth sports and writes poems and plays. Dr. Morrell has influenced the development of *my*Perspectives in Assessment, Writing & Research, Student Engagement, and Collaborative Learning.

Elfrieda Hiebert, Ph.D.

is President and CEO of TextProject, a nonprofit that provides resources to support higher reading levels. She is also a research associate at the University of California, Santa Cruz. Dr. Hiebert has worked in the field of early reading acquisition for 45 years, first as a teacher's aide and teacher of primary-level students in California and, subsequently, as a teacher and researcher. Her research addresses how fluency, vocabulary, and knowledge can be fostered through appropriate texts. Dr. Hiebert has influenced the development of *my*Perspectives in Vocabulary, Text Complexity, and Assessment.

"The signature of complex text is challenging vocabulary. In the systems of vocabulary, it's important to provide ways to show how concepts can be made more transparent to students. We provide lessons and activities that develop a strong vocabulary and concept foundation—a foundation that permits students to comprehend increasingly more complex text."

Kelly Gallagher, M.Ed.

teaches at Magnolia High School in Anaheim, California, where he is in his thirty-first year. He is the former co-director of the South Basin Writing Project at California State University, Long Beach. Mr. Gallagher has influenced the development of *my*Perspectives in Writing, Close Reading, and the Role of Teachers.

"The *my*Perspectives classroom is dynamic. The teacher inspires, models, instructs, facilitates, and advises students as they evolve and grow. When teachers guide students through meaningful learning tasks and then pass them ownership of their own learning, students become engaged and work harder. This is how we make a difference in student achievement—by putting students at the center of their learning and giving them the opportunities to choose, explore, collaborate, and work independently."

Jim Cummins, Ph.D.

is a Professor Emeritus in the Department of Curriculum, Teaching and Learning of the University of Toronto. His research focuses on literacy development in multilingual school contexts as well as on the potential roles of technology in promoting language and literacy development. In recent years, he has been working actively with teachers to identify ways of increasing the literacy engagement of learners in multilingual school contexts. Dr. Cummins has influenced the development of *my*Perspectives in English Language Learner and English Language Development support.

"It's critical to give students the opportunity to read a wide range of highly engaging texts and to immerse themselves in exploring powerful ideas and how these ideas are expressed. In *my*Perspectives, we focus on building up students' awareness of how academic language works, which is especially important for English language learners."

UNIT  1 American Voices

UNIT INTRODUCTION

WHOLE-CLASS LEARNING

SMALL-GROUP LEARNING

ESSENTIAL QUESTION: What does it mean to be "American"?

INDEPENDENT LEARNING

These selections can be accessed via the Interactive Student Edition.

PERFORMANCE-BASED ASSESSMENT PREP

PERFORMANCE-BASED ASSESSMENT

UNIT REFLECTION

DIGITAL PERSPECTIVES

- Unit Introduction Videos
- Media Selections
- Modeling Videos
- Selection Audio Recordings

Additional digital resources can be found in:

- Interactive Student Edition
- *my*Perspectives+

INDEPENDENT LEARNING

These selections can be accessed via the Interactive Student Edition.

PERFORMANCE-BASED ASSESSMENT PREP

PERFORMANCE-BASED ASSESSMENT

UNIT REFLECTION

DIGITAL PERSPECTIVES

- Unit Introduction Videos
- Media Selections
- Modeling Videos
- Selection Audio Recordings

Additional digital resources can be found in:

- Interactive Student Edition
- *my*Perspectives+

UNIT 3 The Literature of Civil Rights

UNIT INTRODUCTION

WHOLE-CLASS LEARNING

PERFORMANCE TASK

SMALL-GROUP LEARNING

PERFORMANCE TASK

INDEPENDENT LEARNING

These selections can be accessed via the Interactive Student Edition.

PERFORMANCE-BASED ASSESSMENT PREP

PERFORMANCE-BASED ASSESSMENT

UNIT REFLECTION

DIGITAL PERSPECTIVES

- Unit Introduction Videos
- Media Selections
- Modeling Videos
- Selection Audio Recordings

Additional digital resources can be found in:

- Interactive Student Edition
- *my*Perspectives+

UNIT  Star-Crossed Romances

UNIT INTRODUCTION

WHOLE-CLASS LEARNING

SMALL-GROUP LEARNING

ESSENTIAL QUESTION: Do we determine our own destinies?

INDEPENDENT LEARNING

These selections can be accessed via the Interactive Student Edition.

PERFORMANCE-BASED ASSESSMENT PREP

PERFORMANCE-BASED ASSESSMENT

UNIT REFLECTION

DIGITAL PERSPECTIVES

- Unit Introduction Videos
- Media Selections
- Modeling Videos
- Selection Audio Recordings

Additional digital resources can be found in:

- Interactive Student Edition
- *my*Perspectives+

ESSENTIAL QUESTION: What can we learn from a journey?

INDEPENDENT LEARNING

These selections can be accessed via the Interactive Student Edition.

PERFORMANCE-BASED ASSESSMENT PREP

PERFORMANCE-BASED ASSESSMENT

UNIT REFLECTION

DIGITAL PERSPECTIVES

- Unit Introduction Videos
- Media Selections
- Modeling Videos
- Selection Audio Recordings

Additional digital resources can be found in:

- Interactive Student Edition
- *my*Perspectives+

UNIT  World's End

UNIT INTRODUCTION

 WHOLE-CLASS LEARNING

PERFORMANCE TASK

 SMALL-GROUP LEARNING

PERFORMANCE TASK

ESSENTIAL QUESTION: Why do we try to imagine the future?

INDEPENDENT LEARNING

These selections can be accessed via the Interactive Student Edition.

PERFORMANCE-BASED ASSESSMENT PREP

PERFORMANCE-BASED ASSESSMENT

UNIT REFLECTION

DIGITAL PERSPECTIVES

- Unit Introduction Videos
- Media Selections
- Modeling Videos
- Selection Audio Recordings

Additional digital resources can be found in:

- Interactive Student Edition
- *my*Perspectives+

Standards Overview

The following English Language Arts standards will prepare you to succeed in college and your future career. The College and Career Readiness Anchor Standards define what you need to achieve by the end of high school, and the grade-specific Standards define what you need to know by the end of your current grade level.

The following provides an overview of the Standards.

Standards for Reading

College and Career Readiness Anchor Standards for Reading
Key Ideas and Details **1.** Read closely to determine what the text says explicitly and to make logical inferences from it; cite specific textual evidence when writing or speaking to support conclusions drawn from the text. **2.** Determine central ideas or themes of a text and analyze their development; summarize the key supporting details and ideas. **3.** Analyze how and why individuals, events, and ideas develop and interact over the course of a text.
Craft and Structure **4.** Interpret words and phrases as they are used in a text, including determining technical, connotative, and figurative meanings, and analyze how specific word choices shape meaning or tone. **5.** Analyze the structure of texts, including how specific sentences, paragraphs, and larger portions of the text (e.g., a section, chapter, scene, or stanza) relate to each other and the whole. **6.** Assess how point of view or purpose shapes the content and style of a text.
Integration of Knowledge and Ideas **7.** Integrate and evaluate content presented in diverse formats and media, including visually and quantitatively, as well as in words. **8.** Delineate and evaluate the argument and specific claims in a text, including the validity of the reasoning as well as the relevance and sufficiency of the evidence. **9.** Analyze how two or more texts address similar themes or topics in order to build knowledge or to compare the approaches the authors take.
Range of Reading and Level of Text Complexity **10.** Read and comprehend complex literary and informational texts independently and proficiently.

Grade 9 Reading Standards for Literature
Standard
Key Ideas and Details
Cite strong and thorough textual evidence to support analysis of what the text says explicitly as well as inferences drawn from the text.
Determine a theme or central idea of a text and analyze in detail its development over the course of the text, including how it emerges and is shaped and refined by specific details; provide an objective summary of the text.
Analyze how complex characters (e.g., those with multiple or conflicting motivations) develop over the course of a text, interact with other characters, and advance the plot or develop the theme.
Craft and Structure
Determine the meaning of words and phrases as they are used in the text, including figurative and connotative meanings; analyze the cumulative impact of specific word choices on meaning and tone (e.g., how the language evokes a sense of time and place; how it sets a formal or informal tone).
Analyze how an author's choices concerning how to structure a text, order events within it (e.g., parallel plots), and manipulate time (e.g., pacing, flashbacks) create such effects as mystery, tension, or surprise.
Analyze a particular point of view or cultural experience reflected in a work of literature from outside the United States, drawing on a wide reading of world literature.
Integration of Knowledge and Ideas
Analyze the representation of a subject or a key scene in two different artistic mediums, including what is emphasized or absent in each treatment (e.g., Auden's "Musée des Beaux Arts" and Breughel's *Landscape with the Fall of Icarus*).
Analyze how an author draws on and transforms source material in a specific work (e.g., how Shakespeare treats a theme or topic from Ovid or the Bible or how a later author draws on a play by Shakespeare).
Range of Reading and Text Complexity
By the end of grade 9, read and comprehend literature, including stories, dramas, and poems, in the grades 9–10 text complexity band proficiently, with scaffolding as needed at the high end of the range.

Standards Overview

Grade 9 Reading Standards for Informational Text
Standard
Key Ideas and Details
Cite strong and thorough textual evidence to support analysis of what the text says explicitly as well as inferences drawn from the text.
Determine a central idea of a text and analyze its development over the course of the text, including how it emerges and is shaped and refined by specific details; provide an objective summary of the text.
Analyze how the author unfolds an analysis or series of ideas or events, including the order in which the points are made, how they are introduced and developed, and the connections that are drawn between them.
Craft and Structure
Determine the meaning of words and phrases as they are used in a text, including figurative, connotative, and technical meanings; analyze the cumulative impact of specific word choices on meaning and tone (e.g., how the language of a court opinion differs from that of a newspaper).
Analyze in detail how an author's ideas or claims are developed and refined by particular sentences, paragraphs, or larger portions of a text (e.g., a section or chapter).
Determine an author's point of view or purpose in a text and analyze how an author uses rhetoric to advance that point of view or purpose.
Integration of Knowledge and Ideas
Analyze various accounts of a subject told in different mediums (e.g., a person's life story in both print and multimedia), determining which details are emphasized in each account.
Delineate and evaluate the argument and specific claims in a text, assessing whether the reasoning is valid and the evidence is relevant and sufficient; identify false statements and fallacious reasoning.
Analyze seminal U.S. documents of historical and literary significance (e.g., Washington's Farewell Address, the Gettysburg Address, Roosevelt's Four Freedoms speech, King's "Letter from Birmingham Jail"), including how they address related themes and concepts.
Range of Reading and Text Complexity
By the end of grade 9, read and comprehend literary nonfiction in the grades 9–10 text complexity band proficiently, with scaffolding as needed at the high end of the range.

Standards for Writing

College and Career Readiness Anchor Standards for Writing
Text Types and Purposes **1.** Write arguments to support claims in an analysis of substantive topics or texts, using valid reasoning and relevant and sufficient evidence. **2.** Write informative/explanatory texts to examine and convey complex ideas and information clearly and accurately through the effective selection, organization, and analysis of content. **3.** Write narratives to develop real or imagined experiences or events using effective technique, well-chosen details, and well-structured event sequences.
Production and Distribution of Writing **4.** Produce clear and coherent writing in which the development, organization, and style are appropriate to task, purpose, and audience. **5.** Develop and strengthen writing as needed by planning, revising, editing, rewriting, or trying a new approach. **6.** Use technology, including the Internet, to produce and publish writing and to interact and collaborate with others.
Research to Build and Present Knowledge **7.** Conduct short as well as more sustained research projects based on focused questions, demonstrating understanding of the subject under investigation. **8.** Gather relevant information from multiple print and digital sources, assess the credibility and accuracy of each source, and integrate the information while avoiding plagiarism. **9.** Draw evidence from literary or informational texts to support analysis, reflection, and research.
Range of Writing **10.** Write routinely over extended time frames (time for research, reflection, and revision) and shorter time frames (a single sitting or a day or two) for a range of tasks, purposes, and audiences.

Grade 9 Writing Standards
Standard
Text Types and Purposes
Write arguments to support claims in an analysis of substantive topics or texts, using valid reasoning and relevant and sufficient evidence.
Introduce precise claim(s), distinguish the claim(s) from alternate or opposing claims, and create an organization that establishes clear relationships among claim(s), counterclaims, reasons, and evidence.

Standards Overview

Grade 9 Writing Standards
Standard
Text Types and Purposes (continued)
Develop claim(s) and counterclaims fairly, supplying evidence for each while pointing out the strengths and limitations of both in a manner that anticipates the audience's knowledge level and concerns.
Use words, phrases, and clauses to link the major sections of the text, create cohesion, and clarify the relationships between claim(s) and reasons, between reasons and evidence, and between claim(s) and counterclaims.
Establish and maintain a formal style and objective tone while attending to the norms and conventions of the discipline in which they are writing.
Provide a concluding statement or section that follows from and supports the argument presented.
Write informative/explanatory texts to examine and convey complex ideas, concepts, and information clearly and accurately through the effective selection, organization, and analysis of content.
Introduce a topic; organize complex ideas, concepts, and information to make important connections and distinctions; include formatting (e.g., headings), graphics (e.g., figures, tables), and multimedia when useful to aiding comprehension.
Develop the topic with well-chosen, relevant, and sufficient facts, extended definitions, concrete details, quotations, or other information and examples appropriate to the audience's knowledge of the topic.
Use appropriate and varied transitions to link the major sections of the text, create cohesion, and clarify the relationships among complex ideas and concepts.
Use precise language and domain-specific vocabulary to manage the complexity of the topic.
Establish and maintain a formal style and objective tone while attending to the norms and conventions of the discipline in which they are writing.
Provide a concluding statement or section that follows from and supports the information or explanation presented (e.g., articulating implications or the significance of the topic).
Write narratives to develop real or imagined experiences or events using effective technique, well-chosen details, and well-structured event sequences.
Engage and orient the reader by setting out a problem, situation, or observation, establishing one or multiple point(s) of view, and introducing a narrator and/or characters; create a smooth progression of experiences or events.
Use narrative techniques, such as dialogue, pacing, description, reflection, and multiple plot lines, to develop experiences, events, and/or characters.
Use a variety of techniques to sequence events so that they build on one another to create a coherent whole.

Grade 9 Writing Standards
Standard
Text Types and Purposes (continued)
Use precise words and phrases, telling details, and sensory language to convey a vivid picture of the experiences, events, setting, and/or characters.
Provide a conclusion that follows from and reflects on what is experienced, observed, or resolved over the course of the narrative.
Production and Distribution of Writing
Produce clear and coherent writing in which the development, organization, and style are appropriate to task, purpose, and audience.
Develop and strengthen writing as needed by planning, revising, editing, rewriting, or trying a new approach, focusing on addressing what is most significant for a specific purpose and audience.
Use technology, including the Internet, to produce, publish, and update individual or shared writing products, taking advantage of technology's capacity to link to other information and to display information flexibly and dynamically.
Research to Build and Present Knowledge
Conduct short as well as more sustained research projects to answer a question (including a self-generated question) or solve a problem; narrow or broaden the inquiry when appropriate; synthesize multiple sources on the subject, demonstrating understanding of the subject under investigation.
Gather relevant information from multiple authoritative print and digital sources, using advanced searches effectively; assess the usefulness of each source in answering the research question; integrate information into the text selectively to maintain the flow of ideas, avoiding plagiarism and following a standard format for citation.
Draw evidence from literary or informational texts to support analysis, reflection, and research.
Apply *grades 9–10 Reading standards* to literature (e.g., "Analyze how an author draws on and transforms source material in a specific work [e.g., how Shakespeare treats a theme or topic from Ovid or the Bible or how a later author draws on a play by Shakespeare]").
Apply *grades 9–10 Reading standards* to literary nonfiction (e.g., "Delineate and evaluate the argument and specific claims in a text, assessing whether the reasoning is valid and the evidence is relevant and sufficient; identify false statements and fallacious reasoning").
Range of Writing
Write routinely over extended time frames (time for research, reflection, and revision) and shorter time frames (a single sitting or a day or two) for a range of tasks, purposes, and audiences.

Standards Overview

Standards for Speaking and Listening

College and Career Readiness
Anchor Standards for Speaking and Listening

Comprehension and Collaboration

1. Prepare for and participate effectively in a range of conversations and collaborations with diverse partners, building on others' ideas and expressing their own clearly and persuasively.
2. Integrate and evaluate information presented in diverse media and formats, including visually, quantitatively, and orally.
3. Evaluate a speaker's point of view, reasoning, and use of evidence and rhetoric.

Presentation of Knowledge and Ideas

4. Present information, findings, and supporting evidence such that listeners can follow the line of reasoning and the organization, development, and style are appropriate to task, purpose, and audience.
5. Make strategic use of digital media and visual displays of data to express information and enhance understanding of presentations.
6. Adapt speech to a variety of contexts and communicative tasks, demonstrating command of formal English when indicated or appropriate.

Grade 9 Standards for Speaking and Listening
Standard
Comprehension and Collaboration
Initiate and participate effectively in a range of collaborative discussions (one-on-one, in groups, and teacher-led) with diverse partners on *grades 9–10 topics, texts, and issues*, building on others' ideas and expressing their own clearly and persuasively.
Come to discussions prepared, having read and researched material under study; explicitly draw on that preparation by referring to evidence from texts and other research on the topic or issue to stimulate a thoughtful, well-reasoned exchange of ideas.
Work with peers to set rules for collegial discussions and decision-making (e.g., informal consensus, taking votes on key issues, presentation of alternate views), clear goals and deadlines, and individual roles as needed.
Propel conversations by posing and responding to questions that relate the current discussion to broader themes or larger ideas; actively incorporate others into the discussion; and clarify, verify, or challenge ideas and conclusions.
Respond thoughtfully to diverse perspectives, summarize points of agreement and disagreement, and, when warranted, qualify or justify their own views and understanding and make new connections in light of the evidence and reasoning presented.
Integrate multiple sources of information presented in diverse media or formats (e.g., visually, quantitatively, orally) evaluating the credibility and accuracy of each source.
Evaluate a speaker's point of view, reasoning, and use of evidence and rhetoric, identifying any fallacious reasoning or exaggerated or distorted evidence.
Presentation of Knowledge and Ideas
Present information, findings, and supporting evidence clearly, concisely, and logically such that listeners can follow the line of reasoning and the organization, development, substance, and style are appropriate to purpose, audience, and task.
Make strategic use of digital media (e.g., textual, graphical, audio, visual, and interactive elements) in presentations to enhance understanding of findings, reasoning, and evidence and to add interest.
Adapt speech to a variety of contexts and tasks, demonstrating command of formal English when indicated or appropriate. (See grades 9–10 Language Standards 1 and 3 for specific expectations.)

Standards Overview

Standards for Language

College and Career Readiness Anchor Standards for Language
Conventions of Standard English **1.** Demonstrate command of the conventions of standard English grammar and usage when writing or speaking. **2.** Demonstrate command of the conventions of standard English capitalization, punctuation, and spelling when writing.
Knowledge of Language **3.** Apply knowledge of language to understand how language functions in different contexts, to make effective choices for meaning or style, and to comprehend more fully when reading or listening.
Vocabulary Acquisition and Use **4.** Determine or clarify the meaning of unknown and multiple-meaning words and phrases by using context clues, analyzing meaningful word parts, and consulting general and specialized reference materials, as appropriate. **5.** Demonstrate understanding of figurative language, word relationships, and nuances in word meanings. **6.** Acquire and use accurately a range of general academic and domain-specific words and phrases sufficient for reading, writing, speaking, and listening at the college and career readiness level; demonstrate independence in gathering vocabulary knowledge when considering a word or phrase important to comprehension or expression.

Grade 9 Standards for Language
Standard
Conventions of Standard English
Demonstrate command of the conventions of standard English grammar and usage when writing or speaking.
Use parallel structure.
Use various types of phrases (noun, verb, adjectival, adverbial, participial, prepositional, absolute) and clauses (independent, dependent; noun, relative, adverbial) to convey specific meanings and add variety and interest to writing or presentations.
Demonstrate command of the conventions of standard English capitalization, punctuation, and spelling when writing.
Use a semicolon (and perhaps a conjunctive adverb) to link two or more closely related independent clauses.

Grade 9 Standards for Language
Standard
Conventions of Standard English (continued)
Use a semicolon (and perhaps a conjunctive adverb) to link two or more closely related independent clauses.
Use a colon to introduce a list or quotation.
Spell correctly.
Knowledge of Language
Apply knowledge of language to understand how language functions in different contexts, to make effective choices for meaning or style, and to comprehend more fully when reading or listening.
Write and edit work so that it conforms to the guidelines in a style manual (e.g., *MLA Handbook*, Turabian's *Manual for Writers*) appropriate for the discipline and writing type.
Vocabulary Acquisition and Use
Determine or clarify the meaning of unknown and multiple-meaning words and phrases based on *grades 9–10 reading and content*, choosing flexibly from a range of strategies.
Use context (e.g., the overall meaning of a sentence, paragraph, or text; a word's position or function in a sentence) as a clue to the meaning of a word or phrase.
Identify and correctly use patterns of word changes that indicate different meanings or parts of speech (e.g., *analyze, analysis, analytical; advocate, advocacy*).
Consult general and specialized reference materials (e.g., dictionaries, glossaries, thesauruses), both print and digital, to find the pronunciation of a word or determine or clarify its precise meaning, its part of speech, or its etymology.
Verify the preliminary determination of the meaning of a word or phrase (e.g., by checking the inferred meaning in context or in a dictionary).
Demonstrate understanding of figurative language, word relationships, and nuances in word meanings.
Interpret figures of speech (e.g., euphemism, oxymoron) in context and analyze their role in the text.
Analyze nuances in the meaning of words with similar denotations.
Acquire and use accurately general academic and domain-specific words and phrases, sufficient for reading, writing, speaking, and listening at the college and career readiness level; demonstrate independence in gathering vocabulary knowledge when considering a word or phrase important to comprehension or expression.

Star-Crossed Romances

Do we determine our own direction in life and in love? Or are we simply at the mercy of fate?

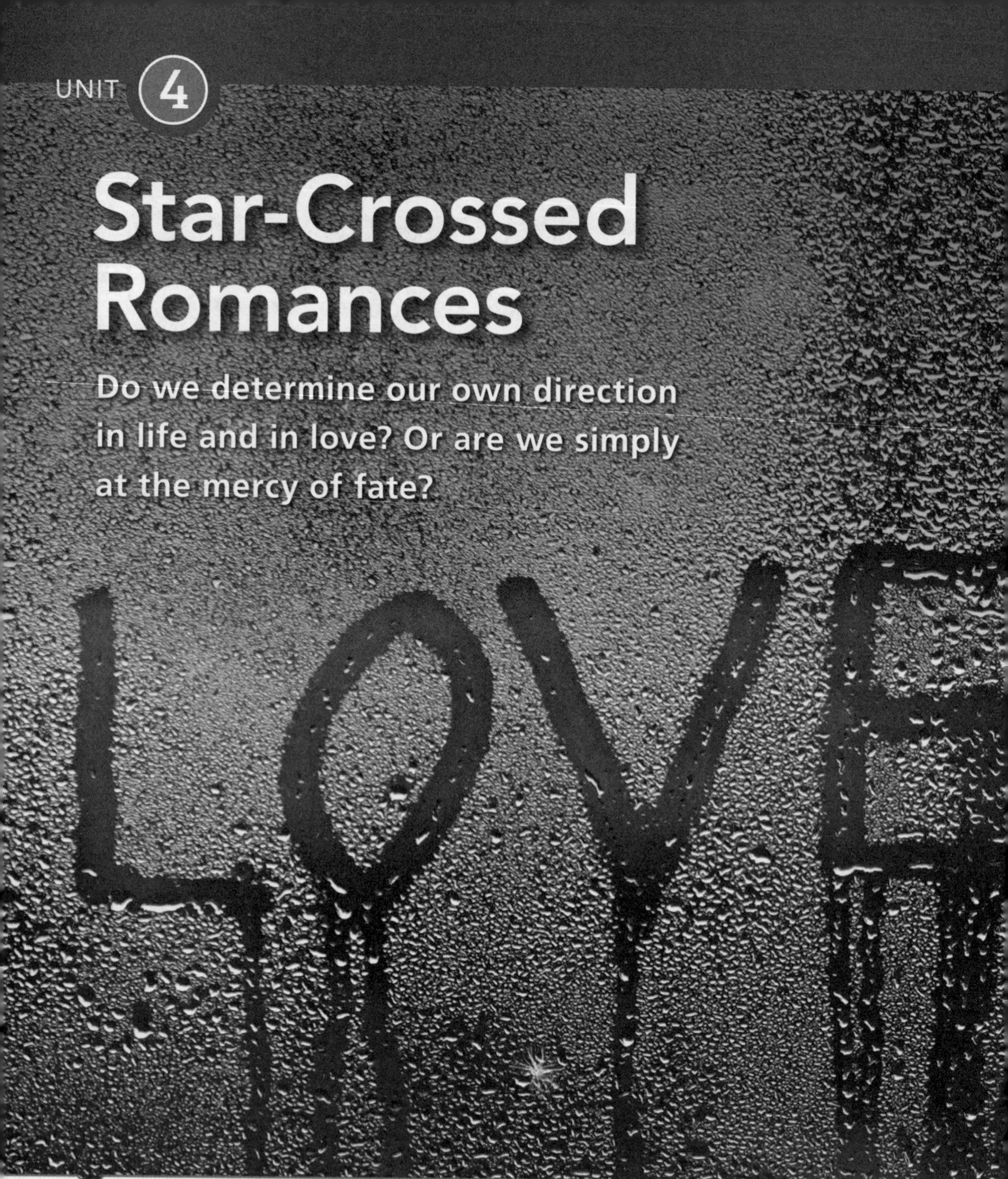

A Modern Take on *Romeo and Juliet*

Discuss It How can a centuries-old love story remain relevant for modern audiences?

Write your response before sharing your ideas.

UNIT INTRODUCTION

ESSENTIAL QUESTION: **Do we determine our own destinies?**

LAUNCH TEXT
ARGUMENT MODEL
Romeo and Juliet: A Tragedy? Or Just a Tragic Misunderstanding?

WHOLE-CLASS LEARNING

COMPARE

LITERATURE AND CULTURE

Historical Context
The Tragedy of Romeo and Juliet

ANCHOR TEXT: DRAMA

The Tragedy of Romeo and Juliet
William Shakespeare

Act I
Act II
Act III
Act IV
Act V

▸ MEDIA CONNECTION: Romeo and Juliet

ANCHOR TEXT: SHORT STORY

Pyramus and Thisbe
Ovid, retold by Edith Hamilton

PERFORMANCE TASK

WRITING FOCUS:
Write an Argument

SMALL-GROUP LEARNING

LITERARY CRITICISM

Romeo and Juliet Is a Terrible Play, and David Leveaux Can't Change That
Alyssa Rosenberg

In Defense of *Romeo and Juliet:* It's Not Childish, It's *About* Childishness
Noah Berlatsky

COMPARE

JOURNALISM

Twenty Years On: The Unfinished Lives of Bosnia's Romeo and Juliet
Gordana Sandić-Hadžihasanović

MEDIA: NEWSCAST

Tragic Romeo and Juliet Offers Bosnia Hope
Nic Robertson

PERFORMANCE TASK

SPEAKING AND LISTENING FOCUS:
Present an Argument

INDEPENDENT LEARNING

MYTH

Popocatepetl and Ixtlaccihuatl
Juliet Piggott Wood

POETRY

Annabel Lee
Edgar Allan Poe

NONFICTION

What's the Rush?: Young Brains Cause Doomed Love
Lexi Tucker

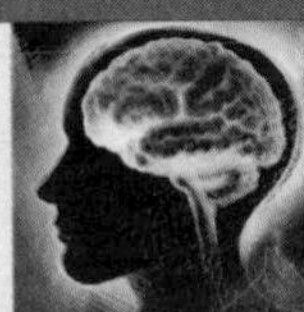

GRAPHIC NOVEL

from William Shakespeare's Romeo & Juliet
artwork by Eli Neugeboren

NEWS ARTICLE

If Romeo and Juliet Had Cell Phones
Misty Harris

PERFORMANCE-BASED ASSESSMENT PREP

Review Evidence for an Argument

PERFORMANCE-BASED ASSESSMENT

Argument: Essay and Multimedia Presentation

PROMPT:
Should the opinions of others affect our own choices or destinies?

Unit Goals

Throughout this unit, you will deepen your understanding of destiny in life and literature by reading, writing, speaking, listening, and presenting. These goals will help you succeed on the Unit Performance-Based Assessment.

Rate how well you meet these goals right now. You will revisit your ratings later when you reflect on your growth during this unit.

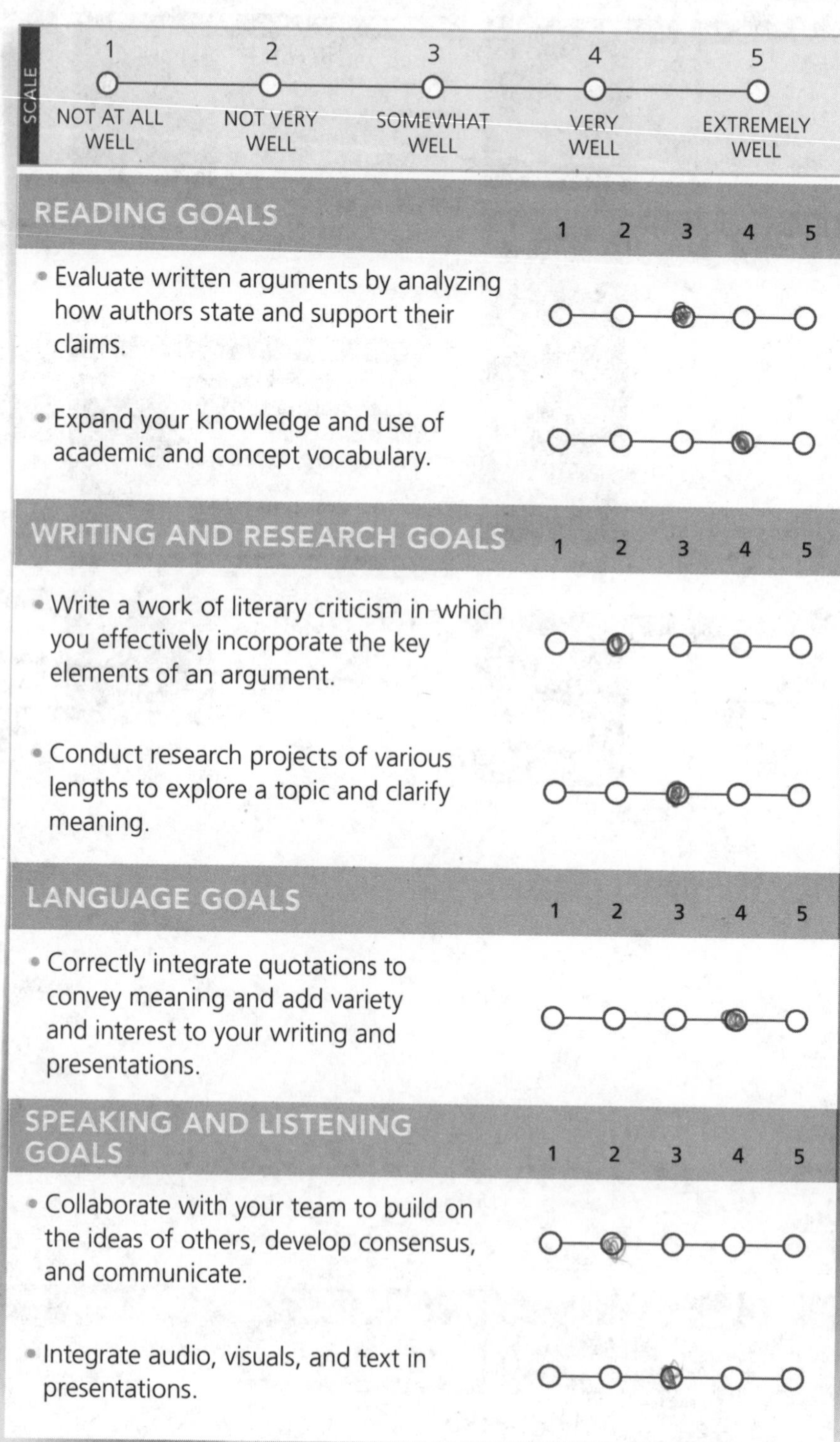

SCALE

1	2	3	4	5
NOT AT ALL WELL	NOT VERY WELL	SOMEWHAT WELL	VERY WELL	EXTREMELY WELL

READING GOALS	1	2	3	4	5
• Evaluate written arguments by analyzing how authors state and support their claims.					
• Expand your knowledge and use of academic and concept vocabulary.					

WRITING AND RESEARCH GOALS	1	2	3	4	5
• Write a work of literary criticism in which you effectively incorporate the key elements of an argument.					
• Conduct research projects of various lengths to explore a topic and clarify meaning.					

LANGUAGE GOALS	1	2	3	4	5
• Correctly integrate quotations to convey meaning and add variety and interest to your writing and presentations.					

SPEAKING AND LISTENING GOALS	1	2	3	4	5
• Collaborate with your team to build on the ideas of others, develop consensus, and communicate.					
• Integrate audio, visuals, and text in presentations.					

STANDARDS

Language
Acquire and use accurately general academic and domain-specific words and phrases, sufficient for reading, writing, speaking, and listening at the college and career readiness level; demonstrate independence in gathering vocabulary knowledge when considering a word or phrase important to comprehension or expression.

Academic Vocabulary: Argument

Academic terms appear in all subjects and can help you read, write, and discuss with more precision. Here are five academic words that will be useful to you in this unit as you analyze and write arguments.

Complete the chart.

1. Review each word, its root, and the mentor sentences.
2. Use the information and your own knowledge to predict the meaning of each word.
3. For each word, list at least two related words.
4. Refer to a dictionary or other resources if needed.

TIP

FOLLOW THROUGH
Study the words in this chart, and highlight them or their forms wherever they appear in the unit.

WORD	MENTOR SENTENCES	PREDICT MEANING	RELATED WORDS
endure ROOT: ***-dur-*** "hard"	1. Just when I thought I couldn't *endure* another minute on the bus, the driver announced that we had arrived. 2. It amazes me that stories from centuries ago continue to *endure*.		endurance; duration
pathos ROOT ***-path-*** "feeling"	1. The novel offers the author's usual blend of humor, drama, and *pathos*. 2. The *pathos* of the drama left audiences in tears.		
compelling ROOT ***-pel-*** "drive"; "push"	1. The jury ruled in favor of the defense because of its *compelling* evidence. 2. When accepting her award, the actress gave a *compelling* speech.		
propose ***-pose-*** "place"	1. At weddings, it is customary for the best man to *propose* a toast to the newly married couple. 2. In his address to Congress, the president will *propose* several new policies and initiatives.		
recurrent ***-curr-*** "run"	1. Hillary has a *recurrent* dream in which she is running and flying at the same time. 2. During the fall, *recurrent* rainstorms led to widespread flooding.		

LAUNCH TEXT | ARGUMENT MODEL

This selection is an example of an **argumentative text,** a type of writing in which an author states and defends a position on a topic. This is the type of writing you will develop in the Performance-Based Assessment at the end of the unit.

As you read, look at the way the writer builds a case. Mark the text to help you answer this question: What is the writer's position, and what evidence supports it?

Romeo and Juliet:
A Tragedy? Or Just a Tragic Misunderstanding?

^ Les Ballets de Monte Carlo, Monaco's national ballet company, performs *Romeo and Juliet* at the London Coliseum in 2015.

NOTES

1 The main characters of William Shakespeare's *Romeo and Juliet* have long inspired audiences' pity. For hundreds of years, people have watched as the two characters meet, fall in love, and—both heartbroken—take their last breaths. While the play's ending is tragic, the famous lovers' deaths are the result of their own impulsive decisions. Romeo and Juliet were not destined to die in each other's arms. That outcome was not inevitable. Instead, their own bad decisions brought them to that terrible point.

2 When the play begins, the city of Verona is being battered by a rivalry between two important families: the House of Montague and the House of Capulet. Swordsmen from both families hurl insults at one another and fight in the streets. Romeo, the son of the head of the Montagues, sneaks into the Capulets' party. Here he sees Juliet, daughter of Capulet, and the two fall head-over-heels in love. Even though their families would never accept their union, they are more than willing to throw away everything to be together—having known each other for barely an evening. Indeed, Juliet says as much of their love:

> It is too rash, too unadvised, too sudden;
> Too like the lightning, which doth cease to be
> Ere one can say it lightens. . . .

3 The sheer lack of care with which they pursue their romance is startling. Neither tries to find a way to reconcile their parents to the idea, or even to flee the city. Instead, they hurriedly marry in secret.

4 As the play continues, the drama of poor judgment unfolds. Juliet's cousin Tybalt goads Romeo to fight. Unwilling to fight a relative of

Juliet's, Romeo refuses. The situation deteriorates further, eventually leading to Romeo's killing of Tybalt. Throughout these events, Romeo simply reacts in the heat of the moment. He is not guided by principle or clear thinking. The result is that he is forced to leave Verona in exile, a situation that sets up the final deadly outcome.

NOTES

5 Juliet is shocked when she hears of Romeo's exile. In another example of startling miscalculation, she chooses to fake her own death in order to escape to be with him. She does not even wait to make sure Romeo knows about her plan. At this point, the play proceeds with a cruel irony that ends with Juliet and Romeo taking their own lives.

6 This play features numerous references to the stars, which symbolize destiny or the absence of human choice and control. These references seem to support the idea that Romeo and Juliet never had any influence over the paths their lives would take. They were destined to meet and destined to die. Indeed, the Prologue calls the two leads "star-cross'd lovers," meaning lovers doomed by the stars, or destiny. Romeo suggests as much before he goes to the party where he first meets Juliet:

> I fear, too early; for my mind misgives
> Some consequence yet hanging in the stars

7 When Romeo hears of Juliet's "death," he cries out against fate: "Then, I defy you, stars!" Yet she is not actually dead, nor is the situation controlled by the stars. Romeo does not know this, but the audience does—Juliet's "death" is not a result of destiny but of her own choices. Despite some instances of pure ill fortune, most of the tragic events are the result of Romeo and Juliet's youthful decisions and haste.

8 In short, Romeo and Juliet were not the victims of destiny. Instead, the two stumbled into their own tragedy. Rather than suffering inevitable doom, they made fatal mistakes. The stars may shine above the events of this play, but that is not the true reason for the tragic outcome.

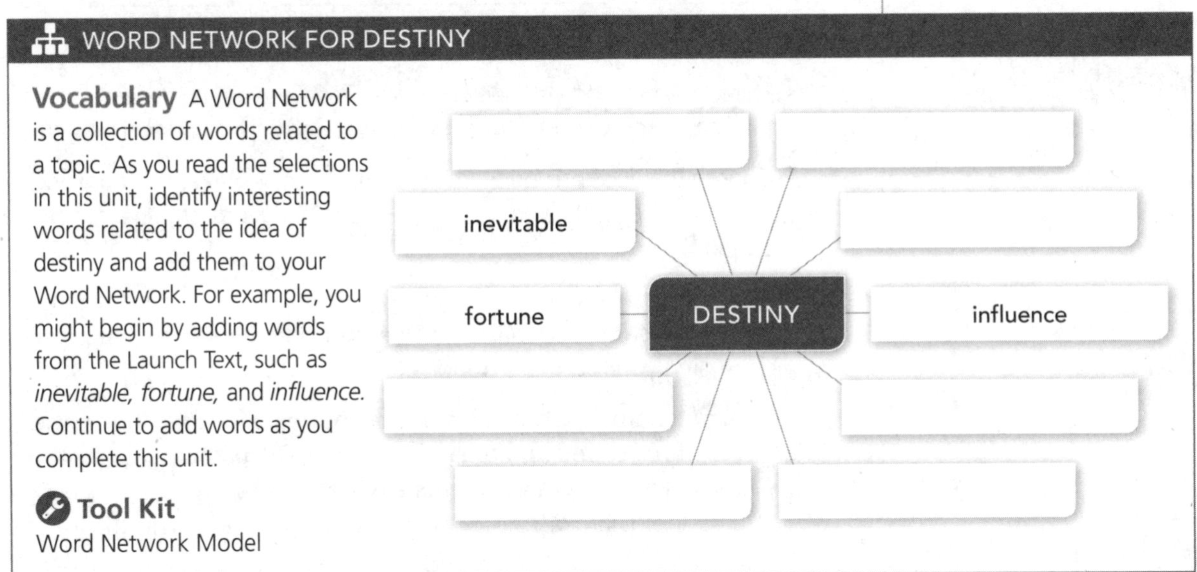

Vocabulary A Word Network is a collection of words related to a topic. As you read the selections in this unit, identify interesting words related to the idea of destiny and add them to your Word Network. For example, you might begin by adding words from the Launch Text, such as *inevitable*, *fortune*, and *influence*. Continue to add words as you complete this unit.

Tool Kit
Word Network Model

Summary

Write a summary of "*Romeo and Juliet:* A Tragedy? Or Just a Tragic Misunderstanding?" A **summary** is a concise, complete, and accurate overview of a text. It should not include a statement of your opinion or an analysis.

Launch Activity

Destiny or Choice? Consider these statements. Check the one that most closely aligns to your point of view. Then, explain your reasoning.

- ☐ The paths we take in life are driven largely by fate.
- ☐ The paths we take in life are determined mostly by others.
- ☐ The paths we take in life are primarily the results of our choices.

- Think of a decision you need to make. Perhaps you are deciding whether to take a up a new sport, strike up a new friendship, or study a new subject.
- Choose the decision you want to make. Then, write down your various options on separate small pieces of paper, one piece of paper for each option.
- Trade your papers with a partner. Discuss all of the options. Then, invite your partner to make your decision for you. Reverse the process, discussing your partner's options.
- After you both have shared your options and decisions, shuffle the pieces of paper and randomly choose one. Discuss how you feel when your decision is made by someone else versus how you feel when you let fate decide. Then, discuss which decision you will actually make.

QuickWrite

Consider class discussions, presentations, the video, and the Launch Text as you think about the prompt. Record your first thoughts here.

PROMPT: **Should the opinions of others affect our own choices or destinies?**

No, I do not think the opinions of others should affect our own choices because they have a free will and if they choose to do something wrong it should not affect us. An example is people say rude things so we can choose not to get hurt.

EVIDENCE LOG FOR STAR-CROSSED ROMANCES

Review your QuickWrite. Summarize your thoughts in one sentence to record in your Evidence Log. Then, record textual details or evidence from "*Romeo and Juliet:* A Tragedy? Or Just a Tragic Misunderstanding?" that support your initial position.

Prepare for the Performance-Based Assessment at the end of the unit by completing the Evidence Log after each selection.

Tool Kit
Evidence Log Model

Title of Text: ____________________ Date: __________

CONNECTION TO PROMPT	TEXT EVIDENCE/DETAILS	ADDITIONAL NOTES/IDEAS

How does this text change or add to my thinking? Date: __________

ESSENTIAL QUESTION:

Do we determine our own destinies?

The idea of destiny was once connected to notions about the stars, which some believed controlled human life. This gave rise to the idea of "star-crossed" lovers—those for whom a sorrowful fate seemed inevitable. While our understanding of the stars has changed, questions about the role destiny plays in our lives remain. You will work with your whole class to explore the idea of destiny. The selections you are going to read present conflicts between destiny and personal choice in two tales of tragic love.

Whole-Class Learning Strategies

Throughout your life, in school, in your community, and in your carer, you will continue to learn and work in large-group environments.

Review these strategies and the actions you can take to practice them as you work with your whole class. Add ideas of your own for each step. Get ready to use these strategies during Whole-Class Learning.

STRATEGY	ACTION PLAN
Listen actively	• Eliminate distractions. For example, put your cell phone away. • Keep your eyes on the speaker. • no side convos
Clarify by asking questions	• If you're confused, other people probably are, too. Ask a question to help your whole class. • If you see that you are guessing, ask a question instead. • write questions down to answer later
Monitor understanding	• Notice what information you already know and be ready to build on it. • Ask for help if you are struggling. • write a summary after every scam
Interact and share ideas	• Share your ideas and answer questions, even if you are unsure. • Build on the ideas of others by adding details or making a connection. • Share your ideas

CONTENTS

^ Queen Elizabeth ruled from 1558 to 1603, but her reign was so successful that the entire Renaissance in England is often called the Elizabethan Age.

Historical Context

Elizabethan England

The Rebirth of Learning Sometime around the year 1350, at the end of the Middle Ages, Italian city-states, such as Venice and Genoa, began to trade extensively with the East. With trade came more knowledge and growing curiosity about the world. Soon, Italy was leading the way in a flowering of European learning known as the Renaissance (REHN uh sons). Commerce, science, and the arts blossomed as people shifted their focus to the interests and pursuits of human life here on earth. The astronomers Copernicus and Galileo questioned long-held beliefs to prove that the world was round and that it circled the sun, not vice versa. Navigators, including Christopher Columbus and Ferdinand Magellan, braved the seas in tiny boats to explore new lands and seek new trade routes. Religious thinkers, such as Martin Luther and John Calvin, challenged the authority of the Roman Catholic Church and spurred the Protestant Reformation. Artists, including Michelangelo and Leonardo da Vinci, painted and sculpted lifelike human beings. Writers, such as Miguel de Cervantes and William Shakespeare, wrote insightfully about complex human personalities in fiction and drama.

The Renaissance in England The Renaissance was slow to come to England. The delay was caused mainly by civil war between two great families, or houses, claiming the English throne—the House of York and the House of Lancaster. The conflict ended in 1485, when Henry Tudor of the House of Lancaster took the throne as King Henry VII. After a successful rule in which English commerce expanded, he was succeeded by his son Henry VIII, whose reign was filled with turmoil. Henry sought a divorce from the Spanish princess Catherine of Aragon so that he could remarry and possibly have a son. He was convinced that only a male would be strong enough to hold the throne. When the Pope refused to grant the divorce, Henry renounced the Roman Catholic Church and made England a Protestant nation. Ironically, his remarriage, to a woman named Anne Boleyn, produced not a son but a daughter, Elizabeth. Even more ironically, when Elizabeth took the throne, she proved to be one of the strongest monarchs that England has ever known.

QUICK INSIGHT

The symbol of the House of York was a white rose, while the symbol of the House of Lancaster was a red rose. For that reason, the civil wars fought between the two houses were called the Wars of the Roses. Shakespeare wrote several plays about English monarchs involved in these conflicts.

The Elizabethan World The reign of Elizabeth I is often seen as a golden age in English history. Treading a moderate and frugal path, Elizabeth brought economic and political stability to the nation, thus allowing commerce and culture to thrive. Advances in mapmaking helped English explorers sail the Old World and claim lands in the New. Practical inventions improved transportation at home. Craft workers created lovely wares for the homes of the wealthy. Musicians composed fine works for the royal court, and literature thrived, peaking with the plays of William Shakespeare.

London became a bustling capital on the busy River Thames (tehmz), where ships from all over the world sailed into port. The city attracted newcomers from the countryside and immigrants from foreign lands. Streets were narrow, dirty, and crowded, but they were also lined with shops where vendors sold merchandise from near and far. English women enjoyed more freedoms than did women elsewhere in Europe, and the class system was more fluid as well. To be sure, those of different ranks led very different lives. Yet even the lowborn were able to attend one of the city's most popular new amusements, the theater.

Elizabeth I and the Spanish Armada

In 1588, King Philip of Spain sent an armada, or fleet of military ships, to invade England. At the time, Spain was the most powerful nation on earth. Nevertheless, the English soundly defeated the invading forces. The victory cemented Elizabeth's popularity with her people. Prior to the battle, the Queen visited her troops to inspire them to fight. Here is a portion of the speech she delivered:

> . . . And therefore I am come amongst you at this time, not as for my recreation or sport, but being resolved, in the midst and heat of the battle, to live or die amongst you all; to lay down, for my God, and for my kingdom and for my people, my honor and my blood, even the dust. I know I have but the body of a weak and feeble woman; but I have the heart of a king, and of a king of England too . . .

England's defeat of the Spanish Armada was a popular subject in fine art for centuries after the events. This print from 1850 shows one artist's imagining of the scene.

Theater in Elizabethan England

Elizabethan audiences included all levels of society, from the "groundlings," who paid a penny entrance fee, to the nobility.

QUICK INSIGHT

Audience members ate and drank while they watched the plays and apparently made a lot of noise. In 1900, archaeologists found the remains of the foundation of the original Globe Theatre. They also found the discarded shells of the many hazelnuts audiences munched on while watching performances.

During the Middle Ages, simple religious plays were performed at inns, in castle halls, and on large wagons at pageants. In early Elizabethan times, acting companies still traveled the countryside to perform their plays. However, the best companies acquired noble patrons, or sponsors, who then invited the troupes to perform in their homes. At the same time, Elizabethan dramatists began to use the tragedies and comedies of ancient Greece and Rome as models for their plays. By the end of the sixteenth century, many talented playwrights had emerged, including Christopher Marlowe, Ben Jonson, and of course, William Shakespeare.

QUICK INSIGHT

During Shakespeare's day, acting companies were entirely male. Women did not perform because it was considered improper. The roles of women were usually played by boys of about eleven, or twelve—that is, before their voices changed.

England's First Theater England's first successful public theater opened in 1576. Known simply as the Theatre, it was built by an actor named James Burbage. Since officials had banned the performance of plays in London, Burbage built his theater in an area called Shoreditch, just outside the London city walls. Some of Shakespeare's earliest plays were first performed here, including *The Tragedy of Romeo and Juliet,* which probably starred James Burbage's son, Richard, as Romeo.

When the lease on the Theatre expired, Richard Burbage, in charge of the company after his father died, decided to move the company to Southwark (SUHTH uhrk), just across the River Thames from London proper. The Shoreditch landlord had been causing problems, and Southwark was emerging as a popular theater district. Using timbers from the old theater building, Burbage had a newer theater built, bigger and better than the one before. It opened in 1599 and was called the Globe. Under that name it would become the most famous theater in the history of the English stage, for many more of Shakespeare's plays were first performed there.

˅ The modern Globe Theatre, rebuilt in the twentieth century a few hundred yards from the original site.

Theater Layout No floor plans of the Theatre or the Globe survive, but people's descriptions and sketches of similar buildings suggest what they were like. They were either round or octagonal, with a central stage open to the sky. This stage stretched out into an area called the pit, where theatergoers called groundlings paid just a penny to stand and watch the play. The enclosure surrounding this open area consisted of two or three galleries, or tiers. The galleries accommodated audience members who paid more to watch the play while under shelter from the elements, and with some distance from the groundlings. The galleries probably also included a few elegant box seats, where members of the nobility could both watch the play and be seen by the masses.

Staging the Play The enclosure directly behind the stage was used not for seating but for staging the play. Actors entered and left the stage from doors at stage level. The stage also had a trap door through which mysterious characters, such as ghosts or witches, could disappear suddenly. Some space above the backstage area was used for storage or dressing rooms. The first gallery, however, was visible to the audience and used as a second stage. It would have been on a second stage like this that the famous balcony scene in *The Tragedy of Romeo and Juliet* was performed.

These open-air theaters did not use artificial light. Instead, performances took place in the afternoon, when it was still light outside. There was also no scenery in the theaters of Shakespeare's day. Instead, the setting for each scene was communicated through dialogue. With no need for set changes, scenes could follow one another in rapid succession. Special effects were simple—smoke might billow at the disappearance of a ghost, for example. By contrast, costumes were often elaborate. The result was a fast-paced, colorful production that lasted about two hours.

The Blackfriars In 1609, Shakespeare's acting company began staging plays in the Blackfriars Theatre as well as the Globe. Located in London proper, the Blackfriars was different from the earlier theaters in which Shakespeare's plays were performed. It was an indoor space with no open area for groundlings. Instead, it relied entirely on a wealthier clientele. It was also one of the first English theaters to use artificial lighting, an innovation that allowed for nighttime performances.

The Globe Theatre

The three-story structure, open to the air, could house as many as 3,000 people in the pit and surrounding galleries.

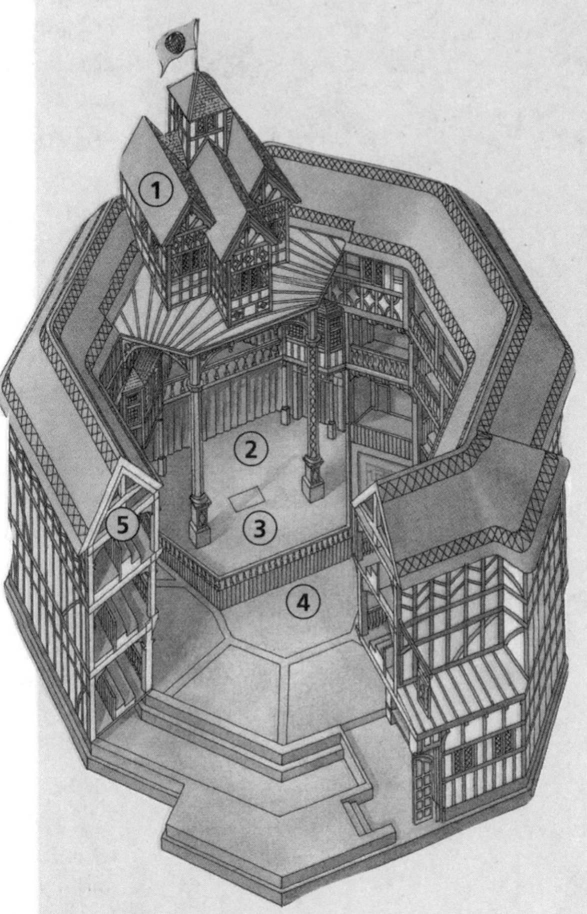

KEY

1. The hut, housing machinery used to lower characters and props to the stage
2. The stage trap, often used for the entrances and exits of special characters, such as ghosts or witches
3. The stage
4. The pit, where groundlings stood to watch the show
5. The galleries

William Shakespeare, Playwright and Poet

Shakespeare's plays and poetry are regarded by many as the finest works ever written in English.

William Shakespeare (1564–1616) is widely revered as one of England's greatest writers. Four centuries after his death, his plays are still read and performed every day. Who was this remarkable author of so many masterpieces? In actual fact, we know very little about him.

From Stratford to London

Shakespeare grew up in Stratford-upon-Avon, a busy market town on the Avon River about 75 miles northwest of London. Church and town records indicate that his mother, Mary Arden, was the daughter of a wealthy farmer who owned the land on which Shakespeare's grandfather lived. Shakespeare's father, John, was a prosperous merchant who also served for a time as Stratford's mayor. Shakespeare most likely went to the local grammar school, where he would have studied Latin and Greek as well as English and world history. He would eventually put all those lessons to use in plays about historical figures, such as Julius Caesar and King Henry IV.

In 1582, when he was eighteen, Shakespeare married a woman named Anne Hathaway and had three children with her, including a set of twins. The next decade of his life is a mystery, but by 1592 he had moved to London, where he gravitated to the theater. Starting off an actor, he soon began writing plays as well. By 1594, he had become the principal playwright of the Lord Chamberlain's Men, the Burbages' acting company. Some of the early plays Shakespeare wrote at this time include the romantic comedy *The Taming of the Shrew* and the romantic tragedy *The Tragedy of Romeo and Juliet.*

Shakespeare was not just a performer and a playwright, however; he was also part owner of the theater company. This meant that he earned money in three ways—from fees for his plays, from his acting salary, and from his share of the company's profits. Those profits rose substantially after the Lord Chamberlain's Men moved to the Globe Theatre, where as many as 3,000 people might attend a single performance. It was at the Globe that many of Shakespeare's later masterpieces premiered, probably beginning with *The Tragedy of Julius Caesar* in 1599.

The King's Players In 1603, Queen Elizabeth I died, and her Scottish cousin took the throne as James I. Partial to the theater, James was particularly supportive of the Lord Chamberlain's Men, which had emerged as one of the two best acting companies in the land. Not only did it have a brilliant playwright in William Shakespeare; it also had a fine actor in Richard Burbage, who starred in most of Shakespeare's plays. In 1606, flattered by the king's patronage, the company changed its name to the King's Men. It is believed that Shakespeare wrote his great Scottish play, *The Tragedy of Macbeth,* to appeal particularly to James I.

Three years later, the King's Men began performing at the Blackfriars Theatre, using the Globe only in summer months. By using this indoor theater in winter, the King's Men further increased profits. The company did so well that Shakespeare was soon able to retire. In 1610, he moved back to Stratford-upon-Avon, buying one of the finest homes in town. He died of unknown causes in 1616.

Shakespeare Says . . .

Shakespeare's impact on the English language has been enormous. Not only did he coin new words and new meanings for old words, but he also used many expressions that have become part of our everyday speech. Here are a few examples.

EXPRESSION AND SOURCE	MEANING
Eat out of house and home *(Henry VI, Part 2)*	Eat so much that it makes the provider poor
For ever and a day *(The Taming of the Shrew)*	Indefinitely; with no end in sight
Give the devil his due *(Henry IV, Part 1)*	Recognize an opponent's achievement
Greek to me *(Julius Caesar)*	Completely unintelligible to me
Green-eyed monster *(Othello)*	Jealousy
In a pickle *(The Tempest)*	In trouble
In stitches *(Twelfth Night)*	Laughing so hard it hurts
Lay it on with a trowel *(As You Like It)*	Flatter excessively
Makes your hair stand on end *(Hamlet)*	Really frightens you
The milk of human kindness *(Macbeth)*	Compassion
A plague on both your houses *(Romeo and Juliet)*	I'm fed up with both sides (in an argument)
Salad days *(Antony and Cleopatra)*	Green, or naïve, youth
Star-crossed lovers *(Romeo and Juliet)*	Ill-fated lovers
Wear your heart upon your sleeve *(Othello)*	Show your love to all
Won't budge an inch *(The Taming of the Shrew)*	Will not give in; stands firm

How to Read Shakespeare

Shakespeare wrote his plays in the language of his time. To the modern ear, however, that language can sound almost foreign. Certain words have changed meaning or fallen out of use. The idioms, slang, and humor of twenty-first-century America are very different from those of Elizabethan England. Even our way of viewing reality has changed. These differences present challenges for modern-day readers of Shakespeare. Here are some strategies for dealing with them.

CHALLENGE: Elizabethan Words

Many words Shakespeare used are now archaic, or outdated. A few types of these words appear here.

TYPE OF WORD	CONTEMPORARY ENGLISH	ELIZABETHAN ENGLISH	EXAMPLE FROM *ROMEO AND JULIET*
pronouns	*you, your, yours*	*thou, thy, thine*	*And if he hear* ***thee, thou*** *wilt anger him. (II.i.22)*
verbs	*come, will, do, has*	*cometh, wilt, doth, hath*	*Verona's summer* ***hath*** *not such a flower. (I.iii.77)*
time words	*morning, evening*	*morrow, even*	*Good* ***morrow****, father. (II.iii.31)*
familiar words used in unfamiliar ways	*if*	*an*	***An*** *I should live a thousand years, / I should never forget it. (I.iii.46–47)*
	fortunate	*happy*	*Oh,* ***happy*** *dagger, / This is thy sheath. (V.iii.182–3)*

STRATEGIES

Familiarize yourself with some of the most common archaic words in Shakespeare.

If a word is completely unfamiliar, look to the marginal notes for a translation. Otherwise, look for clues to the word's meaning in the surrounding text.

CHALLENGE: Elizabethan Syntax

The syntax, or word order, Shakespeare used may also be archaic. In contemporary English, the subject of a sentence usually appears before the verb. Shakespeare often inverts this order, placing the verb before the subject.

Contemporary English Syntax

What do **you** (S) **say** (V)?

Elizabethan English Syntax

What **say** (V) **you** (S)?

STRATEGY

If a sentence uses inverted syntax, identify its subject and verb. Then, rephrase the sentence, placing the subject before the verb.

CHALLENGE: Blank Verse

Shakespeare uses both prose and verse in his plays. The type of verse he wrote is called blank verse. In blank verse, each line has ten syllables, and every unstressed syllable is followed by a stressed one.

> *If* ***ev****er* ***you*** *dis****turb*** *our* ***streets*** *a****gain****,*
> *Your* ***lives*** *shall* ***pay*** *the* ***for****feit* ***of*** *the* ***peace****.* (*Romeo and Juliet,* I.i.87–88)

Often, a single sentence spans more than one line of verse. This is especially true when Shakespeare uses a semicolon to connect two or more clauses.

> *With love's light wings did I o'erperch these walls;*
> *For stony limits cannot hold love out....* (*Romeo and Juliet,* II.ii.66–67)

STRATEGIES

Look for capital letters and end marks to see where sentences begin and end. Read challenging sentences aloud.

When a sentence is made up of two clauses connected by a semicolon, ask yourself how the ideas in the clauses relate to each other.

CHALLENGE: Elizabethan Worldview

In Shakespeare's day, society was rigidly organized. The nobility occupied the top rung of the social ladder, and the uneducated peasantry occupied the bottom. It was difficult, if not impossible, to advance from one social class to another.

The ladder of power also existed within families. Children could not determine their own lives or make their own choices; their parents did so for them. Within a marriage, the husband was the master of his wife.

Elizabethan people expected to live shorter, more difficult lives, and they understood the events of a life to be fated. They did not believe they had the power to shape their own destinies as we do today.

STRATEGY

Keep the Elizabethan worldview in mind as you read. If a character's attitude clashes with your own, try to set aside your own ideas and view the situation through the character's eyes. This will help you understand why the character is behaving or speaking in a certain way.

Close Read the Text

Annotating the text as you read can help you tackle the challenges of Shakespearean language. Here are two sample annotations of an excerpt from Act II, Scene ii of *The Tragedy of Romeo and Juliet*—the famous "balcony scene."

ANNOTATE: Two of Romeo's lines end with a dash. Two of Juliet's sentences include a semicolon.

QUESTION: What do these punctuation marks tell me about how the conversation is unfolding?

CONCLUDE: The dashes tell me that Romeo is being interrupted. The first semicolon shows Juliet changing her mind, and the second semicolon shows her expressing her opinion in yet another way. Juliet's interruptions and ramblings make her seem nervous and flirtatious.

Romeo. Lady, by yonder blessèd moon I vow,
That tips with silver all these fruit-tree tops—
Juliet. O, swear not by the moon, th'inconstant moon,
That monthly changes in her circle orb,
Lest that thy love prove likewise variable.
Romeo. What shall I swear by?
Juliet. Do not swear at all;
Or if thou wilt, swear by thy gracious self,
Which is the god of my idolatry,
And I'll believe thee.
Romeo. Heart's dear love—
Juliet. Well, do not swear. Although I joy in thee,
I have no joy of this contract tonight.
It is too rash, too unadvised, too sudden;
Too like the lightning, which doth cease to be
Ere one can say it lightens.

ANNOTATE: This long, complex sentence uses archaic words and syntax.

QUESTION: What is Juliet really saying?

CONCLUDE: If I paraphrase the sentence using modern-day language, it might read like this: *"Don't swear by the inconstant moon, which changes every month in its orbit, in case your love also proves changeable."* Juliet is saying, "The moon comes and goes. I hope you don't!"

About the Playwright

William Shakespeare (1564–1616) has long been called the greatest writer in the English language. He was born in Stratford-upon-Avon, a town not far from London. In his twenties, he made his name as an actor and a playwright and eventually became a part owner of the Globe theater, where he wrote and produced plays until his late forties. He then retired to the town where he had grown up. For more information, see the Literature and Culture feature.

Tool Kit
First-Read Guide and Model Annotation

STANDARDS
Reading Literature
By the end of grade 9, read and comprehend literature, including stories, dramas, and poems, in the grades 9–10 text complexity band proficiently, with scaffolding as needed at the high end of the range.

The Tragedy of Romeo and Juliet, Act I

Concept Vocabulary

You will encounter the following words as you read Act I of *The Tragedy of Romeo and Juliet*. Before reading, note how familiar you are with each word. Rank the words in order from most familiar (1) to least familiar (3).

WORD	YOUR RANKING
mutiny	
transgression	
heretics	

After completing the first read, come back to the concept vocabulary and review your rankings. Mark changes to your original rankings as needed.

First Read DRAMA

Apply these strategies as you conduct your first read. You will have an opportunity to complete the close-read notes after your first read.

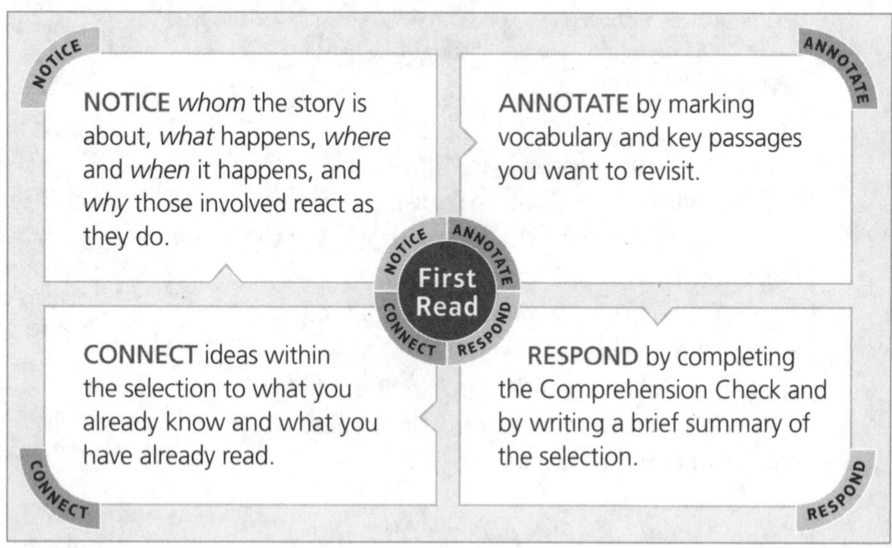
NOTICE
NOTICE *whom* the story is about, *what* happens, *where* and *when* it happens, and *why* those involved react as they do.
ANNOTATE
ANNOTATE by marking vocabulary and key passages you want to revisit.
First Read
NOTICE ANNOTATE CONNECT RESPOND
CONNECT
CONNECT ideas within the selection to what you already know and what you have already read.
RESPOND
RESPOND by completing the Comprehension Check and by writing a brief summary of the selection.

BACKGROUND FOR THE PLAY

Star-Crossed Lovers

Written in 1594 or 1595, when Shakespeare was still a fairly young man, *The Tragedy of Romeo and Juliet* is a play about young love. The basic plot is simple: Two teenagers from feuding families fall in love and marry against their families' wishes, with tragic results. The story is set in Verona, Italy, and is based on an Italian legend that was fairly well known in England at the time.

Shakespeare's Sources Elizabethan writers deeply respected Italy as the birthplace of the Renaissance and often drew on Italian sources for inspiration. In 1562, an English poet named Arthur Brooke wrote *The Tragicall History of Romeus and Juliet*, a long narrative poem based on the Romeo and Juliet legend. Three years later, a prose version of the legend also appeared in England. Scholars believe, however, that Brooke's poem was Shakespeare's chief source.

That poem contains a great deal of moralizing, stressing the disobedience of the young lovers, along with fate, as the cause of their doom. Shakespeare's portrayal of the young lovers is more sympathetic, but he does stress the strong role that fate plays in their tragedy. In fact, at the very start of the play, the Chorus describes Romeo and Juliet as "star-crossed lovers," indicating that their tragic ending is written in the stars, or fated by forces beyond their control.

The Play Through the Centuries Of all the love stories ever written, *The Tragedy of Romeo and Juliet* may well be the most famous. Acting celebrities down through the centuries have played the leading role—Edwin Booth and Ellen Terry in the nineteenth century, for example, and John Gielgud and Judi Dench in the twentieth. There have been dozens of film versions of the play, numerous works of art depicting its scenes, over twenty operatic versions, a famous ballet version by Tchaikovsky. The play is often adapted to reflect the concerns of different eras: *West Side Story*, for example, adapts the story as a musical set amid the ethnic rivalries of 1950s New York City; *Romanoff and Juliet* is a comedy of the Cold War set during the 1960s. One of the most recent popular adaptations was the 1996 film *Romeo + Juliet* starring Leonardo DiCaprio and Claire Danes, which sets the play in the fictional location of Verona Beach, California.

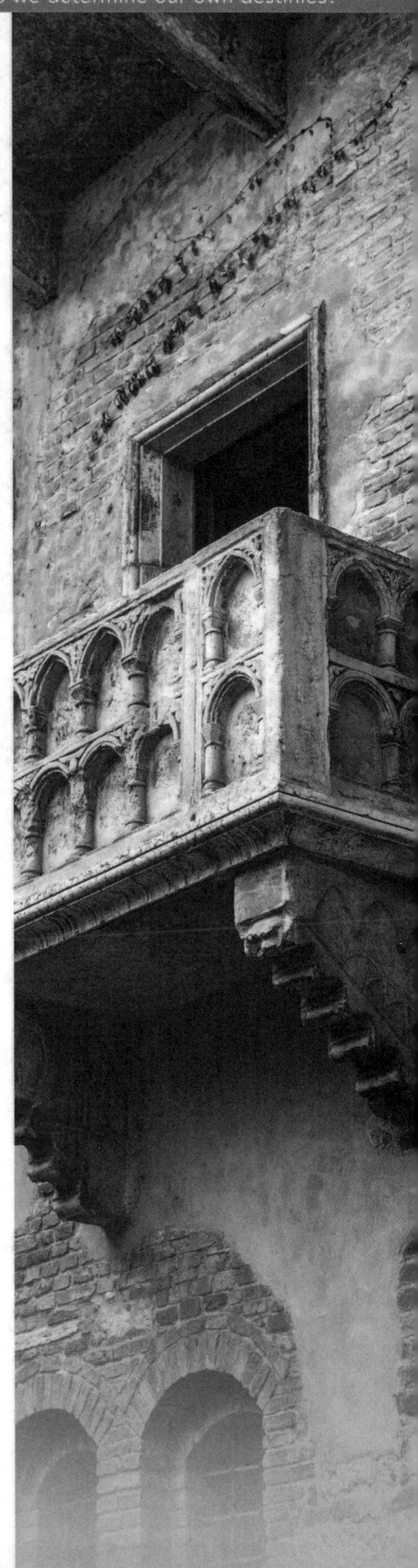

The Tragedy of Romeo and Juliet

Act I

William Shakespeare

Characters

CHORUS

ESCALUS, Prince of Verona

PARIS, a young count, kinsman to the Prince

MONTAGUE

CAPULET

AN OLD MAN, of the Capulet family

ROMEO, son to Montague

MERCUTIO, kinsman to the Prince and friend to Romeo

BENVOLIO, nephew to Montague and friend to Romeo

TYBALT, nephew to Lady Capulet

FRIAR LAWRENCE, Franciscan

FRIAR JOHN, Franciscan

BALTHASAR, servant to Romeo

SAMPSON, servant to Capulet

GREGORY, servant to Capulet

PETER, servant to Juliet's nurse

ABRAM, servant to Montague

AN APOTHECARY

THREE MUSICIANS

AN OFFICER

LADY MONTAGUE, wife to Montague

LADY CAPULET, wife to Capulet

JULIET, daughter to Capulet

NURSE TO JULIET

CITIZENS OF VERONA, Gentlemen and Gentlewomen of both houses, Maskers, Torchbearers, Pages, Guards, Watchmen, Servants, and Attendants

Prologue

Scene: Verona: Mantua

[*Enter* Chorus.]

Chorus. Two households, both alike in dignity,[1]
In fair Verona, where we lay our scene,
From ancient grudge break to new **mutiny**,
Where civil blood makes civil hands unclean.
From forth the fatal loins of these two foes
A pair of star-crossed[3] lovers take their life;
Whose misadventured piteous overthrows[4]
Doth with their death bury their parents' strife.
The fearful passage of their death-marked love,
And the continuance of their parents' rage,
Which, but[5] their children's end, naught could remove,
Is now the two hours' traffic[6] of our stage;
The which if you with patient ears attend,
What here shall miss, our toil shall strive to mend.[7] [*Exit*.]

NOTES

1. **dignity** *n.* high social rank.

mutiny (MYOO tuh nee) *n.* open rebellion against lawful authority, especially by sailors or soldiers against their officers

2. **Where. . . unclean** in which the blood of citizens stains citizens' hands.
3. **star-crossed** ill-fated by the unfavorable positions of the stars.
4. **Whose . . . overthrows** whose unfortunate, sorrowful destruction.
5. **but** except.
6. **two hours' traffic** two hours' business.
7. **What . . . mend** Whatever is unclear in this prologue we actors shall try to clarify in the course of the play.

⌘ ⌘ ⌘

Act I

Scene i • *Verona. A public place.*

[*Enter* Sampson *and* Gregory, *with swords and bucklers,*[1] *of the house of Capulet*.]

Sampson. Gregory, on my word, we'll not carry coals.[2]

Gregory. No, for then we should be colliers.[3]

Sampson. I mean, an we be in choler, we'll draw.[4]

Gregory. Ay, while you live, draw your neck out of collar.[5]

Sampson. I strike quickly, being moved.

Gregory. But thou art not quickly moved to strike.

Sampson. A dog of the house of Montague moves me.

Gregory. To move is to stir, and to be valiant is to stand. Therefore, if thou art moved, thou run'st away.

Sampson. A dog of that house shall move me to stand. I will take the wall[6] of any man or maid of Montague's.

Gregory. That shows thee a weak slave; for the weakest goes to the wall.

Sampson. 'Tis true; and therefore women, being the weaker

1. **bucklers** *n.* small shields.
2. **carry coals** endure insults.
3. **colliers** *n.* sellers of coal.
4. **an . . . draw** if we are angered, we'll draw our swords.
5. **collar** *n.* hangman's noose.
6. **take the wall** assert superiority by walking nearer the houses and therefore farther from the gutter.

vessels, are ever thrust to the wall. Therefore I will push Montague's men from the wall, and thrust his maids to the wall.

Gregory. The quarrel is between our masters and us their men.

Sampson. 'Tis all one, I will show myself a tyrant. When I have fought with the men, I will be cruel with the maids—I will cut off their heads.

Gregory. The heads of the maids?

Sampson. Ay, the heads of the maids or their maidenheads. Take it in what sense thou wilt.

Gregory. They must take it in sense that feel it.

Sampson. Me they shall feel while I am able to stand: and 'tis known I am a pretty piece of flesh.

Gregory. 'Tis well thou art not fish; if thou hadst, thou hadst been Poor John. Draw thy tool![7] Here comes two of the house of Montagues.

[*Enter two other Servingmen,* Abram *and* Balthasar.]

Sampson. My naked weapon is out. Quarrel! I will back thee.

Gregory. How? Turn thy back and run?

Sampson. Fear me not.

Gregory. No, marry. I fear thee!

Sampson. Let us take the law of our sides;[8] let them begin.

Gregory. I will frown as I pass by, and let them take it as they list.[9]

Sampson. Nay, as they dare. I will bite my thumb[10] at them, which is disgrace to them if they bear it.

Abram. Do you bite your thumb at us, sir?

Sampson. I do bite my thumb, sir.

Abram. Do you bite your thumb at us, sir?

Sampson. [*Aside to* Gregory] Is the law of our side if I say ay?

Gregory. [*Aside to* Sampson] No.

Sampson. No, sir, I do not bite my thumb at you, sir, but I bite my thumb, sir.

Gregory. Do you quarrel, sir?

Abram. Quarrel, sir? No, sir.

Sampson. But if you do, sir, I am for you. I serve as good a man as you.

Abram. No better.

Sampson. Well, sir.

[*Enter* Benvolio.]

NOTES

7. **tool** *n.* weapon.

8. **take . . . sides** make sure the law is on our side.

9. **list** please.

10. **bite . . . thumb** make an insulting gesture.

Gregory. [*Aside to* Sampson.] Say "better." Here comes one of my master's kinsmen.

Sampson. Yes, better, sir.

Abram. You lie.

Sampson. Draw, if you be men. Gregory, remember thy swashing blow.[11] [*They fight.*]

Benvolio. Part, fools!
Put up your swords. You know not what you do.
[*Enter* Tybalt.]

Tybalt. What, art thou drawn among these heartless hinds?[12]
Turn thee, Benvolio; look upon thy death.

Benvolio. I do but keep the peace. Put up thy sword,
Or manage it to part these men with me.

Tybalt. What, drawn, and talk of peace! I hate the word
As I hate hell, all Montagues, and thee.
Have at thee, coward! [*They fight.*]

[*Enter an* Officer, *and three or four* Citizens *with clubs or partisans.*[13]]

Officer. Clubs, bills,[14] and partisans! Strike! Beat them down!
Down with the Capulets! Down with the Montagues!

[*Enter old* Capulet *in his gown, and his* Wife.]

Capulet. What noise is this? Give me my long sword, ho!

Lady Capulet. A crutch, a crutch! Why call you for a sword?

Capulet. My sword, I say! Old Montague is come
And flourishes his blade in spite[15] of me.

[*Enter old* Montague *and his* Wife.]

Montague. Thou villain Capulet!—Hold me not; let me go.

Lady Montague. Thou shalt not stir one foot to seek a foe.

[*Enter* Prince Escalus, *with his Train.*[16]]

Prince. Rebellious subjects, enemies to peace,
Profaners[17] of this neighbor-stained steel—
Will they not hear? What, ho! You men, you beasts,
That quench the fire of your pernicious rage
With purple fountains issuing from your veins!
On pain of torture, from those bloody hands
Throw your mistempered[18] weapons to the ground
And hear the sentence of your moved prince.
Three civil brawls, bred of an airy word
By thee, old Capulet, and Montague,
Have thrice disturbed the quiet of our streets
And made Verona's ancient citizens
Cast by their grave beseeming ornaments[19]
To wield old partisans, in hands as old,

NOTES

11. **swashing blow** hard downward swordstroke.

12. **heartless hinds** cowardly servants. *Hind* also means "a female deer."

13. **partisans** *n.* spearlike weapons with broad blades.

14. **bills** *n.* weapons consisting of hook-shaped blades with long handles.

15. **spite** defiance.

16. **Train** *n.* attendants.

17. **Profaners** *n.* those who show disrespect or contempt.

18. **mistempered** *adj.* hardened for a wrong purpose; bad tempered.

19. **Cast . . . ornaments** put aside their dignified and appropriate clothing.

NOTES

20. Cank'red hate rusted from lack of use, to put an end to your malignant feuding.

21. Who . . . abroach? Who reopened this old fight?

22. on . . . part on one side and the other.

23. ware *adj.* aware; wary.

24. covert *n.* hidden place.

25. measuring . . . affections judging his feelings.

26. Which . . . found which wanted to be where there was no one else.

27. Pursued . . . his followed my own mind by not following after Romeo.

28. heavy *adj.* sad; moody.

Cank'red with peace, to part your cank'red hate.[20]
If ever you disturb our streets again,
Your lives shall pay the forfeit of the peace.
For this time all the rest depart away.
You, Capulet, shall go along with me;
And, Montague, come you this afternoon,
To know our further pleasure in this case,
To old Freetown, our common judgment place.
Once more, on pain of death, all men depart.

[*Exit all but* Montague, *his* Wife, *and* Benvolio.]

Montague. Who set this ancient quarrel new abroach?[21]
Speak, nephew, were you by when it began?

Benvolio. Here were the servants of your adversary
And yours, close fighting ere I did approach.
I drew to part them. In the instant came
The fiery Tybalt, with his sword prepared;
Which, as he breathed defiance to my ears,
He swung about his head and cut the winds,
Who, nothing hurt withal, hissed him in scorn.
While we were interchanging thrusts and blows,
Came more and more, and fought on part and part,[22]
Till the prince came, who parted either part.

Lady Montague. O, where is Romeo? Saw you him today?
Right glad I am he was not at this fray.

Benvolio. Madam, an hour before the worshiped sun
Peered forth the golden window of the East,
A troubled mind drave me to walk abroad:
Where, underneath the grove of sycamore
That westward rooteth from the city side,
So early walking did I see your son.
Towards him I made, but he was ware[23] of me
And stole into the covert[24] of the wood.
I, measuring his affections[25] by my own,
Which then most sought where most might not be found,[26]
Being one too many by my weary self,
Pursued my humor not pursuing his,[27]
And gladly shunned who gladly fled from me.

Montague. Many a morning hath he there been seen,
With tears augmenting the fresh morning's dew,
Adding to clouds more clouds with his deep sighs;
But all so soon as the all-cheering sun
Should in the furthest East begin to draw
The shady curtains from Aurora's bed,
Away from light steals home my heavy[28] son
And private in his chamber pens himself,
Shuts up his windows, locks fair daylight out,

And makes himself an artificial night.
Black and portentous[29] must this humor prove
Unless good counsel may the cause remove.

Benvolio. My noble uncle, do you know the cause?

Montague. I neither know it nor can learn of him.

Benvolio. Have you importuned[30] him by any means?

Montague. Both by myself and many other friends;
But he, his own affections' counselor,
Is to himself—I will not say how true—
But to himself so secret and so close,
So far from sounding[31] and discovery,
As is the bud bit with an envious worm
Ere he can spread his sweet leaves to the air
Or dedicate his beauty to the sun.
Could we but learn from whence his sorrows grow,
We would as willingly give cure as know.

[*Enter* Romeo.]

Benvolio. See, where he comes: so please you, step aside;
I'll know his grievance, or be much denied.

Montague. I would thou wert so happy by thy stay,
To hear true shrift.[32] Come, madam, let's away.

[*Exit* Montague *and* Wife.]

Benvolio. Good-morrow, cousin.

Romeo. Is the day so young?

Benvolio. But new struck nine.

Romeo. Ay me! Sad hours seem long.
Was that my father that went hence so fast?

Benvolio. It was. What sadness lengthens Romeo's hours?

Romeo. Not having that which having makes them short.

Benvolio. In love?

Romeo. Out—

Benvolio. Of love?

Romeo. Out of her favor where I am in love.

Benvolio. Alas, that love, so gentle in his view,[33]
Should be so tyrannous and rough in proof![34]

Romeo. Alas, that love, whose view is muffled still,[35]
Should, without eyes, see pathways to his will!
Where shall we dine? O me! What fray was here?
Yet tell me not, for I have heard it all.
Here's much to do with hate, but more with love.[36]
Why, then, O brawling love! O loving hate,
O any thing, of nothing first created!

NOTES

29. portentous *adj.* promising bad fortune.

30. importuned *v.* questioned deeply.

31. sounding *n.* understanding.

32. I . . . shrift I hope you are lucky enough to hear him confess the truth.

33. view *n.* appearance.

34. in proof when experienced.

35. whose . . . still Cupid is traditionally represented as blindfolded.

36. but . . . love loyalty to family and love of fighting in the following lines, Romeo speaks of love as a series of contradictions—a union of opposites.

NOTES

37. **coz** cousin.

transgression (tranz GREHSH uhn) *n.* the act of breaking a law or command, or committing a sin

38. **Which . . . thine** which griefs you will increase by adding your own sorrow to them.

39. **discreet** *adj.* intelligently sensitive.

40. **gall** *n.* a bitter liquid.

41. **Soft!** Wait!

42. **in sadness** seriously.

43. **Dian's wit** the mind of Diana, goddess of chastity.

44. **proof** *n.* armor.

45. **stay** *v.* endure; put up with.

46. **That . . . store** in that her beauty will die with her if she does not marry and have children.

CLOSE READ

ANNOTATE: In lines 200–211, mark words and phrases that relate to war or attacking someone.

QUESTION: What connection do Benvolio and Romeo seem to be making between love and conflict?

CONCLUDE: What do these references suggest about the ways in which the two characters' view love?

O heavy lightness, serious vanity,
Misshapen chaos of well-seeming forms,
Feather of lead, bright smoke, cold fire, sick health,
Still-waking sleep, that is not what it is!
This love feel I, that feel no love in this.
Dost thou not laugh?

Benvolio. No, coz,[37] I rather weep.

Romeo. Good heart, at what?

Benvolio. At thy good heart's oppression.

Romeo. Why, such is love's **transgression**.
Griefs of mine own lie heavy in my breast,
Which thou wilt propagate, to have it prest
With more of thine.[38] This love that thou hast shown
Doth add more grief to too much of mine own.
Love is a smoke raised with the fume of sighs;
Being purged, a fire sparkling in lovers' eyes;
Being vexed, a sea nourished with loving tears.
What is it else? A madness most discreet,[39]
A choking gall,[40] and a preserving sweet.
Farewell, my coz.

Benvolio. Soft![41] I will go along.
And if you leave me so, you do me wrong.

Romeo. Tut! I have lost myself; I am not here;
This is not Romeo, he's some other where.

Benvolio. Tell me in sadness,[42] who is that you love?

Romeo. What, shall I groan and tell thee?

Benvolio. Groan? Why, no;
But sadly tell me who.

Romeo. Bid a sick man in sadness make his will.
Ah, word ill urged to one that is so ill!
In sadness, cousin, I do love a woman.

Benvolio. I aimed so near when I supposed you loved.

Romeo. A right good markman. And she's fair I love.

Benvolio. A right fair mark, fair coz, is soonest hit.

Romeo. Well, in that hit you miss. She'll not be hit
With Cupid's arrow. She hath Dian's wit,[43]
And, in strong proof[44] of chastity well armed,
From Love's weak childish bow she lives uncharmed.
She will not stay[45] the siege of loving terms,
Nor bide th' encounter of assailing eyes,
Nor ope her lap to saint-seducing gold.
O, she is rich in beauty; only poor
That, when she dies, with beauty dies her store.[46]

Benvolio. Then she hath sworn that she will still live chaste?

Romeo. She hath, and in that sparing make huge waste;
For beauty, starved with her severity,
Cuts beauty off from all posterity.[47]
She is too fair, too wise, wisely too fair
To merit bliss by making me despair.[48]
She hath forsworn[49] to love, and in that vow
Do I live dead that live to tell it now.

Benvolio. Be ruled by me; forget to think of her.

Romeo. O, teach me how I should forget to think!

Benvolio. By giving liberty unto thine eyes.
Examine other beauties.

Romeo. 'Tis the way
To call hers, exquisite, in question more.[50]
These happy masks that kiss fair ladies' brows,
Being black put us in mind they hide the fair.
He that is strucken blind cannot forget
The precious treasure of his eyesight lost.
Show me a mistress that is passing fair:
What doth her beauty serve, but as a note
Where I may read who passed that passing fair?[51]
Farewell. Thou canst not teach me to forget.

Benvolio. I'll pay that doctrine, or else die in debt.[52] [*Exit all.*]

NOTES

47. in . . . posterity By denying herself love and marriage, she wastes her beauty, which will not live on in future generations.

48. She . . . despair She is being too good—she will earn happiness in heaven by dooming me to live without her love.

49. forsworn to sworn not to.

50. 'Tis . . . more That way will only make her beauty more strongly present in my mind.

51. who . . . fair who surpassed in beauty that very beautiful woman.

52. I'll . . . debt I will teach you to forget, or else die trying.

⌘ ⌘ ⌘

Scene ii • *A street.*

[*Enter* Capulet, County Paris, *and the* Clown, *Capulet's servant.*]

Capulet. But Montague is bound as well as I,
In penalty alike; and 'tis not hard, I think,
For men so old as we to keep the peace.

Paris. Of honorable reckoning[1] are you both,
And pity 'tis you lived at odds so long.
But now, my lord, what say you to my suit?

Capulet. But saying o'er what I have said before:
My child is yet a stranger in the world,
She hath not seen the change of fourteen years;
Let two more summers wither in their pride
Ere we may think her ripe to be a bride.

Paris. Younger than she are happy mothers made.

Capulet. And too soon marred are those so early made.
Earth hath swallowed all my hopes[2] but she;
She is the hopeful lady of my earth.[3]

1. reckoning *n.* reputation.

2. hopes *n.* children.

3. She . . . earth My hopes for the future rest in her; she will inherit all that is mine.

But woo her, gentle Paris, get her heart;
My will to her consent is but a part.
An she agree, within her scope of choice
Lies my consent and fair according voice.[4]
This night I hold an old accustomed feast,
Whereto I have invited many a guest,
Such as I love; and you among the store,
One more, most welcome, makes my number more.
At my poor house look to behold this night
Earth-treading stars[5] that make dark heaven light.
Such comfort as do lusty young men feel
When well-appareled April on the heel
Of limping Winter treads, even such delight
Among fresh fennel buds shall you this night
Inherit at my house. Hear all, all see,
And like her most whose merit most shall be;
Which, on more view, of many, mine, being one,
May stand in number, though in reck'ning none.[6]
Come, go with me. [*To* Servant, *giving him a paper*]
Go, sirrah, trudge about
Through fair Verona; find those persons out
Whose names are written there, and to them say
My house and welcome on their pleasure stay.[7]

[*Exit with* Paris.]

Servant. Find them out whose names are written here? It is written, that the shoemaker should meddle with his yard and the tailor with his last, the fisher with his pencil and the painter with his nets;[8] but I am sent to find those persons whose names are here writ, and can never find what names the writing person hath here writ. I must to the learned. In good time![9]

[*Enter* Benvolio *and* Romeo.]

Benvolio. Tut, man, one fire burns out another's burning;
One pain is less'ned by another's anguish;
Turn giddy, and be holp by backward turning;[10]
One desperate grief cures with another's languish.
Take thou some new infection to thy eye,
And the rank poison of the old will die.

Romeo. Your plantain leaf[11] is excellent for that.

Benvolio. For what, I pray thee?

Romeo. For your broken shin.

Benvolio. Why, Romeo, art thou mad?

Romeo. Not mad, but bound more than a madman is;
Shut up in prison, kept without my food,
Whipped and tormented and—God-den,[12] good fellow.

NOTES

4. **An . . . voice** If she agrees, I will consent to and agree with her choice.

5. **Earth-treading stars** young ladies.

6. **Which . . . none** If you look at all the young girls, you may see her as merely one among many, and not worth special admiration.

7. **stay** *v.* await.

8. **shoemaker . . . nets** The servant is confusing workers and their tools. He intends to say that people should stick with what they know.

9. **In good time!** Just in time! The servant has seen Benvolio and Romeo, who can read.

10. **Turn . . . turning** If you are dizzy from turning one way, turn the other way.

11. **plantain leaf** used to stop bleeding.

12. **God-den** good afternoon; good evening.

Servant. God gi' go-den. I pray, sir, can you read?

Romeo. Ay, mine own fortune in my misery.

Servant. Perhaps you have learned it without book.
But, I pray, can you read anything you see?

Romeo. Ay, if I know the letters and the language.

Servant. Ye say honestly. Rest you merry.[13]

Romeo. Stay, fellow; I can read. [*He reads the letter.*]
"Signior Martino and his wife and daughters;
County Anselm and his beauteous sisters;
the lady widow of Vitruvio;
Signior Placentio and his lovely nieces;
Mercutio and his brother Valentine;
Mine uncle Capulet, his wife and daughters;
My fair niece Rosaline; Livia;
Signior Valentio and his cousin Tybalt;
Lucio and the lively Helena."
A fair assembly. Whither should they come?

Servant. Up.

Romeo. Whither? To supper?

Servant. To our house.

Romeo. Whose house?

Servant. My master's.

Romeo. Indeed I should have asked you that before.

Servant. Now I'll tell you without asking. My master is the great rich Capulet; and if you be not of the house of Montagues, I pray come and crush a cup of wine. Rest you merry. [*Exit.*]

Benvolio. At this same ancient[14] feast of Capulet's
Sups the fair Rosaline whom thou so loves;
With all the admired beauties of Verona.
Go thither, and with unattainted[15] eye,
Compare her face with some that I shall show,
And I will make thee think thy swan a crow.

Romeo. When the devout religion of mine eye
Maintains such falsehood, then turn tears to fires:
And these, who, often drowned, could never die,
Transparent heretics, be burnt for liars![16]
One fairer than my love? The all-seeing sun
Ne'er saw her match since first the world begun.

Benvolio. Tut! You saw her fair, none else being by,
Herself poised with herself in either eye;[17]
But in that crystal scales[18] let there be weighed
Your lady's love against some other maid

NOTES

13. Rest you merry May God keep you happy—a way of saying farewell.

14. ancient *adj.* long-established; traditional.

15. unattainted *adj.* unprejudiced.

heretics (HEHR uh tihks) *n.* people who hold a different belief from the official belief of their church

16. When . . . liars! When I see Rosaline as just a plain-looking girl, may my tears turn to fire and burn my eyes out!

17. Herself . . . eye Rosaline compared with no one else.

18. crystal scales your eyes.

That I will show you shining at this feast,
And she shall scant show well that now seems best.

Romeo. I'll go along, no such sight to be shown,
But to rejoice in splendor of mine own.[19] [*Exit all.*]

⌘⌘⌘

Scene iii • *A room in Capulet's house.*

[*Enter* Capulet's Wife, *and* Nurse.]

Lady Capulet. Nurse, where's my daughter? Call her forth to me.

Nurse. Now, by my maidenhead at twelve year old,
I bade her come. What, lamb! What, ladybird!
God forbid, where's this girl? What, Juliet!

[*Enter* Juliet.]

Juliet. How now? Who calls?

Nurse. Your mother.

Juliet. Madam, I am here.
What is your will?

Lady Capulet. This is the matter—Nurse, give leave[1] awhile;
We must talk in secret. Nurse, come back again.
I have rememb'red me, thou's hear our counsel.[2]
Thou knowest my daughter's of a pretty age.

Nurse. Faith, I can tell her age unto an hour.

Lady Capulet. She's not fourteen.

Nurse. I'll lay fourteen of my teeth—
And yet, to my teen[3] be it spoken, I have but four—
She's not fourteen. How long is it now
To Lammastide?[4]

Lady Capulet. A fortnight and odd days.[5]

Nurse. Even or odd, of all days in the year,
Come Lammas Eve at night shall she be fourteen.
Susan and she (God rest all Christian souls!)
Were of an age.[6] Well, Susan is with God;
She was too good for me. But, as I said,
On Lammas Eve at night shall she be fourteen;
That shall she, marry; I remember it well.
'Tis since the earthquake now eleven years.
And she was weaned (I never shall forget it),
Of all the days of the year, upon that day;
For I had then laid wormwood to my dug,
Sitting in the sun under the dovehouse wall.
My lord and you were then at Mantua.

NOTES

19. **mine own** my own love; Rosaline.

1. **give leave** Leave us alone.

2. **thou's . . . counsel** You shall hear our conference.

3. **teen** *n.* sorrow.

4. **Lammastide** (LAM uhs tyd) August 1, a holiday celebrating the summer harvest.

5. **A fortnight and odd days** two weeks plus a few days.

6. **Susan . . . age** Susan, the Nurse's child, and Juliet were the same age.

NOTES

Nay, I do bear a brain. But, as I said,
When it did taste the wormwood on the nipple
Of my dug and felt it bitter, pretty fool,
To see it tetchy and fall out with the dug!
Shake, quoth the dovehouse! 'Twas no need, I trow,
To bid me trudge.
And since that time it is eleven years,
For then she could stand high-lone; nay, by th' rood,
She could have run and waddled all about;
For even the day before, she broke her brow;
And then my husband (God be with his soul!
'A was a merry man) took up the child.
"Yea," quoth he, "dost thou fall upon thy face?
Thou wilt fall backward when thou hast more wit;
Wilt thou not, Jule?" and, by my holidam,
The pretty wretch left crying and said "Ay."
To see now how a jest shall come about!
I warrant, and I should live a thousand years,
I never should forget it. "Wilt thou not, Jule?" quoth he,
And, pretty fool, it stinted and said "Ay."

Lady Capulet. Enough of this. I pray thee hold thy peace.

Nurse. Yes, madam. Yet I cannot choose but laugh
To think it should leave crying and say, "Ay."
And yet, I warrant, it had upon it brow
A bump as big as a young cock'rel's stone;
A perilous knock; and it cried bitterly.

CLOSE READ

ANNOTATE: In the Nurse's speech starting on line 16, mark contractions, parenthetical statements, and any other deviations from formal speech.

QUESTION: Why does the Nurse's speech have so many asides and digressions?

CONCLUDE: What overall impression of the Nurse does this speech create?

"Yea," quoth my husband, "fall'st upon thy face?
Thou wilt fall backward when thou comest to age,
Wilt thou not, Jule?" It stinted and said "Ay."

Juliet. And stint thou too. I pray thee, nurse, say I.

Nurse. Peace, I have done. God mark thee to His grace!
Thou wast the prettiest babe that e'er I nursed.
And I might live to see thee married once,
I have my wish.

Lady Capulet. Marry, that "marry" is the very theme
I came to talk of. Tell me, daughter Juliet,
How stands your dispositions to be married?

Juliet. It is an honor that I dream not of.

Nurse. An honor? Were not I thine only nurse,
I would say thou hadst sucked wisdom from thy teat.

Lady Capulet. Well, think of marriage now. Younger than you,
Here in Verona, ladies of esteem,
Are made already mothers. By my count,
I was your mother much upon these years
That you are now a maid.[7] Thus then in brief:
The valiant Paris seeks you for his love.

Nurse. A man, young lady! Lady, such a man
As all the world—Why, he's a man of wax.[8]

Lady Capulet. Verona's summer hath not such a flower.

Nurse. Nay, he's a flower, in faith—a very flower.

Lady Capulet. What say you? Can you love the gentleman?
This night you shall behold him at our feast.
Read o'er the volume of young Paris' face,
And find delight writ there with beauty's pen;
Examine every married lineament,
And see how one another lends content;[9]
And what obscured in this fair volume lies
Find written in the margent[10] of his eyes.
This precious book of love, this unbound lover,
To beautify him only lacks a cover.[11]
The fish lives in the sea, and 'tis much pride
For fair without the fair within to hide.
That book in many's eyes doth share the glory,
That in gold clasps locks in the golden story;
So shall you share all that he doth possess,
By having him making yourself no less.

Nurse. No less? Nay, bigger! Women grow by men.

Lady Capulet. Speak briefly, can you like of Paris' love?

Juliet. I'll look to like, if looking liking move;[12]
But no more deep will I endart mine eye

NOTES

7. **I . . . maid** I was your mother when I was as old as you are now.

8. **he's . . . wax** He's a model of a man.

9. **Examine . . . content** Examine every harmonious feature of his face, and see how each one enhances every other. Throughout this speech, Lady Capulet compares Paris to a book.

10. **margent** *n.* margin. Paris's eyes are compared to the margin of a book, where whatever is not clear in the text (the rest of his face) can be explained by notes.

11. **cover** metaphor for wife.

12. **I'll . . . move** If looking favorably at someone leads to liking him, I will look at Paris in a way that will lead to liking him.

Than your consent gives strength to make it fly.[13]

[*Enter* Servingman.]

Servingman. Madam, the guests are come, supper served up, you called, my young lady asked for, the nurse cursed in the pantry, and everything in extremity. I must hence to wait. I beseech you follow straight. [*Exit.*]

Lady Capulet. We follow thee. Juliet, the County stays.[14]

Nurse. Go, girl, seek happy nights to happy days. [*Exit all.*]

⌘ ⌘ ⌘

Scene iv • *A street.*

[*Enter* Romeo, Mercutio, Benvolio, *with five or six other* Maskers; Torchbearers.]

Romeo. What, shall this speech[1] be spoke for our excuse?
Or shall we on without apology?

Benvolio. The date is out of such prolixity.[2]
We'll have no Cupid hoodwinked with a scarf,
Bearing a Tartar's painted bow of lath,
Scaring the ladies like a crowkeeper,
Nor no without-book prologue, faintly spoke
After the prompter, for our entrance;
But, let them measure us by what they will,
We'll measure them a measure and be gone.

Romeo. Give me a torch. I am not for this ambling.
Being but heavy,[3] I will bear the light.

Mercutio. Nay, gentle Romeo, we must have you dance.

Romeo. Not I, believe me. You have dancing shoes
With nimble soles; I have a soul of lead
So stakes me to the ground I cannot move.

Mercutio. You are a lover. Borrow Cupid's wings
And soar with them above a common bound.

Romeo. I am too sore enpiercèd with his shaft
To soar with his light feathers; and so bound
I cannot bound a pitch above dull woe.
Under love's heavy burden do I sink.

Mercutio. And, to sink in it, should you burden love—
Too great oppression for a tender thing.

Romeo. Is love a tender thing? It is too rough,
Too rude, too boist'rous, and it pricks like thorn.

Mercutio. If love be rough with you, be rough with love.
Prick love for pricking, and you beat love down.

NOTES

13. **But . . . fly** But I will not look harder than what you want me to.

14. **the County stays** The Count, Paris, is waiting.

1. **this speech** Romeo asks whether he and his companions, being uninvited guests, should follow custom by announcing their arrival in a speech.

2. **The . . . prolixity** Such wordiness is outdated. In the following lines, Benvolio says, in sum, "Let us forget about announcing our entrance with a show. The other guests can look over as they see fit. We will dance a while, then leave."

3. **heavy** *adj.* weighed down with sadness.

Give me a case to put my visage[4] in.
A visor for a visor![5] What care I
What curious eye doth quote deformities?[6]
Here are the beetle brows shall blush for me.

Benvolio. Come, knock and enter; and no sooner in
But every man betake him to his legs.[7]

Romeo. A torch for me! Let wantons light of heart
Tickle the senseless rushes[8] with their heels;
For I am proverbed with a grandsire phrase,[9]
I'll be a candleholder, and look on;
The game was ne'er so fair, and I am done.[10]

Mercutio. Tut! Dun's the mouse, the constable's own word![11]
If thou art Dun,[12] we'll draw thee from the mire
Of this sir-reverence love, wherein thou stickest
Up to the ears. Come, we burn daylight, ho!

Romeo. Nay, that's not so.

Mercutio. I mean, sir, in delay
We waste our lights in vain, like lights by day.
Take our good meaning, for our judgment sits
Five times in that ere once in our five wits.[13]

Romeo. And we mean well in going to this masque,
But 'tis no wit to go.

Mercutio. Why, may one ask?

Romeo. I dreamt a dream tonight.

Mercutio. And so did I.

Romeo. Well, what was yours?

Mercutio. That dreamers often lie.

Romeo. In bed asleep, while they do dream things true.

Mercutio. O, then, I see Queen Mab[14] hath been with you.
She is the fairies' midwife, and she comes
In shape no bigger than an agate stone
On the forefinger of an alderman,
Drawn with a team of little atomies[15]
Over men's noses as they lie asleep;
Her wagon spokes made of long spinners'[16] legs,
The cover, of the wings of grasshoppers;
Her traces of the smallest spider web;
Her collars, of the moonshine's wat'ry beams;
Her whip, of cricket's bone; the lash, of film;[17]
Her wagoner, a small gray-coated gnat,
Not half so big as a round little worm
Pricked from the lazy finger of a maid;
Her chariot is an empty hazelnut,
Made by the joiner squirrel or old grub,[18]

NOTES

4. **visage** *n.* mask.
5. **A visor . . . visor!** A mask for a mask—which is what my real face is like!
6. **quote deformities** notice my ugly features.
7. **betake . . . legs** start dancing.
8. **Let . . . rushes** Let fun-loving people dance on the floor coverings.
9. **proverbed . . . phrase** directed by an old saying.
10. **The game . . . done** No matter how much enjoyment may be had, I will not have any.
11. **Dun's . . . word!** Lie low like a mouse—that is what a constable waiting to make an arrest might say.
12. **Dun** proverbial name for a horse.
13. **Take . . . wits** Understand my intended meaning. That shows more intelligence than merely following what your senses perceive.

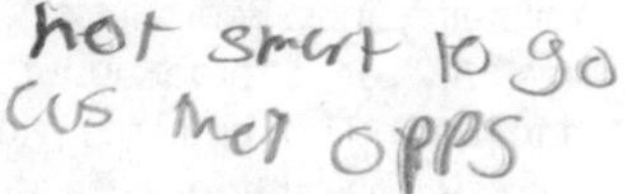

CLOSE READ

ANNOTATE: In lines 43–53, mark lines that one character begins but another ends.

QUESTION: Why does Shakespeare divide lines between characters?

CONCLUDE: How do these divided lines help to convey the nature of the characters' friendship?

14. **Queen Mab** the queen of fairyland.
15. **atomies** *n.* creatures.
16. **spinners** *n.* spiders.
17. **film** *n.* spider's thread.
18. **old grub** insect that bores holes in nuts.

Time out o' mind the fairies' coachmakers.
And in this state she gallops night by night
Through lovers' brains, and then they dream of love;
On courtiers' knees, that dream on curtsies straight;
O'er lawyers' fingers, who straight dream on fees;
O'er ladies' lips, who straight on kisses dream,
Which oft the angry Mab with blisters plagues,
Because their breath with sweetmeats[19] tainted are.
Sometimes she gallops o'er a courtier's nose,
And then dreams he of smelling out a suit;[20]
And sometime comes she with a tithe pig's[21] tail
Tickling a parson's nose as 'a lies asleep,
Then he dreams of another benefice.[22]
Sometime she driveth o'er a soldier's neck,
And then dream he of cutting foreign throats,
Of breaches, ambuscadoes,[23] Spanish blades,
Of healths[24] five fathom deep; and then anon
Drums in his ear, at which he starts and wakes,
And being thus frighted, swears a prayer or two
And sleeps again. This is that very Mab
That plats[25] the manes of horses in the night
And bakes the elflocks[26] in foul sluttish hairs,
Which once untangled much misfortune bodes.
This is the hag, when maids lie on their backs,
That presses them and learns them first to bear,
Making them women of good carriage.[27]
This is she—

Romeo. Peace, peace, Mercutio, peace!
Thou talk'st of nothing.

Mercutio. True, I talk of dreams;
Which are the children of an idle brain,
Begot of nothing but vain fantasy;
Which is as thin of substance as the air,
And more inconstant than the wind, who woos
Even now the frozen bosom of the North
And, being angered, puffs away from thence,
Turning his side to the dew-dropping South.

Benvolio. This wind you talk of blows us from ourselves.
Supper is done, and we shall come too late.

Romeo. I fear, too early; for my mind misgives
Some consequence yet hanging in the stars
Shall bitterly begin his fearful date
With this night's revels and expire the term
Of a despisèd life, closed in my breast,
By some vile forfeit of untimely death.[28]
But he that hath the steerage of my course

NOTES

19. **sweetmeats** *n.* candy.

20. **smelling . . . suit** finding someone who has a petition (suit) for the king and who will pay the courtier to gain the king's favor for the petition.

21. **tithe pig** pig donated to a parson.

22. **benefice** *n.* church appointment that included a guaranteed income.

23. **ambuscadoes** *n.* ambushes.

24. **healths** *n.* toasts ("To your health!").

25. **plats** *n.* tangles.

26. **elflocks** *n.* tangled hair.

27. **carriage** *n.* posture.

28. **my mind . . . death** My mind is fearful that some future event, fated by the stars, shall start to run its course tonight and cut my life short.

NOTES

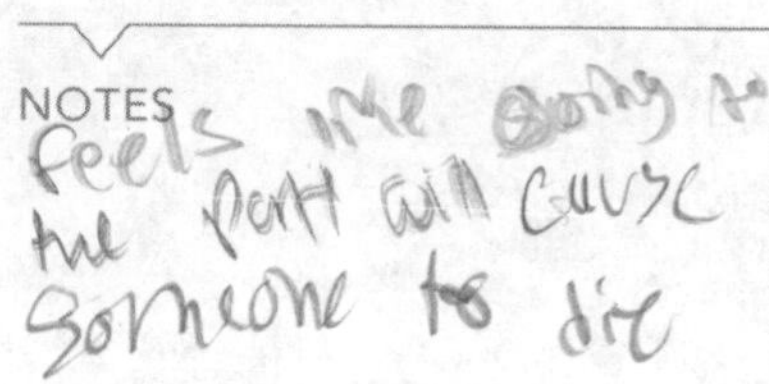

1. **trencher** *n.* wooden platter.

2. **marchpane** *n.* marzipan, a confection made of sugar and almonds.

3. **walk a bout** dance a turn.

4. **makes dainty** hesitates; acts shy.

5. **A hall** clear the floor, make room for dancing.

Direct my sail! On, lusty gentlemen!

Benvolio. Strike, drum.

[*They march about the stage, and retire to one side.*]

⌘ ⌘ ⌘

Scene v • *A hall in Capulet's house.*

[Servingmen *come forth with napkins.*]

First Servingman. Where's Potpan, that he helps not to take away? He shift a trencher![1] He scrape a trencher!

Second Servingman. When good manners shall lie all in one or two men's hands, and they unwashed too, 'tis a foul thing.

First Servingman. Away with the joint-stools, remove the court cupboard, look to the plate. Good thou, save me a piece of marchpane,[2] and, as thou loves me, let the porter let in Susan Grindstone and Nell. Anthony and Potpan!

Second Servingman. Ay, boy, ready.

First Servingman. You are looked for and called for, asked for and sought for, in the great chamber.

Third Servingman. We cannot be here and there too. Cheerly, boys! Be brisk awhile, and the longest liver take all.

[*Exit.*]

[*Enter* Capulet, *his* Wife, Juliet, Tybalt, Nurse, *and all the* Guests *and* Gentlewomen *to the* Maskers.]

Capulet. Welcome, gentlemen! Ladies that have their toes
Unplagued with corns will walk a bout[3] with you.
Ah, my mistresses, which of you all
Will now deny to dance? She that makes dainty,[4]
She I'll swear hath corns. Am I come near ye now?
Welcome, gentlemen! I have seen the day
That I have worn a visor and could tell
A whispering tale in a fair lady's ear,
Such as would please. 'Tis gone, 'tis gone, 'tis gone.
You are welcome, gentlemen! Come, musicians, play.

[*Music plays, and they dance.*]

A hall, a hall![5] Give room! And foot it, girls.
More light, you knaves, and turn the tables up,
And quench the fire; the room is grown too hot.
Ah, sirrah, this unlooked-for sport comes well.
Nay, sit; nay, sit, good cousin Capulet;
For you and I are past our dancing days.

How long is't now since last yourself and I
Were in a mask?

Second Capulet. By'r Lady, thirty years.

Capulet. What, man? 'Tis not so much, 'tis not so much;
'Tis since the nuptial of Lucentio,
Come Pentecost as quickly as it will,
Some-five-and-twenty-years, and then we masked.

Second Capulet. 'Tis more, 'tis more. His son is elder, sir;
His son is thirty.

Capulet. Will you tell me that?
His son was but a ward[6] two years ago.

Romeo. [*To a* Servingman] What lady's that which doth
enrich the hand
Of yonder knight?

Servingman. I know not, sir.

Romeo. O, she doth teach the torches to burn bright!
It seems she hangs upon the cheek of night
As a rich jewel in an Ethiop's ear—
Beauty too rich for use, for earth too dear!
So shows a snowy dove trooping with crows
As yonder lady o'er her fellows shows.
The measure done, I'll watch her place of stand
And, touching hers, make blessèd my rude hand.
Did my heart love till now? Forswear[7] it, sight!
For I ne'er saw true beauty till this night.

Tybalt. This, by his voice, should be a Montague.
Fetch me my rapier, boy. What! Dares the slave
Come hither, covered with an antic face,[8]
To fleer[9] and scorn at our solemnity?
Now, by the stock and honor of my kin,
To strike him dead I hold it not a sin.

Capulet. Why, how now, kinsman? Wherefore storm you so?

Tybalt. Uncle, this is a Montague, our foe,
A villain, that is hither come in spite
To scorn at our solemnity this night.

Capulet. Young Romeo is it?

Tybalt. 'Tis he, that villain Romeo.

Capulet. Content thee, gentle coz,[10] let him alone.
'A bears him like a portly gentleman,[11]
And, to say truth, Verona brags of him
To be a virtuous and well-governed youth.
I would not for the wealth of all this town
Here in my house do him disparagement.[12]
Therefore be patient; take no note of him.

NOTES

6. **ward** *n.* minor.

7. **Forswear** *v.* deny.

8. **antic face** strange, fantastic mask.

9. **fleer** *v.* mock.

10. **coz** a term of address for a relative.

11. **'A . . . gentleman** He behaves like a dignified gentleman.

12. **disparagement** *n.* insult.

It is my will, the which if thou respect,
Show a fair presence and put off these frowns,
An ill-beseeming semblance[13] for a feast.

Tybalt. It fits, when such a villain is a guest.
I'll not endure him.

Capulet. He shall be endured.
What, goodman[14] boy! I say, he shall. Go to![15]
Am I the master here, or you? Go to!
You'll not endure him, God shall mend my soul![16]
You'll make a mutiny among my guests!
You will set cock-a-hoop.[17] You'll be the man!

Tybalt. Why, uncle, 'tis a shame.

Capulet. Go to, go to!
You are a saucy boy. Is't so, indeed?
This trick may chance to scathe you.[18] I know what.
You must contrary me! Marry, 'tis time—
Well said, my hearts!—You are a princox[19]—go!
Be quiet, or—more light, more light!—For shame!
I'll make you quiet. What!—Cheerly, my hearts!

Tybalt. Patience perforce with willful choler meeting[20]
Makes my flesh tremble in their different greeting.
I will withdraw; but this intrusion shall,
Now seeming sweet, convert to bitt'rest gall. [*Exit.*]

Romeo. If I profane with my unworthiest hand
This holy shrine,[21] the gentle sin is this:
My lips, two blushing pilgrims, ready stand
To smooth that rough touch with a tender kiss.

Juliet. Good pilgrim, you do wrong your hand too much,
Which mannerly devotion shows in this;
For saints have hands that pilgrims' hands do touch
And palm to palm is holy palmers'[22] kiss.

Romeo. Have not saints lips, and holy palmers too?

Juliet. Ay, pilgrim, lips that they must use in prayer.

Romeo. O, then, dear saint, let lips do what hands do!
They pray; grant thou, lest faith turn to despair.

Juliet. Saints do not move,[23] though grant for prayers' sake.

Romeo. Then move not while my prayer's effect I take.
Thus from my lips, by thine my sin is purged.

[*Kisses her.*]

Juliet. Then have my lips the sin that they have took.

Romeo. Sin from my lips? O trespass sweetly urged![24]
Give me my sin again. [*Kisses her.*]

NOTES

13. ill-beseeming semblance inappropriate appearance.

14. goodman term of address for someone below the rank of gentleman.

15. Go to! expression of angry impatience.

16. God . . . soul! expression of impatience, equivalent to "God save me!"

17. You will set a cock-a-hoop You want to swagger like a barnyard rooster.

18. This . . . you This trait of yours may turn out to hurt you.

19. princox *n.* rude youngster; wise guy.

20. Patience . . . meeting enforced self-control mixing with strong anger.

21. shrine Juliet's hand

22. palmers *n.* pilgrims who at one time carried palm branches from the Holy Land.

23. move *v.* initiate involvement in earthly affairs.

24. O . . . urged! Romeo is saying, in substance, that he is happy. Juliet calls his kiss a sin, for now he can take it back—by another kiss.

Juliet. You kiss by th' book.[25]

Nurse. Madam, your mother craves a word with you.

Romeo. What is her mother?

Nurse. Marry, bachelor,
Her mother is the lady of the house,
And a good lady, and a wise and virtuous.
I nursed her daughter, that you talked withal.
I tell you, he that can lay hold of her
Shall have the chinks.[26]

Romeo. Is she a Capulet?
O dear account! My life is my foe's debt.[27]

Benvolio. Away, be gone; the sport is at the best.

Romeo. Ay, so I fear; the more is my unrest.

Capulet. Nay, gentlemen, prepare not to be gone;
We have a trifling foolish banquet towards.
Is it e'en so?[28] Why, then, I thank you all.
I thank you, honest gentlemen. Good night.
More torches here! Come on then; let's to bed.
Ah, sirrah, by my fay,[29] it waxes late:
I'll to my rest. [*Exit all but* Juliet *and* Nurse.]

Juliet. Come hither, nurse. What is yond gentleman?

Nurse. The son and heir of old Tiberio.

Juliet. What's he that now is going out of door?

Nurse. Marry, that, I think, be young Petruchio.

Juliet. What's he that follows here, that would not dance?

NOTES

25. by th' book as if you were following a manual of courtly love.

26. chinks *n.* cash.

27. My life . . . debt Since Juliet is a Capulet, Romeo's life is at the mercy of his family.

28. Is . . . so? Is it the case that you really must leave?

29. fay *n.* faith.

NOTES

30. **Prodigious** *adj.* monstrous; foretelling misfortune.

Nurse. I know not.

Juliet. Go ask his name—If he is married,
My grave is like to be my wedding bed.

Nurse. His name is Romeo, and a Montague,
The only son of your great enemy.

Juliet. My only love sprung from my only hate!
Too early seen unknown, and known too late!
Prodigious[30] birth of love it is to me
That I must love a loathèd enemy.

Nurse. What's this? What's this?

Juliet. A rhyme I learnt even now.
Of one I danced withal. [*One calls within,* "Juliet."]

Nurse. Anon, anon!
Come, let's away; the strangers all are gone. [*Exit all.*]

Comprehension Check

Complete the following items after you finish your first read.

1. What is troubling Romeo at the beginning of the play?

Romeo is in love

2. What is Paris's relationship to Juliet?

They are [illegible] feast

3. What does Lord Capulet stop Tybalt from doing at the feast?

he stops tybalt from fighting romeo

4. What does Romeo say a kiss from Juliet will take from him?

his sins

5. **Notebook** Confirm your understanding of the text by writing a summary.

romeo is love sick so he [illegible] the capulets party. he meets Juliet and [illegible]

Close Read the Text

Reread what the Prince says when he finds the Capulets and Montagues quarreling again (Act I, Scene i, lines 77–89). How does the Prince describe the weapons of the citizens of Verona? What does this show about the feud's effect on the community?

THE TRAGEDY OF ROMEO AND JULIET, ACT I

Analyze the Text

CITE TEXTUAL EVIDENCE to support your answers.

Notebook Respond to these questions.

1. (a) What do you know about Romeo's and Juliet's lives at this point in the play? Explain, citing details from the play that support your answer. (b) **Compare and Contrast** How are their circumstances both similar and different? Explain.
2. **Analyze** What threats to Romeo and Juliet's love are evident in Act I? Support your answer with details from the play.
3. (a) What information about the two feuding households is presented in the Prologue? (b) **Connect** How does Juliet's comment in Act I, Scene v, lines 138–141, echo the Prologue? Explain your response.
4. **Essential Question:** ***Do we determine our own destinies?*** What have you learned about destiny by reading Act I of *The Tragedy of Romeo and Juliet*?

Tool Kit
Close-Read Guide and Model Annotation

WORD NETWORK

Add interesting words related to destiny from the text to your Word Network.

LANGUAGE DEVELOPMENT

Concept Vocabulary

mutiny	transgression	heretics

Why These Words? These concept vocabulary words communicate a violation of order or authority. What other words in Act I connect to this concept?

Practice

Notebook Confirm your understanding of these words by using each one in a sentence.

Word Study

Latin Prefix: *trans-* The Latin prefix *trans-* means "across," "beyond," or "through." In the play, Romeo describes his friend's sympathy for him as love's *transgression*. The word suggests that love has crossed a boundary and unfairly involved his friend. Find another word that includes this prefix. Write down the word and its meaning.

STANDARDS

Language
Identify and correctly use patterns of word changes that indicate different meanings or parts of speech.

THE TRAGEDY OF ROMEO AND JULIET, ACT I

Analyze Craft and Structure

Elements of Drama The two most important elements of drama are **dialogue**, the conversation between the characters, and **stage directions**, the notes that describe how the work should be performed. Each plays an important role in conveying meaning in a drama.

In drama, dialogue generally follows the name of the speaker:

> **Benvolio.** My noble uncle, do you know the cause?
> **Montague.** I neither know it nor can learn of him.

Dialogue reveals characters' personalities and relationships, advances the action, and captures the language of the time and place in which a play is set.

Stage directions describe scenes, lighting, sound, and characters' actions. Stage directions are usually italicized and enclosed in brackets or parentheses.

> *Scene i. Verona. A public place.*
> [*Enter* Sampson *and* Gregory, *with swords and bucklers, of the house of Capulet.*]

As you reread portions of the play, notice how the dialogue and stage directions help you "hear" and "see" the action in your mind.

STANDARDS

Reading Literature

- Analyze how complex characters develop over the course of a text, interact with other characters, and advance the plot or develop the theme.
- Analyze how an author's choices concerning how to structure a text, order events within it, and manipulate time create such effects as mystery, tension, or surprise

Practice

CITE TEXTUAL EVIDENCE to support your answers.

Notebook Respond to these questions.

1. Cite two examples of dialogue in Act I, Scene i, that show Benvolio's peace-making personality.
2. Use the chart to analyze what the dialogue among the Nurse, Juliet, and Lady Capulet in Act I, Scene iii, reveals about each character. Record important lines, and determine what those lines reveal about the character speaking them.

CHARACTER	DIALOGUE	WHAT IT REVEALS
Juliet	It's a honer that I dream not of	She doesnt want to got married
Nurse	his name is romeo and a montague	romeo is the enemy
Lady Capulet	the valient paris seeks for his love	She thinks highly of paris

3. **(a)** Identify three examples of stage directions from the text that do more than simply dictate characters' movements on and off stage. **(b)** Explain what each direction shows about the characters and the action.

Author's Style

Figurative Language An **oxymoron** is a figure of speech that combines contradictory, or opposing, ideas. An oxymoron may help create meaning in a text by communicating a complicated truth, or it can simply display an absurd contradiction for effect. The word *bittersweet* is a perfect example; a bittersweet moment combines feelings of happiness and sadness.

In *The Tragedy of Romeo and Juliet*, Shakespeare uses oxymora (the plural form of *oxymoron*) to help communicate characters' feelings.

OXYMORON	MEANING/EFFECT
Romeo. . . . Why, then, O brawling love! O loving hate, O anything, of nothing first created.	These examples of oxymoron show Romeo's conflicting feelings about love and that love can lead to negative feelings.

Read It

Mark examples of oxymoron in this passage from Act I of *The Tragedy of Romeo and Juliet*. Then, describe what they communicate about love and their effect on the text.

DIALOGUE	MEANING/EFFECT
Romeo. . . . O heavy lightness, serious vanity, Misshapen chaos of well-seeming forms, Feather of lead, bright smoke, cold fire, sick health, Still-waking sleep, that is not what it is!	shows how much he emphasized

Write It

Write a paragraph that includes at least two oxymora you made up on your own. Romeo & Juliet is a story very heart breaking

EVIDENCE LOG

Before moving on to a new selection, go to your Evidence Log and record what you learned from Act I of *The Tragedy of Romeo and Juliet.*

STANDARDS

Language
Interpret figures of speech in context and analyze their role in the text.

Playwright

William Shakespeare

The Tragedy of Romeo and Juliet, Act II

Concept Vocabulary

You will encounter the following words as you read Act II of *The Tragedy of Romeo and Juliet.* Before reading, note how familiar you are with each word. Then, rank the words in order from most familiar (1) to least familiar (3).

WORD	YOUR RANKING
cunning	
counterfeit	
confidence	

After completing the first read, come back to the concept vocabulary and review your rankings. Mark changes to your original rankings as needed.

First Read DRAMA

Apply these strategies as you conduct your first read. You will have an opportunity to complete the close-read notes after your first read.

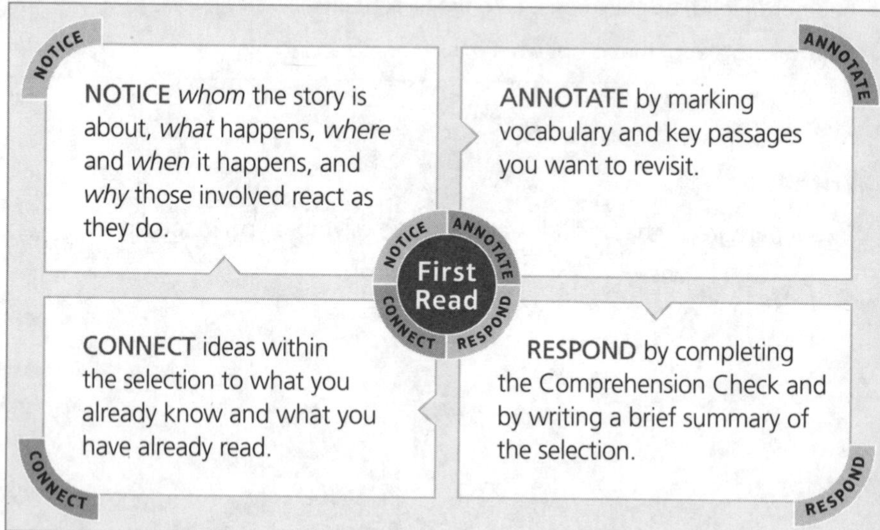
NOTICE
NOTICE *whom* the story is about, *what* happens, *where* and *when* it happens, and *why* those involved react as they do.
ANNOTATE
ANNOTATE by marking vocabulary and key passages you want to revisit.
NOTICE ANNOTATE First Read CONNECT RESPOND
CONNECT ideas within the selection to what you already know and what you have already read.
CONNECT
RESPOND by completing the Comprehension Check and by writing a brief summary of the selection.
RESPOND

Tool Kit
First-Read Guide and Model Annotation

STANDARDS

Reading Literature
By the end of grade 9, read and comprehend literature, including stories, dramas, and poems, in the grades 9–10 text complexity band proficiently, with scaffolding as needed at the high end of the range.

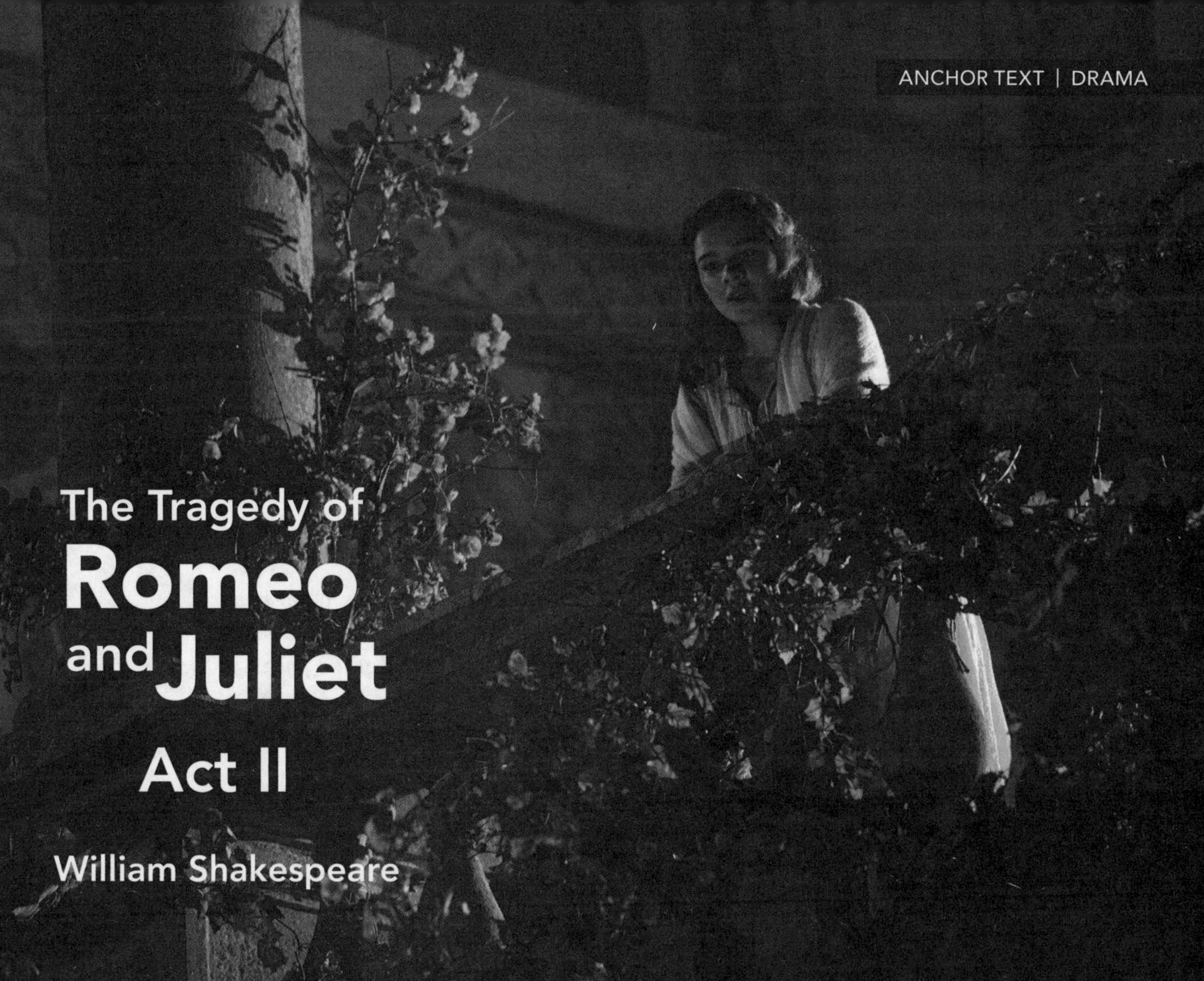

The Tragedy of Romeo and Juliet Act II

William Shakespeare

REVIEW AND ANTICIPATE

Act I reveals a bitter, long-standing feud between the Montagues and the Capulets. It also introduces the play's title characters, who meet at a party and immediately fall in love, only to discover that they come from opposing sides of the feud. As you read Act II, think about the choices Romeo and Juliet make as both their love and the conflicts they face intensify.

Prologue

[*Enter* Chorus.]

Chorus. Now old desire[1] doth in his deathbed lie,
And young affection gapes to be his heir.[2]
That fair[3] for which love groaned for and would die,
With tender Juliet matched, is now not fair.
Now Romeo is beloved and loves again,
Alike bewitched[4] by the charm of looks;
But to his foe supposed he must complain,[5]
And she steal love's sweet bait from fearful hooks.
Being held a foe, he may not have access
To breathe such vows as lovers use to swear,

NOTES

1. **old desire** Romeo's love for Rosaline.
2. **young . . . heir** Romeo's new love for Juliet is eager to replace his love for Rosaline.
3. **fair** beautiful woman (Rosaline).
4. **Alike bewitched** Both Romeo and Juliet are enchanted.
5. **complain** *v.* address his words of love.

And she as much in love, her means much less
 To meet her new belovèd anywhere;
But passion lends them power, time means to meet,
Temp'ring extremities with extreme sweet.[6]
[*Exit.*]

NOTES

6. **Temp'ring . . . sweet** easing their difficulties with great delights.

⌘⌘⌘

Scene i • *Near Capulet's orchard.*

[*Enter* Romeo *alone.*]

Romeo. Can I go forward when my heart is here?
Turn back, dull earth,[1] and find thy center[2] out.
[*Enter* Benvolio *with* Mercutio. Romeo *retires.*]

1. **dull earth** lifeless body.
2. **center** heart, or possibly soul (Juliet).

Benvolio. Romeo! My cousin Romeo! Romeo!

Mercutio. He is wise.
And, on my life, hath stol'n him home to bed.

Benvolio. He ran this way and leapt this orchard wall.
Call, good Mercutio.

Mercutio. Nay, I'll conjure[3] too.
Romeo! Humors! Madman! Passion! Lover!
Appear thou in the likeness of a sigh;
Speak but one rhyme, and I am satisfied!
Cry but "Ay me!" Pronounce but "love" and "dove";
Speak to my gossip[4] Venus one fair word,
One nickname for her purblind son and heir,
Young Abraham Cupid, he that shot so true
When King Cophetua loved the beggar maid!
He heareth not, he stirreth not, he moveth not;
The ape is dead,[5] and I must conjure him.
I conjure thee by Rosaline's bright eyes,
By her high forehead and her scarlet lip,
By her fine foot, straight leg, and quivering thigh,
And the demesnes that there adjacent lie,
That in thy likeness thou appear to us!

3. **conjure** *v.* recite a spell to make Romeo appear.
4. **gossip** *n.* good friend
5. **The ape is dead.** Romeo, like a trained monkey, seems to be playing.

Benvolio. And if he hear thee, thou wilt anger him.

Mercutio. This cannot anger him. 'Twould anger him
To raise a spirit in his mistress' circle
Of some strange nature, letting it there stand
Till she had laid it and conjured it down.
That were some spite; my invocation
Is fair and honest; in his mistress' name,
I conjure only but to raise up him.

Benvolio. Come, he hath hid himself among these trees
To be consorted[6] with the humorous[7] night.
Blind is his love and best befits the dark.

Mercutio. If love be blind, love cannot hit the mark.
Now will he sit under a medlar[8] tree
And wish his mistress were that kind of fruit
As maids call medlars when they laugh alone.
O, Romeo, that she were, O that she were
And open *et cetera*, thou a pop'rin pear!
Romeo, good night. I'll to my truckle bed;[9]
This field bed is too cold for me to sleep.
Come, shall we go?

Benvolio. Go then, for 'tis in vain
To seek him here that means not to be found.
[*Exit with others.*]

⌘ ⌘ ⌘

Scene ii • *Capulet's orchard.*

Romeo. [*Coming forward*] He jests at scars that never felt a wound.
[*Enter* Juliet *at a window.*]
But soft! What light through yonder window breaks?
It is the East, and Juliet is the sun!
Arise, fair sun, and kill the envious moon,
Who is already sick and pale with grief
That thou her maid art far more fair than she.
Be not her maid, since she is envious.
Her vestal livery[1] is but sick and green,
And none but fools do wear it. Cast it off.
It is my lady! O, it is my love!
O, that she knew she were!
She speaks, yet she says nothing. What of that?
Her eye discourses; I will answer it.
I am too bold; 'tis not to me she speaks.
Two of the fairest stars in all the heaven,
Having some business, do entreat her eyes
To twinkle in their spheres[2] till they return.
What if her eyes were there, they in her head?
The brightness of her cheek would shame those stars
As daylight doth a lamp; her eyes in heaven
Would through the airy region stream so bright
That birds would sing and think it were not night.

NOTES

6. **consorted** *v.* associated.

7. **humorous** *adj.* humid; moody, like a lover.

8. **medlar** *n.* applelike fruit.

9. **truckle bed** trundlebed, placed under a larger bed when not in use.

CLOSE READ

ANNOTATE: In lines 2–22, mark words and phrases that relate to brightness and light.

QUESTION: What connection does this language make between Juliet and the skies?

CONCLUDE: What does this famous speech suggest about Romeo's feelings for Juliet?

1. **livery** *n.* clothing or costume worn by a servant.

2. **spheres** *n.* orbits.

NOTES

See how she leans her cheek upon that hand,
O, that I were a glove upon that hand,
That I might touch that cheek!

Juliet. Ay me!

Romeo. She speaks.
O, speak again, bright angel, for thou art
As glorious to this night, being o'er my head,
As is a winged messenger of heaven
Unto the white-upturned wond'ring eyes
Of mortals that fall back to gaze on him
When he bestrides the lazy puffing clouds
And sails upon the bosom of the air.

Juliet. O Romeo. Romeo! Wherefore art thou Romeo?[3]
Deny thy father and refuse they name;
Or, if thou will not, be but sworn my love,
And I'll no longer be a Capulet.

Romeo. [*Aside*] Shall I hear more, or shall I speak at this?

Juliet. 'Tis but thy name that is my enemy.
Thou art thyself, though not[4] a Montague.
What's Montague? It is nor hand, nor foot,
Nor arm, nor face, nor any other part
Belonging to a man. O, be some other name!
What's in a name? That which we call a rose
By any other name would smell as sweet.
So Romeo would, were he not Romeo called,
Retain that dear perfection which he owes[5]
Without that title. Romeo, doff[6] thy name;
And for thy name, which is no part of thee,
Take all myself.

Romeo. I take thee at thy word.
Call me but love, and I'll be new baptized;
Henceforth I never will be Romeo.

Juliet. What man art thou, thus bescreened in night,
So stumblest on my counsel?[7]

Romeo. By a name
I know not how to tell thee who I am.
My name, dear saint, is hateful to myself
Because it is an enemy to thee.
Had I it written, I would tear the word.

Juliet. My ears have yet not drunk a hundred words
Of thy tongue's uttering, yet I know the sound.
Art thou not Romeo, and a Montague?

Romeo. Neither, fair maid, if either thee dislike.

Juliet. How camest thou hither, tell me, and wherefore?
The orchard walls are high and hard to climb,

3. **Wherefore . . . Romeo?** Why are you Romeo—a Montague?

4. **though not** even if you were not.

5. **owes** *v.* owns; possesses.

6. **doff** *v.* remove.

7. **counsel** *n.* secret thoughts.

And the place death, considering who thou art,
If any of my kinsmen find thee here.

Romeo. With love's light wings did I o'erperch[8] these walls;
For stony limits cannot hold love out,
And for what love can do, that dares love attempt.
Therefore thy kinsmen are no stop to me.

Juliet. If they do see thee, they will murder thee.

Romeo. Alack, there lies more peril in thine eye
Than twenty of their swords! Look thou but sweet,
And I am proof[9] against their enmity.

Juliet. I would not for the world they saw thee here.

Romeo. I have night's cloak to hide me from their eyes;
And but[10] thou love me, let them find me here.
My life were better ended by their hate
Than death proroguèd,[11] wanting of thy love.

Juliet. By whose direction found'st thou out this place?

Romeo. By love, that first did prompt me to inquire.
He lent me counsel, and I lent him eyes.
I am no pilot; yet, wert thou as far
As that vast shore washed with the farthest sea,
I should adventure[12] for such merchandise.

Juliet. Thou knowest the mask of night is on my face;
Else would a maiden blush bepaint my cheek
For that which thou hast heard me speak tonight.
Fain would I dwell on form[13]—fain, fain deny
What I have spoke; but farewell compliment![14]
Dost thou love me? I know thou wilt say "Ay";
And I will take thy word. Yet, if thou swear'st,
Thou mayst prove false. At lovers' perjuries,
They say Jove laughs. O gentle Romeo,
If thou dost love, pronounce it faithfully.
Or if thou thinkest I am too quickly won,
I'll frown and be perverse[15] and say thee nay,
So thou wilt woo; but else, not for the world.
In truth, fair Montague, I am too fond,[16]
And therefore thou mayst think my havior light;[17]
But trust me, gentleman, I'll prove more true
Than those that have more **cunning** to be strange.[18]
I should have been more strange, I must confess,
But that thou overheard'st, ere I was ware,
My true-love passion. Therefore pardon me,
And not impute this yielding to light love,
Which the dark night hath so discoverèd.[19]

Romeo. Lady, by yonder blessèd moon I vow,
That tips with silver all these fruit-tree tops—

NOTES

8. **o'erperch** *v.* fly over.

9. **proof** *v.* protected, as by armor.

10. **And but** unless.

11. **proroguèd** (proh ROHG ehd) *v.* postponed.

12. **adventure** *v.* risk a long journey, like a sea adventurer.

13. **Fain . . . form** eagerly would I follow convention (by acting reserved).

14. **compliment** *n.* conventional behavior.

15. **be perverse** act contrary to my true feelings.

16. **fond** *adj.* affectionate.

17. **my havior light** my behavior immodest or unserious.

cunning (KUHN ihng) *n.* skill in deception

18. **strange** *adj.* distant and cold.

19. **discoverèd** *v.* revealed.

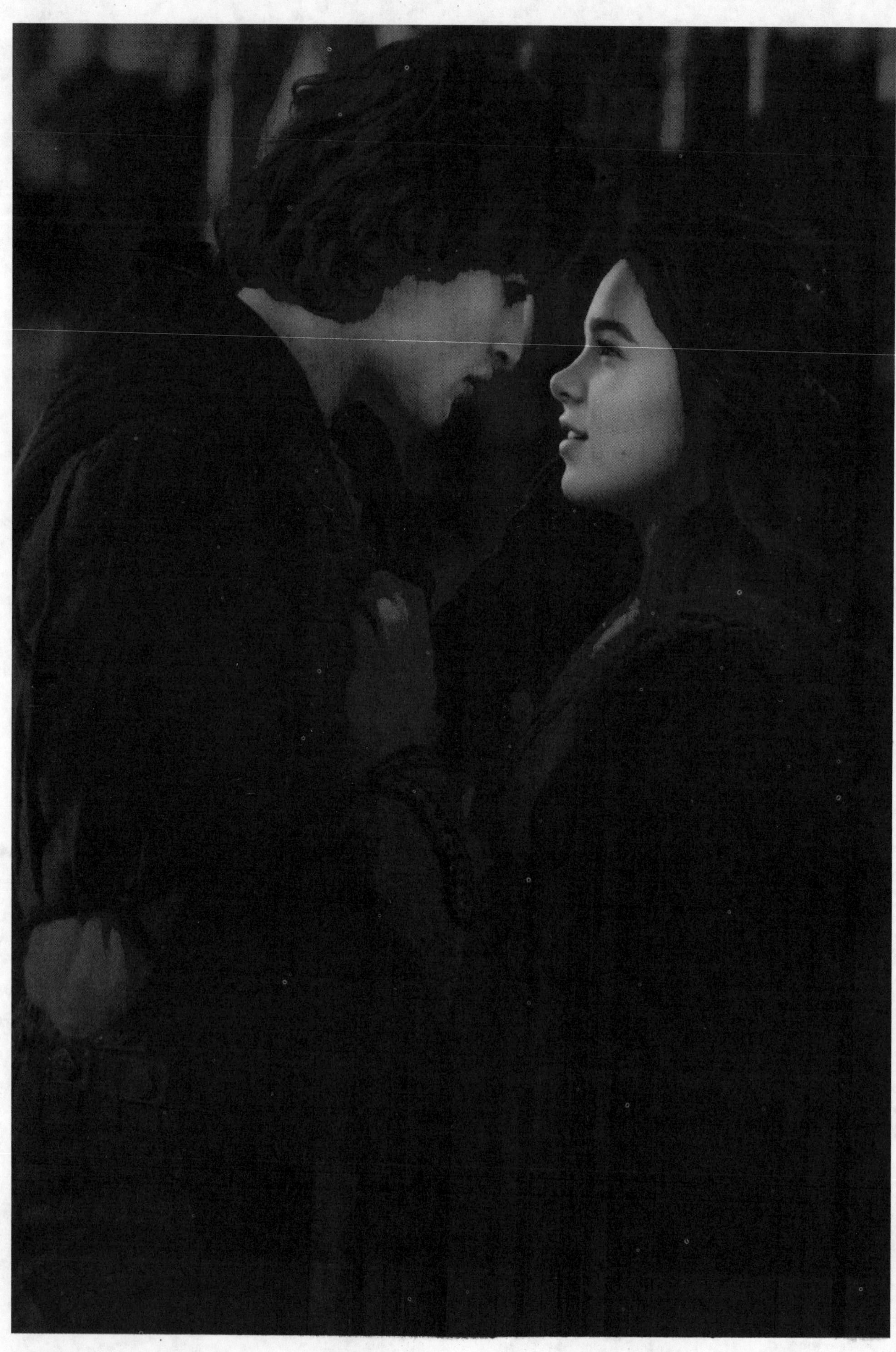

Juliet. O, swear not by the moon, th' inconstant moon,
That monthly changes in her circle orb,
Lest that thy love prove likewise variable.

Romeo. What shall I swear by?

Juliet. Do not swear at all;
Or if thou wilt, swear by thy gracious self,
Which is the god of my idolatry,
And I'll believe thee.

Romeo. If my heart's dear love—

Juliet. Well, do not swear. Although I joy in thee,
I have no joy of this contract[20] tonight.
It is too rash, too unadvised, too sudden;
Too like the lightning, which doth cease to be
Ere one can say it lightens. Sweet, good night!
This bud of love, by summer's ripening breath,
May prove a beauteous flow'r when next we meet.
Good night, good night! As sweet repose and rest
Come to thy heart as that within my breast!

Romeo. O, wilt thou leave me so unsatisfied?

Juliet. What satisfaction canst thou have tonight?

Romeo. Th'exchange of thy love's faithful vow for mine.

Juliet. I gave thee mine before thou didst request it;
And yet I would it were to give again.

Romeo. Wouldst thou withdraw it? For what purpose, love?

Juliet. But to be frank[21] and give it thee again.
And yet I wish but for the thing I have.
My bounty[22] is as boundless as the sea,
My love as deep; the more I give to thee,
The more I have, for both are infinite.

[Nurse *calls within.*]

I hear some noise within. Dear love, adieu!
Anon, good nurse! Sweet Montague, be true.
Stay but a little, I will come again. [*Exit.*]

Romeo. O blessèd, blessèd night! I am afeard,
Being in night, all this is but a dream,
Too flattering-sweet to be substantial.[23]

[*Enter* Juliet *again.*]

Juliet. Three words, dear Romeo, and good night indeed.
If that thy bent[24] of love be honorable,
Thy purpose marriage, send me word tomorrow,
By one that I'll procure to come to thee,
Where and what time thou wilt perform the rite;
And all my fortunes at thy foot I'll lay

NOTES

20. contract *n.* betrothal.

CLOSE READ

ANNOTATE: In lines 116–124, mark repeated words and phrases.

QUESTION: Why do you think Juliet repeats herself so often in this short speech?

CONCLUDE: What is the effect of this repetition?

21. frank *adj.* generous.

22. bounty *n.* what I have to give.

23. substantial *adj.* real.

24. bent *n.* purpose; intention.

NOTES

25. **By and by** at once.

26. **strife** *n.* efforts.

27. **tassel gentle** male falcon.

28. **Bondage is hoarse** Being bound in by my family restricts my speech.

29. **Echo** In classical mythology, the nymph Echo, unable to win the love of Narcissus, wasted away in a cave until nothing was left of her but her voice.

30. **wanton's** spoiled, playful child's.

31. **gyves** (jyvz) *n.* chains.

And follow thee my lord throughout the world.

Nurse. [*Within*] Madam!

Juliet. I come anon.—But if thou meanest not well,
I do beseech thee—

Nurse. [*Within*] Madam!

Juliet. By and by[25] I come.—
To cease thy strife[26] and leave me to my grief.
Tomorrow I will send.

Romeo. So thrive my soul—

Juliet. A thousand times good night! [*Exit.*]

Romeo. A thousand times the worse, to want thy light!
Love goes toward love as schoolboys from their books;
But love from love, toward school with heavy looks.
[*Enter* Juliet *again.*]

Juliet. Hist! Romeo, hist! O for a falc'ner's voice
To lure this tassel gentle[27] back again!
Bondage is hoarse[28] and may not speak aloud,
Else would I tear the cave where Echo[29] lies
And make her airy tongue more hoarse than mine
With repetition of "My Romeo!"

Romeo. It is my soul that calls upon my name.
How silver-sweet sound lovers' tongues by night,
Like softest music to attending ears!

Juliet. Romeo!

Romeo. My sweet?

Juliet. What o'clock tomorrow
Shall I send to thee?

Romeo. By the hour of nine.

Juliet. I will not fail. 'Tis twenty year till then.
I have forgot why I did call thee back.

Romeo. Let me stand here till thou remember it.

Juliet. I shall forget, to have thee still stand there,
Rememb'ring how I love thy company.

Romeo. And I'll stay, to have thee still forget,
Forgetting any other home but this.

Juliet. 'Tis almost morning. I would have thee gone—
And yet no farther than a wanton's[30] bird,
That lets it hop a little from his hand,
Like a poor prisoner in his twisted gyves,[31]
And with a silken thread plucks it back again,
So loving-jealous of his liberty.

Romeo. I would I were thy bird.

Juliet. Sweet, so would I.
Yet I should kill thee with much cherishing.
Good night, good night! Parting is such sweet sorrow
That I shall say good night till it be morrow. [*Exit.*]

Romeo. Sleep dwell upon thine eyes, peace in thy breast!
Would I were sleep and peace, so sweet to rest!
Hence will I to my ghostly friar's[32] close cell,[33]
His help to crave and my dear hap[34] to tell. [*Exit.*]

NOTES

32. **ghostly friar's** spiritual father's.
33. **close cell** small room.
34. **dear hap** good fortune.

⌘⌘⌘

Scene iii • *Friar Lawrence's cell.*

[*Enter* Friar Lawrence *alone, with a basket.*]

Friar. The gray-eyed morn smiles on the frowning night,
Check'ring the eastern clouds with streaks of light;
And fleckèd darkness like a drunkard reels
From forth day's path and Titan's burning wheels.
Now, ere the sun advance his burning eye
The day to cheer and night's dank dew to dry,
I must upfill this osier cage of ours
With baleful weeds and precious-juicèd flowers.
The earth that's nature's mother is her tomb.
What is her burying grave, that is her womb;
And from her womb children of divers kind
We sucking on her natural bosom find,
Many for many virtues excellent,
None but for some, and yet all different.
O, mickle[1] is the powerful grace[2] that lies
In plants, herbs, stones, and their true qualities;
For naught so vile that on the earth doth live
But to the earth some special good doth give;
Nor aught so good but, strained[3] from that fair use,
Revolts from true birth,[4] stumbling on abuse.
Virtue itself turns vice, being misapplied,
And vice sometime by action dignified.
[*Enter* Romeo.]

Within the infant rind[5] of this weak flower
Poison hath residence and medicine power;[6]
For this, being smelt, with that part cheers each part;[7]
Being tasted, stays all senses with the heart.[8]
Two such opposèd kings encamp them still[9]
In man as well as herbs—grace and rude will;
And where the worser is predominant,
Full soon the canker[10] death eats up that plant.

CLOSE READ

ANNOTATE: Mark examples of full rhyme at the ends of lines in the Friar's opening speech.

QUESTION: Why does Shakespeare have the Friar speak in rhymed verse?

CONCLUDE: How does the use of rhyme add to the portrayal of the Friar's character?

1. **mickle** *adj.* great.
2. **grace** *n.* divine power.
3. **strained** *v.* turned away.
4. **Revolts . . . birth** conflicts with its real purpose.
5. **infant rind** tender skin.
6. **and medicine power** and medicinal quality has power.
7. **with . . . part** with that quality—odor—revives each part of the body.
8. **stays . . . heart** kills (stops the working of the five senses along with the heart).
9. **still** *adv.* always.
10. **canker** *n.* destructive caterpillar.

NOTES

11. ***Benedicite!*** God bless you!

12. distemperèd head troubled mind.

13. unstuffed *adj.* not filled with cares.

14. distemp'rature illness.

15. physic (FIHZ ihk) *n.* medicine.

16. My . . . foe my plea also helps my enemy (Juliet, a Capulet).

17. and . . . drift and simple in your speech.

18. Riddling . . . shrift a confusing confession will get you uncertain forgiveness. The Friar means that unless Romeo speaks clearly, he will not get clear and direct advice.

19. And . . . save and we are united in every way, except for (save).

20. brine *n.* salt water (tears).

Romeo. Good morrow, father.

Friar. *Benedicite!*[11]
What early tongue so sweet saluteth me?
Young son, it argues a distemperèd head[12]
So soon to bid good morrow to thy bed.
Care keeps his watch in every old man's eye,
And where care lodges, sleep will never lie;
But where unbruisèd youth with unstuffed[13] brain
Doth couch his limbs, there golden sleep doth reign,
Therefore thy earliness doth me assure
Thou art uproused with some distemp'rature;[14]
Or if not so, then here I hit it right—
Our Romeo hath not been in bed tonight.

Romeo. That last is true. The sweeter rest was mine.

Friar. God pardon sin! Wast thou with Rosaline?

Romeo. With Rosaline, my ghostly father? No.
I have forgot that name and that name's woe.

Friar. That's my good son! But where hast thou been then?

Romeo. I'll tell thee ere thou ask it me again.
I have been feasting with mine enemy,
Where on a sudden one hath wounded me
That's by me wounded. Both our remedies
Within thy help and holy physic[15] lies.
I bear no hatred, blessed man, for, lo,
My intercession likewise steads my foe.[16]

Friar. Be plain, good son, and homely in thy drift.[17]
Riddling confession finds but riddling shrift.[18]

Romeo. Then plainly know my heart's dear love is set
On the fair daughter of rich Capulet;
As mine on hers, so hers is set on mine,
And all combined, save[19] what thou must combine
By holy marriage. When and where and how
We met, we wooed, and made exchange of vow,
I'll tell thee as we pass; but this I pray,
That thou consent to marry us today.

Friar. Holy Saint Francis! What a change is here!
Is Rosaline, that thou didst love so dear,
So soon forsaken? Young men's love then lies
Not truly in their hearts, but in their eyes.
Jesu Maria! What a deal of brine[20]
Hath washed thy sallow cheeks for Rosaline!
How much salt water thrown away in waste
To season love, that of it doth not taste!
The sun not yet thy sighs from heaven clears,
Thy old groans ring yet in mine ancient ears.

Lo, here upon thy cheek the stain doth sit
Of an old tear that is not washed off yet.
If e'er thou wast thyself, and these woes thine,
Thou and these woes were all for Rosaline.
And art thou changed? Pronounce this sentence then:
Women may fall[21] when there's no strength[22] in men.

Romeo. Thou chidst me oft for loving Rosaline.

Friar. For doting,[23] not for loving, pupil mine.

Romeo. And badst[24] me bury love.

Friar. Not in a grave
To lay one in, another out to have.

Romeo. I pray thee chide me not. Her I love now
Doth grace[25] for grace and love for love allow.[26]
The other did not so.

Friar. O, she knew well
Thy love did read by rote, that could not spell.[27]
But come, young waverer, come go with me.
In one respect I'll thy assistant be;
For this alliance may so happy prove
To turn your households' rancor[28] to pure love.

Romeo. O, let us hence! I stand on[29] sudden haste.

Friar. Wisely and slow. They stumble that run fast. [*Exit all.*]

⌘ ⌘ ⌘

Scene iv • *A street.*

[*Enter* Benvolio *and* Mercutio.]

Mercutio. Where the devil should this Romeo be?
Came he not home tonight?

Benvolio. Not to his father's. I spoke with his man.

Mercutio. Why, that same pale hardhearted wench, that Rosaline,
Torments him so that he will sure run mad.

Benvolio. Tybalt, the kinsman to old Capulet,
Hath sent a letter to his father's house.

Mercutio. A challenge, on my life.

Benvolio. Romeo will answer it.

Mercutio. Any man that can write may answer a letter.

Benvolio. Nay, he will answer the letter's master, how he dares, being dared.

NOTES

21. **fall** *v.* be weak or inconstant.
22. **strength** *n.* constancy; stability.
23. **doting** *v.* being infatuated.
24. **badst** *v.* urged.
25. **grace** *n.* favor.
26. **allow** *v.* give.
27. **Thy . . . spell** your love recited words from memory with no understanding of them.
28. **rancor** *n.* hatred.
29. **stand on** insist on.

NOTES

1. **blind bow-boy's butt-shaft** Cupid's blunt arrow.
2. **Prince of Cats** Tybalt, or a variation of it, is the name of the cat in medieval stories of Reynard the Fox.
3. **captain of compliments** master of formal behavior.
4. **as you sing pricksong** with attention to precision.
5. **rests . . . rests** observes all formalities.
6. **button** *n.* exact spot on the opponent's shirt.
7. **first house** finest school of fencing.
8. **the first and second cause** reasons that would cause a gentleman challenge another to a duel.
9. **passado! . . . punto reverso! . . . hay!** lunge . . . backhanded stroke . . . home thrust.
10. **The pox . . . accent** May the plague strike these absurd characters with their phony manners.
11. **these pardon-me's** these men who are always saying "Pardon me."
12. **Without . . . herring** worn out.
13. **numbers** *n.* verses of love poems.

counterfeit (KOWN tuhr fiht) *n.* something made to deceive

14. **slip** *n.* escape. Slip is also a term for a counterfeit coin.

15. **hams** *n.* hips.

Mercutio. Alas, poor Romeo, he is already dead; stabbed with a white wench's black eye; run through the ear with a love song; the very pin of his heart cleft with the blind bow-boy's butt-shaft;[1] and is he a man to encounter Tybalt?

Benvolio. Why, what is Tybalt?

Mercutio. More than Prince of Cats.[2] O, he's the courageous captain of compliments.[3] He fights as you sing pricksong[4]—keeps time, distance, and proportion; he rests his minim rests,[5] one, two, and the third in your bosom! The very butcher of a silk button,[6] a duelist, a duelist! A gentleman of the very first house,[7] of the first and second cause.[8] Ah, the immortal *passado*! The *punto reverso*! The hay![9]

Benvolio. The what?

Mercutio. The pox of such antic, lisping, affecting fantasticoes—these new tuners of accent![10] "By Jesu, a very good blade! A very tall man! A very good whore!" Why, is not this a lamentable thing, grandsir, that we should be thus afflicted with these strange flies, these fashionmongers, these pardon-me's,[11] who stand so much on the new form that they cannot sit at ease on the old bench? O, their bones, their bones!
[*Enter* Romeo.]

Benvolio. Here comes Romeo! Here comes Romeo!

Mercutio. Without his roe, like a dried herring.[12] O flesh, flesh, how art thou fishified! Now is he for the numbers[13] that Petrarch flowed in. Laura, to his lady, was a kitchen wench (marry, she had a better love to berhyme her), Dido a dowdy, Cleopatra a gypsy, Helen and Hero hildings and harlots, Thisbe a gray eye or so, but not to the purpose. Signior Romeo, *bonjour*! there's a French salutation to your French slop. You gave us the **counterfeit** fairly last night.

Romeo. Good morrow to you both. What counterfeit did I give you?

Mercutio. The slip,[14] sir, the slip. Can you not conceive?

Romeo. Pardon, good Mercutio. My business was great, and in such a case as mine a man may strain courtesy.

Mercutio. That's as much as to say, such a case as yours constrains a man to bow in the hams.[15]

Romeo. Meaning, to curtsy.

Mercutio. Thou hast most kindly hit it.

Romeo. A most courteous exposition.

Mercutio. Nay, I am the very pink of courtesy.

Romeo. Pink for flower.

Mercutio. Right.

Romeo. Why, then is my pump[16] well-flowered.

Mercutio. Sure wit, follow me this jest now till thou hast worn out thy pump, that, when the single sole of it is worn, the jest may remain, after the wearing, solely singular.[17]

Romeo. O single-soled jest, solely singular for the singleness![18]

Mercutio. Come between us, good Benvolio! My wits faints.

Romeo. Swits and spurs, swits and spurs; or I'll cry a match.[19]

Mercutio. Nay, if our wits run the wild-goose chase, I am done; for thou hast more of the wild goose in one of thy wits than, I am sure, I have in my whole five. Was I with you there for the goose?

Romeo. Thou wast never with me for anything when thou wast not there for the goose.

Mercutio. I will bite thee by the ear for that jest.

Romeo. Nay, good goose, bite not!

Mercutio. Thy wit is a very bitter sweeting;[20] it is a most sharp sauce.

Romeo. And is it not, then, well served in to a sweet goose?

Mercutio. O, here's a wit of cheveril,[21] that stretches from an inch narrow to an ell broad!

Romeo. I stretch it out for that word "broad," which added to the goose, proves thee far and wide a broad goose.

Mercutio. Why, is not this better now than groaning for love? Now art thou sociable, now art thou Romeo; now art thou what thou art, by art as well as by nature. For this driveling love is like a great natural[22] that runs lolling[23] up and down to hide his bauble[24] in a hole.

Benvolio. Stop there, stop there!

Mercutio. Thou desirest me to stop in my tale against the hair.[25]

Benvolio. Thou wouldst else have made thy tale large.

Mercutio. O, thou art deceived! I would have made it short; for I was come to the whole depth of my tale, and meant indeed to occupy the argument[26] no longer.

Romeo. Here's goodly gear![27]

[*Enter* Nurse *and her Man*, Peter.]

A sail, a sail!

NOTES

16. **pump** *n.* shoe.

17. **when . . . singular** the jest will outwear the shoe and will then be all alone.

18. **O . . . singleness!** O thin joke, unique for only one thing—weakness!

19. **Swits . . . match** Drive your wit harder to beat me or else I will claim victory in this match of word play.

20. **sweeting** *n.* kind of apple.

21. **cheveril** *n.* easily stretched kid leather.

22. **natural** *n.* idiot.

23. **lolling** *v.* with tongue hanging out.

24. **bauble** *n.* toy.

25. **the hair** natural inclination.

26. **occupy the argument** talk about the matter.

27. **goodly gear** good stuff for joking (Romeo sees Nurse approaching).

Mercutio. Two, two! A shirt and a smock.[28]

Nurse. Peter!

Peter. Anon.

Nurse. My fan, Peter.

Mercutio. Good Peter, to hide her face; for her fan's the fairer face.

Nurse. God ye good morrow, gentlemen.

Mercutio. God ye good-den, fair gentlewoman.

Nurse. Is it good-den?

Mercutio. 'Tis no less. I tell ye; for the bawdy hand of the dial is now upon the prick of noon.

Nurse. Out upon you! What a man are you!

Romeo. One, gentlewoman, that God hath made, himself to mar.

Nurse. By my troth, it is well said. "For himself to mar," quoth 'a? Gentlemen, can any of you tell me where I may find the young Romeo?

Romeo. I can tell you; but young Romeo will be older when you have found him than he was when you sought him. I am the youngest of that name, for fault[29] of a worse.

Nurse. You say well.

Mercutio. Yea, is the worst well? Very well took,[30] i' faith! Wisely, wisely.

Nurse. If you be he, sir, I desire some **confidence** with you.

Benvolio. She will endite him to some supper.

Mercutio. A bawd, a bawd, a bawd! So ho!

Romeo. What hast thou found?

Mercutio. No hare, sir; unless a hare, sir, in a lenten pie, that is something stale and hoar ere it be spent.
[*He walks by them and sings.*]

An old hare hoar,
And an old hare hoar,
Is very good meat in Lent;
But a hare that is hoar
Is too much for a score
When it hoars ere it be spent.

Romeo, will you come to your father's? We'll to dinner thither.

Romeo. I will follow you.

Mercutio. Farewell, ancient lady. Farewell, [*singing*] "Lady, lady,[31] lady." [*Exit* Mercutio, Benvolio.]

Nurse. I pray you, sir, what saucy merchant was this that

NOTES

28. **A shirt and a smock** a man and a woman.

29. **fault** *n.* lack.

30. **took** *v.* understood.

confidence (KON fuh duhns) *n.* meeting, especially one held in secret

31. **"Lady . . . lady"** line from an old ballad, "Chaste Susanna."

was so full of his ropery?[32]

Romeo. A gentleman, nurse, that loves to hear himself talk and will speak more in a minute than he will stand to in a month.

Nurse. And 'a[33] speak anything against me, I'll take him down, and 'a were lustier than he is, and twenty such jacks; and if I cannot, I'll find those that shall. Scurvy knave! I am none of his flirt-gills;[34] I am none of his skainsmates.[35] And thou must stand by too, and suffer every knave to use me at his pleasure!

Peter. I saw no man use you at his pleasure. If I had, my weapon should quickly have been out, I warrant you. I dare draw as soon as another man, if I see occasion in a good quarrel, and the law on my side.

Nurse. Now, afore God, I am so vexed that every part about me quivers. Scurvy knave! Pray you, sir, a word; and, as I told you, my young lady bid me inquire you out. what she bid me say, I will keep to myself; but first let me tell ye, if ye should lead her in a fool's paradise, as they say, it were a very gross kind of behavior, as they say; for the gentlewoman is young; and therefore, if you should deal double with her, truly it were an ill thing to be off'red to any gentlewoman, and very weak[36] dealing.

Romeo. Nurse, commend[37] me to thy lady and mistress. I protest unto thee—

Nurse. Good heart, and i' faith I will tell her as much. Lord, Lord, she will be a joyful woman.

Romeo. What wilt thou tell her, nurse? Thou dost not mark me.

Nurse. I will tell her, sir, that you do protest, which, as I take it, is a gentlemanlike offer.

Romeo. Bid her devise
Some means to come to shrift[38] this afternoon;
And there she shall at Friar Lawrence' cell
Be shrived and married. Here is for thy pains.

Nurse. No, truly, sir; not a penny.

Romeo. Go to! I say you shall.

Nurse. This afternoon, sir? Well, she shall be there.

Romeo. And stay, good nurse, behind the abbey wall.
Within this hour my man shall be with thee
And bring thee cords made like a tackled stair.[39]
Which to the high topgallant[40] of my joy
Must be my convoy[41] in the secret night.

NOTES

32. ropery Nurse means "roguery," the talk and conduct of a rascal.

33. 'a he.

34. flirt-gills common girls.

35. skainsmates criminals; cutthroats.

36. weak *adj.* unmanly.

37. commend *v.* convey my respect and best wishes.

38. shrift *n.* confession.

39. tackled stair rope ladder.

40. topgallant *n.* summit.

41. convoy *n.* conveyance.

Farewell. Be trusty, and I'll quit[42] thy pains.
Farewell. Commend me to thy mistress.

Nurse. Now God in heaven bless thee! Hark you, sir.

Romeo. What say'st thou, my dear nurse?

Nurse. Is your man secret? Did you ne'er hear say,
Two may keep counsel, putting one away?[43]

Romeo. Warrant thee my man's as true as steel.

Nurse. Well, sir, my mistress is the sweetest lady. Lord, Lord! When 'twas a little prating[44] thing—O, there is a nobleman in town, one Paris, that would fain lay knife aboard;[45] but she, good soul, had as lieve[46] see a toad, a very toad, as see him. I anger her sometimes, and tell her that Paris is the properer man; but I'll warrant you, when I say so, she looks as pale as any clout[47] in the versal[48] world. Doth not rosemary and Romeo begin both with a letter?

Romeo. Ay, nurse; what of that? Both with an R.

Nurse. Ah, mocker! That's the dog's name.[49] R is for the—No; I know it begins with some other letter; and she hath the prettiest sententious[50] of it, of you and rosemary, that it would do you good to hear it.

Romeo. Commend me to thy lady.

Nurse. Ay, a thousand times. [*Exit* Romeo.] Peter!

Peter. Anon.

Nurse. Before, and apace.[51] [*Exit, after* Peter.]

NOTES

42. quit *v.* reward; pay you back for.

43. Two . . . away Two can keep a secret if one is ignorant, or out of the way.

44. prating *adj.* babbling.

45. fain . . . aboard eagerly seize Juliet for himself.

46. had as lieve would as willingly.

47. clout *n.* cloth.

48. versal world universe.

49. dog's name *R* sounds like a growl.

50. sententious Nurse means "sentences"—clever, wise sayings.

51. Before, and apace Go ahead of me, and quickly.

⌘ ⌘ ⌘

Scene v • *Capulet's orchard.*

[*Enter* Juliet.]

Juliet. The clock struck nine when I did send the nurse;
In half an hour she promised to return.
Perchance she cannot meet him. That's not so.
O, she is lame! Love's heralds should be thoughts,
Which ten times faster glides than the sun's beams
Driving back shadows over low'ring[1] hills.
Therefore do nimble-pinioned doves draw Love.[2]
And therefore hath the wind-swift Cupid wings.
Now is the sun upon the highmost hill
Of this day's journey, and from nine till twelve
Is three long hours; yet she is not come.

1. low'ring *adj.* darkening.

2. Therefore . . . Love therefore, doves with quick wings pull the chariot of Venus, goddess of love.

Had she affections and warm youthful blood,
She would be as swift in motion as a ball;
My words would bandy her[3] to my sweet love,
And his to me.
But old folks, many feign[4] as they were dead—
Unwieldy, slow, heavy and pale as lead.
[*Enter* Nurse *and* Peter.]

O God, she comes! O honey nurse, what news?
Hast thou met with him? Send thy man away.

Nurse. Peter, stay at the gate. [*Exit* Peter.]

Juliet. Now, good sweet nurse—O Lord, why lookest thou sad?
Though news be sad, yet tell them merrily;
If good, thou shamest the music of sweet news
By playing it to me with so sour a face.

Nurse. I am aweary, give me leave[5] awhile.
Fie, how my bones ache! What a jaunce[6] have I!

Juliet. I would thou hadst my bones, and I thy news.
Nay, come, I pray thee speak. Good, good nurse, speak.

Nurse. Jesu, what haste? Can you not stay a while?
Do you not see that I am out of breath?

Juliet. How art thou out of breath when thou hast breath
To say to me that thou art out of breath?
The excuse that thou dost make in this delay
Is longer than the tale thou dost excuse.
Is thy news good or bad? Answer to that.
Say either, and I'll stay the circumstance.[7]
Let me be satisfied, is't good or bad?

Nurse. Well, you have made a simple[8] choice; you know not how to choose a man. Romeo? No, not he. Though his face be better than any man's, yet his leg excels all men's; and for a hand and a foot, and a body, though they be not to be talked on, yet they are past compare. He is not the flower of courtesy, but, I'll warrant him, as gentle as a lamb. Go thy ways, wench; serve God. What, have you dined at home?

Juliet. No, no. But all this I did know before.
What says he of our marriage? What of that?

Nurse. Lord, how my head aches! What a head have I!
It beats as it would fall in twenty pieces.
My back a[9] t'other side—ah, my back, my back!
Beshrew[10] your heart for sending me about
To catch my death with jauncing up and down!

Juliet. I' faith, I am sorry that thou art not well.
Sweet, sweet, sweet nurse, tell me, what says my love?

NOTES

3. **bandy her** send her rapidly.

4. **feign** *v.* act.

5. **give me leave** excuse me; give me a moment's rest.

6. **jaunce** *n.* rough trip.

7. **stay the circumstance** wait for the details.

8. **simple** *adj.* foolish; simpleminded.

CLOSE READ

ANNOTATE: In lines 31–65, mark Juliet's questions to the Nurse about Romeo's intentions.

QUESTION: Why does Shakespeare allow the Nurse to take so long to answer Juliet's question?

CONCLUDE: What is the effect of the Nurse's digressions?

9. **a** on.

10. **Beshrew** shame on.

NOTES

11. **hot** *adj.* impatient; hot-tempered.

12. **Marry . . . trow** Indeed, cool down, I say.

13. **poultice** *n.* remedy.

14. **coil** *n.* disturbance.

15. **wanton** *adj.* excited.

Nurse. Your love says, like an honest gentleman, and a courteous, and a kind, and a handsome, and, I warrant, a virtuous—Where is your mother?

Juliet. Where is my mother? Why, she is within.
Where would she be? How oddly thou repliest!
"Your love says, like an honest gentleman,
'Where is your mother?'"

Nurse. O God's Lady dear!
Are you so hot?[11] Marry come up, I trow.[12]
Is this the poultice[13] for my aching bones?
Henceforth do your messages yourself.

Juliet. Here's such a coil![14] Come, what says Romeo?

Nurse. Have you got leave to go to shrift today?

Juliet. I have.

Nurse. Then hie you hence to Friar Lawrence' cell;
There stays a husband to make you a wife.
Now comes the wanton[15] blood up in your cheeks:
They'll be in scarlet straight at any news.
Hie you to church: I must another way,
To fetch a ladder, by the which your love
Must climb a bird's nest soon when it is dark.
I am the drudge, and toil in your delight:
But you shall bear the burden soon at night.
Go; I'll to dinner; hie you to the cell.

Juliet. Hie to high fortune! Honest nurse, farewell.

[*Exit all.*]

⌘ ⌘ ⌘

Scene vi • *Friar Lawrence's cell.*

[*Enter* Friar Lawrence *and* Romeo.]

1. **That . . . not!** that the future does not punish us with sorrow.

2. **countervail** *v.* equal.

3. **powder** *n.* gunpowder.

Friar. So smile the heavens upon this holy act
That afterhours with sorrow chide us not![1]

Romeo. Amen, amen! But come what sorrow can,
It cannot countervail[2] the exchange of joy
That one short minute gives me in her sight.
Do thou but close our hands with holy words,
Then love-devouring death do what he dare—
It is enough I may but call her mine.

Friar. These violent delights have violent ends
And in their triumph die, like fire and powder,[3]
Which, as they kiss, consume. The sweetest honey

^ Friar Lawrence weds Romeo and Juliet, while the Nurse looks on.

Is loathsome in his own deliciousness
And in the taste confounds[4] the appetite.
Therefore love moderately; long love doth so;
Too swift arrives as tardy as too slow.
[*Enter* Juliet.]
Here comes the lady. O, so light a foot
Will ne'er wear out the everlasting flint.[5]
A lover may bestride the gossamers[6]
That idles in the wanton summer air,
And yet not fall; so light is vanity.[7]

Juliet. Good even to my ghostly confessor.

Friar. Romeo shall thank thee, daughter, for us both.

Juliet. As much to him,[8] else is his thanks too much.

Romeo. Ah, Juliet, if the measure of thy joy
Be heaped like mine, and that thy skill be more
To blazon it,[9] then sweeten with thy breath
This neighbor air, and let rich music's tongue
Unfold the imagined happiness that both
Receive in either by this dear encounter.

Juliet. Conceit, more rich in matter than in words,
Brags of his substance, not of ornament.[10]

NOTES

4. **confounds** *v.* destroys.

5. **flint** *n.* stone.

6. **gossamers** *n.* spider webs.

7. **vanity** *n.* foolish things that cannot last.

8. **As . . . him** the same greeting to him.

9. **and . . . it** and if you are better to proclaim it.

10. **Conceit . . . ornament** Understanding does not need to be dressed up in words.

NOTES

They are but beggars that can count their worth;
But my true love is grown to such excess
I cannot sum up sum of half my wealth.

Friar. Come, come with me, and we will make short work,
For, by your leaves, you shall not stay alone
Till Holy Church incorporate two in one. [*Exit all.*]

Comprehension Check

Complete the following items after you finish your first read.

1. Why does Juliet want Romeo to have a different name?

because he is an montegue and their enemy

2. What items does Friar Lawrence carry in his basket when he first appears in the play?

Flowers, herbs

3. What does Friar Lawrence agree to do for Romeo?

marry him to Juliet

4. In Act II, Scene iv, how is Tybalt described?

good fighter, a fencer

5. Where does Act II, Scene iv, take place?

The Streets

6. **Notebook** Confirm your understanding of the text by writing a summary.

RESEARCH

Research to Clarify Choose at least one unfamiliar detail from the text. Briefly research that detail. In what way does the information you learned shed light on an aspect of the drama?

Close Read the Text

Reread what Mercutio says when Benvolio tells him to call for Romeo in Act II, Scene i, lines 7–21. Mark the word that Mercutio uses to "call" for Romeo. How does it help develop the tone in these lines?

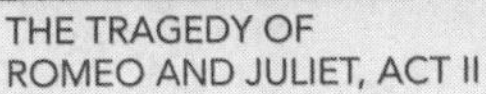

THE TRAGEDY OF ROMEO AND JULIET, ACT II

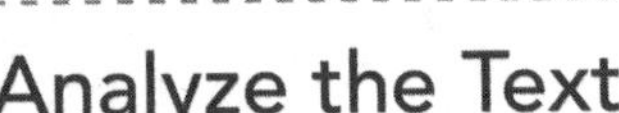

Analyze the Text

CITE TEXTUAL EVIDENCE to support your answers.

Notebook Respond to these questions.

1. (a) When do Romeo and Juliet first mutually declare their love? (b) **Analyze** How does this setting affect what they say to each other?
2. (a) What weakness in Romeo does the Friar point out before agreeing to help? (b) **Compare and Contrast** How do the Friar's motives differ from the couple's motives? Explain your answer based on details from the text.
3. (a) For whom is Juliet waiting in Act II, Scene v? (b) **Analyze** How does she feel as she waits? Use text details to explain your answer.
4. **Essential Question:** ***Do we determine our own destinies?*** What have you learned about destiny by reading Act II of *Romeo and Juliet*?

Tool Kit
Close-Read Guide and Model Annotation

LANGUAGE DEVELOPMENT

Concept Vocabulary

cunning	counterfeit	confidence

Why These Words? These concept vocabulary words relate to secrecy. How does each word contribute to meaning in the text? What other words in the selection connect to this concept?

WORD NETWORK
Add interesting words related to destiny from the text to your Word Network.

Practice

Notebook Confirm your understanding of these words by using each one in a sentence.

Word Study

Notebook **Latin Prefix: *counter-*** The prefix *counter-* comes from the Latin word *contra*, which means "against." In the word *counterfeit*, it is combined with a word part derived from the Latin word *facere*, which means "to make" or "to do." In the word *counterfeit*, *counter-* suggests a substitute, which helps generate its meaning as an "imitation intended to deceive." Using your understanding of the prefix *counter-*, record a definition for each of the following words: *counter*, *counterclaim*, *counterintuitive*.

STANDARDS
Language
Identify and correctly use patterns of word changes that indicate different meanings or parts of speech.

THE TRAGEDY OF ROMEO AND JULIET, ACT II

STANDARDS

Reading Literature
Analyze how an author's choices concerning how to structure a text, order events within it, and manipulate time create such effects as mystery, tension, or surprise.

Analyze Craft and Structure

Poetic Structure **Blank verse** is unrhymed poetry written in a meter called **iambic pentameter**. An **iamb** consists of an unstressed syllable followed by a stressed syllable (˘ ´). In **iambic pentameter,** there are five such units, called "feet," in each line. *Romeo and Juliet* is written mainly in blank verse, as shown here:

M˘ethóught Ĭ héard ă vóice crˇy, "Sléep nˇo móre!" (II,ii,34)

In all of Shakespeare's plays, high-ranking, aristocratic characters speak in blank verse. By contrast, comic characters or those of low rank usually speak in prose, which is writing that is not divided into poetic lines and does not follow a specific meter. These two distinct styles clarify characters' social status and contribute to the tone and mood of their interactions.

Practice

CITE TEXTUAL EVIDENCE to support your answers.

1. Use the chart to mark the stressed syllables in each line. (It may help you to read the lines aloud.) For each line, list the words the meter helps to emphasize. Explain how the emphasis created through meter reflects the character's emotions or conflicts.

Line 1 *from Act II, Scene ii*	**Romeo:** Can I go forward when my heart is here? **Emphasized Words:** **How Emphasis Reflects Character's Emotions or Conflicts:**
Line 33 *from Act II, Scene iv*	**Juliet:** But my true love is grown to such excess. **Emphasized Words:** **How Emphasis Reflects Character's Emotions or Conflicts:**

2. **(a)** Identify the aristocratic and common characters in Act II based on whether they speak in blank verse. **(b)** Why might Shakespeare have chosen blank verse for the dialogue spoken by aristocrats?

Speaking and Listening

Assignment
Work with a partner to choose and analyze a section of dialogue between a commoner and an aristocrat. Present a **dramatic interpretation** of the scene. As you perform the lines, demonstrate the differences between the the commoner's prose speech and the aristocrat's metered speech. After the performance, share your observations about how Shakespeare uses language to suggest character and social status.

1. **Select a Passage** Select an exchange between a commoner and an aristocrat that will work well as a dramatic interpretation. Use the following questions to help you select a passage:
   - What is happening in this passage?
   - How do the characters feel in this passage?
   - How easy or difficult will it be to convey these elements in a dramatic interpretation?
2. **Annotate the Passage** Annotate to better understand what is happening in the passage. Use the following guidelines to help you:
   - Summarize what is happening in the passage.
   - Distinguish between prose and blank verse, and mark the stressed and unstressed syllables in any sections of blank verse.
   - Identify words, phrases, or lines that are funny or convey specific feelings.
3. **Prepare Your Delivery** Practice your performance. Use the following guidelines to plan your delivery:
   - Use emphasis appropriately in both blank verse and prose dialogue.
   - Vary your tone and pace to reflect the characters' emotions or to convey humor.
   - Use facial expressions and gestures to help convey characters' feelings but avoid making them too exaggerated or distracting.
4. **Evaluate Dramatic Interpretations** As your classmates deliver their dramatic interpretations, pay close attention to what they say and do. Use an evaluation guide to analyze their delivery.

PRESENTATION EVALUATION GUIDE

Rate each statement on a scale of 1 (not demonstrated) to 4 (demonstrated).

☐ The speakers conveyed the appropriate actions, if applicable.

☐ The speakers communicated blank verse and prose dialogue appropriately.

☐ The speakers varied their tone and pace appropriately to convey the character's feelings and to convey humor.

☐ The speakers used gestures and other body language effectively to convey the characters' feelings and to convey humor.

EVIDENCE LOG

Before moving on to a new selection, go to your Evidence Log and record what you learned from *The Tragedy of Romeo and Juliet,* Act II.

STANDARDS

Speaking and Listening
- Present information, findings, and supporting evidence clearly, concisely, and logically such that listeners can follow the line of reasoning and the organization, development, substance, and style are appropriate to purpose, audience, and task.
- Adapt speech to a variety of contexts and tasks, demonstrating command of formal English when indicated or appropriate.

Playwright

William Shakespeare

The Tragedy of Romeo and Juliet, Act III

Concept Vocabulary

You will encounter the following words as you read Act III of *The Tragedy of Romeo and Juliet.* Before reading, note how familiar you are with each word. Then, rank the words in order from most familiar (1) to least familiar (3).

WORD	YOUR RANKING
exile	3
banishment	1
pardon	2

After completing the first read, come back to the concept vocabulary and review your rankings. Mark changes to your original rankings as needed.

First Read DRAMA

Apply these strategies as you conduct your first read. You will have an opportunity to complete the close-read notes after your first read.

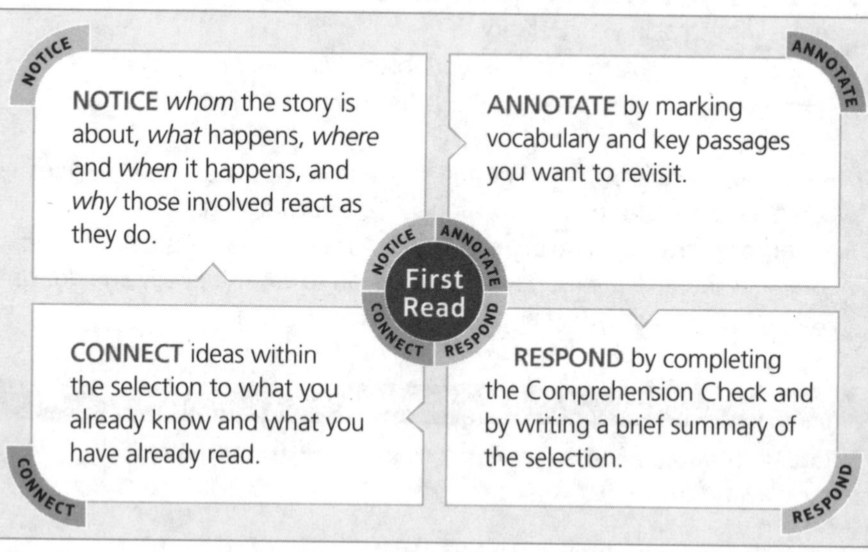
NOTICE
NOTICE *whom* the story is about, *what* happens, *where* and *when* it happens, and *why* those involved react as they do.
ANNOTATE
ANNOTATE by marking vocabulary and key passages you want to revisit.
First Read
NOTICE
ANNOTATE
CONNECT
RESPOND
CONNECT ideas within the selection to what you already know and what you have already read.
RESPOND by completing the Comprehension Check and by writing a brief summary of the selection.
CONNECT
RESPOND

Tool Kit
First-Read Guide and Model Annotation

STANDARDS

Reading Literature
By the end of grade 9, read and comprehend literature, including stories, dramas, and poems, in the grades 9–10 text complexity band proficiently, with scaffolding as needed at the high end of the range.

The Tragedy of Romeo and Juliet Act III

William Shakespeare

REVIEW AND ANTICIPATE

In Act II, Romeo and Juliet express their mutual love and enlist the aid of Juliet's nurse and Friar Lawrence to arrange a secret marriage ceremony. As the act closes, the young couple is about to be married. Before performing the ceremony, the Friar warns, "These violent delights have violent ends. . . ." Consider how this statement might hint at events that will occur in Act III or later in the play.

Scene i • *A public place.*

NOTES

[*Enter* Mercutio, Benvolio, *and* Men.]

Benvolio. I pray thee, good Mercutio, let's retire.
The day is hot, the Capulets abroad.
And, if we meet, we shall not 'scape a brawl,
For now, these hot days, is the mad blood stirring.

Mercutio. Thou are like one of these fellows that, when he enters the confines of a tavern, claps me his sword upon the table and says, "God send me no need of thee!" and by the operation of the second cup draws him on the drawer,[1] when Indeed there is no need.

Benvolio. Am I like such a fellow?

Mercutio. Come, come, thou art as hot as a Jack in thy mood as any in Italy; and as soon moved to be moody, and as soon moody to be moved.[2]

Benvolio. And what to?

Mercutio. Nay, and there were two such, we should have none shortly, for one would kill the other. Thou! Why, thou wilt

1. **and . . . drawer** and by the effect of the second drink, draws his sword against the waiter.

2. **and . . . moved** and as quickly stirred to anger as you are eager to be so stirred.

quarrel with a man that hath a hair more or a hair less in his beard than thou hast. Thou wilt quarrel with a man for cracking nuts, having no other reason but because thou hast hazel eyes. What eye but such an eye would spy out such a quarrel? Thy head is as full of quarrels as an egg is full of meat; and yet thy head hath been beaten as addle[3] as an egg for quarreling. Thou hast quarreled with a man for coughing in the street, because he hath wakened thy dog that hath lain asleep in the sun. Didst thou not fall out with a tailor for wearing his new doublet[4] before Easter? With another for tying his new shoes with old riband?[5] And yet thou wilt tutor me from quarreling![6]

Benvolio. And I were so apt to quarrel as thou art, any man should buy the fee simple[7] of my life for an hour and a quarter.[8]

Mercutio. The fee simple? O simple![9]

[*Enter* Tybalt, Petruchio, *and* Others.]

Benvolio. By my head, here comes the Capulets.

Mercutio. By my heel, I care not.

Tybalt. Follow me close, for I will speak to them.
Gentlemen, good-den. A word with one of you.

Mercutio. And but one word with one of us? Couple it with something; make it a word and a blow.

Tybalt. You shall me find me apt enough to that, sir, and you will give me occasion.[10]

Mercutio. Could you not take some occasion without giving?

Tybalt. Mercutio, thou consortest[11] with Romeo.

Mercutio. Consort?[12] What, dost thou make us minstrels? And thou make minstrels of us, look to hear nothing but discords.[13] Here's my fiddlestick; here's that shall make you dance. Zounds,[14] consort!

Benvolio. We talk here in the public haunt of men.
Either withdraw unto some private place,
Or reason coldly of your grievances,
Or else depart. Here all eyes gaze on us.

Mercutio. Men's eyes were made to look, and let them gaze.
I will not budge for no man's pleasure, I.

[*Enter* Romeo.]

Tybalt. Well, peace be with you, sir. Here comes my man.[15]

Mercutio. But I'll be hanged, sir, if he wears your livery.[16]
Marry, go before to field,[17] he'll be your follower!
Your worship in that sense may call him man.

Tybalt. Romeo, the love I bear thee can afford

NOTES

3. **addle** *adv.* scrambled; crazy.

4. **doublet** *n.* jacket.

5. **riband** *n.* ribbon.

6. **tutor . . . quarreling** instruct me not to quarrel.

7. **fee simple** complete possession.

8. **an hour and a quarter** length of time that a man with Mercutio's fondness for quarreling may be expected to live.

9. **simple!** O stupid!

10. **occasion** *n.* cause; reason.

11. **consortest** *v.* associate with.

12. **Consort** *v.* associate with; *consort* also meant "a group of musicians."

13. **discords** *n.* harsh sounds.

14. **Zounds** exclamation of surprise or anger ("By God's wounds").

15. **man** *n.* man I am looking for; *man* also meant "manservant."

16. **livery** *n.* servant's uniform.

17. **field** *n.* dueling place.

‹ Romeo holds Mercutio back from dueling Tybalt.

NOTES

No better term than this: thou art a villain.[18]

Romeo. Tybalt, the reason that I have to love thee
Doth much excuse the appertaining[19] rage
To such a greeting. Villain am I none.
Therefore farewell. I see thou knowest me not.

Tybalt. Boy, this shall not excuse the injuries
That thou hast done me; therefore turn and draw.

Romeo. I do protest I never injured thee,
But love thee better than thou canst devise[20]
Till thou shalt know the reason of my love;
And so, good Capulet, which name I tender[21]
As dearly as my own, be satisfied

Mercutio. O calm, dishonorable, vile submission!
Alla stoccata[22] carries it away. [*Draws.*]
Tybalt, you ratcatcher, will you walk?

Tybalt. What wouldst thou have with me?

Mercutio. Good King of Cats, nothing but one of your nine lives. That I mean to make bold withal,[23] and, as you shall use me here-after, dry-beat[24] the rest of the eight. Will you pluck your sword out of his pilcher[25] by the ears? Make haste, lest mine be about your ears ere it be out.

Tybalt. I am for you. [*Draws.*]

Romeo. Gentle Mercutio, put thy rapier up.

18. **villain** *n.* low, vulgar person.
19. **appertaining** *adj.* appropriate.
20. **devise** *v.* understand; imagine.
21. **tender** *v.* value.
22. ***Alla stoccata*** at the thrust—Italian fencing term that Mercutio uses as a nickname for Tybalt.
23. **make bold withal** make bold with; take.
24. **dry-beat** *v.* thrash.
25. **pilcher** *n.* scabbard.

Mercutio. Come, sir, your passado! [*They fight.*]

Romeo. Draw, Benvolio; beat down their weapons.
Gentlemen, for shame! Forbear this outrage!
Tybalt, Mercutio, the Prince expressly hath
Forbid this bandying in Verona streets.
Hold, Tybalt! Good Mercutio!

[Tybalt *under* Romeo's *arm thrusts* Mercutio *in, and flies.*]

Mercutio. I am hurt.
A plague a[26] both your houses! I am sped.[27]
Is he gone and hath nothing?

Benvolio. What, art thou hurt?

Mercutio. Ay, ay, a scratch, a scratch. Marry, 'tis enough.
Where is my page? Go, villain, fetch a surgeon. [*Exit* Page.]

Romeo. Courage, man. The hurt cannot be much.

Mercutio. No, 'tis not so deep as a well, nor so wide as
a church door; but 'tis enough, 'twill serve. Ask for
me tomorrow, and you shall find me a grave man. I
am peppered,[28] I warrant, for this world. A plague a
both your houses! Zounds, a dog, a rat, a mouse, a
cat, to scratch a man to death! A braggart, a rogue,
a villain, that fights by the book of arithmetic![29] Why
the devil came you between us? I was hurt under
your arm.

Romeo. I thought all for the best.

Mercutio. Help me into some house, Benvolio,
Or I shall faint. A plague a both your houses!
They have made worms' meat of me. I have it,[30]
And soundly too. Your houses!

[*Exit* Mercutio *and* Benvolio]

Romeo. This gentleman, the Prince's near ally,[31]
My very friend, hath got his mortal hurt
In my behalf—my reputation stained
With Tybalt's slander—Tybalt, that an hour
Hath been my cousin. O sweet Juliet,
Thy beauty hath made me effeminate
And in my temper soft'ned valor's steel!

[*Enter* Benvolio.]

Benvolio. O Romeo, Romeo, brave Mercutio is dead!
That gallant spirit hath aspired[32] the clouds,
Which too untimely here did scorn the earth.

Romeo. This day's black fate on moe[33] days doth depend;[34]
This but begins the woe others must end.

[*Enter* Tybalt.]

NOTES

26. a on.

27. sped *adj.* wounded; done for.

CLOSE READ

ANNOTATE: In lines 90–101, mark examples of Mercutio's wordplay and jokes.

QUESTION: Why does Shakespeare have Mercutio joke around even after he is mortally wounded?

CONCLUDE: What emotional effect does Mercutio's wordplay have in this speech?

28. peppered *adj.* finished off.

29. by . . . arithmetic by formal rules.

30. I have it I have got my deathblow.

31. ally *n.* relative.

32. aspired *v.* climbed to.

33. moe *adj.* more.

34. depend *v.* hang over.

Benvolio. Here comes the furious Tybalt back again.

Romeo. Alive in triumph, and Mercutio slain?
Away to heaven respective[35] lenity,
And fire-eyed fury be my conduct[36] now!
Now, Tybalt, take the "villain" back again
That late thou gavest me; for Mercutio's soul
Is but a little way above our heads,
Staying for thine to keep him company.
Either thou or I, or both, must go with him.

Tybalt. Thou, wretched boy, that didst consort him here,
Shalt with him hence.

Romeo. This shall determine that.

[*They fight.* Tybalt *falls.*]

Benvolio. Romeo, away, be gone!
The citizens are up, and Tybalt slain.
Stand not amazed. The Prince will doom thee death
If thou art taken. Hence, be gone, away!

Romeo. O, I am fortune's fool![37]

Benvolio. Why dost thou stay? [*Exit* Romeo.]

[*Enter* Citizens.]

Citizen. Which way ran he that killed Mercutio?
Tybalt, that murderer, which way ran he?

Benvolio. There lies that Tybalt.

Citizen. Up, sir, go with me.
I charge thee in the Prince's name obey.

[*Enter* Prince, Old Montague, Capulet, *their* Wives, *and all.*]

Prince. Where are the vile beginners of this fray?

Benvolio. O noble Prince, I can discover[38] all
The unlucky manage[39] of this fatal brawl.
There lies the man, slain by young Romeo,
That slew thy kinsman, brave Mercutio.

Lady Capulet. Tybalt, my cousin! O my brother's child!
O Prince! O cousin! Husband! O, the blood is spilled
Of my dear kinsman! Prince, as thou art true,
For blood of ours shed blood of Montague.
O cousin, cousin!

Prince. Benvolio, who began this bloody fray?

Benvolio. Tybalt, here slain, whom Romeo's hand did slay,
Romeo, that spoke him fair, bid him bethink
How nice[40] the quarrel was, and urged withal
Your high displeasure. All this—utterèd
With gentle breath, calm look, knees humbly bowed—

NOTES

35. respective lenity thoughtful mercy.

36. conduct *n.* guide.

37. fool *n.* plaything.

38. discover *v.* reveal.

39. manage *n.* course.

40. nice *adj.* trivial.

NOTES

41. spleen *n.* angry nature.

42. tilts *v.* thrusts.

43. envious *adv.* full of hatred.

44. entertained *v.* considered.

45. His fault . . . Tybalt by killing Tybalt, he did what the law could have done.

exile (EHG zyl) *v.* punish someone by forcing them to leave a place permanently

46. My blood Mercutio was related to the Prince.

47. amerce *v.* punish.

48. attend our will await my decision.

Could not take truce with the unruly spleen[41]
Of Tybalt deaf to peace, but that he tilts[42]
With piercing steel at bold Mercutio's breast;
Who, all as hot, turns deadly point to point,
And, with a martial scorn, with one hand beats
Cold death aside and with the other sends
It back to Tybalt, whose dexterity
Retorts it. Romeo he cries aloud,
"Hold, friends! Friends, part!" and swifter than his tongue,
His agile arm beats down their fatal points,
And 'twixt them rushes; underneath whose arm
An envious[43] thrust from Tybalt hit the life
Of stout Mercutio, and then Tybalt fled;
But by and by comes back to Romeo,
Who had but newly entertained[44] revenge,
And to't they go like lightning; for, ere I
Could draw to part them, was stout Tybalt slain;
And, as he fell, did Romeo turn and fly.
This is the truth, or let Benvolio die.

Lady Capulet. He is a kinsman to the Montague;
Affection makes him false, he speaks not true.
Some twenty of them fought in this black strife,
And all those twenty could but kill one life.
I beg for justice, which thou, Prince, must give.
Romeo slew Tybalt; Romeo must not live.

Prince. Romeo slew him; he slew Mercutio.
Who now the price of his dear blood doth owe?

Montague. Not Romeo, Prince; he was Mercutio's friend;
His fault concludes but what the law should end,
The life of Tybalt.[45]

Prince. And for that offense
Immediately we do **exile** him hence.
I have an interest in your hate's proceeding.
My blood[46] for your rude brawls doth lie a-bleeding;
But I'll amerce[47] you with so strong a fine
That you shall all repent the loss of mine.
I will be deaf to pleading and excuses;
Nor tears nor prayers shall purchase out abuses.
Therefore, use none. Let Romeo hence in haste,
Else, when he is found, that hour is his last.
Bear hence this body and attend our will.[48]
Mercy but murders, pardoning those that kill.

[*Exit with others.*]

⌘⌘⌘

Scene ii • *Capulet's orchard.*

[*Enter* Juliet *alone.*]

Juliet. Gallop apace, you fiery-footed steeds,[1]
Towards Phoebus' lodging![2] Such a wagoner
As Phaëthon[3] would whip you to the west
And bring in cloudy night immediately.
Spread thy close curtain, love-performing night,
That runaways' eyes may wink,[4] and Romeo
Leap to these arms untalked of and unseen.
Lovers can see to do their amorous rites,
And by their own beauties; or, if love be blind,
It best agrees with night. Come, civil night,
Thou sober-suited matron all in black,
And learn me how to lose a winning match,
Played for a pair of stainless maidenhoods.
Hood my unmanned blood, bating in my cheeks,[5]
With thy black mantle till strange[6] love grows bold,
Think true love acted simple modesty,
Come, night; come, Romeo; come, thou day in night;
For thou wilt lie upon the wings of night
Whiter than new snow upon a raven's back.
Come, gentle night; come, loving, black-browed night;
Give me my Romeo; and when I shall die,
Take him and cut him out in little stars,
And he will make the face of heaven so fine
That all the world will be in love with night
And pay no worship to the garish sun.
O, I have bought the mansion of a love,
But not possessed it; and though I am sold,
Not yet enjoyed. So tedious is this day
As is the night before some festival
To an impatient child that hath new robes
And may not wear them. O, here comes my nurse.

[*Enter* Nurse, *with cords.*]

And she brings news; and every tongue that speaks
But Romeo's name speaks heavenly eloquence.
Now, nurse, what news? What hast thou there, the cords
That Romeo bid thee fetch?

Nurse. Ay, ay, the cords.

Juliet. Ay me! What news? Why dost thou wring thy hands?

Nurse. Ah, weraday![7] He's dead, he's dead, he's dead!
We are undone, lady, we are undone!
Alack the day! He's gone, he's killed, he's dead!

NOTES

1. **fiery-footed steeds** horses of the sun god, Phoebus.
2. **Phoebus'** (FEE buhs) **lodging** below the horizon.
3. **Phaëthon** (FAY uh thon) Phoebus' son, who tried to drive his father's horses but was unable to control them.
4. **That runways' eyes may wink** so that the eyes of busybodies may not see.
5. **Hood . . . cheeks** hide the untamed blood that makes me blush.
6. **strange** *adj.* unfamiliar.
7. **Ah, weraday!** alas!

CLOSE READ

ANNOTATE: In lines 1–31 of Scene ii, mark words and phrases that describe the night.

QUESTION: In Juliet's view, what qualities does the night have?

CONCLUDE: How does this language clarify the state of Juliet's emotions?

Juliet. Can heaven be so envious?

Nurse. Romeo can,
Though heaven cannot. O Romeo, Romeo!
Who ever would have thought it? Romeo!

Juliet. What devil art thou that dost torment me thus?
This torture should be roared in dismal hell.
Hath Romeo slain himself? Say thou but "Ay,"[8]
And that bare vowel "I" shall poison more
Than the death-darting eye of cockatrice.
I am not I, if there be such an "Ay,"
Or those eyes' shot[9] that makes thee answer "Ay."
If he be slain, say "Ay"; or if not, "No."
Brief sounds determine of my weal or woe.

Nurse. I saw the wound, I saw it with mine eyes,
(God save the mark![10]) here on his manly breast.
A piteous corse,[11] a bloody piteous corse;
Pale, pale as ashes, all bedaubed in blood,
All in gore-blood. I swounded[12] at the sight.

Juliet. O, break, my heart! Poor bankrout,[13] break at once!
To prison, eyes; ne'er look on liberty!
Vile earth, to earth resign;[14] end motion here,
And thou and Romeo press one heavy bier![15]

Nurse. O Tybalt, Tybalt, the best friend I had!
O courteous Tybalt! Honest gentleman!
That ever I should live to see thee dead!

Juliet. What storm is this that blows so contrary?[16]
Is Romeo slaught'red, and is Tybalt dead?
My dearest cousin, and my dearer lord?
Then, dreadful trumpet, sound the general doom![17]
For who is living, if those two are gone?

Nurse. Tybalt is gone, and Romeo banishèd;
Romeo that killed him, he is banishèd.

Juliet. O God! Did Romeo's hand shed Tybalt's blood?

Nurse. It did, it did! Alas the day, it did!

Juliet. O serpent heart, hid with a flow'ring face!
Did ever dragon keep so fair a cave?
Beautiful tyrant! Fiend angelical!
Dove-feathered raven! Wolvish-ravening lamb!
Despisèd substance of divinest show!
Just opposite to what thou justly seem'st—
A damnèd saint, an honorable villain!
O nature, what hadst thou to do in hell
When thou didst bower the spirit of a fiend
In mortal paradise of such sweet flesh?

NOTES

8. **"Ay"** yes.

9. **eyes' shot** the Nurse's glance.

10. **God save the mark!** May God save us from evil!

11. **corse** *n.* corpse.

12. **swounded** *v.* swooned; fainted.

13. **bankrout** *n.* bankrupt.

14. **Vile . . . resign** let my body return to the earth.

15. **bier** *n.* platform in which a corpse is displayed before burial.

16. **contrary** *adv.* in opposite directions.

17. **dreadful . . . doom** let the trumpet that announces doomsday be sounded.

Was ever book containing such vile matter
So fairly bound? O, that deceit should dwell
In such a gorgeous palace!

Nurse. There's no trust,
No faith, no honesty in men; all perjured,
All forsworn,[18] all naught, all dissemblers.[19]
Ah, where's my man? Give me some aqua vitae.[20]
These griefs, these woes, these sorrows make me old.
Shame come to Romeo!

Juliet. Blistered by thy tongue
For such a wish! He was not born to shame.
Upon his brow shame is ashamed to sit;
For 'tis a throne where honor may be crowned
Sole monarch of the universal earth.
O, what a beast was I to chide at him!

Nurse. Will you speak well of him that killed your cousin?

Juliet. Shall I speak ill of him that is my husband?
Ah, poor my lord, what tongue shall smooth thy name
When I, thy three-hours wife, have mangled it?
But wherefore, villain, didst thou kill my cousin?
That villain cousin would have killed my husband.
Back, foolish tears, back to your native spring!
Your tributary[21] drops belong to woe,
Which you, mistaking, offer up to joy.
My husband lives, that Tybalt would have slain;
And Tybalt's dead, that would have slain my husband.
All this is comfort; wherefore weep I then?
Some word there was, worser than Tybalt's death,
That murd'red me. I would forget it fain;
But O, it presses to my memory
Like damnèd guilty deeds to sinners' minds!
"Tybalt is dead, and Romeo—banishèd."
That "banishèd," that one word "banishèd,"
Hath slain ten thousand Tybalts. Tybalt's death
Was woe enough, if it had ended there;
Or, if sour woe delights in fellowship
And needly will be ranked with[22] other griefs,
Why followed not, when she said "Tybalt's dead,"
Thy father, or thy mother, nay, or both,
Which modern[23] lamentation might have moved?
But with a rearward[24] following Tybalt's death,
"Romeo is banishèd"—to speak that word
Is father, mother, Tybalt, Romeo, Juliet,
All slain, all dead. "Romeo is banishèd"—
There is no end, no limit, no measure, bound,
In that word's death; no words can that woe sound.

NOTES

18. forsworn *v.* are liars.

19. dissemblers *n.* hypocrites.

20. aqua vitae (AK wuh VY tee) brandy.

21. tributary *adj.* contributing; also, honoring.

22. needly . . . with must be accompanied by.

23. modern *adj.* ordinary.

24. rearward *n.* follow up; literally, a rear guard.

NOTES

banishment (BAN ihsh muhnt) *n.* state of having been banished, or exiled

25. wot *v.* know.

1. Affliction . . . parts misery is in love with your attractive qualities.

2. doom *n.* final decision.

3. doomsday *n.* my death.

4. vanished *v.* escaped; came forth.

Where is my father and my mother, nurse?

Nurse. Weeping and wailing over Tybalt's corse.
Will you go to them? I will bring you thither.

Juliet. Wash they his wounds with tears? Mine shall be spent,
When theirs are dry, for Romeo's **banishment**.
Take up those cords. Poor ropes, you are beguiled,
Both you and I, for Romeo is exiled.
He made you for a highway to my bed;
But I, a maid, die maiden-widowèd.
Come, cords; come, nurse. I'll to my wedding bed;
And death, not Romeo, take my maidenhead!

Nurse. Hie to your chamber. I'll find Romeo
To comfort you. I wot[25] well where he is.
Hark ye, your Romeo will be here at night.
I'll to him; he is hid at Lawrence' cell.

Juliet. O, find him! Give this ring to my true knight
And bid him come to take his last farewell. [*Exit with* Nurse.]

⌘⌘⌘

Scene iii • *Friar Lawrence's cell.*

[*Enter* Friar Lawrence.]

Friar. Romeo, come forth; come forth, thou fearful man.
Affliction is enamored of thy parts,[1]
And thou art wedded to calamity.

[*Enter* Romeo.]

Romeo. Father, what news? What is the Prince's doom?
What sorrow craves acquaintance at my hand
That I yet know not?

Friar. Too familiar
Is my dear son with such sour company.
I bring thee tidings of the Prince's doom.[2]

Romeo. What less than doomsday[3] is the Prince's doom?

Friar. A gentler judgment vanished[4] from his lips—
Not body's death, but body's banishment.

Romeo. Ha, banishment? Be merciful, say "death";
For exile hath more terror in his look,
Much more than death. Do not say "banishment."

Friar. Here from Verona art thou banishèd
Be patient, for the world is broad and wide.

Romeo. There is no world without[5] Verona walls,
But purgatory, torture, hell itself.
Hence banishèd is banishèd from the world,
And world's exile is death. Then "banishèd"
Is death mistermed. Calling death "banishèd,"
Thou cut'st my head off with a golden ax
And smilest upon the stroke that murders me.

Friar. O deadly sin! O rude unthankfulness!
Thy fault our law calls death;[6] but the kind Prince,
Taking thy part, hath rushed[7] aside the law,
And turned that black word "death" to "banishment."
This is dear mercy, and thou seest it not.

Romeo. 'Tis torture, and not mercy. Heaven is here,
Where Juliet lives; and every cat and dog
And little mouse, every unworthy thing,
Live here in heaven and may look on her;
But Romeo may not. More validity,[8]
More honorable state, more courtship lives
In carrion flies than Romeo. They may seize
On the white wonder of dear Juliet's hand
And steal immortal blessing from her lips,
Who, even in pure and vestal modesty,
Still blush, as thinking their own kisses sin;
But Romeo may not, he is banishèd.
Flies may do this but I from this must fly;
They are freemen, but I am banishèd.
And sayest thou yet that exile is not death?
Hadst thou no poison mixed, no sharp-ground knife,
No sudden mean[9] of death, though ne'er so mean,[10]
But "banishèd" to kill me—"banishèd"?
O friar, the damnèd use that word in hell;
Howling attends it! How hast thou the heart,
Being a divine, a ghostly confessor,
A sin-absolver, and my friend professed,
To mangle me with that word "banishèd"?

Friar. Thou fond mad man, hear me a little speak.

Romeo. O, thou wilt speak again of banishment.

Friar. I'll give thee armor to keep off that word;
Adversity's sweet milk, philosophy,
To comfort thee, though thou art banishèd.

Romeo. Yet "banishèd"? Hang up philosophy!
Unless philosophy can make a Juliet,
Displant a town, reverse a prince's doom,
It helps not, it prevails not. Talk no more.

Friar. O, then I see that madmen have no ears.

NOTES

5. **without** outside.

6. **Thy fault . . . death** for what you did our law demands the death penalty.

7. **rushed** *v.* pushed.

8. **validity** *v.* value.

9. **mean** *n.* method.

10. **mean** *adj.* humiliating.

NOTES

11. dispute *v.* discuss.

12. estate *n.* condition; situation.

13. By and by! In a minute! (said to the person knocking).

14. simpleness *n.* silly behavior (Romeo does not move).

15. concealed lady secret bride.

Romeo. How should they, when that wise men have no eyes?

Friar. Let me dispute[11] with thee of thy estate.[12]

Romeo. Thou canst not speak of that thou dost not feel.
Wert thou as young as I, Juliet thy love,
An hour but married, Tybalt murderèd,
Doting like me, and like me banishèd,
Then mightst thou speak, then mightst thou tear thy hair,
And fall upon the ground, as I do now,
Taking the measure of an unmade grave.

[*Knock.*]

Friar. Arise, one knocks. Good Romeo, hide thyself.

Romeo. Not I; unless the breath of heartsick groans
Mistlike infold me from the search of eyes. [*Knock.*]

Friar. Hark, how they knock! Who's there? Romeo, arise;
Thou wilt be taken.—Stay awhile!—Stand up; [*Knock.*]
Run to my study.—By and by![13]—God's will,
What simpleness[14] is this.—I come, I come! [*Knock.*]
Who knocks so hard? Whence come you? What's your will?

[*Enter* Nurse.]

Nurse. Let me come in, and you shall know my errand.
I come from Lady Juliet.

Friar. Welcome then.

Nurse. O holy friar, O, tell me, holy friar,
Where is my lady's lord, where's Romeo?

Friar. There on the ground, with his own tears made drunk.

Nurse. O, he is even in my mistress' case,
Just in her case! O woeful sympathy!
Piteous predicament! Even so lies she,
Blubb'ring and weeping, weeping and blubb'ring.
Stand up, stand up! Stand, and you be a man.
For Juliet's sake, for her sake, rise and stand!
Why should you fall into so deep an O?

Romeo. [*Rises.*] Nurse—

Nurse. Ah sir, ah sir! Death's the end of all.

Romeo. Spakest thou of Juliet? How is it with her?
Doth not she think of me an old murderer,
Now I have stained the childhood of our joy
With blood removed but little from her own?
Where is she? And how doth she? And what says
My concealed lady[15] to our canceled love?

Nurse. O, she says nothing, sir, but weeps and weeps;
And now falls on her bed, and then starts up,
And Tybalt calls; and then on Romeo cries,

And then down falls again.

Romeo. As if that name,
Shot from the deadly level[16] of a gun,
Did murder her; as that name's cursèd hand
Murdered her kinsman. O, tell me, friar, tell me,
In what vile part of this anatomy
Doth my name lodge? Tell me, that I may sack[17]
The hateful mansion.

[*He offers to stab himself, and* Nurse *snatches the dagger away.*]

Friar. Hold thy desperate hand.
Art thou a man? Thy form cries out thou art;
Thy tears are womanish, thy wild acts denote
The unreasonable fury of a beast.
Unseemly[18] woman in a seeming man!
And ill-beseeming beast in seeming both![19]
Thou hast amazed me. By my holy order,
I thought thy disposition better tempered.
Hast thou slain Tybalt? Wilt thou slay thyself?
And slay thy lady that in thy life lives,
By doing damnèd hate upon thyself?
Why railest thou on thy birth, the heaven, and earth?
Since birth and heaven and earth, all three do meet
In thee at once; which thou at once wouldst lose.
Fie, fie, thou shamest thy shape, thy love, thy wit,[20]
Which, like a usurer,[21] abound'st in all,
And usest none in that true use indeed
Which should bedeck[22] thy shape, thy love, thy wit,
Thy noble shape is but a form of wax,
Digressing from the valor of a man;
Thy dear love sworn but hollow perjury,
Killing that love which thou hast vowed to cherish;
Thy wit, that ornament to shape and love,
Misshapen in the conduct[23] of them both,
Like powder in a skilless soldier's flask,[24]
Is set afire by thine own ignorance,
And thou dismemb'red with thine own defense.[25]
What, rouse thee, man! Thy Juliet is alive,
For whose dear sake thou wast but lately dead.[26]
There art thou happy.[27] Tybalt would kill thee,
But thou slewest Tybalt. There art thou happy.
The law, that threat'ned death, becomes thy friend
And turns it to exile. There art thou happy.
A pack of blessings light upon thy back;
Happiness courts thee in her best array;
But, like a misbehaved and sullen wench,[28]
Thou puts up[29] thy fortune and thy love.

NOTES

16. level *n.* aim.

17. sack *v.* plunder.

18. Unseemly *adj.* inappropriate (because unnatural).

19. And . . . both! Romeo has inappropriately lost his human nature because he seems like a man and woman combined.

20. wit *n.* mind; intellect.

21. Which, like a usurer who, like a rich money-lender.

22. bedeck *v.* do honor to.

23. conduct *n.* management

24. flask *n.* powder flask.

25. And thou . . . defense The friar is saying that Romeo's mind, which is now irrational, is destroying rather than aiding him.

26. but lately dead only recently declaring yourself dead.

27. happy *adj.* fortunate

28. wench *n.* low, common girl.

29. puts up pouts over.

NOTES

30. watch be set watchmen go on duty.

31. blaze *v.* announce publicly.

pardon (PAHR duhn) *n.* forgiveness for a crime

32. apt unto likely to do.

33. chide *v.* rebuke me (for slaying Tybalt).

34. here . . . state this is your situation.

35. Sojourn *v.* remain.

36. signify *v.* let you know.

Take heed, take heed, for such die miserable.
Go get thee to thy love, as was decreed,
Ascend her chamber, hence and comfort her.
But look thou stay not till the watch be set,[30]
For then thou canst not pass to Mantua,
Where thou shalt live till we can find a time
To blaze[31] your marriage, reconcile your friends,
Beg **pardon** of the Prince, and call thee back
With twenty hundred thousand times more joy
Than thou went'st forth in lamentation.
Go before, nurse. Commend me to thy lady,
And bid her hasten all the house to bed,
Which heavy sorrow makes them apt[32] unto.
Romeo is coming.

Nurse. O Lord, I could have stayed here all the night
To hear good counsel. O, what learning is!
My lord, I'll tell my lady you will come.

Romeo. Do so, and bid my sweet prepare to chide.[33]

[Nurse *offers to go in and turns again.*]

Nurse. Here, sir, a ring she bid me give you, sir.
Hie you, make haste, for it grows very late. [*Exit.*]

Romeo. How well my comfort is revived by this!

Friar. Go hence; good night; and here stands all your state:[34]
Either be gone before the watch is set,
Or by the break of day disguised from hence.
Sojourn[35] in Mantua. I'll find out your man,
And he shall signify[36] from time to time
Every good hap to you that chances here.
Give me thy hand. 'Tis late. Farewell; good night.

Romeo. But that a joy past joy calls out on me,
It were a grief so brief to part with thee.
Farewell. [*Exit all.*]

⌘ ⌘ ⌘

Scene iv • *A room in Capulet's house.*

1. move *v.* discuss your proposal with.

[*Enter old* Capulet, *his* Wife, *and* Paris.]

Capulet. Things have fall'n out, sir, so unluckily
That we have had no time to move[1] our daughter.
Look you, she loved her kinsman Tybalt dearly,
And so did I. Well, we were born to die.
'Tis very late; she'll not come down tonight.

I promise you, but for your company,
I would have been abed an hour ago.

Paris. These times of woe afford no times to woo.
Madam, good night. Commend me to your daughter.

Lady Capulet. I will, and know her mind early tomorrow;
Tonight she's mewed up to her heaviness.[2]

Capulet. Sir, Paris, I will make a desperate tender[3]
Of my child's love. I think she will be ruled
In all respects by me; nay more, I doubt it not.
Wife, go you to her ere you go to bed;
Acquaint her here of my son[4] Paris' love
And bid her (mark you me?) on Wednesday next—
But soft! What day is this?

Paris. Monday, my lord.

Capulet. Monday! Ha, ha! Well, Wednesday is too soon.
A[5] Thursday let it be—a Thursday, tell her,
She shall be married to this noble earl.
Will you be ready? Do you like this haste?
We'll keep no great ado[6]—a friend or two;
For hark you, Tybalt being slain so late,
It may be thought we held him carelessly,[7]
Being our kinsman, if we revel much.
Therefore we'll have some half a dozen friends,
And there an end. But what say you to Thursday?

Paris. My lord, I would that Thursday were tomorrow.

Capulet. Well, get you gone. A Thursday be it then.
Go you to Juliet ere you go to bed;
Prepare her, wife, against[8] this wedding day.
Farewell, my lord.—Light to my chamber, ho!
Afore me,[9] it is so very late
That we may call it early by and by.
Good night. *[Exit all.]*

⌘ ⌘ ⌘

Scene v • *Capulet's orchard.*

[*Enter* Romeo *and* Juliet *aloft.*]

Juliet. Wilt thou be gone? It is not yet near day.
It was the nightingale, and not the lark,
That pierced the fearful hollow of thine ear.
Nightly she sings on yond pomegranate tree.
Believe me, love, it was the nightingale.

NOTES

2. **mewed . . . heaviness** locked up with her sorrow.
3. **desperate tender** risky offer.
4. **son** son-in-law.
5. **A** on.
6. **We'll . . . ado** We will not make a great fuss.
7. **held him carelessly** did not respect him enough.
8. **against** for.
9. **Afore me** indeed (a mild oath).

NOTES

1. **severing** *adj.* parting.
2. **Night's candles** stars.
3. **exhales** *v.* sends out.
4. **reflex . . . brow** reflection of the moon (Cynthia was a name for the moon goddess.).
5. **sharps** *n.* shrill high notes.
6. **division** *n.* melody.
7. **change eyes** exchange eyes (because the lark has a beautiful body with ugly eyes and the toad has an ugly body with beautiful eyes).
8. **affray** *v.* frighten.
9. **hunt's-up** morning song for hunters.
10. **much in years** much older.

Romeo. It was the lark, the herald of the morn;
No nightingale. Look, love, what envious streaks
Do lace the severing[1] clouds in yonder East.
Night's candles[2] are burnt out, and jocund day
Stands tiptoe on the misty mountaintops.
I must be gone and live, or stay and die.

Juliet. Yond light is not daylight; I know it, I.
It is some meteor that the sun exhales[3]
To be to thee this night a torchbearer
And light thee on thy way to Mantua.
Therefore stay yet; thou need'st not to be gone.

Romeo. Let me be ta'en, let me be put to death.
I am content, so thou wilt have it so.
I'll say yon gray is not the morning's eye,
'Tis but the pale reflex of Cynthia's brow;[4]
Nor that is not the lark whose notes do beat
The vaulty heaven so high above our heads.
I have more care to stay than will to go.
Come, death, and welcome! Juliet wills it so.
How is't, my soul? Let's talk; it is not day.

Juliet. It is, it is! Hie hence, be gone, away!
It is the lark that sings so out of tune,
Straining harsh discords and unpleasing sharps.[5]
Some say the lark makes sweet division;[6]
This doth not so, for she divideth us.
Some say the lark and loathèd toad change eyes;[7]
O, now I would they had changed voices too,
Since arm from arm that voice doth us affray,[8]
Hunting thee hence with hunt's-up[9] to the day.
O, now be gone! More light and light it grows.

Romeo. More light and light—more dark and dark our woes.

[*Enter* Nurse.]

Nurse. Madam!

Juliet. Nurse?

Nurse. Your lady mother is coming to your chamber.
The day is broke; be wary, look about. [*Exit.*]

Juliet. Then, window, let day in, and let life out.

Romeo. Farewell, farewell! One kiss, and I'll descend.

[*He goeth down.*]

Juliet. Art thou gone so, love-lord, ay husband-friend?
I must hear from thee every day in the hour,
For in a minute there are many days.
O, by this count I shall be much in years[10]
Ere I again behold my Romeo!

Romeo. Farewell!
I will omit no opportunity
That may convey my greetings, love, to thee.

Juliet. O, think'st thou we shall ever meet again?

Romeo. I doubt it not; and all these woes shall serve
For sweet discourses[11] in our times to come.

Juliet. O God, I have an ill-divining[12] soul!
Methinks I see thee, now thou art so low,
As one dead in the bottom of a tomb.
Either my eyesight fails, or thou lookest pale.

Romeo. And trust me, love, in my eye so do you.
Dry sorrow drinks our blood.[13] Adieu, adieu! [*Exit.*]

Juliet. O Fortune, Fortune! All men call thee fickle.
If thou art fickle, what dost thou[14] with him
That is renowned for faith? Be fickle, Fortune,
For then I hope thou wilt not keep him long
But send him back.

[*Enter* Mother.]

Lady Capulet. Ho, daughter! Are you up?

Juliet. Who is't that calls? It is my lady mother.
Is she not down so late,[15] or up so early?
What unaccustomed cause procures her hither?[16]

Lady Capulet. Why, how now, Juliet?

Juliet. Madam, I am not well.

Lady Capulet. Evermore weeping for your cousin's death?
What, wilt thou wash him from his grave with tears?
An if thou couldst, thou couldst not make him live.
Therefore have done. Some grief shows much of love;
But much of grief shows still some want of wit.

Juliet. Yet let me weep for such a feeling[17] loss.

Lady Capulet. So shall you feel the loss, but not the friend
Which you weep for.

Juliet. Feeling so the loss,
I cannot choose but ever weep the friend.

Lady Capulet. Well, girl, thou weep'st not so much for his death
As that the villain lives which slaughtered him.

Juliet. What villain, madam?

Lady Capulet. That same villain Romeo.

Juliet. [*Aside.*] Villain and he be many miles asunder.[18]—
God pardon him! I do, with all my heart;
And yet no man like he doth grieve my heart.

Lady Capulet. That is because the traitor murderer lives.

NOTES

11. **discourses** *n.* conversations.

12. **ill-divining** *adj.* predicting evil.

13. **Dry sorrow . . . blood** It was once believed that sorrow drained away the blood.

14. **dost thou** do you have to do.

15. **Is she . . . late** Has she stayed up so late?

16. **What . . . hither?** What unusual reason brings her here?

17. **feeling** *adj.* deeply felt.

18. **asunder** *adj.* apart.

NOTES

Juliet. Ay, madam, from the reach of these my hands,
Would none but I might venge my cousin's death!

Lady Capulet. We will have vengeance for it, fear thou not.
Then weep no more. I'll send to one in Mantua,
Where that same banished runagate[19] doth live,
Shall give him such unaccustomed dram[20]
That he shall soon keep Tybalt company;
And then I hope thou wilt be satisfied.

Juliet. Indeed I never shall be satisfied
With Romeo till I behold him—dead[21]—
Is my poor heart so for a kinsman vexed.
Madam, if you could find out but a man
To bear a poison, I would temper[22] it,
That Romeo should, upon receipt thereof,
Soon sleep in quiet. O, how my heart abhors
To hear him named and cannot come to him,
To wreak[23] the love I bore my cousin
Upon his body that hath slaughtered him!

Lady Capulet. Find thou the means, and I'll find such a man.
But now I'll tell thee joyful tidings, girl.

Juliet. And joy comes well in such a needy time.
What are they, I beseech your ladyship?

Lady Capulet. Well, well, thou hast a careful[24] father, child;
One who, to put thee from thy heaviness,
Hath sorted out[25] a sudden day of joy
That thou expects not nor I looked not for.

Juliet. Madam, in happy time![26] What day is that?

Lady Capulet. Marry, my child, early next Thursday morn
The gallant, young, and noble gentleman,
The County Paris, at Saint Peter's Church,
Shall happily make thee there a joyful bride.

Juliet. Now by Saint Peter's Church, and Peter too,
He shall not make me there a joyful bride!
I wonder at this haste, that I must wed
Ere he that should be husband comes to woo.
I pray you tell my lord and father, madam,
I will not marry yet; and when I do, I swear
It shall be Romeo, whom you know I hate,
Rather than Paris. These are news indeed!

Lady Capulet. Here comes your father. Tell him so yourself,
And see how he will take it at your hands.

[*Enter* Capulet *and* Nurse.]

Capulet. When the sun sets the earth doth drizzle dew,
But for the sunset of my brother's son
It rains downright.
How now? A conduit,[27] girl? What, still in tears?

19. **runagate** *n.* renegade; runaway.
20. **unaccustomed dram** unexpected dose of poison.
21. **dead** Juliet is deliberately ambiguous here. Her mother thinks *dead* refers to Romeo. But Juliet is using the word with the following line, in reference to her heart.
22. **temper** *v.* mix; weaken.
23. **wreak** (reek) *v.* avenge; express.
24. **careful** *adj.* considerate
25. **sorted out** selected.
26. **in happy time** just in time.
27. **conduit** *n.* water pipe.

CLOSE READ

ANNOTATE: In lines 94–124, mark Juliet's uses of double meanings and puns.

QUESTION: Why does Shakespeare construct Juliet's lines so that she never directly lies?

CONCLUDE: What purpose does such wordplay, even at critical moments such as this, serve?

^ Juliet, the Nurse, and Lady Capulet speak in private.

Evermore show'ring? In one little body
Thou counterfeits a bark,[28] a sea, a wind:
For still thy eyes, which I may call the sea,
Do ebb and flow with tears; the bark thy body is,
Sailing in this salt flood; the winds, thy sighs,
Who, raging with thy tears and they with them,
Without a sudden calm will overset
Thy tempest-tossèd body. How now, wife?
Have you delivered to her our decree?

Lady Capulet. Ay, sir; but she will none, she gives you
thanks.[29]
I would the fool were married to her grave!

Capulet. Soft! Take me with you,[30] take me with you, wife.
How? Will she none? Doth she not give us thanks?
Is she not proud?[31] Doth she not count her blest,
Unworthy as she is, that we have wrought[32]
So worthy a gentleman to be her bride?

Juliet. Not proud you have, but thankful that you have.
Proud can I never be of what I hate,
But thankful even for hate that is meant love.

Capulet. How, how, how, how, chopped-logic?[33] What is this?
"Proud"—and "I thank you"—and "I thank you not"—
And yet "not proud"? Mistress minion[34] you,
Thank me no thankings, nor proud me no prouds,
But fettle[35] your fine joints 'gainst Thursday next
To go with Paris to Saint Peter's Church,

NOTES

28. bark *n.* boat.

29. she will none . . . thanks she will have nothing to do with it, thank you.

30. Soft! Take . . . you Wait a minute. Let me understand you.

31. proud *adj.* pleased.

32. wrought *v.* arranged.

33. chopped-logic contradictory, unsound thought and speech.

34. Mistress minion Miss Uppity; overly proud.

35. fettle *v.* prepare.

NOTES

36. **hurdle** *n.* sled on which prisoners were taken to their execution.

37. **greensickness carrion** anemic lump of flesh.

38. **baggage** *n.* naughty girl.

39. **tallow-face** wax-pale face.

40. **hilding** *n.* worthless person.

41. **rate** *v.* scold; berate.

42. **Smatter . . . go!** Go chatter with the other old women.

43. **gravity** *v.* wisdom.

44. **God's bread!** By the holy Eucharist!

45. **demesnes** (dih MAYNZ) *n.* property.

46. **parts** *n.* qualities.

47. **puling** *adj.* whining.

48. **mammet** *n.* doll.

49. **in . . . tender** when good fortune is offered her.

50. **advise** *v.* consider.

Or I will drag thee on a hurdle[36] thither.
Out, you greensickness carrion![37] Out, you baggage![38]
You tallow-face![39]

Lady Capulet. Fie, fie! What, are you mad?

Juliet. Good father, I beseech you on my knees,
Hear me with patience but to speak a word.

Capulet. Hang thee, young baggage! Disobedient wretch!
I tell thee what—get thee to church a Thursday
Or never after look me in the face.
Speak not, reply not, do not answer me!
My fingers itch. Wife, we scarce thought us blest
That God had lent us but this only child;
But now I see this one is one too much,
And that we have a curse in having her.
Out on her, hilding![40]

Nurse. God in heaven bless her!
You are to blame, my lord, to rate[41] her so.

Capulet. And why, my Lady Wisdom? Hold your tongue,
Good Prudence. Smatter with your gossips, go![42]

Nurse. I speak no treason.

Capulet. O, God-i-god-en!

Nurse. May not one speak?

Capulet. Peace, you mumbling fool!
Utter your gravity[43] o'er a gossip's bowl,
For here we need it not.

Lady Capulet. You are too hot.

Capulet. God's bread![44] It makes me mad.
Day, night; hour, tide, time; work, play;
Alone, in company; still my care hath been
To have her matched; and having now provided
A gentleman of noble parentage,
Of fair demesnes,[45] youthful, and nobly trained,
Stuffed, as they say, with honorable parts,[46]
Proportioned as one's thought would wish a man—
And then to have a wretched puling[47] fool,
A whining mammet,[48] in her fortune's tender,[49]
To answer "I'll not wed, I cannot love;
I am too young, I pray you pardon me"!
But, and you will not wed, I'll pardon you!
Graze where you will, you shall not house with me.
Look to't, think on't; I do not use to jest.
Thursday is near; lay hand on heart, advise:[50]
And you be mine, I'll give you to my friend;
And you be not, hang, beg, starve, die in the streets,
For, by my soul, I'll ne'er acknowledge thee,

Nor what is mine shall never do thee good.
Trust to't. Bethink you. I'll not be forsworn.[51] [*Exit.*]

Juliet. Is there no pity sitting in the clouds
That sees into the bottom of my grief?
O sweet my mother, cast me not away!
Delay this marriage for a month, a week;
Or if you do not, make the bridal bed
In that dim monument where Tybalt lies.

Lady Capulet. Talk not to me, for I'll not speak a word.
Do as thou wilt, for I have done with thee. [*Exit.*]

Juliet. O God!—O nurse, how shall this be prevented?
My husband is on earth, my faith in heaven.[52]
How shall that faith return again to earth
Unless that husband send it me from heaven
By leaving earth?[53] Comfort me, counsel me.
Alack, alack, that heaven should practice stratagems[54]
Upon so soft a subject as myself!
What say'st thou? Hast thou not a word of joy?
Some comfort, nurse.

Nurse. Faith, here it is.
Romeo is banished; and all the world to nothing[55]
That he dares ne'er come back to challenge[56] you;
Or if he do, it needs must be by stealth.
Then, since the case so stands as now it doth,
I think it best you married with the County.
O, he's a lovely gentleman!
Romeo's a dishclout to him.[57] An eagle, madam,
Hath not so green, so quick, so fair an eye
As Paris hath. Beshrew my very heart,
I think you are happy in this second match,
For it excels your first; or if it did not,
Your first is dead—or 'twere as good he were
As living here and you no use of him.

Juliet. Speak'st thou from thy heart?

Nurse. And from my soul too; else beshrew them both.

Juliet. Amen!

Nurse. What?

Juliet. Well, thou hast comforted me marvelous much.
Go in; and tell my lady I am gone,
Having displeased my father, to Lawrence' cell,
To make confession and to be absolved.[58]

Nurse. Marry, I will; and this is wisely done. [*Exit.*]

Juliet. Ancient damnation![59] O most wicked fiend!
Is it more sin to wish me thus forsworn,
Or to dispraise my lord with that same tongue

NOTES

51. forsworn *v.* made to violate my promise.

52. my faith in heaven my marriage vow is recorded in heaven.

53. leaving earth dying.

54. stratagems *n.* tricks; plots.

55. all . . . nothing the odds are overwhelming.

56. challenge *v.* claim.

57. a dishclout to him a dishcloth compared with him.

58. absolved *v.* receive forgiveness for my sins.

59. Ancient damnation! Old devil!

NOTES

60. Thou . . . twain You will from now on be separated from my trust

Which she hath praised him with above compare
So many thousand times? Go, counselor!
Thou and my bosom henceforth shall be twain.[60]
I'll to the friar to know his remedy.
If all else fail, myself have power to die. [*Exit.*]

Comprehension Check

Complete the following items after you finish your first read.

1. Why does Romeo refuse to fight with Tybalt?

2. In what two ways is Romeo the cause of Mercutio's death?

3. What punishment could the Prince have ordered for Romeo? What punishment did he order?

4. **Notebook** Confirm your understanding of the text by writing a summary.

RESEARCH

Research to Clarify Choose at least one unfamiliar detail from the text. Briefly research that detail. In what way does the information you learned shed light on an aspect of the play?

Close Read the Text

Reread Benvolio's description of the two fights that lead to Mercutio's and Tybalt's deaths (Act III, Scene i, lines 150–173). Mark words and phrases that describe specific details about the actions of Romeo and Tybalt. Based on these details, what is Benvolio trying to convey in his account to the Prince?

THE TRAGEDY OF ROMEO AND JULIET, ACT III

Analyze the Text

CITE TEXTUAL EVIDENCE to support your answers.

Notebook Respond to these questions.

1. (a) How and why does Romeo kill Tybalt? (b) **Interpret** What does Romeo mean when he says, after killing Tybalt, "I am fortune's fool"?
2. (a) **Analyze** Describe the conflicting emotions Juliet feels when the Nurse reports Tybalt's death and Romeo's punishment. (b) **Compare and Contrast** In what ways are Romeo's and Juliet's reactions to Romeo's banishment similar and different? Explain.
3. (a) **Paraphrase** When you **paraphrase**, you restate a text in your own words. Paraphrase Romeo's thoughts in Act III, Scene iii, lines 29–51. (b) **Criticize** How would you describe Romeo's response in these lines?
4. **Essential Question:** What have you learned about destiny by reading Act III of *The Tragedy of Romeo and Juliet*?

Tool Kit
Close-Read Guide and Model Annotation

LANGUAGE DEVELOPMENT

Concept Vocabulary

exile	banishment	pardon

Why These Words? These concept vocabulary words relate to punishment and forgiveness. How does each word contribute to meaning in the text? What other words in the selection connect to this concept?

WORD NETWORK

Add interesting words related to destiny from the text to your Word Network.

Practice

Notebook Confirm your understanding of these words by using each one in a sentence.

Word Study

Notebook **Latin Prefix: ex-** In the word *exile,* the Latin prefix *ex-* means "away" or "out of." In the play, Romeo is exiled, which means he must go away from his home city. Using your understanding of the prefix *ex-*, record a definition for each of the following words: *extract*, *excavate*, *export*, *extension*.

STANDARDS.

Language
Identify and correctly use patterns of word changes that indicate different meanings or parts of speech.

THE TRAGEDY OF ROMEO AND JULIET, ACT III

Analyze Craft and Structure

Dramatic Structures In most plays, the dramatic action takes place primarily through **dialogue**—the conversations between characters. Some playwrights use specialized dialogue in the form of these types of **dramatic speeches:**

- **Soliloquy:** a lengthy speech in which a character—usually alone on the stage—expresses his or her true thoughts or feelings.
- **Aside:** a brief remark, often addressed to the audience and unheard by the other characters.
- **Monologue:** a lengthy speech by one character. Unlike a soliloquy or an aside, a monologue is addressed to other characters.

STANDARDS

Reading Literature
Analyze how an author's choices concerning how to structure a text, order events within it, and manipulate time create such effects as mystery, tension, or surprise.

Practice

CITE TEXTUAL EVIDENCE to support your answers.

Notebook Respond to these questions.

1. (a) What thoughts and feelings does Juliet express in the soliloquy that opens Scene ii of Act III? (b) When Juliet makes an allusion to Phoebus and Phaëthon, what is she hoping will happen? Explain.
2. What criticisms of Romeo does the Friar express in his Act III, Scene iii monologue beginning, "Hold thy desperate hand"? Cite details from the monologue in your response.
3. (a) In Act III, Scene v, when her mother refers to Romeo as a villain, Juliet utters the aside, "Villain and he be many miles asunder." What does she mean by this? (b) Why does Juliet speak only to the audience? Explain.
4. Complete the chart to analyze Mercutio's dialogue in Act III, Scene i. (a) In the first row, write the remark regarding the Montagues and the Capulets that Mercutio makes three times as he is dying. (b) In the second row, explain what Mercutio means by this exclamation. (c) In the third row, explain how his remark reinforces ideas set forth in the play's Prologue.

MERCUTIO'S DIALOGUE
MEANING
EXPLANATION

Writing to Sources

Writings about literature may be called critical writing, literary criticism, or responses to literature. In most literary criticism, you will need to combine explanatory writing with argument. Your aim is to both explain your interpretation of a text and present it in a convincing, persuasive way.

Assignment

Write a **dual character study** in which you show how two characters in the play provide strong contrasts for one another. A character who provides a strong contrast to another character is called a **foil**.

- The foil is usually a secondary character who presents contrasts to a main character.
- The presence of the foil serves to emphasize the main character's distinctive qualities. If a main character is gentle, the foil is aggressive.

In this assignment, consider writing about the following sets of characters:

Romeo and Tybalt / Benvolio and Mercutio

You may also choose another pair of characters that you think work as foils. Regardless of the pair you choose, make sure to describe both characters' qualities and explain how Shakespeare conveys strong contrasts between the two.

EVIDENCE LOG

Before moving on to a new selection, go to your Evidence Log and record what you learned from *The Tragedy of Romeo and Juliet,* Act III.

Vocabulary Connection In your dual character study, consider including concept vocabulary words.

exile	banishment	pardon

Reflect on Your Writing

After you have written your dual character study, answer these questions.

1. What was the hardest part of creating this dual character study?

2. How might you revise your dual character study to clarify your ideas?

3. **Why These Words?** The words you choose make a difference in your writing. Which words helped you convey contrasts between the two characters in your dual character study?

STANDARDS

Writing

Write informative/ explanatory texts to examine and convey complex ideas, concepts, and information clearly and accurately through the effective selection, organization, and analysis of content.

Playwright

William Shakespeare

The Tragedy of Romeo and Juliet, Act IV

Concept Vocabulary

You will encounter the following words as you read Act IV of *The Tragedy of Romeo and Juliet*. Before reading, note how familiar you are with each word. Then, rank the words in order from most familiar (1) to least familiar (3).

WORD	YOUR RANKING
lamentable	
distressed	
melancholy	

After completing your first read, come back to the concept vocabulary and review your rankings. Mark changes to your original rankings as needed.

Tool Kit
First-Read Guide and Model Annotation

First Read DRAMA

Apply these strategies as you conduct your first read. You will have an opportunity to complete the close-read notes after your first read.

NOTICE *whom* the story is about, *what* happens, *where* and *when* it happens, and *why* those involved react as they do.

ANNOTATE by marking vocabulary and key passages you want to revisit.

CONNECT ideas within the selection to what you already know and what you have already read.

RESPOND by completing the Comprehension Check and by writing a brief summary of the selection.

STANDARDS

Reading Literature
By the end of grade 9, read and comprehend literature, including stories, dramas, and poems, in the grades 9–10 text complexity band proficiently, with scaffolding as needed at the high end of the range.

The Tragedy of Romeo and Juliet

William Shakespeare

Act IV

REVIEW AND ANTICIPATE

Romeo and Juliet are married for only a few hours when disaster strikes. In Act III, Juliet's cousin Tybalt kills Mercutio, and then Romeo kills Tybalt. This leads to Romeo's banishment from Verona. To make matters worse, Juliet's parents are determined to marry her to Paris. As you read Act IV, consider the passions and conflicts that motivate Romeo and Juliet as their situation becomes increasingly desperate.

Scene i • *Friar Lawrence's cell.*

[*Enter* Friar Lawrence *and* County Paris.]

Friar. On Thursday, sir? The time is very short.

Paris. My father[1] Capulet will have it so,
And I am nothing slow to slack his haste.[2]

Friar. You say you do not know the lady's mind.
Uneven is the course;[3] I like it not.

Paris. Immoderately she weeps for Tybalt's death,
And therefore have I little talked of love;
For Venus smiles not in a house of tears.
Now, sir, her father counts it dangerous
That she do give her sorrow so much sway,
And in his wisdom hastes our marriage
To stop the inundation[4] of her tears,
Which, too much minded[5] by herself alone,
May be put from her by society.
Now do you know the reason of this haste.

NOTES

1. **father** future father-in-law.
2. **I . . . haste** I will not slow him down by being slow myself.
3. **Uneven . . . course** irregular is the plan.
4. **inundation** *n.* flood.
5. **minded** *v.* thought about.

NOTES

6. That's . . . text That is a certain truth.

CLOSE READ

ANNOTATE: In lines 18–38, mark speeches that are no more than one sentence in length.

QUESTION: Why is Paris and Juliet's conversation composed primarily of short lines?

CONCLUDE: How does this scene make the audience feel about Paris?

7. price *n.* value.

8. before their spite before the harm that the tears did.

9. entreat . . . alone ask to have this time to ourselves.

10. shield *v.* forbid.

11. past . . . wits beyond the ability of my mind to find a remedy.

12. prorogue (proh ROHG) *v.* delay.

13. presently *adv.* at once.

Friar. [*Aside*] I would I knew not why it should be slowed.—
Look, sir, here comes the lady towards my cell.
[*Enter* Juliet.]

Paris. Happily met, my lady and my wife!

Juliet. That may be, sir, when I may be a wife.

Paris. That "may be" must be, love, on Thursday next.

Juliet. What must be shall be.

Friar. That's a certain text.[6]

Paris. Come you to make confession to this father?

Juliet. To answer that, I should confess to you.

Paris. Do not deny to him that you love me.

Juliet. I will confess to you that I love him.

Paris. So will ye, I am sure, that you love me.

Juliet. If I do so, it will be of more price,[7]
Being spoke behind your back, than to your face.

Paris. Poor soul, thy face is much abused with tears.

Juliet. The tears have got small victory by that,
For it was bad enough before their spite.[8]

Paris. Thou wrong'st it more than tears with that report.

Juliet. That is no slander, sir, which is a truth;
And what I spake, I spake it to my face.

Paris. Thy face is mine, and thou hast sland'red it.

Juliet. It may be so, for it is not mine own.
Are you at leisure, holy father, now,
Or shall I come to you at evening mass?

Friar. My leisure serves me, pensive daughter, now.
My lord, we must entreat the time alone.[9]

Paris. God shield[10] I should disturb devotion!
Juliet, on Thursday early will I rouse ye.
Till then, adieu, and keep this holy kiss. [*Exit.*]

Juliet. O, shut the door, and when thou hast done so,
Come weep with me—past hope, past cure, past help!

Friar. O Juliet, I already know thy grief;
It strains me past the compass of my wits.[11]
I hear thou must, and nothing may prorogue[12] it,
On Thursday next be married to this County.

Juliet. Tell me not, friar, that thou hearest of this,
Unless thou tell me how I may prevent it.
If in thy wisdom thou canst give no help,
Do thou but call my resolution wise
And with this knife I'll help it presently.[13]
God joined my heart and Romeo's, thou our hands;

And ere this hand, by thee to Romeo's sealed,
Shall be the label to another deed,[14]
Or my true heart with treacherous revolt
Turn to another, this shall slay them both.
Therefore, out of thy long-experienced time,
Give me some present counsel; or, behold,
'Twixt my extremes and me[15] this bloody knife
Shall play the umpire, arbitrating[16] that
Which the commission of thy years and art
Could to no issue of true honor bring.[17]
Be not so long to speak. I long to die
If what thou speak'st speak not of remedy.

Friar. Hold, daughter. I do spy a kind of hope,
Which craves[18] as desperate an execution
As that is desperate which we would prevent.
If, rather than to marry County Paris,
Thou hast the strength of will to slay thyself,
Then is it likely thou wilt undertake
A thing like death to chide away this shame,
That cop'st with death himself to scape from it;[19]
And, if thou darest, I'll give thee remedy.

Juliet. O, bid me leap, rather than marry Paris,
From off the battlements of any tower,
Or walk in thievish ways,[20] or bid me lurk
Where serpents are; chain me with roaring bears,
Or hide me nightly in a charnel house,[21]
O'ercovered quite with dead men's rattling bones,
With reeky[22] shanks and yellow chapless[23] skulls;
Or bid me go into a new-made grave
And hide me with a dead man in his shroud—
Things that, to hear them told, have made me tremble—
And I will do it without fear or doubt,
To live an unstained wife to my sweet love.

Friar. Hold, then. Go home, be merry, give consent
To marry Paris. Wednesday is tomorrow.
Tomorrow night look that thou lie alone;
Let not the nurse lie with thee in thy chamber.
Take thou this vial, being then in bed,
And this distilled liquor drink thou off;
When presently through all thy veins shall run
A cold and drowsy humor,[24] for no pulse
Shall keep his native[25] progress, but surcease;[26]
No warmth, no breath, shall testify thou livest;
The roses in thy lips and cheeks shall fade
To wanny ashes,[27] thy eyes' windows[28] fall
Like death when he shuts up the day of life;
Each part, deprived of supple government,[29]

NOTES

14. **Shall . . . deed** shall give the seal of approval to another marriage contract.

15. **'Twixt . . . me** between my misfortunes and me.

16. **arbitrating** *v.* deciding.

17. **Which . . . bring** which the authority that derives from your age and ability could not solve honorably.

18. **craves** *v.* requires.

19. **That cop'st . . . it** that bargains with death itself to escape from it.

20. **thievish ways** roads where criminals lurk.

21. **charnel house** vault for bones removed from graves to be reused.

22. **reeky** *adj.* foul-smelling.

23. **chapless** *adj.* jawless.

24. **humor** *n.* fluid; liquid.

25. **native** *adj.* natural.

26. **surcease** *v.* stop.

27. **wanny ashes** to the color of pale ashes.

28. **eyes' windows** eyelids.

29. **supple government** ability for maintaining motion.

Shall, stiff and stark and cold, appear like death;
And in this borrowed likeness of shrunk death
Thou shalt continue two-and-forty hours,
And then awake as from a pleasant sleep.
Now, when the bridegroom in the morning comes
To rouse thee from thy bed, there art thou dead.
Then, as the manner of our country is,
In thy best robes uncovered on the bier[30]
Thou shalt be borne to that same ancient vault
Where all the kindred of the Capulets lie.
In the meantime, against[31] thou shalt awake,
Shall Romeo by my letters know our drift;[32]
And hither shall he come: and he and I
Will watch thy waking, and that very night
Shall Romeo bear thee hence to Mantua.
And this shall free thee from this present shame,
If no inconstant toy[33] nor womanish fear,
Abate thy valor[34] in the acting it.

Juliet. Give me, give me! O, tell not me of fear!

Friar. Hold! Get you gone, be strong and prosperous
In this resolve. I'll send a friar with speed
To Mantua, with my letters to thy lord.

Juliet. Love give me strength! and strength shall help afford.
Farewell, dear father. [*Exit with* Friar.]

⌘⌘⌘

Scene ii • *Hall in Capulet's house.*

[*Enter* Father Capulet, Mother, Nurse, *and* Servingmen, *two or three.*]

Capulet. So many guests invite as here are writ.
[*Exit a* Servingman.]
Sirrah, go hire me twenty cunning[1] cooks.

Servingman. You shall have none ill, sir; for I'll try[2] if they can lick their fingers.

Capulet. How canst thou try them so?

Servingman. Marry, sir, 'tis an ill cook that cannot lick his own fingers.[3] Therefore he that cannot lick his fingers goes not with me.

Capulet. Go, begone.

[*Exit* Servingman.]

We shall be much unfurnished[4] for this time.
What, is my daughter gone to Friar Lawrence?

NOTES

30. uncovered on the bier (bihr) displayed on the funeral platform.

31. against *adv.* before.

32. drift *n.* purpose; plan.

33. inconstant toy passing whim.

34. Abate thy valor Lessen your courage.

1. cunning *adj.* skillful.

2. try *v.* test.

3. 'tis . . . fingers It is a bad cook who will not taste his own cooking.

4. unfurnished *adj.* unprepared.

Nurse. Ay, forsooth.[5]

Capulet. Well, he may chance to do some good on her.
A peevish self-willed harlotry it is.[6]

[*Enter* Juliet.]

Nurse. See where she comes from shrift with merry look.

Capulet. How now, my headstrong! Where have you been
gadding?

Juliet. Where I have learnt me to repent the sin
Of disobedient opposition
To you and your behests,[7] and am enjoined
By holy Lawrence to fall prostrate[8] here
To beg your pardon. Pardon, I beseech you!
Henceforward I am ever ruled by you.

Capulet. Send for the County. Go tell him of this.
I'll have this knot knit up tomorrow morning.

Juliet. I met the youthful lord at Lawrence' cell
And gave him what becomèd[9] love I might,
Not stepping o'er the bounds of modesty.

Capulet. Why, I am glad on't. This is well. Stand up.
This is as't should be. Let me see the County.
Ay, marry, go, I say, and fetch him hither.
Now, afore God, this reverend holy friar,
All our whole city is much bound[10] to him.

Juliet. Nurse, will you go with me into my closet[11]
To help me sort such needful ornaments[12]
As you think fit to furnish me tomorrow?

Lady Capulet. No, not till Thursday. There is time enough.

Capulet. Go, nurse, go with her. We'll to church tomorrow.
[*Exit* Juliet *and* Nurse.]

Lady Capulet. We shall be short in our provision.[13]
'Tis now near night.

Capulet. Tush, I will stir about,
And all things shall be well, I warrant thee, wife.
Go thou to Juliet, help to deck up her.[14]
I'll not to bed tonight; let me alone.
I'll play the housewife for this once. What, ho![15]
They are all forth; well, I will walk myself
To County Paris, to prepare up him
Against tomorrow. My heart is wondrous light,
Since this same wayward girl is so reclaimed.
[*Exit with* Mother.]

⌘ ⌘ ⌘

NOTES

5. **forsooth** *adv.* in truth.

6. **A peevish . . . it is** It is the ill-tempered, selfish behavior of a woman without good breeding.

7. **behests** *v.* requests.

8. **fall prostrate** lie face down in humble submission.

9. **becomèd** *adj.* suitable; proper.

10. **bound** *adj.* indebted.

11. **closet** *n.* private room.

12. **ornaments** *n.* clothes.

13. **short . . . provision** lacking time for preparation.

14. **deck up her** dress her; get her ready.

15. **What, ho!** Capulet is calling one of his servants.

NOTES

1. **orisons** (AWR uh zuhnz) *n.* prayers.

2. **state** *n.* condition.

3. **cross** *adj.* selfish; disobedient.

4. **culled** *v.* chosen.

5. **behoveful** *adj.* desirable; appropriate.

CLOSE READ

ANNOTATE: In lines 15–58, mark the questions Juliet asks that include the word *if*.

QUESTION: Why does Shakespeare have Juliet ask this series of questions?

CONCLUDE: What does this series of questions show about Juliet's state of mind as she prepares to drink the potion?

6. **minist'red** *v.* given me.

7. **tried** *v.* proved.

8. **conceit** *n.* idea; thought.

Scene iii • *Juliet's chamber.*

[*Enter* Juliet *and* Nurse.]

Juliet. Ay, those attires are best: but, gentle nurse,
I pray thee, leave me to my self tonight;
For I have need of many orisons[1]
To move the heavens to smile upon my state,[2]
Which, well thou knowest, is cross[3] and full of sin.

[*Enter* Lady Capulet.]

Lady Capulet. What, are you busy, ho? Need you my help?

Juliet. No, madam; we have culled[4] such necessaries
As are behoveful[5] for our state tomorrow.
So please you, let me now be left alone,
And let the nurse this night sit up with you;
For I am sure you have your hands full all
In this so sudden business.

Lady Capulet. Good night.
Get thee to bed, and rest; for thou hast need.

[*Exit* Lady Capulet *and* Nurse.]

Juliet. Farewell! God knows when we shall meet again.
I have a faint cold fear thrills through my veins
That almost freezes up the heat of life.
I'll call them back again to comfort me.
Nurse!—What should she do here?
My dismal scene I needs must act alone.
Come, vial.
What if this mixture do not work at all?
Shall I be married then tomorrow morning?
No, no! This shall forbid it. Lie thou there.

[*Lays down a dagger.*]

What if it be a poison which the friar
Subtly hath minist'red[6] to have me dead,
Lest in this marriage he should be dishonored
Because he married me before to Romeo?
I fear it is; and yet methinks it should not,
For he hath still been tried[7] a holy man.
How if, when I am laid into the tomb,
I wake before the time that Romeo
Come to redeem me? There's a fearful point!
Shall I not then be stifled in the vault,
To whose foul mouth no healthsome air breathes in,
And there die strangled ere my Romeo comes?
Or, if I live, is it not very like
The horrible conceit[8] of death and night,
Together with the terror of the place—
As in a vault, an ancient receptacle

NOTES

Where for this many hundred years the bones
Of all my buried ancestors are packed;
Where bloody Tybalt, yet but green in earth,[9]
Lies fest'ring in his shroud; where, as they say,
At some hours in the night spirits resort—
Alack, alack, is it not like[10] that I,
So early waking—what with loathsome smells,
And shrieks like mandrakes[11] torn out of the earth,
That living mortals, hearing them, run mad—
O, if I wake, shall I not be distraught,[12]
Environed[13] with all these hideous fears,
And madly play with my forefathers' joints,
And pluck the mangled Tybalt from his shroud,
And, in this rage, with some great kinsman's bone
As with a club dash out my desp'rate brains?
O, look! Methinks I see my cousin's ghost
Seeking out Romeo, that did spit his body
Upon a rapier's point. Stay, Tybalt, stay!
Romeo, Romeo, Romeo, I drink to thee!
[*She falls upon her bed, within the curtains.*]

9. **green in earth** newly entombed.

10. **like** *adv.* likely.

11. **mandrakes** *n.* plants with forked roots that resemble human legs. The mandrake was believed to shriek when uprooted and cause the hearer to go mad.

12. **distraught** *adj.* insane.

13. **Environed** *v.* surrounded.

⌘ ⌘ ⌘

Scene iv • *Hall in Capulet's house.*

[*Enter* Lady of The House *and* Nurse.]

Lady Capulet. Hold, take these keys and fetch more spices, nurse.

Nurse. They call for dates and quinces[1] in the pastry.[2]

[*Enter old* Capulet.]

Capulet. Come, stir, stir, stir! The second cock hath crowed,
The curfew bell hath rung, 'tis three o'clock,

1. **quinces** *n.* golden, apple-shaped fruits.

2. **pastry** *n.* baking room.

Look to the baked meats, good Angelica;[3]
Spare not for cost.

Nurse. Go, you cotquean,[4] go,
Get you to bed! Faith, you'll be sick tomorrow
For this night's watching.[5]

Capulet. No, not a whit. What, I have watched ere now
All night for lesser cause, and ne'er been sick.

Lady Capulet. Ay, you have been a mouse hunt[6] in your time;
But I will watch you from such watching now.
[*Exit* Lady *and* Nurse.]

Capulet. A jealous hood, a jealous hood![7]
[*Enter three or four* Fellows *with spits and logs and baskets.*]
Now, fellow,
What is there?

First Fellow. Things for the cook, sir; but I know not what.

Capulet. Make haste, make haste. [*Exit* First Fellow.] Sirrah, fetch drier logs.
Call Peter; he will show thee where they are.

Second Fellow. I have a head, sir, that will find out logs
And never trouble Peter for the matter.

Capulet. Mass,[8] and well said; a merry whoreson, ha!
Thou shalt be loggerhead.[9]
[*Exit* Second Fellow, *with the others.*]
Good faith, 'tis day.
The County will be here with music straight,
For so he said he would. [*Play music.*]
I hear him near.
Nurse! Wife! What, ho! What, nurse, I say!
[*Enter* Nurse.]
Go waken Juliet; go and trim her up.
I'll go and chat with Paris. Hie, make haste,
Make haste! The bridegroom he is come already;
Make haste, I say. [*Exit.*]

⌘ ⌘ ⌘

Scene v • *Juliet's chamber.*

Nurse. Mistress! What, mistress! Juliet! Fast,[1] I warrant her, she.
Why, lamb! Why, lady! Fie, you slugabed![2]
Why, love, I say! Madam; Sweetheart! Why, bride!
What, not a word? You take your pennyworths now;
Sleep for a week; for the next night, I warrant,

NOTES

3. **Angelica** this is probably the Nurse's name.
4. **cotquean** (KOT kween) *n.* man who does housework.
5. **watching** *adj.* staying awake.
6. **mouse hunt** woman chaser.
7. **jealous hood** jealousy.
8. **Mass** by the Mass (an oath).
9. **loggerhead** blockhead.

CLOSE READ

ANNOTATE: Mark details in both spoken lines and stage directions of Scene iv that relate to food, joy, and anticipation.

QUESTION: Why does Shakespeare present such a happy scene?

CONCLUDE: What are the effects of positioning this scene right after Scene iii in which Juliet drinks the potion?

1. **Fast** fast asleep.
2. **slugabed** sleepyhead.

The County Paris hath set up his rest,
That you shall rest but little. God forgive me!
Marry, and amen. How sound is she asleep!
I must needs wake her. Madam, madam, madam!
Ay, let the County take you in your bed;
He'll fright you up, i' faith. Will it not be?

[*Draws aside the curtains.*]

What, dressed, and in your clothes, and down again?[3]
I must needs wake you. Lady! Lady! Lady!
Alas, alas! Help, help! My lady's dead!
O weraday that ever I was born!
Some aqua vitae, ho! My lord! My lady!
[*Enter* Lady Capulet.]

Lady Capulet. What noise is here?

Nurse. O **lamentable** day!

Lady Capulet. What is the matter?

Nurse. Look, look! O heavy day!

Lady Capulet. O me, O me! My child, my only life!
Revive, look up, or I will die with thee!
Help, help! Call help.

[*Enter* Capulet.]

Capulet. For shame, bring Juliet forth; her lord is come.

Nurse. She's dead, deceased; she's dead, alack the day!

Lady Capulet. Alack the day, she's dead, she's dead, she's dead!

Capulet. Ha! Let me see her. Out alas! She's cold,
Her blood is settled, and her joints are stiff;
Life and these lips have long been separated.
Death lies on her like an untimely frost
Upon the sweetest flower of all the field.

Nurse. O lamentable day!

Lady Capulet. O woeful time!

Capulet. Death, that hath ta'en her hence to make me wail,
Ties up my tongue and will not let me speak.

[*Enter* Friar Lawrence *and the* County Paris, *with* Musicians.]

Friar. Come, is the bride ready to go to church?

Capulet. Ready to go, but never to return.
O son, the night before thy wedding day
Hath Death lain with thy wife. There she lies,
Flower as she was, deflowered by him.
Death is my son-in-law, Death is my heir;
My daughter he hath wedded. I will die,

NOTES

3. down again back in bed.

lamentable (luh MEHN tuh buhl) *adj.* grievous; mournful; sorrowful

NOTES

4. solace *v.* find comfort.

5. Beguiled *adj.* cheated.

distressed (dihs TREHST) *adj.* full of anxiety and suffering

6. Uncomfortable *adj.* painful, upsetting.

7. solemnity *n.* solemn rites.

8. Confusion's . . . confusions The remedy for this calamity is not to be found in these outcries.

9. well *adj.* blessed in heaven.

10. rosemary *n.* evergreen herb signifying love and remembrance.

11. fond nature mistake-prone human nature.

12. Yet . . . merriment While human nature causes us to weep for Juliet, reason should cause us to be happy (since she is in heaven).

13. ordainèd festival planned to be part of a celebration.

And leave him all. Life, living, all is Death's.

Paris. Have I thought, love, to see this morning's face,
And doth it give me such a sight as this?

Lady Capulet. Accursed, unhappy, wretched, hateful day!
Most miserable hour that e'er time saw
In lasting labor of his pilgrimage!
But one, poor one, one poor and loving child,
But one thing to rejoice and solace[4] in,
And cruel Death hath catched it from my sight.

Nurse. O woe! O woeful, woeful, woeful day!
Most lamentable day, most woeful day,
That ever ever I did yet behold!
O day, O day, O day! O hateful day!
Never was seen so black a day as this.
O woeful day! O woeful day!

Paris. Beguiled,[5] divorcèd, wrongèd, spited, slain!
Most detestable Death, by thee beguiled,
By cruel, cruel thee quite overthrown.
O love! O life!—not life, but love in death!

Capulet. Despised, **distressed**, hated, martyred, killed!
Uncomfortable[6] time, why cam'st thou now
To murder, murder our solemnity?[7]
O child! O child! My soul, and not my child!
Dead art thou—alack, my child is dead,
And with my child my joys are burièd!

Friar. Peace, ho, for shame! Confusion's cure lives not
In these confusions.[8] Heaven and yourself
Had part in this fair maid—now heaven hath all,
And all the better is it for the maid.
Your part in her you could not keep from death,
But heaven keeps his part in eternal life.
The most you sought was her promotion,
For 'twas your heaven she should be advanced;
And weep ye now, seeing she is advanced
Above the clouds, as high as heaven itself?
O, in this love, you love your child so ill
That you run mad, seeing that she is well.[9]
She's not well married that lives married long,
But she's best married that dies married young.
Dry up your tears, and stick your rosemary[10]
On this fair corse, and, as the custom is,
And in her best array bear her to church;
For though fond nature[11] bids us all lament,
Yet nature's tears are reason's merriment.[12]

Capulet. All things that we ordainèd festival[13]
Turn from their office to black funeral—

Our instruments to **melancholy** bells,
Our wedding cheer to a sad burial feast,
Our solemn hymns to sullen dirges[14] change;
Our bridal flowers serve for a buried corse;
And all things change them to the contrary.

Friar. Sir, go you in; and, madam, go with him;
And go, Sir Paris. Everyone prepare
To follow this fair corse unto her grave.
The heavens do low'r[15] upon you for some ill;
Move them no more by crossing their high will.
[*Exit, casting rosemary on her and shutting the curtains. The* Nurse *and* Musicians *remain.*]

First Musician. Faith, we may put up our pipes and be gone.

Nurse. Honest good fellows, ah, put up, put up!
For well you know this is a pitiful case.[16] [*Exit.*]

First Musician. Ay, by my troth, the case may be amended.
[*Enter* Peter.]

Peter. Musicians, O, musicians, "Heart's ease," "Heart's ease"!
O, and you will have me live, play "Heart's ease."

First Musician. Why "Heart's ease"?

Peter. O, musicians, because my heart itself plays "My heart is full."
O, play me some merry dump[17] to comfort me.

First Musician. Not a dump we! 'Tis no time to play now.

Peter. You will not, then?

First Musician. No.

Peter. I will then give it you soundly.

First Musician. What will you give us?

Peter. No money, on my faith, but the gleek.[18] I will give you[19] the minstrel.[20]

First Musician. Then I will give you the serving-creature.

Peter. Then will I lay the serving-creature's dagger on your pate.
I will carry no crotchets.[21] I'll re you, I'll fa you. Do you note me?

First Musician. And you re us and fa us, you note us.

Second Musician. Pray you put up your dagger, and put out your wit.

Peter. Then have at you with my wit! I will dry-beat you with an iron wit, and put up my iron dagger. Answer me like men.
"When griping grief the heart doth wound,
And doleful dumps the mind oppress,
Then music with her silver sound"—

NOTES

melancholy (MEHL uhn kol ee) *adj.* sad and depressed

14. **dirges** *n.* funeral hymns.

15. **low'r** *v.* frown.

16. **case** *n.* situation; instrument case.

17. **dump** *n.* sad tune.

18. **gleek** *n.* scornful speech.

19. **give you** call you.

20. **minstrel** a contemptuous term (as opposed to "musician").

21. **crochets** *n.* whims; quarter notes.

NOTES

22. **cry you mercy** beg your pardon.

Why "silver sound"? Why "music with her silver sound?" What say you, Simon Catling?

First Musician. Marry, sir, because silver hath a sweet sound.

Peter. Pretty! What say you, Hugh Rebeck?

Second Musician. I say "silver sound" because musicians sound for silver.

Peter. Pretty too! What say you, James Soundpost?

Third Musician. Faith, I know not what to say.

Peter. O, I cry you mercy,[22] you are the singer. I will say for you. It is "music with her silver sound" because musicians have no gold for sounding.

"Then music with her silver sound
With speedy help doth lend redress." [*Exit.*]

First Musician. What a pestilent knave is this same!

Second Musician. Hang him, Jack! Come, we'll in here, tarry for the mourners, and stay dinner. [*Exit with others.*]

Comprehension Check

Complete the following items after you finish your first read.

1. What is Juliet prepared to do rather than marry Paris?

2. Why does Juliet tell her father she is willing to marry Paris?

3. What happens when Juliet drinks the potion?

4. **Notebook** Confirm your understanding of the text by writing a summary.

RESEARCH

Research to Clarify Choose at least one unfamiliar detail from the text. Briefly research that detail. In what way does the information you learned shed light on an aspect of the play?

Close Read the Text

Reread lines 13–20 of Act IV, Scene iii. Mark words and phrases that describe Juliet's thoughts and feelings after the Nurse and Lady Capulet leave. Based on these details, how does Juliet feel about what she is preparing to do?

THE TRAGEDY OF ROMEO AND JULIET, ACT IV

Analyze the Text

CITE TEXTUAL EVIDENCE to support your answers.

Notebook Respond to these questions.

1. (a) What is Friar Lawrence's plan for Juliet? (b) **Analyze** Why do you think Juliet trusts the Friar? Explain your answer using details from the text.
2. (a) What three fears about taking the potion does Juliet reveal in her soliloquy in Act IV, Scene iii? (b) **Interpret** What does the soliloquy reveal about her personality? Explain your response and support it with details from the text.
3. (a) **Summarize** Juliet's words in Act IV, Scene i, lines 50–59. (b) **Interpret** What do Juliet's words indicate about her view of the situation that she finds herself in?
4. **Essential Question:** ***Do we determine our own destinies?*** What have you learned about destiny by reading Act IV of *The Tragedy of Romeo and Juliet*?

Tool Kit
Close-Read Guide and Model Annotation

WORD NETWORK
Add interesting words related to destiny from the text to your Word Network.

LANGUAGE DEVELOPMENT

Concept Vocabulary

lamentable	distressed	melancholy

Why These Words? The concept vocabulary words relate to feelings of sadness. What other words in the selection connect to this concept?

Practice

Notebook Confirm your understanding of these words by using each one in a sentence.

Word Study

Notebook Latin Root: *-stress-* The word *distressed* contains the root *-stress-*. This root comes from a Latin word, *stringere*, which means "to draw tight." The roots *-strict-*, in the word *constrict,* and *-strain-* in the word *constrain,* also come from *stringere*. Find several other words that contain *-stress-*, *-strict-*, or *-strain-*. Record the words and their meanings.

STANDARDS.
Language
- Identify and correctly use patterns of word changes that indicate different meanings or parts of speech.
- Demonstrate understanding of figurative language, word relationships, and nuances in word meanings.

THE TRAGEDY OF ROMEO AND JULIET, ACT IV

Analyze Craft and Structure

Dramatic Elements The author of a drama may include an element known as dramatic irony. **Dramatic irony** is a contradiction between what a character thinks and what the audience knows to be true. Dramatic irony engages the audience emotionally because it allows tension and suspense to build as the audience waits for the truth to be revealed to the characters. An excellent example of dramatic irony is the scene in which Juliet's family prepares for her wedding celebration while the audience knows that she is lying "dead" in the other room.

In Shakespearean drama, tension and suspense is sometimes broken, at least temporarily, by the use of comic elements such as these:

- **Comic relief** is the introduction of a humorous character or situation into an otherwise tragic sequence of events to lighten the mood and offer the audience some emotional relief.
- A **pun** is a play on words involving either one word that has two different meanings or two words that sound alike but have different meanings. For example, the dying Mercutio makes a pun using the two different meanings of the word *grave*: "Ask for me tomorrow, and you shall find me a grave man."

STANDARDS

Reading Literature
Analyze how an author's choices concerning how to structure a text, order events within it, and manipulate time create such effects as mystery, tension, or surprise.

Language
Interpret figures of speech in context and analyze their role in the text.

Practice

CITE TEXTUAL EVIDENCE to support your answers.

Notebook **Respond to these questions.**

1. Reread Act IV, Scene i, lines 18–43. In what way is Juliet's encounter with Paris in Friar Lawrence's cell an instance of dramatic irony?
2. (a) Based on Capulet's statement in Act IV, Scene iv, line 25, what does the character think? What does the audience know? Record each detail in the chart.
   (b) Use the completed chart to explain why Capulet's statement is an example of dramatic irony. How does this example of dramatic irony build tension and suspense?

WHAT CHARACTER THINKS	WHAT AUDIENCE KNOWS

3. Explain the key role that dramatic irony plays in Act IV, Scene v, lines 1–95.
4. (a) How does Capulet's encounter with the fellows in Act IV, Scene iv, lines 13–21 represent a moment of comic relief? (b) Does this moment effectively lighten the mood? Use text details to support your opinion.
5. Explain the pun in the Nurse's exchange with the First Musician in Act IV, Scene v, lines 97–98. How is the conversation that follows among the musicians and Peter an instance of comic relief? Explain.

Speaking and Listening

Assignment

Hold a **classroom debate** to resolve this question: *Is Juliet's drinking of the potion a brave act or a foolish act?*

- Each debater presents an oral response to the question, stating a claim and supporting it with relevant details from the text.
- A panel of judges or the class as a whole can evaluate the arguments and decide which has the most effective support.

1. **Develop Your Claim and Identify Support** Use the text details you identified to determine how you would respond to the question. Write a clear statement of your claim on a sheet of paper. Then, identify several pieces of supporting evidence from Act IV. Take detailed notes on how each piece of evidence supports your claim.
2. **Develop Your Response** Use your notes to develop your oral response. Decide what points you will make in your response and in what order you will present them.
3. **Prepare Your Delivery** Practice delivering your oral response to the judges. Include the following performance techniques to make your argument convincing:
    - Speak clearly, in an appropriate tone, and at an appropriate volume and rate.
    - Use appropriate facial expressions and gestures to convey your conviction.
    - Maintain regular eye contact with the audience.
4. **Evaluate Responses** Listen carefully as your classmates deliver their responses. Use an evaluation guide like the one shown to evaluate their responses.

EVALUATION GUIDE

Rate each statement on a scale of 1 (not demonstrated) to 4 (demonstrated).

☐ The claim was clearly stated in the response.

☐ The claim was supported with relevant text evidence.

☐ The debater communicated his or her ideas clearly and convincingly.

☐ The debater used appropriate facial expressions, gestures, and eye contact.

EVIDENCE LOG

Before moving on to a new selection, go to your Evidence Log and record what you learned from *The Tragedy of Romeo and Juliet,* Act IV.

STANDARDS

Writing

Write arguments to support claims in an analysis of substantive topics or texts, using valid reasoning and relevant and sufficient evidence.

Speaking and Listening

Present information, findings, and supporting evidence clearly, concisely, and logically such that listeners can follow the line of reasoning and the organization, development, substance, and style are appropriate to purpose, audience, and task.

Playwright

William Shakespeare

The Tragedy of Romeo and Juliet, Act V

Concept Vocabulary

You will encounter the following words as you read Act V of *The Tragedy of Romeo and Juliet.* Before reading, note how familiar you are with each word. Then, rank the words in order from most familiar (1) to least familiar (6).

WORD	YOUR RANKING
desperate	
meager	
misery	
penury	

After completing your first read, come back to the concept vocabulary and review your rankings. Mark changes to your original rankings as needed.

First Read DRAMA

Apply these strategies as you conduct your first read. You will have an opportunity to complete the close-read notes after your first read.

NOTICE *whom* the story is about, *what* happens, *where* and *when* it happens, and *why* those involved react as they do.

ANNOTATE by marking vocabulary and key passages you want to revisit.

CONNECT ideas within the selection to what you already know and what you have already read.

RESPOND by completing the Comprehension Check and by writing a brief summary of the selection.

First Read: NOTICE, ANNOTATE, CONNECT, RESPOND

Tool Kit
First-Read Guide and Model Annotation

STANDARDS

Reading Literature
By the end of grade 9, read and comprehend literature, including stories, dramas, and poems in the grades 9–10 text complexity band proficiently, with scaffolding as needed at the end of the range.

The Tragedy of Romeo and Juliet Act V

William Shakespeare

REVIEW AND ANTICIPATE

To prevent her marriage to Paris, Juliet has taken the Friar's potion, which has placed her in a temporary, deathlike sleep. As Act V begins, her unsuspecting family plans her funeral. Meanwhile, the Friar has sent a messenger to Romeo in Mantua, where he is living in exile. The Friar plans to tell Romeo of the ruse so that he may return and rescue Juliet from the family tomb. As you read Act V, consider how much of the Friar's plan is built on somewhat rickety foundations.

Scene i • *Mantua. A Street.*

[*Enter* Romeo.]

Romeo. If I may trust the flattering truth of sleep,[1]
My dreams presage[2] some joyful news at hand.
My bosom's lord[3] sits lightly in his throne,
And all this day an unaccustomed spirit
Lifts me above the ground with cheerful thoughts.
I dreamt my lady came and found me dead
(Strange dream that gives a dead man leave to think!)
And breathed such life with kisses in my lips

NOTES

1. **flattering . . . sleep** pleasing illusions of dreams.
2. **presage** *v.* foretell.
3. **bosom's lord** heart.

NOTES

4. **shadows** *n.* dreams; unreal images.

5. **Capels' monument** the Capulets' burial vault.

6. **presently took post** immediately set out on horseback.

7. **office** *n.* duty.

8. **import / Some misadventure** suggest some misfortune.

desperate (DEHS puhr iht) *adj.* driven to action by a loss of hope

9. **apothecary** (uh POTH uh kehr ee) *n.* one who prepares and sells drugs and medicines.

10. **In tatt'red . . . simples** in torn clothing, with overhanging eyebrows, sorting out herbs.

meager (MEE guhr) *adj.* extremely thin

misery (MIHZ uhr ee) *n.* condition of great wretchedness

11. **beggarly account** small number.

12. **cakes of roses** pressed rose petals (used for perfume).

penury (PEHN yuhr ee) *n.* destitution or poverty

That I revived and was an emperor.
Ah me! How sweet is love itself possessed,
When but love's shadows[4] are so rich in joy!

[*Enter* Romeo's Man, Balthasar, *booted.*]

News from Verona! How now, Balthasar?
Dost thou not bring me letters from the friar?
How doth my lady? Is my father well?
How fares my Juliet? That I ask again,
For nothing can be ill if she be well.

Man. Then she is well, and nothing can be ill.
Her body sleeps in Capels' monument,[5]
And her immortal part with angels lives.
I saw her laid low in her kindred's vault
And presently took post[6] to tell it you.
O, pardon me for bringing these ill news,
Since you did leave it for my office,[7] sir.

Romeo. Is it e'en so? Then I defy you, stars!
Thou knowest my lodging. Get me ink and paper
And hire post horses. I will hence tonight.

Man. I do beseech you, sir, have patience.
Your looks are pale and wild and do import
Some misadventure.[8]

Romeo. Tush, thou art deceived.
Leave me and do the thing I bid thee do.
Hast thou no letters to me from the friar?

Man. No, my good lord.

Romeo. No matter. Get thee gone.
And hire those horses. I'll be with thee straight.

[*Exit* Balthasar.]

Well, Juliet, I will lie with thee tonight.
Let's see for means. O mischief, thou art swift
To enter in the thoughts of **desperate** men!
I do remember an apothecary,[9]
And hereabouts 'a dwells, which late I noted
In tatt'red weeds, with overwhelming brows,
Culling of simples.[10] **Meager** were his looks,
Sharp **misery** had worn him to the bones;
And in his needy shop a tortoise hung,
An alligator stuffed, and other skins
Of ill-shaped fishes; and about his shelves
A beggarly account[11] of empty boxes,
Green earthen pots, bladders, and musty seeds,
Remnants of packthread, and old cakes of roses[12]
Were thinly scattered, to make up a show.
Noting this **penury** to myself I said,

"And if a man did need a poison now
Whose sale is present death in Mantua,
Here lives a caitiff[13] wretch would sell it him."
O, this same thought did but forerun my need,
And this same needy man must sell it me.
As I remember, this should be the house.
Being holiday, the beggar's shop is shut.
What, ho! Apothecary!

[*Enter* Apothecary.]

Apothecary. Who calls so loud?

Romeo. Come hither, man. I see that thou art poor.
Hold, there is forty ducats.[14] Let me have
A dram of poison, such soon-speeding gear[15]
As will disperse itself through all the veins
That the life-weary taker may fall dead,
And that the trunk[16] may be discharged of breath
As violently as hasty powder fired
Doth hurry from the fatal cannon's womb.

Apothecary. Such mortal drugs I have; but Mantua's law
Is death to any he that utters[17] them.

Romeo. Art thou so bare and full of wretchedness
And fearest to die? Famine is in thy cheeks,
Need and oppression starveth in thy eyes,
Contempt and beggary hangs upon thy back:
The world is not thy friend, nor the world's law;
The world affords no law to make thee rich;
Then be not poor, but break it and take this.

Apothecary. My poverty but not my will consents.

Romeo. I pay thy poverty and not thy will.

Apothecary. Put this in any liquid thing you will
And drink it off, and if you had the strength
Of twenty men, it would dispatch you straight.

Romeo. There is thy gold—worse poison to men's souls,
Doing more murder in this loathsome world,
Than these poor compounds[18] that thou mayst not sell.
I sell thee poison; thou hast sold me none.
Farewell. Buy food and get thyself in flesh.
Come, cordial[19] and not poison, go with me
To Juliet's grave; for there must I use thee. [*Exit all.*]

⌘ ⌘ ⌘

NOTES

13. caitiff *adj.* miserable.

14. ducats (DUHK uhts) *n.* gold coins.

15. soon-speeding gear fast-working stuff.

16. trunk *n.* body.

17. utters *v.* sells.

CLOSE READ

ANNOTATE: In lines 75–86, mark phrases in which Romeo redefines a word to mean its opposite.

QUESTION: Why does Romeo's dialogue contain so many reversals of meaning?

CONCLUDE: What do these reversals show about Romeo's emotional and mental state?

18. compounds *n.* mixtures.

19. cordial *n.* health-giving drink.

NOTES

1. **associate** *v.* accompany.

2. **nice** *adj.* trivial.

3. **full of charge, / Of dear import** urgent and important.

4. **beshrew** *v.* blame.

5. **accidents** *n.* happenings.

1. **aloof** *adv.* apart.

Scene ii • *Friar Lawrence's cell.*

[*Enter* Friar John, calling Friar Lawrence.]

John. Holy Franciscan friar, brother, ho!

[*Enter* Friar Lawrence.]

Lawrence. This same should be the voice of Friar John.
Welcome from Mantua. What says Romeo?
Or, if his mind be writ, give me his letter.

John. Going to find a barefoot brother out,
One of our order, to associate[1] me
Here in this city visiting the sick,
And finding him, the searchers of the town,
Suspecting that we both were in a house
Where the infectious pestilence did reign,
Sealed up the doors, and would not let us forth,
So that my speed to Mantua there was stayed.

Lawrence. Who bare my letter, then, to Romeo?

John. I could not send it—here it is again—
Nor get a messenger to bring it thee,
So fearful were they of infection.

Lawrence. Unhappy fortune! By my brotherhood,
The letter was not nice,[2] but full of charge,
Of dear import;[3] and the neglecting it
May do much danger. Friar John, go hence,
Get me an iron crow and bring it straight
Unto my cell.

John. Brother, I'll go and bring it thee. [*Exit.*]

Lawrence. Now must I to the monument alone.
Within this three hours will fair Juliet wake.
She will beshrew[4] me much that Romeo
Hath had no notice of these accidents;[5]
But I will write again to Mantua,
And keep her at my cell till Romeo come—
Poor living corse, closed in a dead man's tomb! [*Exit.*]

⌘ ⌘ ⌘

Scene iii • *A churchyard; in it a monument belonging to the Capulets.*

[*Enter* Paris *and his* Page *with flowers and sweet water.*]

Paris. Give me thy torch, boy. Hence, and stand aloof.[1]
Yet put it out, for I would not be seen.

Under yond yew trees lay thee all along[2]
Holding thy ear close to the hollow ground.
So shall no foot upon the churchyard tread
(Being loose, unfirm, with digging up of graves)
But thou shalt hear it. Whistle then to me,
As signal that thou hearest something approach.
Give me those flowers. Do as I bid thee, go.

Page. [*Aside*] I am almost afraid to stand alone
Here in the churchyard; yet I will adventure.[3] [*Retires.*]

Paris. Sweet[4] flower, with flowers thy bridal bed I strew
(O woe! thy canopy is dust and stones)
Which with sweet water nightly I will dew;
Or, wanting that, with tears distilled by moans.
The obsequies[5] that I for thee will keep
Nightly shall be to strew thy grave and weep. [Boy *whistles.*]
The boy gives warning something doth approach.
What cursed foot wanders this way tonight
To cross[6] my obsequies and true love's rite?
What, with a torch? Muffle me, night, awhile. [*Retires.*]

[*Enter* Romeo, *and* Balthasar *with a torch, a mattock, and a crow of iron.*]

Romeo. Give me that mattock and the wrenching iron.
Hold, take this letter. Early in the morning
See thou deliver it to my lord and father.
Give me the light. Upon thy life I charge thee,
Whate'er thou hearest or seest, stand all aloof
And do not interrupt me in my course.
Why I descend into this bed of death
Is partly to behold my lady's face,
But chiefly to take thence from her dead finger
A precious ring—a ring that I must use
In dear employment.[7] Therefore hence, be gone.
But if thou, jealous,[8] dost return to pry
In what I farther shall intend to do,
By heaven, I will tear thee joint by joint
And strew this hungry churchyard with thy limbs.
The time and my intents are savage-wild,
More fierce and more inexorable[9] far
Than empty[10] tigers or the roaring sea.

Balthasar. I will be gone, sir, and not trouble ye.

Romeo. So shalt thou show me friendship. Take thou that.
Live, and be prosperous; and farewell, good fellow.

Balthasar. [*Aside*] For all this same, I'll hide me hereabout.
His looks I fear, and his intents I doubt. [*Retires.*]

NOTES

2. **lay . . . along** lie down flat.

3. **adventure** *v.* chance it.

4. **sweet** *adj.* perfumed.

5. **obsequies** (OB suh kweez) *n.* memorial ceremonies.

6. **cross** *v.* interrupt.

7. **dear employment** important business.

8. **jealous** *adj.* curious.

9. **inexorable** *adj.* uncontrollable.

10. **empty** *adj.* hungry.

NOTES

11. maw *n.* stomach.

12. despite *n.* scorn.

13. apprehend *v.* seize; arrest.

14. conjurations *n.* solemn appeals.

15. felon *n.* criminal.

16. peruse *v.* look over.

17. betossèd *adj.* upset.

18. attend *v.* give attention to.

19. lanthorn (LAN tuhrn) *n.* windowed structure on top of a room to admit light; also, a lantern.

20. feasting presence chamber fit for celebration.

Romeo. Thou detestable maw,[11] thou womb of death,
Gorged with the dearest morsel of the earth,
Thus I enforce thy rotten jaws to open,
And in despite[12] I'll cram thee with more food.

[Romeo *opens the tomb.*]

Paris. This is that banished haughty Montague
That murd'red my love's cousin—with which grief
It is supposed the fair creature died—
And here is come to do some villainous shame
To the dead bodies. I will apprehend[13] him.
Stop thy unhallowèd toil, vile Montague!
Can vengeance be pursued further than death?
Condemnèd villain, I do apprehend thee.
Obey, and go with me; for thou must die.

Romeo. I must indeed; and therefore came I hither.
Good gentle youth, tempt not a desp'rate man.
Fly hence and leave me. Think upon these gone;
Let them affright thee. I beseech thee, youth,
Put not another sin upon my head
By urging me to fury. O, be gone!
By heaven, I love thee better than myself,
For I come hither armed against myself.
Stay not, be gone. Live, and hereafter say
A madman's mercy bid thee run away.

Paris. I do defy thy conjurations.[14]
And apprehend thee for a felon[15] here.

Romeo. Wilt thou provoke me? Then have at thee, boy!
[*They fight.*]

Page. Lord, they fight! I will go call the watch.

[*Exit.* Paris *falls.*]

Paris. O, I am slain! If thou be merciful,
Open the tomb, lay me with Juliet. [*Dies.*]

Romeo. In faith, I will. Let me peruse[16] this face.
Mercutio's kinsman, noble County Paris!
What said my man when my betossèd[17] soul
Did not attend[18] him as we rode? I think
He told me Paris should have married Juliet.
Said he not so, or did I dream it so?
Or am I mad, hearing him talk of Juliet,
To think it was so? O, give me thy hand,
One writ with me in sour misfortune's book!
I'll bury thee in a triumphant grave.
A grave? O, no, a lanthorn,[19] slaught'red youth,
For here lies Juliet, and her beauty makes
This vault a feasting presence[20] full of light.

Death, lie thou there, by a dead man interred.

[*Lays him in the tomb.*]

How oft when men are at the point of death
Have they been merry! Which their keepers[21] call
A lightning before death. O, how may I
Call this a lightning? O my love, my wife!
Death, that hath sucked the honey of thy breath,
Hath had no power yet upon thy beauty.
Thou art not conquered. Beauty's ensign[22] yet
Is crimson in thy lips and in thy cheeks,
And death's pale flag is not advancèd there.
Tybalt, liest thou there in thy bloody sheet?
O, what more favor can I do to thee
Than with that hand that cut thy youth in twain
To sunder[23] his that was thine enemy?
Forgive me, cousin! Ah, dear Juliet,
Why art thou yet so fair? Shall I believe
That unsubstantial Death is amorous,[24]
And that the lean abhorrèd monster keeps
Thee here in dark to be his paramour?
For fear of that I still will stay with thee
And never from this pallet[25] of dim night
Depart again. Here, here will I remain
With worms that are thy chambermaids. O, here
Will I set up my everlasting rest
And shake the yoke of inauspicious[26] stars
From this world-wearied flesh. Eyes, look your last!
Arms, take your last embrace! And, lips, O you
The doors of breath, seal with a righteous kiss
A dateless[27] bargain to engrossing[28] death!
Come, bitter conduct;[29] come, unsavory guide!
Thou desperate pilot,[30] now at once run on
The dashing rocks thy seasick weary bark!
Here's to my love! [*Drinks.*] O true apothecary!
Thy drugs are quick. Thus with a kiss I die. [*Falls.*]

[*Enter* Friar Lawrence, *with lanthorn, crow, and spade.*]

Friar. Saint Francis be my speed![31] How oft tonight
Have my old feet stumbled[32] at graves! Who's there?

Balthasar. Here's one, a friend, and one that knows you well.

Friar. Bliss be upon you! Tell me, good my friend,
What torch is yond that vainly lends his light
To grubs[33] and eyeless skulls? As I discern,
It burneth in the Capels' monument.

Balthasar. It doth so, holy sir; and there's my master,
One that you love.

NOTES

21. keepers *n.* jailers.

CLOSE READ

ANNOTATE: In lines 92–120, mark points at which Romeo speaks of death as having human qualities or speaks to death as though it is a person.

QUESTION: Why does Romeo speak of and to death in this way?

CONCLUDE: What is the effect of Romeo's conversation with death?

22. ensign *n.* banner.

23. sunder *v.* cut off.

24. amorous *adj.* full of love.

25. pallet *n.* bed.

26. inauspicious *adj.* promising misfortune.

27. dateless *adj.* eternal.

28. engrossing *adj.* all-encompassing.

29. conduct *n.* guide (poison).

30. pilot *n.* captain (Romeo himself).

31. speed *n.* help.

32. stumbled *v.* stumbling was thought to be a bad omen.

33. grubs *v.* worms.

NOTES

Friar. Who is it?

Balthasar. Romeo.

Friar. How long hath he been there?

Balthasar. Full half an hour.

Friar. Go with me to the vault.

Balthasar. I dare not, sir.
My master knows not but I am gone hence,
And fearfully did menace me with death
If I did stay to look on his intents.

Friar. Stay then; I'll go alone. Fear comes upon me.
O, much I fear some ill unthrifty[34] thing.

Balthasar. As I did sleep under this yew tree here,
I dreamt my master and another fought,
And that my master slew him.

Friar. Romeo!
Alack, alack, what blood is this which stains
The stony entrance of this sepulcher?
What mean these masterless[35] and gory swords
To lie discolored by this place of peace? [*Enters the tomb.*]
Romeo! O, pale! Who else? What, Paris too?
And steeped in blood? Ah, what an unkind[36] hour
Is guilty of this lamentable chance!
The lady stirs. [Juliet *rises.*]

Juliet. O comfortable[37] friar! Where is my lord?
I do remember well where I should be,
And there I am. Where is my Romeo?

Friar. I hear some noise. Lady, come from that nest
Of death, contagion, and unnatural sleep.

34. unthrifty *adj.* unlucky.

35. masterless *adj.* discarded (without masters).

36. unkind *adj.* unnatural.

37. comfortable *adj.* comforting.

A greater power than we can contradict
Hath thwarted our intents. Come, come away.
Thy husband in thy bosom there lies dead;
And Paris too. Come, I'll dispose of thee
Among a sisterhood of holy nuns.
Stay not to question, for the watch is coming.
Come, go, good Juliet. I dare no longer stay.

Juliet. Go, get thee hence, for I will not away. [*Exit* Friar.]
What's here? A cup, closed in my truelove's hand?
Poison, I see, hath been his timeless[38] end.
O churl![39] Drunk all, and left no friendly drop
To help me after? I will kiss thy lips.
Haply some poison yet doth hang on them
To make me die with a restorative.[40] [*Kisses him.*]
Thy lips are warm!

Chief Watchman. [*Within*] Lead, boy. Which way?

Juliet. Yea, noise? Then I'll be brief. O happy[41] dagger!
[*Snatches* Romeo's *dagger.*]
This is thy sheath; there rust, and let me die.
[*She stabs herself and falls.*]

[*Enter* Paris' Boy *and* Watch.]

Boy. This is the place. There, where the torch doth burn.

Chief Watchman. The ground is bloody. Search about the churchyard.
Go, some of you; whoe'er you find attach.[42]
[*Exit some of the* Watch.]
Pitiful sight! Here lies the County slain;
And Juliet bleeding, warm, and newly dead,
Who here hath lain this two days burièd.
Go, tell the Prince; run to the Capulets;
Raise up the Montagues; some others search.
[*Exit others of the* Watch.]
We see the ground[43] whereon these woes do lie,
But the true ground of all these piteous woes
We cannot without circumstance descry.[44]

[*Enter some of the* Watch, *with* Romeo's Man, Balthasar.]

Second Watchman. Here's Romeo's man. We found him in the churchyard.

Chief Watchman. Hold him in safety till the Prince come hither.

[*Enter* Friar Lawrence *and another* Watchman.]

Third Watchman. Here is a friar that trembles, sighs and weeps.
We took this mattock and this spade from him
As he was coming from this churchyard's side.

Chief Watchman. A great suspicion! Stay the friar too.

NOTES

38. timeless *adj.* untimely; too soon.

39. churl *n.* rude fellow.

40. restorative *n.* medicine.

41. happy *adj.* convenient; opportune.

42. attach *v.* arrest.

43. ground *n.* cause.

44. without circumstance descry see clearly without details.

NOTES

45. **house** *n.* sheath.

46. **liege** (leej) *n.* lord.

47. **mouth of outrage** violent cries.

48. **general . . . woes** leader in your sorrow.

49. **let . . . patience** be patient in the face of misfortune.

50. **direful** *adj.* terrible.

51. **impeach and purge** accuse and declare blameless.

[*Enter the* Prince *and* Attendants.]

Prince. What misadventure is so early up,
That calls our person from our morning rest?

[*Enter* Capulet *and his* Wife *with others.*]

Capulet. What should it be, that is so shrieked abroad?

Lady Capulet. O, the people in the street cry "Romeo,"
Some "Juliet," and some "Paris"; and all run
With open outcry toward our monument.

Prince. What fear is this which startles in your ears?

Chief Watchman. Sovereign, here lies the County Paris slain;
And Romeo dead; and Juliet, dead before,
Warm and new killed.

Prince. Search, seek, and know how this foul murder comes.

Chief Watchman. Here is a friar, and slaughtered Romeo's man,
With instruments upon them fit to open
These dead men's tombs.

Capulet. O heavens! O Wife, look how our daughter bleeds!
This dagger hath mista'en, for, lo, his house[45]
Is empty on the back of Montague,
And it missheathèd in my daughter's bosom!

Lady Capulet. O me, this sight of death is as a bell
That warns my old age to a sepulcher.

[*Enter* Montague *and others.*]

Prince. Come, Montague; for thou art early up
To see thy son and heir more early down.

Montague. Alas, my liege,[46] my wife is dead tonight!
Grief of my son's exile hath stopped her breath.
What further woe conspires against mine age?

Prince. Look, and thou shalt see.

Montague. O thou untaught! What manners is in this,
To press before thy father to a grave?

Prince. Seal up the mouth of outrage[47] for a while,
Till we can clear these ambiguities
And know their spring, their head, their true descent;
And then will I be general of your woes[48]
And lead you even to death. Meantime forbear,
And let mischance be slave to patience.[49]
Bring forth the parties of suspicion.

Friar. I am the greatest, able to do least,
Yet most suspected, as the time and place
Doth make against me, of this direful[50] murder;
And here I stand, both to impeach and purge[51]

Myself condemnèd and myself excused.

Prince. Then say at once what thou dost know in this.

Friar. I will be brief, for my short date of breath[52]
Is not so long as is a tedious tale.
Romeo, there dead, was husband to that Juliet;
And she, there dead, that's Romeo's faithful wife.
I married them; and their stol'n marriage day
Was Tybalt's doomsday, whose untimely death
Banished the new-made bridegroom from this city;
For whom, and not for Tybalt, Juliet pined.
You, to remove that siege of grief from her,
Betrothed and would have married her perforce
To County Paris. Then comes she to me
And with wild looks bid me devise some mean
To rid her from this second marriage,
Or in my cell there would she kill herself.
Then gave I her (so tutored by my art)
A sleeping potion; which so took effect
As I intended, for it wrought on her
The form of death. Meantime I writ to Romeo
That he should hither come as[53] this dire night
To help to take her from her borrowed grave,
Being the time the potion's force should cease,
But he which bore my letter, Friar John,
Was stayed by accident, and yesternight
Returned my letter back. Then all alone
At the prefixèd hour of her waking
Came I to take her from her kindred's vault;
Meaning to keep her closely[54] at my cell
Till I conveniently could send to Romeo.
But when I came, some minute ere the time
Of her awakening, here untimely lay
The noble Paris and true Romeo dead.
She wakes; and I entreated her come forth
And bear this work of heaven with patience;
But then a noise did scare me from the tomb,
And she, too desperate, would not go with me.
But, as it seems, did violence on herself.
All this I know, and to the marriage
Her nurse is privy;[55] and if aught in this
Miscarried by my fault, let my old life
Be sacrificed some hour before his time
Unto the rigor[56] of severest law.

Prince. We still have known thee for a holy man.
Where's Romeo's man? What can he say to this?

Balthasar. I brought my master news of Juliet's death;
And then in post he came from Mantua

NOTES

52. date of breath term of life.

53. as on.

54. closely *adv.* hidden; secretly.

55. privy *adj.* secretly informed about.

56. rigor *n.* strictness.

NOTES

57. **made your master** was your master doing.

58. **winking at** closing my eyes to.

59. **brace** *n.* pair (Mercutio and Paris).

60. **jointure** *n.* wedding gift; marriage settlement.

61. **rate** *n.* value.

62. **enmity** *n.* hostility.

63. **glooming** *adj.* cloudy; gloomy.

To this same place, to this same monument.
This letter he early bid me give his father,
And threat'ned me with death, going in the vault,
If I departed not and left him there.

Prince. Give me the letter. I will look on it.
Where is the County's page that raised the watch?
Sirrah, what made your master[57] in this place?

Boy. He came with flowers to strew his lady's grave;
And bid me stand aloof, and so I did.
Anon comes one with light to ope the tomb;
And by and by my master drew on him;
And then I ran away to call the watch.

Prince. This letter doth make good the friar's words,
Their course of love, the tidings of her death;
And here he writes that he did buy a poison
Of a poor 'pothecary and therewithal
Came to this vault to die and lie with Juliet.
Where be these enemies? Capulet, Montague,
See what a scourge is laid upon your hate,
That heaven finds means to kill your joys with love.
And I, for winking at[58] your discords too,
Have lost a brace[59] of kinsmen. All are punished.

Capulet. O brother Montague, give me thy hand.
This is my daughter's jointure,[60] for no more
Can I demand.

Montague. But I can give thee more;
For I will raise her statue in pure gold,
That whiles Verona by that name is known,
There shall no figure at such rate[61] be set
As that of true and faithful Juliet.

Capulet. As rich shall Romeo's by his lady's lie—
Poor sacrifices of our enmity![62]

Prince. A glooming[63] peace this morning with it brings.
The sun for sorrow will not show his head.
Go hence, to have more talk of these sad things;
Some shall be pardoned, and some punishèd;
For never was a story of more woe
Than this of Juliet and her Romeo.

⌘ ⌘ ⌘

MEDIA CONNECTION

Romeo and Juliet

Discuss It Choose and listen to a scene from Act V of the L.A. Theatre Works production of *The Tragedy of Romeo and Juliet*. As you listen, consider specific ways in which the actors modify their voices and time their deliveries to convey nuances of emotion. Do you find their interpretations of the characters accurate and convincing?

Write your response before sharing your ideas with the class.

Comprehension Check

Complete the following items after you finish your first read.

1. How does Romeo get the apothecary to sell him the poison?

2. How was Friar John prevented from delivering Friar Lawrence's letter to Romeo?

3. What is Paris doing at the Capulet vault?

4. **Notebook** Confirm your understanding of the text by writing a summary.

RESEARCH

Research to Clarify Choose at least one unfamiliar detail from the text. Briefly research that detail. In what way does the information you learned shed light on an aspect of the play?

Research to Explore This play may spark your curiosity to read more. Briefly research whether the Montagues and Capulets were real families. You may want to share what you discover with the class.

THE TRAGEDY OF ROMEO AND JULIET, ACT V

Close Read the Text

1. This model, from Act V, Scene iii, lines 286–295, shows two sample annotations, along with questions and conclusions. Close read the passage and find another detail to annotate. Then, write a question and your conclusion.

ANNOTATE: The Prince uses this word to describe Romeo's and Juliet's deaths.

QUESTION: Why does the author use this word to describe their deaths?

CONCLUDE: This word helps emphasize that their deaths serve as a punishment for the feud between the Capulets and Montagues.

Prince. This letter doth make good the friar's words, / Their course of love, the tidings of her death; / And here he writes that he did buy a poison / Of a poor 'pothecary and therewithal / Came to this vault to die and lie with Juliet. / Where be these enemies? Capulet, Montague, / See what a scourge is laid upon your hate, / That heaven finds means to kill your joys with love. / And I, for winking at your discords too, / Have lost a brace of kinsmen. All are punished.

ANNOTATE: These two words are opposites.

QUESTION: Why does the author include these words in the Prince's description of Romeo's and Juliet's death?

CONCLUDE: They help create irony. Romeo and Juliet die for their love for each other, not the hatred that has been bred between their families.

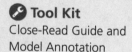

Tool Kit
Close-Read Guide and Model Annotation

2. For more practice, go back into the text, and complete the close-read notes.

3. Revisit a section of the text you found important during your first read. Read this section closely, and **annotate** what you notice. Ask yourself **questions** such as "Why did the author make this choice?" What can you **conclude**?

Analyze the Text

CITE TEXTUAL EVIDENCE to support your answers.

Notebook Respond to these questions.

1. (a) **Interpret** In Act V, Scene i, why does Romeo exclaim, "Then I defy you, stars"? (b) **Analyze** In what way are Romeo's words consistent with what you know of his character? Explain.

2. **Analyze** What does Paris's visit to Juliet's tomb suggest about his feelings for her?

3. **Essential Question:** ***Do we determine our own destinies?*** What have you learned about determining one's own destiny by reading Act V of *The Tragedy of Romeo and Juliet*?

STANDARDS

Reading Literature

- Analyze how complex characters develop over the course of a text, interact with other characters, and advance the plot or develop the theme.
- Analyze how an author's choices concerning how to structure a text, order events within it, and manipulate time create such effects as mystery, tension, or surprise.

Analyze Craft and Structure

Tragedy A **tragedy** is a drama in which the main character, who is of noble stature, meets with great misfortune. Often, the hero's **motives**, or reasons for his or her actions, are good but misguided, and the hero suffers a tragic fate that may seem undeserved. Although tragedies are sad, they also show the nobility of the human spirit.

In Shakespearean tragedies, the hero's doom is the result of fate, a tragic flaw, or a combination of both.

- **Fate** is a destiny over which the hero has little or no control. In some Shakespearean tragedies, errors, the poor judgment of others, or accidents can be interpreted as the workings of fate.
- A **tragic flaw** is a personality defect, such as jealousy, that contributes to the hero's choices and, thus, to his or her tragic downfall.

Practice

CITE TEXTUAL EVIDENCE to support your answers.

Notebook **Respond to these questions.**

1. (a) What is the Friar's motive for helping Romeo and Juliet? (b) To what extent is he responsible for their tragedy?"
2. (a) Who was responsible for Romeo and Juliet's need for secrecy? (b) To what extent was that a cause of their tragedy?
3. Use the chart below to identify elements that contribute to the play's tragic ending. Consider aspects of Romeo's and Juliet's personalities and elements of fate. Explain which element you think is most responsible for the story's tragic outcome. Support your answer with specific details you gathered.

ROMEO'S AND JULIET'S PERSONALITIES	
ROMEO	JULIET
ELEMENTS OF FATE	

THE TRAGEDY OF
ROMEO AND JULIET, ACT V

Concept Vocabulary

desperate	meager	penury	misery

Why These Words? These concept words relate to poverty. Romeo describes the apothecary's apearance as *meager* and says that *misery* has "worn him to the bones." Romeo's observations convince him that the apothecary is poor and will be willing to sell him poison, even though it is illegal.

1. Romeo uses the word *desperate* to describe himself. How does this help the reader understand his actions?

2. What other words in the selection connect to this concept?

Practice

Notebook The concept words appear in Act V of *The Tragedy of Romeo and Juliet*.

1. Use each word in a sentence that demonstrates your understanding of the word's meaning.
2. Work with two classmates, and take turns reading your sentences aloud, leaving out the concept vocabulary words. Have members of your group guess the missing words. Keep taking turns until you each have read all four of your sentences.

WORD NETWORK

Add interesting words related to destiny from the text to your Word Network.

Word Study

Word Families A group of words that share the same root make up a **word family**. The word *desperate*, for example, is part of a word family that includes *despair* and *desperation*. Recognizing that an unfamiliar word may be in the same word family as a familiar word can help you determine its meaning.

1. Identify yet another word that belongs to the same word family as *desperate*, *despair*, and *desperation*.

2. Identify a word that belongs to the same word family as *misery*.

STANDARDS

Language

- Demonstrate command of the conventions of standard English grammar and usage when writing or speaking.
- Use parallel structure.
- Demonstrate understanding of figurative language, word relationships, and nuances in word meanings.

Conventions

Parallelism The use of similar grammatical forms or patterns to express ideas of equal significance is known as **parallelism**. Parallelism creates rhythm and balance in sentences and makes the relationship between ideas in a sentence clear. Shakespeare uses parallelism in Juliet's speech about Romeo's name.

> What's Montague? It is nor hand, nor foot
> Nor arm, nor face, nor any other part
> Belonging to man. O, be some other name!

These lines would be unbalanced and less powerful if they did not include parallel phrases.

Nonparallel: Our work today focused on drafting, reviewing, and to revise a letter.

Parallel: Our work today focused on drafting, reviewing, and revising a letter.

SAMPLE PARALLEL STRUCTURE	
In a Series	The athlete has sharp eyes**,** strong hands**, and** deft fingers. Sarah walks**,** bikes**, or** drives to the store on Sundays.
In a Comparison	I like listening to music better **than** watching movies.
With a Coordinating Conjunction	The French **and** the Spanish have rich histories. Laura will pick up her dry cleaning **and** mail a package.
With a Correlative Conjunction	You can **either** walk to the store **or** ride your bike to the store.

Read It

Mark the parallel words or phrases in each sentence.

1. It is easy to see Romeo's romanticism, Mercutio's courage, and Benvolio's loyalty in *The Tragedy of Romeo and Juliet*.
2. Juliet tries to be both a good daughter and a faithful wife.
3. Friar Lawrence advises Romeo and comforts Juliet.

Write It

Notebook Write a paragraph that includes at least three examples of parallelism. In each example, underline the parallel words or phrases.

THE TRAGEDY OF ROMEO AND JULIET, ACT V

Writing to Sources

Persuasive writing is a type of argumentation that emphasizes emotions over logic. Indeed, some types of persuasion, such as advertising, include no credible support for a position and rely solely on emotional appeals. That is not the type of persuasion you will write in this activity.

Assignment

Imagine that your school is putting on a play and the students are responsible for deciding which one to perform. Write a **persuasive letter** to your fellow students in which you either encourage them to select *The Tragedy of Romeo and Juliet* or urge them to choose a different play.

- Begin by drafting three to five reasons why you think the student body should or should not choose *The Tragedy of Romeo and Juliet.*
- Provide convincing support for your position. All evidence should be relevant and sufficient to support your claims.
- Recognize that others may feel differently, and explain why your position is preferable.
- Revise to address readers' concerns, create parallelism, and incorporate powerful language.

Vocabulary and Conventions Connection Include several of the concept vocabulary words in your letter. Also, remember to use parallelism in your sentences to provide balance, rhythm, and clarity.

desperate	meager	misery	penury

Reflect on Your Writing

After you have written your persuasive letter, answer these questions.

1. How did writing this letter help you better understand the play's central ideas and themes?

2. What was the most challenging part of writing your letter?

3. **Why These Words?** The words you choose make a difference in your writing. Which words did you choose to add power to your letter?

STANDARDS

Writing
Write arguments to support claims in an analysis of substantive topics or texts, using valid reasoning and relevant and sufficient evidence.

Speaking and Listening
Present information, findings, and supporting evidence clearly, concisely, and logically such that listeners can follow the line of reasoning and the organization, development, substance, and style are appropriate to purpose, audience, and task.

Speaking and Listening

Assignment

Listen to a scene or act from *The Tragedy of Romeo and Juliet* as presented by L.A. Theatre Works. Then, evaluate the section of the production you heard, and share a **performance review** as a podcast or classroom presentation. Follow these steps to complete the assignment.

1. **Take Notes** As you listen to the performance, take notes about what you hear so that you can cite specific evidence in your review. Use the following questions to guide you as you take notes on the performance:
   - How does the audio performance compare with the text?
   - What do the actors do to bring their characters to life?
   - How does the music contribute to the impact of the performance?
   - What would you have done differently if you were directing an audio version of *The Tragedy of Romeo and Juliet*?
2. **Plan Your Podcast or Presentation** After you listen to the performance, use your notes to draft your review.
   - Write an overall evaluation of the performance, which you will support with your analysis of its key elements.
   - Identify key elements of the performance and offer an analysis of each element.
3. **Record Your Podcast or Deliver Your Presentation** When you have finished writing your review, record your podcast or deliver your presentation.
4. **Evaluate Reviews** As your classmates deliver their reviews, listen attentively. Use the evaluation guide below to analyze their delivery.

PRESENTATION EVALUATION GUIDE

Rate each statement on a scale of 1 (not demonstrated) to 4 (demonstrated).

☐ The podcast or presentation conveys the reviewer's evaluation and supporting ideas clearly.

☐ The podcast or presentation is well organized.

☐ PODCAST: The speaker uses tone and pace appropriately.

☐ PRESENTATION: The presenter uses eye contact and gestures appropriately.

EVIDENCE LOG

Before moving on to a new selection, go to your Evidence Log and record what you learned from Act V of *The Tragedy of Romeo and Juliet.*

STANDARDS

Reading Literature

Analyze the representation of a subject or a key scene in two different artistic mediums, including what is emphasized or absent in each treatment.

THE TRAGEDY OF ROMEO AND JULIET

Comparing Texts

You will now read the short story "Pyramus and Thisbe." First, complete the first-read and close-read activities. Then, compare the way in which an archetypal, or universal, theme is presented in both the story and Shakespeare's *The Tragedy of Romeo and Juliet.*

PYRAMUS AND THISBE

About the Author

Educated in Rome, **Ovid** (43 B.C.–A.D. 17) began his career writing poems about love and became both popular and successful. For an unknown reason, he fell out of favor with the Emperor Augustus, who banished the poet from Rome. Even though Ovid spent the rest of his life in a remote fishing village, his influence only grew after his death and continues to this day.

Tool Kit
First-Read Guide and Model Annotation

STANDARDS
Reading Literature
By the end of grade 9, read and comprehend literature, including stories, dramas, and poems, in the grades 9–10 text complexity band proficiently, with scaffolding as needed at the end of the range.

Pyramus and Thisbe

Concept Vocabulary

You will encounter the following words as you read "Pyramus and Thisbe." Before reading, note how familiar you are with each word. Then, rank the words in order from most familiar (1) to least familiar (3).

WORD	YOUR RANKING
forbidden	
steal	
tryst	

After completing your first read, come back to the concept vocabulary and review your rankings. Mark changes to your original rankings as needed.

First Read FICTION

Apply these strategies as you conduct your first read. You will have an opportunity to complete the close-read notes after your first read.

NOTICE *whom* the story is about, *what* happens, *where* and *when* it happens, and *why* those involved react the way they do.

ANNOTATE by marking vocabulary and key passages you want to revisit.

CONNECT ideas within the selection to what you already know and what you have already read.

RESPOND by completing the Comprehension Check and by writing a brief summary of the selection.

First Read: NOTICE · ANNOTATE · CONNECT · RESPOND

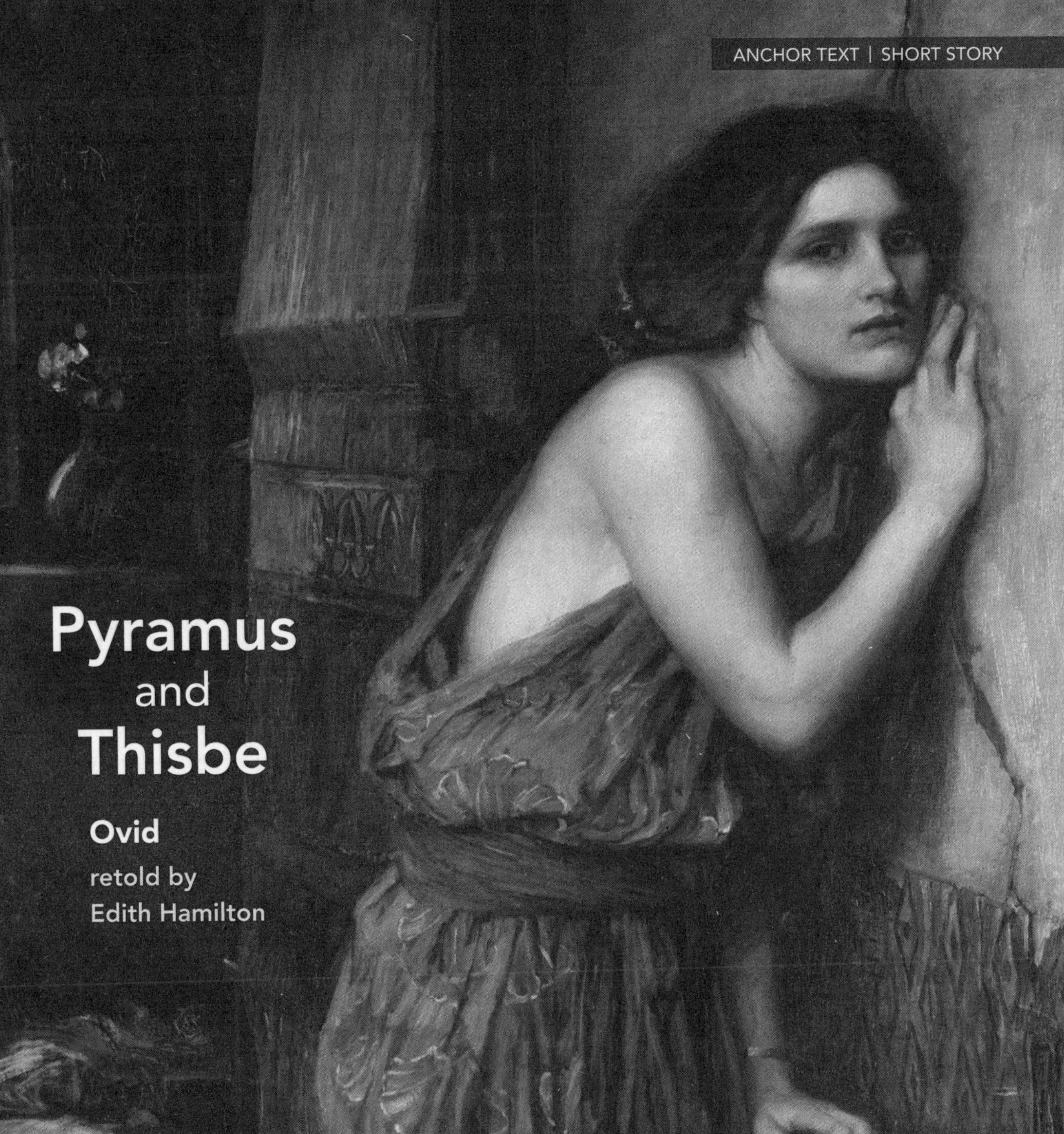

Pyramus and Thisbe

Ovid

retold by Edith Hamilton

BACKGROUND

The tale of Pyramus and Thisbe appears in Book IV of *Metamorphoses,* Ovid's greatest achievement. A poem of nearly 12,000 lines, it tells a series of stories beginning with the creation of the world and ending with the death of Julius Caesar. In each story, someone or something undergoes a transformation. The entire work reads as one long, uninterrupted tale.

NOTES

1 Once upon a time the deep red berries of the mulberry tree were white as snow. The change in color came about strangely and sadly. The death of two young lovers was the cause.

2 Pyramus and Thisbe, he the most beautiful youth and she the loveliest maiden of all the East, lived in Babylon, the city of Queen

NOTES

forbidden (fuhr BIHD uhn) *adj.* prevented or prohibited

CLOSE READ

ANNOTATE: In paragraph 3, mark the spoken dialogue.

QUESTION: Why does the author choose to let the characters speak for themselves at this point?

CONCLUDE: What is the effect of hearing these lines from Pyramus and Thisbe directly?

steal (steel) *v.* move in a way that is secret or quiet

Semiramis, in houses so close together that one wall was common to both. Growing up thus side by side they learned to love each other. They longed to marry, but their parents forbade. Love, however, cannot be **forbidden**. The more that flame is covered up, the hotter it burns. Also love can always find a way. It was impossible that these two whose hearts were on fire should be kept apart.

3 In the wall both houses shared there was a little chink. No one before had noticed it, but there is nothing a lover does not notice. Our two young people discovered it and through it they were able to whisper sweetly back and forth. Thisbe on one side, Pyramus on the other. The hateful wall that separated them had become their means of reaching each other. "But for you we could touch, kiss," they would say. "But at least you let us speak together. You give a passage for loving words to reach loving ears. We are not ungrateful." So they would talk, and as night came on and they must part, each would press on the wall kisses that could not go through to the lips on the other side.

4 Every morning when the dawn had put out the stars, and the sun's rays had dried the hoarfrost on the grass, they would **steal** to the crack and, standing there, now utter words of burning love and now lament their hard fate, but always in softest whispers. Finally a day came when they could endure no longer. They decided that that very night they would try to slip away and steal out through the city into the open country where at last they could be together in freedom. They agreed to meet at a well-known place, the Tomb of Ninus, under a tree there, a tall mulberry full of snow-white berries, near which a cool spring bubbled up. The plan pleased them and it seemed to them the day would never end.

5 At last the sun sank into the sea and night arose. In the darkness Thisbe crept out and made her way in all secrecy to the tomb. Pyramus had not come; still she waited for him, her love making her bold. But of a sudden she saw by the light of the moon a lioness. The fierce beast had made a kill; her jaws were bloody and she was coming to slake her thirst in the spring. She was still far enough away for Thisbe to escape, but as she fled she dropped her cloak. The lioness came upon it on her way back to her lair and she mouthed it and tore it before disappearing into the woods. That is what Pyramus saw when he appeared a few minutes later. Before him lay the bloodstained shreds of the cloak and clear in the dust were the tracks of the lioness. The conclusion was inevitable. He never doubted that he knew all. Thisbe was dead. He had let his love, a tender maiden,

come alone to a place full of danger, and not been there first to protect her. "It is I who killed you," he said. He lifted up from the trampled dust what was left of the cloak and kissing it again and again carried it to the mulberry tree. "Now," he said, "you shall drink my blood too." He drew his sword and plunged it into his side. The blood spurted up over the berries and dyed them a dark red.

6 Thisbe, although terrified of the lioness, was still more afraid to fail her lover. She ventured to go back to the tree of the **tryst**, the mulberry with the shining white fruit. She could not find it. A tree was there, but not one gleam of white was on the branches. As she stared at it, something moved on the ground beneath. She started back shuddering. But in a moment, peering through the shadows, she saw what was there. It was Pyramus, bathed in blood and dying. She flew to him and threw her arms around him. She kissed his cold lips and begged him to look at her, to speak to her. "It is I, your Thisbe, your dearest," she cried to him. At the sound of her name he opened his heavy eyes for one look. Then death closed them.

7 She saw his sword fallen from his hand and beside it her cloak stained and torn. She understood all. "Your own hand killed you," she said, "and your love for me. I too can be brave. I too can love. Only death would have had the power to separate us. It shall not have that power now." She plunged into her heart the sword that was still wet with his life's blood.

8 The gods were pitiful at the end, and the lovers' parents too. The deep red fruit of the mulberry is the everlasting memorial of these true lovers, and one urn holds the ashes of the two whom not even death could part. ❧

NOTES

tryst (trihst) *n.* secret romantic meeting

Comprehension Check

Complete the following items after you finish your first read.

1. Who is keeping Pyramus and Thisbe from seeing one another?

2. How are Pyramus and Thisbe able to communicate?

3. Why is Thisbe at the tomb where she meets the lion?

4. **Notebook** Confirm your understanding of the text by writing a summary.

RESEARCH

Research to Clarify Choose at least one unfamiliar detail from the text. Briefly research that detail. In what way does the information you learned shed light on an aspect of the story?

Research to Explore This story may spark your curiosity to read more. Briefly research other stories or plays that may have been inspired by the story of Pyramus and Thisbe. You may want to share what you discover with the class.

Close Read the Text

Reread paragraph 5 of "Pyramus and Thisbe." Mark words and phrases that describe what Pyramus does after finding Thisbe's bloody cloak. How do these details contribute to the mood of the scene?

PYRAMUS AND THISBE

Analyze the Text

CITE TEXTUAL EVIDENCE to support your answers.

Notebook Respond to these questions.

1. (a) **Interpret** What does "The more that flame is covered up, the hotter it burns" mean? (b) **Analyze** What effect does the author create by comparing love to a fire?
2. (a) Identify at least three events after Thisbe reaches the Ninus' tomb that together cause the tragedy. (b) **Evaluate** Does it make sense for Pyramus to come to the conclusion that Thisbe is dead? Explain.
3. (a) What happens to the mulberries in the tree by the tomb? (b) **Analyze** How does the story explain the color of mulberries today?
4. **Essential Question** *Do we determine our own destinies?* What have you learned about destiny from reading this story?

Tool Kit
Close-Read Guide and Model Annotation

LANGUAGE DEVELOPMENT

Concept Vocabulary

forbidden	steal	tryst

Why These Words? These concept vocabulary words connote, or are associated with, encounters with risk and secrecy. How does each word contribute to meaning in the text? What other words in the selection connect to this concept?

Add interesting words related to destiny from the text to your Word Network.

Practice

Notebook Confirm your understanding of these words by using each one in a sentence.

Word Study

Notebook **Multiple-Meaning Words** Many English words have multiple meanings, or more than one distinct definition. For example, the word *steal* has several different meanings. In paragraph 4 of "Pyramus and Thisbe," it means "to move quietly." However, it can also mean "to take illegally." Find two other multiple-meaning words in the short story. Record the words, and list two definitions for each.

STANDARDS
Language
Demonstrate understanding of figurative language, word relationships, and nuances in word meanings.

THE TRAGEDY OF ROMEO AND JULIET

PYRAMUS AND THISBE

STANDARDS

Reading Literature
Analyze how an author draws on and transforms source material in a specific work.

Writing
- Write informative/explanatory texts to examine and convey complex ideas, concepts, and information clearly and accurately through the effective selection, organization, and analysis of content.
- Apply *grades 9–10 Reading standards* to literature.

Writing to Compare

The play and short story you have read in this section center on similar types of characters and plots. In fact, Ovid's story is a foundational source for *The Tragedy of Romeo and Juliet*. Now, deepen your understanding of the texts by comparing and writing about them.

Assignment

An **archetype** is a plot, character, image, symbol, pattern, or setting that appears in literature from all cultures and time periods. The **theme** of a literary work is its central idea, message, or insight about life.

- **Archetypal themes** are ideas about life that are expressed across cultures and time periods. Ill-fated love is one archetypal theme.
- An archetypal theme may also be referred to as a **universal theme**.

Write an **analytical essay** in which you examine the presentation of the archetypal theme of ill-fated love in Shakespeare's *The Tragedy of Romeo and Juliet* and Ovid's "Pyramus and Thisbe." Explain which elements of Ovid's story are used and transformed in Shakespeare's tragic drama.

Prewriting

Analyze the Texts Works of literature can differ for a variety of reasons in their presentations of the same archetypal theme. The values of the work's era, the author's purpose, and the author's culture and language may affect how a writer presents a universal theme. Use the chart to identify similarities and differences between Ovid's "Pyramus and Thisbe" and Shakespeare's *The Tragedy of Romeo and Juliet.*

	SIMILARITIES	DIFFERENCES
Characters		
Settings		
Obstacles Characters Face		
Story Events		

Notebook Respond to these questions.

1. How does the transformation of the mulberry tree at the end of Ovid's tale reflect Roman culture and religion?
2. What kind of memorial, if any, exists for Romeo and Juliet at the end of Shakespeare's play?

Drafting

Write a statement of purpose. Determine the specific purpose, or goal, of your essay. Then, write a statement of purpose that you can use in your introduction. Include both the authors' names and titles in your statement. Complete this sentence to get started:

Statement of Purpose: In this essay, I will analyze _________________ and show how ______________________________
____
____.

Organize your ideas. In this essay, you need to identify similarities and differences between two works. You also need to consider how Shakespeare drew on elements of Ovid's story to write his play. Decide whether you wish to focus more on the similarities or the differences between the two works. Then, focus your essay by emphasizing the elements you feel matter the most.

Identify passages to use as evidence. Use your Prewriting notes to identify specific passages from the play and the story to use in your essay.

Example Passage: ____
Point it will Support:

Example Passage: ____
Point it will Support:

Example Passage: ____
Point it will Support:

Example Passage: ____
Point it will Support:

Provide other supporting details. In addition to example passages, you may include other types of evidence:

- **Summaries,** or brief retellings of the events of a text, can give readers necessary background information. However, make sure not to confuse a summary with deeper analysis and explanation of your ideas.
- **Paraphrases,** or restatements of a text in your own words, can help you clarify someone else's ideas. In this essay, you may want to use paraphrases that interpret Shakespearean language.

Review, Revise and Edit

Once you are done drafting, reread your essay. Make sure your have supported your ideas with clear reasons and evidence. Review each paragraph, marking the main idea. Then, mark sentences that support that idea. If there are sentences that do not support or develop the main idea, consider deleting or rewriting them.

EVIDENCE LOG

Before moving on to a new selection, go to your Evidence Log and record what you have learned from *The Tragedy of Romeo and Juliet* and "Pyramus and Thisbe."

WRITING TO SOURCES

- THE TRAGEDY OF ROMEO AND JULIET
- PYRAMUS AND THISBE

Write an Argument

You've read a play and a short story that deal with tragic love. In *The Tragedy of Romeo and Juliet*, two lovers attempt to marry despite a long-standing feud between their families. In "Pyramus and Thisbe," one of the inspirations for *The Tragedy of Romeo and Juliet*, two lovers attempt to cross boundaries in order to be together.

Assignment

Use your knowledge of *The Tragedy of Romeo and Juliet* and "Pyramus and Thisbe" to choose and defend a position on the topic of destiny. Based on those two texts, write an argument in the form of **literary criticism** in response to this question:

Which has a greater impact on the characters in these texts: destiny or personal choices?

Tool Kit
Student Model of an Argument

ACADEMIC VOCABULARY

As you craft your argument, consider using some of the academic vocabulary you learned in the beginning of this unit.

endure
pathos
compelling
propose
recurrent

Elements of Literary Criticism

One form of argumentative writing is literary criticism.

Literary criticism explores the meaning and techniques of literary works. Like other forms of argument, literary criticism requires the development of a logical line of reasoning and the support of ideas with precise, relevant text evidence.

Effective literary criticism contains these elements:

- an analysis of the work, including its content, organization, and style
- a thesis statement, or precise claim, that expresses your interpretation of the work
- inclusion of a counterclaim, or alternate interpretation, and a discussion of why it is less accurate or less well-supported than your claim(s)
- textual evidence that supports your interpretation
- a logical organization, including a conclusion that follows from and validates your claim
- a formal style and objective tone appropriate for the purpose and audience
- error-free grammar, including standard conventions for the inclusion of quotations

Model Literary Criticism For a model of a well-crafted literary criticism, see the Launch Text, "*Romeo and Juliet*: A Tragedy? Or Just a Tragic Misunderstanding?"

Challenge yourself to find all of the elements of an effective literary criticism in the text. You will have an opportunity to review these elements as you prepare to write your own literary criticism.

STANDARDS

Writing
- Write arguments to support claims in an analysis of substantive topics or texts, using valid reasoning and relevant and sufficient evidence.
- Write routinely over extended time frames and shorter time frames for a range of tasks, purposes, and audiences.

Prewriting / Planning

Write a Working Thesis Now that you have read and thought about the selections, write a sentence in which you state your "working" **thesis,** an initial position on the question posed in this assignment. As you continue to write, you may revise your thesis or even change it entirely.

Thesis: ____

____.

Consider Possible Counterclaims Remember that part of your task is to address **counterclaims,** or opposing positions. Complete these sentences to address a counterclaim. Think about reasons and evidence you can use to defend your position.

Another possible interpretation is ____________________________.

However, the majority of the text evidence points to ____________________________.

Writing for a Purpose All literary criticism shares similar goals:

- **making connections** within or between works, or between a work of literature and its historical and cultural context
- **making distinctions** or showing differences between elements of a single work or aspects of two or more works
- **achieving insights** that were not apparent from a superficial reading

Gather Evidence These types of evidence you can use in your literary criticism:

- **details from the text:** important ideas from the text that you can describe in your own words
- **quotations from the text:** the exact words of the text, when they are especially relevant or powerful

In the Launch Text, the writer uses both types of evidence as support. For example, the writer uses a quotation from Juliet to demonstrate her awareness of her of own impulsiveness:

Even though their families would never accept their union, they are more than willing to throw away everything to be together—having known each other for barely an evening. Indeed, Juliet says as much of their love:

It is too rash, too unadvised, too sudden;
Too like the lightning, which doth cease to be
Ere one can say "It lightens."

Connect Across Texts As you write, use evidence from both texts to develop your claims. Support your ideas with exact quotations from the texts, paraphrases of the texts, or evidence from secondary sources. Consult a style manual to confirm how to incorporate quotations, paraphrases, or outside evidence into your essay correctly.

EVIDENCE LOG

Review your Evidence Log and identify key details you may want to cite in your literary criticism.

STANDARDS

Writing

- Introduce precise claim(s), distinguish the claim(s) from alternate or opposing claims, and create an organization that establishes clear relationships among claim(s), counterclaims, reasons, and evidence.
- Develop claim(s) and counterclaims fairly, supplying evidence for each while pointing out the strengths and limitations of both in a manner that anticipates the audience's knowledge level and concerns.

Language

Write and edit work so that it conforms to the guidelines in a style manual appropriate for the discipline and writing type.

Drafting

Choose an Effective Organization The organization of an essay is the order in which information is assembled. Organization is especially important in an argumentative essay. A solid organizational structure can help you to unfold a clear analysis and keep your reader on track.

Each section of your literary criticism should connect directly to your main claim and contain sufficient text evidence to support it. Reread the first paragraph of the Launch Text and identify the author's thesis, or claim. Then, read paragraphs 2 and 3. Notice how the writer organizes thoughts and supporting evidence. The writer describes the action of the play, uses, a direct quotation to clarify, and follows the quotation with the the connected argument.

Next, revisit paragraphs 6 and 7 and the different organizational style the author uses. In this section, the author presents an opinion first, followed by quotations to support the argument.

STANDARDS

Reading Literature
Cite strong and thorough textual evidence to support analysis of what the text says explicitly as well as inferences drawn from the text.

Writing
Develop claim(s) and counterclaims fairly, supplying evidence for each while pointing out the strengths and limitations of both in a manner that anticipates the audience's knowledge level and concerns.

Organize Your Argument

Before you draft your essay, use this graphic organizer to identify the points you would like to make, and then find support from the text. Each of your points should be a reason that clearly supports your thesis. Do not include any points that you cannot support with multiple pieces of evidence from each text. Likewise, select evidence from the texts that you can use to address a possible counterclaim in a persuasive way that your audience will understand.

	SUPPORT FROM THE TEXTS
Reason 1	
Counterclaim	
Response to counterclaim	
Reason 2	
Reason 3	

Write a First Draft Use your graphic organizer to write your first draft. Be sure to address the assignment completely by proposing and supporting a clear claim regarding the two texts. Make connections and draw distinctions between the texts. Share the insights you have achieved by reading the texts closely and in relation to each other.

LANGUAGE DEVELOPMENT: CONVENTIONS

Supporting Argument: Using Quotations

Text-based analysis and evaluation, such as literary criticism, requires a lot of evidence from sources. **Direct quotations** are passages taken word for word from a work of literature. **Indirect quotations** are paraphrases, or restatements of the ideas in a text. You will use both in your writing.

Setting and Punctuating Direct Quotations All direct quotations in the running text must be enclosed in quotation marks. A comma usually precedes a direct quotation, but sometimes a colon precedes it. Make sure that periods and commas are included inside closing quotation marks. Question marks and exclamation points should be included inside the closing quotation marks only if they are part of the quotation.

Read It

Short Direct Quotations When including a direct quotation that will take up fewer than three lines of your essay, surround it with quotation marks.

> *When Romeo hears of Juliet's "death," he cries out against fate: "Then, I defy you, stars!"*

Block Indentation Use block indentation whenever a direct quotation is four or more lines long, or when you are quoting multiple lines of dialogue from a drama. Introduce such a quotation with a colon, and do not use quotation marks.

> *Romeo suggests as much before he goes to the party where he first meets Juliet:*
>
> > *I fear, too early: for my mind misgives*
> > *Some consequence yet hanging in the stars*

Indirect Quotations Use an indirect quotation, or paraphrase, when a restatement of dialogue or events will suffice. Because indirect quotations are paraphrases of the text, you should not put them in quotation marks.

> *Juliet is shocked when she hears of Romeo's exile.*

Write It

Revisit *The Tragedy of Romeo and Juliet* and "Pyramus and Thisbe," and mark passages you would like to include in your essay. Use this chart to record how you will incorporate the evidence into your writing.

SOURCE TEXT TITLE	PARAGRAPH OR LINE NUMBER	TYPE OF QUOTE: RUNNING, BLOCK, OR INDIRECT

STANDARDS

Writing

- Develop claim(s) and counterclaims fairly, supplying evidence for each while pointing out the strengths and limitations of both in a manner that anticipates the audience's knowledge level and concerns.
- Use words, phrases and clauses to link the major sections of the text, create cohesion, and clarify the relationships between claim(s) and reasons, between reasons and evidence, and between claim(s) and counterclaims.

Language

Use a colon to introduce a list or quotation.

Revising

Evaluating Your Draft

Use the checklist to evaluate the effectiveness of your first draft. Then, use your evaluation and the instruction on this page to guide your revision.

FOCUS AND ORGANIZATION	EVIDENCE AND ELABORATION	CONVENTIONS
☐ Introduces a thesis consisting of a claim about the texts. ☐ Distinguishes the thesis from opposing claims. ☐ Provides a conclusion that follows from the introduction and argument presented. ☐ Establishes a logical organization and situates evidence appropriately to support the thesis and reasons. ☐ Uses words, phrases, and clauses to clarify the relationships between and among ideas.	☐ Develops the thesis fully by analyzing, comparing, contrasting, and offering insights about multiple texts. ☐ Provides adequate quotations and paraphrases for each major idea. ☐ Uses vocabulary and word choice that are appropriate for the audience and purpose.	☐ Attends to the norms and conventions of the discipline, especially the correct use and punctuation of quotations. ☐ Establishes and maintains a formal style and an objective tone.

WORD NETWORK

Include interesting words from your Word Network in your literary criticism.

Revising for Focus and Organization

Checking for Understanding Revising is an excellent time to clarify your arguments and support with your audience in mind. If your audience is not knowledgeable about your topic, you may have to revise to define unfamiliar terms for your readers. If your audience is more sophisticated, you can go straight to making sure you carefully outline the strengths and limitation of claims and counterclaims. For example, you might point out where there is not enough evidence to support a specific counterclaim.

Revising for Evidence and Elaboration

Style Literary criticism is written in a formal style even though you are sharing your own original interpretations of the selections. Review your draft. Delete phrases such as "I believe that" and "My interpretation is." Replace them with straightforward claims and explanations, such as "The quote shows . . ."

Revise to Eliminate Unnecessary Information Reread your draft, looking for any words or phrases that are either imprecise or unnecessary. Here are some steps to help you revise ideas and better support your thesis:

- Underline your thesis or claim and the main idea of each paragraph.
- Highlight sentences that do not support your thesis.
- Consider adding or revising details to make a tighter connection to your main idea.
- Eliminate any details that do not clearly contribute to your analysis.

STANDARDS

Writing

- Establish and maintain a formal style and objective tone while attending to the norms and conventions of the discipline in which they are writing.
- Provide a concluding statement or section that follows from and supports the argument presented.

PEER REVIEW

Exchange papers with a classmate. Use the checklist to evaluate your classmate's literary criticism and provide supportive feedback.

1. Is the thesis clear? Is it obvious what reasons support the thesis?

☐ yes ☐ no If no, explain what confused you.

2. Is the thesis supported by evidence from both texts?

☐ yes ☐ no If no, point out what needs additional support.

3. Did the literary criticism present the writer's own analysis and insight?

☐ yes ☐ no If no, write a brief note explaining what you thought was missing.

4. What is the strongest part of your classmate's paper? Why?

____

____

____

____

Editing and Proofreading

Edit for Conventions Reread your draft for accuracy and consistency. Correct errors in grammar and word usage. When using a direct quotation, make sure that a comma or colon is used to introduce the quotation and that periods and commas are included within the quotation marks.

Proofread for Accuracy Read your draft carefully, looking for errors in spelling and punctuation. Specifically, check the spelling of words in direct quotations. Because *The Tragedy of Romeo and Juliet* and "Pyramus and Thisbe" are older texts, the spelling of the words may be different from the modern spelling. Check the source material for the exact spelling used in the text.

Publishing and Presenting

Create a final version of your essay. Share it with your class so that your classmates can read it and make comments. In turn, review and comment on your classmates' work. Which insights do you find particularly interesting? Which interpretation is the most common? Which is the least common? Consider the ways in which other students' essays are both similar to and different from your own. Always maintain a polite and respectful tone when commenting.

Reflecting

Think about what you learned while writing your literary criticism. What could you do differently the next time you engage in literary criticism to make the writing experience easier and to make your argument stronger?

OVERVIEW: SMALL-GROUP LEARNING

ESSENTIAL QUESTION:

Do we determine our own destinies?

In both literature and life, questions about who or what is responsible when things go terribly wrong can be painful. You will read selections that examine whether tragic outcomes result from personal decisions or destiny in both fiction and real life. You will work in a group to continue your exploration of the concept of destiny.

Small-Group Learning Strategies

Throughout your life, in school, in your community, and in your career, you will continue to learn and work with others.

Look at these strategies and the actions you can take to practice them as you work in teams. Add ideas of your own for each step. Use these strategies during Small-Group Learning.

STRATEGY	ACTION PLAN
Prepare	• Complete your assignments so that you are prepared for group work. • Organize your thinking so you can contribute to your group's discussions. •
Participate fully	• Make eye contact to signal that you are listening and taking in what is being said. • Use text evidence when making a point. •
Support others	• Build off ideas from others in your group. • Invite others who have not yet spoken to join the discussion. •
Clarify	• Paraphrase the ideas of others to ensure that your understanding is correct. • Ask follow-up questions. •

CONTENTS

COMPARE

PERFORMANCE TASK

SPEAKING AND LISTENING FOCUS

Present an Argument

The Small-Group readings feature nonfiction writings about tragic love stories, both fictional and real. After reading, your group will plan and deliver a multimedia presentation about the reasons people are drawn to tales of tragic destiny.

Working as a Team

1. **Take a Position** In your group, discuss the following question:

   Is luck another way to talk about destiny? Or are luck and destiny totally different concepts?

   As you take turns sharing your positions, be sure to provide reasons for your ideas. After all group members have shared, discuss some of the ways in which characters or people in real life can be lucky or unlucky.

2. **List Your Rules** As a group, decide on the rules that you will follow as you work together. Samples are provided; add two more of your own. You may add or revise rules based on your experience together.

   - Everyone should participate in group discussions.
   - People should not interrupt.
   - ______________________________
   - ______________________________

3. **Apply the Rules** Practice working as a group. Share what you have learned about destiny. Make sure each person in the group contributes. Take notes and be prepared to share with the class one thing that you heard from another member of your group.

4. **Name Your Group** Choose a name that reflects the unit topic.

   Our group's name: ______________________________

5. **Create a Communication Plan** Decide how you want to communicate with one another. For example, you might use online collaboration tools, email, or instant messaging.

   Our group's decision: ______________________________

Making a Schedule

First, find out the due dates for the Small-Group activities. Then, preview the texts and activities with your group, and make a schedule for completing the tasks.

SELECTION	ACTIVITIES	DUE DATE
Romeo and Juliet Is a Terrible Play, and David Leveaux Can't Change That In Defense of *Romeo and Juliet:* It's Not Childish, It's *About* Childishness		
Twenty Years On: The Unfinished Lives of Bosnia's Romeo and Juliet		
Tragic Romeo and Juliet Offers Bosnia Hope		

Working on Group Projects

As your group works together, you'll find it more effective if each person has a specific role. Different projects require different roles. Before beginning a project, discuss the necessary roles, and choose one for each group member. Here are some possible roles; add your own ideas.

Project Manager: monitors the schedule and keeps everyone on task

Researcher: organizes research activities

Recorder: takes notes during group meetings

____

____

____

____

____

LITERARY CRITICISM

Romeo and Juliet Is a Terrible Play, and David Leveaux Can't Change That

In Defense of *Romeo and Juliet*: It's Not Childish, It's *About* Childishness

Concept Vocabulary

As you perform your first read of these two articles, you will encounter the following words.

intrigued	credulity	indignation

Context Clues If these words are unfamiliar to you, try using **context clues**—other words and phrases that appear in a text—to help you determine their meanings. There are various types of context clues that you may encounter as you read.

Synonyms: This salad is delicious—absolutely **delectable**.

Restatement of Idea: I could give the idea no **credence**. I simply couldn't believe it.

Contrast of Ideas and Topics: Helga is usually responsible, but this time she was completely **unreliable**.

Apply your knowledge of context clues and other vocabulary strategies to determine the meanings of unfamiliar words you encounter during your first read.

First Read NONFICTION

Apply these strategies as you conduct your first read. You will have an opportunity to complete a close read after your first read.

NOTICE the general ideas of each text. *What* is it about? *Who* is involved?

ANNOTATE by marking vocabulary and key passages you want to revisit.

CONNECT ideas within the selection to what you already know and what you have already read.

RESPOND by completing the Comprehension Check and by writing a brief summary of each selection.

First Read: NOTICE, ANNOTATE, RESPOND, CONNECT

STANDARDS

Reading Informational Text
By the end of grade 9, read and comprehend literary nonfiction in the grades 9–10 text complexity band proficiently, with scaffolding as needed at the high end of the range.

Language
Use context as a clue to the meaning of a word or phrase.

About the Authors

Originally from Massachusetts, **Alyssa Rosenberg** (b. 1984) attended Yale University. She has contributed to many publications, including the *New York Times*, *New York*, the *Daily Beast*, the *New Republic*, and *Salon*. She has been the culture editor at ThinkProgress.com, a columnist at WomenandHollywood.com, and a pop-culture blogger at the *Washington Post*.

Noah Berlatsky (b. 1971) has been working as a freelance writer and editor for more than 20 years. He serves as editor for a comics and culture website. His work has appeared in the *Atlantic*, *Salon*, the *Awl*, *Slate*, and the *Chicago Reader*, as well as other popular blogs and websites. He has also been featured on National Public Radio's news program *All Things Considered*.

Backgrounds

Romeo and Juliet Is a Terrible Play, and David Leveaux Can't Change That

In her critique of David Leveaux's 2013 production of *The Tragedy of Romeo and Juliet*, Alyssa Rosenberg discusses the level of immaturity displayed by the characters in Shakespeare's original play, and how the play holds up when viewed with modern sensibilities.

In Defense of *Romeo and Juliet*: It's Not Childish, It's *About* Childishness

After Alyssa Rosenberg's critique of *The Tragedy of Romeo and Juliet* received a strong reader reaction, Noah Berlatsky responded by describing his experience as an adult rereading the play about young lovers.

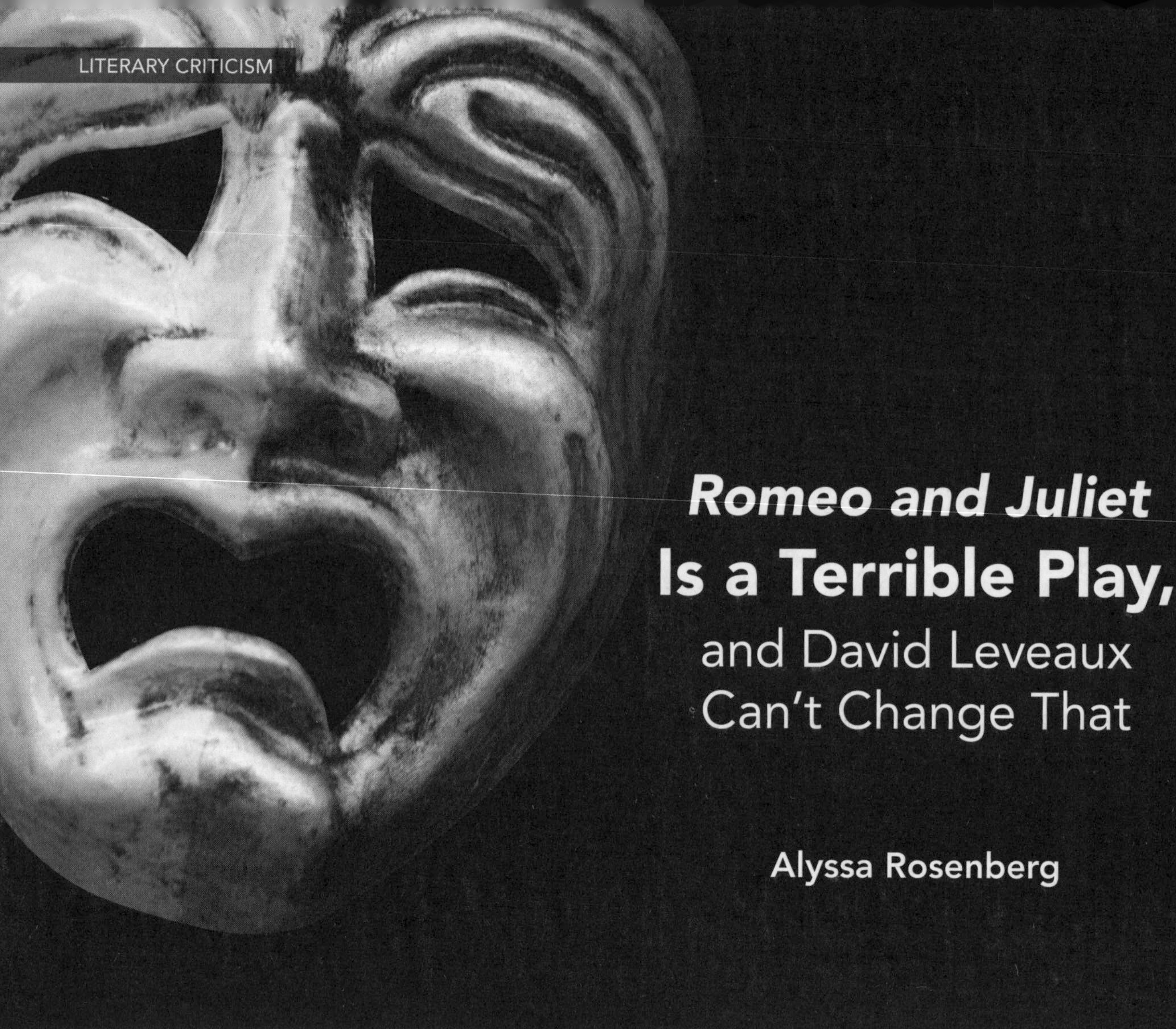

Romeo and Juliet Is a Terrible Play, and David Leveaux Can't Change That

Alyssa Rosenberg

NOTES

1 A new, interracial production of *Romeo and Juliet* arrives on Broadway this September, starring Orlando Bloom and Condola Rashad. Director David Leveaux decided to cast the lovers' families in alignment with their races, resulting in a much more diverse production. So why am I not cheering?

2 Because, despite the fact that its latest staging features a 36-year-old actor and a 26-year-old actress, *Romeo and Juliet*—a play about children—is full of terrible, deeply childish ideas about love. And as much as I want to see more interracial couples in pop culture and more diverse casts on stage and screen, I don't want to see them cast in material that is so horribly depressing.

3 *Romeo and Juliet* itself hasn't aged well. The story follows Juliet Capulet, who is 13 when she meets Romeo Montague at a party, falls head over heels in love with him, and marries him within a day of meeting him. Romeo's age isn't specified in the play, but the quickness with which he throws over a former flame for Juliet

doesn't suggest a particularly mature man. Maybe this works on the page, when we're not forced to watch actors and actresses who are clearly in their 20s and 30s behave like early teenagers. But the effect is embarrassing and unsettling for today's theater audiences, perhaps already fretting over suspended adolescence and stunted millennials.

NOTES

4 Update the play to match the aged-up actors in the two main roles, and the plot still doesn't make a lot of sense. Why are the families fighting? What was the inciting incident? The absence of a reason does mean that adaptations can fill in space that Shakespeare left behind, making the warring parties Puerto Rican and Polish-American, for instance, or Israeli and Palestinian. But even then, having the two lovers kill themselves through a series of misunderstandings doesn't translate well in a setting that takes any sort of modern communications for granted. And it's hard to believe the couple, no matter how lovelorn, would lack the patience to wait 24 hours to get hitched—not to mention the savvy to check up on a bad report from Verona.

5 But beyond that, the vision of Romeo and Juliet's deaths uniting their families is an adolescent fantasy of death solving all problems, a "won't they miss me when I'm gone" pout. There's a reason that, in the best modern riff on *Romeo and Juliet*, *West Side Story*, Maria lives after Tony's death to shame the Sharks and the Jets, her survival a seal on the truce between them. Dying is easy. Living to survive the consequences of your actions and to do the actual work of reconciliation is the hard part. An interracial *Romeo and Juliet* is nice, but black actors and actresses deserve richer roles than Romeo and Juliet. ❧

LITERARY CRITICISM

In Defense of *Romeo and Juliet*: It's Not Childish, It's *About* Childishness

Noah Berlatsky

NOTES

Mark context clues or indicate another strategy you used that helped you determine meaning.

intrigued (ihn TREEGD) *v.*

MEANING:

credulity (kruh DYOO luh tee) *n.*

MEANING:

1 I haven't read *Romeo and Juliet* since I was in high school 25 years ago. High school is, of course, a time of rampaging hormones and extravagant romantic angst; in theory, the perfect life moment to read *Romeo and Juliet*. In practice . . . eh. I think my favorite character was Mercutio. I thought he was funny.

2 I just reread the play last week, inspired by Alyssa Rosenberg's declaration at *Slate* that "*Romeo and Juliet* is a terrible play." The comments section erupted in howls of outrage . . . but I was **intrigued**. Suddenly, I was curious to find out what I thought of a work I hadn't revisited in more than two decades.

3 Rosenberg argued that "*Romeo and Juliet*—a play about children—is full of terrible, deeply childish ideas about love." Juliet, Rosenberg reminds us, is 13. If you cast someone that age in the role now, the result is queasy. If you cast someone older, you end up with an adult actor behaving like she's a tween. Romeo's age is uncertain, but a lot of what he does is immature, and adolescent as well. The lovers' haste to marry strains **credulity**—it seems (though Rosenberg doesn't quite say this) like a childish fantasy of love at first sight. Similarly, the reconciliation of the lovers' warring families upon their demise reads for Rosenberg as "an adolescent fantasy of death solving all problems."

4 Adolescent or not, though, I sure enjoyed reading it this time through. Romeo and Juliet's first meeting, for example, all by itself validates the romantic comedy genre.

Romeo. [*To* Juliet] If I profane with my unworthiest hand
This holy shrine, the gentle fine is this:
My lips, two blushing pilgrims, ready stand
To smooth that rough touch with a tender kiss.

Juliet. Good pilgrim, you do wrong your hand too much,
Which mannerly devotion shows in this;
For saints have hands that pilgrims' hands do touch,
And palm to palm is holy palmers' kiss.

Romeo. Have not saints lips, and holy palmers too?

Juliet. Ay, pilgrim, lips that they must use in prayer.

NOTES

5 That is some searingly saucy banter, there. "Ay, pilgrim, lips that they must use in prayer" has to be one of the archest lines in all of literature. I'm with Romeo. I'd fall in love with that.

6 In short, now that I'm an adult, I appreciate the young lovers a good bit more than I did when I was their age. This may be counterintuitive . . . but it also seems to be one of the main points of the play itself.

7 A number of Rosenberg's commenters noted that *Romeo and Juliet* is deliberately about young love. This is no doubt true. But the play is also, and insistently, about age. The fact that Juliet is 13, for example, is not just mentioned once. It comes up again and again. Moreover, the first time Juliet appears on stage, her aged comic Nurse launches into a rambling anecdote about when her charge was a toddler, an anecdote that Juliet clearly finds both tedious and embarrassing. Juliet's youth, then, is adamantly established, and also adamantly presented as a source of fascination for the elderly.

8 Old/young remains an obsession throughout the play—but that obsession does not, interestingly, work in any single way. Sometimes, being young means being rash and changeable, as when Romeo switches his hyperbolic affections from Rosaline to Juliet. Sometimes, it means being a hope for the future—as when the Friar marries the couple to try to end the feud between Montagues and Capulets. There are passages where old and young are presented as almost different species, as when Juliet irritably declaims, ". . . old folks, many feign as they were dead; / Unwieldy, slow, heavy and pale as lead."

9 And then there are moments where it seems like old and young don't really act all that differently. Juliet's hasty marriage to Romeo, for example, isn't much more precipitous than Lord Capulet's sudden decision to marry her to Paris. And Romeo's affections aren't any more changeable than those of the Nurse, who, having cheerfully helped Juliet marry Romeo, just as cheerfully advises her to forget that first marriage and turn polyandrist[1] by wedding as her father wishes.

10 Rosenberg might argue that even the adults behave like kids in *Romeo and Juliet* because the play itself is childish. But . . . is Capulet really childish? Is the Nurse? Surely, you don't have to be young

1. **polyandrist** (POL ee an drihst) *n.* one who has two or more husbands at the same time.

NOTES

Mark context clues or indicate another strategy you used that helped you determine meaning.

indignation (ihn dihg NAY shuhn) *n.*

MEANING:

to be precipitate or fickle. Adults behave like children with some frequency. And . . . vice versa.

11 For *Romeo and Juliet*, in other words, youth and age seem less like solid, immutable categories than like tropes. They're devices manipulated by Juliet or Romeo to give force to their sense of **indignation** or specialness. Or manipulated by the Nurse to give force to her affection and nostalgia. Or manipulated by Shakespeare to sweep (adults?) into a romantic swoon. Or manipulated by Rosenberg, to denigrate[2] that same swooning. From this perspective, the point of the play isn't so much the exhilaration of young love or the dunderheadedness of young love. Rather (as often with Shakespeare) the point is the language itself: the dazzling, disturbing rhetorical force of old/young, corrupt/innocent, experienced/naïve.

12 Rosenberg claims that *Romeo and Juliet* is dated because of the uncomfortable way its childishness, and its child protagonists, sit in our contemporary culture. I'd argue, though, that that uncomfortableness is not a contemporary addition, but is instead one of the things Shakespeare was writing about to begin with. At that first flirtatious meeting, for example, Romeo is masked with friends at a Capulet party. Old Capulet, seeing the maskers, reminisces about when he used to do the same.

Capulet. What, man! 'tis not so much, 'tis not so much:
'Tis since the nuptials of Lucentio,
Come pentecost as quickly as it will,
Some five and twenty years; and then we mask'd.

Second Capulet. 'Tis more, 'tis more, his son is elder, sir;
His son is thirty.

Capulet. Will you tell me that?
His son was but a ward two years ago.

Romeo. [*To a* Servingman] What lady is that, which doth enrich the hand
Of yonder knight?

13 Capulet slips back through time . . . and when he stops slipping, it is Romeo who speaks and goes to woo Juliet. Capulet was Romeo, Romeo is Capulet—and so, by substitution, the lover of the daughter is the father. The mask is a device not so much to enable young love, as to enable the old to imagine young love.

14 In *Romeo and Juliet* play-acting with the categories of adult and child can lead to exhilarating delight, pleasurably moralistic revulsion and, sometimes, to tragedy. If, in our own day, we have pushed the onset of adulthood past the tweens, past the teens, and even to some degree up into the 20s—that makes the play's insights and its sometimes exasperating perversities more relevant, not less. ❧

2. **denigrate** (DEHN uh grayt) *v.* disparage; insult.

Comprehension Check

Complete the following items after you finish your first read. Review and clarify details with your group.

ROMEO AND JULIET IS A TERRIBLE PLAY

1. What does Rosenberg like about the new production of *The Tragedy of Romeo and Juliet* that she is describing?

2. Why does she object to the ages of the actors?

3. What is Rosenberg's main criticism of the play?

IN DEFENSE OF *ROMEO AND JULIET*

1. How much time has passed since the author initially read *The Tragedy of Romeo and Juliet?*

2. How does Berlatsky feel about the play now that he is an adult?

3. In Berlatsky's opinion, what makes the play's insights more relevant today?

4. **Notebook** Confirm your understanding by writing a summary of each text.

RESEARCH

Research to Explore Choose something that interested you from one of the texts, and formulate a research question.

SOURCES

- *ROMEO AND JULIET* IS A TERRIBLE PLAY, AND DAVID LEVEAUX CAN'T CHANGE THAT
- IN DEFENSE OF *ROMEO AND JULIET*: IT'S NOT CHILDISH, IT'S *ABOUT* CHILDISHNESS

Close Read the Text

With your group, revisit sections of the texts you marked during your first read. **Annotate** what you notice. What **questions** do you have? What can you **conclude**?

Analyze the Text

CITE TEXTUAL EVIDENCE to support your answers.

Complete the activities.

1. **Review and Clarify** With your group, reread paragraph 3 of "*Romeo and Juliet* is a Terrible Play." Why does the author focus on the ages of the main characters and the actors who portray them?
2. **Present and Discuss** Now, work with your group to share the passages from "*Romeo and Juliet* is a Terrible Play" and "In Defense of *Romeo and Juliet*" that you found especially important. Take turns presenting your passages. Discuss what you notice in the texts, the questions you asked, and the conclusions you reached.
3. **Essential Question** ***Do we determine our own destinies?*** How have these articles contributed to your thinking about destiny? Discuss with your group.

TIP

GROUP DISCUSSION
Start a discussion by expressing your opinion. Then, try to support your opinion with evidence from the article or examples from the play.

LANGUAGE DEVELOPMENT

Concept Vocabulary

intrigued	credulity	indignation

Why These Words? The three concept vocabulary words are related. With your group, determine what the words have in common. Write your ideas, and add another word that fits the category.

WORD NETWORK
Add interesting words related to destiny from the texts to your Word Network.

Practice

Notebook Confirm your understanding of each vocabulary word by using it in a sentence. Use context clues to help make the meanings clear.

Word Study

Notebook **Latin Root: *-cred-*** The concept vocabulary word *credulity* contains the Latin root *-cred-*, meaning "believe."

1. Write a definition for the word *credulity* that demonstrates how the Latin root *-cred-* contributes to its meaning.
2. Write definitions for these words that also contain the Latin root *-cred-*: *incredible*, *credentials*, *accredited*. Consult a dictionary if needed.

STANDARDS

Reading Informational Text
Delineate and evaluate the argument and specific claims in a text, assessing whether the reasoning is valid and the evidence is relevant and sufficient; identify false statements and fallacious reasoning.

Language
Identify and correctly use patterns of word changes that indicate different meanings or parts of speech.

Analyze Craft and Structure

Argumentative Text A **criticism** is a type of argumentative writing in which the author expresses an opinion about a created work, such as a book, a film, or a performance. Both "*Romeo and Juliet* Is a Terrible Play" and "In Defense of *Romeo and Juliet*" are examples of criticism.

Effective critical writing includes evidence to support the writer's position and to convince readers that his or her evaluation of the work is valid and correct. Many works of criticism include the following elements:

- background about the work and its significance
- related points about a work's strengths or weaknesses
- relevant and strong examples, quotations, facts, and other evidence presented in a knowledgeable, convincing way
- consideration of opposing points of view or counterclaims; By acknowledging other positions, a writer shows that other claims have been considered, but ultimately his or her argument is the most valid.

COLLABORATION

It can be helpful to discuss your thoughts with a partner before writing them. Your partner can help by asking you clarifying questions. Together, you can expand the writing.

CITE TEXTUAL EVIDENCE to support your answers.

Practice

Gather information about the arguments that the two articles present by responding to the questions in the chart. Share your responses with the group.

	Romeo and Juliet Is a Terrible Play	In Defense of *Romeo and Juliet*
What is the writer's argument?		
What reasons and evidence does the writer present?		
Is the evidence relevant and sufficient to convince readers? Explain.		
Does the writer effectively acknowledge counterclaims? Explain.		

SOURCES

- *ROMEO AND JULIET* IS A TERRIBLE PLAY, AND DAVID LEVEAUX CAN'T CHANGE THAT
- IN DEFENSE OF *ROMEO AND JULIET*: IT'S NOT CHILDISH, IT'S *ABOUT* CHILDISHNESS

Author's Style

Organization Writers use **transitions**, or words and phrases that clarify the relationships between ideas, to help organize a text. To create clear paragraphs, transitions can connect ideas and examples or create contrasts within or between sentences. Writers also use transitions to connect paragraphs with related ideas.

For example, in paragraph 2 of "*Romeo and Juliet* is a Terrible Play," Rosenberg uses the transitional word *because* to connect the rhetorical question "So why am I not cheering?" with her answer. With the word *because*, Rosenberg signals a cause-and-effect relationship; the fact that Rosenberg is not cheering about the new casting of *The Tragedy of Romeo and Juliet* is caused by the fact that she believes the play to be "full of terrible, deeply childish ideas about love."

Below are more examples of types of relationships and the transitional words and phrases writers use to establish those relationships.

Comparison: similarly, in comparison, likewise
Contrast: on the other hand, in contrast, however
Cause and Effect: because, inasmuch as, as a result
Addition: also, and, furthermore, in addition
Introducing: for example, for instance, particularly
Summary: in short, to sum up, all in all

STANDARDS

Reading Informational Text
Analyze how the author unfolds an analysis or series of ideas or events, including the order in which the points are made, how they are introduced and developed, and the connections that are drawn between them.

Writing
Use appropriate and varied transitions and sentence structures to link the major sections of the text, create cohesion, and clarify the relationships among ideas and concepts.

Read It

Work individually. Use this chart to identify the transition in each passage from "In Defense of *Romeo and Juliet.*" Explain what relationship the transition shows. When you have finished, discuss with your group.

SELECTION PASSAGE	TRANSITION	TYPE OF RELATIONSHIP
Similarly, the reconciliation of the lovers' warring families upon their demise reads for Rosenberg as "an adolescent fantasy of death solving all problems." (paragraph 3)		
Romeo and Juliet's first meeting, for example, all by itself validates the romantic comedy. (paragraph 4)		
In short, now that I'm an adult, I appreciate the young lovers a good bit more than I did when I was their age. (paragraph 6)		

Write It

Notebook Rewrite each passage in your notebook. Replace the transition with another one that has the same meaning.

Writing to Sources

Join the conversation between Rosenberg and Berlatsky by writing responses to these two essays about Shakespeare's play *The Tragedy of Romeo and Juliet*.

Assignment

Remember that **criticism** texts are argumentative texts that express opinions about created works. Write your own criticism using one of the following choices. Your text should include **claims**, or statements that express a position, and evidence that supports these claims. To strengthen your writing, address and refute opposing opinions, called **counterclaims**. Once you have completed the writing, present your work to the class.

☐ **Reader Comments** Write comments that could be posted to the blog and website on which these essays appeared. Respond to their ideas and add your own, using textual evidence to support your response.

☐ **Speaker Invitation** Write letters to Rosenberg and Berlatsky, inviting them to participate in a school-sponsored Shakespeare festival. State specific reasons you want to include them and support each reason by citing evidence from these essays.

☐ **Proposal for Anthology** Write a proposal to create an anthology of critical writings about *The Tragedy of Romeo and Juliet*. Explain whether you wish to include or omit the essays by Rosenberg and Berlatsky.

Analyze Arguments Think carefully about the qualities of each article that worked and did not work as an argument before you write your own criticism. Consult your chart from the Analyze Craft and Structure page to help you analyze the argument in each text. Use the chart below to help you organize your thoughts.

	WHAT WORKED	WHAT DID NOT WORK
Rosenberg		
Berlatzky		

Clarify Ideas and Evidence Use the information you recorded in the chart to determine your claims about each text. Then, identify at least two reasons that support your claim. Finally, identify textual evidence that supports each reason. Discuss your ideas with your group and use their feedback to help you draft your criticism text.

TIP

COLLABORATION

If you are writing a negative comment about someone's writing, be sure to remain polite, especially when you are online. Rude comments reflect badly on the commenter.

EVIDENCE LOG

Before moving on to a new selection, go to your Evidence Log and record what you learned from "*Romeo and Juliet* Is a Terrible Play" and "In Defense of *Romeo and Juliet.*"

STANDARDS

Reading Informational Text
Delineate and evaluate the argument and specific claims in a text, assessing whether the reasoning is valid and the evidence is relevant and sufficient; identify false statements and fallacious reasoning.

Writing
Introduce precise claim(s), distinguish the claim(s) from alternate or opposing claims, and create an organization that establishes clear relationships among claim(s), counterclaims, reasons, and evidence.

TWENTY YEARS ON: THE UNFINISHED LIVES OF BOSNIA'S ROMEO AND JULIET

Comparing Text to Media

In this lesson, you will compare two pieces of journalism—one print and one digital. First, you will complete the first-read and close-read activities for the piece of print journalism. The work you do with your group on this selection will help prepare you for the comparing task.

TRAGIC ROMEO AND JULIET OFFERS BOSNIA HOPE

About the Author

The journalism of **Gordana Sandić-Hadžihasanović** has focused on the plight of refugees. In her program named "I Don't Want Another's, I Want My Own," she interviews approximately 100 refugees about their histories and their attempts to return to their former lives.

Twenty Years On: The Unfinished Lives of Bosnia's Romeo and Juliet

Concept Vocabulary

As you perform your first read of "Twenty Years On: The Unfinished Lives of Bosnia's Romeo and Juliet," you will encounter these words.

besieged **surrounding** **intervened**

Base Words If these words are unfamiliar to you, analyze each one to see whether it contains a base word you know. Here is an example of how to apply the strategy.

Unfamiliar Word: *senseless*

Familiar "Inside" Word: *sense*, with meanings including "good reason."

Context: This modern-day "Romeo and Juliet" showed the tragic and **senseless** destruction of the city.

Conclusion: The author thinks that the war did not need to happen. *Senseless* might mean "without a good reason."

Apply your knowledge of base words and other vocabulary strategies to determine the meanings of unfamiliar words you encounter during your first read.

First Read NONFICTION

Apply these strategies as you conduct your first read. You will have an opportunity to complete a close read after your first read.

NOTICE

NOTICE the general ideas of the text. *What* is it about? *Who* is involved?

ANNOTATE

ANNOTATE by marking vocabulary and key passages you want to revisit.

NOTICE ANNOTATE First Read CONNECT RESPOND

CONNECT ideas within the selection to what you already know and what you have already read.

CONNECT

RESPOND by completing the Comprehension Check and by writing a brief summary of the selection.

RESPOND

STANDARDS

Reading Informational Text
By the end of grade 9, read and comprehend literary nonfiction in the grades 9–10 text complexity band proficiently, with scaffolding as needed at the high end of the range.

Language
Identify and correctly use patterns of word changes that indicate different meanings or parts of speech.

Twenty Years On: The Unfinished Lives of Bosnia's Romeo and Juliet

Gordana Sandić-Hadžihasanović

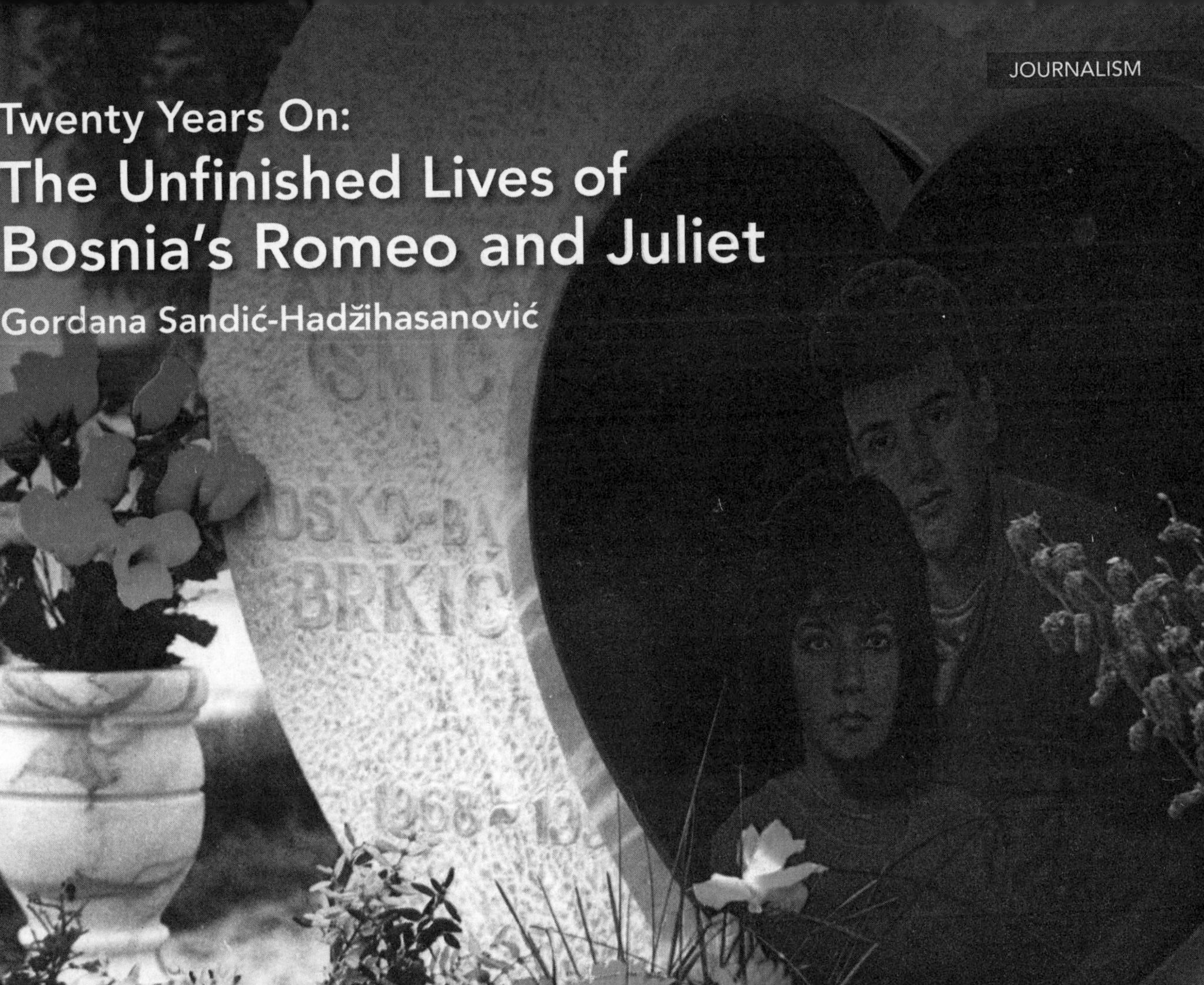

BACKGROUND

The Bosnian Civil War began in 1992 when Bosnia and Herzegovina, a small country in southeastern Europe, voted for independence from the former Yugoslavia. The primary rival groups included the mostly Christian Serbs and mostly Muslim Bosniaks. The country's capital, Sarajevo, was under siege for nearly four years.

SARAJEVO– The story of Bosko Brkic and Admira Ismic ended with two short bursts from a sniper's rifle on a Sarajevo bridge the afternoon of May 19, 1993.

2 Bosko, a 24-year-old ethnic Serb, was killed instantly. Admira, his 25-year-old Bosniak girlfriend, was fatally wounded. She crawled to Bosko and, after about 10 minutes, died with him.

3 One eyewitness described the scene in an interview years later.

4 "The girl was carrying a bag and waving it. They were running and holding hands. It looked like she was dancing," the witness said.

NOTES

NOTES

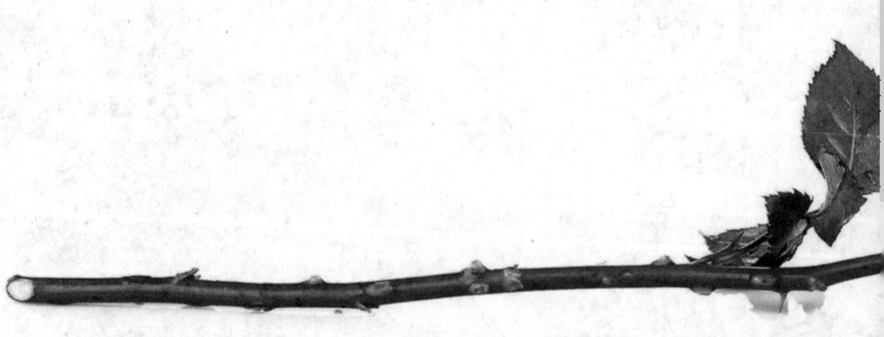

Mark base words or indicate another strategy you used that helped you determine meaning.

besieged (bih SEEJD) *adj.*

MEANING:

surrounding (suh ROWN dihng) *adj.*

MEANING:

"Suddenly, I heard the rifle shots. They fell to the ground, embracing each other."

5 The bodies remained in the no-man's land of **besieged** Sarajevo for nearly four days before Serbian forces **surrounding** the city sent some Muslim prisoners to gather them.

6 Both sides blamed the other for breaking the shaky cease-fire under which the star-crossed lovers were trying to escape the siege. No definitive conclusions were ever reached.

"Each Other and a Dream"

7 The story flashed around the world in a now-famous dispatch by Reuters correspondent Kurt Schork. For millions around the world, this modern-day "Romeo and Juliet," a love destroyed by the hatred that surrounded it, brought home the tragedy and senselessness of the destruction of Bosnia-Herzegovina's capital.

8 Twenty years later, the classic Yugoslav rock band Zabranjeno Pusenje (No Smoking) has issued a new song and video called starkly "Bosko and Admira," a piece suffused with the sadness and dashed hopes of the original story:

The times get worse around them; they had no chance.
But difficult times always bring great romance.
They weren't from the same tribe, nor did they have the same god.
But they had each other and a dream of escaping out from under it all.

9 "This is [a] well-known Sarajevo story—about Sarajevo's Romeo and Juliet, about Bosko and Admira, young people killed in the war who were trying to find a place for their love and their freedom," Zabranjeno Pusenje front man Davor Sucic tells RFE/RL's Balkan Service. "This is a symbolic story, very relevant, even today. After so many years of peace we are still searching for love and freedom in

NOTES

this country. In this story, I found a lot of things in common with life today and what is happening to us now."

10 The video was directed by Croatian Zare Batinovic, who tells RFE/RL about the challenges of making the film of a story so intimately tied to a city—the prewar, multiethnic Sarajevo—that essentially no longer exists.

11 "The theme is here. Everyone knows the story," Batinovic says. "So many years have been passed, and it was not easy to evoke the Sarajevo of the 1990s."

Haunting Question

12 If Bosnia's capital little resembles the scarred Sarajevo of 1993, it also remains far from the smiling, confident city that hosted the Winter Olympics in 1984, the year that Bosko and Admira first kissed at a New Year's party at the age of 16.

13 Admira's parents say they plan nothing special to mark the anniversary of their daughter's death beyond visiting the graves and leaving flowers. Her father, Zijo Ismic, still wrestles with the forces that swept over his daughter, his city, his country.

14 "War **intervened** in love—that's the problem," Ismic says. "In such situations, the laws of love do not exist. Only the laws of war."

15 Bosko's mother, Rada Brkic, left Sarajevo during the war and never returned, unable to face the familiar streets and neighborhoods where Bosko and Admira lived and loved.

16 She tells RFE/RL that she tries not to dwell too much on the fact that her son's killers were never identified.

17 "I don't think too much about the person who killed them," she says. "But if I ever saw him, I'd ask: 'Why did you do it?' That's all."

18 Bosko and Admira are buried in Sarajevo's Lion Cemetery along with thousands of other victims of the siege. Schork, who told their story, was killed while on assignment in Sierra Leone in 2000. Half of his ashes were buried next to the grave of Bosko and Admira. ❧

Mark base words or indicate another strategy you used that helped you determine meaning.

intervened (ihn tuhr VEEND) *v.*

MEANING:

Comprehension Check

Complete the following items after you finish your first read. Review and clarify details with your group.

1. What were Bosko and Admira trying to do when they were shot?

2. What was taking place in the city of Sarajevo during this time period?

3. What happened twenty years later to remind people of Bosko and Admira?

4. **Notebook** Confirm your understanding of the text by writing a summary of the article.

RESEARCH

Research to Explore Choose something that interested you from the text, and formulate a research question.

Close Read the Text

With your group, revisit sections of the text you marked during your first read. What do you **notice**? What **questions** do you have? What can you **conclude**?

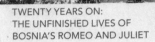

TWENTY YEARS ON: THE UNFINISHED LIVES OF BOSNIA'S ROMEO AND JULIET

Analyze the Text

CITE TEXTUAL EVIDENCE to support your answers.

Notebook Complete the activities.

1. **Review and Clarify** With your group, reread paragraphs 1–4 of the text. Discuss with your group the exact events of the afternoon of May 19, 1993. What insight does the eyewitness provide?
2. **Present and Discuss** Now, work with your group to share the passages from the text that you found especially important. Take turns presenting your passages. Discuss what you notice in the text, the questions you asked, and the conclusions you reached.
3. **Essential Question:** ***Do we determine our own destinies?*** What has this text taught you about destiny?

GROUP DISCUSSION

Ask questions to spur discussion. When many members of a group are asking and answering questions, the group is able to come up with more ideas than if only one person is offering ideas.

LANGUAGE DEVELOPMENT

Concept Vocabulary

beseiged **surrounding** **intervened**

Why These Words? The three concept vocabulary words are related. With your group, determine what the words have in common. Write your ideas, and add another word that fits the category.

Add interesting words related to destiny from the text to your Word Network.

Practice

Notebook Confirm your understanding of the concept vocabulary words from the text by using them in sentences. Share your sentences with members of your group.

Word Study

Notebook **Latin Prefix: *inter-*** The word *intervened* begins with the Latin prefix *inter-*, which means "between" or "among." Complete these activities, and discuss your answers with your group.

1. The Latin root *-ven-* means "to come." Using this fact, write a definition for *intervened* that shows your understanding of the prefix *inter-*.

2. Infer the meaning of *intercultural*, and write a definition. Use a dictionary to verify your answer.

STANDARDS

Language

- Identify and correctly use patterns of word changes that indicate different meanings or parts of speech.
- Verify the preliminary determination of the meaning of a word or phrase.

TWENTY YEARS ON: THE UNFINISHED LIVES OF BOSNIA'S ROMEO AND JULIET

Analyze Craft and Structure

Journalism News articles and broadcasts make up an important part of journalism, a type of nonfiction writing that focuses on current events and nonfiction subjects of general interest to the public. **Feature articles**, such as "Twenty Years On," are a type of journalism that focuses on a specific event or situation.

Effective journalism grabs readers' attention and emphasizes the most important information in a news story. To do this, the author must first answer the basic questions *who, what, where, when,* and *why* of a story. Authors may answer most of the questions in the first few paragraphs, or lead paragraphs, but they may use the rest of the article to address the *why* questions, since the answer may be more complex. As they answer the *why* questions, authors often include quotations from eyewitnesses or other people related to the story. Authors may also include a paragraph that summarizes the important details and the significance of the event in a "nutshell" paragraph. Finally, authors will conclude with a memorable ending, such as a poignant quotation or a statement that challenges readers to think about what the event may mean for the future. This variety of organizational elements helps journalists convey information logically while also conveying the importance of an event or situation.

TIP

GROUP DISCUSSION
Sometimes facts that are stated simply can be more powerful and memorable than facts that are stated in a complicated or highly descriptive way.

Practice

CITE TEXTUAL EVIDENCE to support your answers.

Use the chart to analyze the various elements of a feature article. Then, share your ideas with your group.

FEATURE ARTICLE ELEMENT	DETAILS EMPHASIZED
Headline	
Lead Paragraph(s)	
Basic Questions *Who, What, When, Where,* and *Why*	
Quotations	
Nutshell Paragraph	
Ending	

STANDARDS
Reading Informational Text
Analyze in detail how an author's ideas or claims are developed and refined by particular sentences, paragraphs, or larger portions of a text.

Conventions

Using Phrases to Add Variety Writers may use various types of phrases to clarify the logical relationships among ideas and to add variety to their writing. Two of those types of phrases are appositive phrases and absolute phrases.

An **appositive** is a group of words that identifies, renames, or explains a noun or pronoun. An **appositive phrase** is an appositive along with its own modifiers. An appositive or appositive phrase usually appears directly after the word it is modifying.

An **absolute phrase** features a noun or pronoun and its modifiers. Often, the modifiers include a participle or participial phrase. Rather than modifying an individual word, an absolute phrase modifies an entire clause or sentence.

To strengthen your writing, when two separate sentences are closely related, consider revising to combine them using an appositive phrase or an absolute phrase. This chart shows two examples of this type of revision.

WEAKER WRITING	REVISION USING A PHRASE
Romeo and Juliet is a play by William Shakespeare. It has the archetypal theme of ill-fated love.	Appositive Phrase: *Romeo and Juliet*, **a play by William Shakespeare**, has ill-fated love as a theme.
Bosko and Admira's legend lives long after their death. They are a reminder of senseless loss for the people of Sarajevo.	Absolute Phrase: **Their legend living long after their death**, Bosko and Admira are a reminder of senseless loss for the people of Sarajevo.

EVIDENCE LOG

Before moving on to a new selection, go to your evidence log and record what you've learned from *Twenty Years On: The Unfinished Lives of Bosnia's Romeo and Juliet.*

STANDARDS

Language
Use various types of phrases and clauses to convey specific meanings and add variety and interest to writing or presentations.

Read It

Work individually. Use this chart to identify the appositive phrase or absolute phrase in each sentence.

SENTENCE	APPOSITIVE PHRASE	ABSOLUTE PHRASE
The story of Bosko and Admira takes place in Sarajevo, a town torn by civil war in the early 1990s.		
Their hearts filled with love, Bosko and Admira crossed the bridge between the two halves of the city.		
Zabranjeno Pusenje, a Yugoslav rock band, recently wrote a song about Bosko and Admira.		
Many of its buildings rebuilt, the city remains in the shadow of the war.		

Write It

Notebook In your notebook, write one sentence about the article. In your sentence, include either an appositive phrase or an absolute phrase.

TWENTY YEARS ON

Comparing Text to Media

The video "Tragic Romeo and Juliet Offers Bosnia Hope" is from Cable News Network's website. While viewing this selection, you will analyze the differences between how written text and video can tell a story.

TRAGIC ROMEO AND JULIET OFFERS BOSNIA HOPE

About the Narrator

With over twenty years' experience, CNN's Senior International Correspondent **Nic Robertson** (b. 1962) has had a decorated career. He has reported from the war-torn regions of Iraq, Libya, Afghanistan, Yugoslavia, Pakistan, Lebanon, Sudan, and Northern Ireland, among others. His work has won many prestigious awards, including Emmys, Peabodys, and the duPont Award.

Tragic Romeo and Juliet Offers Bosnia Hope

Media Vocabulary

These terms will be useful to you as you analyze, discuss, and write about news videos.

Human Interest Story: story that focuses on the personal issues of people	• Human interest stories are often told in a more emotional way than other news stories. • These stories encourage the viewer or listener to identify with the subjects of the stories. • These stories may deal with difficult situations faced by individuals or the achievements of individuals.
Establishing Shot: shot that shows the context of a scene in a film or video	• An establishing shot is often a long shot that shows where a scene takes place.
Reporter Stand-Ups: shot that shows a reporter looking into the camera and delivering information about a story	• Often, reporter stand-ups appear at or near the beginning or the end of a film or video.
Montage: group of images shown quickly, one after another, to create a single impression	• Montages are often used when a director has access to only still images of a person or event. • Montages can be very effective in communicating the personality of a person or the nature of a relationship.

First Review MEDIA: VIDEO

Apply these strategies as you conduct your first review.

WATCH *who* speaks, *what* they say, and *how* they say it.

NOTE elements that you find interesting and want to revisit.

First Review

CONNECT ideas in the video to other media you've experienced, texts you've read, or images you've seen.

RESPOND by completing the Comprehension Check at the end.

STANDARDS

Reading Informational Text
Analyze various accounts of a subject told in different mediums, determining which details are emphasized in each account.

Language
Acquire and use accurately general academic and domain-specific words and phrases, sufficient for reading, writing, speaking and listening at the college and career readiness level; demonstrate independence in gathering vocabulary knowledge when considering a word or phrase important to comprehension or expression.

Tragic Romeo and Juliet Offers Bosnia Hope

Nic Robertson

BACKGROUND

During the Bosnian Civil War, the Serbs and the Yugoslav army attacked areas with large Bosniak populations, including the capital city, Sarajevo, in order to control the region. The attack also served as a means of what could be described as "ethnic cleansing." By the end of the war in 1995, about 100,000 people had been killed.

NOTES

Comprehension Check

Complete the following items after you finish your first review. Review and clarify details with your group.

1. Through whose eyes does the newscast show Bosko and Admira?

2. Describe the setting in the reporter stand-up shot near the beginning of the newscast.

3. Why could only one parent attend Bosko and Admira's funeral?

4. **Notebook** Confirm your understanding by writing a summary of the newscast.

Close Review

With your group, revisit the video and your first-review notes. Record any new observations that seem important. What **questions** do you have? What can you **conclude**?

TRAGIC ROMEO AND JULIET OFFERS BOSNIA HOPE

Analyze the Media

CITE TEXTUAL EVIDENCE to support your answers.

Complete the activities.

1. **Present and Discuss** How does the first shot in the newscast establish a sense of memory and the past? How does this shot convey a sense of loss? Discuss your thoughts with your group.
2. **Review and Synthesize** With your group, review the entire newscast. What does the newscast convey about tragedy, and about hope? Support your ideas with evidence from the media.
3. **Essential Question:** ***Do we determine our own destinies?*** What has this newscast taught you about destiny? Support your ideas with evidence from the newscast, then discuss them with your group.

WORD NETWORK

Add interesting words related to destiny from the video to your Word Network.

LANGUAGE DEVELOPMENT

Media Vocabulary

human interest story	reporter stand-ups
establishing shot	montage

Use the media vocabulary words and phrases in your responses to the questions.

1. How would you describe the opening of the newscast?
2. How would you describe the camera shot that takes place on the bridge?
3. How does the newscast give viewers an idea of what Bosko and Admira were like together?

STANDARDS

Language
Acquire and use accurately general academic and domain-specific words and phrases, sufficient for reading, writing, speaking, and listening at the college and career readiness level; demonstrate independence in gathering vocabulary knowledge when considering a word or phrase important to comprehension or expression.

TWENTY YEARS ON: THE UNFINISHED LIVES OF BOSNIA'S ROMEO AND JULET

TRAGIC ROMEO AND JULIET OFFERS BOSNIA HOPE

Writing to Compare

You have watched a work of broadcast journalism and read a news article about Bosko and Admira—Sarajevo's "Romeo and Juliet." Now, analyze the texts and consider how the medium, or form, in which the information is delivered affects what you learn and feel about the subject.

Assignment

Write an **argument** in which you compare and contrast the two works of journalism, considering the information each provides and how that information is presented. Explain whether one medium presents more or different facts than the other; delivers information in a more compelling way; or offers richer insights. Choose one of these options.

- ☐ an **email** to a fellow student in which you offer advice about whether to use the article, the video, or both in a presentation
- ☐ an **opinion article** for a website that analyzes the effects of war on individuals
- ☐ a **blog post** that recommends either the article or the video to readers interested in nonfiction about ill-fated love

Analyze the Texts

Notebook Work together to complete the activity and respond to the questions.

Compare Forms of Journalism Gather details from both works of journalism. Identify facts both reports provide. Briefly describe how those facts are presented. Some of the ways in which information can be presented are listed here. Using your observations of the two works, add your own categories to the list.

- reporter relates the information directly
- provides information in an interview
- quotes from another source
- provides information in a camera shot without words
- suggests through descriptive language but does not state directly

1. (a) What information appears in the article but not in the newscast? (b) What information appears in the newscast but not in the article?

2. Which facts or other information appear in both the newscast and the article but are presented differently? Explain.

3. Using your observations, explain the advantages and disadvantages of telling a news story in broadcast form versus print form.

STANDARDS

Reading Informational Text
Analyze various accounts of a subject told in different mediums determining which details are emphasized in each account.

Writing
Write arguments to support claims in an analysis of substantive topics or texts, using valid reasoning and relevant and sufficient evidence.

Planning and Prewriting

Categorize Information and Write a Thesis Work independently to plan and draft your argument. First, review the notes you took as a group. Organize details and observations into logical categories. For example, you might group together one set of details related to facts and another set related to emotional impact. Then, write a working thesis, or claim:

Working Thesis: ______________________________

____

____

Drafting

Provide Varied Details For every claim you make, include evidence to support your ideas.

- **Exact quotations** can illustrate a speaker's attitude.
- **Examples** can help readers visualize a reporter's actions or word choice.
- **Paraphrases,** or restatements in your own words, can help clarify others' ideas.

Establish a Structure Follow this guide to plan the order of your ideas and supporting details.

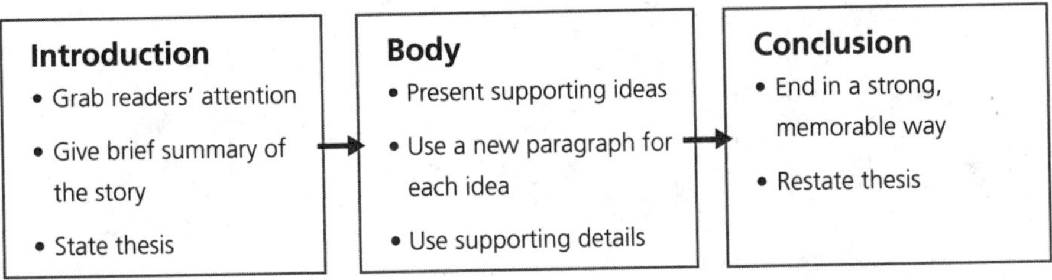

Introduction
• Grab readers' attention
• Give brief summary of the story
• State thesis
Body
• Present supporting ideas
• Use a new paragraph for each idea
• Use supporting details
Conclusion
• End in a strong, memorable way
• Restate thesis

Consider Audience Judge your audience's familiarity with the news story and use that judgment to determine how much background information to include.

Review and Revise

Share your writing with your group and review one another's work. Ask for feedback about the clarity of your organization and the strength of your supporting details. Use the feedback to improve any elements that are unclear or ineffective.

EVIDENCE LOG

Before moving on to a new selection, go to your Evidence Log and record what you've learned from "Twenty Years On: The Unfinished Lives of Sarajevo's Romeo and Juliet" and "Tragic Romeo and Juliet Offers Bosnia Hope."

SOURCES

- *ROMEO AND JULIET* IS A TERRIBLE PLAY, AND DAVID LEVEAUX CAN'T CHANGE THAT
- IN DEFENSE OF *ROMEO AND JULIET*: IT'S NOT CHILDISH, IT'S *ABOUT* CHILDISHNESS
- TWENTY YEARS ON: THE UNFINISHED LIVES OF BOSNIA'S ROMEO AND JULIET
- TRAGIC ROMEO AND JULIET OFFERS BOSNIA HOPE

Present an Argument

Assignment

You have read two works of literary criticism about *The Tragedy of Romeo and Juliet,* and you have also read and viewed accounts of a true-life "Romeo and Juliet." Work with your group to develop and refine a **multimedia presentation** that addresses this question:

What is compelling about stories in which people face a tragic destiny?

Plan With Your Group

Analyze the Text With your group, discuss the various factors that make these kinds of tragic love stories compelling. Why do they hold our attention? What do we learn from them? Use the chart to list your ideas. For each selection, identify examples from the text that help explain each story's significance. Then, come to a consensus about why star-crossed romances have such a profound impact on audiences.

TITLE	WHY IS TRAGIC DESTINY COMPELLING?
Romeo and Juliet Is a Terrible Play, and David Leveaux Can't Change That	
In Defense of *Romeo and Juliet*: It's Not Childish, It's *About* Childishness	
Twenty Years On: The Unfinished Lives of Sarajevo's Romeo and Juliet	
Tragic Romeo and Juliet Offers Bosnia Hope	

Gather Evidence and Media Examples Scan the selections to record specific examples that support your group's claim. Then, brainstorm for types of media you can use to illustrate or elaborate on each example. Consider photographs, illustrations, music, charts, graphs, and video clips that relate to the topic of tragic destiny. For instance, you might use a clip of a tragic scene from a movie or a show that is especially gripping. Allow each group member to make suggestions.

STANDARDS

Speaking and Listening

Present information, findings, and supporting evidence clearly, concisely, and logically such that listeners can follow the line of reasoning and the organization, development, substance, and style are appropriate to purpose, audience, and task.

Organize Your Ideas As a group, create a clear statement regarding the appeal of tragic stories. Then, organize your evidence in a logical way, supporting your claim. Choose presentation techniques that will make it clear which point each piece of evidence is related to. Use a storyboard to plan the order of speakers and your use of media.

Rehearse With Your Group

Practice With Your Group As you deliver your portion of the presentation, use this checklist to evaluate the effectiveness of your group's first run-through.

CONTENT	USE OF MEDIA	PRESENTATION TECHNIQUES
☐ The presentation presents a clear claim. ☐ Main ideas are supported with evidence from the texts in Small-Group Learning.	☐ The media support the claim. ☐ Media are used evenly throughout the presentation. ☐ Equipment functions properly.	☐ Media are visible and audible. ☐ Transitions are smooth. ☐ The speaker uses eye contact and speaks clearly.

Fine Tune the Content Review the assignment to make sure that your presentation answers the question completely and with sufficient supporting text evidence.

Improve Your Use of Media Make sure that all included media serve a clear purpose. Vary your use of media as much as possible: alternate video clips with audio, quotations from text, or illustrations. Finally, determine what devices you will need to present your multimedia and check their availability.

Brush Up on Your Presentation Techniques Practice your presentation often so that you are entirely familiar with the material and comfortable responding to questions.

Present and Evaluate

When you present as a group, be sure that each member has taken into account each of the checklist items. As you watch other groups, evaluate how well they meet requirements on the checklist.

STANDARDS

Speaking and Listening
Make strategic use of digital media in presentations to enhance understanding of findings, reasoning, and evidence and to add interest.

OVERVIEW: INDEPENDENT LEARNING

ESSENTIAL QUESTION:

Do we determine our own destinies?

Throughout history and across all cultures people have had to overcome many struggles to be with their true loves. In this section, you complete your study of star-crossed romances by exploring an additional selection related to the topic. You'll then share what you learn with classmates. To choose a text, follow these steps.

Look Back Think about the selections you have already studied. What more do you want to know about the topic of star-crossed romance?

Look Ahead Preview the texts by reading the descriptions. Which one seems most interesting and appealing to you?

Look Inside Take a few minutes to scan the text you chose. Choose a different one if this text doesn't meet your needs.

Independent-Learning Strategies

Throughout your life, in school, in your community, and in your career, you will need to rely on yourself to learn and work on your own. Review these strategies and the actions you can take to practice them during Independent Learning. Add ideas of your own for each category.

STRATEGY	ACTION PLAN
Create a schedule	• Understand your goals and deadlines. • Make a plan for what to do each day. •
Practice what you've learned	• Use first-read and close-read strategies to deepen your understanding. • After you read, evaluate the usefulness of the evidence to help you understand the topic. • Consider the quality and reliability of the source. •
Take notes	• Record important ideas and information. • Review your notes before preparing to share with a group. •

CONTENTS

Choose one selection. Selections are available online only.

MYTH

Popocatepetl and Ixtlaccihuatl

Juliet Piggott Wood

The Mexican myth of a princess and her lover, kept apart from her stubborn father, the emperor.

POETRY

Annabel Lee

Edgar Allan Poe

Can death keep lovers apart?

NONFICTION

What's the Rush?: Young Brains Cause Doomed Love

Lexi Tucker

Could brain chemistry be to blame for Romeo and Juliet's demise?

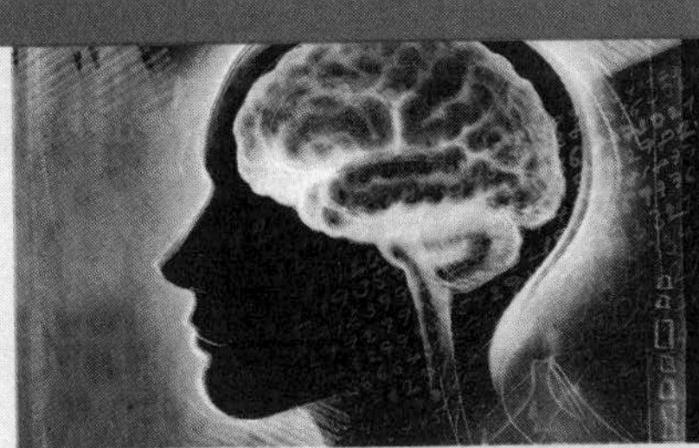

MEDIA: GRAPHIC NOVEL

William Shakespeare's Romeo & Juliet

artwork by Eli Neugeboren

Romeo and Juliet has been adapted for stage and screen countless times, but how would it look as a comic book?

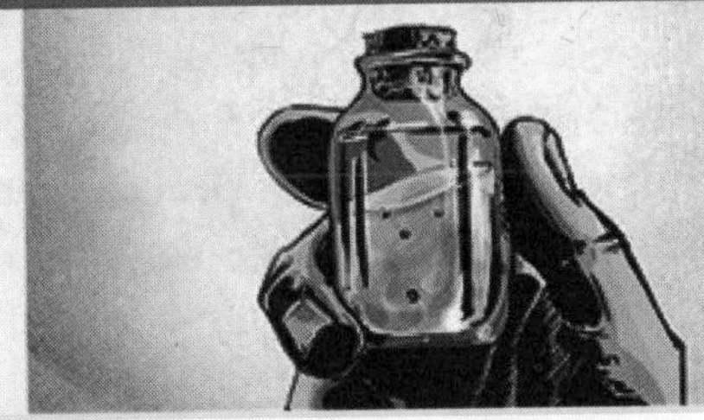

NEWS ARTICLE

If Romeo and Juliet Had Cell Phones

Misty Harris

Could a simple text message have saved the doomed lovers?

PERFORMANCE-BASED ASSESSMENT PREP

Review Evidence for an Argument

Complete your Evidence Log for the unit by evaluating what you've learned and synthesizing the information you have recorded.

First-Read Guide

Tool Kit
First-Read Guide and Model Annotation

Use this page to record your first-read ideas.

Selection Title: ______________________________

NOTICE

NOTICE new information or ideas you learn about the unit topic as you first read this text.

ANNOTATE

ANNOTATE by marking vocabulary and key passages you want to revisit.

NOTICE ANNOTATE First Read CONNECT RESPOND

CONNECT ideas within the selection to other knowledge and the selections you have read.

RESPOND by writing a brief summary of the selection.

CONNECT

RESPOND

STANDARD

Reading Read and comprehend complex literary and informational texts independently and proficiently.

Close-Read Guide

Tool Kit
Close-Read Guide and Model Annotation

Use this page to record your close-read ideas.

Selection Title: ____________________

Close Read the Text

Revisit sections of the text you marked during your first read. Read these sections closely and **annotate** what you notice. Ask yourself **questions** about the text. What can you **conclude**? Write down your ideas.

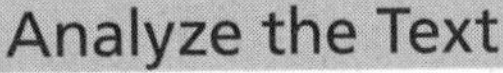

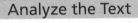

Analyze the Text

Think about the author's choices of patterns, structure, techniques, and ideas included in the text. Select one and record your thoughts about what this choice conveys.

QuickWrite

Pick a paragraph from the text that grabbed your interest. Explain the power of this passage.

STANDARD

Reading Read and comprehend complex literary and informational texts independently and proficiently.

EVIDENCE LOG

Go to your Evidence Log and record what you learned from the text you read.

Share Your Independent Learning

Prepare to Share

Do we determine our own destinies?

Even when you read or learn something independently, you can continue to grow by sharing what you have learned with others. Reflect on the text you explored independently and write notes about its connection to the unit. In your notes, consider why this text belongs in this unit.

Learn from Your Classmates

Discuss It Share your ideas about the text you explored on your own. As you talk with your classmates, jot down ideas that you learn from them.

Reflect

Review your notes, and underline the most important insight you gained from these writing and discussion activities. Explain how this idea adds to your understanding of the topic of star-crossed romances.

Review Evidence for an Argument

At the beginning of this unit, you took a position on the following question:

Should the opinions of others affect our own choices or destinies?

EVIDENCE LOG

Review your Evidence Log and your QuickWrite from the beginning of the unit. Has your position changed?

☐ YES	☐ NO
Identify at least three pieces of evidence that convinced you to change your mind.	Identify at least three pieces of evidence that reinforced your initial position:
1.	**1.**
2.	**2.**
3.	**3.**

State your position now: ____________________

____

____

Identify a possible counterclaim: ____________________

____

____

Evaluate the Strength of Your Evidence Do you have enough evidence to support your claim? Do you have enough evidence to refute a counterargument? If not, make a plan.

☐ Do more research ☐ Talk with my classmates

☐ Reread a selection ☐ Ask an expert

☐ Other: ____________________

STANDARDS

Writing

- Introduce precise claim(s), distinguish the claim(s) from alternate or opposing claims, and create an organization that establishes clear relationships among claim(s), counterclaims, reasons, and evidence.

SOURCES

- WHOLE-CLASS SELECTIONS
- SMALL-GROUP SELECTIONS
- INDEPENDENT LEARNING

WORD NETWORK

As you write and revise your argumentative essay, use your Word Network to help vary your word choices.

STANDARDS

Writing

- Introduce precise claim(s), distinguish the claim(s) from alternate or opposing claims, and create an organization that establishes clear relationships among claim(s), counterclaims, reasons, and evidence.
- Develop claim(s) and counterclaims fairly, supplying evidence for each while pointing out the strengths and limitations of both in a manner that anticipates the audience's knowledge level and concerns.
- Draw evidence from literary or informational texts to support analysis, reflection, and research.
- Write routinely over extended time frames and shorter time frames for a range of tasks, purposes, and audiences.

PART 1

Writing to Sources: Argument

In this unit, you read about people, both real and fictional, who were kept apart from their lovers because of forces they could not control. Sometimes forbidden love can overcome the obstacles of society, but oftentimes it cannot.

Assignment

Write an argument in the form of a short piece of **literary criticism** that explores how the selections in this unit address the following question:

Should the opinions of others affect our own choices or destinies?

Propose and defend a claim about two or more texts you read in this unit. Acknowledge and address a counterclaim, or possible alternate interpretation of the works. Integrate text evidence from each of the selections you address in your essay and build a compelling argument.

Reread the Assignment Review the assignment to be sure you fully understand it. The task may reference some of the academic words presented at the beginning of the unit. Be sure you understand each of the words given below in order to complete the assignment correctly.

Academic Vocabulary

endure	compelling	recurrent
pathos	propose	

Review the Elements of Literary Criticism Before you begin writing, read the Literary Criticism Rubric. Once you have completed your first draft, check it against the rubric. If one or more of the elements is missing or not as strong as it could be, revise your essay to add or strengthen that component.

Literary Criticism Rubric

	Focus and Organization	Evidence and Elaboration	Conventions
4	The introduction is engaging and establishes the claim in a compelling way. Establishes a clear relationship between the texts and the topic of the assignment. Writer's insights and analysis progress logically, and include a variety of sentence transitions. The conclusion demonstrates deep comprehension and evaluation of the texts.	Sources of evidence are comprehensive and specific and contain relevant information. Textual analysis is supported with appropriate use of direct and indirect quotations. Uses vocabulary strategically and appropriately for the audience and purpose.	The conventions of standard English are used consistently throughout the entire essay. The tone of the essay is formal and objective.
3	The introduction is engaging and establishes the claim. Establishes some relationship between the texts and the topic of the assignment. Writer's insights and analysis progress logically, and include appropriate sentence transitions. The conclusion demonstrates deep comprehension of the texts.	Some direct and indirect quotations are supplied to support textual analysis. Uses vocabulary that is generally appropriate for the audience and purpose.	The conventions of standard English are used throughout most of the essay. The tone of the essay is mostly formal and objective.
2	The introduction establishes the claim. Establishes some similarities or differences between the texts. Writer's insights and analysis progress logically. Transition words and phrases are used. The conclusion demonstrates comprehension of the texts.	Some relevant evidence is used to support textual analysis. Uses vocabulary that is somewhat appropriate for the audience and purpose.	The conventions of standard English are sometimes used in the essay. The tone of the essay is occasionally formal and objective.
1	The claim is not clearly stated. Relationship between the texts, or between the texts and the topic, is not established. Writer's insights and analysis are unclear or hard to follow. Transition words and phrases are not present. The conclusion does not demonstrate comprehension of the texts.	Does not include significant analysis of the texts. Does not include supporting evidence for analysis. The vocabulary is limited or ineffective.	The conventions of standard English are rarely or never used in the essay. The tone of the essay is largely informal.

SOURCES

- WHOLE-CLASS SELECTIONS
- SMALL-GROUP SELECTIONS
- INDEPENDENT LEARNING SELECTION

STANDARDS

Speaking and Listening

- Present information, findings, and supporting evidence clearly, concisely, and logically such that listeners can follow the line of reasoning and the organization, development, substance, and style are appropriate to purpose, audience, and task.
- Make strategic use of digital media in presentations to enhance understanding of findings, reasoning, and evidence and to add interest.
- Adapt speech to a variety of contexts and tasks, demonstrating command of formal English when indicated or appropriate.

PART 2

Speaking and Listening: Multimedia Presentation

Assignment

After completing the final draft of your literary criticism essay, use it as the foundation for a three-to five-minute multimedia presentation.

Your presentation should consist of more than just reading your essay aloud. Take the following steps to make your presentation lively and engaging.

- Go back to your essay and annotate the claim and most important text evidence from your introduction, body paragraphs, and conclusion.
- Choose audio clips and visuals, such as photographs and video, to support your presentation. Mark your text to note audio and visual cues.
- Refer to your annotated text to guide your presentation and keep it focused.
- Deliver your presentation with conviction, speak with adequate volume, and maintain eye contact with your audience.

Review the Multimedia Presentation Rubric The criteria by which your multimedia presentation will be evaluated appear in the rubric below. Review these criteria before presenting to ensure that you are prepared.

	Content	Use of Media	Presentation Techniques
3	Presentation clearly introduces and supports a claim about the texts and their relationship to the prompt. A counterclaim is acknowledged and refuted. Main claim is well-supported by relevant evidence from multiple sources.	Media has obvious connection to the topic and provides support for the speaker's claim.	Speaker demonstrates understanding of the content and presents it in a way that is easy to understand and engaging. Speaker uses appropriate eye contact, volume, and rate of speech throughout the presentation.
2	Presentation introduces and supports a claim. A counterclaim is mentioned. Main claim is supported by some relevant evidence.	Media is relevant to the claim.	Speaker demonstrates understanding of the content. Speaker uses appropriate eye contact, volume, and rate of speech during some of the presentation.
1	Presentation includes a claim and a counterclaim. Evidence from sources is included.	Media is not present, or is irrelevant.	Speaker does not demonstrate understanding of the content. Speaker does not use appropriate eye contact, volume, or rate of speech.

Reflect on the Unit

Now that you've completed the unit, take a few moments to reflect on your learning. Use the guidelines below to think about where you succeeded, what skills and strategies helped you, and where you can continue to grow in the future.

Reflect on the Unit Goals

Look back at the goals at the beginning of the unit. Use a different colored pen to rate yourself again. Think about readings and activities that contributed the most to the growth of your understanding. Record your thoughts.

Reflect on the Learning Strategies

Discuss It Write a reflection on whether you were able to improve your learning based on your Action Plans. Think about what worked, what didn't, and what you might do to keep working on these strategies. Record your ideas before a class discussion.

Reflect on the Text

Choose a selection that you found challenging, and explain what made it difficult.

Explain something that surprised you about a text in the unit.

Which activity taught you the most about star-crossed romances? What did you learn?

Journeys of Transformation

Why are we drawn to seek new horizons?

What do we learn when we go?

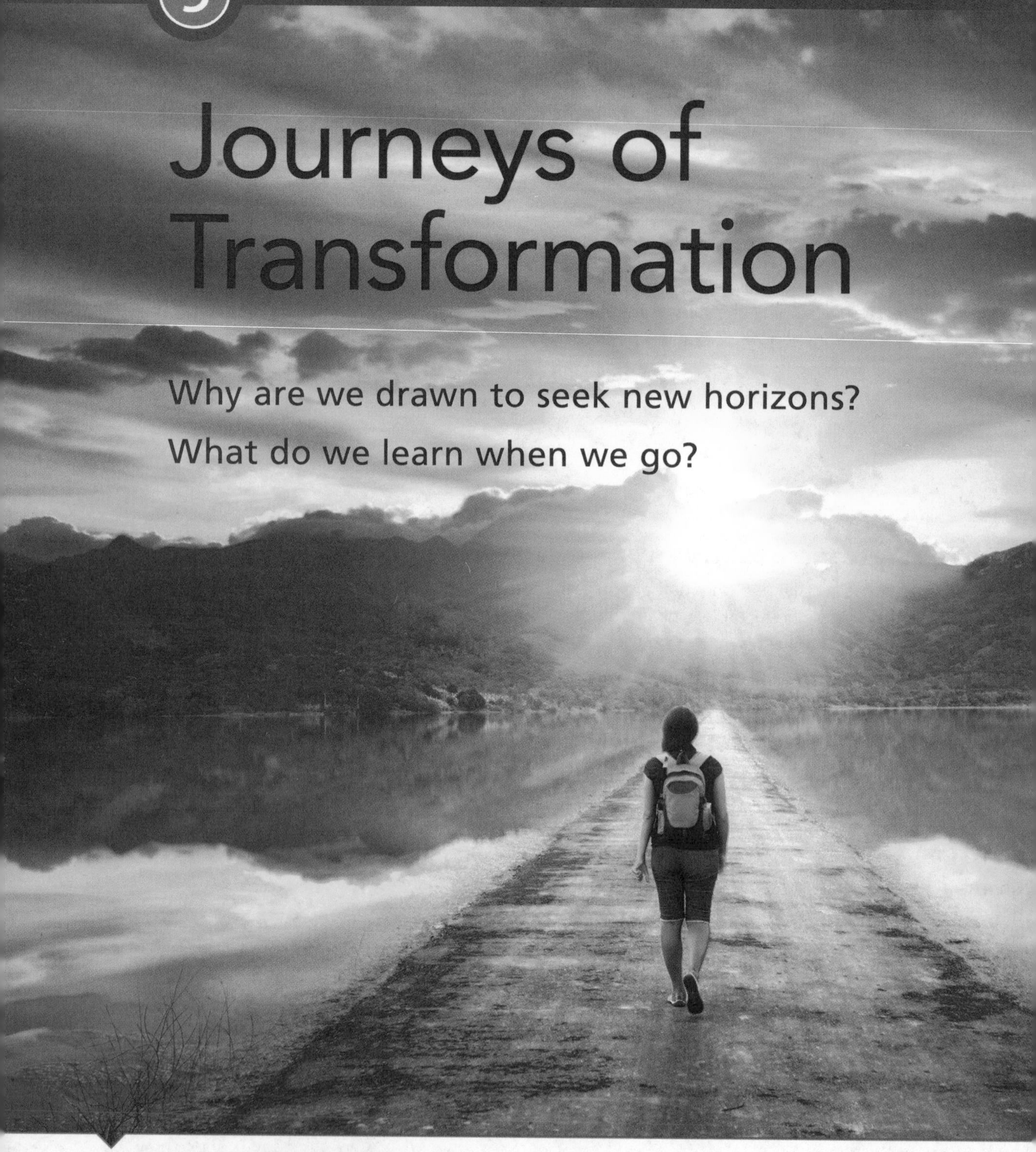

Misty Copeland's Hard-Fought Journey to Ballet Stardom

Discuss It What are the challenges that most people face during their journey to adulthood?

Write your response before sharing your ideas.

UNIT 5

UNIT INTRODUCTION

ESSENTIAL QUESTION: **What can we learn from a journey?**

LAUNCH TEXT
EXPLANATORY MODEL
Gone and Back Again: A Traveler's Advice

WHOLE-CLASS LEARNING

LITERATURE AND CULTURE
Historical Context
The Odyssey

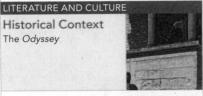

COMPARE

ANCHOR TEXT: EPIC POEM
from the **Odyssey, Part 1**
Homer
translated by Robert Fitzgerald

ANCHOR TEXT: EPIC POEM
from the **Odyssey, Part 2**
Homer
translated by Robert Fitzgerald

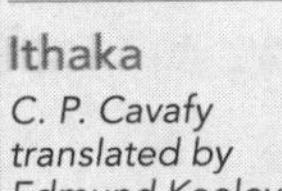

MEDIA: GRAPHIC NOVEL
from **The Odyssey: A Graphic Novel**
Gareth Hinds

FUNCTIONAL WORKPLACE DOCUMENT
Application for a Mariner's License
United States Government

PERFORMANCE TASK
WRITING FOCUS:
Write an Explanatory Essay

SMALL-GROUP LEARNING

SHORT STORY
The Return
Ngugi wa Thiong'o

INTERVIEW
from **The Hero's Adventure**
from The Power of Myth
Joseph Campbell and Bill Moyers

POETRY COLLECTION 1
Courage
Anne Sexton

Ithaka
C. P. Cavafy
translated by Edmund Keeley and Philip Sherrard

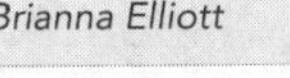

from **The Narrow Road of the Interior**
Matsuo Bashō
translated by Helen Craig McCullough

PERFORMANCE TASK
SPEAKING AND LISTENING FOCUS:
Deliver a Multimedia Presentation

INDEPENDENT LEARNING

POETRY COLLECTION 2
The Road Not Taken
Robert Frost

Your World
Georgia Douglas Johnson

SHORT STORY
The Ugly Duckling
Hans Christian Andersen

MEDIA: PHOTO ESSAY
Thirteen Epic Animal Migrations That Prove Just How Cool Mother Nature Is
Brianna Elliott

MEMOIR
from **Wild**
Cheryl Strayed

PERFORMANCE-BASED ASSESSMENT PREP
Review Evidence for an Explanatory Essay

PERFORMANCE-BASED ASSESSMENT

Explanatory Text: Essay and Podcast

PROMPT:
When does the journey matter more than the destination?

Unit Goals

Throughout the unit you will deepen your perspective of journeys by reading, writing, speaking, listening, and presenting. These goals will help you succeed on the Unit Performance-Based Assessment.

Rate how well you meet these goals right now. You will revisit your ratings later when you reflect on your growth during this unit.

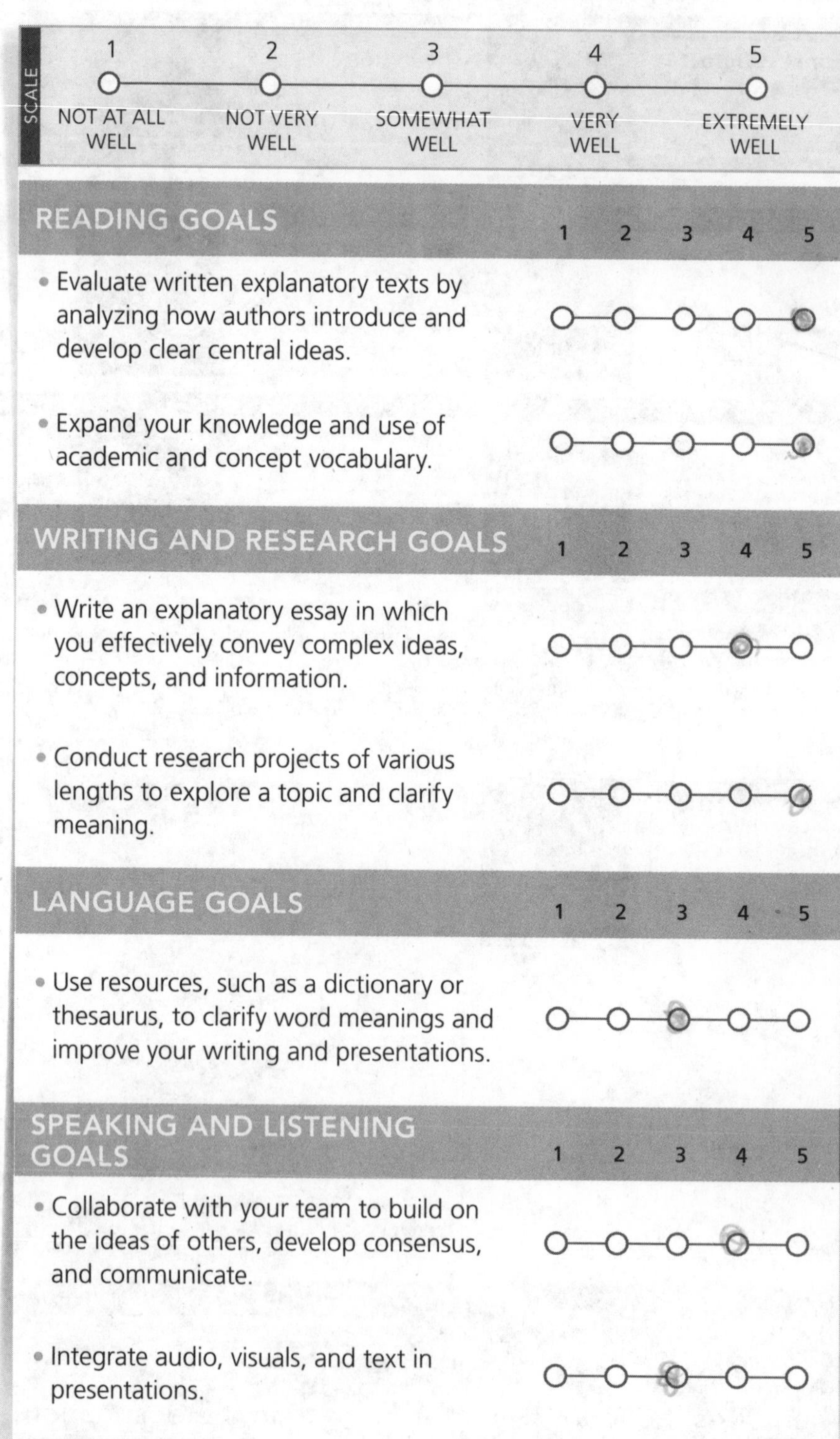

SCALE

1 NOT AT ALL WELL — 2 NOT VERY WELL — 3 SOMEWHAT WELL — 4 VERY WELL — 5 EXTREMELY WELL

READING GOALS	1	2	3	4	5
• Evaluate written explanatory texts by analyzing how authors introduce and develop clear central ideas.					
• Expand your knowledge and use of academic and concept vocabulary.					

WRITING AND RESEARCH GOALS	1	2	3	4	5
• Write an explanatory essay in which you effectively convey complex ideas, concepts, and information.					
• Conduct research projects of various lengths to explore a topic and clarify meaning.					

LANGUAGE GOALS	1	2	3	4	5
• Use resources, such as a dictionary or thesaurus, to clarify word meanings and improve your writing and presentations.					

SPEAKING AND LISTENING GOALS	1	2	3	4	5
• Collaborate with your team to build on the ideas of others, develop consensus, and communicate.					
• Integrate audio, visuals, and text in presentations.					

STANDARDS

Language

Acquire and use accurately general academic and domain-specific words and phrases, sufficient for reading, writing, speaking, and listening at the college and career readiness level; demonstrate independence in gathering vocabulary knowledge when considering a word or phrase important to comprehension or expression.

Academic Vocabulary: Explanatory Text

Academic terms appear in all subjects and can help you read, write, and discuss with more precision. Here are five academic words that will be useful to you in this unit as you analyze and write explanatory texts.

Complete the chart.

1. Review each word, its root, and the mentor sentences.
2. Use the information and your own knowledge to predict the meaning of each word.
3. For each word, list at least two related words.
4. Refer to a dictionary or other resources if needed.

FOLLOWING THROUGH
Study the words in this chart, and highlight them or their forms wherever they appear in the unit.

WORD	MENTOR SENTENCES	PREDICT MEANING	RELATED WORDS
voluntary ROOT: ***-vol-*** "wish"; "will"	**1.** Cindy made a *voluntary* contribution to the charity because she supported its mission. **2.** The teacher told us that the project was *voluntary* and could be done for extra credit.	Willing or committed to do something	voluntarily; volunteer
elucidate ROOT: ***-luc-*** "light"	**1.** Alex was not quite clear about the story's theme, but Aliyah's essay helped to *elucidate* the concept. **2.** Current research is helping both to *elucidate* the problems and to find solutions.		
expedite ROOT: ***-ped-*** "foot"	**1.** In order to make our deadlines, we need to *expedite* matters by splitting up the work. **2.** As soon as she was in office, the senator began to *expedite* the projects she had promised her supporters.	Speed up things	Quick and reckless
subsequent ROOT: ***-sequ-*** "follow"	**1.** The baseball team won the first game but lost the *subsequent* game. **2.** The editors were able to make corrections in *subsequent* editions of the book.		
procedure ROOT: ***-ced-/ceed-*** "move"; "go"	**1.** The doctor performed the *procedure* on the patient very carefully. **2.** Barry first learned the *procedure* for lining up when he joined our classroom.		

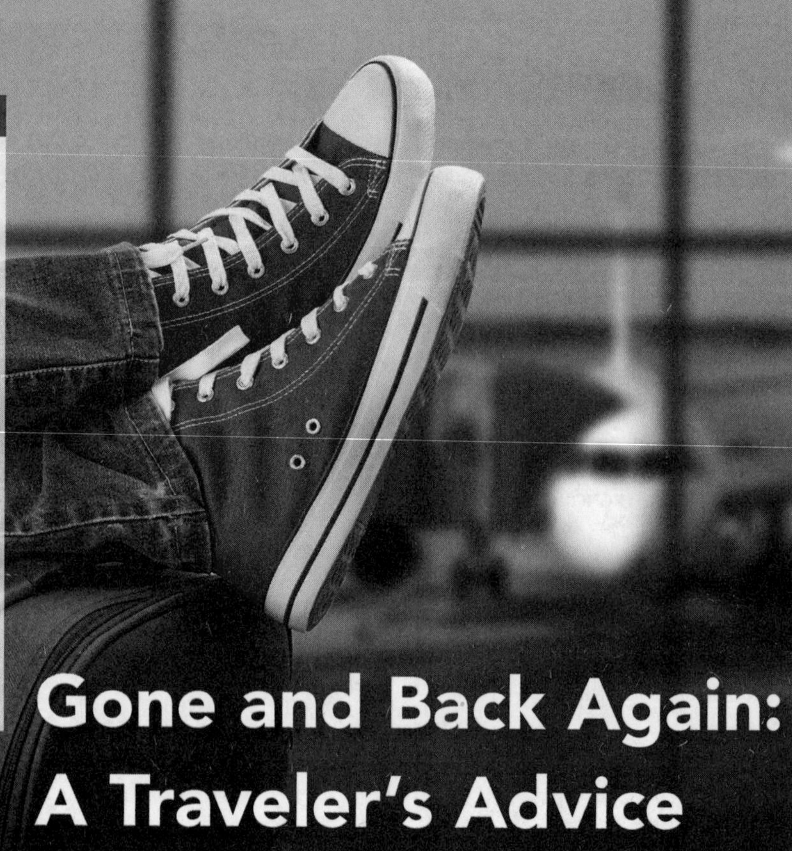

LAUNCH TEXT | EXPLANATORY MODEL

This selection is an example of an **explanatory text,** a type of writing in which the author presents information, discusses ideas, or explains a process. This is the type of writing you will develop in the Performance-Based Assessment at the end of the unit.

As you read, think about how the writer describes the events listed. Mark the text to help you answer this question: How does the order in which the details appear help the reader understand the thesis?

Gone and Back Again: A Traveler's Advice

NOTES

1 Let common sense guide you before you travel and you'll have a better trip. Consider the businesslike details first. Down the road, rich rewards will follow.

2 If you're leaving the country, you'll need backups of all essential documents. Keep both digital and physical copies of your passport, visas, driver's license, birth certificate, health insurance card, serial numbers, and important phone numbers. You may be too young to have some of these items, but if you can read this you're old enough to assist in preparation. Anything can be lost or stolen. Backups might just save you a great deal of international grief.

3 Talk yourself into packing less stuff. The more journeys you take, the sooner you'll discover you don't need as many items as you think. Traveling light makes it easier and faster to get from one place to another, with a more manageable load to lug around. If you really must have a second black sweater, you can probably buy it on the fly.

4 Smart preparations also include shopping wisely from home. There is a wide world of online options for bargain transportation and lodging. Save your money for the experiences you'll be seeking once you get out of your rented bed. Or do a little digging and win major points from your loved ones by helping them save a few bucks.

5 And once you get there, get up early. The light is lovely in the morning. You'll have more tourist attractions to yourself while the layabouts are snoring into their pillows. And you'll run less risk of running into bad experiences: scam artists and other bad actors tend to keep late hours.

6 There is far more practical ground to cover before you take to the skies, the seas, or the road. Do your homework. You'll know you've earned a passing grade when you're having the time of your life.

7 To make the most of your travels, it will also pay to pack a positive attitude. Keep in mind the following suggestions that apply more to what is in your head and heart than your luggage or hip pocket.

8 Keep an open mind. You'll be encountering people whose lifestyles are different from yours. You stop learning when you start judging, and you close yourself off to new experiences. Embrace possibility. Seek opportunity. Ask questions in a spirit of respectful goodwill. There's common ground to be found, no matter where you go.

9 Get lost deliberately. The natives know the cheapest places to eat; the least crowded beaches; the byways and backwaters that are less traveled, that have their own histories and unlikely charms. Hit the pavement on foot. Follow your feet. Stay safe, but seek the unexpected.

10 Slow down occasionally. Take a seat on a park bench or a set of stone steps and watch the local parade go by. The scents and the shades, the tone and feel of a place start to reveal themselves when you put down your guidebook and your smart phone. You never know when you'll be making a memory. Open your senses and let the setting in.

11 And remember to smile, easily and often. In so doing, you will be communicating in the fundamental global language that opens us all up to new people and new experiences. Anna Quindlen said, "The life you have led doesn't need to be the only life you have." Vital moments in that life may be around the next corner. There's no better way to reach out toward those moments than with a hopeful grin.

12 Be prepared. Have fun. The world is ready when you are. Don't forget your toothbrush. ❧

NOTES

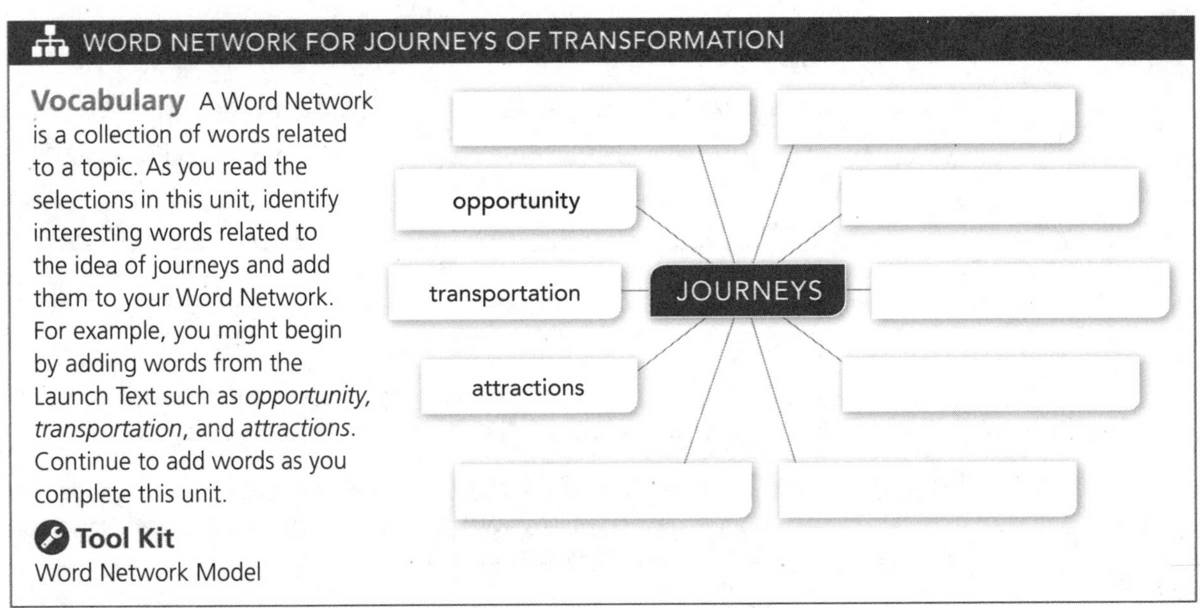

WORD NETWORK FOR JOURNEYS OF TRANSFORMATION
Vocabulary A Word Network is a collection of words related to a topic. As you read the selections in this unit, identify interesting words related to the idea of journeys and add them to your Word Network. For example, you might begin by adding words from the Launch Text such as *opportunity*, *transportation*, and *attractions*. Continue to add words as you complete this unit.
Tool Kit
Word Network Model
opportunity
transportation
JOURNEYS
attractions

Summary

Write a summary of "Gone and Back Again: A Traveler's Advice." A **summary** is a concise, complete, and accurate overview of a text. It should not include a statement of your opinion or an analysis.

Launch Activity

Round Table Consider this statement: **The best way to travel is by train.**

- Record your position on the statement and explain your thinking.

  ☐ Agree ☐ Disagree

- Form a group with like-minded students.
- If you agree with the statement, work together to list reasons that support your position. Identify as many reasons as possible.
- If you disagree with the statement, work together to list reasons that support your point of view. For example, you might consider the purpose for a journey, as well as a traveler's age and interests.
- After your discussion, have a representative present a two- to three-minute summary of the group's ideas.

QuickWrite

Consider class discussions, presentations, the video, and the Launch Text as you think about the prompt. Record your first thoughts here.

PROMPT: **When does the journey matter more than the destination?**

EVIDENCE LOG FOR JOURNEYS OF TRANSFORMATION

Review your QuickWrite. Summarize your thoughts in one sentence to record in your Evidence Log. Then, record textual details or evidence from "Gone and Back Again: A Traveler's Advice" that support your thinking.

Prepare for the Performance-Based Assessment at the end of the unit by completing the Evidence Log after each selection.

Evidence Log Model

Title of Text: ____________ Date: ________

CONNECTION TO PROMPT	TEXT EVIDENCE/DETAILS	ADDITIONAL NOTES/IDEAS

How does this text change or add to my thinking? Date: ________

OVERVIEW: WHOLE-CLASS LEARNING

ESSENTIAL QUESTION:

What can we learn from a journey?

A journey that opens our eyes to something new can take place in an instant or over a lifetime. You will work with your whole class to explore the story of an epic journey and to consider what it says about all journeys. These selections present insights into journeys and their deeper meanings.

Whole-Class Learning Strategies

Throughout your life, in school, in your community, and in your career, you will continue to learn and work in large-group environments.

Review these strategies and the actions you can take to practice them as you work with your whole class. Add ideas of your own for each step. Get ready to use these strategies during Whole-Class Learning.

STRATEGY	ACTION PLAN
Listen actively	• Eliminate distractions. For example, put your cell phone away. • Keep your eyes on the speaker. • Practicy listenins
Clarify by asking questions	• If you're confused, other people probably are, too. Ask a question to help your whole class. • If you see that you are guessing, ask a question instead. • write down questions
Monitor understanding	• Notice what information you already know and be ready to build on it. • Ask for help if you are struggling. • Search for what your looking for
Interact and share ideas	• Share your ideas and answer questions, even if you are unsure. • Build on the ideas of others by adding details or making a connection. • ask about your Ideas

CONTENTS

LITERATURE AND CULTURE

Historical Context

The *Odyssey*

What is it about Greek mythology and culture that has fascinated people throughout history?

COMPARE

ANCHOR TEXT: EPIC POEM

from the Odyssey, Part 1

Homer, translated by Robert Fitzgerald

How much can one man endure as he tries to return home?

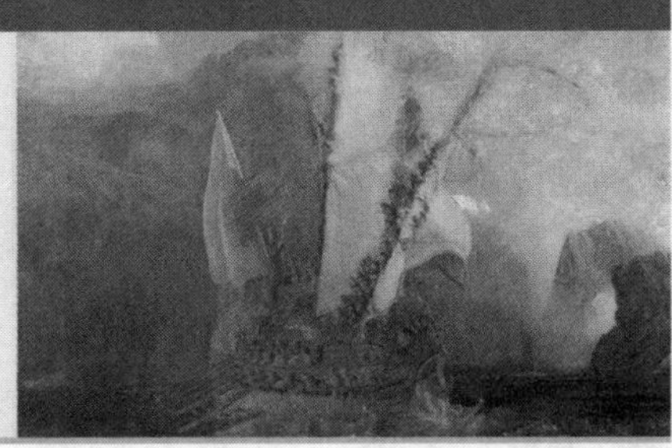

ANCHOR TEXT: EPIC POEM

from the Odyssey, Part 2

Homer, translated by Robert Fitzgerald

After an absence of twenty years, what changes will a man find when he returns home?

MEDIA: GRAPHIC NOVEL

from The Odyssey: A Graphic Novel

Gareth Hinds

Can a traveler trying to find his way home get help in the Land of the Dead?

FUNCTIONAL WORKPLACE DOCUMENT

Application for a Mariner's License

United States Government

It takes more than just will or desire to operate a ship on the open sea.

PERFORMANCE TASK

WRITING FOCUS

Write an Explanatory Essay

The Whole-Class readings illustrate the obstacles one of literature's greatest travelers faces as he struggles to get back home. After reading, you will write an explanatory essay about the personal strengths and weaknesses that shape our journeys.

^ The photograph above shows a reconstruction of one wall of The Palace of Minos at Knossos, Crete.

Historical Context

Ancient Greece

The world of ancient Greece included the Greek mainland, dipping down from continental Europe, and western Asia Minor, the Asian part of present-day Turkey. It also included hundreds of islands in the Aegean (ee JEE uhn) Sea, the arm of the Mediterranean Sea between mainland Greece and Asia Minor, and in the Ionian (y OH nee uhn) Sea, the arm of the Mediterranean to the west of mainland Greece. Odysseus, the legendary hero of Homer's *Odyssey*, was said to be the ruler of Ithaca, one of the western islands.

The Minoans and Mycenaeans Nearly a thousand years before Odysseus would have lived, Greek civilization rose to greatness on Crete, another island south of the mainland. By about 2000 B.C., a sophisticated society called the Minoan (mih NOH uhn) civilization had developed on Crete. Judging by the archaeological evidence, the Minoans produced elegant stone palaces and fine carvings and metalwork. They also developed a writing system, preserved on a few hundred of the clay tablets on which they wrote. Scholars call that writing system Linear A and have yet to decipher it.

For several centuries, Minoan civilization dominated the Greek world. Then, in about 1450 B.C., it collapsed rather suddenly, perhaps due to earthquakes and invasion. With the weakening of Minoan culture, the Mycenaeans (my suh NEE uhnz) became the dominant force in the Greek world. Originating on mainland Greece, the Mycenaeans had swept south and into Crete. Strongly influenced by Minoan civilization, the Mycenaeans too had a palace culture, an economy based on trade, and a writing system that mostly used clay tablets. Evidence of their writing is found in Knossos and Chania on Crete as well as in Mycenae, Pylos, and Thebes, three of their mainland strongholds. Because the Mycenaeans spoke an archaic, or older, form of Greek, scholars have been able to decipher their writing, known as Linear B. It was used primarily to keep palace records.

QUICK INSIGHT

Sir Arthur Evans, the British archaeologist who worked extensively on Crete, named Minoan civilization for King Minos (MY nos), a ruler of Crete in Greek mythology.

Legendary Conflicts The writing and archaeological remains suggest early cities with large central palaces and thick protective walls, each ruled by a *wanax*, or king. Others in society included priests, slaves, workers in trades or crafts, administrative officials, and a warrior class. The Mycenaens wore armor in battle, in which they engaged with apparent frequency. Their warfare with Troy, on the northwest coast of Asia Minor, has become one of the most famous military venues of all time—the Trojan War. If there really was a King Odysseus, he would have been a key player in that conflict.

Scholars date the Trojan War to somewhere around 1200 B.C. Shortly thereafter, Mycenaean civilization collapsed as the Greek world fell into chaos and confusion. For some three hundred years, writing seems to have disappeared in what is often called the Greek Dark Ages. Then, in about 850 B.C., Greece began emerging from this darkness, spurred by flourishing trade throughout the Mediterranean region. Along with the economic boom came a resurgence of the arts and learning that peaked with the epic poems of Homer. These poems—the *Iliad* and the *Odyssey*—chronicle the Trojan War and the subsequent adventures of the hero Odysseus.

The Rise of City-States After Homer's time, Greek civilization grew more organized and sophisticated. Smaller communities organized as city-states—cities that functioned independently, as countries do. Among them were Sparta, known for its military prowess, and Athens, the birthplace of democracy. Through rivalries sometimes led to warfare among city-states, the Greeks still recognized their common heritage as *Hellenes*, as they usually called themselves by that time. They coordinated efforts to defend against their common enemies, such as the Persians. They participated in the Olympic games, which records indicate began in 776 B.C. Together, too, they saw the works of Homer as pillars of their heritage, two great epics that celebrated their common past and its heroes.

QUICK INSIGHT

The Greek word for "city-state" is *polis,* the origin of our words *metropolis* and *politics.*

Ancient Greece included mainland territories and hundreds of islands clustered in the Aegean and Ionian Seas. Odysseus' kingdom of Ithaca is a small island in the Ionian Sea.

Greek Mythology and Customs

All aspects of Greek culture reflected belief in the Olympian gods.

Ancient Greek religion was based on a belief in many gods. Zeus was king of the gods; Hera, his beautiful and powerful wife. Other gods and goddesses were associated with different aspects of nature or human behavior. The most important ones were said to dwell on Mount Olympus, the tallest mountain in Greece, where Zeus sat on a throne of gold.

The Titans Are Overthrown The early poet Hesiod (HEE see uhd) wrote a mythic account of the origin of the gods in *Theogony*, a work the Greeks revered almost as much as Homer's epics. According to that origin myth, first there was Chaos, a dark, empty void. Out of chaos came the Earth, personified as the goddess Gaea. The Earth generated the skies, personified as the god Uranus, who with Gaea produced the giant gods known as Titans. Cronus, the chief Titan, ruled the universe until he was displaced by his three sons, who split the universe among them. Zeus, the most powerful of these sons, became ruler of the heavens. His brother Poseidon became ruler of the seas. The third brother, Hades, became ruler of he underworld, a dark region also called Hades, which was inhabited by the dead.

The Greek gods were powerful, but they were not all-powerful: even Zeus had to bow to fate. The gods displayed many human qualities and were often vengeful and quarrelsome. They were also quick to punish human beings guilty of hubris (HYOO brihs), or excessive pride. To appease the gods, human beings performed sacrifices, which often involved the killing of animals. In the *Odyssey*, Odysseus makes several sacrifices to plead for divine aid on his journey home.

Celebrating the Gods The Greeks worshipped the gods in temples dedicated to many gods or just one. The Parthenon in Athens, for instance, was a temple dedicated to the goddess Athena. The Greeks also celebrated their gods at great festivals such as the Olympic games, which were dedicated to Zeus.

The Greeks believed in prophecy, which they associated with the god Apollo. In the *Odyssey*, Odysseus journeys all the way to the underworld to consult the blind prophet Tiresias (ty REE see uhs), who continues to have the gift of prophecy even though he has died. The Greeks also believed in myths, stories about gods and heroes that they used to explain the world around them. The *Iliad* and the *Odyssey* drew on these myths; however, for future generations of ancient Greeks, Homer's two epics—like Hesiod's *Theogony*—took on the aura of myths themselves.

› a statue of the Greek goddess Athena

Gods in Greek Mythology

^ Zeus, or Jupiter

You may be more familiar with the Roman names for the Greek gods. The ancient Romans accepted Greek mythology, but they had their own names for its gods and heroes. For example, they called Odysseus *Ulysses*. For each Greek god listed below, the Roman equivalent is also given.

GREEK NAME	DESCRIPTION	ROMAN NAME
Zeus (zoos)	king of the gods and ruler of the heavens	*Jupiter*, sometimes called *Jove*
Hera (HEHR uh)	wife of Zeus and goddess of married women	*Juno*
Poseidon (poh SY duhn)	god of the sea	*Neptune*
Aphrodite (af ruh DY tee)	goddess of love and beauty	*Venus*
Ares (AIR eez)	god of war	*Mars*
Apollo (uh POL oh)	god of prophecy and music; also called Phoebus (FEE buhs)	*Apollo*
Artemis (AHR tuh mihs)	goddess of the hunt and the moon	*Diana*
Athena (uh THEE nuh)	goddess of wisdom, skills, and war	*Minerva*
Hephaestus (hee FEHS tuhs)	god of fire and metalwork	*Vulcan*
Hermes (HUR meez)	god of commerce and cunning; messenger of the gods	*Mercury*
Demeter (dih MEE tuhr)	goddess of the harvest	*Ceres* (SEER eez)
Dionysus (dy uhn Y suhs)	god of wine and revelry, also called Bacchus (BAK uhs)	*Dionysus* or *Bacchus*
Hestia (HEHS tee uh)	goddess of home and hearth	*Vesta*
Helios (HEE lee os)	sun god	*Sol*
Uranus (YOO ruh nuhs)	sky god supplanted by his son Cronus	*Uranus*
Gaea (JEE uh)	earth goddess and mother of the Titans and Cyclopes	*Tellus* or *Terra*
Cronus (KROH nuhs)	Titan who ruled the universe before his son Zeus dethroned him	*Saturn*
Rhea (REE uh)	wife of Cronus and mother of Zeus	*Cybele* (SIHB uh lee)
Cyclops (SY klops)	any one of three Titans who forged thunderbolts for Zeus; plural, Cyclopes (sy KLOH peez)	
The Fates	three goddesses who wove the threads of each person's life; Clotho (KLOH thoh) spun the thread; Lachesis (LAK ih sihs) measured out the amount of thread; Atropos (A truh pohs) snipped the thread	
The Muses (MYOO zihz)	nine goddesses who presided over the arts and sciences, including Calliope (kuh LY uh pee), the Muse of epic poetry	

Homer, Epic Poet

The poems attributed to Homer still influence literature and culture today.

Homer is the legendary poet credited with writing the *Iliad* and the *Odyssey*. These epics, known for their sweeping scope, gripping stories, and vivid style, have captured readers' imaginations for almost 3,000 years.

Was there really a Homer? No one can prove his existence with any certainty, for no authentic record of Homer's life exists. Tradition has it that he was born in Ionia in western Asia Minor, perhaps on the island of Chios, and that he was blind. The location is not unreasonable, for Ionia was a center of poetry and learning, where eastern and western cultures met and new intellectual currents were born. Descriptions of Asia Minor in the *Iliad* and the *Odyssey* contain plot elements found in the world's first known epic, *Gilgamesh*, which by Homer's era had traveled from Mesopotamia (present-day Iraq) to become familiar in Asia Minor. For example, the hero *Gilgamesh* visits the underworld, just like the hero of the *Odyssey*; he also has a very good friend who is killed, just like Achilles has in the *Iliad*.

Most efforts to date Homer's life place him somewhere between 850 and 750 B.C. As a Greek oral poet, it is unlikely he lived much later, for by then writing had been reintroduced to Greek culture. The details in Homer's epics make clear that the poems were orally composed and that the *Iliad* was written first—probably some years before the *Odyssey*. The two epics differ in style: the *Iliad* is a single long, highly dramatic narrative, while the *Odyssey* is episodic and reads more like an adventure novel than a drama. For these reasons, some scholars even speculate that the epics were composed by two different poets.

Inspiring Poems Whatever the truth about Homer may be, no one disputes the quality of the two epics with which he is credited. The ancient Greeks revered the *Iliad* and the *Odyssey*. They recited the poems at religious festivals and had children memorize them in school. All the Greek writers and philosophers who came after Homer drew on the two epics. Their influence spread to Rome and beyond, and they became foundational works of western literature. Even in modern times, great works from James Joyce's *Ulysses* to Derek Walcott's *Omeros* have been directly inspired by Homer's verse.

The Epic Form

An **epic** is a long narrative poem that relates important events in the history or folklore of the culture that produced it. Its central character, or epic hero, is a larger-than-life person who embodies traits that the culture values. Typical among those characteristics are physical strength, bravery, high birth, fame, and effective skills as a leader and in a battle.

The *Iliad* and the *Odyssey* influenced virtually all the great western epics that followed them. From the *Aeneid*, the great epic of ancient Rome, to *Beowulf*, the foundational epic of Old English; from *The Divine Comedy*, the masterful epic by the Italian poet Dante, to *Paradise Lost*, the brilliant epic by Britain's John Milton—all had Homer's epics as models. Literary devices in Homer's epics are often imitated in these later works, even though many of the later epics were not orally composed. Influential literary devices found in Homer's epics include the following:

- **Opening invocation to the Muse:** The speaker of the poem asks the Muse for inspiration.
- **Starting the story *in medias res*,** or "in the middle of things": Beginning (after the invocation) with action instead of background information helps capture audience attention.
- **Lofty style:** Elegant language stresses the nobility of the subject.
- **Objective tone:** By keeping an emotional distance, the poet focuses attention on the story.
- **Meter,** or a fixed rhythmic pattern: A strong meter helps the oral poet remember the lines. In the original Greek, the *Odyssey* uses *hexameter*, or six beats to a line, which helps create a fast pace.
- **Epithet,** a characterizing phrase for a person, place, or thing: Recurring epithets are easy to remember and can help fill out the meter. Some examples of Homer's epithets include "rosy-fingered dawn" and "son of Laertes," for Odysseus.
- **Epic simile,** a long comparison over many lines: Such similes were another way to fill out the meter and aid the poet's memory.

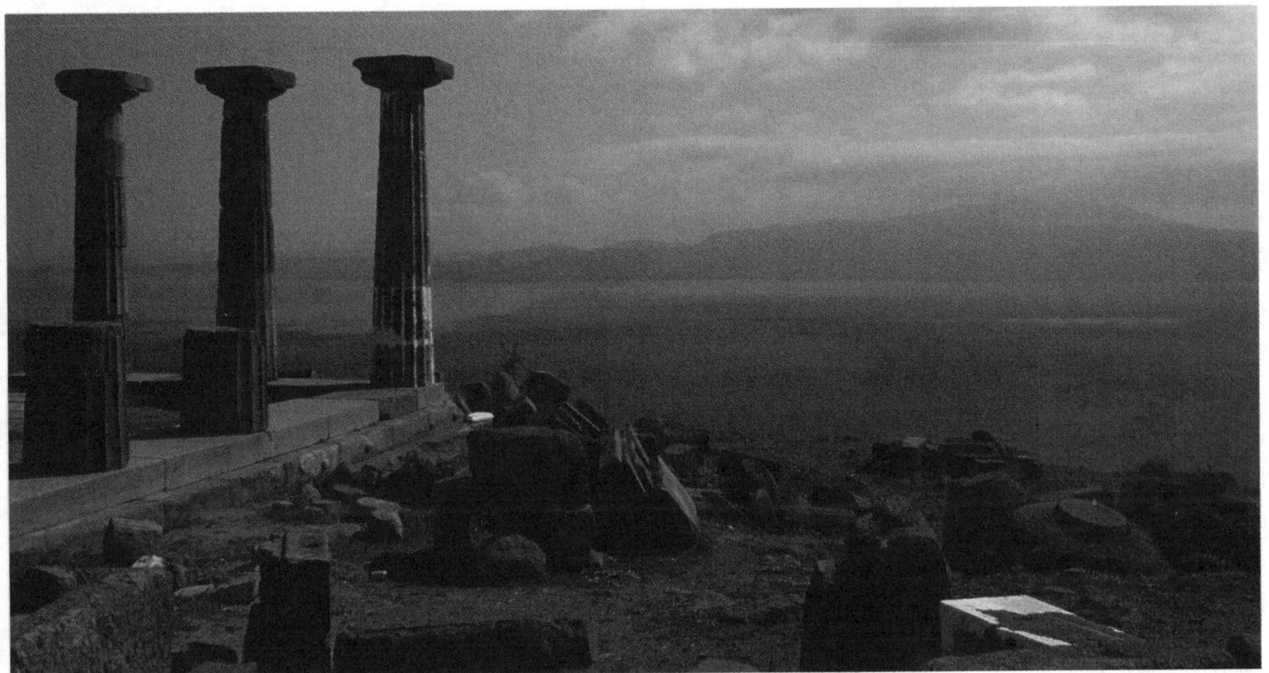

^ A view from the ruins of the Temple of Athena in Turkey, on the Acropolis of Assos.

About the Poet

Homer (approx. 850–750 B.C.) is credited with writing the *Iliad* and the *Odyssey*. For almost 3,000 years, these epic poems have captured readers' imaginations and inspired countless works of art and literature.

from the Odyssey, Part 1

Concept Vocabulary

You will encounter the following words as you read Part I of the *Odyssey*. Before reading, note how familiar you are with each word. Then, rank the words in order from most familiar (1) to least familiar (6).

WORD	YOUR RANKING
plundered	to steal
fugitives	Did a crime and is w
avenge	to get revenge
dispatched	to send out
ventured	to go out of your c
tactics	to plan

After completing the first read, come back to the concept vocabulary and review your rankings. Mark changes to your original rankings as needed.

First Read EPIC POEM

Apply these strategies as you conduct your first read. You will have an opportunity to complete the close-read notes after your first read.

NOTICE

NOTICE *whom* the story is about, *what* happens, *where* and *when* it happens, and *why* those involved react as they do.

ANNOTATE

ANNOTATE by marking vocabulary and key passages you want to revisit.

NOTICE ANNOTATE First Read CONNECT RESPOND

CONNECT ideas within the selection to what you already know and what you have already read.

CONNECT

RESPOND by completing the Comprehension Check and by writing a brief summary of the selection.

RESPOND

Tool Kit
First-Read Guide and Model Annotation

STANDARDS

Reading Literature
By the end of grade 9, read and comprehend literature, including stories, dramas, and poems, in the grades 9–10 text complexity band proficiently, with scaffolding as needed at the high end of the range.

BACKGROUND

The Trojan War

In the *Iliad*, Homer focuses on the final year of the Trojan War; in the *Odyssey*, he tells what happened to one of the key warriors afterward.

It Begins With Strife According to legend, the Trojan War began when Eris, goddess of strife, brought among the gods a golden apple inscribed "To the fairest." Hera, Athena, and Aphrodite all wanted that apple. They asked Paris, son of the king of Troy, to decide which of them deserved it. Each tried to bribe him: Hera offered power; Athena, wisdom; and Aphrodite, the world's most beautiful woman. The famous Judgment of Paris was that Aphrodite was the fairest. Soon, on a diplomatic mission to Sparta, Paris met Helen, the world's most beautiful woman and Sparta's queen. With Aphrodite's help, the two fell in love and eloped. When Menelaus (mehn uh LAY uhs), king of Sparta, could not persuade the Trojans to send his wife, Helen, back, he went to his brother Agamemnon, who called on all the Greek rulers to honor a pact and go to Troy to fight to bring Helen home. The Greeks agreed and sailed to Troy. They laid siege to the city but for ten long years could not breach its impregnable walls.

War Crimes and Punishment Agamemnon might have been a more powerful king and Achilles (uh KIHL eez) a superior warrior, but Odysseus, king of Ithaca, was cleverest of them all. He devised a scheme in which the Greeks left a great wooden horse outside the walls of Troy and tricked the Trojans into taking it inside. That night, the Greeks hiding inside the horse—Odysseus among them—slipped out, unlocked the gates of the city, and allowed their fellow warriors to come swarming in to defeat the Trojans and sack the city. The fighting was brutal and destructive. King Priam (PRY uhm), Paris's father, for example, was killed while he was praying. The Greeks' behavior angered many of the gods, who made their voyages home very difficult.

Odysseus was no exception. Following the Greek victory, he set sail for Ithaca but encountered a series of perilous misadventures that made his journey last ten years. It is this difficult, adventure-filled journey that Homer's *Odyssey* recounts.

ANCHOR TEXT | EPIC POEM

from the Odyssey

Homer

translated by Robert Fitzgerald

Part I
The Adventures of Odysseus

CHARACTERS

Alcinous (al SIHN oh uhs)—king of the Phaeacians, to whom Odysseus tells his story

Odysseus (oh DIHS ee uhs)—king of Ithaca

Calypso (kuh LIHP soh)—sea goddess who loves Odysseus

Circe (SUR see)—enchantress who helps Odysseus

Zeus (zoos)—king of the gods

Apollo (uh POL oh)—god of music, poetry, prophecy, and medicine

Agamemnon (ag uh MEHM non)—king and leader of Greek forces

Poseidon (poh SY duhn)—god of sea, earthquakes, horses, and storms at sea

Athena (uh THEE nuh)—goddess of wisdom, skills, and warfare

Polyphemus (pol ih FEE muhs)—the Cyclops who imprisons Odysseus

Laertes (lay UR teez)—Odysseus' father

Cronus (KROH nuhs)—Titan ruler of the universe; father of Zeus

Perimedes (pehr uh MEE deez)—member of Odysseus' crew

Eurylochus (yoo RIHL uh kuhs)—another member of the crew

Tiresias (ty REE see uhs)—blind prophet who advises Odysseus

Persephone (puhr SEHF uh nee)—wife of Hades

Telemachus (tuh LEHM uh kuhs)—Odysseus and Penelope's son

Sirens (SY ruhnz)—creatures whose songs lure sailors to their deaths

Scylla (SIHL uh)—sea monster of gray rock

Charybdis (kuh RIHB dihs)—enormous and dangerous whirlpool

Lampetia (lahm PEE shuh)—nymph

Hermes (HUR meez)—herald and messenger of the gods

Eumaeus (yoo MEE uhs)—old swineherd and friend of Odysseus

Antinous (ant IHN oh uhs)—leader among the suitors

Eurynome (yoo RIHN uh mee)—housekeeper for Penelope

Penelope (puh NEHL uh pee)—Odysseus' wife

Eurymachus (yoo RIH muh kuhs)—suitor

Amphinomus (am FIHN uh muhs)—suitor

In the opening verses, Homer addresses the muse of epic poetry. He asks her help in telling the tale of Odysseus.

Sing in me, Muse,[1] and through me tell the story
of that man skilled in all ways of contending,
the wanderer, harried for years on end,
after he **plundered** the stronghold
on the proud height of Troy.[2]
He saw the townlands
and learned the minds of many distant men,
and weathered many bitter nights and days
in his deep heart at sea, while he fought only
to save his life, to bring his shipmates home.
But not by will nor valor could he save them.
for their own recklessness destroyed them all—

NOTES

1. **Muse** (myooz) any one of the nine goddesses of the arts.

plundered (PLUHN duhrd) *v.* took something by force

2. **Troy** city in northwest Asia Minor; site of the Trojan War.

NOTES

3. Helios (HEE lee ohs) sun god.

4. Zeus (zoos) king of the gods.

5. Laertes (LAY ur teez)

6. guile (gyl) *n.* craftiness; cunning.

7. Ithaca (IHTH uh kuh) island off the west coast of Greece.

8. Calypso (kuh LIHP soh) sea goddess who loved Odysseus.

9. Circe (SUR see) of Aeaea (EE ee uh)

10. Ilium (IHL ee uhm) Troy.

11. Cicones (sih KOH neez)

children and fools, they killed and feasted on
the cattle of Lord Helios,[3] the Sun,
and he who moves all day through heaven
took from their eyes the dawn of their return.
Of these adventures, Muse, daughter of Zeus,[4]
tell us in our time, lift the great song again.

Sailing From Troy

Ten years after the Trojan War, Odysseus departs from the goddess Calypso's island. He arrives in Phaeacia, ruled by Alcinous. Alcinous offers a ship to Odysseus and asks him to tell of his adventures.

"I am Laertes'[5] son, Odysseus.
Men hold me
formidable for guile[6] in peace and war:
this fame has gone abroad to the sky's rim.

My home is on the peaked sea-mark of Ithaca[7]
under Mount Neion's wind-blown robe of leaves,
in sight of other islands—Dulichium,
Same, wooded Zacynthus—Ithaca
being most lofty in that coastal sea,
and northwest, while the rest lie east and south.
A rocky isle, but good for a boy's training;
I shall not see on earth a place more dear,
though I have been detained long by Calypso,[8]
loveliest among goddesses, who held me
in her smooth caves to be her heart's delight,
as Circe of Aeaea,[9] the enchantress,
desired me, and detained me in her hall.
But in my heart I never gave consent.
Where shall a man find sweetness to surpass
his own home and his parents? In far lands
he shall not, though he find a house of gold.

What of my sailing, then, from Troy?
What of those years
of rough adventure, weathered under Zeus?
The wind that carried west from Ilium[10]
brought me to Ismarus, on the far shore,
a strongpoint on the coast of Cicones.[11]
I stormed that place and killed the men who fought.
Plunder we took, and we enslaved the women,
to make division, equal shares to all—
but on the spot I told them: 'Back, and quickly!

Out to sea again!' My men were mutinous,[12]
fools, on stores of wine. Sheep after sheep
they butchered by the surf, and shambling cattle,
feasting,—while **fugitives** went inland, running
to call to arms the main force of Cicones.
This was an army, trained to fight on horseback
or, where the ground required, on foot. They came
with dawn over that terrain like the leaves
and blades of spring. So doom appeared to us,
dark word of Zeus for us, our evil days.
My men stood up and made a fight of it—
backed on the ships, with lances kept in play,
from bright morning through the blaze of noon
holding our beach, although so far outnumbered;
but when the sun passed toward unyoking time,
then the Achaeans,[13] one by one, gave way.
Six benches were left empty in every ship
that evening when we pulled away from death.
And this new grief we bore with us to sea:
our precious lives we had, but not our friends.
No ship made sail next day until some shipmate
had raised a cry, three times, for each poor ghost
unfleshed by the Cicones on that field.

The Lotus-Eaters

Now Zeus the lord of cloud roused in the north
a storm against the ships, and driving veils
of squall moved down like night on land and sea.
The bows went plunging at the gust; sails
cracked and lashed out strips in the big wind.
We saw death in that fury, dropped the yards,
unshipped the oars, and pulled for the nearest lee:[14]
then two long days and nights we lay offshore
worn out and sick at heart, tasting our grief,
until a third Dawn came with ringlets shining.
Then we put up our masts, hauled sail, and rested,
letting the steersmen and the breeze take over.

I might have made it safely home, that time,
but as I came round Malea the current
took me out to sea, and from the north
a fresh gale drove me on, past Cythera.
Nine days I drifted on the teeming sea
before dangerous high winds. Upon the tenth
we came to the coastline of the Lotus-Eaters,
who live upon that flower. We landed there
to take on water. All ships' companies

NOTES

12. mutinous (MYOO tuh nuhs) *adj.* rebellious.

fugitives (FYOO juh tihvz) *n.* group of persons who have run away from danger

CLOSE READ

ANNOTATE: In lines 53–57, mark the words Odysseus uses to describe the enemy army.

QUESTION: What is he expressing about what he and his men felt?

CONCLUDE: How threatening did the enemy appear to Odysseus?

13. Achaeans (uh KEE uhnz) Greeks; here, Odysseus' men.

14. lee *n.* area sheltered from the wind.

NOTES

mustered alongside for the mid-day meal.
Then I sent out two picked men and a runner
to learn what race of men that land sustained.
They fell in, soon enough, with Lotus-Eaters,
who showed no will to do us harm, only
offering the sweet Lotus to our friends—
but those who ate this honeyed plant, the Lotus,
never cared to report, nor to return:
they longed to stay forever, browsing on
that native bloom, forgetful of their homeland.
I drove them, all three wailing, to the ships,
tied them down under their rowing benches,
and called the rest: 'All hands aboard;
come, clear the beach and no one taste
the Lotus, or you lose your hope of home.'
Filing in to their places by the rowlocks
my oarsmen dipped their long oars in the surf,
and we moved out again on our sea faring.

The Cyclops

In the next land we found were Cyclopes,[15]
giants, louts, without a law to bless them.
In ignorance leaving the fruitage of the earth in mystery
to the immortal gods, they neither plow
nor sow by hand, nor till the ground, though grain—
wild wheat and barley—grows untended, and
wine-grapes, in clusters, ripen in heaven's rains.
Cyclopes have no muster and no meeting,
no consultation or old tribal ways,
but each one dwells in his own mountain cave
dealing out rough justice to wife and child,
indifferent to what the others do. . . .

As we rowed on, and nearer to the mainland,
at one end of the bay, we saw a cavern
yawning above the water, screened with laurel,
and many rams and goats about the place
inside a sheepfold—made from slabs of stone
earthfast between tall trunks of pine and rugged
towering oak trees.

A prodigious[16] man
slept in this cave alone, and took his flocks
to graze afield—remote from all companions,
knowing none but savage ways, a brute
so huge, he seemed no man at all of those

15. Cyclopes (SY kloh peez) *n.* plural form of Cyclops (SY klops), race of giants with one eye in the middle of the forehead.

16. prodigious (proh DIHJ uhs) *adj.* enormous.

who eat good wheaten bread; but he seemed rather
a shaggy mountain reared in solitude.
We beached there, and I told the crew
to stand by and keep watch over the ship:
as for myself I took my twelve best fighters
and went ahead. I had a goatskin full
of that sweet liquor that Euanthes' son,
Maron, had given me. He kept Apollo's[17]
holy grove at Ismarus; for kindness
we showed him there, and showed his wife and child,
he gave me seven shining golden talents[18]
perfectly formed, a solid silver winebowl,
and then this liquor—twelve two-handled jars
of brandy, pure and fiery. Not a slave
in Maron's household knew this drink; only
he, his wife, and the storeroom mistress knew;
and they would put one cupful—ruby-colored,
honey-smooth—in twenty more of water,
but still the sweet scent hovered like a fume
over the winebowl. No man turned away
when cups of this came round.

A wineskin full
I brought along, and victuals[19] in a bag,
for in my bones I knew some towering brute
would be upon us soon—all outward power,
a wild man, ignorant of civility.

We climbed, then, briskly to the cave. But Cyclops
had gone afield, to pasture his fat sheep,
so we looked round at everything inside:
a drying rack that sagged with cheeses, pens
crowded with lambs and kids,[20] each in its class:
firstlings apart from middlings, and the 'dewdrops,'
or newborn lambkins, penned apart from both.
And vessels full of whey[21] were brimming there—
bowls of earthenware and pails for milking.
My men came pressing round me, pleading:

'Why not
take these cheeses, get them stowed, come back,
throw open all the pens, and make a run for it?
We'll drive the kids and lambs aboard. We say
put out again on good salt water!'

Ah,
how sound that was! Yet I refused. I wished
to see the cave man, what he had to offer—

NOTES

17. **Apollo** (uh POL oh) god of music, poetry, prophecy, and medicine.

18. **talents** units of money in ancient Greece.

19. **victuals** (viht uhlz) *n.* food or other provisions.

20. **kids** young goats.

21. **whey** (hway) *n.* thin, watery part of milk separated from the thicker curds.

NOTES

no pretty sight, it turned out, for my friends.
We lit a fire, burnt an offering,
and took some cheese to eat; then sat in silence
around the embers, waiting. When he came
he had a load of dry boughs[22] on his shoulder
to stoke his fire at suppertime. He dumped it
with a great crash into that hollow cave,
and we all scattered fast to the far wall.
Then over the broad cavern floor he ushered
the ewes he meant to milk. He left his rams
and he-goats in the yard outside, and swung
high overhead a slab of solid rock
to close the cave. Two dozen four-wheeled wagons,
with heaving wagon teams, could not have stirred
the tonnage of that rock from where he wedged it
over the doorsill. Next he took his seat
and milked his bleating ewes. A practiced job
he made of it, giving each ewe her suckling;
thickened his milk, then, into curds and whey,
sieved out the curds to drip in withy[23] baskets,
and poured the whey to stand in bowls
cooling until he drank it for his supper.
When all these chores were done, he poked the fire,
heaping on brushwood. In the glare he saw us.

'Strangers,' he said, 'who are you? And where from?
What brings you here by seaways—a fair traffic?
Or are you wandering rogues, who cast your lives
like dice, and ravage other folk by sea?'

We felt a pressure on our hearts, in dread
of that deep rumble and that mighty man.
But all the same I spoke up in reply:
'We are from Troy, Achaeans, blown off course
by shifting gales on the Great South Sea;
homeward bound, but taking routes and ways
uncommon: so the will of Zeus would have it.
We served under Agamemnon,[24] son of Atreus—
the whole world knows what city
he laid waste, what armies he destroyed.
It was our luck to come here; here we stand,
beholden for your help, or any gifts
you give—as custom is to honor strangers.
We would entreat you, great Sir, have a care
for the gods' courtesy; Zeus will **avenge**
the unoffending guest.'

22. **boughs** (bowz) *n.* tree branches.

CLOSE READ

ANNOTATE: In lines 178–180, mark the verb Odysseus uses to tell how he and his men moved away from Cyclops.

QUESTION: What kind of creature does that verb evoke?

CONCLUDE: What comparison does it suggest between Cyclops and Odysseus and his men?

23. **withy** (WIHTH ee) *adj.* made from tough, flexible twigs.

24. **Agamemnon** (ag uh MEHM non) king who led the Greek army during the Trojan War.

avenge (uh VEHNJ) *v.* to get revenge

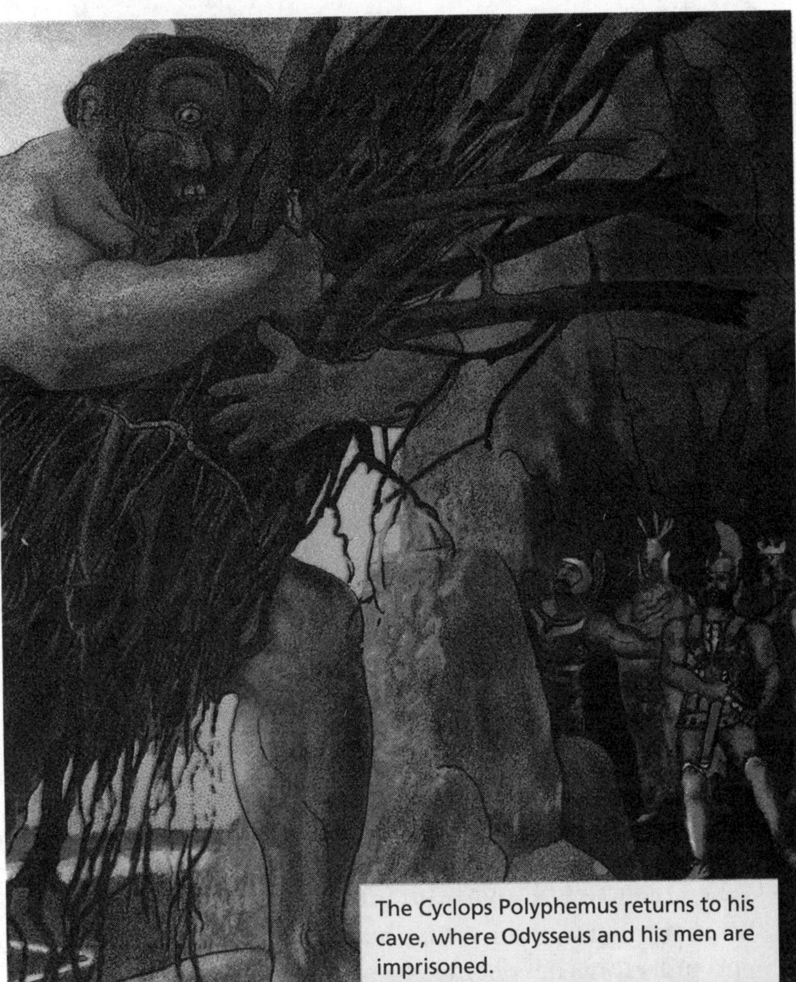
The Cyclops Polyphemus returns to his cave, where Odysseus and his men are imprisoned.

NOTES

He answered this
from his brute chest, unmoved:

'You are a ninny,
or else you come from the other end of nowhere,
telling me, mind the gods! We Cyclopes
care not a whistle for your thundering Zeus
or all the gods in bliss; we have more force by far.

I would not let you go for fear of Zeus—
you or your friends—unless I had a whim[25] to.
Tell me, where was it, now, you left your ship—
around the point, or down the shore, I wonder?'

He thought he'd find out, but I saw through this,
And answered with a ready lie:

'My ship?
Poseidon[26] Lord, who sets the earth a-tremble,
broke it up on the rocks at your land's end.
A wind from seaward served him, drove us there.
We are survivors, these good men and I.'

25. **whim** *n.* sudden thought or wish to do something.

26. **Poseidon** (poh SY duhn) god of the sea, earthquakes, horses, and storms at sea.

NOTES

Neither reply nor pity came from him,
but in one stride he clutched at my companions
and caught two in his hands like squirming puppies
to beat their brain out, spattering the floor.
Then he dismembered them and made his meal,
gaping and crunching like a mountain lion—
everything: innards, flesh, and marrow bones.
We cried aloud, lifting our hands to Zeus,
powerless, looking on at this, appalled;
but Cyclops went on filling up his belly
with manflesh and great gulps of whey,
then lay down like a mast among his sheep.
My heart beat high now at the chance of action,
and drawing the sharp sword from my hip I went
along his flank to stab him where the midriff
holds the liver. I had touched the spot
when sudden fear stayed me: if I killed him
we perished there as well, for we could never
move his ponderous doorway slab aside.
So we were left to groan and wait for morning.

When the young Dawn with fingertips of rose
lit up the world, the Cyclops built a fire
and milked his handsome ewes, all in due order,
putting the sucklings to the mothers. Then,
his chores being all **dispatched**, he caught
another brace[27] of men to make his breakfast,
and whisked away his great door slab
to let his sheep go through—but he, behind,
reset the stone as one would cap a quiver.[28]
There was a din[29] of whistling as the Cyclops
rounded his flock to higher ground, then stillness.
And now I pondered how to hurt him worst,
if but Athena[30] granted what I prayed for.
Here are the means I thought would serve my turn:

a club, or staff, lay there along the fold—
an olive tree, felled green and left to season[31]
for Cyclops' hand. And it was like a mast
a lugger[32] of twenty oars, broad in the beam—
a deep-sea-going craft—might carry:
so long, so big around, it seemed. Now I
chopped out a six foot section of this pole
and set it down before my men, who scraped it;
and when they had it smooth, I hewed again
to make a stake with pointed end. I held this
in the fire's heart and turned it, toughening it,

dispatched (dihs PACHT) *v.* finished something quickly

27. brace *n.* pair.

28. cap a quiver (KWIHV uhr) close a case holding arrows.

29. din *n.* loud, continuous noise; uproar.

30. Athena (uh THEE nuh) goddess of wisdom, skills, and warfare.

31. felled green and left to season chopped down and exposed to the weather to age the wood.

32. lugger *n.* small sailing vessel.

then hid it, well back in the cavern, under
one of the dung piles in profusion there.
Now came the time to toss for it: who **ventured**
along with me? whose hand could bear to thrust
and grind that spike in Cyclops' eye, when mild
sleep had mastered him? As luck would have it,
the men I would have chosen won the toss—
four strong men, and I made five as captain.

At evening came the shepherd with his flock,
his woolly flock. The rams as well, this time,
entered the cave: by some sheepherding whim—
or a god's bidding—none were left outside.
He hefted his great boulder into place
and sat him down to milk the bleating ewes
in proper order, put the lambs to suck,
and swiftly ran through all his evening chores.
Then he caught two more men and feasted on them.
My moment was at hand, and I went forward
holding an ivy bowl of my dark drink,
looking up, saying:

'Cyclops, try some wine.
Here's liquor to wash down your scraps of men.
Taste it, and see the kind of drink we carried
under our planks. I meant it for an offering
if you would help us home. But you are mad,
unbearable, a bloody monster! After this,
will any other traveler come to see you?'

He seized and drained the bowl, and it went down
so fiery and smooth he called for more:

'Give me another, thank you kindly. Tell me,
how are you called? I'll make a gift will please you.
Even Cyclopes know the wine grapes grow
out of grassland and loam in heaven's rain,
but here's a bit of nectar and ambrosia!'[33]

Three bowls I brought him, and he poured them down.
I saw the fuddle and flush come over him,
then I sang out in cordial tones:

'Cyclops,
you ask my honorable name? Remember
the gift you promised me, and I shall tell you.
My name is Nohbdy: mother, father, and friends,
everyone calls me Nohbdy.'

NOTES

ventured (VEHN chuhrd) *v.* tried something dangerous

33. **nectar** (NEHK tuhr) **and ambrosia** (am BROH zhuh) drink and food of the gods.

NOTES

And he said:
'Nohbdy's my meat, then, after I eat his friends.
Others come first. There's a noble gift, now.'

Even as he spoke, he reeled and tumbled backward,
his great head lolling to one side; and sleep
took him like any creature. Drunk, hiccuping,
he dribbled streams of liquor and bits of men.

Now, by the gods, I drove my big hand spike
deep in the embers, charring it again,
and cheered my men along with battle talk
to keep their courage up: no quitting now.
The pike of olive, green though it had been,
reddened and glowed as if about to catch.
I drew it from the coals and my four fellows
gave me a hand, lugging it near the Cyclops
as more than natural force nerved them; straight
forward they sprinted, lifted it, and rammed it
deep in his crater eye, and leaned on it
turning it as a shipwright tums a drill
in planking, having men below to swing
the two-handled strap that spins it in the groove.
So with our brand we bored[34] that great eye socket
while blood ran out around the red-hot bar.
Eyelid and lash were seared; the pierced ball
hissed broiling, and the roots popped.

In a smithy
one sees a white-hot axehead or an adze
plunged and wrung in a cold tub, screeching steam—
the way they make soft iron hale and hard—:
just so that eyeball hissed around the spike.
The Cyclops bellowed and the rock roared round him,
and we fell back in fear. Clawing his face
he tugged the bloody spike out of his eye,
threw it away, and his wild hands went groping:
then he set up a howl for Cyclopes
who lived in caves on windy peaks nearby.
Some heard him; and they came by divers[35] ways
to clump around outside and call:

'What ails you,
Polyphemus?[36] Why do you cry so sore
in the starry night? You will not let us sleep.
Sure no man's driving off your flock? No man
has tricked you, ruined you?'

34. bored *v.* made a hole in.

35. divers *adj.* several; various.

36. Polyphemus (pol ih FEE muhs)

Out of the cave
the mammoth Polyphemus roared in answer:

'Nohbdy, Nohbdy's tricked me, Nohbdy's ruined me!'

To this rough shout they made a sage[37] reply:

'Ah well, if nobody has played you foul
there in your lonely bed, we are no use in pain
given by great Zeus. Let it be your father,
Poseidon Lord, to whom you pray.'

So saying
they trailed away. And I was filled with laughter
to see how like a charm the name deceived them.
Now Cyclops, wheezing as the pain came on him,
fumbled to wrench away the great doorstone
and squatted in the breach with arms thrown wide
for any silly beast or man who bolted—
hoping somehow I might be such a fool.
But I kept thinking how to win the game:
death sat there huge; how could we slip away?
I drew on all my wits, and ran through **tactics**,
reasoning as a man will for dear life,
until a trick came—and it pleased me well.
The Cyclops' rams were handsome, fat, with heavy
fleeces, a dark violet.

Three abreast
I tied them silently together, twining
cords of willow from the ogre's bed;
then slung a man under each middle one
to ride there safely, shielded left and right.

So three sheep could convey each man. I took
the woolliest ram, the choicest of the flock,
and hung myself under his kinky belly,
pulled up tight, with fingers twisted deep
in sheepskin ringlets for an iron grip.
So, breathing hard, we waited until morning.

When Dawn spread out her fingertips of rose
the rams began to stir, moving for pasture,
and peals of bleating echoed round the pens
where dams with udders full called for a milking.
Blinded, and sick with pain from his head wound,
the master stroked each ram, then let it pass,
but my men riding on the pectoral[38] fleece
the giant's blind hands blundering never found.

NOTES

37. sage *adj.* wise.

CLOSE READ

ANNOTATE: Mark the verbs Odysseus uses to describe the actions of Cyclops in the sentence beginning on line 366.

QUESTION: What do these verbs suggest about Cyclops' condition?

CONCLUDE: What does this reveal about Cyclops' pain, anger, and remaining strength?

tactics (TAK tihks) *n.* military procedures

38. pectoral (PEHK tuh ruhl) *adj.* located in or on the chest.

The Cyclops fails to notice the men hidden under the ram.

Last of them all my ram, the leader, came,
weighted by wool and me with my meditations.
The Cyclops patted him, and then he said:

'Sweet cousin ram, why lag behind the rest
in the night cave? You never linger so,
but graze before them all, and go afar
to crop sweet grass, and take your stately way
leading along the streams, until at evening
you run to be the first one in the fold.
Why, now, so far behind? Can you be grieving
over your Master's eye? That carrion rogue[39]
and his accurst companions burnt it out
when he had conquered all my wits with wine.
Nohbdy will not get out alive, I swear.
Oh, had you brain and voice to tell
where he may be now, dodging all my fury!
Bashed by this hand and bashed on this rock wall
his brains would strew the floor, and I should have
rest from the outrage Nohbdy worked upon me.'

He sent us into the open, then. Close by,
I dropped and rolled clear of the ram's belly,
going this way and that to untie the men.
With many glances back, we rounded up
his fat, stiff-legged sheep to take aboard,
and drove them down to where the good ship lay.

We saw, as we came near, our fellows' faces
shining; then we saw them turn to grief
tallying those who had not fled from death.
I hushed them, jerking head and eyebrows up,
and in a low voice told them: 'Load this herd:
move fast, and put the ship's head toward the breakers.'
They all pitched in at loading, then embarked
and struck their oars into the sea. Far out,
as far off shore as shouted words would carry,
I sent a few back to the adversary:
'O Cyclops! Would you feast on my companions?
Puny, am I, in a cave man's hands?
How do you like the beating that we gave you,
you damned cannibal? Eater of guests
under your roof! Zeus and the gods have paid you!'

The blind thing in his doubled fury broke
a hilltop in his hands and heaved it after us.
Ahead of our black prow it struck and sank
whelmed in a spuming geyser, a giant wave

NOTES

39. carrion (KAR ee uhn) **rogue** (rohg) repulsive scoundrel.

NOTES

that washed the ship stern foremost back to shore.
I got the longest boathook out and stood
fending us off, with furious nods to all
to put their backs into a racing stroke—
row, row, or perish. So the long oars bent
kicking the foam sternward, making head
until we drew away, and twice as far.
Now when I cupped my hands I heard the crew
in low voices protesting:

'Godsake, Captain!
Why bait the beast again? Let him alone!'

'That tidal wave he made on the first throw
all but beached us.'

'All but stove us in!'
'Give him our bearing with your trumpeting,
he'll get the range and lob a boulder.'

'Aye
He'll smash our timbers and our heads together!'
I would not heed them in my glorying spirit,
but let my anger flare and yelled:

'Cyclops,
if ever mortal man inquire
how you were put to shame and blinded, tell him
Odysseus, raider of cities, took your eye:
Laertes' son, whose home's on Ithaca!'

At this he gave a mighty sob and rumbled:
'Now comes the weird[40] upon me, spoken of old.
A wizard, grand and wondrous, lived here—Telemus,[41]
a son of Eurymus;[42] great length of days
he had in wizardry among the Cyclopes,
and these things he foretold for time to come:
my great eye lost, and at Odysseus' hands.
Always I had in mind some giant, armed
in giant force, would come against me here.
But this, but you—small, pitiful, and twiggy—
you put me down with wine, you blinded me.
Come back, Odysseus, and I'll treat you well,
praying the god of earthquake[43] to befriend you—
his son I am, for he by his avowal
fathered me, and, if he will, he may
heal me of this black wound—he and no other
of all the happy gods or mortal men.'

CLOSE READ

ANNOTATE: Mark the punctuation in lines 448–454.

QUESTION: What does this punctuation indicate?

CONCLUDE: What does the poet accomplish by letting the reader hear the crew's own voices for the first time?

40. weird *n.* fate or destiny.

41. Telemus (tehl EH muhs)

42. Eurymus (yoo RIHM uhs)

43. god of earthquake Poseidon.

Few words I shouted in reply to him:

'If I could take your life I would and take
your time away, and hurl you down to hell!
The god of earthquake could not heal you there!'

At this he stretched his hands out in his darkness
toward the sky of stars, and prayed Poseidon:

'O hear me, lord, blue girdler of the islands,
if I am thine indeed, and thou art father:
grant that Odysseus, raider of cities, never
see his home: Laertes' son, I mean,
who kept his hall on Ithaca. Should destiny
intend that he shall see his roof again
among his family in his father land,
far be that day, and dark the years between.

Let him lose all companions, and return
under strange sail to bitter days at home.'
In these words he prayed, and the god heard him.
Now he laid hands upon a bigger stone
and wheeled around, titanic for the cast,
to let it fly in the black-prowed vessel's track.
But it fell short, just aft the steering oar,
and whelming seas rose giant above the stone
to bear us onward toward the island.

There
as we ran in we saw the squadron waiting,
The trim ships drawn up side by side, and all
our troubled friends who waited, looking seaward.
We beached her, grinding keel in the soft sand,
and waded in, ourselves, on the sandy beach.
Then we unloaded all the Cyclops' flock
to make division, share and share alike,
only my fighters voted that my ram,
the prize of all, should go to me. I slew him
by the seaside and burnt his long thighbones
to Zeus beyond the storm cloud, Cronus'[44] son,
who rules the world. But Zeus disdained my offering;
destruction for my ships he had in store
and death for those who sailed them, my companions.
Now all day long until the sun went down
we made our feast on mutton and sweet wine,
till after sunset in the gathering dark
we went to sleep above the wash of ripples.

NOTES

44. Cronus (KROH nuhs) Titan who was ruler of the universe until he was overthrown by his son Zeus.

NOTES

When the young Dawn with fingertips of rose
touched the world, I roused the men, gave orders
to man the ships, cast off the mooring lines;
and filing in to sit beside the rowlocks
oarsmen in line dipped oars in the gray sea.
So we moved out, sad in the vast offing,[45]
having our precious lives, but not our friends.

The Land of the Dead

Odysseus and his men sail to Aeolia, where Aeolus,[46] king of the winds, sends Odysseus on his way with a gift: a sack containing all the winds except the favorable west wind. When they are near home, Odysseus' men open the sack, letting loose a storm that drives them back to Aeolia. Aeolus casts them out, having decided that they are detested by the gods. They sail for seven days and arrive in the land of the Laestrygonians,[47] a race of cannibals. These creatures destroy all of Odysseus' ships except the one he is sailing in.

Odysseus and his reduced crew escape and reach Aeaea, the island ruled by the sorceress-goddess Circe. She transforms half of the men into swine. Protected by a magic herb, Odysseus demands that Circe change his men back into human form. Before Odysseus departs from the island a year later, Circe informs him that in order to reach home he must journey to the land of the dead, Hades, and consult the blind prophet Tiresias.

We bore down on the ship at the sea's edge
and launched her on the salt immortal sea,
stepping our mast and spar in the black ship;
embarked the ram and ewe and went aboard
in tears, with bitter and sore dread upon us.
But now a breeze came up for us astern—
a canvas-bellying landbreeze, hale shipmate
sent by the singing nymph with sunbright hair;[48]
so we made fast the braces, took our thwarts,
and let the wind and steersman work the ship
with full sail spread all day above our coursing,
till the sun dipped, and all the ways grew dark
upon the fathomless unresting sea.

By night
our ship ran onward toward the Ocean's bourne,
the realm and region of the Men of Winter,
hidden in mist and cloud. Never the flaming
eye of Helios lights on those men

45. offing *n.* distant part of the sea visible from the shore.

46. Aeolia (ee OH lee uh) . . . **Aeolus** (EE uh luhs)

47. Laestrygonians (lehs trih GOH nee uhnz)

48. singing nymph . . . hair Circe.

at morning, when he climbs the sky of stars,
nor in descending earthward out of heaven;
ruinous night being rove over those wretches.
We made the land, put ram and ewe ashore,
and took our way along the Ocean stream
to find the place foretold for us by Circe.
There Perimedes and Eurylochus[49]
pinioned[50] the sacred beasts. With my drawn blade
I spaded up the votive[51] pit, and poured
libations[52] round it to the unnumbered dead:
sweet milk and honey, then sweet wine, and last
clear water; and I scattered barley down.
Then I addressed the blurred and breathless dead,
vowing to slaughter my best heifer for them
before she calved, at home in Ithaca,
and burn the choice bits on the altar fire;
as for Tiresias,[53] I swore to sacrifice
a black lamb, handsomest of all our flock.
Thus to assuage the nations of the dead
I pledged these rites, then slashed the lamb and ewe,
letting their black blood stream into the wellpit.
Now the souls gathered, stirring out of Erebus,[54]
brides and young men, and men grown old in pain,
and tender girls whose hearts were new to grief;
many were there, too, torn by brazen lanceheads,
battle-slain, bearing still their bloody gear.
From every side they came and sought the pit
with rustling cries; and I grew sick with fear.
But presently I gave command to my officers
to flay those sheep the bronze cut down, and make
burnt offerings of flesh to the gods below—
to sovereign Death, to pale Persephone.[55]
Meanwhile I crouched with my drawn sword to keep
the surging phantoms from the bloody pit
till I should know the presence of Tiresias.

One shade came first—Elpenor, of our company,
who lay unburied still on the wide earth
as we had left him—dead in Circe's hall,
untouched, unmourned, when other cares compelled us.
Now when I saw him there I wept for pity
and called out to him:

'How is this, Elpenor,
how could you journey to the western gloom
swifter afoot than I in the black lugger?'
He sighed, and answered:

NOTES

49. **Perimedes** (pehr uh MEE deez) **and Eurylochus** (yoo RIHL uh kuhs)

50. **pinioned** (PIHN yuhnd) *v.* confined or shackled.

51. **votive** (VOHT ihv) *adj.* done to fulfill a vow or express thanks.

52. **libations** (ly BAY shuhnz) *n.* wine or other liquids poured upon the ground as a sacrifice or offering.

53. **Tiresias** (ty REE see uhs)

54. **Erebus** (EHR uh buhs) dark region under the earth through which the dead pass before entering realm of Hades.

55. **Persephone** (puhr SEHF uh nee)

NOTES

'Son of great Laertes,
Odysseus, master mariner and soldier,
bad luck shadowed me, and no kindly power;
ignoble death I drank with so much wine.
I slept on Circe's roof, then could not see
the long steep backward ladder, coming down,
and fell that height. My neckbone, buckled under,
snapped, and my spirit found this well of dark.
Now hear the grace I pray for, in the name
of those back in the world, not here—your wife
and father, he who gave you bread in childhood,
and your own child, your only son, Telemachus,[56]
long ago left at home.

When you make sail
and put these lodgings of dim Death behind,
you will moor ship, I know, upon Aeaea Island;
there, O my lord, remember me, I pray,
do not abandon me unwept, unburied,
to tempt the gods' wrath, while you sail for home;
but fire my corpse, and all the gear I had,
and build a cairn[57] for me above the breakers—
an unknown sailor's mark for men to come.
Heap up the mound there, and implant upon it
the oar I pulled in life with my companions.'

He ceased and I replied:

'Unhappy spirit,
I promise you the barrow and the burial.'

So we conversed, and grimly, at a distance,
with my long sword between, guarding the blood,
while the faint image of the lad spoke on.
Now came the soul of Anticlea, dead,
my mother, daughter of Autolycus,[58]
dead now, though living still when I took ship
for holy Troy. Seeing this ghost I grieved,
but held her off, through pang on pang of tears,
till I should know the presence of Tiresias.
Soon from the dark that prince of Thebes[59] came forward
bearing a golden staff; and he addressed me:

'Son of Laertes and the gods of old,
Odysseus, master of landways and seaways,
why leave the blazing sun, O man of woe,
to see the cold dead and the joyless region?
Stand clear, put up your sword;
let me but taste of blood, I shall speak true.'

56. Telemachus (tuh LEHM uh kuhs)

57. cairn (kairn) *n.* conical heap of stones built as a monument.

58. Autolycus (aw TOL ih kuhs)

59. Thebes (theebz)

At this I stepped aside, and in the scabbard
let my long sword ring home to the pommel silver,
as he bent down to the somber blood. Then spoke
the prince of those with gift of speech:

'Great captain,
a fair wind and the honey lights of home
are all you seek. But anguish lies ahead;
the god who thunders on the land prepares it,
not to be shaken from your track, implacable,
in rancor for the son whose eye you blinded.
One narrow strait may take you through his blows:
denial of yourself, restraint of shipmates.
When you make landfall on Thrinacia first
and quit the violet sea, dark on the land
you'll find the grazing herds of Helios
by whom all things are seen, all speech is known.
Avoid those kine,[60] hold fast to your intent,
and hard seafaring brings you all to Ithaca.
But if you raid the beeves, I see destruction
for ship and crew. Though you survive alone,
bereft of all companions, lost for years,
under strange sail shall you come home, to find
your own house filled with trouble: insolent men
eating your livestock as they court your lady.
Aye, you shall make those men atone in blood!
But after you have dealt out death—in open
combat or by stealth—to all the suitors,
go overland on foot, and take an oar,
until one day you come where men have lived
with meat unsalted, never known the sea,
nor seen seagoing ships, with crimson bows
and oars that fledge light hulls for dipping flight.
The spot will soon be plain to you, and I
can tell you how: some passerby will say,
"What winnowing fan is that upon your shoulder?"
Halt, and implant your smooth oar in the turf
and make fair sacrifice to Lord Poseidon:
a ram, a bull, a great buck boar; turn back,
and carry out pure hecatombs[61] at home
to all wide heaven's lords, the undying gods,
to each in order. Then a seaborne death
soft as this hand of mist will come upon you
when you are wearied out with rich old age,
your country folk in blessed peace around you.
And all this shall be just as I foretell.'

NOTES

CLOSE READ

ANNOTATE: In lines 632–637, mark the words that describe Odysseus' home and the words that describe what is in his future.

QUESTION: What do these contrasting words express?

CONCLUDE: What can you conclude about Odysseus' goal and what will happen before he reaches it?

60. kine (kyn) *n.* cattle.

61. hecatombs (HEHK uh tohmz) *n.* large-scale sacrifices to the gods in ancient Greece; often, the slaughter of 100 cattle at one time.

NOTES

This nineteenth-century painting by John William Waterhouse shows the Sirens as bird-women, which echoes ancient Greek portrayals of these figures.

The Sirens

Odysseus returns to Circe's island. The goddess reveals his course to him and gives advice on how to avoid the dangers he will face: the Sirens, who lure sailors to their destruction; the Wandering Rocks, sea rocks that destroy even birds in flight: the perils of the sea monster Scylla and, nearby, the whirlpool Charybdis;[62] *and the cattle of the sun god, which Tiresias has warned Odysseus not to harm.*

As Circe spoke, Dawn mounted her golden throne,
and on the first rays Circe left me, taking
her way like a great goddess up the island.
I made straight for the ship, roused up the men
to get aboard and cast off at the stern.
They scrambled to their places by the rowlocks
and all in line dipped oars in the gray sea.
But soon an offshore breeze blew to our liking—
a canvas-bellying breeze, a lusty shipmate
sent by the singing nymph with sunbright hair.
So we made fast the braces, and we rested,
letting the wind and steersman work the ship.
The crew being now silent before me, I
addressed them, sore at heart:

62. Charybdis (kuh RIHB dihs)

NOTES

'Dear friends,
more than one man, or two, should know those things
Circe foresaw for us and shared with me,
so let me tell her forecast: then we die
with our eyes open, if we are going to die,
or know what death we baffle if we can. Sirens
weaving a haunting song over the sea
we are to shun, she said, and their green shore
all sweet with clover; yet she urged that I
alone should listen to their song. Therefore
you are to tie me up, tight as a splint,
erect along the mast, lashed to the mast,
and if I shout and beg to be untied,
take more turns of the rope to muffle me.'

I rather dwelt on this part of the forecast,
while our good ship made time, bound outward down
the wind for the strange island of Sirens.

Then all at once the wind fell, and a calm
came over all the sea, as though some power
lulled the swell.

The crew were on their feet
briskly, to furl the sail, and stow it; then,

NOTES

CLOSE READ

ANNOTATE: In lines 719–744, mark the end words of the lines of several stanzas of the Sirens' song.

QUESTION: What do you notice about these words in relation to each other?

CONCLUDE: How does this contribute to a sense of the Sirens' music?

each in place, they poised the smooth oar blades
and sent the white foam scudding by. I carved
a massive cake of beeswax into bits
and rolled them in my hands until they softened—
no long task, for a burning heat came down
from Helios, lord of high noon. Going forward
I carried wax along the line, and laid it
thick on their ears. They tied me up, then, plumb
amidships, back to the mast, lashed to the mast,
and took themselves again to rowing. Soon,
as we came smartly within hailing distance,
the two Sirens, noting our fast ship
off their point, made ready, and they sang:

This way, oh turn your bows,
Achaea's glory,
As all the world allows—
Moor and be merry.

Sweet coupled airs we sing.
No lonely seafarer
Holds clear of entering
Our green mirror.

Pleased by each purling note
Like honey twining
From her throat and my throat,
Who lies a-pining?

Sea rovers here take joy
Voyaging onward,
As from our song of Troy
Graybeard and rower-boy
Goeth more learnèd.

All feats on that great field
In the long warfare,
Dark days the bright gods willed,
Wounds you bore there,

Argos' old soldiery[63]
On Troy beach teeming,
Charmed out of time we see.
No life on earth can be
Hid from our dreaming.

The lovely voices in ardor appealing over the water
made me crave to listen, and I tried to say
'Untie me!' to the crew, jerking my brows;

63. **Argos' old soldiery** soldiers from Argos, a city in ancient Greece.

but they bent steady to the oars. Then Perimedes
got to his feet, he and Eurylochus,
and passed more line about, to hold me still.
So all rowed on, until the Sirens
dropped under the sea rim, and their singing
dwindled away.

My faithful company
rested on their oars now, peeling off
the wax that I had laid thick on their ears;
then set me free.

Scylla and Charybdis

But scarcely had that island
faded in blue air than I saw smoke
and white water, with sound of waves in tumult—
a sound the men heard, and it terrified them.
Oars flew from their hands; the blades went knocking
wild alongside till the ship lost way,
with no oar blades to drive her through the water.
Well, I walked up and down from bow to stern,
trying to put heart into them, standing over
every oarsman, saying gently,

'Friends,
have we never been in danger before this?
More fearsome, is it now, than when the Cyclops
penned us in his cave? What power he had!
Did I not keep my nerve, and use my wits
to find a way out for us?

Now I say
by hook or crook this peril too shall be
something that we remember.

Heads up, lads!
We must obey the orders as I give them.
Get the oar shafts in your hands, and lay back
hard on your benches; hit these breaking seas.
Zeus help us pull away before we founder.
You at the tiller, listen, and take in
all that I say—the rudders are your duty;
keep her out of the combers and the smoke;[64]
steer for that headland; watch the drift, or we
fetch up in the smother, and you drown us.'

NOTES

64. the combers and the smoke large waves that break on the beach and the ocean spray.

An artist's rendering of the two terrors—Charybdis (the whirlpool) and Scylla (the monster).

That was all, and it brought them round to action.
But as I sent them on toward Scylla,[65] I
told them nothing, as they could do nothing.
They would have dropped their oars again, in panic,
to roll for cover under the decking. Circe's
bidding against arms had slipped my mind,
so I tied on my cuirass[66] and took up
two heavy spears, then made my way along
to the foredeck—thinking to see her first from there,
the monster of the gray rock, harboring
torment for my friends. I strained my eyes
upon the cliffside veiled in cloud, but nowhere
could I catch sight of her.

And all this time,
in travail,[67] sobbing, gaining on the current,
we rowed into the strait—Scylla to port
and on our starboard beam Charybdis, dire
gorge[68] of the salt seatide. By heaven! when she
vomited, all the sea was like a cauldron
seething over intense fire, when the mixture
suddenly heaves and rises.

The shot spume
soared to the landside heights, and fell like rain.
But when she swallowed the sea water down
we saw the funnel of the maelstrom,[69] heard
the rock bellowing all around, and dark

NOTES

65. Scylla (SIHL uh)

66. cuirass (kwih RAS) *n.* armor for the upper body.

67. travail (truh VAYL) *n.* very hard work.

68. gorge (gawrj) *n.* throat or gullet.

69. maelstrom (MAYL struhm) *n.* large, violent whirlpool.

sand raged on the bottom far below.
My men all blanched against the gloom, our eyes
were fixed upon that yawning mouth in fear
of being devoured.

Then Scylla made her strike,
whisking six of my best men from the ship.
I happened to glance aft at ship and oarsmen
and caught sight of their arms and legs, dangling
high overhead. Voices came down to me
in anguish, calling my name for the last time.

A man surfcasting on a point of rock
for bass or mackerel, whipping his long rod
to drop the sinker and the bait far out,
will hook a fish and rip it from the surface
to dangle wriggling through the air:

so these
were borne aloft in spasms toward the cliff.

She ate them as they shrieked there, in her den,
in the dire grapple, reaching still for me—
and deathly pity ran me through
at that sight—far the worst I ever suffered,
questing the passes of the strange sea.

We rowed on.
The Rocks were now behind; Charybdis, too,
and Scylla dropped astern.

The Cattle of the Sun God

In the small hours of the third watch, when stars
that shone out in the first dusk of evening
had gone down to their setting, a giant wind
blew from heaven, and clouds driven by Zeus
shrouded land and sea in a night of storm;
so, just as Dawn with fingertips of rose
touched the windy world, we dragged our ship
to cover in a grotto, a sea cave
where nymphs had chairs of rock and sanded floors.
I mustered all the crew and said:

'Old shipmates,
our stores are in the ship's hold, food and drink;
the cattle here are not for our provision,
or we pay dearly for it.

NOTES

CLOSE READ

ANNOTATE: Mark the words in lines 815–820 that describe a sports activity.

QUESTION: Why does Homer liken this activity to Scylla's actions?

CONCLUDE: What does this comparison suggest about Scylla's power?

NOTES

70. **Olympus** (oh LIHM puhs) Mount Olympus, home of the gods.

71. **Lord of Noon** Helios.

Fierce the god is
who cherishes these heifers and these sheep:
Helios; and no man avoids his eye.'

To this my fighters nodded. Yes. But now
we had a month of onshore gales, blowing
day in, day out—south winds, or south by east.
As long as bread and good red wine remained
to keep the men up, and appease their craving,
they would not touch the cattle. But in the end,
when all the barley in the ship was gone,
hunger drove them to scour the wild shore
with angling hooks, for fishes and sea fowl,
whatever fell into their hands; and lean days
wore their bellies thin.

The storms continued.
So one day I withdrew to the interior
to pray the gods in solitude, for hope
that one might show me some way of salvation.
Slipping away, I struck across the island
to a sheltered spot, out of the driving gale.
I washed my hands there, and made supplication
to the gods who own Olympus,[70] all the gods—
but they, for answer, only closed my eyes
under slow drops of sleep.

Now on the shore Eurylochus
made his insidious plea:

'Comrades,' he said,
'You've gone through everything; listen to what I say.
All deaths are hateful to us, mortal wretches,
but famine is the most pitiful, the worst
end that a man can come to.

Will you fight it?
Come, we'll cut out the noblest of these cattle
for sacrifice to the gods who own the sky;
and once at home, in the old country of Ithaca,
if ever that day comes—
we'll build a costly temple and adorn it
with every beauty for the Lord of Noon.[71]
But if he flares up over his heifers lost,
wishing our ship destroyed, and if the gods
make cause with him, why, then I say: Better
open your lungs to a big sea once for all
than waste to skin and bones on a lonely island!'

Thus Eurylochus; and they murmured 'Aye!'
trooping away at once to round up heifers.
Now, that day tranquil cattle with broad brows
were grazing near, and soon the men drew up
around their chosen beasts in ceremony.
They plucked the leaves that shone on a tall oak—
having no barley meal—to strew the victims,
performed the prayers and ritual, knifed the kine
and flayed each carcass, cutting thighbones free
to wrap in double folds of fat. These offerings,
with strips of meat, were laid upon the fire.
Then, as they had no wine, they made libation
with clear spring water, broiling the entrails first;
and when the bones were burnt and tripes shared,
they spitted the carved meat.
Just then my slumber
left me in a rush, my eyes opened,
and I went down the seaward path. No sooner
had I caught sight of our black hull, than savory
odors of burnt fat eddied around me;
grief took hold of me, and I cried aloud:

'O Father Zeus and gods in bliss forever,
you made me sleep away this day of mischief!
O cruel drowsing, in the evil hour!
Here they sat, and a great work they contrived.'[72]
Lampetia[73] in her long gown meanwhile
had borne swift word to the Overlord of Noon:
'They have killed your kine.'
And the Lord Helios
burst into angry speech amid the immortals:

'O Father Zeus and gods in bliss forever,
punish Odysseus' men! So overweening,
now they have killed my peaceful kine, my joy
at morning when I climbed the sky of stars,
and evening, when I bore westward from heaven.
Restitution or penalty they shall pay—
and pay in full—or I go down forever
to light the dead men in the underworld.'

Then Zeus who drives the stormcloud made reply:
'Peace, Helios: shine on among the gods,
shine over mortals in the fields of grain.
Let me throw down one white-hot bolt, and make
splinters of their ship in the winedark sea.'

NOTES

72. contrived *v.* thought up; devised.

73. Lampetia (lam PEE shuh) a nymph.

NOTES

74. Hermes (HUR meez) *n.* god who serves as herald and messenger of the other gods.

75. beeves (beevz) *n.* alternate plural form of "beef."

76. petrels (PEH truhlz) *n.* small, dark sea birds.

—Calypso later told me of this exchange,
as she declared that Hermes[74] had told her.
Well, when I reached the sea cave and the ship,
I faced each man, and had it out; but where
could any remedy be found? There was none.
The silken beeves[75] of Hellos were dead.
The gods, moreover, made queer signs appear:
cowhides began to crawl, and beef, both raw
and roasted, lowed like kine upon the spits.

Now six full days my gallant crew could feast
upon the prime beef they had marked for slaughter
from Hellos' herd; and Zeus, the son of Cronus,
added one fine morning.

All the gales
had ceased, blown out, and with an offshore breeze
we launched again, stepping the mast and sail,
to make for the open sea. Astern of us
the island coastline faded, and no land
showed anywhere, but only sea and heaven,
when Zeus Cronion piled a thunderhead
above the ship, while gloom spread on the ocean.
We held our course, but briefly. Then the squall
struck whining from the west, with gale force, breaking
both forestays, and the mast came toppling aft
along the ship's length, so the running rigging
showered into the bilge.

On the afterdeck
the mast had hit the steersman a slant blow
bashing the skull in, knocking him overside,
as the brave soul fled the body, like a diver.
With crack on crack of thunder, Zeus let fly
a bolt against the ship, a direct hit,
so that she bucked, in reeking fumes of sulphur,
and all the men were flung into the sea.
They came up 'round the wreck, bobbing awhile
like petrels[76] on the waves.

No more seafaring
homeward for these, no sweet day of return;
the god had turned his face from them.

I clambered
fore and aft my hulk until a comber
split her, keel from ribs, and the big timber
floated free; the mast, too, broke away.

A backstay floated dangling from it, stout
rawhide rope, and I used this for lashing
mast and keel together. These I straddled,
riding the frightful storm.

Nor had I yet
seen the worst of it: for now the west wind
dropped, and a southeast gale came on—one more
twist of the knife—taking me north again,
straight for Charybdis. All that night I drifted,
and in the sunrise, sure enough, I lay
off Scylla mountain and Charybdis deep.
There, as the whirlpool drank the tide, a billow
tossed me, and I sprang for the great fig tree,
catching on like a bat under a bough.
Nowhere had I to stand, no way of climbing,
The root and bole[77] being far below, and far
above my head the branches and their leaves,
massed, overshadowing Charybdis pool.
But I clung grimly, thinking my mast and keel
would come back to the surface when she spouted.

And ah! how long, with what desire, I waited!
till, at the twilight hour, when one who hears
and judges pleas in the marketplace all day
between contentious men, goes home to supper,
the long poles at last reared from the sea.

Now I let go with hands and feet, plunging
straight into the foam beside the timbers,
pulled astride, and rowed hard with my hands
to pass by Scylla. Never could I have passed her
had not the Father of gods and men,[78] this time,
kept me from her eyes. Once through the strait,
nine days I drifted in the open sea
before I made shore, buoyed up by the gods,
upon Ogygia[79] Isle. The dangerous nymph
Calypso lives and sings there, in her beauty,
and she received me, loved me.

But why tell
the same tale that I told last night in hall
to you and to your lady? Those adventures
made a long evening, and I do not hold
with tiresome repetition of a story."

NOTES

77. bole (bohl) *n.* tree trunk.

78. Father . . . men Zeus.

79. Ogygia (o JIHJ ee uh)

Comprehension Check

Complete the following items after you finish your first read.

1. Why does Odysseus leave home?

2. Why does Cyclops live alone in a cave?

3. Why does Odysseus go to Hades, the land of the dead?

4. To whom does Odysseus speak in the land of the dead?

5. **Notebook** Confirm your understanding of the text by writing a summary.

RESEARCH

Research to Clarify Choose at least one unfamiliar detail from the text. Briefly research that detail. In what way does the information you learned shed light on an aspect of the epic?

Research to Explore This epic poem may spark your curiosity to learn more. Briefly research one of the locations mentioned in the poem. You may want to share what you discover with the class.

Close Read the Text

Reread Cyclops' prayer to Poseidon (lines 484–493). Mark his initial request and his alternative request. How do these two requests reflect ancient Greek beliefs about the gods' involvement in the mortal world?

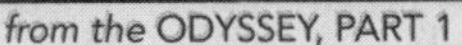

from the ODYSSEY, PART 1

Analyze the Text

CITE TEXTUAL EVIDENCE to support your answers.

Notebook Respond to these questions.

1. (a) What does Odysseus want more than anything else?
   (b) **Analyze** How does this goal give structure to the epic?
2. (a) What two aspects of the life of Cyclopes make Odysseus think that they are uncivilized before he interacts with one?
   (b) **Compare and Contrast** How are the lives of Cyclopes different from the lives of Odysseus and his men?
3. (a) How does Eurylochus convince Odysseus' men to kill Helios' cattle?
   (b) **Analyze** What value do you think Eurylochus is appealing to in his argument?
4. **Essential Question:** *What can we learn from a journey?* What have you learned about the power of journeys by reading Part 1 of the *Odyssey*?

Tool Kit
Close-Read Guide and Model Annotation

LANGUAGE DEVELOPMENT

Concept Vocabulary

plundered	avenge	ventured
fugitives	dispatched	tactics

Why These Words? These concept vocabulary words relate to actions during war. How does each word contribute to meaning in the text? What other words in the selection connect to this concept?

Practice

Notebook Confirm your understanding of these words from the text by using them in a paragraph. Include context clues that hint at each word's meaning.

WORD NETWORK

Add interesting words related to journeys from the text to your Word Network.

Word Study

Notebook **Word Parts** Many English words are formed by adding prefixes, suffixes, or both to existing words. The word *tactic*, for example, is a noun that means "action planned to achieve a certain purpose." Frequently appearing in military contexts, it is often used in the plural. Knowing the meaning of *tactic* can help you figure out that a *tactician* is a person who plans actions to accomplish certain tasks, a valuable person in a war. Divide the following words into their word parts, and use the word parts to write a definition for each word: *marvelous*, *consultation*, *frightful*.

STANDARDS

Language

- Identify and correctly use patterns of word changes that indicate different meanings or parts of speech.
- Demonstrate understanding of figurative language, word relationships, and nuances in word meanings.

from the ODYSSEY, PART 1

STANDARDS

Reading Literature

- Analyze how complex characters develop over the course of a text, interact with other characters, and advance the plot or develop the theme.
- Analyze how an author's choices concerning how to structure a text, order events within it, and manipulate time create such effects as mystery, tension, or surprise.
- Analyze a particular point of view or cultural experience reflected in a work of literature from outside the United States, drawing on a wide reading of world literature.

Analyze Craft and Structure

Oral Tradition Storytellers and poets of long ago did not write down the tales they told. Instead, they learned the stories and poems of their culture from others and recited them from memory. The term **oral tradition** refers to the literature that was passed down through the ages by word of mouth. Eventually, these spoken stories and poems were retold in writing.

One form of literature that has come from the oral tradition is the **epic**, a long narrative poem that is central to a culture's national identity. The narrative in an epic centers around an **epic hero**, a larger-than-life character who possesses traits that his society values most highly.

Traditional epics like the *Odyssey* use certain plot devices, or structures, that both provide information and allow the story to unfold in an exciting way. Many epics begin ***in medias res***, which means "in the middle of things." Major events occurred before the action of the poem begins, and the audience is thrust into the middle of the story. The hero's adventures are often recounted in a **flashback**, a scene that interrupts a narrative to relate earlier events.

Practice

CITE TEXTUAL EVIDENCE to support your answers.

Notebook Respond to these questions.

1. In this epic, the hero Odysseus recounts his own adventures. In what way does this affect your reaction to the events he describes? Cite an example from the text to support your response.
2. Odysseus recounts most of the action in Part 1 in the form of a flashback. List the events of Part 1 in chronological order, beginning with the end of the Trojan War.
3. (a) Using the chart, identify three actions that Odysseus performs. (b) For each action, identify the character trait that it reveals. (c) Using the results of your analysis, explain which character traits the ancient Greeks admired most.

ACTION	CHARACTER TRAIT

Speaking and Listening

Assignment

With two classmates, write and deliver a **conversation** among ordinary Greeks discussing Odysseus' exploits. Each character's statements should reflect ancient Greek values shown in Part I of the *Odyssey*.

1. **Develop Your Characters** Decide each character's traits and attitude toward Odysseus. For example, one character may admire Odysseus, while another may be critical of his leadership. One may know Odysseus well, while another may have barely heard of him.

Use the chart to make notes about your characters and their attitudes. Each description should include the character's name, age, occupation, and other important information, such as whether he or she knows Odysseus personally.

	FIRST CHARACTER	SECOND CHARACTER	THIRD CHARACTER
Description			
Attitude toward Odysseus			

2. **Plan Your Conversation** As a group, agree on an overall plan for the conversation, but leave room for improvisation.
3. **Prepare Your Delivery** Practice your conversation with your group. Use the following techniques to help communicate ideas clearly and to make your conversation entertaining.
   - As you speak, use verbal techniques—such as varied tone, volume, and pace—to convey different emotions and to make your conversation realistic.
   - In addition, use nonverbal techniques—such as gestures, facial expressions, and eye contact—to help convey your ideas.
4. **Evaluate Conversations** As your classmates deliver their conversations, watch and listen attentively. Use an evaluation guide like the one shown to analyze their delivery.

EVALUATION GUIDE

Rate each statement on a scale of 1 (not demonstrated) to 4 (demonstrated).

☐ The speakers clearly conveyed their characters' traits.

☐ The speakers clearly conveyed their characters' attitudes toward Odysseus.

☐ The speakers used verbal techniques effectively.

☐ The speakers used nonverbal techniques effectively.

TIP

COLLABORATION

One of the rules of improvisation is that you must respond to what your fellow actor says or does, even if it's not what you planned. Remember that as you are presenting your conversation.

EVIDENCE LOG

Before moving on to a new selection, go to your Evidence Log and record what you learned from Part 1 of the *Odyssey*.

STANDARDS

Speaking and Listening

- Initiate and participate effectively in a range of collaborative discussions with diverse partners on *grades 9-10 topics, texts, and issues,* building on others' ideas and expressing their own clearly and persuasively.
- Come to discussions prepared, having read and researched material under study; explicitly draw on that preparation by referring to evidence from texts and other research on the topic or issue to stimulate a thoughtful, well-reasoned exchange of ideas.
- Work with peers to set rules for collegial discussions and decision-making, clear goals and deadlines, and individual roles as needed.

About the Poet

Homer (approx. 850–750 B.C.) is credited with writing the *Iliad* and the *Odyssey*. For almost 3,000 years, these epic poems have captured readers' imaginations and inspired countless works of art and literature.

from the Odyssey, Part 2

Concept Vocabulary

You will encounter the following words as you read the *Odyssey*, Part 2. Before reading, note how familiar you are with each word. Then, rank the words in order from most familiar (1) to least familiar (6).

WORD	YOUR RANKING
craft	
dissemble	
incredulity	
bemusing	
guise	
deceived	

After completing the first read, come back to the concept vocabulary and review your rankings. Mark changes to your original rankings as needed.

Tool Kit
First-Read Guide and Model Annotation

First Read EPIC POEM

Apply these strategies as you conduct your first read. You will have an opportunity to complete the close-read notes after your first read.

NOTICE *whom* the story is about, *what* happens, *where* and *when* it happens, and *why* those involved react as they do.

ANNOTATE by marking vocabulary and key passages you want to revisit.

CONNECT ideas within the selection to what you already know and what you have already read.

RESPOND by completing the Comprehension Check and by writing a brief summary of the selection.

First Read: NOTICE, ANNOTATE, CONNECT, RESPOND

STANDARDS

Reading Literature
By the end of grade 9, read and comprehend literature, including stories, dramas, and poems, in the grades 9–10 text complexity band proficiently, with scaffolding as needed at the high end of the range.

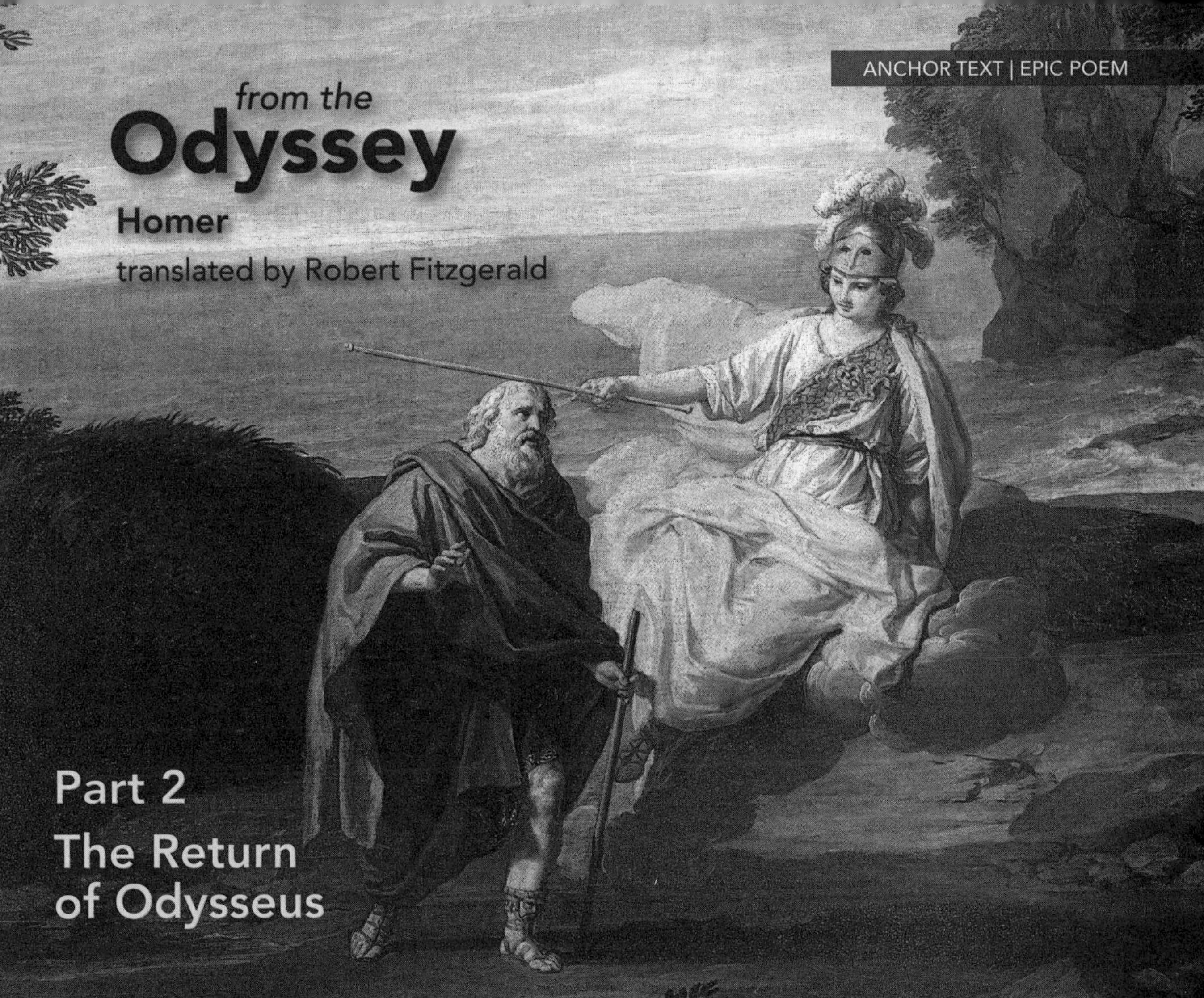

BACKGROUND

The Greek concept of hospitality, *xenia,* was very important in Greek culture and plays a role in Odysseus' tale. Some scholars believe that this value is based on Greek religious belief. Since the Greek gods could take multiple earthly forms, there was always the possibility that the stranger at the door was a god in disguise. Thus, Greeks opened their homes to strangers. In Part 2, as Odysseus returns home, it is clear that this cultural practice has created some problems.

"Twenty years gone, and I am back again . . ."

Odysseus has finished telling his story to the Phaeacians. The next day, young Phaeacian noblemen conduct him home by ship. He arrives in Ithaca after an absence of twenty years. The goddess Athena appears and informs him of the situation at home. Numerous suitors, believing Odysseus to be dead, have been continually seeking the hand of his wife, Penelope, in marriage, while overrunning Odysseus' palace and enjoying themselves at Penelope's expense. Moreover, they are plotting to

NOTES

murder Odysseus' son, Telemachus, before he can inherit his father's lands. Telemachus, who, like Penelope, still hopes for his father's return, has journeyed to Pylos and Sparta to learn what he can about his father's fate. Athena disguises Odysseus as a beggar and directs him to the hut of Eumaeus,[1] *his old and faithful swineherd. While Odysseus and Eumaeus are eating breakfast, Telemachus arrives. Athena then appears to Odysseus.*

NOTES

1. ***Eumaeus*** (yoo MEE uhs)

. . . From the air
she walked, taking the form of a tall woman,
handsome and clever at her **craft**, and stood
beyond the gate in plain sight of Odysseus,
unseen, though, by Telemachus, unguessed,
for not to everyone will gods appear.
Odysseus noticed her; so did the dogs,
who cowered whimpering away from her. She only
nodded, signing to him with her brows,
a sign he recognized. Crossing the yard,
he passed out through the gate in the stockade
to face the goddess. There she said to him:
"Son of Laertes and the gods of old,
Odysseus, master of landways and seaways,
dissemble to your son no longer now.
The time has come: tell him how you together
will bring doom on the suitors in the town.
I shall not be far distant then, for I
myself desire battle."

craft (kraft) *n.* activity that requires skill

dissemble (dih SEHM buhl) *v.* put on an appearance or disguise

CLOSE READ

ANNOTATE: Mark the indications of a direct quotation in lines 1004–1015.

QUESTION: Why does Homer choose to provide Athena's direct words in this passage rather than summarize her speech to Odysseus?

CONCLUDE: What does this speech suggest about the relationship between gods and mortals, especially Odysseus?

Saying no more,
she tipped her golden wand upon the man,
making his cloak pure white, and the knit tunic
fresh around him. Lithe and young she made him,
ruddy with sun, his jawline clean, the beard
no longer gray upon his chin. And she
withdrew when she had done.

Then Lord Odysseus
reappeared—and his son was thunderstruck.
Fear in his eyes, he looked down and away
As though it were a god, and whispered:

"Stranger,
you are no longer what you were just now!
Your cloak is new; even your skin! You are
one of the gods who rule the sweep of heaven!
Be kind to us, we'll make you fair oblation[2]
and gifts of hammered gold. Have mercy on us!"

2. **oblation** (ob LAY shuhn) *n.* offering to a god.

The noble and enduring man replied:

"No god. Why take me for a god? No, no.
I am that father whom your boyhood lacked
and suffered pain for lack of. I am he."

Held back too long, the tears ran down his cheeks
as he embraced his son.
Only Telemachus,
uncomprehending, wild
with **incredulity** cried out:
"You cannot
be my father Odysseus! Meddling spirits
conceived this trick to twist the knife in me!
No man of woman born could work these wonders
by his own craft, unless a god came into it
with ease to turn him young or old at will.
I swear you were in rags and old,
and here you stand like one of the immortals!"

Odysseus brought his ranging mind to bear
and said:
"This is not princely, to be swept
away by wonder at your father's presence.
No other Odysseus will ever come,
for he and I are one, the same; his bitter
fortune and his wanderings are mine.
Twenty years gone, and I am back again
on my own island.
As for my change of skin,
that is a charm Athena, Hope of Soldiers,
uses as she will; she has the knack
to make me seem a beggar man sometimes
and sometimes young, with finer clothes about me.
It is no hard things for the gods of heaven
to glorify a man or bring him low."

When he had spoken, down he sat.
Then, throwing
his arms around this marvel of a father
Telemachus began to weep. Salt tears
rose from the wells of longing in both men,
and cries burst from both as keen and fluttering
as those of the great taloned hawk,
whose nestlings farmers take before they fly.
So helplessly they cried, pouring out tears,
and might have gone on weeping so till sundown,
had not Telemachus said:

NOTES

incredulity (ihn kruh DYOO luh tee) *n.* doubt

CLOSE READ

ANNOTATE: In lines 1048–1050, mark words relating to the concept of identity.

QUESTION: Why do you think Homer places such emphasis on the idea of identity?

CONCLUDE: How do these words emphasize Odysseus' message to his son?

NOTES

3. **cutter** *n.* small, swift ship or boat carried aboard a large ship to transport personnel or supplies.

4. **in their prime** in the best or most vigorous stage of their lives.

"Dear father! Tell me
what kind of vessel put you here ashore
on Ithaca? Your sailors, who were they?
I doubt you made it, walking on the sea!"

Then said Odysseus, who had borne the barren sea:

"Only plain truth shall I tell you, child.
Great seafarers, the Phaeacians, gave me passage
as they give other wanderers. By night
over the open ocean, while I slept,
they brought me in their cutter,[3] set me down
on Ithaca, with gifts of bronze and gold
and stores of woven things. By the gods' will
these lie all hidden in a cave. I came
to this wild place, directed by Athena,
so that we might lay plans to kill our enemies.
Count up the suitors for me, let me know
what men at arms are there, how many men.
I must put all my mind to it, to see
if we two by ourselves can take them on
or if we should look round for help."

Telemachus
replied:
"O father, all my life your fame
as a fighting man has echoed in my ears—
your skill with weapons and the tricks of war—
but what you speak of is a staggering thing,
beyond imagining, for me. How can two men
do battle with a houseful in their prime?[4]
For I must tell you this is no affair
of ten or even twice ten men, but scores,
throngs of them. You shall see, here and now.
The number from Dulichium alone
is fifty-two picked men, with armorers,
a half dozen; twenty-four came from Same,
twenty from Zacynthus; our own island
accounts for twelve, high-ranked, and their retainers,
Medon the crier, and the Master Harper,
besides a pair of handymen at feasts.
If we go in against all these
I fear we pay in salt blood for your vengeance.
You must think hard if you would conjure up
the fighting strength to take us through."

Odysseus
who had endured the long war and the sea
answered:

"I'll tell you now.
Suppose Athena's arm is over us, and Zeus
her father's, must I rack my brains for more?"

Clearheaded Telemachus looked hard and said:

"Those two are great defenders, no one doubts it,
but throned in the serene clouds overhead;
other affairs of men and gods they have
to rule over."

And the hero answered:
"Before long they will stand to right and left of us
in combat, in the shouting, when the test comes—
our nerve against the suitors' in my hall.
Here is your part: at break of day tomorrow
home with you, go mingle with our princes.
The swineherd later on will take me down
the port-side trail—a beggar, by my looks,
hangdog and old. If they make fun of me
in my own courtyard, let your ribs cage up
your springing heart, no matter what I suffer,
no matter if they pull me by the heels
or practice shots at me, to drive me out.
Look on, hold down your anger. You may even
plead with them, by heaven! in gentle terms
to quit their horseplay—not that they will heed you,
rash as they are, facing their day of wrath.
Now fix the next step in your mind.

Athena,
counseling me, will give me word, and I
shall signal to you, nodding: at that point
round up all armor, lances, gear of war
left in our hall, and stow the lot away
back in the vaulted storeroom. When the suitors
miss those arms and question you, be soft
in what you say: answer:

'I thought I'd move them
out of the smoke. They seemed no longer those
bright arms Odysseus left us years ago
when he went off to Troy. Here where the fire's
hot breath came, they had grown black and drear.
One better reason, too, I had from Zeus:
suppose a brawl starts up when you are drunk,

NOTES

CLOSE READ

ANNOTATE: In lines 1120–1132, mark the words Odysseus uses to tell his son what he should do if the suitors abuse Odysseus.

QUESTION: What do these words suggest about Telemachus' emotions?

CONCLUDE: How do these words express Odysseus' sense of his son's love for him?

NOTES

you might be crazed and bloody one another,
and that would stain your feast, your courtship.
Tempered
iron can magnetize a man.'
Say that.
But put aside two broadswords and two spears
for our own use, two oxhide shields nearby
when we go into action. Pallas Athena
and Zeus All-Provident will see you through,
bemusing our young friends.
Now one thing more.
If son of mine you are and blood of mine,
let no one hear Odysseus is about.
Neither Laertes, nor the swineherd here,
nor any slave, nor even Penelope.

bemusing (bih MYOOZ ihng) *adj.* confusing; bewildering

But you and I alone must learn how far
the women are corrupted; we should know
how to locate good men among our hands
the loyal and respectful, and the shirkers[5]
who take you lightly, as alone and young."

5. **shirkers** (SHURK uhrz) *n.* people who get out of doing what needs to be done.

Argus

Odysseus heads for town with Eumaeus. Outside the palace, Odysseus's old dog, Argus, is lying at rest as his long-absent master approaches.

While he spoke
an old hound, lying near, pricked up his ears
and lifted up his muzzle. This was Argus,
trained as a puppy by Odysseus,
but never taken on a hunt before
his master sailed for Troy. The young men, afterward,
hunted wild goats with him, and hare, and deer,
but he had grown old in his master's absence.
Treated as rubbish now, he lay at last
upon a mass of dung before the gates—
manure of mules and cows, piled there until
fieldhands could spread it on the king's estate.
Abandoned there, and half destroyed with flies,
old Argus lay.
But when he knew he heard
Odysseus's voice nearby, he did his best

to wag his tail, nose down, with flattened ears,
having no strength to move nearer his master.
And the man looked away,
wiping a salt tear from his cheek; but he
hid this from Eumaeus. Then he said:

"I marvel that they leave this hound to lie
here on the dung pile;
he would have been a fine dog, from the look of him,
though I can't say as to his power and speed
when he was young. You find the same good build
in house dogs, table dogs landowners keep
all for style."
And you replied, Eumaeus:

"A hunter owned him—but the man is dead
in some far place. If this old hound could show
the form he had when Lord Odysseus left him,
going to Troy, you'd see him swift and strong.
He never shrank from any savage thing
he'd brought to bay in the deep woods; on the scent
no other dog kept up with him. Now misery
has him in leash. His owner died abroad,
and here the women slaves will take no care of him.
You know how servants are: without a master
they have no will to labor, or excel.
For Zeus who views the wide world takes away
half the manhood of a man, that day
he goes into captivity and slavery."

Eumaeus crossed the court and went straight forward
into the megaron[6] among the suitors:
but death and darkness in that instant closed
the eyes of Argus, who had seen his master,
Odysseus, after twenty years.

NOTES

CLOSE READ

ANNOTATE: In lines 1185–1196, mark adjectives and nouns Odysseus and Eumaeus use to describe the dog as he once was.

QUESTION: What do these words have in common?

CONCLUDE: How do they emphasize the sadness of the dog now?

6. **megaron** (MEHG uh ron) *n.* great, central hall of the house, usually containing a center hearth.

Penelope, Odysseus' wife, in her home overrun with suitors.

The Suitors

Still disguised as a beggar, Odysseus enters his home. He is confronted by the haughty[7] suitor Antinous.[8]

But here Antinous broke in, shouting:

"God!

What evil wind blew in this pest?

Get over,

stand in the passage! Nudge my table, will you?
Egyptian whips are sweet
to what you'll come to here, you nosing rat,
making your pitch to everyone!
These men have bread to throw away on you
because it is not theirs. Who cares? Who spares
another's food, when he has more than plenty?"

With guile Odysseus drew away, then said:

"A pity that you have more looks than heart.
You'd grudge a pinch of salt from your own larder
to your own handyman. You sit here, fat
on others' meat, and cannot bring yourself
to rummage out a crust of bread for me!"

Then anger made Antinous' heart beat hard,
and, glowering under his brows, he answered:

"Now!

You think you'll shuffle off and get away
after that impudence?[9] Oh, no you don't!"

The stool he let fly hit the man's right shoulder
on the packed muscle under the shoulder blade—
like solid rock, for all the effect one saw.
Odysseus only shook his head, containing
thoughts of bloody work, as he walked on,
then sat, and dropped his loaded bag again
upon the door sill. Facing the whole crowd
he said, and eyed them all:

"One word only,

my lords, and suitors of the famous queen.
One thing I have to say.
There is no pain, no burden for the heart
when blows come to a man, and he defending
his own cattle—his own cows and lambs.

NOTES

7. **haughty** (HAWT ee) *adj.* arrogant.

8. **Antinous** (an TIHN oh uhs)

9. **impudence** (IHM pyoo duhns) *n.* quality of being shamelessly bold; disrespectfulness

Here it was otherwise. Antinous
hit me for being driven on by hunger—
how many bitter seas men cross for hunger!
If beggars interest the gods, if there are Furies[10]
pent in the dark to avenge a poor man's wrong, then may
Antinous meet his death before his wedding day!"
Then said Eupeithes's son, Antinous:
"Enough.
Eat and be quiet where you are, or shamble elsewhere,
unless you want these lads to stop your mouth
pulling you by the heels, or hands and feet,
over the whole floor, till your back is peeled!"

But now the rest were mortified, and someone
spoke from the crowd of young bucks to rebuke him:

"A poor show, that—hitting this famished tramp—
bad business, if he happened to be a god.
You know they go in foreign **guise**, the gods do,
looking like strangers, turning up
in towns and settlements to keep an eye
on manners, good or bad."
But at this notion
Antinous only shrugged.
Telemachus,
after the blow his father bore, sat still
without a tear, though his heart felt the blow.
Slowly he shook his head from side to side,
containing murderous thoughts.
Penelope
on the higher level of her room had heard
the blow, and knew who gave it. Now she murmured:

"Would god you could be hit yourself, Antinous—
hit by Apollo's bowshot!"

And Eurynome[11]
her housekeeper, put in:

"He and no other?
If all we pray for came to pass, not one
would live till dawn!"

Her gentle mistress said:

"Oh, Nan, they are a bad lot; they intend
ruin for all of us; but Antinous

NOTES

10. Furies (FYUR eez) *n.* three terrible female spirits who punish the doers of unavenged crimes.

guise (gyz) *n.* outward appearance

CLOSE READ

ANNOTATE: In lines 1261–1270, mark the noun that appears three times. Then, mark its synonym, which appears twice.

QUESTION: What does this repetition emphasize?

CONCLUDE: How does deliberate use of repetition help reveal the feelings of Odysseus' son and wife?

11. Eurynome (yoo RIHN uhm ee)

appears a blacker-hearted hound than any.
Here is a poor man come, a wanderer,
driven by want to beg his bread, and everyone
in hall gave bits, to cram his bag—only
Antinous threw a stool, and banged his shoulder!"

So she described it, sitting in her chamber
among her maids—while her true lord was eating.
Then she called in the forester and said:

"Go to that man on my behalf, Eumaeus,
and send him here, so I can greet and question him.
Abroad in the great world, he may have heard
rumors about Odysseus—may have known him!"

NOTES

Penelope

In the evening, Penelope interrogates the old beggar.

"Friend, let me ask you first of all:
who are you, where do you come from, of what nation
and parents were you born?"
And he replied:
"My lady, never a man in the wide world
should have a fault to find with you. Your name
has gone out under heaven like the sweet
honor of some god-fearing king, who rules
in equity over the strong: his black lands bear
both wheat and barley, fruit trees laden bright,
new lambs at lambing time—and the deep sea
gives great hauls of fish by his good strategy,
so that his folk fare well.

O my dear lady,
this being so, let it suffice to ask me
of other matters—not my blood, my homeland.
Do not enforce me to recall my pain.
My heart is sore; but I must not be found
sitting in tears here, in another's house:
it is not well forever to be grieving.
One of the maids might say—or you might think—
I had got maudlin over cups of wine."

NOTES

12. carriage *n.* posture.

13. Zacynthus (za SIHN thuhs)

14. Ruses (ROOZ ihz) *n.* tricks.

deceived (dih SEEVD) *v.* lied to; tricked

CLOSE READ

ANNOTATE: In the stanza beginning on line 1335, mark the words having to do with time and duration.

QUESTION: What do these words emphasize in Penelope's story?

CONCLUDE: How do they confirm her fidelity to Odysseus?

And Penelope replied:

"Stranger, my looks,
my face, my carriage,[12] were soon lost or faded
when the Achaeans crossed the sea to Troy,
Odysseus my lord among the rest.
If he returned, if he were here to care for me,
I might be happily renowned!
But grief instead heaven sent me—years of pain.
Sons of the noblest families on the islands,
Dulichium, Same, wooded Zacynthus,[13]
with native Ithacans, are here to court me,
against my wish; and they consume this house.
Can I give proper heed to guest or suppliant
or herald on the realm's affairs?

How could I?
wasted with longing for Odysseus, while here
they press for marriage.

Ruses[14] served my turn
to draw the time out—first a close-grained web
I had the happy thought to set up weaving
on my big loom in hall. I said, that day:
'Young men—my suitors, now my lord is dead,
let me finish my weaving before I marry,
or else my thread will have been spun in vain.
It is a shroud I weave for Lord Laertes
When cold Death comes to lay him on his bier.
The country wives would hold me in dishonor
if he, with all his fortune, lay unshrouded.'
I reached their hearts that way, and they agreed.
So every day I wove on the great loom,
but every night by torchlight I unwove it;
and so for three years I **deceived** the Achaeans.

But when the seasons brought a fourth year on,
as long months waned, and the long days were spent,
through impudent folly in the slinking maids
they caught me—clamored up to me at night;
I had no choice then but to finish it.
And now, as matters stand at last,
I have no strength left to evade a marriage,
cannot find any further way; my parents
urge it upon me, and my son
will not stand by while they eat up his property.
He comprehends it, being a man full-grown,
able to oversee the kind of house
Zeus would endow with honor.

But you too
confide in me, tell me your ancestry.
You were not born of mythic oak or stone."

Penelope again asks the beggar to tell about himself. He makes up a tale in which Odysseus is mentioned and declares that Penelope's husband will soon be home.

"You see, then, he is alive and well, and headed
homeward now, no more to be abroad
far from his island, his dear wife and son.
Here is my sworn word for it. Witness this,
god of the zenith, noblest of the gods,[15]
and Lord Odysseus's hearthfire, now before me:
I swear these things shall turn out as I say.
Between this present dark and one day's ebb,
after the wane, before the crescent moon,
Odysseus will come."

NOTES

15. **god of the zenith, noblest of the gods** Zeus.

The Challenge

Pressed by the suitors to choose a husband from among them, Penelope says she will marry the man who can string Odysseus's bow and shoot an arrow through twelve ax handle sockets. The suitors try and fail. Still in disguise, Odysseus asks for a turn and gets it.

And Odysseus took his time,
turning the bow, tapping it, every inch,
for borings that termites might have made
while the master of the weapon was abroad.
The suitors were now watching him, and some
jested among themselves:

"A bow lover!"

"Dealer in old bows!"

"Maybe he has one like it
at home!"

"Or has an itch to make one for himself."

"See how he handles it, the sly old buzzard!"

And one disdainful suitor added this:
"May his fortune grow an inch for every inch he bends it!"

NOTES

CLOSE READ

ANNOTATE: In lines 1378–1383, mark words that indicate or describe sounds.

QUESTION: Why do you think the poet uses these words?

CONCLUDE: How do these words intensify the description of the action?

16. **nocked** set an arrow into the bowstring.

But the man skilled in all ways of contending,
satisfied by the great bow's look and heft,
like a musician, like a harper, when
with quiet hand upon his instrument
he draws between his thumb and forefinger
a sweet new string upon a peg: so effortlessly
Odysseus in one motion strung the bow.
Then slid his right hand down the cord and plucked it,
so the taut gut vibrating hummed and sang
a swallow's note.
                              In the hushed hall it smote the suitors
and all their faces changed. Then Zeus thundered
overhead, one loud crack for a sign.
And Odysseus laughed within him that the son
of crooked-minded Cronus had flung that omen down.
He picked one ready arrow from his table
where it lay bare: the rest were waiting still
in the quiver for young men's turn to come.
He nocked[16] it, let it rest across the handgrip,
And drew the string and grooved butt of the arrow,
Aiming from where he sat upon the stool.

                                                            Now flashed
arrow from twanging bow clean as a whistle
through every socket ring, and grazed not one,
to thud with heavy brazen head beyond.
                                                            Then quietly
Odysseus said:

                                        "Telemachus, the stranger
you welcomed in your hall has not disgraced you.
I did not miss, neither did I take all day
stringing the bow. My hand and eye are sound,
not so contemptible as the young men say.
The hour has come to cook their lordships' mutton—
supper by daylight. Other amusements later,
with song and harping that adorn a feast."

He dropped his eyes and nodded, and the prince
Telemachus, true son of King Odysseus,
belted his sword on, clapped hand to his spear,
and with a clink and glitter of keen bronze
stood by his chair, in the forefront near his father.

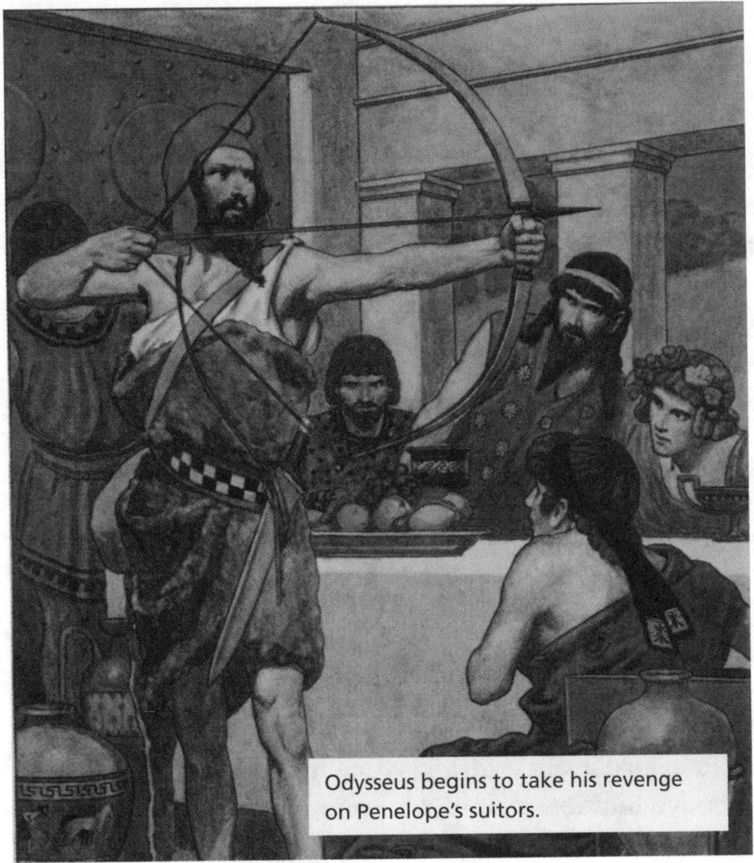
Odysseus begins to take his revenge on Penelope's suitors.

NOTES

Odysseus' Revenge

Now shrugging off his rags the wiliest[17] fighter of the islands
leapt and stood on the broad doorsill, his own bow in his hand.
He poured out at his feet a rain of arrows from the quiver
and spoke to the crowd:

"So much for that. Your clean-cut game is over.
Now watch me hit a target that no man has hit before,
if I can make this shot. Help me, Apollo."

He drew to his fist the cruel head of an arrow for Antinous
just as the young man leaned to lift his beautiful drinking cup,
embossed, two-handled, golden: the cup was in his fingers:
the wine was even at his lips: and did he dream of death?
How could he? In that revelry[18] amid his throng of friends
who would imagine a single foe—though a strong foe indeed—
could dare to bring death's pain on him and darkness on his eyes?
Odysseus's arrow hit him under the chin
and punched up to the feathers through his throat.

17. **wiliest** (WYL ee uhst) *adj.* craftiest; slyest.

CLOSE READ

ANNOTATE: In lines 1412–1414, mark adjectives that describe the drinking cup.

QUESTION: Why do you think the poet describes the cup in such detail and with these words?

CONCLUDE: How does the description heighten the effect of Odysseus' action?

18. **revelry** (REHV uhl ree) *n.* noisy partying.

NOTES

19. **Eurymachus** (yoo RIH muh kuhs)

Backward and down he went, letting the winecup fall
from his shocked hand. Like pipes his nostrils jetted
crimson runnels, a river of mortal red,
and one last kick upset his table
knocking the bread and meat to soak in dusty blood.
Now as they craned to see their champion where he lay
the suitors jostled in uproar down the hall,
everyone on his feet. Wildly they turned and scanned
the walls in the long room for arms; but not a shield,
not a good ashen spear was there for a man to take and
throw.
All they could do was yell in outrage at Odysseus:

"Foul! to shoot at a man! That was your last shot!"
"Your own throat will be slit for this!"
"Our finest lad is down!
You killed the best on Ithaca."
"Buzzards will tear your eyes out!"

For they imagined as they wished—that it was a wild shot,
an unintended killing—fools, not to comprehend
they were already in the grip of death.
But glaring under his brows Odysseus answered:

"You yellow dogs, you thought I'd never make it
home from the land of Troy. You took my house to
plunder . . .
You dared bid for my wife while I was still alive.
Contempt was all you had for the gods who rule wide
heaven,
contempt for what men say of you hereafter.
Your last hour has come. You die in blood."

As they all took this in, sickly green fear
pulled at their entrails, and their eyes flickered
looking for some hatch or hideaway from death.
Eurymachus[19] alone could speak. He said:

"If you are Odysseus of Ithaca come back,
all that you say these men have done is true.
Rash actions, many here, more in the countryside.
But here he lies, the man who cause them all.
Antinous was the ringleader, he whipped us on
to do these things. He cared less for a marriage
than for the power Cronion has denied him
As king of Ithaca. For that
he tried to trap your son and would have killed him.
He is dead now and has his portion. Spare

your own people. As for ourselves, we'll make
restitution of wine and meat consumed,
and add, each one, a tithe of twenty oxen
with gifts of bronze and gold to warm your heart.
Meanwhile we cannot blame you for your anger."

Odysseus glowered under his black brows
and said:
"Not for the whole treasure of your fathers,
all you enjoy, lands, flocks, or any gold
put up by others, would I hold my hand.
There will be killing till the score is paid.
You forced yourselves upon this house. Fight your way out,
or run it, if you think you'll escape death.
I doubt one man of you skins by."

They felt their knees fail, and their hearts—but heard
Eurymachus for the last time rallying them.
"Friends," he said, "the man is implacable.
Now that he's got his hands on bow and quiver
he'll shoot from the big doorstone there
until he kills us to the last man.
Fight, I say,
let's remember the joy of it. Swords out!
Hold up your tables to deflect his arrows.
After me, everyone: rush him where he stands.
If we can budge him from the door, if we can pass
into the town, we'll call out men to chase hm.
This fellow with his bow will shoot no more."

He drew his own sword as he spoke, a broadsword of fine bronze,
honed like a razor on either edge. Then crying hoarse and loud
he hurled himself at Odysseus. But the kingly man let fly
an arrow at that instant, and the quivering feathered butt
sprang to the nipple of his breast as the barb stuck in his liver.
The bright broadsword clanged down. He lurched and fell aside,
pitching across his table. His cup, his bread and meat,
were spilt and scattered far and wide, and his head slammed on the ground.
Revulsion, anguish in his heart, with both feet kicking out,
he downed his chair, while the shrouding wave of mist closed on his eyes.
Amphinomus now came running at Odysseus,
broadsword naked in his hand. He thought to make

NOTES

CLOSE READ

ANNOTATE: Mark the first two sentences of the stanza that begins on line 1484.

QUESTION: How are these lines different from those that go before them?

CONCLUSION: Why do you think the poet made this change when beginning a description of the battle?

NOTES

the great soldier give way at the door.
But with a spear throw from behind Telemachus hit him
between the shoulders, and the lancehead drove
clear through his chest. He left his feet and fell
forward, thudding, forehead against the ground.
Telemachus swerved around him, leaving the long dark spear
planted in Amphinomus. If he paused to yank it out
someone might jump him from behind or cut him down with a sword
at the moment he bent over. So he ran—ran from the tables
to his father's side and halted, panting, saying:

"Father let me bring you a shield and spear,
a pair of spears, a helmet.
I can arm on the run myself: I'll give
outfits to Eumaeus and this cowherd.
Better to have equipment."

Said Odysseus:
"Run then, while I hold them off with arrows
as long as the arrows last. When all are gone
if I'm alone they can dislodge me."

Quick
upon his father's word Telemachus
ran to the room where spears and armor lay.
He caught up four light shields, four pairs of spears,
four helms of war high-plumed with flowing manes,
and ran back, loaded down to his father's side.
He was the first to pull a helmet on
and slide his bare arm in a buckler strap.
The servants armed themselves, and all three took their stand
beside the master of battle.

While he had arrows
he aimed and shot, and every shot brought down
one of his huddling enemies.
But when all barbs had flown from the bowman's fist,
he leaned his bow in the bright entryway
beside the door, and armed: a four-ply shield
hard on his shoulder, and a crested helm,
horsetailed, nodding stormy upon his head,
then took his tough and bronze-shod spears. . . .

Aided by Athena, Odysseus, Telemachus, Eumaeus, and other faithful herdsmen kill all the suitors.

And Odysseus looked around him, narrow-eyed,
for any others who had lain hidden
while death's black fury passed.

In blood and dust
he saw that crowd all fallen, many and many slain.

Think of a catch that fishermen haul in to a half-moon bay
in a fine-meshed net from the whitecaps of the sea:
how all are poured out on the sand, in throes for the salt sea,
twitching their cold lives away in Helios' fiery air:
so lay the suitors heaped on one another.

Penelope's Test

Penelope tests Odysseus to prove he really is her husband.

Greathearted Odysseus, home at last,
was being bathed now by Eurynome
and rubbed with golden oil, and clothed again
in a fresh tunic and a cloak. Athena
lent him beauty, head to foot. She made him
taller, and massive, too, with crisping hair
in curls like petals of wild hyacinth
but all red-golden. Think of gold infused
on silver by a craftsman, whose fine art
Hephaestus[20] taught him, or Athena: one
whose work moves to delight: just so she lavished
beauty over Odysseus' head and shoulders.
He sat then in the same chair by the pillar,
facing his silent wife, and said:

"Strange woman,
the immortals of Olympus made you hard,
harder than any. Who else in the world
would keep aloof as you do from her husband
if he returned to her from years of trouble,
cast on his own land in the twentieth year?

Nurse, make up a bed for me to sleep on.
Her heart is iron in her breast."

Penelope
spoke to Odysseus now. She said:

NOTES

20. **Hephaestus** (hee FEHS tuhs) god of fire and metalworking.

NOTES

This illustration shows Odysseus' return to Penelope after an absence of twenty years.

"Strange man,
if man you are . . . This is no pride on my part
nor scorn for you—not even wonder, merely.
I know so well how you—how he—appeared
boarding the ship for Troy. But all the same . . .

Make up his bed for him, Eurycleia.
Place it outside the bedchamber my lord
built with his own hands. Pile the big bed
with fleeces, rugs, and sheets of purest linen."

With this she tried him to the breaking point,
and he turned on her in a flash raging:

"Woman, by heaven you've stung me now!
Who dared to move my bed?
No builder had the skill for that—unless
a god came down to turn the trick. No mortal
in his best days could budge it with a crowbar.
There is our pact and pledge, our secret sign,
built into that bed—my handiwork
and no one else's!

NOTES

An old trunk of olive
grew like a pillar on the building plot,
and I laid out our bedroom round that tree,
lined up the stone walls, built the walls and roof,
gave it a doorway and smooth-fitting doors.
Then I lopped off the silvery leaves and branches,
hewed and shaped that stump from the roots up
into a bedpost, drilled it, let it serve
as model for the rest. I planed them all,
inlaid them all with silver, gold, and ivory,
and stretched a bed between—a pliant web
of oxhide thongs dyed crimson.
There's our sign!
I know no more. Could someone else's hand
have sawn that trunk and dragged the frame away?"

Their secret! as she heard it told, her knees
grew tremulous and weak, her heart failed her.
With eyes brimming tears she ran to him,
throwing her arms around his neck, and kissed him,
murmuring:

NOTES

"Do not rage at me, Odysseus!
No one ever matched your caution! Think
what difficulty the gods gave: they denied us
life together in our prime and flowering years,
kept us from crossing into age together.
Forgive me, don't be angry. I could not
welcome you with love on sight! I armed myself
long ago against the frauds of men,
impostors who might come—and all those many
whose underhanded ways bring evil on! . . .
But here and now, what sign could be so clear
as this of our own bed?
No other man has ever laid eyes on it—
only my own slave, Actoris, that my father
sent with me as a gift—she kept our door.
You make my stiff heart know that I am yours."

Now from his breast into his eyes the ache
of longing mounted, and he wept at last,
his dear wife, clear and faithful, in his arms,
longed for as the sunwarmed earth is longed for by a swimmer
spent in rough water where his ship went down
under Poseidon's blows, gale winds and tons of sea.
Few men can keep alive through a big surf
to crawl, clotted with brine, on kindly beaches
in joy, in joy, knowing the abyss[21] behind:
and so she too rejoiced, her gaze upon her husband,
her white arms round him pressed as though forever.

21. **abyss** (uh BIHS) *n.* ocean depths.

The Ending

Odysseus is reunited with his father. Athena commands that peace prevail between Odysseus and the relatives of the slain suitors. Odysseus has regained his family and his kingdom.

Comprehension Check

Complete the following items after you finish your first read.

1. After twenty years, how does Odysseus finally get home?

2. What are Antinous and the others doing in Odysseus' house?

3. What test does Penelope use to choose a husband from among the suitors?

4. **Notebook** Confirm your understanding of the text by writing a summary.

RESEARCH

Research to Explore This epic poem may spark your curiosity to read more. Briefly research other works by Homer. You may want to share what you discover with the class.

Close Read the Text

1. This model, from lines 1116–1132 of the text, shows two sample annotations, along with questions and conclusions. Close read the passage and find another detail to annotate. Then, write a question and your conclusion.

ANNOTATE · QUESTION · Close Read · CONCLUDE

ANNOTATE: Odysseus describes in vivid language what Telemachus should do if the suitors mistreat his father.

QUESTION: What effect does the author's use of vivid language have on the reader?

CONCLUDE: The vivid language helps the reader imagine how Telemachus will feel.

Here is your part: at break of day tomorrow / home with you, go mingle with our princes. / The swineherd later on will take me down / the port-side trail—a beggar, by my looks, / hangdog and old. If they make fun of me / in my own courtyard, let your ribs cage up / your springing heart, no matter what I suffer, / no matter if they pull me by the heels or practice shots at me, to drive me out.

ANNOTATE: This phrase is repeated.

QUESTION: Why does the author repeat the phrase *no matter?*

CONCLUDE: The repetition emphasizes the many types of injustices that Odysseus is likely to face when the suitors mistreat him.

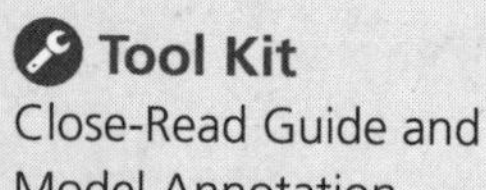

Tool Kit
Close-Read Guide and Model Annotation

2. For more practice, go back into the text and complete the close-read notes.

3. Revisit a section of the text you found important during your first read. Read this section closely, and **annotate** what you notice. Ask yourself **questions** such as "Why did the author make this choice?" What can you **conclude**?

Analyze the Text

CITE TEXTUAL EVIDENCE to support your answers.

Notebook Respond to these questions.

1. (a) Describe Antinous' treatment of Odysseus. (b) **Analyze** Why does Odysseus provoke Antinous to behave badly?

2. (a) What reasons does Odysseus give for taking revenge on the suitors? (b) **Interpret** Did Odysseus care more about what the suitors had stolen from him or about how they offended his honor? Explain.

3. **Essential Question** *What can we learn from a journey?* What have you learned about what a journey can teach people by reading this epic poem?

STANDARDS

Reading Literature
Analyze a particular point of view or cultural experience reflected in a work of literature from outside the United States, drawing on a wide reading of world literature.

Analyze Craft and Structure

Figurative Language Literature from the oral tradition is full of vivid language that made the works memorable and brought characters, settings, and events alive for listeners. **Figurative language** is language that is used imaginatively rather than literally. There are many types of figurative language, including metaphors, similes, and personification. A special form of simile—the epic simile—is particularly important in Homer's writing.

- A **simile** is a comparison of two fundamentally different things using the words *like* or *as*. For example, you might say that someone's eyes are "as blue as the sky." Similes usually suggest some quality other than the one that is directly stated. In this case, the simile suggests that the eyes are also lovely, like the sky. The same quality of loveliness would not be implied if the eyes were compared to a blue mailbox.
- An **epic simile** is an elaborate simile that may continue for several lines. Unlike a regular simile, which draws a relatively limited comparison and creates a single image, an epic simile might recall an entire place or story. In lines 1061–1065 of Part 2, the poet uses an epic simile to describe the cries of Odysseus and Telemachus when they are reunited.

> Telemachus began to weep. Salt tears
> rose from the wells of longing in both men,
> and cries burst from both as keen and fluttering
> as those of the great taloned hawk,
> whose nestlings farmers take before they fly.

Practice

CITE TEXTUAL EVIDENCE to support your answers.

Notebook Respond to these questions.

1. (a) Reread the epic simile in lines 1535–1539. Identify the two things being compared. (b) Explain why this is an effective simile.
2. (a) Use the chart to analyze the epic simile in lines 1613–1623. (b) Explain how Odysseus' feelings are like those of the swimmer.

THINGS BEING COMPARED	DETAILS OF SIMILE	PURPOSE

from the ODYSSEY, PART 2

Concept Vocabulary

craft	incredulity	guise
dissemble	bemusing	deceived

Why These Words? These concept words relate to ideas about honesty and dishonesty. When Athena tells Odysseus, "*dissemble* to your son no longer," she is telling him to stop pretending that he is a beggar and let his son know the truth. When Homer tells us that Telemachus is "wild with *incredulity*," he is saying that Telemachus cannot believe what Odysseus is telling him.

1. How does the concept vocabulary help readers understand the various layers of pretending and lying in Part 2 of the *Odyssey*?

2. What other words in the selection connect to the concepts of honesty and dishonesty?

Practice

Notebook The concept vocabulary words appear in Part 2 of the *Odyssey*.

1. Use each concept word in a sentence that demonstrates your understanding of the word's meaning.
2. In three of your sentences, challenge yourself to replace the concept word with one or two synonyms. How does the word change affect the meaning of your sentence? For example, which sentence is more descriptive?

WORD NETWORK

Add interesting words related to journeys from the text to your Word Network.

Word Study

Latin Root: *-sem- -sim-* The Latin root *-sim-* means "seem" or "like." In a few instances, such as in the word *dissemble*, the root is spelled with an *e* rather than an *i*.

1. Write a definition of *dissemble* based on your understanding of its root and context clues from the text.

2. Define these words that contain the same root: *resemble*, *similar*, *simulation*. Use a dictionary to verify your definitions.

STANDARDS

Language

- Demonstrate command of the conventions of standard English grammar and usage when writing or speaking.
- Apply knowledge of language to understand how language functions in different contexts, to make effective choices for meaning or style, and to comprehend more fully when reading or listening.
- Identify and correctly use patterns of word changes that indicate different meanings or parts of speech.

Author's Style

Word Order The order of words in a sentence varies from language to language, but it is usually very predictable within a language. In English, the subject of a sentence usually precedes the verb, unless the sentence is a question. Adjectives usually precede the nouns they modify. Adverbs usually follow the verbs they modify.

Most people do not notice word order unless it is changed. Poets often invert words, or reverse their positions, for the sake of meter, rhyme, or emphasis. The reversal of the normal word order in a sentence is known as **inverted word order.**

Both Homer and Robert Fitzgerald, the translator of this version of the epic, sometimes use inverted word order. One of the reasons Fitzgerald's translation of the *Odyssey* is easier to read than other translations is that he does not use inverted word order very often. When he does, he has a purpose. For example, line 1145 states, "One better reason, too, I had from Zeus." In this line, Fitzgerald emphasizes "one better reason" by putting it first.

Read It

Use this chart to identify the word or phrase in each passage from the *Odyssey* that is not in the predictable order.

PASSAGE	WORDS NOT IN PREDICTABLE ORDER
Lithe and young she made him, *ruddy with sun, his jawline clean, the beard* *no longer gray upon his chin.* *(lines 1018–1020)*	
When he had spoken, down he sat. *(line 1059)*	
They seemed no longer those *bright arms Odysseus left us years ago* *when he went off to Troy.* *(lines 1141–1143)*	
Now flashed *arrow from twanging bow clean as a whistle* *through every socket ring, and grazed not one,* *to thud with heavy brazen head beyond.* *(lines 1389–1392)*	

Write It

Notebook Rewrite each passage in the chart so that the words are in the usual order. Consider how the rewritten passages are different and whether they have the same power.

from the ODYSSEY, PART 2

Writing to Sources

A biography is a type of informative text in which the writer tells the life story of another person. Writers of biographies often include narrative elements such as character development, descriptions of settings, and plot sequences to capture and hold the reader's attention.

Assignment

Write a short **biography** of Odysseus based on details presented in the *Odyssey*. Include the basic facts of the hero's life and adventures, including his important relationships, and hold your reader's attention by describing dramatic situations in detail. Use the following guidelines:

- List events from the *Odyssey* that are suitable for your biography. Focus on events that reveal the character of Odysseus.
- Include quotations from the epic to add detail and depth.
- Share your biography with classmates, and compare the events you each chose to include. In your discussion, consider what makes some events more significant than others.
- Based on your discussion with classmates, consider whether your version of Odysseus' life is complete, accurate, and interesting to readers. Revise your work as needed.

Vocabulary and Conventions Connection Include several of the concept vocabulary words in your biography. Consider using inverted word order at certain points in your biography to call the reader's attention to significant events in Odysseus' life.

craft	incredulity	guise
dissemble	bemusing	deceived

Reflect on Your Writing

After you have written your biography, answer these questions.

1. How do you think writing your biography strengthened your understanding of the epic?

2. What advice would you give to another student writing a biography of a heroic figure?

3. **Why These Words?** The words you choose make a difference in your writing. Which words did you specifically choose to add power to your biography?

STANDARDS

Writing

Produce clear and coherent writing in which the development, organization, and style are appropriate to task, purpose, and audience.

Speaking and Listening

- Initiate and participate effectively in a range of collaborative discussions with diverse partners on *grades 9–10 topics, texts, and issues,* building on others' ideas and expressing their own clearly and persuasively.
- Evaluate a speaker's point of view, reasoning, and use of evidence and rhetoric, identifying any fallacious reasoning or exaggerated or distorted evidence.

Speaking and Listening

Assignment

Conduct a **debate** to decide whether Odysseus should be prosecuted for the murders of Penelope's suitors.

- Volunteers should make up opposing teams. One team will argue the affirmative—that Odysseus should be prosecuted—and the other will argue the negative. Each team will present an oral argument, stating its position and supporting it with text evidence.
- A panel of judges or the class as a whole can evaluate the arguments and decide which one has the most effective support.

First, reread the selection. Identify specific text details that relate to the murder of the suitors. Then, follow these steps to complete the assignment.

1. **State and Support the Position** Both affirmative and negative teams should prepare clear position statements and support these statements with strong reasons and relevant evidence from Part 2 of the *Odyssey*.
2. **Refute the Opposing Position** Both teams should also prepare arguments against the opposing team's position, using strong reasons and relevant text evidence to refute the position.
3. **Develop the Argument** Consider how to best organize the information in the argument. Plan to include an introduction to the issue, a body that conveys the main argument, and a conclusion that summarizes the position.
4. **Prepare Your Delivery** Practice delivering the oral argument to the judges. Include the following performance techniques to make the argument convincing:
   - Speak clearly, in an appropriate tone, and at an appropriate volume and rate.
   - Use appropriate facial expressions and gestures to convey your conviction.
5. **Evaluate Responses** Listen carefully as each team delivers its argument. Use an evaluation guide like the one shown to evaluate the argument.

EVALUATION GUIDE

Rate each statement on a scale of 1 (not demonstrated) to 5 (demonstrated).

☐ The position was clearly stated in the oral argument.

☐ The position was supported with relevant text evidence.

☐ The opposing team's position was clearly stated and effectively refuted.

☐ Debaters used appropriate facial expressions, gestures, and eye contact.

EVIDENCE LOG

Before moving on to a new selection, go to your Evidence Log and record what you learned from Part 2 of the *Odyssey*.

Comparing Texts

The illustrations on the following pages are taken from *The Odyssey: A Graphic Novel*, by Gareth Hinds. While reviewing this selection, you will consider how verbal and visual texts tell a story in different ways.

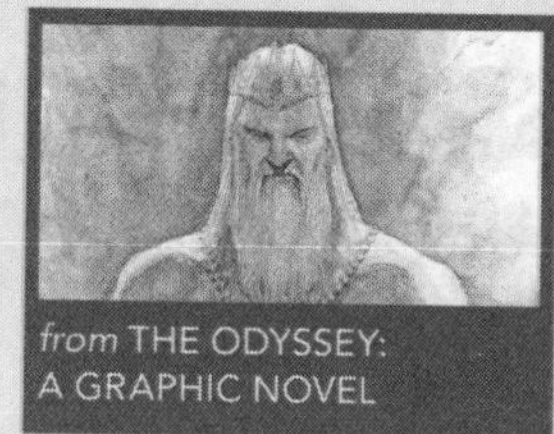

About the Author

Gareth Hinds (b. 1971) grew up in Vermont as a self-described "nerdy kid" who drew a lot and was fascinated by mixed martial arts. After graduating from the Parsons School of Design in New York, Hinds began working on video games before turning his attention to writing and illustrating graphic novels, including *Beowulf, King Lear, The Merchant of Venice*, and *Romeo and Juliet*. He is a recipient of the Boston Public Library's "Literary Lights for Children" award.

from The Odyssey: A Graphic Novel

Media Vocabulary

The following words or concepts will be useful to you as you analyze, discuss, and write about graphic novels.

panel: one of the drawings on a page, usually framed by a border	• A single panel usually contains one piece of the action or one bit of information.
splash: large, full-page illustration	• Often, a splash is used to begin a story. • A splash used within a story adds emphasis and visual impact.
tier: row of panels	• A tier can contain several panels or just one.
gutter: space between panels	• A gutter indicates change of place, time, or action.
caption: words in a separate box	• A caption is usually used to contain the words of the narrator, the person who is telling the story.
speech bubble: rounded shape containing a character's words	• The speech bubble usually has a small tail that points to the character that is speaking.

First Review MEDIA: GRAPHIC NOVEL

Apply these strategies as you conduct your first review. You will have an opportunity to complete a close review after your first read.

LOOK

LOOK at each image and determine *whom* or *what* it portrays.

NOTE

NOTE elements in each panel that you find interesting and want to revisit.

First Review (LOOK, NOTE, RESPOND, CONNECT)

CONNECT

CONNECT details in the images to other media you've experienced, texts you've read, or images you've seen.

RESPOND

RESPOND by completing the Comprehension Check and by writing a brief summary of the selection.

STANDARDS

Reading Literature

By the end of grade 9, read and comprehend literature, including stories, dramas, and poems, in the grades 9–10 text complexity band proficiently, with scaffolding as needed at the high end of the range.

Language

Acquire and use accurately general academic and domain-specific words and phrases, sufficient for reading, writing, speaking, and listening at the college and career readiness level; demonstrate independence in gathering vocabulary knowledge when considering a word or phrase important to comprehension or expression.

BACKGROUND

Necromancy, or communication with the dead, appears in ancient myths as a way to see into the future or learn how to fulfill a challenging task. In this excerpt, Odysseus has followed the witch-goddess Circe's advice and has traveled to the western edge of the world to summon the spirit of the old prophet Tiresias, in order to ask him how he can return home to Ithaca.

1
"Just spread your sail," Circe told me, "and the north wind will carry you directly to the black shore."
2
"Beach your ship and go inland, looking for the lake where the river of fire and the river of tears meet."
3
"Dig a trench there on the shore, a forearm's length on each side, and sacrifice a black lamb and a young goat."

4 "The spirits of the dead will soon appear, drawn by the smell of blood. Have your men quickly burn the carcasses in sacrifice to the twelve gods, while you draw your sword and stand over the trench. You may see spirits you know, but let none touch the blood until Tiresias appears. Question him about your journey, and he will tell you everything."

5

Elpenor? How did you get here? You were with us yesterday!
Captain, it was my ill luck that brought me here, more swiftly than your black ship.

6

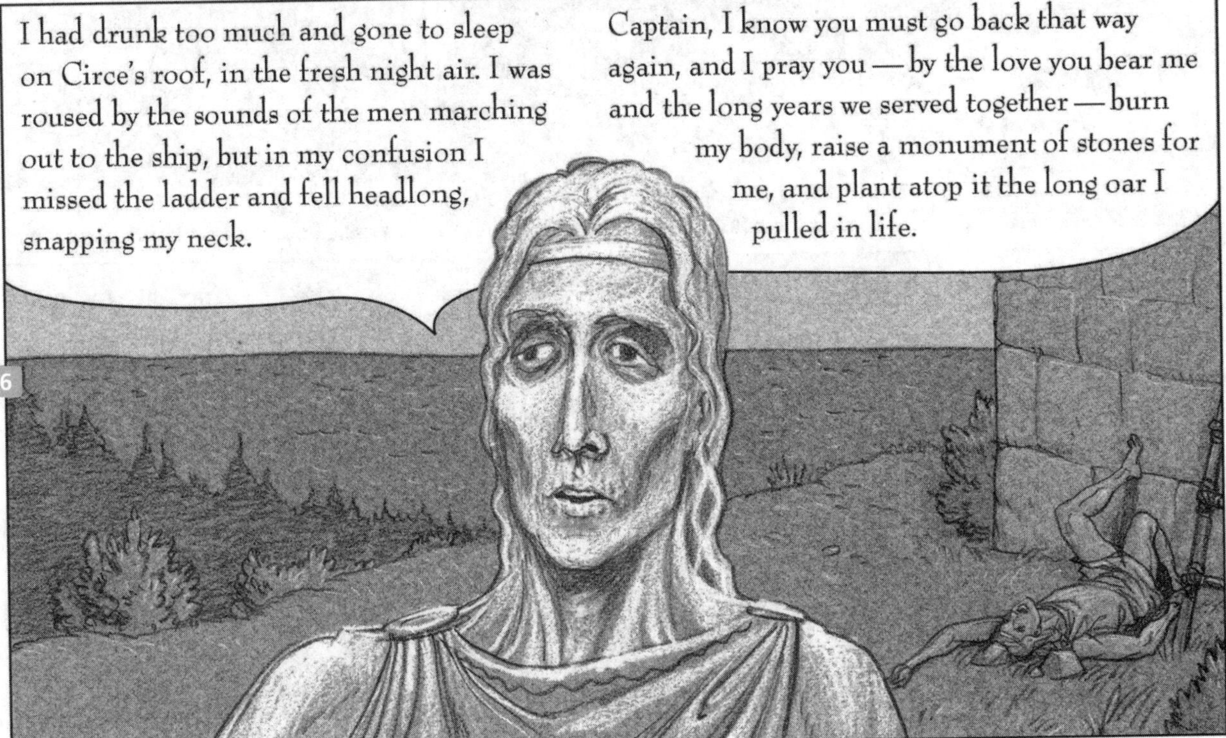

I had drunk too much and gone to sleep on Circe's roof, in the fresh night air. I was roused by the sounds of the men marching out to the ship, but in my confusion I missed the ladder and fell headlong, snapping my neck.
Captain, I know you must go back that way again, and I pray you — by the love you bear me and the long years we served together — burn my body, raise a monument of stones for me, and plant atop it the long oar I pulled in life.

I promised him, and his spirit faded back into the darkness. But then came another shade I knew too well: Anticleia, my own beloved mother, who had still lived when I sailed for Troy.

7

The sight broke my heart, but I kept my sword out, and she held back from it, until finally I saw the man I sought.

8

Tiresias.

9

10

11

So. Great Odysseus.

12

You come to me for prophecy and advice. You want to know how you can return home to your beloved island of Ithaca.

Yes, great sage. Tell me what you see. How can I complete the journey?

13

You can only reach your home by disciplining yourself and your men.
Heed my words. You must not touch the cattle of Helios, the sun god, who sees all! If you leave those sacred beasts unharmed, your ship and all your crew will reach Ithaca safely.
But if you allow your men to kill any of Helios's cattle, then your ship and crew will be destroyed, and you will suffer more long years at sea. You'll return at last, but under a strange sail, unrecognized at home, and your palace overrun by enemies— suitors who seek to eat up your flocks and claim your wife.
Once you have killed these men, whether in open combat or by stealth, and put your house in order, you must take your oar with you and travel inland until you reach a country where men know nothing of ships or the sea. You will know you've reached the place when a stranger asks you what is on your shoulder and thinks it a flail or some tool for threshing grain.
There you must plant your oar and make a rich sacrifice to Lord Poseidon — a ram, a bull, and a breeding boar — asking his forgiveness for putting out the eye of his son Polyphemus. Then return home and make rich sacrifices to all the gods in turn. If you do this, then death will come upon you peacefully in old age, with your loved ones around you.

Comprehension Check

Complete the following items after you finish your first read.

1. Why does Odysseus go to the Land of the Dead?

2. What brings the spirits of the dead to Odysseus?

3. What does Tiresias say that Odysseus and his men must not do?

4. **Notebook** Confirm your understanding of the text by writing a summary.

RESEARCH

Research to Clarify Choose at least one unfamiliar detail from the text. Briefly research that detail. In what way does the information you learned shed light on an aspect of the story?

Research to Explore This graphic novel may spark your curiosity to learn more. Briefly research one of the mythological beings mentioned in the story. You may want to share what you discover with the class.

Close Review

Review the splash (last panel) in this excerpt from the graphic novel. How has the artist divided Tiresias' advice to Odysseus? How is the meaning of Tiresias' words reflected in the images? How do text and images work together to communicate Tiresias' message?

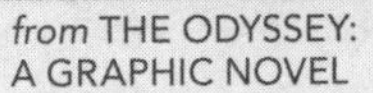

from THE ODYSSEY: A GRAPHIC NOVEL

Analyze the Media

CITE TEXTUAL EVIDENCE to support your answers.

Notebook **Respond to these questions.**

1. **Interpret** When Circe tells Odysseus that the north wind will carry his ship to the black shore, what does she mean by "the black shore"?
2. (a) **Interpret** What is the effect of using black and white drawings to portray the land of the dead? (b) **Analyze** Why do you think the author depicts the blood in color?
3. (a) In each of panels 1–3, which detail of Circe's advice has the artist chosen to depict? (b) **Analyze** What effect does this choice have on the pacing, or speed, of the story?
4. **Essential Question:** ***What can we learn from a journey?*** What have you learned about journeys by reading the graphic novel of the *Odyssey*?

LANGUAGE DEVELOPMENT

Media Vocabulary

panel	**tier**	**caption**
splash	**gutter**	**speech bubble**

Use the vocabulary words in your responses to the questions.

1. Where does Odysseus begin narrating the story?
2. How does the artist use different elements to depict Tiresias' drinking the blood? What effect do these elements have?
3. How does the artist emphasize the importance of Tiresias' prophecy and advice?

WORD NETWORK

Add interesting words related to journeys from the text to your Word Network.

STANDARDS

Language
Acquire and use accurately general academic and domain-specific words and phrases, sufficient for reading, writing, speaking, and listening at the college and career readiness level; demonstrate independence in gathering vocabulary knowledge when considering a word or phrase important to comprehension or expression.

from the ODYSSEY

from THE ODYSSEY: A GRAPHIC NOVEL

Writing to Compare

You have read a variety of scenes from Homer's *Odyssey* and looked at a graphic novel version of one of those scenes. Now, deepen your understanding of the texts by comparing and writing about them.

Assignment

An **adaptation** is a work of art that is based on another work of art. A novel or comic book is adapted as a film, for example, or a poem is adapted as a story. When creating an adaptation, an artist must decide which details from the original to include in the new work, as well as how to include them. Write a **review** of the graphic novel in which you examine the choices Gareth Hinds made in adapting the scene in the land of the dead from Homer's *Odyssey*. Evaluate how well Hinds captures the scene.

Prewriting

Analyze the Texts Use the chart to identify details from the graphic novel that relate to characters, settings, actions, conflicts, and imagery present in the poem.

	EPIC POEM	GRAPHIC NOVEL
Characters' appearances, words, and actions		
Settings		
Conflicts		
Imagery		

Notebook Respond to these questions.

1. Is Hinds's adaptation of the scene faithful, or true, to the original? Why or why not?
2. Does Hinds's adaptation add something new to Homer's work? Explain.
3. **(a)** Does Hinds's artwork do justice to the poem? **(b)** Is his organization of the text effective? Explain.
4. Does Hinds's adaptation enhance Homer's work or diminish it? Explain.

STANDARDS

Reading Literature

- Analyze the representation of a subject or a key scene in two different artistic mediums, including what is emphasized or absent in each treatment.
- Analyze how an author draws on and transforms source material in a specific work.

Writing

- Introduce precise claim(s), distinguish the claim(s) from alternate or opposing claims, and create an organization that establishes clear relationships among claim(s), counterclaims, reasons, and evidence.
- Apply *grades 9–10 Reading standards* to literature.

Drafting

Write a Rough Outline Organize your ideas in a rough outline. Start with a working claim, or thesis, in which you express your evaluation of Hinds's adaptation. Then, list three reasons that support your evaluation. Be specific. Write a possible counterclaim, or alternative opinion. Add one strong reason that refutes that claim. Finally, consider how you might conclude your review in a memorable way.

Working Claim: ______________________________

____

Three Supporting Reasons:

1. ______________________________

2. ______________________________

3. ______________________________

Counterclaim: ______________________________

______________________________.

Answer to Counterclaim: ______________________________

______________________________.

Conclusion:

____

______________________________.

As you write, you may modify your claim, reasons, or the entire outline to better reflect your ideas.

Use Precise Language Use precise words to describe colors or other visual elements of the adaptation. In addition, use the Media Vocabulary you studied to refer to specific elements of the adaptation. Terms such as *panel*, *splash*, *tier*, and *speech bubble* will help you be more precise in your evaluation.

Review, Revise, and Edit

Once you are done drafting, reread your review. Make sure you have supported your ideas with clear reasons and evidence. Review each paragraph, marking the main idea. Then, mark sentences that support that idea. If there are sentences that do not support or develop the main idea, consider deleting or rewriting them.

EVIDENCE LOG

Before moving on to a new selection, go to your Evidence Log and record what you have learned from the *Odyssey* and *The Odyssey: A Graphic Novel.*

Application for a Mariner's License

Workplace Vocabulary

The following words or concepts will be useful to you as you analyze, discuss, and write about functional workplace documents.

Applicant Information: data about a person applying for a job	• Applicant information may include the person's name, social security number, birth date, and other forms of personal data.
Check Box: place on a form to indicate "yes," signifying that a certain statement is true	• Applicants place a check mark or the letter *X* in the check box to indicate "yes." • Applicants should leave a box unchecked if the statement does not apply or is not true.
Privacy Statement: statement from an institution that guarantees personal information will not be given out	• By law, an institution is not allowed to give out information such as medical records, financial records, military records, and social security numbers. • The privacy statement ensures that an applicant's personal information will stay confidential.

First Read FUNCTIONAL WORKPLACE DOCUMENT

Apply these strategies as you conduct your first read. You will have the opportunity to complete a close read after your first read.

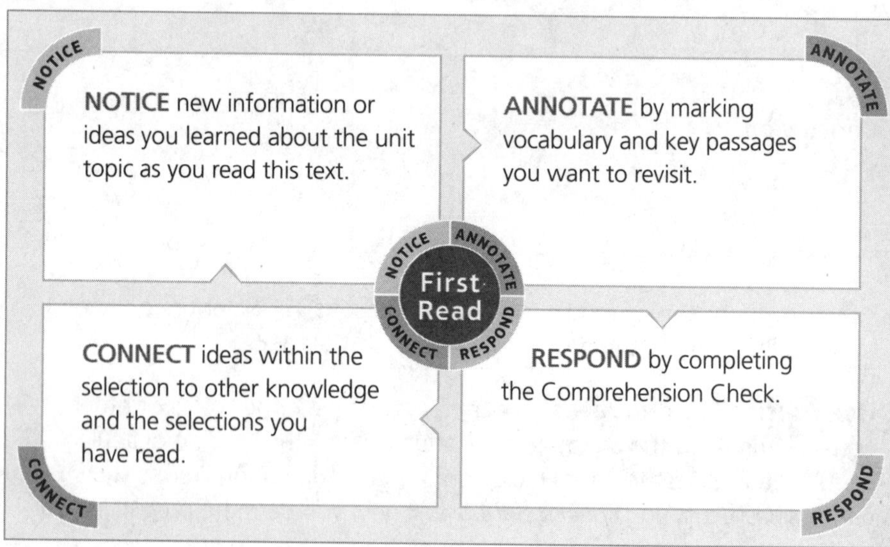

STANDARDS

Language
Acquire and use accurately general academic and domain-specific words and phrases, sufficient for reading, writing, speaking, and listening at the college and career readiness level; demonstrate independence in gathering vocabulary knowledge when considering a word or phrase important to comprehension or expression.

Application for a Mariner's License

BACKGROUND

Merchant Marines are civilians working for private shipping companies but are licensed and overseen by the government. During wartime and disasters, the U.S. Merchant Marine may be called upon to support the U.S. Navy by carrying troops and equipment. The U.S. Coast Guard issues merchant mariner licenses and requires that mariners be physically capable of handling shipboard tasks. Those seeking jobs as merchant mariners are required to complete this application.

NOTES

U.S. DEPARTMENT OF HOMELAND SECURITY U.S. COAST GUARD CG-719K/E Rev. (01-09)	**Merchant Mariner Application for Entry Level Ratings**

Section I – Applicant Information

Name of Applicant:		
Height:	Eye Color:	Gender:
Weight:	Hair Color:	Distinguishing Marks:

Section II – Physical Ability Certification

An applicant for an Entry Level Rating [ordinary seaman, wiper, or steward's department (food handler)] is not required to complete a physical examination, but they must have the agility, strength, and flexibility to complete the following shipboard tasks and related physical abilities as described in the table below:

Shipboard Task, Function, Event, or Condition	*Related Physical Ability*	*The applicant attests that he or she . . .*
Routine movement on slippery, uneven and unstable surfaces.	Maintain balance (equilibrium).	Has no disturbance in sense of balance.
Routine access between levels.	Climb up and down vertical ladders and stairways.	Is able, without assistance, to climb up and down vertical ladders and stairways.
Routine movement between spaces and compartments.	Step over high doorsills and coamings, and move through restricted accesses.	Is able, without assistance, to stepover a doorsill or coaming of 24 inches (61 centimeters) in height. Able to move through a restricted opening of 24 inches.
Open and close watertight doors, hand cranking systems, open/close valve.	Manipulate mechanical devices using manual and digital dexterity, and strength.	Is able, without assistance, to open and close watertight doors that may weigh up to 55 pounds (25 kilograms). Should be able to move hands/arms to open and close valve wheels in vertical and horizontal directions; rotate wrists to turn handles. Reach above shoulder height.
Handle ship's stores.	Lift, pull, push and carry a load.	Is able, without assistance, to lift at least a 40-pound (18.1-kilogram) load off the ground, and to carry, push or pull the same load.
General vessel maintenance.	Crouch (lowering height by bending knees); kneel (placing knees on ground); and stoop (lowering height by bending at the waist). Use hand tools such as spanners, valve wrenches, hammers, screwdrivers, pliers.	Is able, without assistance, to grasp, lift and manipulate various common shipboard tools.
Emergency response procedures, including escape from smoke-filled spaces.	Crawl (the ability to move the body with hands and knees); feel (the ability to handle or touch to examine or determine differences in texture and temperature).	Is able, without assistance, to crouch, keel and crawl, and to distinguish differences in texture and temperature by feel.
Stand a routine watch.	Stand a routine watch.	Is able, without assistance, to intermittently stand on feet for up to four hours with minimal rest periods.
React to visual alarms and instructions, emergency response procedures.	Distinguish an object or shape at a certain distance.	Fulfills the eyesight standards for the merchant mariner credential(s) applied for.
React to audible alarms and instructions, emergency response procedures.	Hear a specified decibel (dB) sound at a specified frequency.	Fulfills the hearing capacity standards for the merchant mariner credential(s) applied for.
Make verbal reports or call attention to suspicious or emergency conditions.	Describe immediate surroundings and activities, and pronounce words clearly.	Is capable of normal conversation.
Participate in firefighting activities.	Be able to carry and handle fire hoses and fire extinguishers.	Is able, without assistance, to pull an uncharged 1.5 inch diameter, 50' fire hose with nozzle to full extension, and to lift a charged 1.5 inch diameter fire hose to fire fighting position.
Abandon ship.	Use survival equipment.	Has the agility, strength and range of motion to put on a personal flotation device and exposure suit without assistance from another individual.

Place an X in the appropriate block below.

☐ I have the physical strength, agility, and flexibility to perform **all** of the items listed above.	☐ I do **NOT** have the physical strength, agility, and flexibility to perform one or more of the items listed above.

Comments:

Please list any experience or additional information you feel would help you qualify as a Merchant Mariner of Entry Level Ranking:

Section III – Applicants Signature

I certify that all information provided by me is complete and true to the best of my knowledge X ______________________ Signature of Applicant	Date

Description of the requirements for Certificate of Fitness

For a vessel to be operated safely, it is essential that the crewmembers be physically fit and free of debilitating illness and injury. The seafaring life is arduous, often hazardous, and the availability of medical assistance or treatment is generally minimal. As the international trend toward smaller crews continues, the ability of each crewmember to perform his or her routine duties and respond to emergencies becomes even more critical.

All mariners should be capable of living and working in cramped spaces, frequently in adverse weather causing violent evolutions such as fire-fighting or launching lifeboats or life rafts. Members of the deck and engine department must be capable of physical labor, climbing and handling moderate weights (30-60 pounds).

PRIVACY ACT STATEMENT

As required, the following information is provided when supplying personal information to the United States Coast Guard.

1. The principal purpose for which the information provided in this application is used is to determine if an applicant is physically capable of performing their duties.
2. The routine uses which may be made of this information:
   a. This form becomes a part of the applicant's file as documentary evidence that regulatory physical requirements have been satisfied and that the applicant is physically competent to hold a credential.
   b. The information becomes part of the total credential file and is subject to review by Federal agency casualty investigators.
   c. This information may be used by the United States Coast Guard and an Administrative Law Judge in determining causation of marine casualties and appropriate suspension and revocation action.
3. Disclosure of this information is voluntary, but failure to provide this information will result in non-issuance of a credential.

Comprehension Check

Complete the following items after you finish your first read.

1. What kind of position is the application for?

2. Which federal department issues this application?

3. What tasks must an applicant be able to do, in general, according to the table in Section II of the application?

4. To what is an applicant attesting by signing Section III of the application?

WORKPLACE VOCABULARY

Use these words as you discuss and write about the document.

applicant information
check box
privacy statement

WORD NETWORK

Add interesting words related to journeys from the application to your Word Network.

STANDARDS

Reading Informational Text

- Cite strong and thorough textual evidence to support analysis of what the text says explicitly as well as inferences drawn from the text.
- Analyze in detail how an author's ideas or claims are developed and refined by particular sentences, paragraphs, or larger portions of a text.

Close Read the Text

Go over the application again. **Annotate** details that you notice. What **questions** do you still have? What can you **conclude**?

Analyze the Text

CITE TEXTUAL EVIDENCE to support your answers.

Notebook Respond to these questions.

1. **(a) Infer** Review the table in Section II of the application. What dangers might a mariner face on board a ship? **(b) Speculate** How do you think shipboard procedures have changed since Homer's time?

2. **Speculate** Given what you know about Odysseus, how likely is it that his application would be accepted? Explain.

3. **(a) Connect** What skills must an applicant have in order to participate in firefighting activities? **(b) Analyze** What other situations and skills noted in the document relate to potentially life-threatening conditions on board a ship? Explain.

4. **Essential Question:** *What can we learn from a journey?* What have you learned about journeys by reading this application?

Writing to Sources

Assignment

Complete the **job application** for a mariner's license as if you were Odysseus.

- Fill in all relevant information. Use your knowledge of Odysseus to speculate about such things as height, weight, and "distinguishing marks."
- Pay special attention to the box that asks the applicant to list any experience or additional information that would help him or her qualify as a merchant mariner.
  - Which kinds of experiences should Odysseus include to show that he has good judgment and strong character?
  - Think back to Odysseus' battles with the Cyclops, Scylla and Charybdis, the suitors, and others.
  - Keep in mind that Odysseus should present himself in the most positive way possible to increase his chances of being accepted.

APPLICATION FOR A MARINER'S LICENSE

Speaking and Listening

Assignment

With a partner, role-play a **job interview** in which Odysseus is applying for a job in the Merchant Marine.

- Have one partner play the role of Odysseus and the other partner the role of the interviewer.
- Work out the specifics of the job for which Odysseus is applying. Is he applying to be an ordinary sailor or a deck officer? Does he seek a special position?
- The interviewer should prepare questions ahead of time. Here are some sample questions.
  - Why are you seeking this particular job? What makes you especially qualified for the job?
  - What kinds of life experiences have you had that would help you with this job?
  - How do you get along with other people? What kinds of leadership and problem-solving abilities do you bring to the job?
  - Describe a difficult situation you faced in your life. How did you handle it? What skills did you need to use?

EVIDENCE LOG

Before moving on to a new selection, go to your Evidence Log and record what you learned from the application.

WRITING TO SOURCES

- *from the* ODYSSEY
- *from* THE ODYSSEY: A GRAPHIC NOVEL
- APPLICATION FOR A MARINER'S LICENSE

Write an Explanatory Essay

You've read sections of the *Odyssey*, as well as a graphic novel version, and filled out an application for a mariner's license. Each text deals with the concept of a journey in its own way. In the *Odyssey* text and graphic novel, Odysseus encounters challenges as he sails on his journey home from Troy. In the application for a mariner's license, readers learn what mariners need to know and do while at sea. Now you will use your knowledge of these texts to write an explanatory essay about the requirements of journeys.

Assignment

Use your knowledge of the *Odyssey*, the graphic novel, and the application for a mariner's license to inform readers about journeys at sea and explain what they would need to know in order to survive. Write a brief **explanatory essay** in which you refer to ideas from the texts and answer this question:

How are personal strengths and weaknesses magnified during the course of a journey at sea?

Tool Kit
Student Model of an Explanatory Text

ACADEMIC VOCABULARY

As you craft your explanatory text, consider using some of the academic vocabulary you learned at the beginning of the unit.

voluntary
elucidate
expedite
subsequent
procedure

Elements of an Explanatory Text

An **explanatory text** describes and summarizes information gathered from a number of sources on a concept.

An effective explanatory text includes these elements:

- a clear thesis statement about the topic
- facts and evidence from a variety of credible sources
- a clear introduction, body, and conclusion
- precise word choices that suit your audience and purpose
- a clear, logical organizational structure that supports the topic and purpose
- correct spelling, grammar, a formal style, and an objective tone

Model Explanatory Text For a model of a well-crafted explanatory text, see the Launch Text, "Gone and Back Again: A Traveler's Advice."

Challenge yourself to find all of the elements of an effective explanatory text in the Launch Text. You will have an opportunity to review these elements as you prepare to write your own explanatory text.

STANDARDS

Writing
- Write informative/explanatory texts to examine and convey complex ideas, concepts, and information clearly and accurately through the effective selection, organization, and analysis of content.
- Write routinely over extended time frames and shorter time frames for a range of tasks, purposes, and audiences.

Prewriting / Planning

Write a Clear Thesis Now that you have read and thought about the selections, write a sentence in which you state your **thesis**, an informative statement that addresses how personal strengths and weaknesses affect sailors' journeys. As you continue to write, you may revise your thesis or even change it entirely. For now, it will help you choose how to organize your ideas and determine how to select facts, details, and information from sources to develop them.

Thesis: ____

____.

Gather Evidence Once you have a thesis that can guide your thinking, look through the selections and your notes for evidence that supports your thesis. You will be using the following types of evidence:

- **concrete details:** facts or definitions, physical descriptions of people or characters, actions, or settings in the selection
- **quotations:** lines copied from a text to provide direct support for a main idea

Use the chart to help you organize evidence. A sample of each type of evidence has been provided.

SELECTION	DETAILS/QUOTATIONS	CONNECTION TO THESIS
from the Odyssey	The survival of Odysseus and the sailors is threatened by Charybdis, a massive whirlpool.	
from The Odyssey: A Graphic Novel	"Yes, great sage. Tell me what you see. How can I complete the journey?"	
Application for a Mariner's License	Mariners need to be able to crouch, or squat with bent knees.	

Connect Across Texts As you write your explanatory text, you will be using evidence from multiple texts to explain what traits are necessary for a successful journey. Include evidence from both *Odyssey* texts and the mariner's license application to support your thesis. It can be helpful to use one piece of evidence as your main point in a paragraph, then develop or explain it with another piece of evidence. For the mariner's license application, you may want to pull direct quotes from the document, then write hypothetically, or in an imagined way, about whether the characters from the *Odyssey* would or would not be successful as mariners today.

EVIDENCE LOG

Review your Evidence Log and identify key details you may want to cite in your explanatory essay.

STANDARDS

Writing

- Introduce a topic, organize complex ideas, concepts, and information to make important connections and distinctions; include formatting, graphics, and multimedia when useful to aiding comprehension.
- Develop the topic with well-chosen, relevant, and sufficient facts, extended definitions, concrete details, quotations, or other information and examples appropriate to the audience's knowledge of the topic.

Drafting

Organize Your Ideas Once you have gathered your evidence, create an organizational plan. You may use a standard outline or a graphic organizer, such as the one shown. Most explanatory essays include three parts:

INTRODUCTION	BODY PARAGRAPH	BODY PARAGRAPH	CONCLUSION
State topic •	Present idea •	Present idea •	Restate topic and thesis, show implications or significance of topic • •
	Develop idea with evidence from one source •	Develop idea with evidence from one source •	
State main ideas about topic • •	Develop idea with evidence from another source •	Develop idea with evidence from another source •	
	Clarify connection between evidence from multiple sources •	Clarify differences between evidence from multiple sources •	

- the **introduction**, in which you introduce the topic and state your thesis
- the **body**, in which you develop the topic with relevant evidence, details, quotations, and examples
- the **conclusion**, in which you readdress your thesis and summarize your ideas about the topic

In the introduction, preview your information. Notice how the Launch Text sets up its thesis, followed by the two major ideas it will address:

> Let common sense guide you before you travel and you'll have a better trip. Consider the businesslike details first. Down the road, rich rewards will follow.

Each paragraph of the body contains an idea that develops or explains some aspect of your thesis, followed by evidence that relates to the idea.

> Traveling light makes it easier and faster to get from one place to another, with a more manageable load to lug around. If you really must have a second black sweater, you can probably buy it on the fly.

In the conclusion, restate your thesis and summarize the information that you have shared. Notice how the Launch Text wraps up its major points.

> Be prepared. Have fun. The world is ready when you are. Don't forget your toothbrush.

Write a First Draft Use your graphic organizer to write your first draft. Remember to write with your thesis in mind. Use your evidence to develop the topic. Keep your structure simple and logical for ease of reading.

STANDARDS

Writing

Introduce a topic, organize complex ideas, concepts, and information to make important connections and distinctions; include formatting, graphics, and multimedia when useful to aiding comprehension.

LANGUAGE DEVELOPMENT: AUTHOR'S STYLE

Check for Accuracy: Using a Dictionary and Thesaurus

A **dictionary** provides information to help writers use words correctly, including a word's pronunciation, part of speech, and meaning.

A **thesaurus** lists synonyms and antonyms. Use it to find the exact word to fit your meaning and to vary your word choice. A thesaurus can also help you locate words that have the same **denotation**, or dictionary definition, but have different **connotations**, or shades of meaning.

Many types of dictionaries and thesauruses can be found in the reference section of your library. You may also find them online and as mobile applications.

Read It

These sentences from the Launch Text use terms the author may have had to look up in a dictionary:

- *If you're leaving the country, you'll need* **backups** *of all essential documents.* **("*Backup*" is an important word in the Launch Text. Consider how the meaning of backup might change if it is broken into two separate words.)**
- *You'll have more tourist attractions to yourself while the* **layabouts** *are snoring into their pillows.* **("*Layabouts*" is a way of calling people "lazy." Think about how the writer could confirm that layabouts is one word.)**

These sentences from the Launch Text use terms the author may have found in a thesaurus to add variety and interest to the text.

- *You'll be* **encountering** *people whose lifestyles are different from yours.* **("Encountering" is a synonym for "meeting" that has a more dramatic effect.)**
- *Get lost* **deliberately. ("Deliberately" is another way of saying "on purpose.")**

TIP

SPELLING

Be sure you are checking your spelling as you are writing.

- If you are using a word processing program on a computer, check to see if the autocorrect and spellcheck are enabled.
- If a word is confusing to you, check the spelling before you forget. Be sure the source you are using is valid.

Write It

Notebook Practice using dictionaries and thesauruses in the following activities:

- Use a thesaurus to find a synonym for three words in the following sentence from the Launch Text: *Traveling light makes it easier and faster to get from one place to another, with a more manageable load to lug around.* Explain the differences in connotations between the original word and the synonym. Why do you think the author chose the original word rather than the synonym?
- Use a dictionary to find the correct meaning, origin, and part of speech of the word *vital* in this sentence from the Launch Text:

  Vital moments in that life may be around the next corner.

STANDARDS

Writing

Use precise language and domain-specific vocabulary to manage the complexity of the topic.

Language

- Spell correctly.
- Consult general and specialized reference materials, both print and digital, to find the pronunciation of a word or determine or clarify its precise meaning, its part of speech, or its etymology.

Revising

Evaluating Your Draft

Use the following checklist to evaluate the effectiveness of your draft. Then, use your evaluation and the instruction on this page to guide your revision.

FOCUS AND ORGANIZATION	EVIDENCE AND ELABORATION	CONVENTIONS
☐ Introduces the topic and thesis.	☐ Develops the thesis and supplies evidence.	☐ Attends to the norms and conventions of the discipline, especially accurate word choice.
☐ Provides a conclusion that follows from the thesis and the body paragraphs.	☐ Provides adequate examples for each major idea.	☐ Is free from errors in spelling and punctuation.
☐ Establishes a logical organization that suits the topic and purpose for writing.	☐ Uses vocabulary and word choices that are appropriate for the audience and purpose.	
☐ Uses transitional words, phrases, and clauses to clarify the relationships between and among ideas.	☐ Establishes and maintains a formal style and an objective tone.	

WORD NETWORK

Include interesting words from your Word Network in your explanatory essay.

Revising for Focus and Organization

Logical Organization Reread your explanatory essay. Does the introduction properly introduce the topic and thesis? Does each paragraph of the body contain an idea related to the topic and thesis? Is that idea followed by examples from the text to further develop the topic? Do you use appropriate transitions, such as *although, in contrast,* and *similarly* to show the relationships between ideas and maintain a smooth flow between paragraphs? Does the essay end with a conclusion that readdresses the thesis and summarizes the most important ideas from the essay?

Revising for Evidence and Elaboration

Depth of Support Review your draft. Did you use examples from the texts when needed? Did the examples you used connect the concepts you wished to explain to the reader?

Tone Remember to consider your **tone**, your attitude toward the audience or subject. Because informative texts present information on a subject to the reader, they have a formal and authoritative tone. Apply the following steps to create and maintain a formal tone:

- Avoid slang and abbreviations, and limit the use of contractions.
- Choose precise words.
- Generally, avoid the use of idioms, which tend to be less formal in tone.
- Refer to places, people, or formal concepts by their proper names.

STANDARDS

Writing

- Use appropriate and varied transitions to link the major sections of the text, create cohesion, and clarify the relationships among complex ideas and concepts.
- Establish and maintain a formal style and objective tone while attending to the norms and conventions of the discipline in which they are writing.

PEER REVIEW

Exchange papers with a classmate. Use the checklist to evaluate your classmate's explanatory essay and provide supportive feedback.

1. Is the thesis clear?
   ☐ yes ☐ no If no, explain what confused you.
2. Are ideas clearly stated and supported by facts and examples?
   ☐ yes ☐ no If no, point out what needs more support.
3. Does the conclusion readdress the thesis and summarize key ideas about the topic?
   ☐ yes ☐ no If no, write a brief note explaining what you thought was missing.
4. What is the strongest part of your classmate's paper? Why?

____

____

____

____

Editing and Proofreading

Edit for Conventions Reread your draft for accuracy and consistency. Correct errors in grammar and word usage. Check your use of tense. When writing an explanatory essay about literature, use the present tense.

Proofread for Accuracy Read your draft carefully, looking for errors in spelling and punctuation. Check your spelling by consulting a dictionary.

Publishing and Presenting

Create a final version of your essay. Share it with your class so that your classmates can read it and make comments. In turn, review and comment on your classmates' work. Consider the ways in which other students' explanatory texts are both similar to and different from your own. Always maintain a polite and respectful tone when commenting.

Reflecting

Think about what you learned by writing an explanatory text. What could you do differently the next time to make the writing experience easier and to make your information more interesting? For example, you might discuss the topic with a classmate before your start writing.

STANDARDS

Writing
Produce clear and coherent writing in which the development, organization, and style are appropriate to task, purpose, and audience.

Language
- Spell correctly.
- Consult general and specialized reference materials, both print and digital, to find the pronunciation of a word or determine or clarify its precise meaning, its part of speech, or its etymology.

OVERVIEW: SMALL-GROUP LEARNING

ESSENTIAL QUESTION:

What can we learn from a journey?

Adventurers do not need planes, boats, or cars to go out in the world. They do not even need to leave their seats in order to begin a journey. You will work in a group to continue your exploration of the concept of journeys.

Small-Group Learning Strategies

Throughout your life, in school, in your community, and in your career, you will continue to learn and work with others.

Look at these strategies and the actions you can take to practice them as you work in teams. Add ideas of your own for each step. Use these strategies during Small-Group Learning.

STRATEGY	ACTION PLAN
Prepare	• Complete your assignments so that you are prepared for group work. • Organize your thinking so you can contribute to your group's discussions. •
Participate fully	• Make eye contact to signal that you are listening and taking in what is being said. • Use text evidence when making a point. •
Support others	• Build off ideas from others in your group. • Invite others who have not yet spoken to join the discussion. •
Clarify	• Paraphrase the ideas of others to ensure that your understanding is correct. • Ask follow-up questions. •

CONTENTS

SHORT STORY

The Return

Ngugi wa Thiong'o

After five years as a political prisoner, how will Kamau be welcomed back to his village?

INTERVIEW

from The Hero's Adventure

from The Power of Myth

Joseph Campbell and Bill Moyers

Is the hero's journey one we all experience?

POETRY COLLECTION 1

Courage *Anne Sexton*

Ithaka *C. P. Cavafy, translated by Edmund Keeley and Philip Sherrard*

from The Narrow Road of the Interior

Matsuo Bashō, translated by Helen Craig McCullough

In what ways is life itself a journey into the unknown?

PERFORMANCE TASK

SPEAKING AND LISTENING FOCUS

Deliver a Multimedia Presentation

The Small-Group readings feature journeys that are physical or emotional or both. After reading, your group will plan and deliver a multimedia presentation about journeys that involve no travel.

Working as a Team

1. **Take a Position** In your group, discuss the following question:

   Why are some people reluctant to make a journey?

   As you take turns sharing your positions, be sure to provide reasons that support your ideas. After all group members have shared, discuss some of the reasons people have for their choices to start—or to avoid—a travel adventure.

2. **List Your Rules** As a group, decide on the rules that you will follow as you work together. Samples are provided; add two more of your own. You may add or revise rules based on your experience together.

   - Everyone should participate in group discussions.
   - People should not interrupt.
   - ______________________________
     ____
   - ______________________________
     ____

3. **Apply the Rules** Practice working as a group. Share what you have learned about journeys. Make sure each person in the group contributes. Take notes, and be prepared to share with the class one thing that you heard from another member of your group.

4. **Name Your Group** Choose a name that reflects the unit topic.

   Our group's name: ______________________________

5. **Create a Communication Plan** Decide how you want to communicate with one another. For example, you might use online collaboration tools, email, or instant messaging.

   Our group's decision: ______________________________

   ____

Making a Schedule

First, find out the due dates for the small-group activities. Then, preview the texts and activities with your group, and make a schedule for completing the tasks.

SELECTION	ACTIVITIES	DUE DATE
The Return		
from The Hero's Adventure		
Courage Ithaka *from* The Narrow Road of the Interior		

Working on Group Projects

As your group works together, you'll find it more effective if each person has a specific role. Different projects require different roles. Before beginning a project, discuss the necessary roles, and choose one for each group member. Here are some possible roles; add your own ideas.

Project Manager: monitors the schedule and keeps everyone on task

Researcher: organizes research activities

Recorder: takes notes during group meetings

About the Author

Ngugi wa Thiong'o (b. 1938) was born in Kenya and as a young boy lived through the Mau Mau Rebellion. His first play, *The Black Hermit*, was a major success. His unsparing but accurate account of life in the dictatorship of postcolonial Kenya, *Petals of Blood*, landed him in prison in 1977. After his release, the government reissued a warrant for his arrest. Ngugi chose exile instead, and fled to the United States. Ngugi has received numerous honors and taught at a number of major universities.

STANDARDS

Reading Literature
By the end of grade 9, read and comprehend literature, including stories, dramas, and poems, in the grades 9–10 text complexity band proficiently, with scaffolding as needed at the high end of the range.

Language
- Determine or clarify the meaning of unknown and multiple-meaning words and phrases based on *grades 9–10 reading and content*, choosing flexibly from a range of strategies.
- Identify and correctly use patterns of word changes that indicate different meanings or parts of speech.

The Return

Concept Vocabulary

As you perform your first read of "The Return," you will encounter the following words.

sprawling **serpentine** **compact**

Base Words If these words are unfamiliar to you, analyze each one to see whether it contains a base word you know. Then, use your knowledge of the "inside" word and any prefix or suffix, along with context, to determine a meaning for the concept word. Here is an example of how to apply the strategy.

Unfamiliar Word: *detainee*

Familiar "Inside" Word: *detain*, which means "keep" or "confine."

Context: One day he was working next to another **detainee** from Muranga.

Conclusion: *Detainee* is referring to a person in this sentence. It might mean "one who has been detained, or confined."

Apply your knowledge of base words and other vocabulary strategies to determine the meanings of unfamiliar words you encounter during your first read.

First Read FICTION

Apply these strategies as you conduct your first read. You will have an opportunity to complete a close read after your first read.

NOTICE *whom* the story is about, *what* happens, *where* and *when* it happens, and *why* those involved react as they do.

ANNOTATE by marking vocabulary and key passages you want to revisit.

CONNECT ideas within the selection to what you already know and what you have already read.

RESPOND by completing the Comprehension Check and by writing a brief summary of the selection.

SHORT STORY

The Return

Ngugi wa Thiong'o

BACKGROUND

The British colonial government controlled Kenya, the setting of this story, from the late nineteenth century until 1963. In 1952, this government declared a state of emergency in order to violently suppress the Mau Mau Rebellion, an anti-British uprising by the Gikuyu ethnic group. Over 20,000 Gikuyu were imprisoned by the government, and over 10,000 people lost their lives during the fighting.

1 The road was long. Whenever he took a step forward, little clouds of dust rose, whirled angrily behind him, and then slowly settled again. But a thin train of dust was left in the air, moving like smoke. He walked on, however, unmindful of the dust and ground under his feet. Yet with every step he seemed more and more conscious of the hardness and apparent animosity of the road. Not that he looked down; on the contrary, he looked straight ahead as if he would, any time now, see a familiar object that would hail him as a friend and tell him that he was near home. But the road stretched on.

2 He made quick, springing steps, his left hand dangling freely by the side of his once white coat, now torn and worn out. His right hand, bent at the elbow, held onto a string tied to a small bundle on his slightly drooping back. The bundle, well wrapped with a cotton cloth that had once been printed with red flowers now faded out, swung from side to side in harmony with the rhythm of his steps. The bundle held the bitterness and hardships of the years spent in detention camps. Now and then he looked at the sun on its homeward journey. Sometimes he darted quick side-glances at the small hedged strips of land which, with their sickly-looking crops, maize, beans, and peas, appeared much as everything else did—unfriendly. The whole country was dull and seemed weary. To Kamau, this was nothing new. He remembered that, even before the Mau Mau emergency, the overtilled Gikuyu holdings wore haggard looks in contrast to the **sprawling** green fields in the settled area.

3 A path branched to the left. He hesitated for a moment and then made up his mind. For the first time, his eyes brightened a little as he went along the path that would take him down the valley and then

NOTES

Mark base words or indicate another strategy you used that helped you determine meaning.

sprawling (SPRAWL ihng) *adj.*

MEANING:

NOTES

Mark base words or indicate another strategy you used that helped you determine meaning.

serpentine (SUR puhn teen) *adj.*

MEANING:

to the village. At last home was near and, with that realization, the faraway look of a weary traveler seemed to desert him for a while. The valley and the vegetation along it were in deep contrast to the surrounding country. For here green bush and trees thrived. This could only mean one thing: Honia River still flowed. He quickened his steps as if he could scarcely believe this to be true till he had actually set his eyes on the river. It was there; it still flowed. Honia, where so often he had taken a bath, plunging stark naked into its cool living water, warmed his heart as he watched its **serpentine** movement around the rocks and heard its slight murmurs. A painful exhilaration passed all over him and for a moment he longed for those days. He sighed. Perhaps the river would not recognize in his hardened features that same boy to whom the riverside world had meant everything. Yet as he approached Honia, he felt more akin to it than he had felt to anything else since his release.

4 A group of women were drawing water. He was excited, for he could recognize one or two from his ridge. There was the middle-aged Wanjiku, whose deaf son had been killed by the Security Forces just before he himself was arrested. She had always been a darling of the village, having a smile for everyone and food for all. Would they receive him? Would they give him a "hero's welcome"? He thought so. Had he not always been a favorite all along the ridge? And had he not fought for the land? He wanted to run and shout: "Here I am. I have come back to you." But he desisted. He was a man.

5 "Is it well with you?" A few voices responded. The other women, with tired and worn features, looked at him mutely as if his greeting was of no consequence. Why! Had he been so long in the camp? His spirits were damped as he feebly asked: "Do you not remember me?" Again they looked at him. They stared at him with cold, hard looks; like everything else, they seemed to be deliberately refusing to know or own him. It was Wanjiku who at last recognized him. But there was neither warmth nor enthusiasm in her voice as she said, "Oh, is it you, Kamau? We thought you—" She did not continue. Only now he noticed something else—surprise? fear? He could not tell. He saw their quick glances dart at him and he knew for certain that a secret from which he was excluded bound them together.

6 "Perhaps I am no longer one of them!" he bitterly reflected. But they told him of the new village. The old village of scattered huts spread thinly over the ridge was no more.

7 He left them, feeling embittered and cheated. The old village had not even waited for him. And suddenly he felt a strong nostalgia for his old home, friends and surroundings. He thought of his father, mother and—and—he dared not think about her. But for all that, Muthoni, just as she had been in the old days, came back to his mind. His heart beat faster. He felt desire and a warmth thrilled through him. He quickened his step. He forgot the village women as he remembered his wife. He had stayed with her for a mere two weeks;

then he had been swept away by the colonial forces. Like many others, he had been hurriedly screened and then taken to detention without trial. And all that time he had thought of nothing but the village and his beautiful woman.

8 The others had been like him. They had talked of nothing but their homes. One day he was working next to another detainee from Muranga.[1] Suddenly the detainee, Njoroge, stopped breaking stones. He sighed heavily. His worn-out eyes had a faraway look.

9 "What's wrong, man? What's the matter with you?" Kamau asked.

10 "It is my wife. I left her expecting a baby. I have no idea what has happened to her."

11 Another detainee put in: "For me, I left my woman with a baby. She had just been delivered. We were all happy. But on the same day, I was arrested . . ."

12 And so they went on. All of them longed for one day—the day of their return home. Then life would begin anew.

13 Kamau himself had left his wife without a child. He had not even finished paying the bride price. But now he would go, seek work in Nairobi, and pay off the remainder to Muthoni's parents. Life would indeed begin anew. They would have a son and bring him up in their own home. With these prospects before his eyes, he quickened his steps. He wanted to run—no, fly to hasten his return. He was now nearing the top of the hill. He wished he could suddenly meet his brothers and sisters. Would they ask him questions? He would, at any rate, not tell them all: the beating, the screening, and the work on roads and in quarries with an askari[2] always nearby ready to kick him if he relaxed. Yes. He had suffered many humiliations, and he had not resisted. Was there any need? But his soul and all the vigor of his manhood had rebelled and bled with rage and bitterness.

14 One day these wazungu[3] would go!

15 One day his people would be free! Then, then—he did not know what he would do. However, he bitterly assured himself no one would ever flout his manhood again.

16 He mounted the hill and then stopped. The whole plain lay below. The new village was before him—rows and rows of **compact** mud huts, crouching on the plain under the fast-vanishing sun. Dark blue smoke curled upward from various huts, to form a dark mist that hovered over the village. Beyond, the deep, blood-red sinking sun sent out fingerlike streaks of light that thinned outward and mingled with the gray mist shrouding the distant hills.

17 In the village, he moved from street to street, meeting new faces. He inquired. He found his home. He stopped at the entrance to the yard and breathed hard and full. This was the moment of his return home. His father sat huddled up on a three-legged stool. He was now very aged and Kamau pitied the old man. But he had been spared—yes, spared to see his son's return—

1. **Muranga** (moo RAHN gah) town in Kenya.
2. **askari** (ahs KAH ree) *n.* local soldier employed by the British Empire in colonial Africa.
3. **wazungu** (wah ZOON goo) *n.* people of European descent.

NOTES

Mark base words or indicate another strategy you used that helped you determine meaning.

compact (kuhm PAKT) *adj.*

MEANING:

NOTES

18 "Father!"

19 The old man did not answer. He just looked at Kamau with strange vacant eyes. Kamau was impatient. He felt annoyed and irritated. Did he not see him? Would he behave like the women Kamau had met by the river?

20 In the street, naked and half-naked children were playing, throwing dust at one another. The sun had already set and it looked as if there would be moonlight.

21 "Father, don't you remember me?" Hope was sinking in him. He felt tired. Then he saw his father suddenly start and tremble like a leaf. He saw him stare with unbelieving eyes. Fear was discernible in those eyes. His mother came, and his brothers too. They crowded around him. His aged mother clung to him and sobbed hard.

22 "I knew my son would come. I knew he was not dead."

23 "Why, who told you I was dead?"

24 "That Karanja, son of Njogu."

25 And then Kamau understood. He understood his trembling father. He understood the women at the river. But one thing puzzled him: he had never been in the same detention camp with Karanja. Anyway he had come back. He wanted now to see Muthoni. Why had she not come out? He wanted to shout, "I have come, Muthoni; I am here." He looked around. His mother understood him. She quickly darted a glance at her man and then simply said:

26 "Muthoni went away."

27 Kamau felt something cold settle in his stomach. He looked at the village huts and the dullness of the land. He wanted to ask many questions but he dared not. He could not yet believe that Muthoni had gone. But he knew by the look of the women at the river, by the look of his parents, that she was gone.

28 "She was a good daughter to us," his mother was explaining. "She waited for you and patiently bore all the ills of the land. Then Karanja came and said that you were dead. Your father believed him. She believed him too and keened[4] for a month. Karanja constantly paid us visits. He was of your Rika,[5] you know. Then she got a child. We could have kept her. But where is the land? Where is the food? Ever since land consolidation,[6] our last security was taken away. We let Karanja go with her. Other women have done worse—gone to town. Only the infirm and the old have been left here."

29 He was not listening; the coldness in his stomach slowly changed to bitterness. He felt bitter against all, all the people including his father and mother. They had betrayed him. They had leagued against him, and Karanja had always been his rival. Five years was admittedly not a short time. But why did she go? Why did they allow her to go? He wanted to speak. Yes, speak and denounce

4. **keened** *v.* wailed in mourning.
5. **Rika** (REE kah) *n.* group of Gikuyu children that are the same age.
6. **land consolidation** British policy of seizing Gikuyu land to make large farms for cash crops.

everything—the women by the river, the village, and the people who dwelled there. But he could not. This bitter thing was choking him.

30 "You—you gave my own away?" he whispered.

31 "Listen, child, child . . ."

32 The big yellow moon dominated the horizon. He hurried away bitter and blind, and only stopped when he came to the Honia River.

33 And standing at the bank, he saw not the river, but his hopes dashed on the ground instead. The river moved swiftly, making ceaseless monotonous murmurs. In the forest the crickets and other insects kept up an incessant buzz. And above, the moon shone bright. He tried to remove his coat, and the small bundle he had held onto so firmly fell. It rolled down the bank and before Kamau knew what was happening, it was floating swiftly down the river. For a time he was shocked and wanted to retrieve it. What would he show his—Oh, had he forgotten so soon? His wife had gone. And the little things that had so strangely reminded him of her and that he had guarded all those years, had gone! He did not know why, but somehow he felt relieved. Thoughts of drowning himself dispersed. He began to put on his coat, murmuring to himself, "Why should she have waited for me? Why should all the changes have waited for my return?" ❧

NOTES

Comprehension Check

Complete the following items after you finish your first read. Review and clarify details with your group.

1. Where has Kamau been for the five years preceding the events in the story?

2. Where is Kamau going as the story begins?

3. How does Kamau's mother feel about Kamau's wife, Muthoni?

4. **Notebook** To confirm your understanding, write a summary of the story.

RESEARCH

Research to Clarify Choose an unfamiliar detail from the text. Briefly research that detail. How has the information you learned shed light on an aspect of the story?

THE RETURN

TIP

GROUP DISCUSSION

As your group discusses the story, try to build upon each other's ideas so that you can deepen your understanding of the text.

Close Read the Text

With your group, revisit sections of the text you marked during your first read. **Annotate** details that you notice. What **questions** do you have? What can you **conclude**?

Analyze the Text

CITE TEXTUAL EVIDENCE to support your answers.

Complete the activities.

1. **Review and Clarify** With your group, reread paragraphs 4–6. Discuss the reaction to Kamau that the three women at the river have. What is the "secret" that he feels is binding them together?
2. **Present and Discuss** Work with your group to share other key passages from the selection. What passage did you focus on? What made you choose this particular passage? Take turns presenting your choices.
3. **Essential Question:** ***What can we learn from a journey?*** What has this selection taught you about journeys? Discuss with your group.

LANGUAGE DEVELOPMENT

Concept Vocabulary

sprawling **serpentine** **compact**

Why These Words? The three concept vocabulary words are related. With your group, determine what the words have in common. How do these word choices enhance the impact of the text?

Practice

Notebook Confirm your understanding of these words from the text by using them in sentences. Provide context clues to each word's meaning.

WORD NETWORK

Add interesting words related to journeys from the text to your Word Network.

Word Study

Latin Suffix: *-ine* In "The Return," the author describes the Honia River's movement as *serpentine*. The word *serpentine* ends with the Latin suffix *-ine*, which means "of," "like," or "related to." The suffix appears in many adjectives that describe animals or animal-like qualities. For instance, you may be familiar with *canine*, meaning "related to dogs."

1. Explain why the word *serpentine* may be a fitting word to describe a river.
2. Use a college-level dictionary to look up these words that end with the suffix *-ine: bovine, leonine, porcine.* Write the animal to which each word refers.

STANDARDS

Reading Literature

- Analyze how an author's choices concerning how to structure a text, order events within it, and manipulate time create such effects as mystery, tension, or surprise.
- Analyze a particular point of view or cultural experience reflected in a work of literature from outside the United States, drawing on a wide reading of world literature.

Language

- Identify and correctly use patterns of word changes that indicate different meanings or parts of speech.
- Demonstrate understanding of figurative language, word relationships, and nuances in word meanings.

Analyze Craft and Structure

Author's Choices: Plot Devices Short story authors draw on various literary devices to build suspense and add meaning to their narratives. Two essential devices in "The Return" are *foreshadowing* and *situational irony.*

Foreshadowing is the use of clues carefully placed throughout a story that hint at later events. For example, in "The Return," the strange behavior of the women at the river raises questions in readers' minds about how Kamau will be received at home. These clues help to pull readers through the story, and make the sequence of events feel logical and unified.

Situational irony also plays with readers' expectations. **Situational irony** occurs when events in a story directly challenge readers' or characters' expectations. Authors use situational irony to interest and surprise readers and to emphasize and deepen meaning.

CITE TEXTUAL EVIDENCE to support your answers.

Practice

With your group, review "The Return" to identify elements of foreshadowing and situational irony in the story. Then, individually, complete the charts to understand how foreshadowing sets up expectations that affect situational irony. Finally, gauge the impact of situational irony on what the story says about homecomings.

FORESHADOWING IN "THE RETURN"		
STORY CLUES	QUESTIONS RAISED	WHAT THE CLUES SUGGEST

SITUATIONAL IRONY IN "THE RETURN"		
EXPECTATIONS	WHAT ACTUALLY HAPPENS	CONNECTION TO THE STORY'S MEANING

THE RETURN

Conventions

Active and Passive Voice The **voice** of a verb indicates whether the subject is performing the action or is being acted upon. A verb is in the **active voice** if its subject performs the action. A verb is in the **passive voice** if its action is performed upon the subject. A passive verb is always a verb phrase made from a form of *to be* plus the past participle of a verb—for instance, *is eaten, has been deceived,* or *will be sung*.

Passive Voice: The mouse <u>was trapped</u> by the cat.

Active Voice: The cat <u>trapped</u> the mouse.

The active voice tends to be more direct and economical. However, the passive voice does have two important uses. Writers use the passive voice to emphasize the receiver of an action rather than the performer. They also use the passive voice to point out the receiver of an action when the performer is not important or not easily identified.

Read It

Work individually. Read each of these passages from "The Return." Mark each verb or verb phrase. Then, write whether the passage is in the active voice or the passive voice. When you are done, discuss your answers with your group. Resolve any differences in your answers.

1. But a thin train of dust was left in the air. . . .

2. The bundle held the bitterness and hardships of the years. . . .

3. And suddenly he felt a strong nostalgia for his old home, friends and surroundings.

4. Ever since land consolidation, our last security was taken away.

5. The big yellow moon dominated the horizon.

Write It

Notebook Work individually. Write two sentences about "The Return" in the passive voice. Then, revise those sentences so that they are in the active voice. When you are done, share your sentences with your group. Discuss the effect your revisions had on the impact of your sentences.

STANDARDS

Writing
Write informative/explanatory texts to examine and convey complex ideas, concepts, and information clearly and accurately through the effective selection, organization, and analysis of content.

Language
Demonstrate command of the conventions of standard English grammar and usage when writing or speaking.

Writing to Sources

Assignment

Writing can help you understand and explain your response to a story. Choose from the following projects.

- ☐ Write a **chat board post** in which you explain your response to the story. Identify the moment or moments that had the greatest impact on you, and explain the reasons they were effective. You may assume that your readers have read the story.
- ☐ "The Return" presents many details specific to the Kenyan cultural experience. Do these details make the story more or less universal? Support your answer by writing a **short essay** explaining the effect of specific details on the reader.
- ☐ Imagine that you are a film director. Draft an **adaptation proposal** for the story to create a short film. Describe the devices you will use to reflect specific effects achieved by the author.

Project Plan Before you begin, make a list of the tasks you will need to accomplish in order to complete your chosen assignment. Develop your central idea and write it so that it will guide the rest of your work. Review the selection or conduct research as needed to complete the tasks you have listed. Then, assign individual group members to each task. Finally, determine how you will make decisions about choices of images, text, and the overall design of your project.

Sensory Details Words and phrases that appeal to the senses have a strong impact on readers. Similarly, film writers choose images and sounds for the impact they will have on the audience. Use the chart below to record some sensory details you want to be sure to use in your writing.

SENSORY DETAIL	EFFECT ON READER/AUDIENCE

EVIDENCE LOG

Before moving on to a new selection, go to your Evidence Log and record what you learned from "The Return."

About the Authors

Joseph Campbell (1904–1987) At the age of seven, Joseph Campbell attended Buffalo Bill's Wild West show and became enamored with all things Native American. His curiosity led him to an interest in anthropology and English literature. Through those disciplines, Campbell developed new insights into heroes and myths, which he shared in his acclaimed book *The Hero With a Thousand Faces*.

Bill Moyers (b. 1934) A publisher, writer, press secretary, presidential assistant, deputy director of the Peace Corps, and broadcast journalist, Bill Moyers has expanded the tradition of television journalism to include not only political discussion but also conversations with some of the world's leading thinkers. Moyers worked for both CBS and PBS starting in the 1970s, and he continues to work for PBS.

from The Hero's Adventure

Concept Vocabulary

As you perform your first read of the excerpt from "The Hero's Adventure," you will encounter these words.

infantile psyche dependency

Context Clues To infer the meaning of an unfamiliar word, look to its context—the words and sentences that surround it.

Example: Sammy complained that he was experiencing **vertigo** and could not seem to get his balance.

Explanation: The underlined context clues provide hints that *vertigo* means "state of being dizzy or off balance."

Example: The senator told his **constituents,** "If you vote for me in the next election, I will make our state great again!"

Explanation: The underlined context clues help you to infer that *constituents* refers to the people who are able to vote for the senator and determine his reelection. *Constituents* must mean "people represented by a public official."

Apply your knowledge of context clues and other vocabulary strategies to determine the meanings of unfamiliar words you encounter during your first read.

First Read NONFICTION

Apply these strategies as you conduct your first read. You will have an opportunity to complete a close read after your first read.

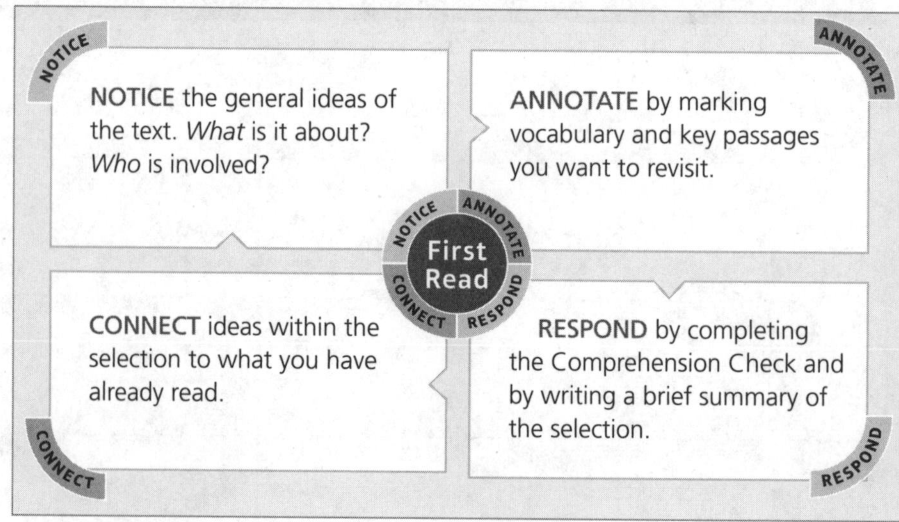

NOTICE
NOTICE the general ideas of the text. *What* is it about? *Who* is involved?
ANNOTATE
ANNOTATE by marking vocabulary and key passages you want to revisit.
First Read
CONNECT ideas within the selection to what you have already read.
RESPOND by completing the Comprehension Check and by writing a brief summary of the selection.
CONNECT
RESPOND

STANDARDS

Reading Informational Text
By the end of grade 9, read and comprehend literary nonfiction in the grades 9–10 text complexity band proficiently, with scaffolding as needed at the high end of the range.

Language
Use context as a clue to the meaning of a word or phrase.

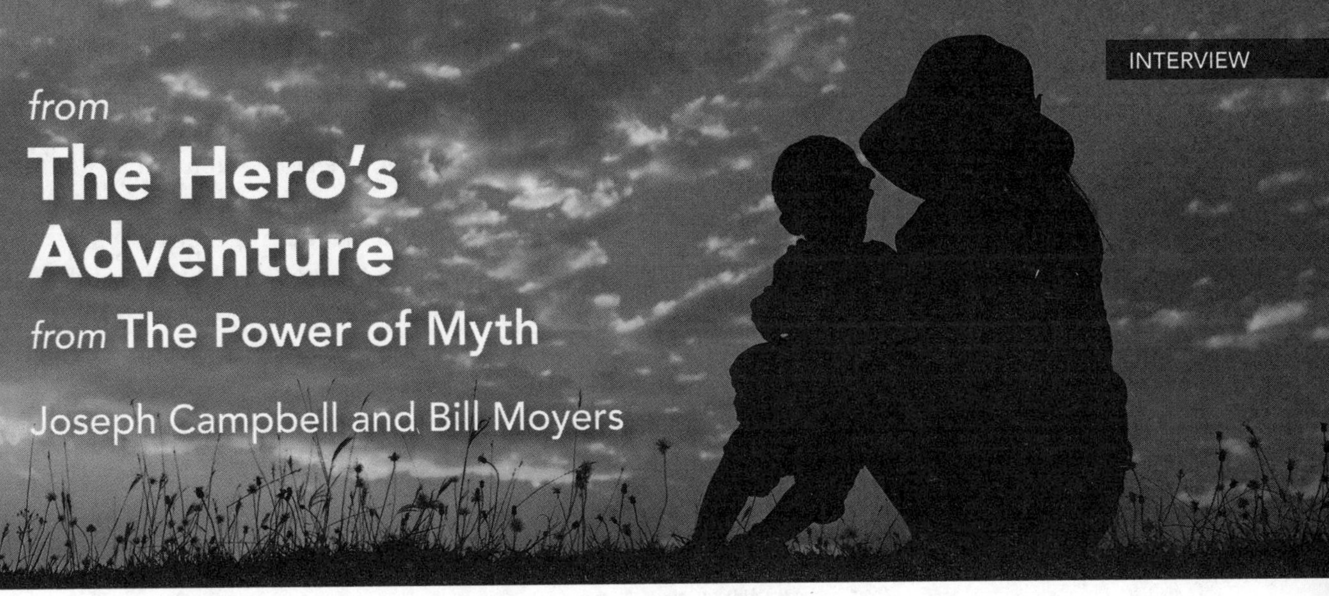

INTERVIEW

from
The Hero's Adventure
from The Power of Myth
Joseph Campbell and Bill Moyers

BACKGROUND

Joseph Campbell first published his theories about the structure of myth in his 1949 book *The Hero With A Thousand Faces*. In it, he describes the monomyth, a single central myth that he believes is present in all human societies. This interview is a brief excerpt of a famous series of conversations between Campbell and Bill Moyers.

1 **Moyers:** Why are there so many stories of the hero in mythology?

2 **Campbell:** Because that's what's worth writing about. Even in popular novels, the main character is a hero or heroine who has found or done something beyond the normal range of achievement and experience. A hero is someone who has given his or her life to something bigger than oneself.

3 **Moyers:** So in all of these cultures, whatever the local costume the hero might be wearing, what is the deed?

4 **Campbell:** Well, there are two types of deed. One is the physical deed, in which the hero performs a courageous act in battle or saves a life. The other kind is the spiritual deed, in which the hero learns to experience the supernormal range of human spiritual life and then comes back with a message.

5 The usual hero adventure begins with someone from whom something has been taken, or who feels there's something lacking in the normal experiences available or permitted to the members of his society. This person then takes off on a series of adventures beyond the ordinary, either to recover what has been lost or to discover some life-giving elixir. It's usually a cycle, a going and a returning.

6 But the structure and something of the spiritual sense of this adventure can be seen already anticipated in the puberty or initiation rituals of early tribal societies, through which a child is compelled to give up its childhood and become an adult—to die, you might say, to its **infantile** personality and **psyche** and come back as a responsible adult. This is a fundamental psychological transformation that everyone has to undergo. We are in childhood in a condition of **dependency** under someone's protection and supervision for some

NOTES

Mark context clues or indicate another strategy you used that helped you determine meaning.

infantile (IHN fuhn tyl) *adj.*

MEANING:

psyche (SY kee) *n.*

MEANING:

dependency (dih PEHN duhn see) *n.*

MEANING:

NOTES

fourteen to twenty-one years—and if you're going on for your Ph.D., this may continue to perhaps thirty-five. You are in no way a self-responsible, free agent, but an obedient dependent, expecting and receiving punishments and rewards. To evolve out of this position of psychological immaturity to the courage of self-responsibility and assurance requires a death and a resurrection. That's the basic motif of the universal hero's journey—leaving one condition and finding the source of life to bring you forth into a richer or mature condition.

7 **Moyers:** So even if we happen not to be heroes in the grand sense of redeeming society, we still have to take that journey inside ourselves, spiritually and psychologically.

8 **Campbell:** That's right. Otto Rank in his important little book *The Myth of the Birth of the Hero* declares that everyone is a hero in birth, where he undergoes a tremendous psychological as well as physical transformation, from the condition of a little water creature living in a realm of amniotic fluid into an air-breathing mammal which ultimately will be standing. That's an enormous transformation, and had it been consciously undertaken, it would have been, indeed, a heroic act. And there was a heroic act on the mother's part, as well, who had brought this all about.

9 **Moyers:** Then heroes are not all men?

10 **Campbell:** Oh, no. The male usually has the more conspicuous role, just because of the conditions of life. He is out there in the world, and the woman is in the home. But among the Aztecs, for example, who had a number of heavens to which people's souls would be assigned according to the conditions of their death, the heaven for warriors killed in battle was the same for mothers who died in childbirth. Giving birth is definitely a heroic deed, in that it is the giving over of oneself to the life of another.

11 **Moyers:** Don't you think we've lost that truth in this society of ours, where it's deemed more heroic to go out into the world and make a lot of money than it is to raise children?

12 **Campbell:** Making money gets more advertisement. You know the old saying: if a dog bites a man, that's not a story, but if a man bites a dog, you've got a story there. So the thing that happens and happens and happens, no matter how heroic it may be, is not news. Motherhood has lost its novelty, you might say.

13 **Moyers:** That's a wonderful image, though—the mother as hero.

14 **Campbell:** It has always seemed so to me. That's something I learned from reading these myths.

15 **Moyers:** It's a journey—you have to move out of the known, conventional safety of your life to undertake this.

16 **Campbell:** You have to be transformed from a maiden to a mother. That's a big change, involving many dangers.

17 **Moyers:** And when you come back from your journey, with the child, you've brought something for the world.

18 **Campbell:** Not only that, you've got a life job ahead of you. Otto Rank makes the point that there is a world of people who think that their heroic act in being born qualifies them for the respect and support of their whole community.

19 **Moyers:** But there's still a journey to be taken after that.

20 **Campbell:** There's a large journey to be taken, of many trials.

21 **Moyers:** What's the significance of the trials, and tests, and ordeals of the hero?

22 **Campbell:** If you want to put it in terms of intentions, the trials are designed to see to it that the intending hero should be really a hero. Is he really a match for this task? Can he overcome the dangers? Does he have the courage, the knowledge, the capacity, to enable him to serve? ❧

NOTES

Comprehension Check

Complete the following items after you finish your first read. Review and clarify details with your group.

1. How does Campbell define a hero?

2. What are the two types of deeds that make up the hero's journey?

3. Describe the main stages in a typical hero's adventure.

4. **Notebook** Write a five-sentence summary of "The Hero's Adventure."

RESEARCH

Research to Clarify Choose at least one unfamiliar detail from the text. Briefly research that detail. In what way does the information you learned shed light on an aspect of the interview?

from THE HERO'S ADVENTURE

Close Read the Text

With your group, revisit sections of the text you marked during your First Read. **Annotate** details that you notice. What **questions** do you have? What can you **conclude**?

Analyze the Text

CITE TEXTUAL EVIDENCE to support your answers.

Complete the activities.

1. **Review and Clarify** With your group, reread paragraphs 4–8 of the interview. Discuss the idea that "everyone is a hero." Does this concept grant dignity to every individual, or does it weaken the idea of heroism?

2. **Present and Discuss** Now, work with your group to share the passages from the selection that you found especially important. Discuss what you notice in the selection, what questions you asked, and what conclusions you reached.

3. **Essential Question:** ***What can we learn from a journey?*** What has this text taught you about journeys? Discuss with your group.

TIP

GROUP DISCUSSION

Consider "trying on" opinions that are different from your own by expressing and defending opposite viewpoints as clearly and strongly as possible. This technique can help you understand other points of view and may lead you to modify or expand your own response.

LANGUAGE DEVELOPMENT

Concept Vocabulary

infantile **psyche** **dependency**

Why These Words? The three concept vocabulary words are related. With your group, determine what the words have in common. Write your ideas, and add another word that fits the category.

Practice

Notebook Confirm your understanding of these words by writing sentences as a team. One group member begins with a single word. Take turns adding one word at a time until you have a complete sentence that uses one concept vocabulary word. Evaluate the sentence as a group to make sure the word is used correctly. Repeat for the other two concept vocabulary words.

WORD NETWORK

Add interesting words related to journeys from the text to your Word Network.

Word Study

Notebook **Etymology: Greek Names** A word's origins are called its **etymology**. The word *psyche* comes from a name from Greek mythology. Psyche was a young woman who fell in love with the god Eros. As a result of their relationship, she became closely identified with the soul—a connection still reflected in the meaning of the English word *psyche*.

1. Research the etymology of each of these other words that come from Greek mythology: *draconian, herculean, iridescent, lethargic.*

2. Share with your group information about the original Greek names, and discuss how the words' origins are reflected in their English meanings.

STANDARDS

Reading Informational Text
Analyze how the author unfolds an analysis or series of ideas or events, including the order in which the points are made, how they are introduced and developed, and the connections that are drawn between them.

Language
- Consult general and specialized reference materials, both print and digital, to find the pronunciation of a word or determine or clarify its precise meaning, its part of speech, or its etymology.
- Demonstrate understanding of figurative language, word relationships, and nuances in word meanings.

Analyze Craft and Structure

Development of Ideas An **interview** is an exchange of ideas between an interviewer and an expert or someone who has had a unique experience. The basic structure of an interview is the **Q&A** (question-and-answer) **format**. A good interviewer does not simply follow a script of prepared questions, wait for an answer, and proceed to the next question. Instead, interviewers use different types of questions and statements to create a fluid exchange of ideas. The interviewer builds on and clarifies the interviewee's ideas during the conversation, resulting in a smooth progression of anecdotes and ideas that informs and engages the audience. In most cases, interviews are edited for organization and consistency before publication.

Interviews may include these techniques to develop and communicate ideas:

- **Follow-up questions** build on the interview subject's response, clarifying and deepening answers.
- **Restatements,** or paraphrases, help an interviewer make sure the audience understands the main point the interviewee is communicating.
- **Clarifications** focus on a specific part of a response, sometimes simplifying the original idea and other times providing more detail.

COLLABORATION
When analyzing the structure of a text as a group, have each group member scan the text for one technique or strategy. Then, share your analyses to draw conclusions about which strategies are used most frequently and most effectively.

Practice

CITE TEXTUAL EVIDENCE to support your answers.

Working as a group, use the chart to analyze how ideas are introduced and developed in "The Hero's Adventure." Cite an example of each technique listed. Then, explain how the technique is used to introduce, build on, or clarify an idea.

TECHNIQUE	EXAMPLES	EXPLANATION
Initial Question		
Follow-Up Question		
Restatement		
Clarification		

from THE HERO'S ADVENTURE

Conventions

Gerunds and Gerund Phrases A **gerund** is a form of a verb that ends in *-ing* and acts as a noun. A **gerund phrase** is a gerund and its modifiers, objects, or complements, all acting together as a noun.

This box shows examples of the ways a gerund or gerund phrase can function in a sentence. The gerunds are italicized, and the gerund phrases are underlined.

Subject: *Surfing* is Heather's hobby.

Direct Object: Yan enjoys *floating* slowly down the river.

Predicate Noun: Ahmed's greatest talent is *playing* the piano.

Object of a Preposition: Wei never gets tired of *playing* boardgames.

Appositive Phrase: I am putting off the worst chore, *cleaning* the kitchen.

Read It

Work individually. Read these sentences from "The Hero's Adventure." In the chart, identify each gerund phrase and its function in the sentence. Discuss your answers with your group.

SENTENCE	GERUND PHRASE	FUNCTION
So even if we happen not to be heroes in the grand sense of redeeming society . . . (paragraph 7)		
Making money gets more advertisement. (paragraph 7)		
. . . it is the giving over of oneself to the life of another. (paragraph 10)		
That's the basic motif of the universal hero's journey—leaving one condition. . . . (paragraph 6)		

Write It

Notebook Write a paragraph summarizing what Campbell and Moyers talked about in the interview. In your paragraph, use at least two gerund phrases.

STANDARDS

Writing

- Conduct short as well as more sustained research projects to answer a question or solve a problem; narrow or broaden the inquiry when appropriate; synthesize multiple sources on the subject, demonstrating understanding of the subject under investigation.
- Draw evidence from literary or informational texts to support analysis, reflection, and research.

Language

- Demonstrate command of the conventions of standard English grammar and usage when writing or speaking.
- Use various types of phrases and clauses to convey specific meanings and add variety and interest to writing or presentations.

Research

Assignment

With your group, create a **multimedia presentation** in which you incorporate charts, images, video, music, or any other media that help convey your ideas effectively to explain a subject. Choose from the following options:

- ☐ Research and present the "origin story" of a hero from literature, film, television, or another narrative choice. Incorporate Campbell's theories about what heroism is.
- ☐ Joseph Campbell's philosophy is often summarized in his quote "Follow your bliss." Research what Campbell means by this quotation and consider whether or not this belief is consistent with the ideas he expresses in the interview.
- ☐ Moyers and Campbell discuss one way that women can be heroes. Research three different cultural perspectives on female heroes and relate them to the concept of the hero's journey.

EVIDENCE LOG

Before moving on to a new selection, go to your Evidence Log and record what you learned from "The Hero's Adventure."

Project Plan Make a list of tasks that your group will need to carry out. Assign individual group members to carry out each task. Determine how you will obtain or create multimedia items for your presentation, which may include text, charts, images, video, music, and other media. Use this chart to organize your plans.

Working Title: ______________________________

TASK	WHO	QUESTIONS TO ASK

Practice Practice your presentation before you present it to your class. Include the following performance techniques to help you achieve the desired effect.

- Speak clearly and comfortably without rushing.
- Vary the tone and pitch of your voice in order to convey meaning and add interest. Avoid speaking in a flat, monotone style.
- Use appropriate and effective body language. Maintain eye contact to keep your audience's attention.
- Ensure that you can present your media smoothly, without technical problems.

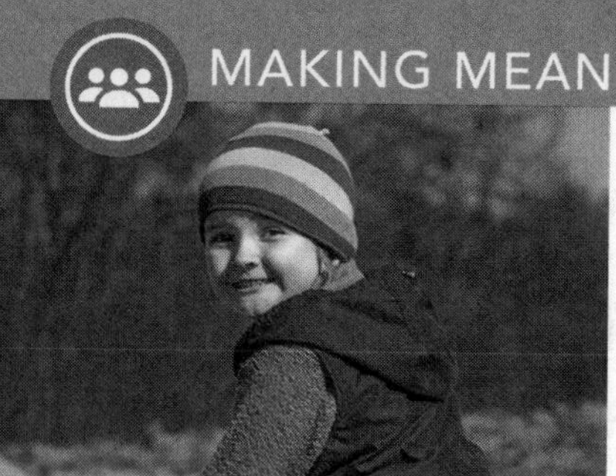

POETRY COLLECTION 1

Courage

Ithaka

from The Narrow Road of the Interior

Concept Vocabulary

As you perform your first read of these three poems, you will encounter the following words.

awesome	destined	eternal

Context Clues If these words are unfamiliar to you, try using context clues to help you determine their meanings. There are various types of context clues that you may encounter as you read.

Synonyms: The house was terribly shabby, really **dilapidated**.

Restatement of Ideas: The **convoluted** explanation confused the children, who were not accustomed to someone speaking in a rambling, disconnected way.

Contrast of Ideas: I really like to stay home, but she gets **wanderlust** every time she sees a train.

Apply your knowledge of context clues and other vocabulary strategies to determine the meanings of unfamiliar words you encounter during your first read. If necessary, verify the meaning you infer using a dictionary.

First Read POETRY

Apply these strategies as you conduct your first read. You will have an opportunity to complete a close read after your first read.

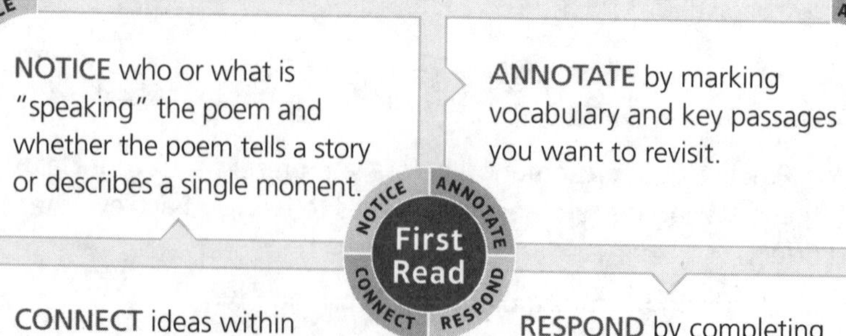

NOTICE
NOTICE who or what is "speaking" the poem and whether the poem tells a story or describes a single moment.
ANNOTATE
ANNOTATE by marking vocabulary and key passages you want to revisit.
NOTICE ANNOTATE First Read CONNECT RESPOND
CONNECT ideas within the selection to what you already know and what you have already read.
RESPOND by completing the Comprehension Check.
CONNECT
RESPOND

STANDARDS

Reading Literature
By the end of grade 9, read and comprehend literature, including stories, dramas, and poems, in the grades 9–10 text complexity band proficiently, with scaffolding as needed at the high end of the range.

Language
- Use context as a clue to the meaning of a word or phrase.
- Verify the preliminary determination of the meaning of a word or phrase.

About the Poets

Anne Sexton (1928–1974) had a difficult childhood growing up in Massachusetts. She attended boarding school, married at nineteen to a soldier serving in the Korean War, and later found work as a model. Sexton's work is considered to be part of the "confessional" movement in American poetry. Emerging in the 1950s and including poets such as Sylvia Plath and John Berryman, confessional poetry emphasized intensely personal experiences in a way not previously seen in American literature.

Of Greek descent, **C. P. Cavafy** (1863–1933) was born in Egypt to parents who worked in the import-export business. After the death of his father, Cavafy's family relocated to Liverpool, England, where Cavafy spent most of his teenage years. An obscure poet during his lifetime, Cavafy is now regarded as one of Greece's greatest writers.

Widely regarded as the seventeenth-century master of haiku, **Matsuo Bashō** (1644–1694) became interested in literature as a child and soon began writing poems in collaboration with others. After losing his home to a fire, Basho walked over 1,200 miles for more than five months and described his travels in some of his best-known poems, including "Travelogue of Weather-Beaten Bones."

Backgrounds

Courage

Anne Sexton's life and work were intimately tied together. She struggled with mental illness but found in poetry a way to confront and release her fears. Perhaps it was her daily struggle with fear that inspired this poem about courage.

Ithaka

Ithaka (or Ithaca), a part of Greece, is a real island in the Ionian sea. It is also the fabled island home to which Odysseus, the epic hero of the *Odyssey*, struggles to return. It is this second meaning that drives the symbolism of this poem.

from The Narrow Road of the Interior

This is an excerpt from Bashō's famous *haibun*, a classical Japanese form of literature that combines elements of prose with *haiku*. Haiku are unrhymed verses arranged into three lines of five, seven, and five syllables. The haiku poet often uses a striking image from nature to convey a strong emotion.

Courage

Anne Sexton

It is in the small things we see it.
The child's first step,
as **awesome** as an earthquake.
The first time you rode a bike,
wallowing up the sidewalk.
The first spanking when your heart
went on a journey all alone.
When they called you crybaby
or poor or fatty or crazy
and made you into an alien,
you drank their acid
and concealed it.
Later,
if you faced the death of bombs and bullets
you did not do it with a banner,
you did it with only a hat to
cover your heart.
You did not fondle the weakness inside you
though it was there.
Your courage was a small coal
that you kept swallowing.
If your buddy saved you
and died himself in so doing,
then his courage was not courage,
it was love; love as simple as shaving soap.
Later,
if you have endured a great despair,
then you did it alone,
getting a transfusion from the fire,
picking the scabs off your heart,
then wringing it out like a sock.
Next, my kinsman, you powdered your sorrow,
you gave it a back rub
and then you covered it with a blanket
and after it had slept a while
it woke to the wings of the roses
and was transformed.
Later,
when you face old age and its natural conclusion
your courage will still be shown in the little ways,
each spring will be a sword you'll sharpen,
those you love will live in a fever of love,
and you'll bargain with the calendar
and at the last moment
when death opens the back door
you'll put on your carpet slippers
and stride out.

NOTES

Mark context clues or indicate another strategy you used that helped you determine meaning.

awesome (AW suhm) *adj.*

MEANING:

POETRY

Ithaka

C. P. Cavafy

translated by Edmund Keeley and Philip Sherrard

NOTES

As you set out for Ithaka
hope the voyage is a long one,
full of adventure, full of discovery.
Laistrygonians[1] and Cyclops,
angry Poseidon—don't be afraid of them:
you'll never find things like that on your way
as long as you keep your thoughts raised high,
as long as a rare excitement
stirs your spirit and your body.
Laistrygonians and Cyclops,
wild Poseidon—you won't encounter them
unless you bring them along inside your soul,
unless your soul sets them up in front of you.

1. **Laistrygonians** (lehs trih GOH nee uhnz) cannibals who destroy all of Odysseus' ships except his own and kill the crews.

Hope the voyage is a long one.
May there be many a summer morning when,
with what pleasure, what joy,
you come into harbors seen for the first time;
may you stop at Phoenician trading stations
to buy fine things,
mother of pearl and coral, amber and ebony,
sensual perfume of every kind—
as many sensual perfumes as you can;
and may you visit many Egyptian cities
to gather stores of knowledge from their scholars.

Keep Ithaka always in your mind.
Arriving there is what you are **destined** for.
But do not hurry the journey at all.
Better if it lasts for years,
so you are old by the time you reach the island,
wealthy with all you have gained on the way,
not expecting Ithaka to make you rich.

Ithaka gave you the marvelous journey.
Without her you would not have set out.
She has nothing left to give you now.

And if you find her poor, Ithaka won't have fooled you.
Wise as you will have become, so full of experience,
you will have understood by then what these Ithakas mean.

NOTES

Mark context clues or indicate another strategy you used that helped you determine meaning.

destined (DEHS tihnd) *adj.*

MEANING:

POETRY

from

The Narrow Road of the Interior

Matsuo Bashō
translated by Helen Craig McCullough

1 The sun and the moon are **eternal** voyagers; the years that come and go are travelers too. For those whose lives float away on boats, for those who greet old age with hands clasping the lead ropes of horses, travel is life, travel is home. And many are the men of old who have perished as they journeyed.

2 I myself fell prey to wanderlust some years ago, desiring nothing better than to be a vagrant cloud scudding before the wind. Only last autumn, after having drifted along the seashore for a time, had I swept away the old cobwebs from my dilapidated riverside hermitage. But the year ended before I knew it, and I found myself looking at hazy spring skies and thinking of crossing Shirakawa Barrier.[1] Bewitched by the god of restlessness, I lost my peace of mind; summoned by the spirits of the road, I felt unable to settle down to anything. By the time I had mended my torn trousers, put a new cord on my hat, and cauterized my legs with moxa,[2] I was thinking only of the moon at Matsushima.[3] I turned over my dwelling to others, moved to a house belonging to Sanpū,[4] and affixed the initial page of a linked-verse sequence to one of the pillars at my cottage.

kusa no to mo
sumikawaru yo zo
hana no ie

Even my grass-thatched hut
will have new occupants now:
a display of dolls.

NOTES

Mark context clues or indicate another strategy you used that helped you determine meaning.

eternal (ih TUR nuhl) *adj.*

MEANING:

1. **Shirakawa** (shee rah kah wah) **Barrier** ancient gate between the northern and southern regions of Honshu, the largest island of Japan.
2. **moxa** *n.* traditional medicine treatment similar to acupuncture, using burning herbs.
3. **Matsushima** (mah tsoo shee mah) group of Japanese islands known for their scenic views.
4. **Sanpū** (sahn poo) Sanpū Sugiyama, patron of Matsuo Bashō.

Comprehension Check

Complete the following items after you finish your first read. Review and clarify details with your group.

COURAGE

1. When the speaker of the poem says "you," is it meant to refer to only the readers' experiences—or the speaker's experiences as well? How do you know?

2. What effect does name calling have on its targets, according to the speaker?

3. According to the speaker, how does sorrow affect those who suffer a great loss?

ITHAKA

1. How does the speaker believe the traveler should react when encountering Cyclops and Poseidon?

2. What type of journey does the speaker hope the traveler has?

3. What does the speaker say will make the traveler wealthy?

from THE NARROW ROAD OF THE INTERIOR

1. In what way are the sun, the moon, and time similar to the speaker?

2. What does restlessness prevent the speaker from doing?

3. What becomes of the first page of verse the speaker writes after moving to a new home?

RESEARCH

Research to Explore The Cavafy and Bashō pieces may spark your curiosity to learn more. Briefly research a location mentioned in one of the poems. How does your newfound knowledge add to your appreciation of the text?

POETRY COLLECTION 1

Close Read the Text

With your group, revisit sections of the text you marked during your first read. **Annotate** details that you notice. What **questions** do you have? What can you **conclude**?

Analyze the Text

CITE TEXTUAL EVIDENCE to support your answers.

Complete the activities.

1. **Review and Clarify** With your group, reread the first stanzas of "Courage" and "Ithaka." Discuss the way the two speakers talk about the journey of life. What specific events does each speaker mention?
2. **Present and Discuss** Now, work with your group to share the passages from the text that you found especially important. Take turns presenting your passages. Discuss what you notice in the text, what questions you asked, and what conclusions you reached.
3. **Essential Question:** *What can we learn from a journey?* What have these texts taught you about journeys? Discuss with your group.

TIP

GROUP DISCUSSION

Some group members may have good contributions to make to the discussion but find it difficult to speak up. To make sure that you hear all the best ideas, reach out to quieter group members by asking them questions.

LANGUAGE DEVELOPMENT

Concept Vocabulary

awesome **destined** **eternal**

Why These Words? The three concept vocabulary words are related. With your group, determine what the words have in common. Write your ideas, and add another word that fits the category.

Practice

Notebook Confirm your understanding of these words from the text by using all three of them in a single sentence. Try several variations. Use context clues to help you make the meanings clear.

WORD NETWORK

Add interesting words related to journeys from the text to your Word Network.

Word Study

Anglo-Saxon Suffix: *-some* In "Courage," the speaker describes a child's first step as "awesome as an earthquake." The word *awesome* ends with the Anglo-Saxon suffix *-some*, which means "causing," "tending to," or "to a considerable degree" and is used to form adjectives from nouns, verbs, and other adjectives.

1. Write a definition for the word *awesome* that demonstrates your understanding of the suffix *-some*.

2. Write definitions for these words ending with the suffix *-some: troublesome, fearsome, quarrelsome*. Consult a dictionary if necessary.

STANDARDS

Language

- Identify and correctly use patterns of word changes that indicate different meanings or parts of speech.
- Demonstrate understanding of figurative language, word relationships, and nuances in word meaning.

Analyze Craft and Structure

Figurative Language Language used imaginatively rather than literally is referred to as **figurative language**. Its meaning is not what it appears to be. To say that a person's smile is "as warm as the sun," is not to say that a thermometer put next to his or her face would register thousands of degrees. This phrase means that the person's smile makes you feel good, the way a nice, warm, sunny day does. Figurative language often compares two things—like the sun and the smile—that are essentially different. Simile and metaphor are two examples of this.

- A **simile** is a comparison that uses a connecting word, either *like* or *as.* The example given above of the sun and the smile is a simile.
- A **metaphor** is a comparison that does not use a connecting word. Instead, the comparison is either implied or directly stated: "All the world's a stage."
- An **extended metaphor** is also called a **sustained metaphor**. It involves a metaphorical comparison that is developed through multiple references and layers of meaning.

Figurative language is especially useful for poets because it allows them to express complex emotions and ideas in vivid, powerful ways.

CITE TEXTUAL EVIDENCE to support your answers.

Practice

Working individually, use this chart to record and analyze three metaphors or similes from the poems. Compare and discuss your responses with your group

METAPHOR OR SIMILE	THINGS COMPARED	EFFECT ON THE READER

POETRY COLLECTION 1

Author's Style

Point of View The **point of view** of a piece of literature is the perspective from which a story or poem is narrated, spoken, or told. The point of view affects every aspect of a story or poem. The two most familiar and commonly used points of view are **first person** and **third person**. In first-person point of view, the narrator or speaker is a character in the story or poem who uses pronouns such as *I*, *me*, *we*, and *us* and **reflexive pronouns** such as *myself*. In third-person point of view, the narrator or speaker is a voice outside the work who uses third-person pronouns such as *he*, *she*, *they*, *them*, *him*, and *her*. A first-person narrator/speaker may refer to other characters using third-person pronouns, but a third-person narrator/speaker will never use a first-person pronoun.

The more unusual **second-person** narrator/speaker uses **direct address**, speaking directly to the reader and using second-person pronouns such as *you* and *your*. This point of view is rarely used in fiction, but it is often used in advertisements, handbooks, and song lyrics. It is frequently used in poetry. It focuses attention not on the person writing or speaking, and not on a character in a story, but on the person being spoken to.

First-person point of view: "I stepped around the corner and saw my destiny."

Second-person point of view: "You need to hold your hand very steady."

Third-person point of view: "He watched the sun fade from the sky."

Read It

Work individually. Use this chart to identify the point of view used in each of the poems. Quote evidence from the poems to support your choice.

SELECTION	POINT OF VIEW	EVIDENCE
Courage		
Ithaka		
The Narrow Road of the Interior		

Write It

Notebook Write a paragraph using either the first-person or the second-person point of view.

STANDARDS

Reading Literature
Determine the meaning of words and phrases as they are used in the text, including figurative and connotative meanings; analyze the cumulative impact of specific word choices on meaning and tone.

Language
Demonstrate command of the conventions of standard English grammar and usage when writing or speaking.

Speaking and Listening

Assignment

With your group, explore the ideas expressed in "Courage," "Ithaka," and "The Narrow Road of the Interior." Choose from the following options.

- ☐ **Nomination** Imagine that you are on a committee that will present student achievers with an engraved plaque featuring a poem. Discuss which of these poems you would recommend and why. You might also consider whether to include the entire poem or only a section.
- ☐ **Debate** Are some ideas better expressed through poetry than through prose? Choose your position, and defend it with examples from the poems.
- ☐ **Radio Broadcast** Present a radio show in which a caller asks for advice on a specific life issue. Respond with advice supported by a key theme or message of one of the poems. Quote relevant lines, and give examples.

Project Plan After you have selected an option, work with your group to determine what additional preparation is necessary. Review your group's rules for discussion: What methods do you have in place for taking and holding the floor? How do you ensure that diverse perspectives are represented in discussion? Decide how you will assign discussion roles to group members, and use this chart to record the responsibilities of each.

DISCUSSION ROLE	TASKS	GROUP MEMBER

EVIDENCE LOG

Before moving on to a new selection, go to your Evidence Log and record what you learned from "Courage," "Ithaka," and "The Narrow Road of the Interior."

STANDARDS

Speaking and Listening
Initiate and participate effectively in a range of collaborative discussions with diverse partners on grades 9–10 topics, texts, and issues, building on others' ideas and expressing their own clearly and persuasively.

SOURCES

- THE RETURN
- *from* THE HERO'S ADVENTURE
- COURAGE
- ITHAKA
- *from* THE NARROW ROAD OF THE INTERIOR

Deliver a Multimedia Presentation

Assignment

You have read a short story, an interview, and three poems that deal with different perspectives of journeys. Work with your group to develop, refine, and present a **multimedia presentation** in which you explain your answer to this question:

What different types of journeys are there, and how can they transform someone?

Plan with Your Group

Analyze the Text With your group, analyze the question, and decide how you will define the key terms *journeys* and *transform*. This will help you create a precise thesis on the topic of personal transformation and develop your ideas with evidence from the selections.

Next, discuss key information and themes at work in the selections you have read. Think about how each writer presents the idea of a journey. Make sure that your group expands its thinking beyond just physical journeys. Identify specific examples from the selections to support your group's ideas. Use a graphic organizer to list your ideas and textual evidence.

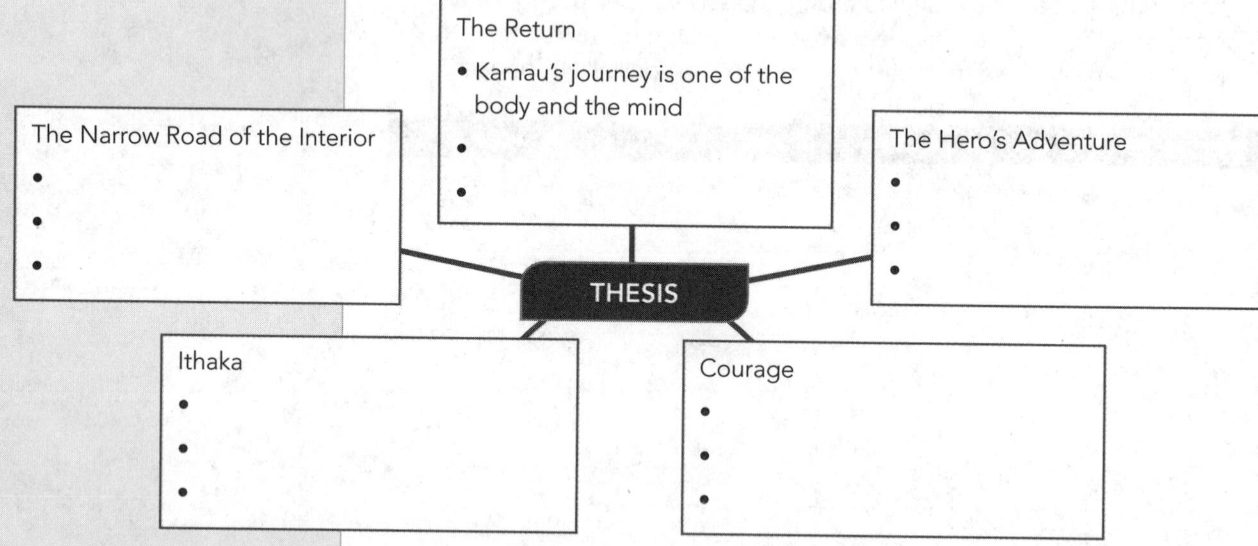

Gather Evidence and Media Examples As a group, brainstorm for types of media you can use to illustrate each example. Consider photographs, paintings or drawings, music, charts, graphs, and video. Next, make a research plan. Each group member should be assigned pieces of media to acquire. If possible, use your local library or media center. After you have gathered your text evidence and media, determine what equipment your presentation will require.

STANDARDS

Speaking and Listening
Present information, findings, and supporting evidence clearly, concisely and logically such that listeners can follow the line of reasoning and the organization, development, substance, and style are appropriate to purpose, audience, and task

Organize Your Ideas As a group, organize the script for your presentation. You may use the Multimedia Presentation Script shown here. Decide who will do what job in each part of the presentation. Also note when multimedia will be used.

MULTIMEDIA PRESENTATION SCRIPT		
	Media Cues	Script
Presenter 1		
Presenter 2		
Presenter 3		

Rehearse with Your Group

Practice with Your Group Use this checklist to evaluate the effectiveness of your group's first run-through. Then, use your evaluation and the instructions here to guide your revision.

CONTENT	USE OF MEDIA	PRESENTATION TECHNIQUES
☐ The presentation presents a clear thesis. ☐ Main ideas are supported with evidence from the texts in Small-Group Learning.	☐ The media support the thesis. ☐ The media communicate key ideas. ☐ Media are used evenly throughout the presentation. ☐ Equipment functions properly.	☐ Media are visible and audible. ☐ Transitions between media segments are smooth. ☐ The speaker uses eye contact and speaks clearly.

Fine-Tune the Content To make your explanation of the topic clearer or more thorough, you may need to go back into the texts to find more support for your main ideas. Alternately, you may need to add or replace some of your multimedia content. Check with your group to identify key details that are not clear to listeners. Find new or additional examples, definitions, or quotations to include.

Improve Your Use of Media Double-check that everything is in working order and make a back-up plan in case your equipment fails. If the media are not well distributed through the presentation, work to change the pacing.

Make sure you consider your audience and their interest level with your use of media. For instance, media can often add drama or visual interest to a wordy description.

Present and Evaluate

When you present as a group, be sure that each member has taken into account each of the checklist items. As you watch other groups, evaluate how well they meet the requirements on the checklist.

STANDARDS

Speaking and Listening

- Make strategic use of digital media in presentations to enhance understanding of findings, reasoning, and evidence and to add interest.
- Adapt speech to a variety of contexts and tasks, demonstrating a command of formal English when indicated or appropriate.

OVERVIEW: INDEPENDENT LEARNING

ESSENTIAL QUESTION:

What can we learn from a journey?

Reading about others' journeys can help us reflect on our own. In this section, you will complete your study of journeys of transformation by exploring an additional selection related to the topic. You'll then share what you learn with classmates. To choose a text, follow these steps.

Look Back Think about the selections you have already studied. What more do you want to know about the topic of journeys of transformation?

Look Ahead Preview the texts by reading the descriptions. Which one seems most interesting and appealing to you?

Look Inside Take a few minutes to scan the text you chose. Choose a different one if this text doesn't meet your needs.

Independent Learning Strategies

Throughout your life, in school, in your community, and in your career, you will need to rely on yourself to learn and work on your own. Review these strategies and the actions you can take to practice them during Independent Learning. Add ideas of your own to each category.

STRATEGY	ACTION PLAN
Create a schedule	• Understand your goals and deadlines. • Make a plan for what to do each day. •
Practice what you have learned	• Use first-read and close-read strategies to deepen your understanding. • After you read, evaluate the usefulness of the evidence to help you understand the topic. • Consider the quality and reliability of the source. •
Take notes	• Record important ideas and information • Review your notes before preparing to share with a group. •

CONTENTS

Choose one selection. Selections are available online only.

POETRY COLLECTION 2

The Road Not Taken

Robert Frost

Your World

Georgia Douglas Johnson

What can we find when we explore the unknown?

SHORT STORY

The Ugly Duckling

Hans Christian Andersen

Where we begin and where we end can be quite different.

MEDIA: PHOTO ESSAY

Thirteen Epic Animal Migrations That Prove Just How Cool Mother Nature Is

Brianna Elliott

What guides animals on their migrations of hundreds and even thousands of miles?

MEMOIR

from Wild

Cheryl Strayed

Can a hiker overcome the obstacles of both the trail and her own self-doubt to finish her journey?

PERFORMANCE-BASED ASSESSMENT PREP

Review Evidence for an Explanatory Essay

Complete your Evidence Log for the unit by evaluating what you have learned and synthesizing the information you have recorded.

First-Read Guide

Tool Kit
First-Read Guide and Model Annotation

Use this page to record your first-read ideas.

Selection Title: ______________________

NOTICE

NOTICE new information or ideas you learn about the unit topic as you first read this text.

ANNOTATE

ANNOTATE by marking vocabulary and key passages you want to revisit.

NOTICE ANNOTATE First Read CONNECT RESPOND

CONNECT ideas within the selection to other knowledge and the selections you have read.

RESPOND by writing a brief summary of the selection.

CONNECT

RESPOND

STANDARD

Reading Read and comprehend complex literary and informational texts independently and proficiently.

Close-Read Guide

Tool Kit
Close-Read Guide and Model Annotation

Use this page to record your close-read ideas.

Selection Title: ______________________________

Close Read the Text

Revisit sections of the text you marked during your first read. Read these sections closely and **annotate** what you notice. Ask yourself **questions** about the text. What can you **conclude**? Write down your ideas.

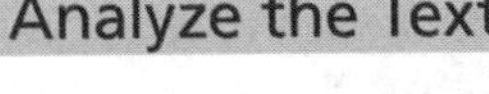

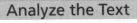

Analyze the Text

Think about the author's choices of patterns, structure, techniques, and ideas included in the text. Select one and record your thoughts about what this choice conveys.

QuickWrite

Pick a paragraph from the text that grabbed your interest. Explain the power of this passage.

STANDARD

Reading Read and comprehend complex literary and informational texts independently and proficiently.

EVIDENCE LOG

Go to your Evidence Log and record what you learned from the text you read.

Share Your Independent Learning

Prepare to Share

What can we learn from a journey?

Even when you read or learn something independently, you can continue to grow by sharing what you have learned with others. Reflect on the text you explored independently, and write notes about its connection to the unit. In your notes, consider why this text belongs in this unit.

Learn From Your Classmates

Discuss It Share your ideas about the text you explored on your own. As you talk with your classmates, jot down ideas that you learn from them.

Reflect

Review your notes, and underline the most important insight you gained from these writing and discussion activities. Explain how this idea adds to your understanding of the topic of journeys of transformation.

STANDARDS

Speaking and Listening
Initiate and participate effectively in a range of collaborative discussions with diverse partners on grades 9-10 *topics, texts, and issues,* building on others' ideas and expressing their own clearly and persuasively.

Review Evidence for an Explanatory Essay

At the beginning of the unit, you wrote a response to the following question:

When does the journey matter more than the destination?

EVIDENCE LOG

Review your Evidence Log and your QuickWrite from the beginning of the unit. Did you learn anything new?

☐ YES	☐ NO
Identify at least three ideas, definitions, or examples that stood out to you related to the topic of journeys of transformation.	Identify at least three ideas, definitions, or examples that reinforced your original ideas related to journeys of transformation.
1.	**1.**
2.	**2.**
3.	**3.**

Identify a fact or detail that relates to one of your revised ideas about journeys of transformation: ______________________________

____

Develop your thoughts into a topic sentence for an explanatory essay. Complete this sentence starter:

The journey matters more than the destination when

____

Evaluate Your Evidence Consider what information you learned. Did the texts you read expand your knowledge? If not, make a plan.

☐ Do more research
☐ Talk with my classmates
☐ Reread a selection
☐ Ask an expert
☐ Other: ______________________________

STANDARDS

Writing

Write informative/ explanatory texts to examine and convey ideas, concepts, and information clearly and accurately through the effective selection, organization, and analysis of content.

SOURCES

- WHOLE-CLASS SELECTIONS
- SMALL-GROUP SELECTIONS
- INDEPENDENT LEARNING

PART 1

Writing to Sources: Explanatory Essay

In this unit, you read about the journeys of various people and characters. When they reached their destination, these characters learned something new about themselves and the world.

Assignment

Write an explanatory essay in which you examine a topic and convey ideas, concepts, procedures, and information related to the following question:

When does the journey matter more than the destination?

Use relevant evidence from at least three of the selections you read and researched in this unit to elucidate your ideas. Ensure that you introduce your topic, develop the topic with sufficient facts, details, and quotes, and use appropriate and varied transitions.

Reread the Assignment Review the assignment to be sure you fully understand it. The task may reference some of the academic words presented at the beginning of the unit. Be sure you understand each of the words here in order to complete the assignment correctly.

Academic Vocabulary

voluntary	expedite	procedure
elucidate	subsequent	

Review the Elements of Effective Explanatory Essays

Before you begin writing, review the Explanatory Rubric. Once you have completed your first draft, check it against the rubric. If one or more of the elements is missing or not as strong as it could be, revise your essay to add or strengthen that component.

WORD NETWORK

As you write and revise your explanatory text, use your Word Network to help vary your word choices.

STANDARDS

Writing

- Write informative/explanatory texts to examine and convey complex ideas, concepts, and information clearly and accurately through the effective selection, organization, and analysis of content.
- Write routinely over extended time frames and shorter time frames for a range of tasks, purposes, and audiences.

Explanatory Rubric

	Focus and Organization	Evidence and Elaboration	Conventions
4	The introduction engages the reader and states a thesis in a very effective way. The essay's organization is clear and well-suited to its topic. The conclusion summarizes ideas and offers fresh insight into the thesis.	The tone of the essay is always formal and objective. The topic is developed with well-chosen, relevant, and sufficient facts, extended definitions, concrete details, quotations, or other information appropriate to the audience's knowledge of the topic. The language is always precise and appropriate for the audience and purpose.	The essay consistently uses standard English conventions of usage and mechanics. Transitions are appropriately varied to link major sections of the text, create cohesion, and clarify the relationships among complex ideas and concepts.
3	The introduction engages the reader and sets forth the thesis. The essay's organization is mostly clear and suited to its topic. The conclusion offers some insight into the claim and summarizes ideas.	The tone of the essay is mostly formal and objective. The topic is mostly developed with well-chosen, relevant, and sufficient facts, extended definitions, concrete details, quotations, or other information appropriate to the audience's knowledge of the topic. The language is mostly precise and appropriate for the audience and purpose.	The essay demonstrates general accuracy in standard English conventions of usage and mechanics. Transitions are mostly varied to link major sections of the text, create cohesion, and clarify the relationships among complex ideas and concepts.
2	The introduction states a thesis, but does not engage the reader. The essay's organization is sometimes unclear and does not fully support its topic. The conclusion restates information.	The tone of the essay switches from formal to informal at times. The topic is developed with adequate relevant facts, definitions, details, quotations, or other information appropriate to the audience's knowledge of the topic. The language is rarely precise and appropriate for the audience and purpose.	The essay contains some mistakes in standard English conventions of usage and mechanics. Transitions are sometimes used to link major sections of the text, create cohesion, and clarify the relationships among complex ideas and concepts, but are sometimes used incorrectly.
1	The introduction does not state a thesis. The essay does not have a logical organization. The conclusion does not summarize ideas, or is missing completely.	The tone of the essay is informal and expresses personal opinions. The topic is developed primarily with opinions; contains no well-chosen, relevant, and sufficient facts, definitions, details, quotations, or other information appropriate to the audience's knowledge of the topic. The language is imprecise and confusing to the audience.	The essay contains many mistakes in standard English conventions of usage and mechanics. The essay lacks appropriate transitions.

PART 2

Speaking and Listening: Podcast

Assignment

After completing the final draft of your explanatory essay, use it as the foundation for a three- to five-minute **podcast**.

Take the following steps to make your podcast lively and engaging. If possible, record your podcast and distribute it within your school.

- Podcasts come in many different forms. Choose the type that you find interesting. Some examples include: interviews, individual or multiple people telling a story, or a performance of a dramatic scene.
- Choose one of the supporting details from your explanatory essay, and expand upon it with greater description of the characters, events, and settings. Consider using sound effects or other media to enhance your podcast.

STANDARDS

Speaking and Listening

Present information, findings, and supporting evidence clearly, concisely, and logically such that listeners can follow the line of reasoning and the organization, development, substance, and style are appropriate to purpose, audience, and task.

Review the Rubric The criteria by which your oral podcast will be evaluated appear in this rubric. Review these criteria before presenting to ensure that you are prepared.

	Content	Use of Media	Presentation Technique
3	The podcast has a clear focus that is well developed with details. The language is always precise and appropriate for the audience and purpose. The podcast has a clear, logical organization that suits its overall purpose.	The speaker uses time very effectively by spending the right amount of time on each part. Sound effects, recorded audio, and other media effectively develop and clarify the topic and ideas.	The speaker(s) engages the listener with dialogue relevant to the thesis. The speaker(s) speaks clearly and at an appropriate pace. The speaker(s) presents with strong conviction and energy.
2	The podcast has a clear focus that is supported with some details. The language is sometimes precise and appropriate for the audience and purpose. The podcast has a somewhat effective organizational structure.	The speaker uses time effectively by spending the right amount of time on most parts. Sound effects, recorded audio, and other media mostly develop and clarify the topic and ideas.	The speaker(s) provides some support of the thesis, but is occasionally off-topic. The speaker(s) mostly speaks clearly and at an appropriate pace. The speaker(s) presents with some conviction and energy.
1	The podcast lacks a clear focus. The language is not precise or appropriate for the audience and purpose. The podcast has no organizational structure.	The speaker does not allot time effectively. Sound effects, recorded audio, and other media fail to develop and clarify the topic and ideas.	The speaker(s) does not support the thesis. The speaker(s) does not speak clearly or at an appropriate pace. The speaker(s) lack energy.

Reflect on the Unit

Now that you've completed the unit, take a few moments to reflect on your learning. Use the questions below to think about where you succeeded, what skills and strategies helped you, and where you can continue to grow in the future.

Reflect on the Unit Goals

Look back at the goals at the beginning of the unit. Use a different colored pen to rate yourself again. Think about readings and activities that contributed the most to the growth of your understanding. Record your thoughts.

Reflect on the Learning Strategies

Discuss It Write a reflection on whether you were able to improve your learning based on your Action Plans. Think about what worked, what didn't, and what you might do to keep working on these strategies. Record your ideas before a class discussion.

Reflect on the Text

Choose a selection that you found challenging, and explain what made it difficult.

Explain something that surprised you about a text in the unit.

Which activity taught you the most about journeys of transformation? What did you learn?

STANDARDS

Speaking and Listening
Present information, findings, and supporting evidence clearly, concisely, and logically such that listeners can follow the line of reasoning and the organization, development, substance, and style are appropriate to purpose, audience, and task.

World's End

What draws us to imagine doomsday scenarios? And why are they so entertaining?

"Doomsday" Plane Ready for Nuclear Attack

Discuss It Should the government keep a "Doomsday" plane or similar resource in continuous operation?

UNIT INTRODUCTION

ESSENTIAL QUESTION: **Why do we try to imagine the future?**

LAUNCH TEXT
NARRATIVE MODEL
Dream's Winter

WHOLE-CLASS LEARNING

ANCHOR TEXT: SHORT STORY

By the Waters of Babylon
Stephen Vincent Benét

ANCHOR TEXT: SHORT STORY

There Will Come Soft Rains
Ray Bradbury

PERFORMANCE TASK

WRITING FOCUS:
Write a Narrative

SMALL-GROUP LEARNING

MAGAZINE ARTICLE

The Nuclear Tourist
George Johnson

POETRY COLLECTION 1

the beginning of the end of the world
Lucille Clifton

The Powwow at the End of the World
Sherman Alexie

A Song on the End of the World
Czeslaw Milosz

COMPARE

MEDIA: RADIO BROADCAST

from Radiolab: War of the Worlds
NPR

MAGAZINE ARTICLE

The Myth of the *War of the Worlds* Panic
Jefferson Pooley and Michael Socolow

PERFORMANCE TASK

SPEAKING AND LISTENING FOCUS:
Create a Podcast

INDEPENDENT LEARNING

GOVERNMENT WEBSITE ARTICLE

Preparedness 101: Zombie Apocalypse
Ali S. Khan

NEWS ARTICLE

The Secret Bunker Congress Never Used
NPR

MEDIA: IMAGE GALLERY

The End of the World Might Just Look Like This
Megan Gambino

POETRY COLLECTION 2

Fire and Ice
Robert Frost

Perhaps the World Ends Here
Joy Harjo

MEDIA: NEWSCAST

A Visit to the Doomsday Vault
60 Minutes

PERFORMANCE-BASED ASSESSMENT PREP

Review Notes for a Narrative

PERFORMANCE-BASED ASSESSMENT

Narrative: Short Story and Dramatic Reading

PROMPT:
Which matters more—the present or the future?

Unit Goals

Throughout this unit, you will deepen your understanding of literature about the future by reading, writing, speaking, presenting, and listening. These goals will help you succeed on the Unit Performance-Based Assessment.

Rate how well you meet these goals right now. You will revisit your ratings later when you reflect on your growth during this unit.

SCALE	1	2	3	4	5
	NOT AT ALL WELL	NOT VERY WELL	SOMEWHAT WELL	VERY WELL	EXTREMELY WELL

READING GOALS	1	2	3	4	5
• Evaluate written narratives by analyzing how authors craft their stories.	O	O	O	O	O
• Expand your knowledge and use of academic and concept vocabulary.	O	O	O	O	O

WRITING AND RESEARCH GOALS	1	2	3	4	5
• Write a narrative to convey an experience or event using effective techniques, well-chosen details, and well-structured sequences.	O	O	O	O	O
• Conduct research projects of various lengths to explore a topic and clarify meaning.	O	O	O	O	O

LANGUAGE GOALS	1	2	3	4	5
• Use adverbial and other types of clauses to convey precise meaning and add sentence variety to your writing and presentations.	O	O	O	O	O

SPEAKING AND LISTENING GOALS	1	2	3	4	5
• Collaborate with your team to build on the ideas of others, develop consensus, and communicate.	O	O	O	O	O
• Integrate audio, visuals, and text in presentations.	O	O	O	O	O

STANDARDS

Language

Acquire and use accurately general academic and domain-specific words and phrases, sufficient for reading, writing, speaking, and listening at the college and career readiness level; demonstrate independence in gathering vocabulary knowledge when considering a word or phrase important to comprehension or expression.

Academic Vocabulary: Narrative

Academic terms appear in all subjects and can help you read, write, and discuss with more precision. Here are five academic words that will be useful to you in this unit as you analyze and write narratives.

Complete the chart.

1. Review each word, its root, and the mentor sentences.
2. Use the information and your own knowledge to predict the meaning of each word.
3. For each word, list at least two related words.
4. Refer to a dictionary or other resources if needed.

TIP

FOLLOW THROUGH

Study the words in this chart, and highlight them or their forms wherever they appear in the unit.

WORD	MENTOR SENTENCES	PREDICT MEANING	RELATED WORDS
innovate ROOT: ***-nov-*** "new"	**1.** American musicians have shown that they can *innovate* and create new musical forms. **2.** When you work on a project, *innovate* and avoid repeating the same old ideas.		innovation; innovative; innovatively
technique ROOT: ***-tech-*** "skill"; "craft"	**1.** The statue demonstrates the artist's impressive *technique* and skill in working with marble. **2.** A singer's emotional power can be more important than vocal *technique*.		
depiction ROOT: ***-pict-*** "paint"	**1.** The new president's vision for America is a *depiction* of peace, equality, and prosperity. **2.** Your proposal for the new playground should include some sort of *depiction*, such as a drawing or map.		
introspective ROOT: ***-spec-*** "see"	**1.** Amanda likes action stories more than *introspective* dramas. **2.** Michaela's father worries that she is too *introspective* and thinks too much.		
conjecture ROOT: ***-jec-*** "throw"	**1.** Any notion of what might happen in the future is just *conjecture*. **2.** I can only *conjecture* that Willis will do well because he studied so hard.		

LAUNCH TEXT | NARRATIVE MODEL

This selection is an example of a **narrative text,** a type of writing in which the author tells a story. This is the type of writing you will develop in the Performance-Based Assessment at the end of the unit.

As you read, think about how the writer uses the elements of character, time, and setting. Mark the text to help you answer the question: How do specific details add to the portrayal of characters and events?

Dream's Winter

NOTES

1 Chase sat with his back to the old dead tree, scratching at a patch of hard, blackened earth with his compass.

2 "So what do you dream of, kid?"

3 The Tribe on the Hill operates the way a football team did, back when there was such a thing. They're an elite unit, comprised of specialists. It wasn't long ago they took me in. They were impressed with my skills as a sneak: I got through two and a half layers of security before they nabbed me, nine paces from the Shed.

4 They accepted me because I'm a good shot—with a rock, a makeshift spear, or a rifle. But they're not about to trust me with the latter. I wouldn't expect them to.

5 Chase is a scrounge. He has status here. I don't. One wrong word, one errant move, and they could throw me back down the hill, to waste away from starvation and thirst.

6 So I stared at a pill bug on its back, little gray legs flailing, trying to right itself. I'm not touching this one, or that one either.

7 Chase has a face that seems hacked out of flint, like an actor whose name I can't remember. He's old enough to be my father, I guess. That kind of thing doesn't matter like it used to.

8 "I dream of snow," he said, staring at me. Looking past me. I stretched my legs. The pill bug stopped scrabbling.

9 "Kids playing in snow," he said. "Rosy cheeks. Little smiles. Like the kids on the old soup cans."

10 The bug turned itself over. It started to run, then got near my left foot and stopped.

NOTES

11 "I'm watching them through a tall, narrow window," he said. Out of the corner of my eye, I saw him bend his head. I think he wanted me to look up. His eyes were so dark they seemed to be all pupils. They're too bright for my liking, but not harsh.

12 "My dining room used to have windows like that. Do you remember dining rooms, kid?"

13 I lifted my heel so it was poised above the bug. Roly-polies, they also call them. It curled into a ball, its shell a series of overlapping blackish-brown wedges.

14 "Then there's the flash," Chase said. "Boom!" Something shook in the pit of my gut, from down beneath uneasiness and hunger.

15 "Then it goes black," he said. "I stare out the window. I can still hear the kids. I can't see them. They're saying something. Whispering and laughing. For the life of me, I can't make it out."

16 He stood up. I flicked the bug away. Pill bugs have blue blood. I remember reading that a few years ago in a book I pulled out of a ditch, but I didn't need to see this proved.

17 Chase tried driving his stick into the crusty earth, as if he were planting a flag. It snapped at a weak spot. He studied the broken end protruding from his fist as if it were trying to tell him something.

18 "I used to wake up in a sweat every time I heard the bang," he said. "Now I don't. Now I stay in the dream, straining... straining in sleep, to hear what those kids out there are saying."

19 I looked up at him. His mouth had gone small, pulled to one side. He chewed at his inner lip. His eyes were wet. He tried to make them steely.

20 "The water bottles come out in a while," he said. "Be ready. No one's going to call you."

21 My foot had missed the bug. It took off, following Chase, as if it heard and understood about the water.

22 John Carradine. That's the actor's name. I think I might have read that somewhere too. ❧

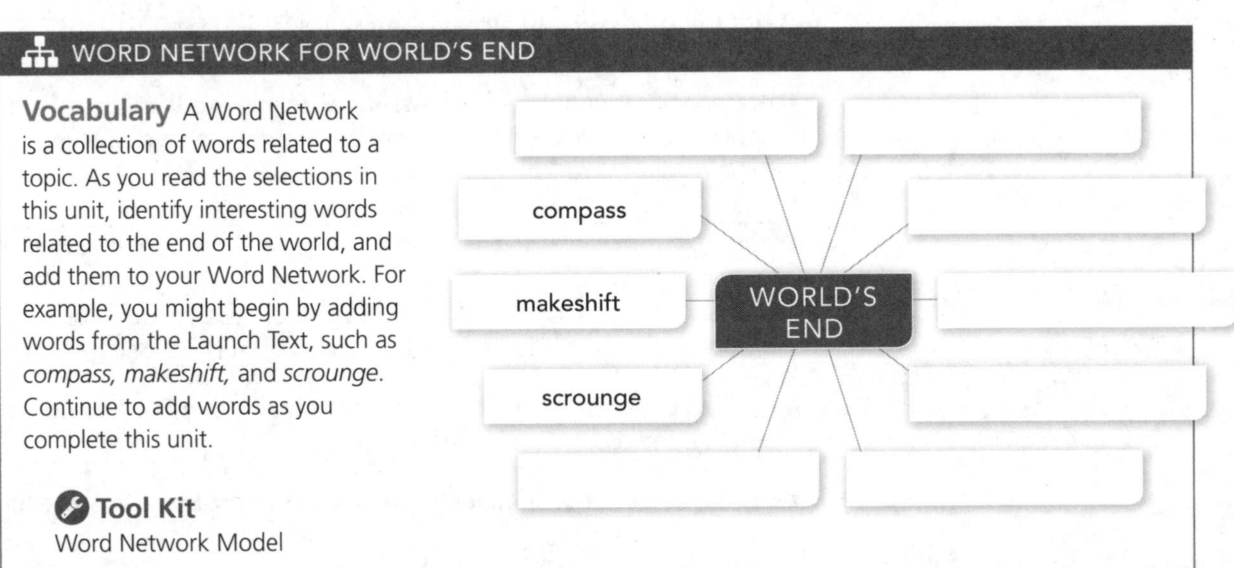

Vocabulary A Word Network is a collection of words related to a topic. As you read the selections in this unit, identify interesting words related to the end of the world, and add them to your Word Network. For example, you might begin by adding words from the Launch Text, such as *compass, makeshift,* and *scrounge*. Continue to add words as you complete this unit.

Tool Kit
Word Network Model

Summary

Write a summary of "Dream's Winter." A **summary** is a concise, complete, and accurate overview of a text. It should not include a statement of your opinion or an analysis.

Launch Activity

Conduct a Small-Group Discussion Consider this question: **Is it possible to imagine the end of the world?**

- Record your thoughts on the question in relation to the Launch Text, books you have read, and movies or programs you have watched. Explain your thinking.
- Gather in small groups. Each group should discuss the question, and group members should explain their thoughts and reasoning.
- Bring all the small groups together, and have a representative from each describe the group's responses.
- Discuss as a class the different responses. Is it possible to imagine the end of the world? Why or why not?

QuickWrite

Consider class discussions, presentations, the video, and the Launch Text as you think about the prompt. Record your first thoughts here.

PROMPT: **Which matters more—the present or the future?**

EVIDENCE LOG FOR WORLD'S END

Review your QuickWrite. Summarize your thoughts in one sentence to record in your Evidence Log. Then, record textual details or evidence from "Dream's Winter" that support your thinking.

Prepare for the Performance-Based Assessment at the end of the unit by completing the Evidence Log after each selection.

Tool Kit
Evidence Log Model

Title of Text: ______________________ Date: __________

CONNECTION TO PROMPT	TEXT EVIDENCE/DETAILS	ADDITIONAL NOTES/IDEAS

How does this text change or add to my thinking? Date: __________

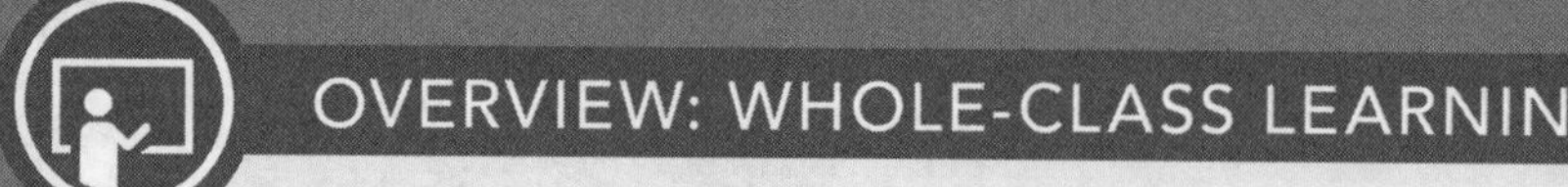

ESSENTIAL QUESTION:

Why do we try to imagine the future?

Human beings are curious. We are explorers, unwilling to step back and let questions remain unanswered. Yet, there are limits to what we can know. For example, we cannot visit the future, no matter how hard we try. Instead, in literature, in movies, and in science, we work to imagine it. The stories that we tell as a result are sometimes reassuring and sometimes frightening. As you read, you will work with your whole class to explore literary visions of the world's end. The selections you are going to read present two writers' conceptions of a troubled future.

Whole-Class Learning Strategies

Throughout your life, in school, in your community, and in your career, you will continue to learn and work in large-group environments.

Review these strategies and the actions you can take to practice them as you work with your whole class. Add ideas of your own for each category.

STRATEGY	ACTION PLAN
Listen actively	• Eliminate distractions. For example, put your cellphone away. • Keep your eyes on the speaker. •
Clarify by asking questions	• If you're confused, other people probably are, too. Ask a question to help your whole class. • If you see that you are guessing, ask a question instead. •
Monitor understanding	• Notice what information you already know and be ready to build on it. • Ask for help if you are struggling. •
Interact and share ideas	• Share your ideas and answer questions, even if you are unsure. • Build on the ideas of others by adding details or making a connection. •

CONTENTS

ANCHOR TEXT: SHORT STORY

By the Waters of Babylon

Stephen Vincent Benét

What will John find when he travels to the Dead Places?

ANCHOR TEXT: SHORT STORY

There Will Come Soft Rains

Ray Bradbury

In the aftermath of destruction, what do we leave behind?

PERFORMANCE TASK

WRITING FOCUS

Write a Narrative

The Whole-Class readings illustrate the world after catastrophe has struck. After reading, you will write your own narrative about the world that remains in the wake of a similar catastrophe.

About the Author

Stephen Vincent Benét (1898–1943) and his two siblings were clearly influenced by their father's love of literature, as they all grew up to be writers. Much of Benét's work centers on American history and folklore, including his most famous story, "The Devil and Daniel Webster," and his epic poem about the Civil War, *John Brown's Body.* The latter work won the Pulitzer Prize in 1929. At the time of his death, Benét was at work on a second epic poem, *Western Star,* which he planned to write as a narrative that would span five books. He finished only the first volume, which posthumously won him a second Pulitzer Prize when it was published in 1944.

Tool Kit

First-Read Guide and Model Annotation

STANDARDS

Reading Literature
By the end of grade 9, read and comprehend literature, including stories, dramas, and poems, in the grades 9–10 text complexity band proficiently, with scaffolding as needed at the high end of the range.

By the Waters of Babylon

Concept Vocabulary

You will encounter the following words as you read "By the Waters of Babylon." Before reading, note how familiar you are with each word. Then, rank the words in order from most familiar (1) to least familiar (6).

WORD	YOUR RANKING
purified	
bade	
stern	
fasting	
customs	
summoned	

After completing the first read, come back to the concept vocabulary and review your rankings. Mark changes to your original rankings as needed.

First Read FICTION

Apply these strategies as you conduct your first read. You will have an opportunity to complete the close-read notes after your first read.

NOTICE *whom* the story is about, *what* happens, *where* and *when* it happens, and *why* those involved react as they do.

ANNOTATE by marking vocabulary and key passages you want to revisit.

CONNECT ideas within the selection to what you already know and what you have already read.

RESPOND by completing the Comprehension Check and by writing a brief summary of the selection.

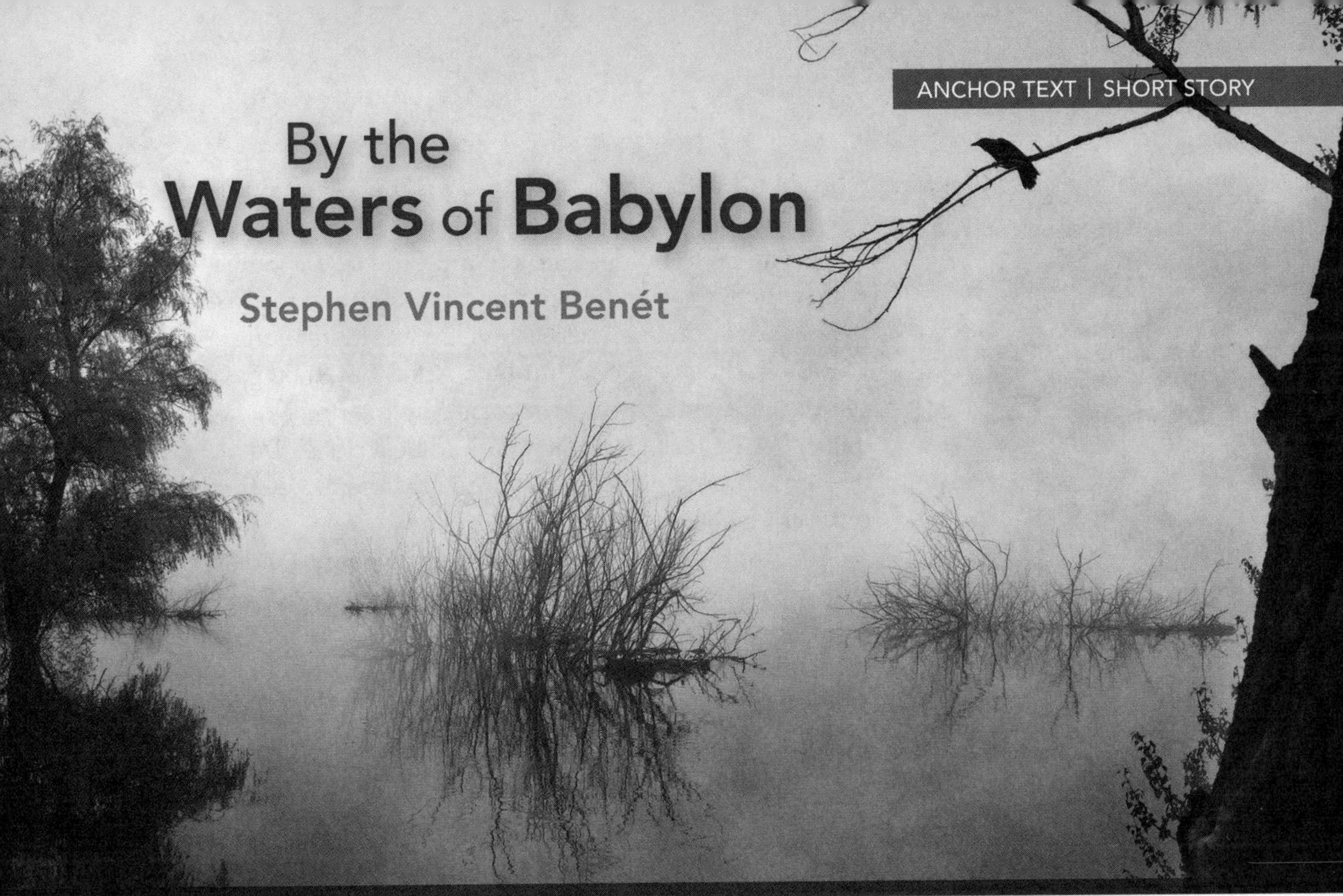

By the Waters of Babylon

Stephen Vincent Benét

BACKGROUND

Stephen Vincent Benét published this story in 1937, just after the devastating bombing of Guernica in Spain, in which hundreds of defenseless civilians were killed. During this time, people were afraid of the increasingly destructive power of modern weaponry. A few short years after this story was published, World War II would erupt, and the nuclear bomb would be invented. The title of the story is an allusion, or reference, to a line from Psalm 137, which describes the yearning of the Jews for their homeland after they were exiled by the Babylonians.

1 The north and the west and the south are good hunting ground, but it is forbidden to go east. It is forbidden to go to any of the Dead Places except to search for metal, and then he who touches the metal must be a priest or the son of a priest. Afterwards, both the man and the metal must be **purified**! These are the rules and the laws: they are well made. It is forbidden to cross the great river and look upon the place that was the Place of the Gods—this is most strictly forbidden. We do not even say its name though we know its name. It is there that spirits live, and demons—it is there that there are the ashes of the Great Burning. These things are forbidden—they have been forbidden since the beginning of time.

2 My father is a priest; I am the son of a priest. I have been in the Dead Places near us, with my father—at first, I was afraid. When my father went into the house to search for the metal, I stood by the door and my heart felt small and weak. It was a dead man's house, a spirit house. It did not have the smell of man, though there were old bones in a corner. But it is not fitting that a priest's son should show fear. I looked at the bones in the shadow and kept my voice still.

NOTES

purified (PYUR uh fyd)
v. cleaned by removing harmful or unwanted materials or qualities

CLOSE READ

ANNOTATE: In paragraph 1, mark a key word that the narrator repeats.

QUESTION: What emotional quality or **tone** does this repetition create?

CONCLUDE: What does this repeated word suggest about the narrator and his society?

NOTES

bade (bayd) *v.* past tense of *bid;* requested

stern (sturn) *adj.* strict; severe

3 Then my father came out with the metal—a good, strong piece. He looked at me with both eyes but I had not run away. He gave me the metal to hold—I took it and did not die. So he knew that I was truly his son and would be a priest in my time. That was when I was very young—nevertheless, my brothers would not have done it, though they are good hunters. After that, they gave me the good piece of meat and the warm corner by the fire. My father watched over me—he was glad that I should be a priest. But when I boasted or wept without a reason, he punished me more strictly than my brothers. That was right.

4 After a time, I myself was allowed to go into the dead houses and search for metal. So I learned the ways of those houses—and if I saw bones, I was no longer afraid. The bones are light and old—sometimes they will fall into dust if you touch them. But that is a great sin.

5 I was taught the chants and the spells—I was taught how to stop the running of blood from a wound and many secrets. A priest must know many secrets—that was what my father said. If the hunters think we do all things by chants and spells, they may believe so—it does not hurt them. I was taught how to read in the old books and how to make the old writings—that was hard and took a long time. My knowledge made me happy—it was like a fire in my heart. Most of all, I liked to hear of the Old Days and the stories of the gods. I asked myself many questions that l could not answer, but it was good to ask them. At night, I would lie awake and listen to the wind—it seemed to me that it was the voice of the gods as they flew through the air.

6 We are not ignorant like the Forest People—our women spin wool on the wheel, our priests wear a white robe. We do not eat grubs from the tree, we have not forgotten the old writings, although they are hard to understand. Nevertheless, my knowledge and my lack of knowledge burned in me—I wished to know more. When I was a man at last, I came to my father and said, "It is time for me to go on my journey. Give me your leave."

7 He looked at me for a long time, stroking his beard, then he said at last, "Yes. It is time." That night, in the house of the priesthood, I asked for and received purification. My body hurt but my spirit was a cool stone. It was my father himself who questioned me about my dreams.

8 He **bade** me look into the smoke of the fire and see—I saw and told what I saw. It was what I have always seen—a river, and, beyond it, a great Dead Place and in it the gods walking. I have always thought about that. His eyes were **stern** when I told him—he was no longer my father but a priest. He said, "This is a strong dream."

9 "It is mine," I said, while the smoke waved and my head felt light. They were singing the Star song in the outer chamber and it was like the buzzing of bees in my head.

10 He asked me how the gods were dressed and I told him how they were dressed. We know how they were dressed from the book, but

I saw them as if they were before me. When I had finished, he threw the sticks three times and studied them as they fell.

11 "This is a very strong dream," he said. "It may eat you up."

12 "I am not afraid," I said and looked at him with both eyes. My voice sounded thin in my ears but that was because of the smoke.

13 He touched me on the breast and the forehead. He gave me the bow and the three arrows.

14 "Take them," he said. "It is forbidden to travel east. It is forbidden to cross the river. It is forbidden to go to the Place of the Gods. All these things are forbidden."

15 "All these things are forbidden," I said, but it was my voice that spoke and not my spirit. He looked at me again.

16 "My son," he said. "Once I had young dreams. If your dreams do not eat you up, you may be a great priest. If they eat you, you are still my son. Now go on your journey."

17 I went **fasting**, as is the law. My body hurt, but not my heart. When the dawn came, I was out of sight of the village. I prayed and purified myself, waiting for a sign. That sign was an eagle. It flew east.

18 Sometimes signs are sent by bad spirits. I waited again on the flat rock, fasting, taking no food. I was very still—I could feel the sky above me and the earth beneath. I waited till the sun was beginning to sink. Then three deer passed in the valley, going east—they did not mind me or see me. There was a white fawn with them—a very great sign.

19 I followed them, at a distance, waiting for what would happen. My heart was troubled about going east, yet I knew that I must go. My head hummed with my fasting—I did not even see the panther spring upon the white fawn. But, before I knew it, the bow was in my hand. I shouted and the panther lifted his head from the fawn. It is not easy to kill a panther with one arrow but the arrow went through his eye and into his brain. He died as he tried to spring—he rolled over, tearing at the ground. Then I knew I was meant to go east—I knew that was my journey. When the night came, I made my fire and roasted meat.

20 It is eight suns' journey to the east and a man passes by many Dead Places. The Forest People are afraid of them but I am not. Once I made my fire on the edge of a Dead Place at night and, next morning, in the dead house, I found a good knife, little rusted. That was small to what came afterward, but it made my heart feel big. Always when I looked for game, it was in front of my arrow, and twice I passed hunting parties of the Forest People without their knowing. So I knew my magic was strong and my journey clean, in spite of the law.

21 Toward the setting of the eighth sun, I came to the banks of the great river. It was half-a-day's journey after I had left the god-road—we do not use the god-roads now for they are falling apart into great blocks of stone, and the forest is safer going. A long way off, I had seen the water through trees but the trees were thick. At last, I came out upon an open place at the top of a cliff. There was the

NOTES

CLOSE READ

ANNOTATE: In paragraphs 13–16, mark examples of repetition.

QUESTION: Why has the author chosen to repeat words and word patterns?

CONCLUDE: What overall effect does the use of repetition create?

fasting (FAS tihng) *v.* intentionally not eating, often for religious or spiritual reasons

NOTES

great river below, like a giant in the sun. It is very long, very wide. It could eat all the streams we know and still be thirsty. Its name is Ou-dis-sun, the Sacred, the Long. No man of my tribe had seen it, not even my father, the priest. It was magic and I prayed.

22 Then I raised my eyes and looked south. It was there, the Place of the Gods.

23 How can I tell you what it was like—you do not know. It was there, in the red light, and they were too big to be houses. It was there with the red light upon it, mighty and ruined. I knew that in another moment the gods would see me. I covered my eyes with my hands and crept back into the forest.

24 Surely, that was enough to do, and live. Surely it was enough to spend the night upon the cliff. The Forest People themselves do not come near. Yet, all through the night, I knew that I should have to cross the river and walk in the places of the gods, although the gods ate me up. My magic did not help me at all and yet there was a fire in my bowels, a fire in my mind. When the sun rose I thought, "My journey has been clean. Now I will go home from my journey." But, even as I thought so, I knew I could not. If I went to the place of the gods, I would surely die, but, if I did not go, I could never be at peace with my spirit again. It is better to lose one's life than one's spirit, if one is a priest and the son of a priest.

If I went to the place of the gods, I would surely die, . . .

25 Nevertheless, as I made the raft, the tears ran out of my eyes. The Forest People could have killed me without a fight, if they had come upon me then, but they did not come. When the raft was made, I said the sayings for the dead and painted myself for death. My heart was cold as a frog and my knees like water, but the burning in my mind would not let me have peace. As I pushed the raft from the shore, I began my death song—I had the right. It was a fine song.

"I am John, son of John," I sang. "My people are the Hill People. They are the men.
I go into the Dead Places but I am not slain.
I take the metal from the Dead Places but I am not blasted.
I travel upon the god-roads and am not afraid. E-yah! I have killed the panther. I have killed the fawn!
E-yah! I have come to the great river. No man has come there before.
It is forbidden to go east, but I have gone, forbidden to go on the great river, but I am there.
Open your hearts, you spirits, and hear my song.
Now I go to the Place of the Gods. I shall not return.
My body is painted for death and my limbs weak, but my heart is big as I go to the Place of the Gods!"

CLOSE READ

ANNOTATE: In paragraph 25, mark contrasting details in John's song.

QUESTION: Why has the author chosen to emphasize contrasting ideas?

CONCLUDE: What can you conclude about John from his song?

26 All the same, when I came to the Place of the Gods. I was afraid, afraid. The current of the great river is very strong—it gripped my

raft with its hands. That was magic, for the river itself is wide and calm. I could feel evil spirits about me, in the bright morning: I could feel their breath on my neck as I was swept down the stream. Never have I been so much alone—I tried to think of my knowledge, but it was a squirrel's heap of winter nuts. There was no strength in my knowledge any more, and I felt small and naked as a new-hatched bird—alone upon the great river, the servant of the gods.

27 Yet, after a while, my eyes were opened and I saw both banks of the river—I saw that once there had been god-roads across it, though now they were broken and fallen like broken vines. Very great they were, and wonderful and broken—broken in the time of the Great Burning when the fire fell out of the sky. And always the current took me nearer to the Place of the Gods, and the huge ruins rose before my eyes.

28 I do not know the **customs** of rivers—we are the People of the Hills. I tried to guide my raft with the pole but it spun around, I thought the river meant to take me past the Place of the Gods and out into the Bitter Water of the legends. I grew angry then—my heart felt strong. I said aloud, "I am a priest and the son of a priest!" The gods heard me—they showed me how to paddle with the pole on one side of the raft. The current changed itself—I drew near to the Place of the Gods.

29 When I was very near, my raft struck and turned over. I can swim in our lakes—I swam to the shore. There was a great spike or rusted metal sticking out into the river—I hauled myself up upon it and sat there, panting. I had saved my bow and two arrows and the knife I found in the Dead Place but that was all. My raft went whirling downstream toward the Bitter Water. I looked after it, and thought if it had trod me under, at least I would be safely dead. Nevertheless, when I had dried my bow-string and restrung it, I walked forward to the Place of the Gods.

30 It felt like ground underfoot; it did not burn me. It is not true what some of the tales say, that the ground there burns forever, for I have been there. Here and there were the marks and stains of the Great Burning, on the ruins, that is true. But they were old marks and old stains. It is not true either, what some of our priests say, that it is an island covered with fogs and enchantments. It is not. It is a great Dead Place—greater than any Dead Place we know. Everywhere in it there are god-roads, though most are cracked and broken. Everywhere there are the ruins of the high towers of the gods.

31 How shall I tell what I saw? I went carefully, my strung bow in my hand, my skin ready for danger. There should have been the wailings of spirits and the shrieks of demons, but there were not. It was very silent and sunny where I had landed—the wind and the rain and the birds that drop seeds had done their work—the grass grew in the cracks of the broken stone. It is a fair island—no wonder the gods built there. If I had come there, a god, I also would have built.

NOTES

customs (KUHS tuhmz) *n.* traditions; actions that are commonly done by a group of people

CLOSE READ

ANNOTATE: Mark the first sentence in paragraphs 31, 32, and 33.

QUESTION: Why does the narrator start each paragraph with the same question?

CONCLUDE: What is the narrator trying to communicate about his experience by asking these questions?

NOTES

32 How shall I tell what I saw? The towers are not all broken—here and there one still stands, like a great tree in a forest, and the birds nest high. But the towers themselves look blind, for the gods are gone. I saw a fish-hawk, catching fish in the river. I saw a little dance of white butterflies over a great heap of broken stones and columns. I went there and looked about me—there was a carved stone with cut-letters, broken in half. I can read letters but I could not understand these. They said UBTREAS. There was also the shattered image of a man or a god. It had been made of white stone and he wore his hair tied back like a woman's. His name was ASHING, as I read on the cracked half of a stone. I thought it wise to pray to ASHING, though I do not know that god.

33 How shall I tell what I saw? There was no smell of man left, on stone or metal. Nor were there many trees in that wilderness of stone. There are many pigeons, nesting and dropping in the towers—the gods must have loved them, or, perhaps, they used them for sacrifices. There are wild cats that roam the god-roads, green-eyed, unafraid of man. At night they wail like demons, but they are not demons. The wild dogs are more dangerous, for they hunt in a pack, but them I did not meet till later. Everywhere there are the carved stones carved with magical numbers or words.

34 I went North—I did not try to hide myself. When a god or a demon saw me, then I would die, but meanwhile I was no longer afraid. My hunger for knowledge burned in me—there was so much that I could not understand. After a while, I knew that my belly was hungry. I could have hunted for my meat, but I did not hunt. It is known that the gods did not hunt as we do—they got their food from enchanted boxes and jars. Sometimes these are still found in the Dead Places—once, when I was a child and foolish, I opened such a jar and tasted it and found the food sweet. But my father found out and punished me for it strictly, for, often, that food is death. Now, though, I had long gone past what was forbidden, and I entered the likeliest towers, looking for the food of the gods.

35 I found it at last in the ruins of a great temple in the mid-city. A mighty temple it must have been, for the roof was painted like the sky at night with its stars—that much I could see, though the colors were faint and dim. It went down into great caves and tunnels— perhaps they kept their slaves there. But when I started to climb down, I heard the squeaking of rats, so I did not go—rats are unclean, and there must have been many tribes of them, from the squeaking. But near there, I found food, in the heart of a ruin, behind a door that still opened. I ate only the fruits from the jar—they had a very sweet taste. There was drink, too, in bottles of glass— the drink of the gods was strong and made my head swim. After I had eaten and drunk, I slept on the top of a stone, my bow at my side.

36 When I woke, the sun was low. Looking down from where I lay, I saw a dog sitting on his haunches. His tongue was hanging out of his mouth; he looked as if he were laughing. He was a big dog,

NOTES

with a gray-brown coat, as big as a wolf. I sprang up and shouted at him but he did not move—he just sat there as if he were laughing. I did not like that. When I reached for a stone to throw, he moved swiftly out of the way of the stone. He was not afraid of me; he looked at me as if I were meat. No doubt I could have killed him with an arrow, but I did not know if there were others. Moreover, night was falling.

37 I looked about me—not far away there was a great broken god-road, leading North. The towers were high enough, but not so high, and while many of the dead-houses were wrecked, there were some that stood. I went toward this god-road, keeping to the heights of the ruins, while the dog followed. When I had reached the god-road. I saw that there were others behind him. If I had slept later, they would have come upon me asleep and torn out my throat. As it was, they were sure enough of me; they did not hurry. When I went into the dead-house, they kept watch at the entrance—doubtless they thought they would have a fine hunt. But a dog cannot open a door and I knew from the books, that the gods did not like to live on the ground but on high.

38 I had just found a door I could open when the dogs decided to rush. Ha! They were surprised when I shut the door in their faces—it was a good door, of strong metal. I could hear their foolish baying beyond it, but I did not stop to answer them. I was in darkness—I found stairs and climbed. There were many stairs, turning around till my head was dizzy. At the top was another door—I found the knob and opened it. I was in a long small chamber—on one side of it was a bronze door that could not be opened, for it had no handle. Perhaps there was a magic word to open it, but l did not have the word. I turned to the door in the opposite side of the wall. The lock of it was broken and I opened it and went in.

CLOSE READ

ANNOTATE: In paragraphs 36–38, mark details that characterize or describe the dogs.

QUESTION: Why does the author provide so much detail about John's encounter with the dogs?

CONCLUDE: What can you conclude about the ways in which John's world differs from that of the reader?

NOTES

39 Within, there was a place of great riches. The god who lived there must have been a powerful god. The first room was a small anteroom—I waited there for some time, telling the spirits of the place that I came in peace and not as a robber. When it seemed to me that they had had time to hear me, I went on. Ah, what riches! Few, even, of the windows had been broken—it was all as it had been. The great windows that looked over the city had not been broken at all though they were dusty and streaked with many years. There were coverings on the floors, the colors not greatly faded, and the chairs were soft, and deep. There were pictures upon the walls, very strange, very wonderful—I remember one of a bunch of flowers in a jar—if you came close to it, you could see nothing but bits of color, but if you stood away from it, the flowers might have been picked yesterday. It made my heart feel strange to look at this picture—and to look at the figure of a bird, in some hard clay, on a table and see it so like our birds. Everywhere there were books and writings, many in tongues that I could not read. The god who lived there must have been a wise god and full of knowledge. I felt I had right there, as I sought knowledge also.

Everywhere there were books and writings, many in tongues that I could not read.

40 Nevertheless, it was strange. There was a washing-place but no water—perhaps the gods washed in air. There was a cooking-place but no wood, and though there was a machine to cook food, there was no place to put fire in it. Nor were there candles or lamps—there were things that looked like lamps but they had neither oil nor wick. All these things were magic, but I touched them and lived—the magic had gone out of them. Let me tell one thing to show. In the washing-place, a thing said "Hot" but it was not hot to the touch—another thing said "Cold" but it was not cold. This must have been a strong magic but the magic was gone. I do not understand—they had ways—I wish that I knew.

41 It was close and dry and dusty in their house of the gods. I have said the magic was gone but that is not true—it had gone from the magic things but it had not gone from the place. I felt the spirits about me, weighing upon me. Nor had I ever slept in a Dead Place before—and yet, tonight, I must sleep there. When I thought of it, my tongue felt dry in my throat, in spite of my wish for knowledge. Almost I would have gone down again and faced the dogs, but I did not.

42 I had not gone through all the rooms when the darkness fell. When it fell, I went back to the big room looking over the city and made fire. There was a place to make fire and a box with wood in it, though I do not think they cooked there. I wrapped myself in a floorcovering and slept in front of the fire—I was very tired.

43 Now I tell what is very strong magic. I woke in the midst of the night. When I woke, the fire had gone out and I was cold. It seemed to me that all around me there were whisperings and voices. I closed my eyes to shut them out. Some will say that I slept again, but I do not think that I slept. I could feel the spirits drawing my spirit out of my body as a fish is drawn on a line.

44 Why should I lie about it? I am a priest and the son of a priest. If there are spirits, as they say, in the small Dead Places near us, what spirits must there not be in that great Place of the Gods? And would not they wish to speak? After such long years? I know that I felt myself drawn as a fish is drawn on a line. I had stepped out of my body—I could see my body asleep in front of the cold fire, but it was not I. I was drawn to look out upon the city of the gods.

45 It should have been dark, for it was night, but it was not dark. Everywhere there were lights—lines of lights—circles and blurs of light—ten thousand torches would not have been the same. The sky itself was alight—you could barely see the stars for the glow in the sky. I thought to myself "This is strong magic" and trembled. There was a roaring in my ears like the rushing of rivers. Then my eyes grew used to the light and my ears to the sound. I knew that I was seeing the city as it had been when the gods were alive.

46 That was a sight indeed—yes, that was a sight: I could not have seen it in the body—my body would have died. Everywhere went the gods, on foot and in chariots—there were gods beyond number and counting, and their chariots blocked the streets. They had turned night to day for their pleasure—they did not sleep with the sun. The noise of their coming and going was the noise of many waters. It was magic what they could do—it was magic what they did.

47 I looked out of another window—the great vines of their bridges were mended and the god-roads went East and West. Restless, restless, were the gods and always in motion! They burrowed tunnels under rivers—they flew in the air. With unbelievable tools they did giant works—no part of the earth was safe from them, for, if they wished for a thing, they **summoned** it from the other side of the world. And always, as they labored and rested, as they feasted and made love, there was a drum in their ears—the pulse of the giant city, beating and beating like a man's heart.

48 Were they happy? What is happiness to the gods? They were great, they were mighty, they were wonderful and terrible. As I looked upon them and their magic, I felt like a child—but a little more, it seemed to me, and they would pull down the moon from the sky. I saw them with wisdom beyond wisdom and knowledge beyond knowledge. And yet not all they did was well done—even I could see that—and yet their wisdom could not but grow until all was peace.

49 Then I saw their fate come upon them and that was terrible past speech. It came upon them as they walked the streets of their city. I have been in the fights with the Forest People—I have seen men die. But this was not like that. When gods war with gods, they use weapons we do not know. It was fire falling out of the sky and a mist that poisoned. It was the time of the Great Burning and the Destruction. They ran about like ants in the streets of their city—poor gods, poor gods! Then the towers began to fall. A few escaped—yes, a few. The legends tell it. But, even after the city had become a Dead Place, for

NOTES

summoned (SUHM uhnd) *v.* ordered someone or something to come to a place

NOTES

many years the poison was still in the ground. I saw it happen, I saw the last of them die. It was darkness over the broken city, and I wept.

50 All this, I saw. I saw it as I have told it, though not in the body. When I woke in the morning. I was hungry, but I did not think first of my hunger, for my heart was perplexed and confused. I know the reason for the Dead Places but I did not see why it had happened. It seemed to me it should not have happened, with all the magic they had. I went through the house looking for an answer. There was so much in the house I could not understand—and yet I am a priest and the son of a priest. It was like being on one side of the great river, at night, with no light to show the way.

51 Then I saw the dead god. He was sitting in his chair, by the window, in a room I had not entered before and, for the first moment, I thought that he was alive. Then I saw the skin on the back of his hand—it was like dry leather. The room was shut, hot and dry—no doubt that had kept him as he was. At first I was afraid to approach him—then the fear left me. He was sitting looking out over the city—he was dressed in the clothes of the gods. His age was neither young nor old—I could not tell his age. But there was wisdom in his face and great sadness. You could see that he would have not run away. He had sat at his window, watching his city die—then he himself had died. But it is better to lose one's life than one's spirit— and you could see from the face that his spirit had not been lost. I knew that if I touched him, he would fall into dust—and yet, there was something unconquered in the face.

CLOSE READ

ANNOTATE: Mark the uses of dashes and commas in paragraph 51, and take note of the groupings of words contained within dashes.

QUESTION: Why do you think the author has chosen to create sentences that sometimes break off into new thoughts that are separated by dashes?

CONCLUDE: What effect does the author's choice create? In what way does this choice help you better understand the narrator?

52 That is all of my story, for then I knew he was a man—I knew then that they had been men, neither gods nor demons. It is a great knowledge, hard to tell and believe. They were men—they went a dark road, but they were men. I had no fear after that—I had no fear going home, though twice I fought off the dogs and once I was hunted for two days by the Forest People. When I saw my father again, I prayed and was purified. He touched my lips and my breast, he said, "You went a boy. You come back a man and a priest." I said, "Father, they were men! I have been to the Place of the Gods and seen it! Now slay me, if it is the law—but still I know they were men."

53 He looked at me out of both eyes. He said, "The law is not always the same shape—you have done what you have done. I could not have done it in my time but you come after me. Tell!"

54 I told and he listened. After that, I wished to tell all the people but he showed me otherwise. He said, "Truth is a hard deer to hunt. If you eat too much truth at once, you may die of the truth. It was not idly that our fathers forbade the Dead Places." He was right—it is better the truth should come little by little. I have learned that, being a priest. Perhaps, in the old days, they ate knowledge too fast.

55 Nevertheless, we make a beginning. It is not for the metal alone we go to the Dead Places now—there are the books and the writings. They are hard to learn. And the magic tools are broken—but we can look at them and wonder. At least, we make a beginning. And, when

I am chief priest we shall go beyond the great river. We shall go to the Place of the Gods—the place newyork—not one man but a company. We shall look for the images of the gods and find the god ASHING and the others—the gods Lincoln and Biltmore[1] and Moses.[2] But they were men who built the city, not gods or demons. They were men. I remember the dead man's face. They were men who were here before us. We must build again. ❧

NOTES

1. **Biltmore** hotel in New York City.
2. **Moses** Robert Moses (1888–1981), former New York City municipal official who oversaw many large construction projects.

Comprehension Check

Complete the following items after you finish your first read.

1. After what type of event is this story set?

2. What sets the narrator and his father apart from the people surrounding them?

3. How does the narrator arrive at his insight about who the gods of the Dead Places were?

4. What advice about sharing knowledge does John's father give him at the end of the story?

5. **Notebook** To confirm your understanding, write a summary of the story.

RESEARCH

Research to Clarify Choose at least one unfamiliar detail from the text. Briefly research that detail. In what way does the information you learned shed light on an aspect of the story?

Research to Explore Benét wrote this story in response to the bombing of the Basque town of Guernica on April 26, 1937, during the Spanish Civil War. Conduct research to find out more about this event and consider how it influenced Benét's story. Share your findings and conclusions with the class.

BY THE WATERS OF BABYLON

Close Read the Text

1. This model, from paragraph 1 of the text, shows two sample annotations, along with questions and conclusions. Close read the passage, and find another detail to annotate. Then, write a question and your conclusion.

ANNOTATE • QUESTION • Close Read • CONCLUDE

ANNOTATE: These words are repeated.

QUESTION: What effect does the repetition create?

CONCLUDE: The repetition gives the text a formal, solemn, and religious tone.

It is there that spirits live, and demons—it is there that there are the ashes of the Great Burning. These things are forbidden—they have been forbidden since the beginning of time.

ANNOTATE: These words are capitalized.

QUESTION: What does the capitalization tell a reader?

CONCLUDE: The capitalization shows that this event has become one of historical significance for the narrator's people.

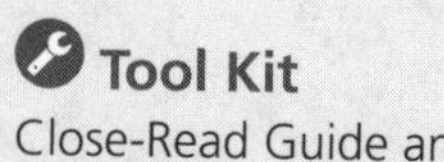

Tool Kit
Close-Read Guide and Model Annotation

2. For more practice, go back into the text, and complete the close-read notes.
3. Revisit a section of the text you found important during your first read. Read this section closely, and **annotate** what you notice. Ask yourself **questions** such as "Why did the author make this choice?" What can you **conclude**?

Analyze the Text

CITE TEXTUAL EVIDENCE to support your answers.

Notebook Respond to these questions.

1. (a) In paragraph 6, what word does John, one of the Hill People, use to describe the Forest People? (b) **Make Inferences** What does this suggest about how the Hill People view the Forest People?
2. (a) What does John compare his knowledge to in paragraph 26? (b) **Interpret** How does this metaphor help you understand how John feels at this point in the story?
3. (a) **Summarize** In paragraph 51, what does John observe about the "dead god"? (b) **Analyze** Why do these observations free John from fear?
4. (a) What phrase does John repeat in the beginning of paragraph 52? (b) **Interpret** What does this repetition suggest about his realizations in that particular moment? Explain.
5. **Essential Question:** *Why do we try to imagine the future?* What have you learned about world's end literature from reading this story?

STANDARDS

Reading Literature

- Analyze how an author's choices concerning how to structure a text, order events within it, and manipulate time create such effects as mystery, tension, or surprise.
- Cite strong and thorough textual evidence to support analysis of what the text says explicitly as well as inferences drawn from the text.

Analyze Craft and Structure

Author's Choices: Narrative Elements Fiction writers choose a specific **narrative point of view**, or vantage point, from which to tell a story. In "By the Waters of Babylon," Stephen Vincent Benét uses a first-person narrator, John, who is a character in the story and speaks in the first person, using the pronoun *I*.

Benét's use of the first-person point of view in this story contributes to the development of **dramatic irony**, a device that involves a contrast between what a character thinks to be true and what the reader knows to be true. In this story, readers can see the meaning in certain details, such as the name of the river John crosses, but John himself cannot. The first-person point of view allows the reader to connect textual clues to build an understanding of events that John only realizes later.

Practice

CITE TEXTUAL EVIDENCE to support your answers.

Notebook **Respond to these questions.**

1. **(a)** Reread paragraphs 1 and 2. How does the author introduce the narrative point of view? **(b)** How might the narrative be different if told by a third-person narrator who is not a character in the story?
2. Record in the chart examples of dramatic irony by comparing John's beliefs with the reader's understanding.

WHAT JOHN BELIEVES	WHAT THE READER KNOWS

3. At what point in the story does John's understanding catch up to the reader's? Explain.
4. **(a)** How does the use of dramatic irony in this story suggest the loss of knowledge that may occur when a civilization fails? **(b)** What does this irony suggest about our own understanding of past civilizations?

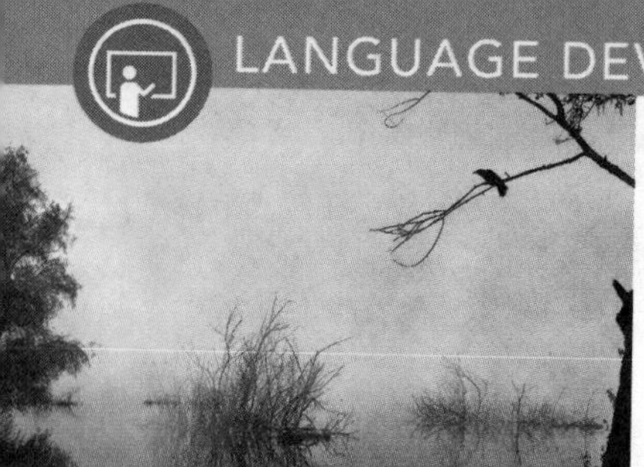

BY THE WATERS OF BABYLON

Concept Vocabulary

purified	stern	customs
bade	fasting	summoned

Why These Words? These concept words all help to describe the elaborate ceremonies and rituals that John's people have created. For example, in the opening paragraph, the narrator explains that metal gathered from the Dead Places must be *purified*, or cleansed. Later, John mentions that he "asked for and received purification" before his solo journey. The idea of purification has religious connotations, emphasizing the removal of unclean or impure thoughts, as well as physical poisons.

1. How does the concept vocabulary help readers understand John's culture?
2. What other words in the selection connect to this concept?

Practice

Notebook The concept words appear in "By the Waters of Babylon."

1. Demonstrate your understanding of the concept words' meanings by using each word in a sentence to answer these questions.
   - How might you tell whether or not a material has been *purified*?
   - If you *bade* another person to take action to resolve a problem, what is it that you did?
   - How might a *stern* teacher act toward students?
   - How might you feel after *fasting* for 24 hours?
   - What are two *customs* that reflect your cultural heritage?
   - If you *summoned* your dog, what would you expect the animal to do?
2. Create fill-in-the-blank puzzles for others to solve. First, write a sentence that demonstrates the meaning of each concept word. Then, rewrite each sentence, but replace the concept word with a blank. Challenge your classmates to fill in the missing words.

WORD NETWORK

Add interesting words related to the world's end from the text to your Word Network.

Word Study

Word Families A **word family** is a group of words that share the same origin or that were all formed from a common base word. For instance, the words *purified* and *purification,* which appear in "By the Waters of Babylon," are part of the same word family as the word *pure.*

1. Identify two other words that belong to the same word family as *purified, purification,* and *pure.*
2. Identify two words that belong to the same word family as *customs.*

STANDARDS

Reading Literature
Analyze how complex characters develop over the course of a text, interact with other characters, and advance the plot or develop the theme.

Language
- Demonstrate command of the conventions of standard English capitalization, punctuation, and spelling when writing.
- Identify and correctly use patterns of word changes that indicate different meanings or parts of speech.
- Demonstrate understanding of figurative language, word relationships, and nuances in word meanings.

Author's Style

Character Development Benét uses a variety of elements to develop the character of John, the narrator of "By the Waters of Babylon." The author's choices help readers understand both John's personality and the culture that helped form it.

ELEMENT	EXAMPLE	ANALYSIS
Punctuation: marks (other than letters) that are used to organize writing and make its meaning clear	*These things are forbidden—they have been forbidden since the beginning of time.* (paragraph 1)	The use of a dash (—) emphasizes the connection between ideas and creates the feeling that John is truly speaking the story.
Diction: a writer's or speaker's word choice—the type of vocabulary, the vividness of the language, and the appropriateness of the words	*It did not have the smell of man, though there were old bones in a corner. But it is not fitting that a priest's son should show fear.* (paragraph 2)	John's vocabulary is relatively limited. He uses formal diction characterized by an absence of contractions, which suggests that John is unfamiliar with colloquial language. It might also suggest that he is concerned with presenting himself correctly and does not use language carelessly.
Syntax: the way that words are organized, such as their order in a sentence or phrase	*He gave me the metal to hold—I took it and did not die.* (paragraph 3)	John speaks in simple sentences that reflect his formality and might suggest a lack of familiarity or comfort with informal language.

Read It

1. Mark the punctuation in this excerpt from paragraph 5 of "By the Waters of Babylon." How does the author use this punctuation to develop John's character?

   I was taught the chants and the spells—I was taught how to stop the running of blood from a wound and many secrets. A priest must know many secrets—that was what my father said. If the hunters think we do all things by chants and spells, they may believe so—it does not hurt them.

2. Read John's "death song" in paragraph 26 aloud. Listen carefully to John's diction and syntax. Explain how the diction and syntax in his "fine song" help you understand and appreciate both John's character and his culture.

Write It

Notebook Revise the punctuation, diction, and syntax in this paragraph to make it sound more like John's narration in "By the Waters of Babylon."

> Everyone's always telling me I need to follow the rules, but I know better. I'm sure that I was totally right to travel east, even though everybody says you shouldn't go there. It was definitely worth it even though I can't share what I learned now that I'm back home. The others can't handle the truth right now, but maybe someday they'll be ready.

BY THE WATERS OF BABYLON

Writing to Sources

A great story ends with a satisfying conclusion that resolves the main conflicts. However, some narratives leave questions open for readers to interpret. Writing a sequel can help readers imagine the events that take place after a story is over.

Assignment

Write a **sequel** that begins after the last sentence of "By the Waters of Babylon." Consider these questions as you plan your writing:

- What happens when John rejoins his people?
- What truths does he begin to share with them, and how does he do so?
- What does John's community do with this new knowledge? How do they change their culture and start to rebuild?
- How might John's people avoid repeating the errors of the past?

Your sequel should include:

- A clear narrative with a beginning, a middle, and an end
- Realistic dialogue that reflects characters' personalities
- Detailed descriptions of characters, settings, and events
- Pacing that speeds up or slows down the action

Vocabulary and Style Connection Include several of the concept vocabulary words in your sequel to show how rituals changed for John's people after the end of the story. Develop characters through careful choices in diction, syntax, and punctuation.

purified	stern	customs
bade	fasting	summoned

STANDARDS

Writing

- Write narratives to develop real or imagined experiences or events using effective technique, well-chosen details, and well-structured event sequences.
- Use narrative techniques, such as dialogue, pacing, description, reflection, and multiple plot lines, to develop experiences, events, and/or characters.

Speaking and Listening

- Integrate multiple sources of information presented in diverse media or formats evaluating the credibility and accuracy of each source.
- Present information, findings, and supporting evidence clearly, concisely and logically such that listeners can follow the line of reasoning and the organization, development, substance, and style are appropriate to purpose, audience, and task.
- Make strategic use of digital media in presentations to enhance understanding of findings, reasoning, and evidence and to add interest.

Reflect on Your Writing

After you have written your sequel, answer these questions.

1. How did writing a sequel help you understand and appreciate the events of the original story?

2. What details from the original story helped you create an effective sequel?

3. **Why These Words?** The words you choose make a difference in your writing. Which words did you use to achieve a specific effect in your sequel?

Speaking and Listening

Assignment

Create and present a **multimedia timeline** of the story that includes information about events that took place before the beginning of John's narration. Include images, videos, audio, or other media elements in your timeline to enhance your audience's understanding of the events. First, reread the selection. Then, follow these steps to complete the assignment.

1. **Identify and Order Events** First, list the key story events. Then, look for clues in the story that tell what happened in the past and how those events affected the society in which John lives during the time of the story. List these "prequel" events. Finally, order the events chronologically.
2. **Write Timeline Labels** After you identify and order events, write concise timeline labels to describe them. Most events should be described in one sentence. Consider how to shorten long labels without losing crucial details.
3. **Select Appropriate Media** Review each timeline event, and consider which type of media element would best support it. Remember, you will be presenting your entire timeline, so make sure that individual media elements are relatively short.
4. **Prepare Your Delivery** Practice presenting your completed timeline. Consider how to pace your presentation. Develop a planning script that shows how much time you will spend discussing each event. Remember to include the time needed to screen videos or play audio recordings.
5. **Evaluate Timelines** As your classmates share their timelines, listen attentively. Use the evaluation guide to analyze their timelines.

EVALUATION GUIDE

Rate each statement on a scale of 1 (not demonstrated) to 4 (demonstrated).

☐ The timeline includes, in chronological order, key events from before and during the action of the story.

☐ Events are described briefly and clearly.

☐ Media elements effectively support the timeline.

☐ The presenter used time wisely and fully explained each event.

EVIDENCE LOG

Before moving on to a new selection, go to your Evidence Log and record what you learned from "By the Waters of Babylon."

About the Author

Ray Bradbury (1920–2012) developed a fascination with horror movies and futuristic fantasies. As a teenager, he decided to become a writer and to use fiction to "live forever." He published his first novel, *The Martian Chronicles*, in 1950, and his novel *Fahrenheit 451* became an instant bestseller when it was published in 1953. In 2007, Bradbury won a special Pulitzer Prize for his "distinguished, prolific, and deeply influential career as an unmatched author of science fiction and fantasy."

Tool Kit

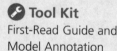

First-Read Guide and Model Annotation

STANDARDS

Reading Literature

By the end of grade 9, read and comprehend literature, including stories, dramas, and poems, in the grades 9–10 text complexity band proficiently, with scaffolding as needed at the high end of the range.

There Will Come Soft Rains

Concept Vocabulary

You will encounter the following words as you read "There Will Come Soft Rains." Before reading, note how familiar you are with each word. Then, rank the words in order from most familiar (1) to least familiar (6).

WORD	YOUR RANKING
chimed	
attending	
delicately	
fluttered	
manipulated	
tremulous	

After completing the first read, come back to the concept vocabulary and review your rankings. Mark changes to your original rankings as needed.

First Read FICTION

Apply these strategies as you conduct your first read. You will have an opportunity to complete the close-read notes after your first read.

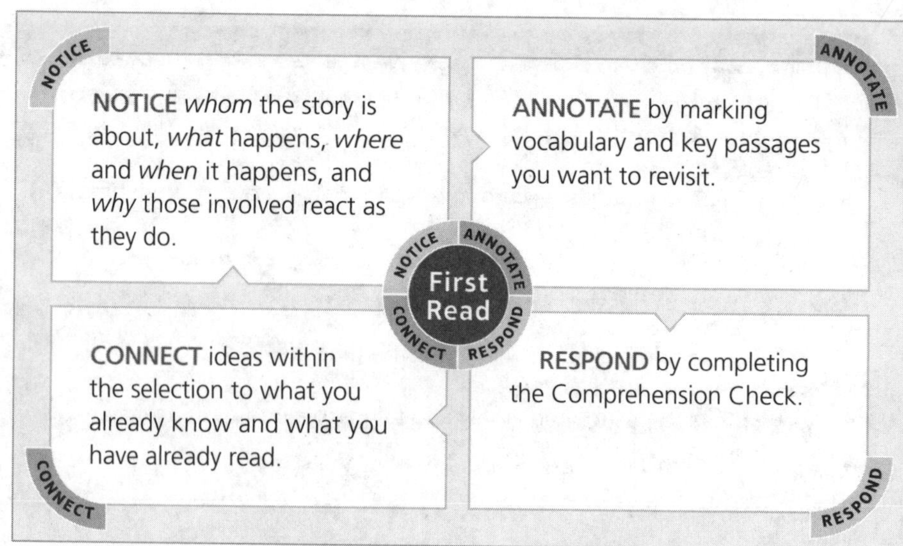
NOTICE
NOTICE *whom* the story is about, *what* happens, *where* and *when* it happens, and *why* those involved react as they do.
ANNOTATE
ANNOTATE by marking vocabulary and key passages you want to revisit.
First Read
NOTICE
ANNOTATE
CONNECT
RESPOND
CONNECT ideas within the selection to what you already know and what you have already read.
RESPOND by completing the Comprehension Check.
CONNECT
RESPOND

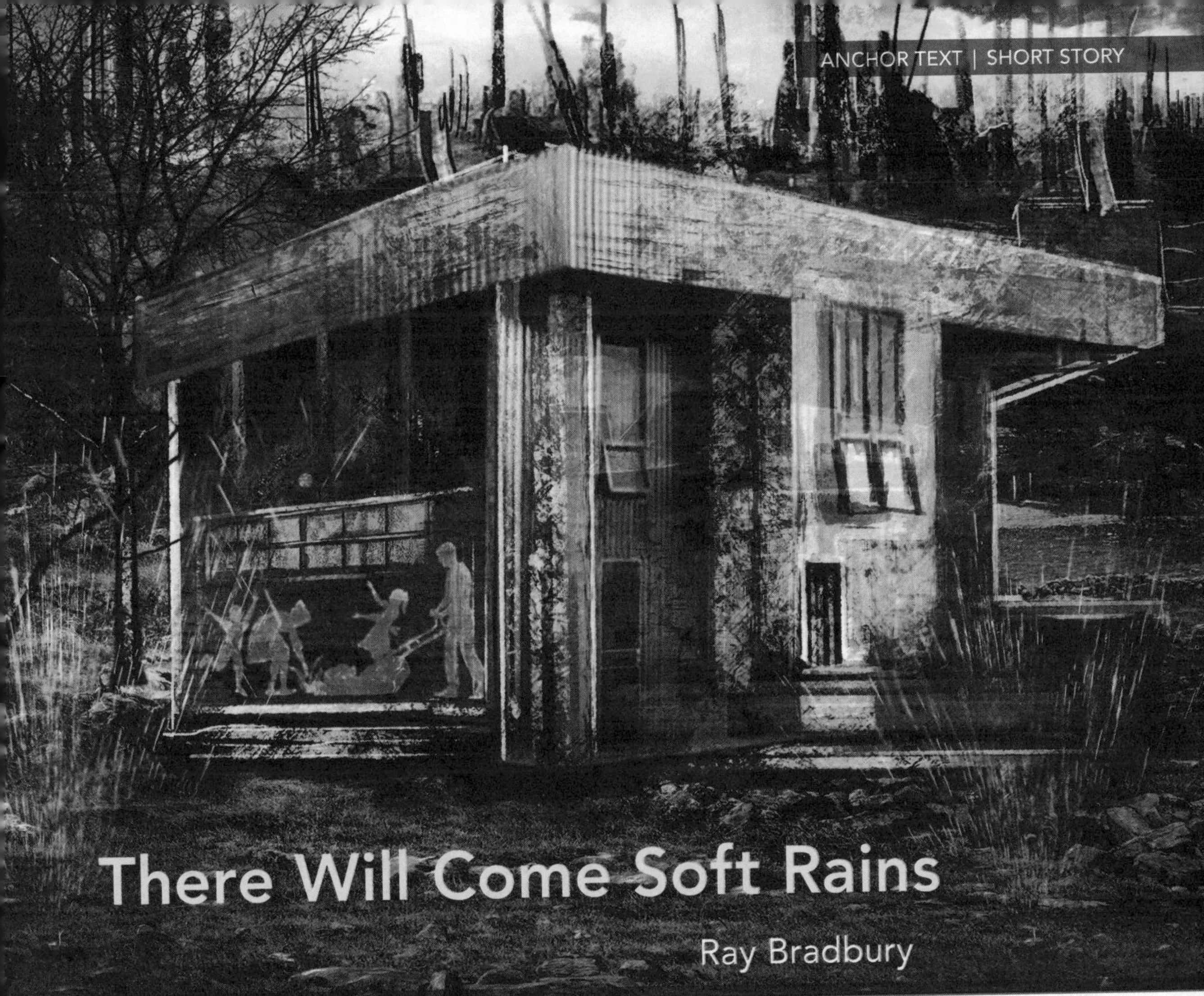

There Will Come Soft Rains

Ray Bradbury

BACKGROUND

This story was written in 1950 during a period known as the Cold War, a mostly non-military conflict that occurred between the United States and the Soviet Union. Each side became increasingly focused on developing more nuclear weapons to discourage the other side from using its own bombs. This, coupled with the fact that the United States had dropped two atomic bombs on Japan during World War II, created a widespread fear of nuclear war.

1 In the living room the voice-clock sang, *Tick-tock, seven o'clock, time to get up, time to get up, seven o'clock!* as if it were afraid nobody would. The morning house lay empty. The clock ticked on, repeating and repeating its sounds into the emptiness. *Seven-nine, breakfast time, seven-nine!*

2 In the kitchen the breakfast stove gave a hissing sigh and ejected from its warm interior eight pieces of perfectly browned toast, eight eggs sunnyside up, sixteen slices of bacon, two coffees, and two cool glasses of milk.

3 "Today is August 4, 2026," said a second voice from the kitchen ceiling, "in the city of Allendale, California." It repeated the date three times for memory's sake. "Today is Mr. Featherstone's birthday.

NOTES

CLOSE READ

ANNOTATE: In paragraph 1, mark examples of sing-song language.

QUESTION: Why does the author include this language in the opening scene?

CONCLUDE: What mood, or emotional quality, does the sing-song language create?

NOTES

Today is the anniversary of Tilita's marriage. Insurance is payable, as are the water, gas, and light bills."

4 Somewhere in the walls, relays clicked, memory tapes glided under electric eyes.

5 *Eight-one, tick-tock, eight-one o'clock, off to school, off to work, run, run, eight-one!* But no doors slammed, no carpets took the soft tread of rubber heels. It was raining outside. The weather box on the front door sang quietly: "Rain, rain, go away; rubbers, raincoats for today . . ." And the rain tapped on the empty house, echoing.

chimed (chymd) *v.* rang; made the sound of a bell

6 Outside, the garage **chimed** and lifted its door to reveal the waiting car. After a long wait the door swung down again.

7 At eight-thirty the eggs were shriveled and the toast was like stone. An aluminum wedge scraped them into the sink, where hot water whirled them down a metal throat which digested and flushed them away to the distant sea. The dirty dishes were dropped into a hot washer and emerged twinkling dry.

8 *Nine-fifteen*, sang the clock, *time to clean*.

9 Out of warrens in the wall, tiny robot mice darted. The rooms were acrawl with the small cleaning animals, all rubber and metal. They thudded against chairs, whirling their mustached runners, kneading the rug nap, sucking gently at hidden dust. Then, like mysterious invaders, they popped into their burrows. Their pink electric eye faded. The house was clean.

10 *Ten o'clock*. The sun came out from behind the rain. The house stood alone in a city of rubble and ashes. This was the one house left standing. At night the ruined city gave off a radioactive glow which could be seen for miles.

11 *Ten-fifteen*. The garden sprinklers whirled up in golden founts, filling the soft morning air with scatterings of brightness. The water pelted windowpanes, running down the charred west side where the house had been burned evenly free of its white paint. The entire west face of the house was black, save for five places. Here the silhouette[1] in paint of a man mowing a lawn. Here, as in a photograph, a woman bent to pick flowers. Still farther over, their images burned on wood in one titanic instant, a small boy, hands flung into the air; higher up, the image of a thrown ball, and opposite him a girl, hand raised to catch a ball which never came down.

CLOSE READ

ANNOTATE: Mark the words in paragraphs 11 and 12 that describe the "five spots of paint."

QUESTION: How do these descriptions differ from the earlier descriptions of the house?

CONCLUDE: What idea does the author emphasize by carefully selecting sensory language?

12 The five spots of paint—the man, the woman, the children, the ball—remained. The rest was a thin charcoaled layer.

13 The gentle sprinkler rain filled the garden with falling light.

14 Until this day, how well the house had kept its peace. How carefully it had inquired, "Who goes there? What's the password?" and, getting no answer from the lonely foxes and whining cats, it had shut up its windows and drawn shades in an old-maidenly preoccupation with self-protection which bordered on a mechanical paranoia.

1. **silhouette** (sihl uh WEHT) *n.* outline of a figure, filled in with a solid color.

15 It quivered at each sound, the house did. If a sparrow brushed a window, the shade snapped up. The bird, startled, flew off! No, not even a bird must touch the house!

16 The house was an altar with ten thousand attendants, big, small, servicing, **attending**, in choirs. But the gods had gone away, and the ritual of the religion continued senselessly, uselessly.

17 *Twelve noon.*

18 A dog whined, shivering, on the front porch.

19 The front door recognized the dog voice and opened. The dog, once huge and fleshy, but now gone to bone and covered with sores, moved in and through the house, tracking mud. Behind it whirred angry mice, angry at having to pick up mud, angry at inconvenience.

20 For not a leaf fragment blew under the door but what the wall panels flipped open and the copper scrap rats flashed swiftly out. The offending dust, hair, or paper, seized in miniature steel jaws, was raced back to the burrows. There, down tubes which fed into the cellar, it was dropped into the sighing vent of an incinerator which sat like evil Baal[2] in a dark corner.

21 The dog ran upstairs, hysterically yelping to each door, at last realizing, as the house realized, that only silence was here.

22 It sniffed the air and scratched the kitchen door. Behind the door, the stove was making pancakes which filled the house with a rich baked odor and the scent of maple syrup.

23 The dog frothed at the mouth, lying at the door, sniffing, its eyes turned to fire. It ran wildly in circles, biting at its tail, spun in a frenzy, and died. It lay in the parlor for an hour.

24 *Two o'clock,* sang a voice.

25 **Delicately** sensing decay at last, the regiments of mice hummed out as softly as blown gray leaves in an electrical wind.

26 *Two-fifteen.*

27 The dog was gone.

28 In the cellar, the incinerator glowed suddenly and a whirl of sparks leaped up the chimney.

29 *Two thirty-five.*

30 Bridge tables sprouted from patio walls. Playing cards **fluttered** onto pads in a shower of pips. Glasses manifested on an oaken bench with egg salad sandwiches. Music played.

31 But the tables were silent and the cards untouched.

32 At four o'clock the tables folded like great butterflies back through the paneled walls.

33 *Four-thirty.*

34 The nursery walls glowed.

35 Animals took shape: yellow giraffes, blue lions, pink antelopes, lilac panthers cavorting in crystal substance. The walls were glass. They looked out upon color and fantasy. Hidden films clocked though the well-oiled sprockets, and the walls lived. The nursery

2. **Baal** (BAY uhl) ancient Near Eastern deity, later associated with evil.

NOTES

attending (uh TEHND ihng) *adj.* being present; taking care of things

delicately (DEHL uh kiht lee) *adv.* carefully; with grace and gentleness

fluttered (FLUH tuhrd) *v.* waved gently

NOTES

manipulated (muh NIHP yuh layt ihd) *v.* managed or controlled through clever moves

tremulous (TREHM yuh luhs) *adj.* trembling; quivering; timid; fearful

floor was woven to resemble a crisp cereal meadow. Over this ran aluminum roaches and iron crickets, and in the hot still air butterflies of delicate red tissue wavered among the sharp aroma of animal spoors![3] There was the sound like a great matted yellow hive of bees within a dark bellows, the lazy bumble of a purring lion. And there was the patter of okapi[4] feet and the murmur of a fresh jungle rain, like other hoofs falling upon the summer-starched grass. Now the walls dissolved into distances of parched weed, mile on mile, and warm endless sky. The animals drew away into thorn brakes and water holes.

36 It was the children's hour.

37 *Five o'clock.* The bath filled with clear hot water.

38 *Six, seven, eight o'clock.* The dinner dishes **manipulated** like magic tricks, and in the study a click. In the metal stand opposite the hearth a fire now blazed up warmly.

39 *Nine o'clock.* The beds warmed their hidden circuits, for nights were cool here.

40 *Nine-five.* A voice spoke from the study ceiling:

41 "Mrs. McClellan, which poem would you like this evening?"

42 The house was silent.

43 The voice said at last, "Since you express no preference, I shall select a poem at random." Quiet music rose to back the voice. "Sara Teasdale. As I recall, your favorite . . .

44 *There will come soft rains and the smell of the ground,*
And swallows circling with their shimmering sound;

And frogs in the pools singing at night,
And wild plum trees in **tremulous** *white;*

Robins will wear their feathery fire,
Whistling their whims on a low fence-wire;

And not one will know of the war, not one
Will care at last when it is done.

Not one would mind, neither bird nor tree,
If mankind perished utterly;

And Spring herself, when she woke at dawn
Would scarcely know that we were gone."

45 The fire burned on the stone hearth. The empty chairs faced each other between the silent walls, and the music played.

46 At ten o'clock the house began to die.

47 The wind blew. A falling tree bough crashed through the kitchen window. Cleaning solvent, bottled, shattered over the stove. The room was ablaze in an instant!

48 "Fire!" screamed a voice. The house lights flashed, water pumps shot water from the ceilings. But the solvent spread on the linoleum,

3. **spoors** (spurz) *n.* droppings of wild animals.
4. **okapi** (oh KAH pee) *n.* African animal related to the giraffe but with a much shorter neck.

licking, eating, under the kitchen door, while the voices took it up in chorus: "Fire, fire, fire!"

49 The house tried to save itself. Doors sprang tightly shut, but the windows were broken by the heat and the wind blew and sucked upon the fire.

50 The house gave ground as the fire in ten billion angry sparks moved with flaming ease from room to room and then up the stairs. While scurrying water rats squeaked from the walls, pistoled their water, and ran for more. And the wall sprays let down showers of mechanical rain.

51 But too late. Somewhere, sighing, a pump shrugged to a stop. The quenching rain ceased. The reserve water supply which filled the baths and washed the dishes for many quiet days was gone.

52 The fire crackled up the stairs. It fed upon Picassos and Matisses[5] in the upper halls, like delicacies, baking off the oily flesh, tenderly crisping the canvases into black shavings.

53 Now the fire lay in beds, stood in windows, changed the colors of drapes!

54 And then, reinforcements.

55 From attic trapdoors, blind robot faces peered down with faucet mouths gushing green chemical.

NOTES

5. **Picassos** (pih KAH sohz) **and Matisses** (mah TEES ihz) paintings by the celebrated modern painters Pablo Picasso (1881–1973) and Henri Matisse (1869–1954).

NOTES

56 The fire backed off, as even an elephant must at the sight of a dead snake. Now there were twenty snakes whipping over the floor, killing the fire with a clear cold venom of green froth.

57 But the fire was clever. It had sent flames outside the house, up through the attic to the pumps there. An explosion! The attic brain which directed the pumps was shattered into bronze shrapnel on the beams.

58 The fire rushed back into every closet and felt of the clothes that hung there.

59 The house shuddered, oak bone on bone, its bared skeleton cringing from the heat, its wire, its nerves revealed as if a surgeon had torn the skin off to let the red veins and capillaries quiver in the scalded air. Help, help! Fire! Run, run! Heat snapped mirrors like the first brittle winter ice. And the voices wailed Fire, fire, run, run, like a tragic nursery rhyme, a dozen voices, high, low, like children dying in a forest, alone, alone. And the voices fading as the wires popped their sheathings like hot chestnuts. One, two, three, four, five voices died.

60 In the nursery the jungle burned. Blue lions roared, purple giraffes bounded off. The panthers ran in circles, changing color, and ten million animals, running before the fire, vanished off toward a distant steaming river . . .

CLOSE READ

ANNOTATE: In paragraphs 61 and 63, mark words and phrases that relate to extreme mental states.

QUESTION: What do these words show about the process the house is undergoing?

CONCLUDE: What is the effect of the author's choice to portray the house in this way?

61 Ten more voices died. In the last instant under the fire avalanche, other choruses, oblivious, could be heard announcing the time, playing music, cutting the lawn by remote-control mower, or setting an umbrella frantically out and in the slamming and opening front door, a thousand things happening, like a clock shop when each clock strikes the hour insanely before or after the other, a scene of maniac confusion, yet unity; singing, screaming, a few last cleaning mice darting bravely out to carry the horrid ashes away! And one voice, with sublime disregard for the situation, read poetry aloud all in the fiery study, until all the film spools burned, until all the wires withered and the circuits cracked.

62 The fire burst the house and let it slam flat down, puffing out skirts of spark and smoke.

63 In the kitchen, an instant before the rain of fire and timber, the stove could be seen making breakfasts at a psychopathic rate, ten dozen eggs, six loaves of toast, twenty dozen bacon strips, which, eaten by fire, started the stove working again, hysterically hissing!

64 The crash. The attic smashing into the kitchen and parlor. The parlor into cellar, cellar into subcellar. Deep freeze, armchair, film tapes, circuits, beds, and all like skeletons thrown in a cluttered mound deep under.

65 Smoke and silence. A great quantity of smoke.

66 Dawn showed faintly in the east. Among the ruins, one wall stood alone. Within the wall, a last voice said, over and over again and again, even as the sun rose to shine upon the heaped rubble and steam:

67 "Today is August 5, 2026, today is August 5, 2026, today is . . ." ❧

Comprehension Check

Complete the following items after you finish your first read.

1. What is the daily routine of the automated house?

2. What has happened to the rest of the houses in the neighborhood?

3. What are the five spots of paint on the exterior of the house?

4. By the end of the story, what happens to the house?

5. **Notebook** Create a storyboard that summarizes the sequence of events in "There Will Come Soft Rains."

RESEARCH

Research to Clarify Choose at least one unfamiliar detail from the text. Briefly research that detail. In what way does the information you learned shed light on an aspect of the story?

Research to Explore Bradbury published this story in 1950. Conduct research about modern "smart houses" to find out which of the technologies he described exist today. Share your findings with the class.

THERE WILL COME SOFT RAINS

Close Read the Text

1. This model, from paragraph 5 of the text, shows two sample annotations, along with questions and conclusions. Close read the passage, and find another detail to annotate. Then, write a question and your conclusion.

Close Read — ANNOTATE, QUESTION, CONCLUDE

ANNOTATE: This unusually exact time is repeated in rapid succession.

QUESTION: What effect does the rapid repetition of *"eight-one"* create?

CONCLUDE: It suggests a relentless technology that may be unnecessarily precise and does not allow for flexibility.

Eight-one, tick-tock, eight-one o'clock, off to school, off to work, run, run, eight-one! But no doors slammed, no carpets took the soft tread of rubber heels. It was raining outside. The weather box on the front door sang quietly: "Rain, rain, go away; rubbers, raincoats for today . . ."

ANNOTATE: These sing-song rhymes are childish.

QUESTION: Why does the author include these lines?

CONCLUDE: The house's technology treated all inhabitants, including the adults, like children.

Tool Kit
Close-Read Guide and Model Annotation

2. For more practice, go back into the text, and complete the close-read notes.

3. Revisit a section of the text you found important during your first read. Read this section closely, and **annotate** what you notice. Ask yourself **questions** such as "Why did the author make this choice?" What can you **conclude**?

Analyze the Text

CITE TEXTUAL EVIDENCE to support your answers.

Notebook Respond to these questions.

1. (a) **Analyze** What tone, or attitude, does the automated voice use to address the missing inhabitants? (b) **Draw Conclusions** What idea about technology does this tone suggest?

2. Reread paragraph 16. (a) **Interpret** Who are the "gods" that have gone away? (b) **Contrast** What contrast does this passage set up between the house's behavior and the new reality?

3. (a) **Summarize** In paragraphs 40–42, what personal information is given about one of the house's former inhabitants? (b) **Hypothesize** Why does the author wait until this point in the story to provide specific information about one of the people who lived in the house?

4. **Evaluate** Reread the poem in paragraph 44. Is the story a "retelling" of the poem? Explain.

5. **Essential Question:** *Why do we try to imagine the future?* What have you learned about people's attempts to imagine the future from reading this story?

STANDARDS

Reading Literature
- Determine the meaning of words and phrases as they are used in the text, including figurative and connotative meanings; analyze the cumulative impact of specific word choices on meaning and tone.
- Analyze how an author's choices concerning how to structure a text, order events within it, and manipulate time create such effects as mystery, tension, or surprise.

Language
Demonstrate understanding of figurative language, word relationships, and nuances in word meanings.

Analyze Craft and Structure

Author's Choices: Setting In many stories, the **setting**, or time and place of the action, merely provides a backdrop for the action. However, in stories such as "There Will Come Soft Rains," the setting serves a much more central function. Since there are no living characters in this story, the setting of the automated house also functions as a character through an extended form of **personification**, a figure of speech in which a nonhuman subject is given human characteristics.

Bradbury introduces this device in the opening sentence:

> In the living room the voice-clock sang, *Tick-tock, seven o'clock, time to get up, time to get up, seven o'clock!* as if it were afraid nobody would.

The verb *sang* is usually reserved for humans, not machines. Also, the idea that the house itself has emotions such as fear launches the personification that will be extended and deepened throughout the story.

Practice

CITE TEXTUAL EVIDENCE to support your answers.

Notebook Respond to these questions.

1. (a) Record in the chart specific examples of personification from the story.
   (b) Review each example and write a brief analysis of how it gives a particular human characteristic to the automated house.

EXAMPLE OF PERSONIFICATION	ANALYSIS OF EXAMPLE

2. Review the details in your completed chart. How does the use of personification add to the emotional quality of the story?
3. In what ways is the house personified as a dynamic character—that is, a character who develops during the course of the story?

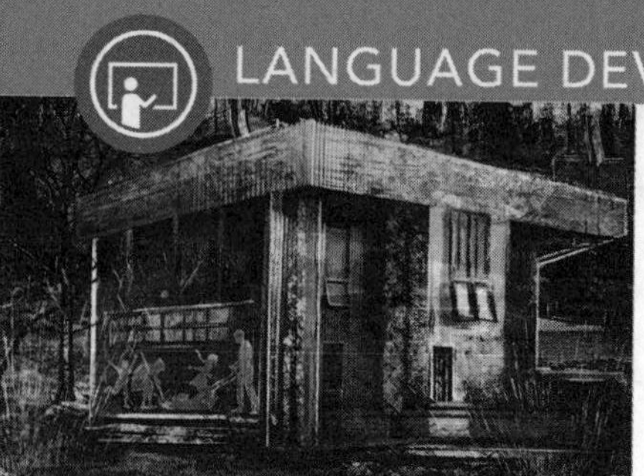

THERE WILL COME SOFT RAINS

Concept Vocabulary

chimed	delicately	manipulated
attending	fluttered	tremulous

Why These Words? These concept words relate to delicacy and carefulness. For example, consider the description "the garage chimed and lifted its door." The verb *chimed* has connotations of softness and grace, suggesting a sound that is more delicate than the loud clang of a bell or an alarm. Later, the house is described as *attending* to chores, suggesting that it is a loyal servant to its inhabitants.

1. How does the concept vocabulary help readers understand both the automated house and the society that created it?

2. What other words in the selection connect to this concept?

Practice

Notebook The concept words appear in "There Will Come Soft Rains."

1. Use each concept word in a sentence that demonstrates your understanding of the word's meaning.
2. Rewrite the sentences, replacing each concept word with a synonym. Exchange sentences with a partner. Identify the synonym in each of your partner's sentences, as well as the concept word that the synonym replaced. Discuss with your partner how each synonym differs slightly in meaning from the concept word that it replaced.

WORD NETWORK

Add interesting words related to the world's end from the text to your Word Network.

Word Study

Latin Root: *-man-* Many English words contain the root *-man-*, which is derived from the Latin word *manus*, meaning "hand." In "There Will Come Soft Rains," the verb *manipulated* means "managed or controlled through clever moves"—as though being moved by skillful hands.

1. Using your knowledge of the root *-man-*, record definitions of the words *manual*, *manuscript*, and *manifest*. Use a college-level dictionary to verify your answers.

2. Use reliable print or online reference materials to find two more words that contain the root *-man-*. Briefly define each one in your own words.

STANDARDS

Language

- Demonstrate command of the conventions of standard English grammar and usage when writing or speaking.
- Use parallel structure.
- Identify and correctly use patterns of word changes that indicate different meanings or parts of speech.
- Verify the preliminary determination of the meaning of a word or phrase.

Author's Style

Parallelism Ray Bradbury uses the literary device of parallelism to describe many events in "There Will Come Soft Rains." **Parallelism** is the use of similar grammatical forms or patterns to express similar ideas. Effective use of parallelism adds rhythm and balance to writing and strengthens connections among ideas.

The chart shows types of parallel elements, along with examples from "There Will Come Soft Rains."

TYPE OF PARALLEL ELEMENT	EXAMPLE
adjectives—words that describe nouns or pronouns	*Animals took shape: yellow giraffes, blue lions, pink antelopes, lilac panthers cavorting in crystal substance.* (paragraph 35)
adverbs—words that modify verbs, adjectives, or other adverbs	*But the gods had gone away, and the ritual of the religion continued senselessly, uselessly.* (paragraph 16)
adjective phrases—groups of words that function as adjectives	*They thudded against chairs, whirling their mustached runners, kneading the rug nap, sucking gently at hidden dust.* (paragraph 9)
adverb phrases—groups of words that function as adverbs	*Until this day, how well the house had kept its peace. How carefully it had inquired, "Who goes there? What's the password?"* (paragraph 14)
verb phrases—main and helping verbs that describe actions	*The offending dust, hair, or paper, seized in miniature steel jaws, was raced back to the burrows. There, down tubes which fed into the cellar, it was dropped into the sighing vent of an incinerator which sat like evil Baal in a dark corner.* (paragraph 20)

Read It

Read this paragraph about "There Will Come Soft Rains." Mark and classify the parallel elements in each sentence.

> The small whirring robots cleaned under rugs, inside drawers, on top of counters, and over doorways. They took care of thinly layered dust, entirely uneaten meals, and almost-imaginary dirt. As they worked, they whistled contentedly, purposefully. When they were done, the house was spotless, gleaming, and empty.

Write It

Notebook Add details to this paragraph, using parallel structures. Include one set of parallel adjectives or adjective phrases and one set of parallel adverbs or verb phrases.

> As night began to fall, the house prepared for dinner. Mechanical arms set the table while kitchen appliances cooked a three-course meal. The dining-room chairs stood empty while each dish was conveyed to the table. Finally, the meal was removed and thrown away.

THERE WILL COME SOFT RAINS

Writing to Sources

Like longer works of fiction, short stories include the narrative elements of character, setting, and plot. However, short stories usually have fewer characters than longer fictional works do, as well as simpler plots, and often just one setting. Short stories also tend to reveal character at a crucial moment rather than developing it over time and through many incidents.

Assignment

Imagine that the house in this story can speak. Write a **short story** in which the house describes a day in the life of its family before the bombs fell. Incorporate details from "There Will Come Soft Rains" that suggest what the house does for its living inhabitants and how it feels while performing these tasks.

Your story should include:

- a clear first-person narrative with a beginning, middle, and end
- precise words and phrases that capture how the house speaks
- relevant descriptive details to explain events
- sensory language that develops the character of the house

Vocabulary and Style Connection Include several of the concept vocabulary words in your story. Also, use parallelism to create detailed descriptions of the routines that the house carries out on the day in which your story takes place.

chimed	delicately	manipulated
attending	fluttered	tremulous

Reflect on Your Writing

After you have written your story, answer these questions.

1. How did writing a story from the house's point of view deepen your understanding of the original story?

2. What details from the story helped you effectively create the voice of the house?

3. **Why These Words?** The words you choose make a difference in your writing. Which words did you use to give the house a specific quality or characteristic?

STANDARDS

Writing

- Write narratives to develop real or imagined experiences or events using effective technique, well-chosen details, and well-structured event sequences.
- Use precise words and phrases, telling details, and sensory language to convey a vivid picture of the experiences, events, setting, and/or characters.

Speaking and Listening

Present information, findings, and supporting evidence clearly, concisely, and logically such that listeners can follow the line of reasoning and the organization, development, substance, and style are appropriate to purpose, audience, and task.

Speaking and Listening

Assignment

Work with a partner to prepare and deliver an **oral recitation and interpretation** of the Sara Teasdale poem included in "There Will Come Soft Rains." Structure your presentation to include:

- an oral recitation of the poem
- an explanation of whether or not the world that Teasdale's poem predicts actually emerges in the story.

First, reread the selection. Then, follow these steps to complete the assignment.

1. **Memorize the Poem** Use the following ideas to help you memorize the poem.
   - Copy the poem, and read it aloud numerous times, varying your tone of voice, the your reading pace, and your speaking volume. Make notes on the poem to mark your most effective choices. For example, you might add double slashes (//) to indicate places where you will pause and underline words you will emphasize.
   - Use the poem's rhythms and rhymes to help you remember the words.
   - Have your partner follow along with your marked-up copy of the poem as you read it aloud so that he or she can tell you if you have dropped, changed, or added any words. Make corrections as needed.
2. **Plan Your Interpretation** Discuss with your partner the interpretation of the poem that you would like to share with the class. Use this question to focus your thinking: Does the poem accurately predict what happens in the story? State your position in writing, and gather supporting evidence from both the poem and the story.
3. **Prepare Your Delivery** Practice reciting the poem from memory and delivering your interpretation of the poem. Include the following performance techniques to make the oral recitation and interpretation compelling.
   - Speak clearly, in an appropriate tone, and at an appropriate volume and rate.
   - Use appropriate facial expressions and gestures to convey the poem's power and your interpretation of the work.
   - Maintain regular eye contact with the audience.
4. **Evaluate Oral Recitations and Interpretations** As your classmates deliver their recitations and interpretations, listen attentively, and take notes. Afterward, write a brief analysis of each classmate's delivery. List specific examples of what each speaker did well and suggestions for how the recitation could be improved.

EVIDENCE LOG

Before moving on to a new selection, go to your Evidence Log and record what you learned from "There Will Come Soft Rains."

WRITING TO SOURCES

- BY THE WATERS OF BABYLON
- THERE WILL COME SOFT RAINS

Write a Narrative

You have read two short stories that address the topic of the end of the world. "By the Waters of Babylon" presents the journey of a young narrator who belongs to a tribe that remains after a catastrophic event has befallen humankind. "There Will Come Soft Rains" describes an ordinary household in the aftermath of an apocalyptic event. Each story deals with the concept of the world's end in its own way. Now you will use what you have learned to write your own narrative about the end of the world.

Assignment

Use your knowledge of "By the Waters of Babylon" and "There Will Come Soft Rains" as inspiration to write a **narrative** that answers this question:

After the end of the world, how do we begin again?

Tool Kit
Student Model of a Narrative

ACADEMIC VOCABULARY

As you craft your narrative, consider using some of the academic vocabulary you learned in the beginning of the unit.

innovate
technique
depiction
introspective
conjecture

Elements of a Narrative

A **narrative** is any type of writing that tells a story, whether it is fiction, nonfiction, poetry, or drama.

An effective narrative connects specific incidents with larger themes and includes these elements:

- an introduction to the characters and the situation they face
- a specific perspective or point of view from which the story is told
- events and characters developed though narrative techniques such as dialogue, pacing, and description
- a smooth and logical sequence of events
- precise words and phrases, descriptive details, and sensory language
- an ending that conveys the significance of story events

Model Narrative For a model of a well-crafted narrative, see the Launch Text, "Dream's Winter."

Challenge yourself to find all of the elements of an effective narrative in the text. You will have an opportunity to review these elements as you prepare to write your own narrative.

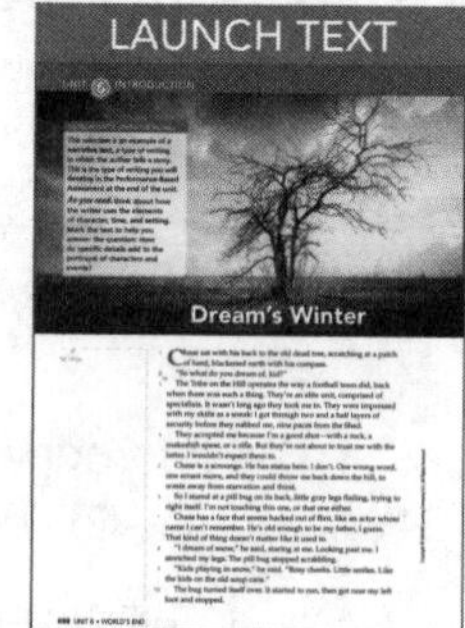

STANDARDS

Writing

- Write narratives to develop real or imagined experiences or events using effective technique, well-chosen details, and well-structured event sequences.
- Write routinely over extended time frames and shorter time frames for a range of tasks, purposes, and audiences.

Prewriting / Planning

Establish a Situation You need to establish a situation at the outset of your narrative to engage and orient the reader. First, review "By the Waters of Babylon" and "There Will Come Soft Rains" to determine how the authors establish the situations in their stories. Then, answer these questions to establish an engaging situation for your own narrative.

- Who are the characters?
- Where and when do the events take place?
- What are the characters trying to achieve?
- What obstacle(s) will they have to overcome to achieve their goal(s)?
- What happens in the end?

Write a sentence describing the situation: ______________________________

____

Establish Point of View A story's **point of view** is the perspective from which it is told. Point of view is determined by what type of **narrator**, or voice, is telling the story. Will your story be told from the point of view of a character that speaks in the first person, or a narrator who is not a story character? Will your story have multiple points of view? Complete this sentence to establish the point of view in your story.

My story will be told from the point of view of ______________________________

Gather Details There are different narrative techniques you can use to develop experiences, events, and characters in your story:

- **dialogue:** conversation between or among characters
- **pacing:** speed at which a narrative unfolds
- **description:** portrait in words of a person, place, or thing

Using a variety of narrative techniques can help you craft a compelling narrative. Brainstorm to generate details to use in dialogue and description. For example, in the Launch Text, the writer uses vivid description to help the reader visualize a character.

> ***Chase has a face that seems hacked out of flint, like an actor whose name I can't remember.***
>
> –"Dream's Winter"

EVIDENCE LOG

Review your Evidence Log and identify key details you may want to cite in your narrative.

STANDARDS

Writing

Engage and orient the reader by setting out a problem, situation, or observation, establishing one or multiple point(s) of view, and introducing a narrator and/or characters; create a smooth progression of experiences or events.

Organize Your Narrative

The sequence of related events in a narrative is known as **plot**. There are five elements of plot:

- the **exposition** introduces the setting, the characters, and the basic situation
- the **rising action** introduces and develops the central conflict, or problem
- the **climax**, or turning point, is the highest point of the action and tension
- the **falling action** shows how the conflict lessens in intensity
- the **resolution** shows how the conflict is resolved, ties up loose ends, and often conveys an insight or change by the main character

Use the graphic organizer to take notes on how you will include the plot elements in your own narrative.

EXPOSITION

RISING ACTION

CLIMAX

FALLING ACTION

RESOLUTION

STANDARDS

Writing

- Use narrative techniques, such as dialogue, pacing, description, reflection, and multiple plot lines, to develop experiences, events, and/or characters.
- Use a variety of techniques to sequence events so that they build on one another to create a coherent whole.

Drafting

Write a First Draft Use your completed graphic organizer to write your first draft. Begin by introducing your narrator and other characters, the situation they face, and the setting. Develop the characters, setting, and plot though narrative techniques such as dialogue, pacing, and description. Aim to present a smooth and logical sequence of events. Use precise words and phrases, descriptive details, and sensory language to make your narrative engaging. End with a resolution that conveys the significance of story events.

LANGUAGE DEVELOPMENT: CONVENTIONS

Add Variety: Use Adverbial Clauses to Combine Sentences

Adverbial Clauses A **clause** is a group of words that contains a subject and a verb. An **adverbial clause** is a type of clause that begins with a subordinating conjunction and functions as an adverb in a sentence. It tells *where, when, in what way, to what extent, how much, under what condition,* or *why.* Adverbial clauses can be used to combine sentences, clarifying the relationships between ideas and adding variety to writing.

Some Common Subordinating Conjunctions

after	as though	since	when
although	because	so that	whenever
as	before	than	where
as if	even though	unless	wherever
as long as	if	until	while

TIP

PUNCTUATION

Make sure to punctuate sentences that contain adverbial clauses correctly. When an adverbial clause begins a sentence, put a comma after the clause.

Read It

These sentences from the Launch Text use adverbial clauses to link related ideas and show the relationship between them.

- *I got through two and a half layers of security* ***before*** *they nabbed me. . . .* **(tells *when*)**
- *They accepted me* ***because*** *I'm a good shot. . . .* **(tells *why*)**
- *Chase tried driving his stick into the crusty earth,* ***as if*** *he were planting a flag.* **(tells *in what way*)**

Write It

As you draft your narrative, think about how you can use adverbial clauses to combine sentences that contain related ideas. First, identify the relationship between the ideas in the sentences. Then, select a subordinating conjunction that clarifies that relationship, and use it to turn information in one sentence into an adverbial clause. Put the adverbial clause at the beginning or end of the combined sentence.

If you want to...	consider using one of these conjunctions.
tell where	*where, wherever*
tell when	*after, before, until, when, whenever, while*
tell in what way	*as, as if, as though*
tell under what condition	*if, unless*
tell why	*because, since, so that*

STANDARDS

Writing

Use precise words, and phrases, telling details, and sensory language to convey a vivid picture of the experiences, events, setting, and/or characters.

Language

Use various types of phrases and clauses to convey specific meanings and add variety and interest to writing or presentations.

Revising

Evaluating Your Draft

Use the following checklist to evaluate the effectiveness of your draft. Then, use your evaluation and the instruction on this page to guide your revision.

FOCUS AND ORGANIZATION	DEVELOPMENT OF IDEAS/ELABORATION	CONVENTIONS
☐ Begins with an introduction that clearly establishes the situation and point of view.	☐ Develops events and characters through narrative techniques such as dialogue, pacing, and description.	☐ Spells all words correctly, using a print or online dictionary as needed.
☐ Organizes the sequence of events smoothly and logically through the use of the five stages of plot.	☐ Includes precise words and phrases, descriptive details, and sensory language to engage the reader.	☐ Attends to the norms and conventions of the discipline, especially the correct use of adverbial clauses in sentences.
☐ Ends with a conclusion that shows the resolution of the conflict and conveys the significance of story events.		

Revising for Focus and Organization

Logical Organization Reread your narrative. Are the events organized smoothly and logically into a coherent whole through the use of the five stages of plot? If not, review the five elements, and determine which ones are missing or could be strengthened in your draft. Revise parts of your narrative as needed.

Revising for Ideas and Elaboration

Use Narrative Techniques Remember that narrative techniques such as dialogue, pacing, and description can help to develop the events and characters in a story. Review your draft and ask yourself these questions:

- Are there sections where adding a conversation between or among characters could convey ideas more clearly? If so, how?
- Are there sections where the speed of the story seems to be too fast or too slow? If so, how can the pacing be improved?
- Are there sections where a person, place, or thing could be described in more detail? What specific details could be included in the description?

Mark these sections in your draft, and revise them as needed.

Use Vivid Details Reread your draft, and mark your use of descriptive details. Ask yourself these questions:

- Have I relied too much on adjectives? If so, would nouns that are more specific work better?
- Have I repeated too many verbs? If so, would varying my choice of verbs or adding adverbs provide more interest and color to my story?

Continue to review your word choices, and revise as needed.

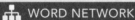

 WORD NETWORK

Include interesting words from your Word Network in your narrative.

STANDARDS

Writing
Use a variety of techniques to sequence events so that they build on one another to create a coherent whole.

Language
- Demonstrate command of the conventions of standard English grammar and usage when writing or speaking.
- Spell correctly.

PEER REVIEW

Exchange papers with a classmate. Use the checklist to evaluate your classmate's narrative and provide supportive feedback.

1. Are the situation and point of view clearly established?

   ☐ yes ☐ no If no, suggest how the writer might clarify them.

2. Is there a clear sequence of events that unfolds smoothly and logically?

   ☐ yes ☐ no If no, explain what confused you.

3. Does the narrative end with a conclusion that conveys the significance of story events?

   ☐ yes ☐ no If no, tell what you think might be missing.

4. What is the strongest part of your classmate's paper? Why?

   ____

   ____

Editing and Proofreading

Edit for Conventions Reread your draft for accuracy and consistency. Correct errors in grammar and word usage. Be sure you have included a variety of sentence structures that add variety and interest to your narrative and reflect your unique voice.

Proofread for Accuracy Read your draft carefully, correcting errors in spelling and punctuation. As you proofread, make sure that any dialogue is enclosed in quotation marks. Review your draft closely for instances of split dialogue—that is, dialogue in which a quotation is split up by additional information, such as the identification of the speaker. Make sure these instances of split dialogue are punctuated correctly with quotation marks.

Publishing and Presenting

Create a final version of your narrative. Share it with a small group so that your classmates can read it and make comments. In turn, review and comment on your classmates' work. As a group, discuss what your narratives have in common and the ways in which they are different. Always maintain a polite and respectful tone when commenting.

Reflecting

Reflect on what you learned as you wrote your narrative. In what ways did writing about imagined experiences and events relating to the end of the world enhance your understanding of the topic? What was the most challenging aspect of composing your narrative? Did you learn something from reviewing the work of others and discussing your narrative with your classmates that might inform your narrative writing process in the future?

OVERVIEW: SMALL-GROUP LEARNING

ESSENTIAL QUESTION:

Why do we try to imagine the future?

Some stories about a doomed future capture people's anxieties about the world right now. You will read selections featuring situations that seem futuristic but affect people in the present. You will work in a group to continue your exploration of literature about the world's end.

Small-Group Learning Strategies

Throughout your life, in school, in your community, and in your career, you will continue to learn and work with others.

Review these strategies and the actions you can take to practice them as you work in teams. Add ideas of your own for each step. Use these strategies during Small-Group Learning.

STRATEGY	ACTION PLAN
Prepare	• Complete your assignments so that you are prepared for group work. • Organize your thinking so you can contribute to your group's discussions. •
Participate fully	• Make eye contact to signal that you are listening and taking in what is being said. • Use text evidence when making a point. •
Support others	• Build off ideas from others in your group. • Invite others who have not yet spoken to join the discussion. •
Clarify	• Paraphrase the ideas of others to ensure that your understanding is correct. • Ask follow-up questions. •

CONTENTS

Working as a Team

1. **Take a Position** In your group, discuss the following question:

   What is one thing people can do today to make the world a better place tomorrow?

   As you take turns sharing your ideas, provide reasons that support them. After all group members have shared, discuss similarities and differences among the various suggestions.

2. **List Your Rules** As a group, decide on the rules that you will follow as you work together. Samples are provided; add two more of your own. You may add or revise rules based on your experience together.

   - Everyone should participate in group discussions.
   - People should not interrupt.
   - ______________________________
     ____
   - ______________________________
     ____

3. **Apply the Rules** Practice working as a group. Share what you have learned about world's end stories. Make sure each person in the group contributes. Take notes and be prepared to share with the class one thing that you heard from another member of your group.

4. **Name Your Group** Choose a name that reflects the unit topic.

   Our group's name: ______________________________

5. **Create a Communication Plan** Decide how you want to communicate with one another. For example, you might use online collaboration tools, email, or instant messaging.

   Our group's decision: ______________________________

   ____

Making a Schedule

First, find out the due dates for the small-group activities. Then, preview the texts and activities with your group, and make a schedule for completing the tasks.

SELECTION	ACTIVITIES	DUE DATE
The Nuclear Tourist		
the beginning of the end of the world The Powwow at the End of the World A Song on the End of the World		
from Radiolab: War of the Worlds The Myth of the *War of the Worlds* Panic		

Working on Group Projects

As your group works together, you'll find it more effective if each person has a specific role. Different projects require different roles. Before beginning a project, discuss the necessary roles, and choose one for each group member. Here are some possible roles; add your own ideas.

Project Manager: monitors the schedule and keeps everyone on task
Researcher: organizes research activities
Recorder: takes notes during group meetings

About the Author

George Johnson (b. 1952) is a science writer who writes for the *New York Times, Slate, National Geographic*, and several other publications. Johnson is the author of nine books, three of which were finalists for the Royal Society Winton Prize for Science Books. In 2014, he won the AAAS Kavli Science Journalism Award for three of his articles.

The Nuclear Tourist

Concept Vocabulary

As you perform your first read of "The Nuclear Tourist," you will encounter these words.

macabre	eerily	specter

Context Clues If these words are unfamiliar to you, try using **context clues**—other words and phrases that appear in a text—to help you determine their meanings. There are various types of context clues that you may encounter as you read.

Synonyms: Extreme **valor** in the face of danger earned the firefighters commendations for bravery.

Elaborating Details: Her parents were **ecstatic** about her grades, heaping praise on her for her excellent work.

Contrast of Ideas: The **immaculate** silverware stood out against the filthy tablecloth and uncleaned plates.

Apply your knowledge of context clues and other vocabulary strategies to determine the meanings of unfamiliar words you encounter during your first read.

First Read NONFICTION

Apply these strategies as you conduct your first read. You will have an opportunity to complete a close read after your first read.

NOTICE the general ideas of the text. *What* is it about? *Who* is involved?

ANNOTATE by marking vocabulary and key passages you want to revisit.

CONNECT ideas within the selection to what you already know and what you have already read.

RESPOND by completing the Comprehension Check and by writing a brief summary of the selection.

First Read: NOTICE, ANNOTATE, CONNECT, RESPOND

STANDARDS

Reading Informational Text
By the end of grade 9, read and comprehend literary nonfiction in the grades 9–10 text complexity band proficiently, with scaffolding as needed at the high end of the range.

Language
Use context as a clue to the meaning of a word or phrase.

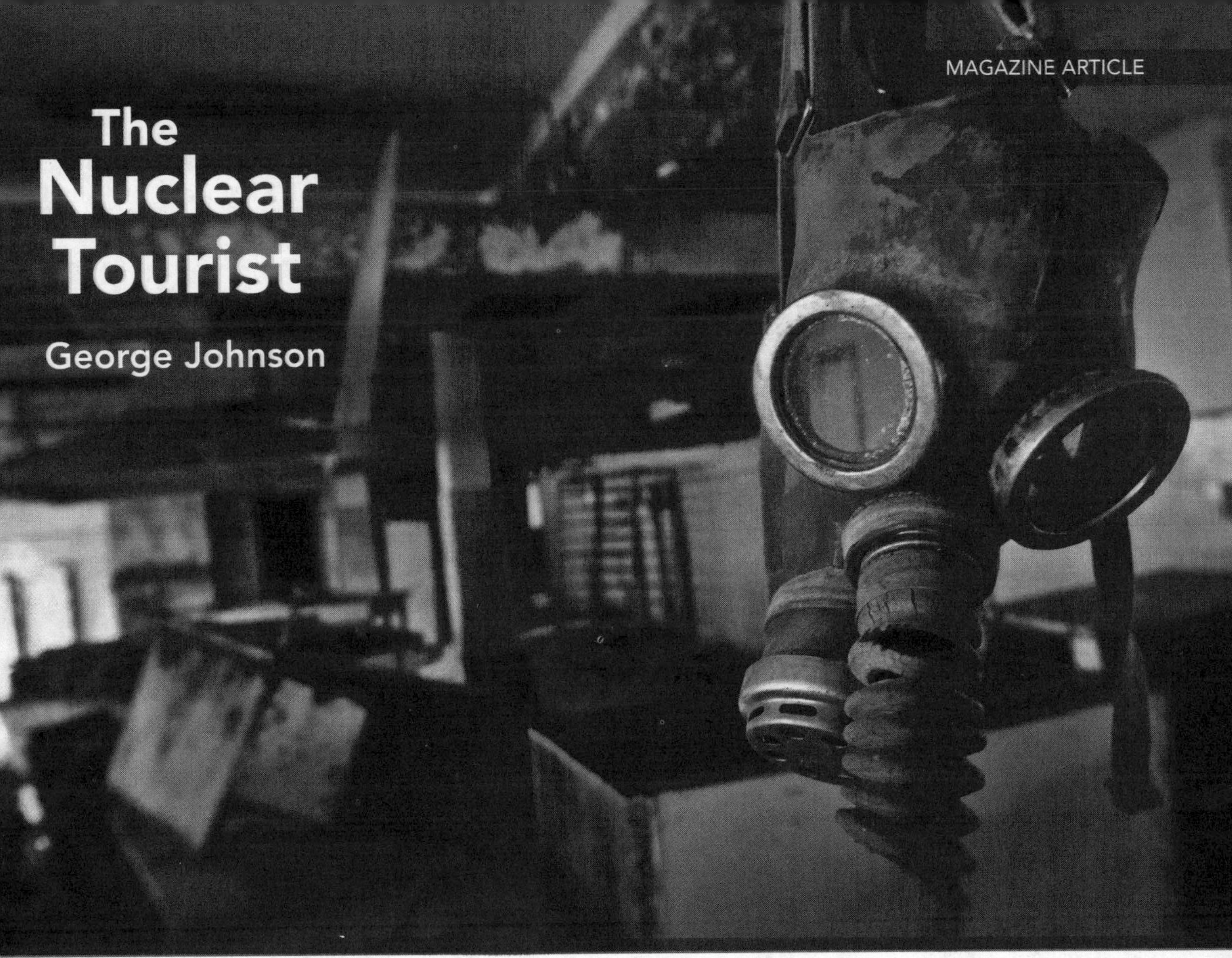

MAGAZINE ARTICLE

The Nuclear Tourist

George Johnson

BACKGROUND

On April 26, 1986, during a routine test, a power surge caused an explosion in one of the reactors at the Chernobyl Nuclear Power Plant in Pripyat, Ukraine. To date, the Chernobyl incident is the worst nuclear power plant disaster in history, exceeding other incidents such as the 1979 Three Mile Island disaster in Pennsylvania. The Chernobyl explosion is one of only two incidents that have been classified as Level 7 events on the International Nuclear Event Scale, the highest possible rating in terms of destruction.

NOTES

1 They say that five sieverts of radiation is enough to kill you, so I was curious to see the reading on my Russian-made dosimeter[1] as our tour van passed into the exclusion zone—the vast, quarantined wilderness that surrounds Chernobyl. Thick stands of pines and birches crowded the roadside as our guide reminded us of the ground rules: Don't pick the mushrooms, which concentrate radionuclides, or risk letting the contaminants into your body by eating or smoking outdoors. A few minutes later we passed the first of the abandoned villages and pulled over to admire a small band of wild Przewalski's horses.[2]

1. **dosimeter** (doh SIHM uh tuhr) *n.* device used to measure the total absorbed dose from radiation exposure.
2. **Przewalski's** (shuh VOL skeez) **horses** endangered wild horses native to central Asia.

NOTES

Mark context clues or indicate another strategy you used that helped you determine meaning.

macabre (muh KAH bruh) *adj.*

MEANING:

2 Twenty-eight years after the explosion of a nuclear reactor at Chernobyl, the zone, all but devoid of people, has been seized and occupied by wildlife. There are bison, boars, moose, wolves, beavers, falcons. In the ghost city of Pripyat, eagles roost atop deserted Soviet-era apartment blocks. The horses—a rare, endangered breed—were let loose here a decade after the accident, when the radiation was considered tolerable, giving them more than a thousand square miles to roam.

3 I glanced at my meter: 0.19 microsieverts per hour—a fraction of a millionth of a single sievert, a measure of radiation exposure. Nothing to worry about yet. The highest levels I had seen so far on my trip to Ukraine were on the transatlantic flight from Chicago—spikes of 3.5 microsieverts per hour as we flew 40,000 feet over Greenland, cosmic rays penetrating the plane and passengers. Scientists studying Chernobyl remain divided over the long-term effects of the radiation on the flora and fauna. So far they have been surprisingly subtle. More threatening to the animals are the poachers, who sneak into the zone with guns.

4 A few minutes later we reached Zalesye, an old farming village, and wandered among empty houses. Broken windows, peeling paint, crumbling plaster. On the floor of one home a discarded picture of Lenin[3]—pointy beard, jutting chin—stared sternly at nothing, and hanging by a cord on a bedroom wall was a child's doll. It had been suspended by the neck as if with an executioner's noose. Outside, another doll sat next to the remains of a broken stroller. These were the first of the **macabre** tributes we saw during our two days in the zone. Dolls sprawling half dressed in cribs, gas masks hanging from trees—tableaux placed by visitors, here legally or otherwise, signifying a lost, quiet horror.

5 Farther down the road we were surprised by an inhabitant. Dressed in a scarf, a red sweater, and a winter vest, Rosalia is one of what officials call the "returnees"—stubborn old people, women mostly, who insist on living out their lives in the place they call home. She seemed happy for the company. Prompted by our guide, she told us of worse hardships. The lands around Chernobyl (or Chornobyl, as it is known in Ukraine) are part of the Pripyat Marshes on the eastern front, where the bloodiest battles of World War II were fought. She remembers the German soldiers and the hardships under Stalin.[4]

6 "You can't see radiation," she said in Ukrainian. Anyway, she added, she is not planning to have children. She lives with five cats. Before we departed, she showed us her vegetable garden and said her biggest problem now is Colorado potato bugs.

3. **Lenin** (LEHN ihn) Vladimir Lenin (1870–1924), leader of the Russian Communist revolution of 1917 and first premier of the Soviet Union.
4. **Stalin** (STAH lihn) Joseph Stalin (1879–1953), leader of the Soviet Union from 1922 to 1953. Under Stalin's rule, the Soviet Union became a world power, but millions of people were imprisoned in labor camps, died from famine, or were executed.

7 There is something deeply rooted in the human soul that draws us to sites of unimaginable disaster. Pompeii, Antietam, Auschwitz, and Treblinka—all **eerily** quiet now. But in the 21st century we hold a special awe for the aftermath of nuclear destruction. The splitting of the atom almost a hundred years ago promised to be the most important human advance since the discovery of fire. Unleashing the forces bound inside atomic nuclei would bring the world nearly limitless energy. Inevitably it was first used in warfare, but after Hiroshima and Nagasaki[5] a grand effort began to provide electricity "too cheap to meter," freeing the world from its dependence on fossil fuels.

8 More than half a century later the swirling symbol of the atom, once the emblem of progress and the triumph of technology, has become a bewitching death's-head, associated in people's minds with destruction and Cold War fear. Every spring visitors head for Stallion Gate in southern New Mexico for an open house at Trinity Site, where the first atomic bomb was detonated—a preview of what was to come when the bombers reached Japan. Monthly tours to the Nevada Test Site in the Mojave Desert, where more than a thousand nuclear weapons were exploded during the Cold War, are booked solid through 2014.

9 Then there is the **specter** of nuclear meltdown. In 2011, Chernobyl, site of the world's worst catastrophe at a nuclear power plant, was officially declared a tourist attraction.

10 Nuclear tourism. Coming around the time of the Fukushima disaster,[6] the idea seems absurd. And that is what drew me, along with the wonder of seeing towns and a whole city—almost 50,000 people lived in Pripyat—that had been abandoned in a rush, left to the devices of nature.

11 Sixty miles away in Kiev, Ukraine's capital city, weeks of bloody demonstrations had led in February to the expulsion of the president and the installation of a new government. In response to the upheaval Russia had occupied Crimea, the peninsula that juts from southern Ukraine into the Black Sea. Russian troops were massing on Ukraine's eastern border. In a crazy way, Chernobyl felt like the safest place to be.

12 The other diehards in the van had come for their own reasons. John, a young man from London, was into "extreme tourism." For his next adventure he had booked a tour of North Korea and was looking into options for bungee jumping from a helicopter. Gavin from Australia and Georg from Vienna were working together on a performance piece about the phenomenon of quarantine. We are used to thinking of sick people quarantined from the general population. Here it was the land itself that was contagious.

13 Of all my fellow travelers, the most striking was Anna, a quiet young woman from Moscow. She was dressed all in black with

NOTES

Mark context clues or indicate another strategy you used that helped you determine meaning.

eerily (EER uh lee) *adv.*

MEANING:

Mark context clues or indicate another strategy you used that helped you determine meaning.

specter (SPEHK tuhr) *n.*

MEANING:

5. **Hiroshima** (hee roh shee mah) **and Nagasaki** (nah gah sah kee) Japanese cities upon which the United States dropped nuclear bombs during World War II.
6. **Fukushima** (foo koo shee mah) **disaster** In 2011, a nuclear power plant in Fukushima, Japan, overheated and leaked radiation after a powerful earthquake and tsunami struck the area.

NOTES

fur-lined boots, her long dark hair streaked with a flash of magenta. It reminded me of radioactivity. This was her third time at Chernobyl, and she had just signed up for another five-day tour later in the year.

14 "I'm drawn to abandoned places that have fallen apart and decayed," she said. Mostly she loved the silence and the wildlife—this accidental wilderness. On her T-shirt was a picture of a wolf.

15 "'Radioactive Wolves'?" I asked. It was the name of a documentary I'd seen on PBS's *Nature* about Chernobyl. "It's my favorite film," she said.

16 In the early hours of April 26, 1986, during a scheduled shutdown for routine maintenance, the night shift at Chernobyl's reactor number four was left to carry out an important test of the safety systems—one delayed from the day before, when a full, more experienced staff had been on hand.

17 Within 40 seconds a power surge severely overheated the reactor, rupturing some of the fuel assemblies and quickly setting off two explosions. The asphalt roof of the plant began burning, and, much more threatening, so did the graphite blocks that made up the reactor's core. A plume of smoke and radioactive debris rose high into the atmosphere and began bearing north toward Belarus and Scandinavia. Within days the fallout had spread across most of Europe.

18 Throughout the night firefighters and rescue crews confronted the immediate dangers—flames, smoke, burning chunks of graphite. What they couldn't see or feel—until hours or days later when the sickness set in—were the invisible poisons. Isotopes of cesium, iodine, strontium, plutonium.[7] The exposures they received totaled as much as 16 sieverts—not micro or milli but whole sieverts, vastly more radiation than a body can bear. From the high-rises of Pripyat, less than two miles away, Chernobyl workers and their families stood on balconies and watched the glow.

19 In the morning—it was the weekend before May Day[8]—they went about their routines of shopping, Saturday morning classes, picnics in the park. It was not until 36 hours after the accident that the evacuation began. The residents were told to bring enough supplies for three to five days and to leave their pets behind. The implication was that after a quick cleanup they would return home. That didn't happen. Crews of liquidators quickly moved in and began bulldozing buildings and burying topsoil. Packs of dogs were shot on sight. Nearly 200 villages were evacuated.

20 The immediate death toll was surprisingly small. Three workers died during the explosion, and 28 within a year from radiation poisoning. But most of the effects were slow in unfolding. So far, some 6,000 people who were exposed as children to irradiated

7. **Isotopes of cesium, iodine, strontium, plutonium** versions of these elements that are radioactive.

8. **May Day** holiday for laborers and the working class celebrated in the Soviet Union and other countries.

An abandoned school in the small city of Pripyat. Evacuated on April 27, 1986, the city remains largely untouched to this day.

milk and other food have had thyroid cancer. Based on data from Hiroshima and Nagasaki, the overall mortality rate from cancer may rise by a few percent among the 600,000 workers and residents who received the highest doses, possibly resulting in thousands of premature deaths.

NOTES

21 After the accident a concrete and steel structure—the sarcophagus—was hastily erected to contain the damaged reactor. As the sarcophagus crumbled and leaked, work began on what has been optimistically named the New Safe Confinement, a 32,000-ton arch, built on tracks so it can be slid into place when fully assembled. Latest estimate: 2017. Meanwhile the cleanup continues. According to plans by the Ukrainian government, the reactors will be dismantled and the site cleared by 2065. Everything about this place seems like science fiction. Will there even be a Ukraine?

22 What I remember most about the hours we spent in Pripyat is the sound and feel of walking on broken glass. Through the dilapidated hospital wards with the empty beds and cribs and the junk-strewn operating rooms. Through the school hallways, treading across mounds of broken-back books. Mounted over the door of an old science class was an educational poster illustrating the spectrum of electromagnetic radiation. Heat to visible light to x-rays and gamma rays—the kind that break molecular bonds and mutate DNA. How abstract that must have seemed to the schoolkids before the evacuation began.

23 In another room gas masks hung from the ceiling and were piled in heaps on the floor. They were probably left there, our guides told us, by "stalkers"—surreptitious visitors who sneak into the zone. At

NOTES

first they came to scavenge, later for the thrill. They drink from the Pripyat River and swim in Pripyat bay, daring the radiation and the guards to get them. A stalker I met later in Kiev said he'd been to Chernobyl a hundred times. "I imagined the zone to be a vast, burnt-out place—empty, horrible," he told me. Instead he found forests and rivers, all this contaminated beauty.

24 Our tour group walked along the edge of a bone-dry public swimming pool, its high dive and racing clock still intact, and across the rotting floor of a gymnasium. Building after building, all decomposing. We visited the ruins of the Palace of Culture, imagining it alive with music and laughter, and the small amusement park with its big yellow Ferris wheel. Walking up 16 flights of steps—more glass crunching underfoot—we reached the top of one of the highest apartment buildings. The metal handrails had been stripped away for salvage. Jimmied doors opened onto gaping elevator shafts. I kept thinking how unlikely a tour like this would be in the United States. It was refreshing really. We were not even wearing hard hats.

25 From the rooftop we looked out at what had once been grand, landscaped avenues and parks—all overgrown now. Pripyat, once hailed as a model Soviet city, a worker's paradise, is slowly being reabsorbed by the earth.

26 We spent the night in the town of Chernobyl. Eight centuries older than Pripyat, it now has the look of a Cold War military base, the center for the endless containment operation. My hotel room with its stark accommodations was like a set piece in a museum of life in Soviet times. One of the guides later told me that the vintage furnishings were salvaged from Pripyat. I wasn't able to confirm that officially. The radiation levels in my room were no greater than what I've measured back home.

27 By the next morning we were becoming almost cavalier about the exposure risk. Standing beneath the remains of a cooling tower, our guide, hurrying us along, exclaimed, "Oh, over here is a high-radiation spot! Let's go see!" as casually as if she were pointing us toward a new exhibit in a wax museum. She pulled up a board covering the hot spot, and we stooped down holding our meters—they were frantically beeping—in a friendly competition to see who could detect the highest amount. My device read 112 microsieverts per hour—30 times as high as I had measured on the flight. We stayed for only a minute.

28 The hottest spot we measured that day was on the blade of a rusting earthmover that had been used to plow under the radioactive topsoil: 186 microsieverts per hour—too high to linger but nothing compared with what those poor firemen and liquidators got.

29 On the drive back to Kiev our guide tallied up our accumulated count—ten microsieverts during the entire weekend visit.

30 I'd probably receive more than that on the flight back home. ❧

Comprehension Check

Complete the following items after you finish your first read. Review and clarify details with your group.

1. What is the exclusion zone?

2. What are some characteristics that draw tourists to areas like Chernobyl?

3. What elements caused the explosion at Chernobyl in 1986?

4. What is the current condition of the towns of Pripyat and Chernobyl?

5. **Notebook** Confirm your understanding of the text by writing a summary.

RESEARCH

Research to Clarify Choose at least one unfamiliar detail from the text. Briefly research that detail. In what way does the information you learned shed light on an aspect of the article?

Research to Explore This essay may spark your curiosity to learn more. Briefly research a topic that interests you. You may want to share what you discover with your group.

THE NUCLEAR TOURIST

Close Read the Text

With your group, revisit sections of the text you marked during your first read. **Annotate** details that you notice. What **questions** do you have? What can you **conclude**?

Analyze the Text

CITE TEXTUAL EVIDENCE to support your answers.

Complete the activities.

1. **Review and Clarify** With your group, reread paragraphs 7–10 of the selection. Do you agree or disagree with the author that "There is something deeply rooted in the human soul" that compels people to visit places like Chernobyl? Explain.

2. **Present and Discuss** Now, work with your group to share the passages from the selection that you found especially important. Discuss what you noticed in the selection, the questions you asked, and the conclusions you reached.

3. **Essential Question:** ***Why do we try to imagine the future?*** What has this article taught you about world's end literature? Discuss with your group.

LANGUAGE DEVELOPMENT

Concept Vocabulary

macabre	eerily	specter

Why These Words? The three concept vocabulary words are related. With your group, determine what the words have in common. Write your ideas, and add another word that fits the category.

Practice

Notebook Write a sentence using each of the concept vocabulary words. How did the words make your sentences more vivid? Discuss.

Word Study

Notebook **Latin Root: *-spec-*** In "The Nuclear Tourist," Johnson explains "the specter of nuclear meltdown." The word *specter* contains the Latin root *-spec-*, meaning "to see" or "to look." Work individually to complete the following activities. Then, discuss your responses with your group.

1. Reread paragraph 22 of "The Nuclear Tourist." Identify a word that contains the root *-spec-*. Look the word up in an online dictionary, and write its definition.

2. Find and write definitions for these words that contain the root *-spec-*: *inspection, spectacles, aspect.*

WORD NETWORK

Add interesting words related to the world's end from the text to your Word Network.

STANDARDS

Reading Informational Text
Cite strong and thorough textual evidence to support analysis of what the text says explicitly as well as inferences drawn from the text.

Language
- Identify and correctly use patterns of word changes that indicate different meanings or parts of speech.
- Consult general and specialized reference materials, both print and digital, to find the pronunciation of a word or determine or clarify its precise meaning, its part of speech, or its etymology.

Analyze Craft and Structure

Literary Nonfiction In literary nonfiction, authors use traditional fiction-writing techniques to bring true stories and real locations to life for readers. **Travel journalism** is a type of literary nonfiction in which the writer describes what it is like to visit a particular place.

Effective travel journalism captures the reader's interest and gives the reader a vivid impression of a specific location or journey. To accomplish this goal, the writer does the following:

- includes fact-based information about the place. This information can include the place's location, how to get there, and key historical events that happened there.
- adds personal observations about the place, such as what the writer saw, heard, felt, tasted, and smelled. These observations are *subjective*, or based on personal opinion, but they also offer an impression of the place beyond what readers may get from straightforward facts.
- employs literary techniques, such as a story-like sequence of events, figurative language, and dialogue. With these literary techniques, writers set the scene for readers, allowing them to imagine what they might see, hear, or experience as if they had traveled with the writer.

Practice

Work independently to analyze elements of travel journalism in "The Nuclear Tourist." Then, discuss your findings with your group.

FEATURE	EXAMPLES FROM THE ARTICLE	HOW THEY HELP READERS IMAGINE CHERNOBYL
fact-based information		
personal observations		
literary techniques		

GROUP DISCUSSION
There is no wrong way to think about a particular place, but travel journalism has to be based on real experiences that happened in that location. Members of your group might have different ideas about similar places. Talk out differing opinions, and learn more about why group members feel a certain way about an area.

THE NUCLEAR TOURIST

Author's Style

Diction Word choice, or **diction,** is a key element of a writer's style, helping to express his or her voice and purpose. A writer's diction also reflects the topic. For example, articles about history will include diction particular to that study. Likewise, writings about science or technology will include **scientific and technical terms,** or words and phrases with precise scientific or technical meanings. Consider passages A and B, both of which are based on paragraph 3 of the article.

Passage A: *I glanced at my device: The dial had moved past zero—this indicated that I was being exposed to some measure of danger. Nothing to worry about yet.*

Passage B: *I glanced at my meter: 0.19 microsieverts per hour—a fraction of a millionth of a single sievert, a measure of radiation exposure. Nothing to worry about yet.*

Passage A provides information, but it is not specific. The reader does not learn what type of danger the author is in nor how he is measuring it. In contrast, Passage B uses scientific and technical terms, such as *radiation exposure* and *sieverts*, that have precise meanings. These terms communicate specific information in an efficient way.

The use of scientific and technical terms allows writers to quantify critical information and make it exact. However, these terms can be challenging for general readers.

STANDARDS

Language

- Apply knowledge of language to understand how language functions in different contexts, to make effective choices for meaning or style, and to comprehend more fully when reading or listening.
- Acquire and use accurately general academic and domain-specific words and phrases, sufficient for reading, writing, speaking, and listening at the college and career readiness level; demonstrate independence in gathering vocabulary knowledge when considering a word or phrase important to comprehension or expression.

Read It

Work individually. Use this chart to record examples of scientific and technical terms from the selection. Define each term by using context clues and verifying definitions in a dictionary. Then, discuss with your group how each term helps the author communicate precise information in an efficient way.

SCIENTIFIC/TECHNICAL TERM	DEFINITION	HOW IT IMPROVES UNDERSTANDING

Write It

Notebook Rewrite the sentences so that each includes a scientific or technical term.

1. My device told me that I had been exposed to some radiation.
2. Our guide told us that we could be harmed just from picking mushrooms, which concentrate poisons.

Research

"The Nuclear Tourist" touches on the effects of Chernobyl and looks at what it was like to visit the area decades after the disaster. Learn more about Chernobyl by completing the following research assignment.

Assignment

With your group, research the Chernobyl disaster. Focus on finding out about what happened before, during, and after the accident.

Once your research is complete, present your findings in one of the following formats. Remember that scientific and technical terms help clarify important concepts, so consider using those terms to support ideas in your writing.

- ☐ Assume the identity of a journalist stationed in the Soviet Union in 1986. Write a series of three **newspaper reports** that correspond to before, during, and after the accident.
- ☐ Assume the identity of a citizen who lives in Chernobyl in 1986. Write three **journal entries** that describe what life was like before, during, and after the accident.
- ☐ Assume the identity of a local government official who lives in Chernobyl in 1986. Write three **reports** that might have been issued by the government before, during, and after the accident.

Project Plan Before you begin, make a list of the tasks you will need to accomplish to complete your research. Then, assign individual group members to each task. Finally, determine how you will make decisions about what sources you will use, what information and details to include, and how you will present your information.

Finding Sources When researching, consult a variety of reliable and trustworthy sources such as newspapers, peer-reviewed magazine and journal articles, encyclopedias, and books written about the subject. When searching on the Internet, look for articles and studies that list their own sources. Then, verify the credibility of those sources. Use the checklist to determine the quality and usefulness of the sources you find. You should be able to check the "Yes" boxes for all sources you choose to use.

Source Checklist

☐ Yes	☐ No	Does the source have a good reputation?
☐ Yes	☐ No	Does the source avoid bias or a political agenda?
☐ Yes	☐ No	Is the content well-written and clearly designed?
☐ Yes	☐ No	Does the source accurately cite information from other sources?
☐ Yes	☐ No	Does the source address questions you have about the subject, either directly or through textual details?

EVIDENCE LOG

Before moving on to a new selection, go to your Evidence Log and record what you learned from "The Nuclear Tourist."

STANDARDS

Writing

- Conduct short as well as more sustained research projects to answer a question or solve a problem; narrow or broaden the inquiry when appropriate; synthesize multiple sources on the subject, demonstrating understanding of the subject under investigation.
- Gather relevant information from multiple authoritative print and digital sources, using advanced searches effectively; assess the usefulness of each source in answering the research question; integrate information into the text selectively to maintain the flow of ideas, avoiding plagiarism and following a standard format for citation.
- Draw evidence from literary or informational texts to support analysis, reflection, and research.

POETRY COLLECTION 1

the beginning of the end of the world

The Powwow at the End of the World

A Song on the End of the World

Concept Vocabulary

As you perform your first read, you will encounter these words.

prayerful	faithless	prophet

Base Words If these words are unfamiliar to you, analyze each one to see whether it contains a base word you know. Then, use your knowledge of the "inside" word, along with context, to determine the meaning of the concept word. Here is an example of how to apply the strategy.

Unfamiliar Word in Context: . . . until [the salmon] arrives in the shallows of a secret bay on the **reservation** where I wait alone.

Familiar "Inside" Word: *reserve*, with meanings including "to save for future use."

Conclusion: The speaker is waiting in a secret area, so *reservation* may refer to land that has been set aside for a specific purpose.

Apply your knowledge of base words and other vocabulary strategies to help you determine the meanings of unfamiliar words you encounter during your first read.

First Read POETRY

Apply these strategies as you conduct your first read. You will have an opportunity to complete a close read after your first read.

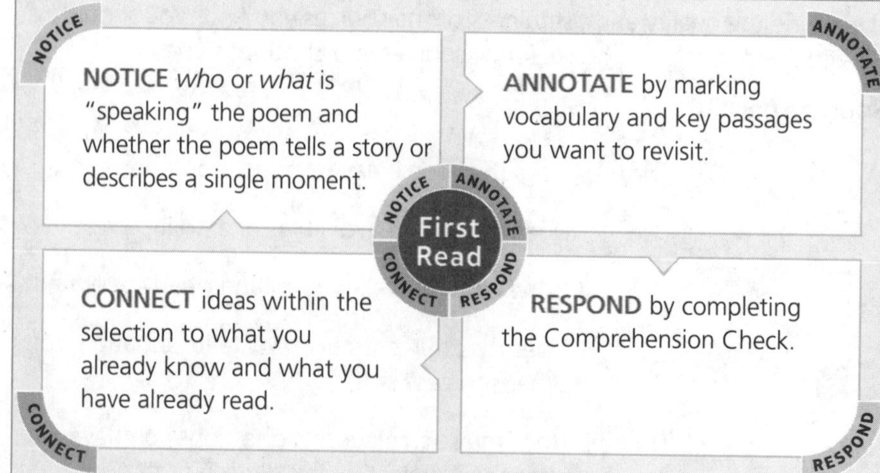

NOTICE
NOTICE *who* or *what* is "speaking" the poem and whether the poem tells a story or describes a single moment.
ANNOTATE
ANNOTATE by marking vocabulary and key passages you want to revisit.
First Read
NOTICE
ANNOTATE
CONNECT
RESPOND
CONNECT ideas within the selection to what you already know and what you have already read.
RESPOND by completing the Comprehension Check.
CONNECT
RESPOND

STANDARDS

Reading Literature
By the end of grade 9, read and comprehend literature, including stories, dramas, and poems, in the grades 9–10 text complexity band proficiently, with scaffolding as needed at the high end of the range.

Language
Identify and correctly use patterns of word changes that indicate different meanings or parts of speech.

About the Poets

Lucille Clifton (1936–2010) grew up in New York State and worked in government agencies until shortly after her first book was published. From there, Clifton authored many critically acclaimed collections of poetry. Her many honors include an Emmy Award, the National Book Award, the Coretta Scott King Award, and the Ruth Lilly Prize for Poetry.

Sherman Alexie (b. 1966) grew up on the Spokane Indian Reservation in Washington State. As a child, Alexie suffered from seizures and spent much of his time in bed reading. After he finished college, his career as a writer took off. Since then, Alexie has won numerous awards for his novels, stories, screenplays, and poems.

Czeslaw Milosz (1911–2004) was born in Lithuania before the revolution brought the Soviets to power in 1918. Milosz spent the World War II years working for underground presses, then came to the United States as an embassy official for the communist Polish government. In 1951, Milosz defected to the United States and began writing books, ultimately receiving the Nobel Prize in 1980.

Backgrounds

the beginning of the end of the world

Cockroaches have been around for 300 million years. They easily outlived the dinosaurs, and time will tell if they will outlast people as well. It is often said that only cockroaches could survive a nuclear war. That may be an exaggeration, but they are resilient creatures—a cockroach can withstand ten times as much radiation as a person can.

The Powwow at the End of the World

The Grand Coulee Dam spans the Columbia River and stands 550 feet tall and over 5,000 feet long. Completed in 1942, the dam was built to provide jobs and generate massive amounts of electricity for the region. However, the dam has been controversial—its creation flooded Native American communities and forced thousands to relocate. Furthermore, the dam has blocked salmon migration and was used to supply energy for the production of the first atomic bombs.

A Song on the End of the World

Warsaw, Poland, was one of many cities devastated by the Nazi regime during World War II. For most of the war, the Nazis occupied the city. Polish Jews were rounded up in ghettos, sent to concentration camps, and executed. In 1944, the Polish Home Army staged an uprising against the Nazis. Civilian casualties were in the hundreds of thousands. The Nazis eventually overcame the uprising and went on to destroy much of the city.

POETRY

the **beginning** of the **end** of the **world**

Lucille Clifton

cockroach population possibly declining
—news report

maybe the morning the roaches
walked into the kitchen
bold with they bad selves
marching up out of the drains
not like soldiers like priests
grim and patient in the sink
and when we ran the water
trying to drown them as if they were
soldiers they seemed to bow their
sad heads for us not at us
and march single file away

maybe then the morning we rose
from our beds as always
listening for the bang of the end
of the world maybe then
when we heard only the tiny tapping
and saw them dark and **prayerful**
in the kitchen maybe then
when we watched them turn from us
faithless at last
and walk in a long line away

NOTES

Mark base words or indicate another strategy you used that helped you determine meaning.

prayerful (PRAIR fuhl) *adj.*

MEANING:

faithless (FAYTH lihs) *adj.*

MEANING:

POETRY

The Powwow at the End of the World

Sherman Alexie

NOTES

I am told by many of you that I must forgive and so I shall
after an Indian woman puts her shoulder to the Grand Coulee Dam
and topples it. I am told by many of you that I must forgive
and so I shall after the floodwaters burst each successive dam
downriver from the Grand Coulee. I am told by many of you
that I must forgive and so I shall after the floodwaters find
their way to the mouth of the Columbia River as it enters the Pacific
and causes all of it to rise. I am told by many of you that I must forgive
and so I shall after the first drop of floodwater is swallowed by that salmon
waiting in the Pacific. I am told by many of you that I must forgive and so I shall
after that salmon swims upstream, through the mouth of the Columbia
and then past the flooded cities, broken dams and abandoned reactors
of Hanford.* I am told by many of you that I must forgive and so I shall

* **Hanford** nuclear production site in southeastern Washington State where the plutonium for the atomic bomb that ended World War II was made.

after that salmon swims through the mouth of the Spokane River
as it meets the Columbia, then upstream, until it arrives
in the shallows of a secret bay on the reservation where I wait alone.
I am told by many of you that I must forgive and so I shall after
that salmon leaps into the night air above the water, throws
a lightning bolt at the brush near my feet, and starts the fire
which will lead all of the lost Indians home. I am told
by many of you that I must forgive and so I shall
after we Indians have gathered around the fire with that salmon
who has three stories it must tell before sunrise: one story will teach us
how to pray; another story will make us laugh for hours;
the third story will give us reason to dance. I am told by many
of you that I must forgive and so I shall when I am dancing
with my tribe during the powwow at the end of the world.

NOTES

POETRY

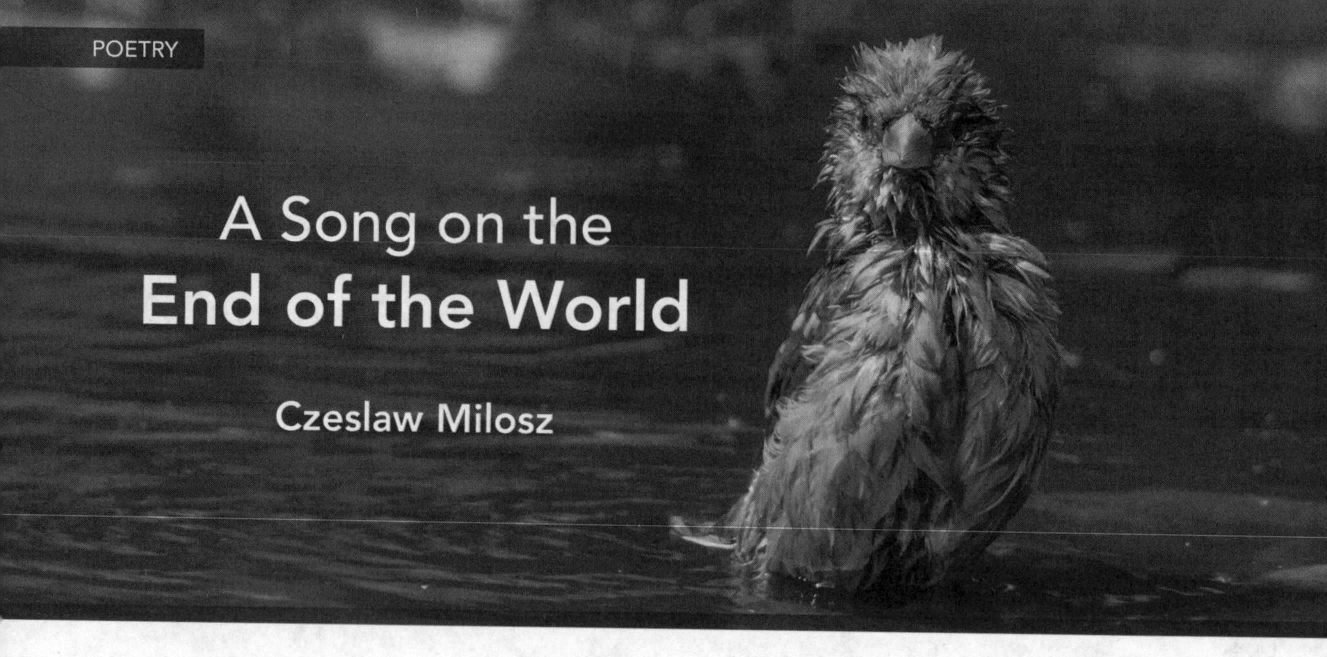

A Song on the End of the World

Czeslaw Milosz

NOTES

On the day the world ends
A bee circles a clover,
A fisherman mends a glimmering net.
Happy porpoises jump in the sea,
By the rainspout young sparrows are playing
And the snake is gold-skinned as it should always be.

On the day the world ends
Women walk through the fields under their umbrellas,
A drunkard grows sleepy at the edge of a lawn,
Vegetable peddlers shout in the street
And a yellow-sailed boat comes nearer the island,
The voice of a violin lasts in the air
And leads into a starry night.

And those who expected lightning and thunder
Are disappointed.
And those who expected signs and archangels' trumps*
Do not believe it is happening now.
As long as the sun and the moon are above,
As long as the bumblebee visits a rose,
As long as rosy infants are born
No one believes it is happening now.

Only a white-haired old man, who would be a **prophet**
Yet is not a prophet, for he's much too busy,
Repeats while he binds his tomatoes:
There will be no other end of the world,
There will be no other end of the world.

Warsaw, 1944

Mark base words or indicate another strategy you used that helped you determine meaning.

prophet (PROF iht) *n.*

MEANING:

* **trumps** trumpets.

Comprehension Check

Complete the following items after you finish your first read. Review and clarify details with your group.

1. How does the speaker try to get rid of the roaches in "the beginning of the end of the world"?

2. What causes the Pacific Ocean to rise in "The Powwow at the End of the World"?

3. In "The Powwow at the End of the World," how will each of the three stories the salmon tells affect listeners?

4. In "A Song on the End of the World," why are some people disappointed?

5. **Notebook** Confirm your understanding by writing a brief description of each poem.

RESEARCH

Research to Clarify Choose at least one unfamiliar detail from one of the poems. Briefly research that detail. In what way does the information you learned shed light on an aspect of the poem?

POETRY COLLECTION 1

GROUP DISCUSSION

Keep in mind that the members of your group have had diverse experiences. Listen to each other's experiences with an open mind. Use empathy so that you can learn from and relate to one another.

Close Read the Text

With your group, revisit sections of the poems you marked during your first read. **Annotate** details that you notice. What **questions** do you have? What can you **conclude**?

Analyze the Text

CITE TEXTUAL EVIDENCE to support your answers.

Complete the activities.

1. **Review and Clarify** With your group, reread "The Powwow at the End of the World." Who or what must the speaker forgive? Under what conditions will the speaker completely forgive? Explain.
2. **Present and Discuss** Now, work with your group to share the passages from the poems that you found especially important. Discuss what you noticed in the poems, the questions you asked, and the conclusions you reached.
3. **Essential Question:** *Why do we try to imagine the future?* What have these poems taught you about world's end literature? Discuss.

LANGUAGE DEVELOPMENT

Concept Vocabulary

prayerful	faithless	prophet

Why These Words? The three concept vocabulary words are related. With your group, determine what the words have in common. Write your ideas, and add another word that fits the category.

WORD NETWORK

Add interesting words related to the world's end from the texts to your Word Network.

Practice

Notebook Use a dictionary to confirm the definitions of these words. Write a sentence using each word. How did these words improve the clarity and meaning of the sentences you wrote? Discuss with your group.

Word Study

Notebook **Anglo-Saxon Suffixes: *-ful* and *-less*** In "the beginning of the end of the world," Clifton uses the words *prayerful* and *faithless*. These two words end in Anglo-Saxon suffixes that have opposite meanings. The suffix *-ful* means "full of" or "having," whereas the suffix *-less* means "without" or "lacking." Many base words can take either suffix, forming a pair of antonyms. Work individually to complete these activities.

1. Using your understanding of these two suffixes, write a definition for the word *faithful*, an antonym of *faithless*.
2. Write a synonym for the word *prideful*. Consult a thesaurus if needed.

STANDARDS

Reading Literature

Determine a theme or central idea of a text and analyze in detail its development over the course of the text, including how it emerges and is shaped and refined by specific details; provide an objective summary of the text.

Language

- Identify and correctly use patterns of word changes that indicate different meanings or parts of speech.
- Consult general and specialized reference materials, both print and digital, to find the pronunciation of a word or determine or clarify its precise meaning, its part of speech, or its etymology.

Analyze Craft and Structure

Theme and Poetic Structure A **theme** is a central idea or message about life revealed through a literary work. Sometimes, poets state themes directly. More often, however, messages are implied. When themes are implied, readers make connections among the events, details, and images in order to figure out the poem's larger message.

One literary element that can reinforce a poem's theme is **poetic structure,** the way in which lines and stanzas of the poem are organized. A **stanza** is a group of lines in a poem that is separated from other stanzas by space. Like a paragraph in prose, a stanza often expresses a single main idea. Poems vary widely in structure. They may have short lines, long lines, short stanzas, long stanzas, and so on. These choices support the flow of the poet's ideas and are clues to the theme.

GROUP DISCUSSION
Discuss each group member's interpretations of the poems. Through this discussion, determine possible themes for each poem. Remember to be respectful of other students' interpretations during discussion.

Practice

CITE TEXTUAL EVIDENCE to support your answers.

Notebook Work with your group to answer the questions.

1. What is the end of the world like in each poem? For example, is it terrible, peaceful, or uneventful? Explain.
2. (a) What message are the cockroaches trying to communicate in Clifton's poem? (b) Do the people understand that message? Explain.
3. Why might Alexie have chosen to use one continuous stanza? What effect does that choice have?
4. Work together to identify elements of each poem that suggest its theme. Capture your notes in the chart. Then, for each poem, propose and discuss possible themes.

	EVENTS	DETAILS/IMAGES	POSSIBLE THEMES
the beginning of the end of the world			
The Powwow at the End of the World			
A Song on the End of the World			

POETRY COLLECTION 1

Author's Style

Use of Language Some poems are organized in set patterns, a quality that is often evident from the way they look. Poetry that follows a defined structure is called formal verse. **Free verse** poems, like those in this collection, are poems that do not follow specific set patterns. While free verse poems may have a looser appearance, they, too, use formal elements, such as sound devices, to build meaning.

Sound devices are uses of language that emphasize the sound relationships among words. Rhyme is one type of sound device, but there are others:

- **Alliteration:** repetition of initial consonant sounds in nearby syllables, particularly stressed syllables (as in ***n**early **n**apping*)
- **Consonance:** repetition of final consonant sounds in stressed syllables that follow different vowel sounds (as in *si**t*** and *ca**t***)
- **Assonance:** repetition of similar vowel sounds in stressed syllables that end with different consonant sounds (as in *s**ea**l* and *m**ee**t*)

All sound devices create musical and emotional effects, heighten the sense of unity in a poem, and emphasize meaning.

Read It

1. Work together to identify examples of alliteration, consonance, and assonance in each of the three poems. Use the chart to gather your observations.

POEM	ALLITERATION	CONSONANCE	ASSONANCE
the beginning of the end of the world			
The Powwow at the End of the World			
A Song on the End of the World			

2. Choose one example from each poem, and explain how it emphasizes meaning, creates a sense of unity, or adds a musical effect.

Write It

Notebook Working independently, write three phrases or poetic lines. Use alliteration in one, consonance in the second, and assonance in the third.

STANDARDS

Reading Literature
Analyze how an author's choices concerning how to structure a text, order events within it, and manipulate time create such effects as mystery, tension, or surprise.

Speaking and Listening

The poems in this collection all relate to the idea of the world's end. Explore this idea further by writing and presenting an original literary work.

Assignment

With your group, choose one of the following prompts. Discuss the poem related to your prompt, and refer to your notes about the author's style and the poem's themes. As a group, use your discussion to craft an original literary piece, which you will deliver in an **oral presentation** to the class.

☐ In "the beginning of the end of the world," the cockroaches are sad for and eventually become disappointed in the speaker. Write a **poem** from the cockroaches' point of view in which they are able to say in words what they cannot communicate in the poem.

☐ In "The Powwow at the End of the World," the speaker says that he or she will forgive when the speaker and all the lost Indians sit around a fire and listen to a salmon tell three stories. Use information from the poem to write and tell the **three stories** that the salmon relates.

☐ In "A Song on the End of the World," what might the disappointed people in the third stanza wish to tell the white-haired prophet? Write a **dialogue** between the two parties that addresses the poem's ideas about the expectations and realities of the end of the world.

Project Plan Before you begin, make a list of the tasks you will need to accomplish in order to complete the assignment. Then, assign individual group members to each task. Finally, determine how you will make decisions about what themes you want to convey, what images and word choice to use, and how you will use literary structure to present your ideas.

Revise Before you present, read your writing aloud as a group. Consider your stylistic choices, and make changes as needed in order to emphasize the words, images, and lines that are the most important to convey the meaning of your work. Make sure all group members have a role to play in the presentation.

Present Once your group is satisfied with your work, practice your presentation, and provide constructive feedback. Strive to make the presentation seamless and smooth.

EVIDENCE LOG

Before moving on to a new selection, go to your Evidence Log and record what you learned from "the beginning of the end of the world," "The Powwow at the End of the World," and "A Song on the End of the World."

STANDARDS

Writing

Write narratives to develop real or imagined experiences or events using effective techniques, well-chosen details, and well-structured event sequences.

Speaking and Listening

- Integrate multiple sources of information presented in diverse media or formats evaluating the credibility and accuracy of each source.
- Present information, findings, and supporting evidence clearly, concisely, and logically such that listeners can follow the line of reasoning and the organization, development, substance, and style are appropriate to purpose, audience, and task.

from RADIOLAB: WAR OF THE WORLDS

Comparing Media to Text

In this lesson, you will compare two different takes on the famous "War of the Worlds" radio broadcast of 1938. First, you will complete the first-review and close-review activities for a clip from an episode of the NPR show *Radiolab*.

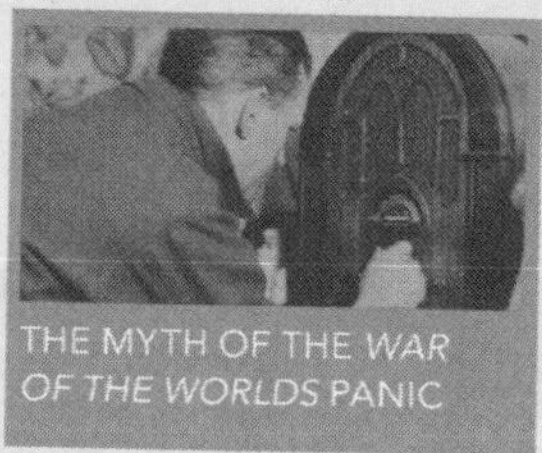
THE MYTH OF THE *WAR OF THE WORLDS* PANIC

About the Narrators

Jad Abumrad (b. 1973) came up with the idea for *Radiolab* while working for the radio station WNYC. He now cohosts the Peabody Award–winning radio program with **Robert Krulwich**, a television and radio journalist with more than 20 years of experience. Each month, more than four million people tune in to listen to the show, which focuses on the intersections of science, philosophy, and human experience.

from Radiolab: War of the Worlds

Media Vocabulary

The following words or concepts will be useful to you as you analyze, discuss, and write about radio broadcasts.

archival audio: sound recorded from radio broadcasts, television shows, or films of past decades	• For historical documentation, archival audio is considered to be a primary source. • Archival audio is converted to and preserved in digital format.
tone: attitude a speaker takes toward a subject	• Tone can vary from friendly, breezy, gentle, or playful to serious, intense, solemn, or even aggressive.
understatement: downplaying a topic to make it seem less important	• Radio show hosts often use understatement to establish a humorous or ironic tone.
banter: friendly exchange between speakers	• Banter often includes wordplay, jokes, and other witty remarks.

First Review MEDIA: AUDIO

Apply these strategies as you conduct your first review. You will have the opportunity to complete a close review after your first review.

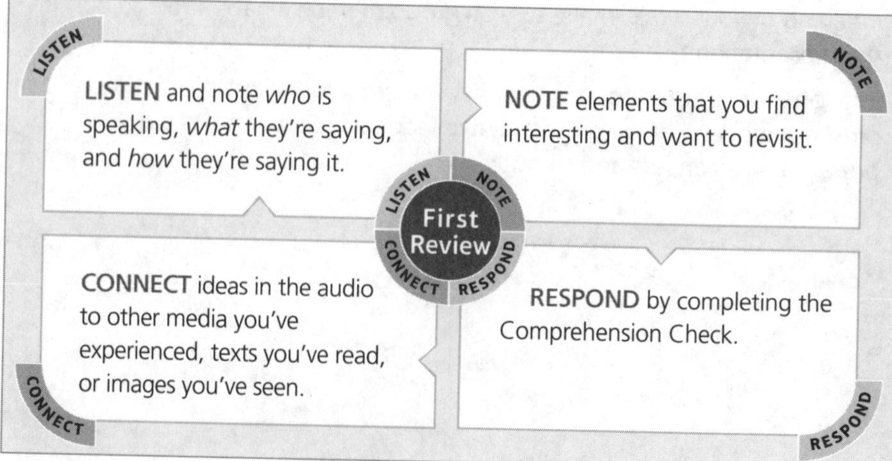

LISTEN
LISTEN and note *who* is speaking, *what* they're saying, and *how* they're saying it.
NOTE
NOTE elements that you find interesting and want to revisit.
First Review
LISTEN NOTE CONNECT RESPOND
CONNECT
CONNECT ideas in the audio to other media you've experienced, texts you've read, or images you've seen.
RESPOND
RESPOND by completing the Comprehension Check.

STANDARDS

Language
Acquire and use accurately general academic and domain-specific words and phrases, sufficient for reading, writing, speaking, and listening at the college and career readiness level; demonstrate independence in gathering vocabulary knowledge when considering a word or phrase important to comprehension or expression.

from Radiolab: War of the Worlds

NPR

BACKGROUND

In the photo, director Orson Welles is seen rehearsing his broadcast of a radio play based on H. G. Wells's classic novel *The War of the Worlds*. The broadcast aired the night before Halloween in 1938, causing a controversy that remains to this day. Starting in the early 1920s, radio was a major source of news and entertainment for many Americans. Radio offered a full array of programs, including music and variety shows, news and journalism, and plays in every genre. The rise in popularity of television during the 1950s pushed radio to the sidelines, but it remains an important media source today.

NOTES

MAKING MEANING

Comprehension Check

Complete the following items after you finish your first listen. Review and clarify details with your group.

1. What is the first indication in the 1938 broadcast that something unusual is taking place?

2. In the 1938 broadcast, where do the Martians land, and what response do Americans have to their landing?

3. **Notebook** According to the *Radiolab* episode, what did newspapers of the time report about the public's response to the 1938 broadcast?

WORD NETWORK

Add interesting words related to the world's end from the broadcast to your Word Network.

Close Review

Listen to the radio broadcast again. What **questions** do you have? What can you **conclude**?

Analyze the Media

Complete the activities.

1. **Present and Discuss** Now, work with your group to share the segments of the broadcast you found especially important. Discuss the questions you asked and the conclusions you reached.

2. **Review and Synthesize** With your group, listen to the segment that describes the innovation that Edward R. Murrow introduced. How do the audio clips help you understand listeners' responses to the broadcast?

3. **Notebook Essential Question:** *Why do we try to imagine the future?* What has this broadcast taught you about world's end literature?

LANGUAGE DEVELOPMENT

Media Vocabulary

understatement **banter** **archival audio** **tone**

Notebook Use these vocabulary words in your responses.

1. What techniques do the hosts use to recreate a listener's experience of Welles's adaptation of H. G. Wells's *The War of the Worlds*?

2. How do the hosts convey their feelings about the broadcast?

STANDARDS

Language

Acquire and use accurately general academic and domain-specific words and phrases, sufficient for reading, writing, speaking, and listening at the college and career readiness level; demonstrate independence in gathering vocabulary knowledge when considering a word or phrase important to comprehension or expression.

Writing to Sources

Assignment

With your group, discuss the central ideas of the clip from the *Radiolab* "War of the Worlds" broadcast, and consider how the hosts convey them to listeners. Then, create a **broadcast outline** in which you trace how the hosts introduce, develop, and support ideas in this section of the show.

from RADIOLAB: WAR OF THE WORLDS

Discuss the Broadcast Listen to the entire excerpt again before you hold your discussion. As you discuss the broadcast, keep in mind that it might not follow a linear structure. The hosts might not state central ideas directly, and you may have to infer them from the hosts' conversation and their use of evidence.

Create an Outline After you have discussed the broadcast with your group, use the chart to create an outline of the key ideas, the ways in which the hosts introduce and develop those ideas, and the evidence they use to support them.

RADIOLAB: WAR OF THE WORLDS	
INTRODUCTION:	
KEY IDEA:	The use of news bulletins in the presentation of "War of the Worlds" made the radio play seem realistic.
Introduction	
Development	
Evidence	
KEY IDEA:	
Introduction	
Development	
Evidence	

EVIDENCE LOG

Before moving on to a new selection, go to your Evidence Log and record what you learned from the *Radiolab* "War of the Worlds" broadcast.

STANDARDS

Reading Informational Text

- Cite strong and thorough textual evidence to support analysis of what the text says explicitly as well as inferences drawn from the text.
- Determine a central idea of a text and analyze its development over the course of the text, including how it emerges and is shaped and refined by specific details; provide an objective summary of the text.
- Analyze how the author unfolds an analysis or series of ideas or events, including the order in which the points are made, how they are introduced and developed, and the connections that are drawn between them.

from RADIOLAB: WAR OF THE WORLDS

Comparing Media to Text

So far, you have been presented with one view of the 1938 "War of the Worlds" broadcast. As you read this next selection, you will consider whether there was more to the "War of the Worlds" broadcast than people have been led to believe.

THE MYTH OF THE *WAR OF THE WORLDS* PANIC

About the Authors

Jefferson Pooley (b. 1976) is the chairman of the Media and Communications department at Muhlenberg College in Allentown, Pennsylvania. He has written widely on consumer culture, as well as on the impact of social media on culture.

Michael J. Socolow (b. 1969) is a media historian who specializes in the analysis of the first radio networks that arose in America during the 1920s and 1930s. Socolow is especially interested in how the early radio networks gained control of popular media and what they did with their control once they obtained it.

The Myth of the *War of the Worlds* Panic

Concept Vocabulary

As you perform your first read of the article, you will encounter these words.

sensationalized **apocryphal** **salient**

Context Clues To infer the meaning of unfamiliar words, analyze how they are used within their context. Consider this line from the selection.

So the papers seized the opportunity presented by Welles' program to ***discredit*** *radio as a source of news.*

- The word *discredit* is used as a verb and consists of the prefix *dis-*, meaning "not," plus the root word *credit*, meaning "to acknowledge or praise."
- Since the newspapers were upset that radio had siphoned off ad revenues, it makes sense that *discredit* means "to insult or dishonor."

First Read NONFICTION

Apply these strategies as you conduct your first read. You will have an opportunity to complete a close read after your first read.

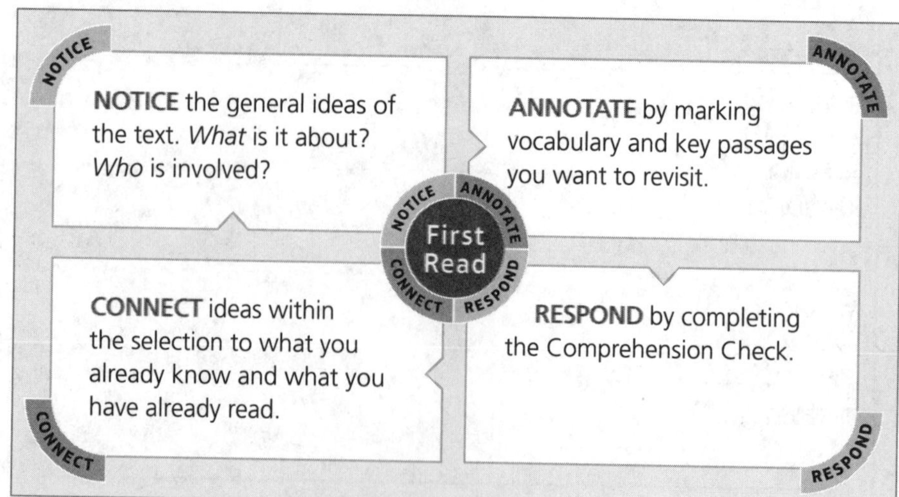

NOTICE
NOTICE the general ideas of the text. *What* is it about? *Who* is involved?
ANNOTATE
ANNOTATE by marking vocabulary and key passages you want to revisit.
NOTICE ANNOTATE First Read CONNECT RESPOND
CONNECT
CONNECT ideas within the selection to what you already know and what you have already read.
RESPOND
RESPOND by completing the Comprehension Check.

STANDARDS

Reading Informational Text
By the end of grade 9, read and comprehend literary nonfiction in the grades 9–10 text complexity band proficiently, with scaffolding as needed at the high end of the range.

Language
Use context as a clue to the meaning of a word or phrase.

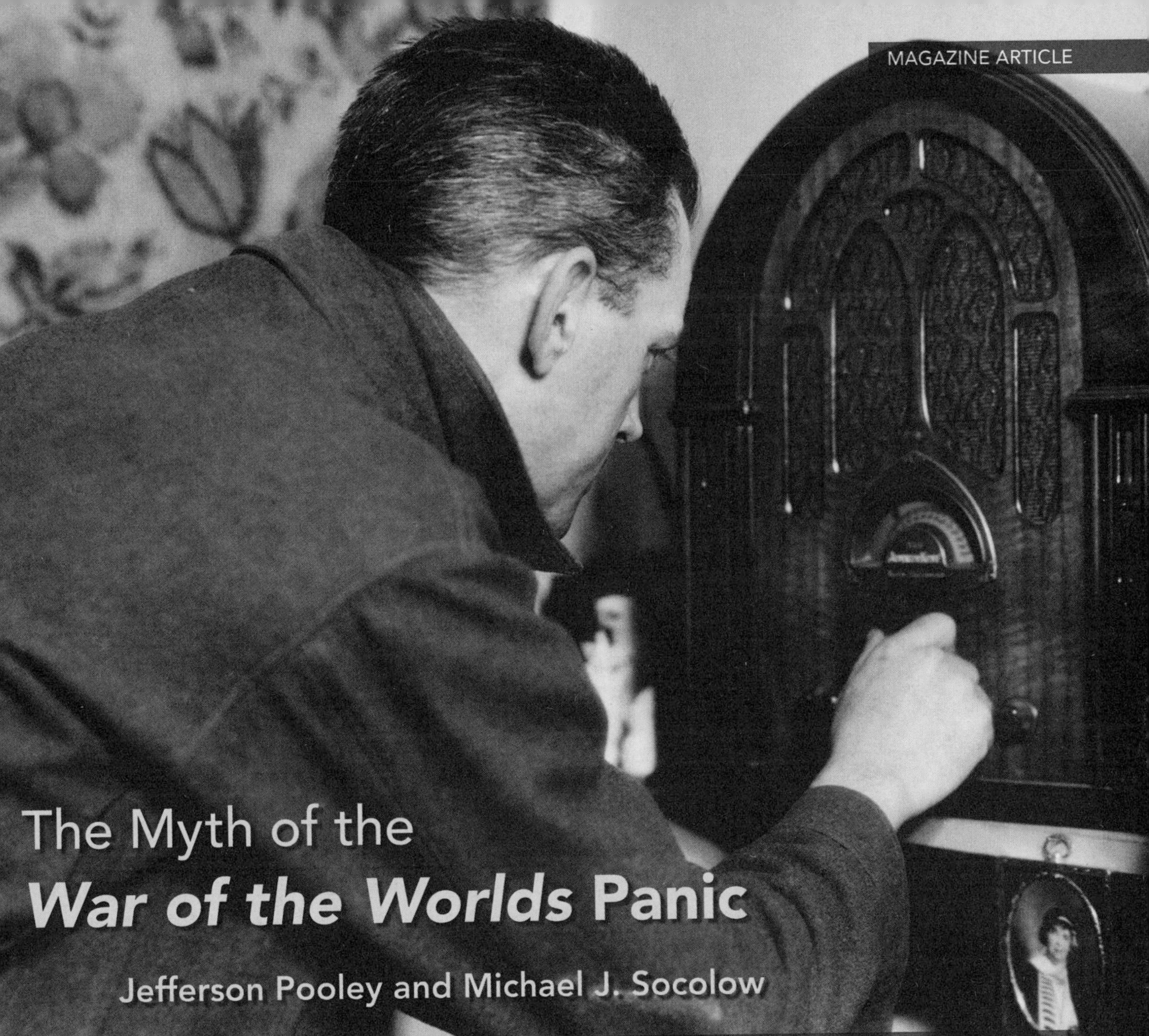

The Myth of the *War of the Worlds* Panic

Jefferson Pooley and Michael J. Socolow

BACKGROUND

H. G. Wells's sensational 1898 novel *The War of the Worlds* was one of the first to depict a Martian invasion of Earth. In 1938, director and actor Orson Welles adapted the novel into a radio play, which was produced to sound like an actual news broadcast instead of a work of fiction. The popular legend is that when the program first aired, many listeners believed a real alien invasion was happening, causing mass panic.

1 How did the story of panicked listeners begin? Blame America's newspapers. Radio had siphoned off advertising revenue from print during the Depression,[1] badly damaging the newspaper industry. So the papers seized the opportunity presented by Welles' program to discredit radio as a source of news. The newspaper industry **sensationalized** the panic to prove to advertisers, and regulators, that radio management was irresponsible and not to be trusted. In an editorial titled "Terror by Radio," the *New York Times*

NOTES

Mark context clues or indicate another strategy you used that helped you determine meaning.

sensationalized (sehn SAY shuh nuh lyzd) *V.*

MEANING:

1. **the Depression** period of economic downturn in the United States that lasted from 1929 through the 1930s.

NOTES

reproached "radio officials" for approving the interweaving of "blood-curdling fiction" with news flashes "offered in exactly the manner that real news would have been given." Warned *Editor and Publisher*, the newspaper industry's trade journal, "The nation as a whole continues to face the danger of incomplete, misunderstood news over a medium which has yet to prove . . . that it is competent to perform the news job."

2 The contrast between how newspaper journalists experienced the supposed panic, and what they reported, could be stark. In 1954, Ben Gross, the *New York Daily News'* radio editor, published a memoir in which he recalled the streets of Manhattan being deserted as his taxi sped to CBS headquarters just as *War of the Worlds* was ending. Yet that observation failed to stop the *Daily News* from splashing the panic story across the cover a few hours later.

Mark context clues or indicate another strategy you used that helped you determine meaning.

apocryphal
(uh POK ruh fuhl) *adj.*
MEANING:

3 From these initial newspaper items on Oct. 31, 1938, the **apocryphal** apocalypse only grew in the retelling. A curious (but predictable) phenomenon occurred: As the show receded in time and became more infamous, more and more people claimed to have heard it. As weeks, months, and years passed, the audience's size swelled to such an extent that you might actually believe most of America was tuned to CBS that night. But that was hardly the case.

4 Far fewer people heard the broadcast—and fewer still panicked—than most people believe today. How do we know? The night the program aired, the C. E. Hooper ratings service telephoned 5,000 households for its national ratings survey. "To what program are you listening?" the service asked respondents. Only 2 percent answered a radio "play" or "the Orson Welles program," or something similar indicating CBS. None said a "news broadcast," according to a summary published in *Broadcasting*. In other words, 98 percent of those surveyed were listening to something else, or nothing at all, on Oct. 30, 1938. This miniscule rating is not surprising. Welles' program was scheduled against one of the most popular national programs at the time—ventriloquist Edgar Bergen's *Chase and Sanborn Hour*, a comedy-variety show.

5 The new PBS documentary allows that, "of the tens of millions of Americans listening to their radios that Sunday evening, few were tuned to the *War of the Worlds*" when it began, due to Bergen's popularity. But the documentary's script goes on to claim that "millions of listeners began twirling the dial" when the opening comedy routine on the *Chase and Sanborn Hour* gave way to a musical interlude. "Just at that moment thousands, hundreds, we don't how many listeners, started to dial-surf, where they landed on the *Mercury Theatre on the Air*,"[2] explained *Radiolab* this weekend. No scholar, however, has ever isolated or extrapolated an actual number of dial twirlers. The data collected was simply not specific

2. ***Mercury Theatre on the Air*** weekly radio show created by Orson Welles that broadcast the "War of the Worlds" radio play.

enough for us to know how many listeners might have switched over to Welles—just as we can't estimate how many people turned their radios off, or switched from *Mercury Theatre on the Air* over to NBC's *Chase and Sanborn Hour* either. (*Radiolab* played the *Chase and Sanborn Hour's* musical interlude for its audience, as if the song itself constituted evidence that people of course switched to Welles' broadcast.)

6 Both *American Experience* and *Radiolab* also omit the **salient** fact that several important CBS affiliates (including Boston's WEEI) pre-empted Welles' broadcast in favor of local commercial programming, further shrinking its audience. CBS commissioned a nationwide survey the day after the broadcast, and network executives were relieved to discover just how few people actually tuned in. "In the first place, most people didn't hear it," CBS's Frank Stanton recalled later. "But those who did hear it, looked at it as a prank and accepted it that way." ❧

NOTES

Mark context clues or indicate another strategy you used that helped you determine meaning.

salient (SAY lee uhnt) *adj.*

MEANING:

Comprehension Check

Complete the following items after you finish your first read. Review and clarify details with your group.

1. According to the authors, what was the size of the audience that listened to the "War of the Worlds" broadcast?

2. According to these authors, the "panic" that took place on the night of the broadcast was greatly exaggerated. Whom do the authors blame for this exaggeration?

3. According to the authors, why is it inaccurate to assume there were a large number of "dial-turners" the night of the incident?

4. What action by some CBS affiliates further reduced the size of Welles's audience that night?

RESEARCH

Research to Clarify Choose at least one unfamiliar detail from the text. Briefly research that detail. In what way does the information you learned shed light on an aspect of the article?

Research to Explore Choose something from the text that interests you, and formulate a research question.

Close Read the Text

With your group, revisit sections of the text you marked during your first read. **Annotate** details that you notice. What **questions** do you have? What can you **conclude**?

THE MYTH OF THE *WAR OF THE WORLDS* PANIC

Analyze the Text

CITE TEXTUAL EVIDENCE to support your answers.

Complete the activities.

1. **Review and Clarify** With your group, reread paragraphs 4 and 6 of the selection. What important pieces of evidence do the authors include to support their claim that the audience for Welles's radio play was much smaller than people believe?
2. **Present and Discuss** Now, work with your group to share the passages from the text that you found especially important. Take turns presenting your passages. Discuss what you noticed in the text, the questions you asked, and the conclusions you reached.
3. **Essential Question:** ***Why do we try to imagine the future?*** What has this article taught you about world's end literature? Discuss with your group.

TIP

GROUP DISCUSSION

Keep in mind that finding the truth in a controversy such as this one can be challenging. Be sure to consider the significance of the data and the historical context the authors offer as you discuss the article.

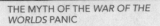

LANGUAGE DEVELOPMENT

Concept Vocabulary

sensationalized **salient** **apocryphal**

Why These Words? The three concept vocabulary words are related. With your group, determine what the words have in common. Write your ideas, and add another word that fits the category.

WORD NETWORK

Add interesting words related to the world's end from the text to your Word Network.

Practice

Notebook Confirm your understanding of these words by using each one in a sentence. Be sure to include context clues that hint at each word's meaning.

Word Study

Notebook **Word Families** Many English words are part of a word family, or a group of words derived from a single base word. The word *sensationalized*, for example, belongs to the family of words derived from *sense*. The word *sense* usually refers to sight, hearing, smell, taste, or touch, but it can also suggest "good judgment" or "meaning that is conveyed." Use your understanding of the word *sense* to determine a definition for the following words: *sensation*, *sensationally*, *nonsense*. Then, use a dictionary to check your definitions.

RADIOLAB: WAR OF THE WORLDS

THE MYTH OF THE *WAR OF THE WORLDS* PANIC

Writing to Compare

You have studied two accounts of Orson Welles's radio play based on H. G. Wells's *The War of the Worlds*. Now, analyze the selections, and consider how the medium of each one shapes its message.

Assignment

Both accounts of the 1938 radio broadcast offer a **claim**, or main idea, supported by **evidence**, or supporting details. Compare and contrast the claims and evidence in each. Then, create a **script** for an audio production that answers the following question: Did the 1938 radio broadcast cause mass hysteria? Choose from the following options:

- ☐ a radio essay
- ☐ a radio play
- ☐ a podcast

Include details from both the *Radiolab* episode and the magazine article in your production. You may deliver your production live or, if possible, record and post it for your class.

Analyze the Texts

Compare the Broadcast and Article With your group, consider how the *Radiolab* episode and the magazine article convey information. Use the chart to identify a claim each selection makes. Then, analyze the types of evidence used to support the claim.

ACCOUNT	CLAIM	TYPES OF EVIDENCE / HOW THEY SUPPORT CLAIM
Radiolab: War of the Worlds		
The Myth of the *War of the Worlds* Panic		

STANDARDS

Reading Informational Text
Analyze various accounts of a subject told in different mediums, determining which details are emphasized in each account.

Writing
Apply *grades 9–10 Reading standards* to literary nonfiction.

Speaking and Listening
Make strategic use of digital media in presentations to enhance understanding of findings, reasoning, and evidence and to add interest.

Notebook Respond to these questions.

1. **(a)** What types of evidence does the radio broadcast include that the magazine article does not? **(b)** What types of evidence does the magazine article include that the radio broadcast does not?
2. In what ways does the medium of each selection affect the types of evidence it uses?
3. Does one account do a better job than the other of supporting its claim? Explain.

Planning and Prewriting

Organize Tasks Make a list of tasks you will have to accomplish as you prepare for the production and then record it or present it live. Assign the tasks to individual group members. You may add to or modify this list as needed.

TASK LIST

Conduct Research: Decide whether you need more information about the 1938 "War of the Worlds" broadcast. If you do, research that content.

Assigned To: ______

Locate Audio Files: Consider whether you need audio files. For example, you may want to use archival recordings from 1930s radio, sound effects, or period music.

Assigned To: ______

Cast the Production: Assign the roles each group member will take on during the recording or live presentation. Consider the following jobs:

Recording Engineer

Assigned To: ______

Narrator / Actors / Hosts

Assigned To: ______

Sound–Effects Person

Assigned To: ______

Write a Working Outline: Prepare a sequence for your content. You may always change it later.

Assigned To: ______

Drafting

Include Cues Write your script in play form, clearly indicating speaking parts, as well as cues to play music or add sound effects.

Answer the Question Your production should be both entertaining and informative. Answer the question posed in the assignment, and draw evidence from both the radio broadcast and the magazine article.

Reviewing and Revising

Make sure your script is clearly organized so that information flows logically and no one is confused about what he or she is saying or doing. If necessary, simplify your use of audio or sound effects to make your presentation more manageable.

EVIDENCE LOG

Before moving on to a new selection, go to your Evidence Log and record what you learned from the *Radiolab* "War of the Worlds" episode and "The Myth of the *War of the Worlds* Panic."

STANDARDS

Writing
- Write arguments to support claims in an analysis of substantive topics or texts, using valid reasoning and relevant and sufficient evidence.
- Draw evidence from literary or informational texts to support analysis, reflection, and research.

Speaking and Listening
- Present information, findings, and supporting evidence clearly, concisely and logically such that listeners can follow the line of reasoning and the organization, development, substance, and style are appropriate to purpose, audience, and task.
- Make strategic use of digital media in presentations to enhance understanding of findings, reasoning, and evidence and to add interest.

SOURCES

- THE NUCLEAR TOURIST
- THE BEGINNING OF THE END OF THE WORLD
- THE POWWOW AT THE END OF THE WORLD
- A SONG ON THE END OF THE WORLD
- *from* RADIOLAB: WAR OF THE WORLDS
- THE MYTH OF THE *WAR OF THE WORLDS* PANIC

Create a Podcast

Assignment

You have read or listened to two magazine articles, three poems, and a radio broadcast that explore how people respond, or might respond, to catastrophic events. Work with your group to develop a podcast that addresses this question:

What do stories about the future say about the present?

Plan With Your Group

Analyze the Text With your group, discuss key ideas and themes from each text. Use the chart to list your ideas. As a group, discuss your notes about the selections. Use these notes to begin your discussion on how stories about the future reflect the present. Then, come to a consensus about which ideas about the present reflected in stories about the future are most significant. You will discuss these ideas in your podcast.

TITLE	KEY IDEAS/THEMES
The Nuclear Tourist	
the beginning of the end of the world	
The Powwow at the End of the World	
A Song on the End of the World	
from Radiolab: War of the Worlds	
The Myth of the *War of the Worlds* Panic	

Gather Evidence and Media Examples Identify specific examples from the selections to support your group's ideas. Then, brainstorm ideas for types of audio you can use to help convey your ideas. Consider using audio clips of actors or authors reading the selections. You may also include your own readings of passages, music, and other sound effects. Allow each group member to make suggestions.

STANDARDS

Speaking and Listening

Present information, findings, and supporting evidence clearly, concisely and logically such that listeners can follow the line of reasoning and the organization, development, substance, and style are appropriate to purpose, audience, and task.

Organize Your Ideas Organize the script for your podcast. Assign roles for each part of the podcast, including the introduction and the conclusion. Allow each member of the team the opportunity to perform. Note when each segment will begin, and record what each speaker will say. Plan where you will place audio clips.

PODCAST SCRIPT		
	Audio	Script
Speaker: 1	1	1
Speaker: 2	2	2
Speaker: 3	3	3

Rehearse With Your Group

Practice with Your Group As you work through the script for your podcast, use this checklist to evaluate the effectiveness of your group's first run-through. Then, use your evaluation and the instruction here to guide your revision.

CONTENT	USE OF AUDIO	PRESENTATION TECHNIQUES
☐ The podcast has a clear introduction, explaining the topic. ☐ The podcast presents clear ideas about the topic. ☐ Ideas are supported with evidence from the texts.	☐ The audio helps communicate key ideas. ☐ Media clips are used appropriately and effectively.	☐ Podcast is audible. ☐ Transitions between speakers' segments and other audio clips are smooth. ☐ Each speaker speaks clearly.

Fine-Tune the Content To make your podcast stronger, you may need to review each speaker's segment to make sure it relates to the prompt. Check with your group to identify key ideas that are not clear to listeners. Find another way to word these ideas.

Improve Your Use of Audio Review all audio clips and sound effects to make sure they communicate key ideas and help create cohesion. Ensure that the equipment is working properly to record and play your podcast.

Brush Up on Your Presentation Techniques Practice reading your script before recording anything. Review your recorded podcast so that you can rerecord anything that is not audible.

Present and Evaluate

Before you play your podcast for the class, be sure that each member has taken into account each of the checklist items. As you listen to other groups' podcasts, evaluate how well they meet requirements on the checklist.

STANDARDS

Speaking and Listening

- Make strategic use of digital media in presentations to enhance understanding of findings, reasoning, and evidence and to add interest.
- Adapt speech to a variety of contexts and tasks, demonstrating command of formal English when indicated or appropriate.

OVERVIEW: INDEPENDENT LEARNING

ESSENTIAL QUESTION:

Why do we try to imagine the future?

Our fears and hopes lead us to prepare for whatever the future may bring. In this section, you will complete your study of world's end literature by exploring an additional selection related to the topic. You'll then share what you learn with classmates. To choose a text, follow these steps.

Look Back Think about the selections you have already studied. What more do you want to know about world's end literature?

Look Ahead Preview the texts by reading the descriptions. Which one seems more interesting and appealing to you?

Look Inside Take a few minutes to scan the text you chose. Choose a different one if this text doesn't meet your needs.

Independent Learning Strategies

Throughout your life, in school, in your community, and in your career, you will need to rely on yourself to learn and work on your own. Review these strategies and the actions you can take to practice them during Independent Learning. Add ideas of your own to each category.

STRATEGY	ACTION PLAN
Create a schedule	• Understand your goals and deadlines. • Make a plan for what to do each day. •
Practice what you have learned	• Use first-read and close-read strategies to deepen your understanding. • After you read, evaluate the usefulness of the evidence to help you understand the topic. • Consider the quality and reliability of the source. •
Take notes	• Record important ideas and information. • Review your notes before preparing to share with a group. •

CONTENTS

Choose one selection. Selections are available online only.

GOVERNMENT WEBSITE ARTICLE

Preparedness 101: Zombie Apocalypse

Ali S. Khan

When the zombie apocalypse arrives, will you be ready?

NEWS ARTICLE

The Secret Bunker Congress Never Used

NPR

What happens when you combine a luxury resort, a giant concrete box, and thirty years of secrets?

MEDIA: IMAGE GALLERY

The End of the World Might Just Look Like This *Megan Gambino*

An artist transforms scientific information into gorgeous images of disaster.

POETRY COLLECTION 2

Fire and Ice *Robert Frost*

Perhaps the World Ends Here *Joy Harjo*

What will the last day look like?

MEDIA: NEWSCAST

A Visit to the Doomsday Vault

60 Minutes

People are making sure the world will bloom again if disaster strikes.

PERFORMANCE-BASED ASSESSMENT PREP

Review Notes for a Narrative

Complete your Evidence Log for the unit by evaluating what you have learned and synthesizing the information you have recorded.

First-Read Guide

Tool Kit
First-Read Guide and Model Annotation

Use this page to record your first-read ideas.

Selection Title: ______________________________

NOTICE

NOTICE new information or ideas you learn about the unit topic as you first read this text.

ANNOTATE

ANNOTATE by marking vocabulary and key passages you want to revisit.

NOTICE ANNOTATE First Read CONNECT RESPOND

CONNECT ideas within the selection to other knowledge and the selections you have read.

RESPOND by writing a brief summary of the selection.

CONNECT

RESPOND

STANDARD

Reading Read and comprehend complex literary and informational texts independently and proficiently.

Close-Read Guide

Tool Kit
Close-Read Guide and Model Annotation

Use this page to record your close-read ideas.

Selection Title: ____________________

Close Read the Text

Revisit sections of the text you marked during your first read. Read these sections closely and **annotate** what you notice. Ask yourself **questions** about the text. What can you **conclude**? Write down your ideas.

ANNOTATE · QUESTION · CONCLUDE — Close Read

Analyze the Text

Think about the author's choices of patterns, structure, techniques, and ideas included in the text. Select one and record your thoughts about what this choice conveys.

QuickWrite

Pick a paragraph from the text that grabbed your interest. Explain the power of this passage.

STANDARD

Reading Read and comprehend complex literary and informational texts independently and proficiently.

Share Your Independent Learning

Prepare to Share

Why do we try to imagine the future?

Even when you read or learn something independently, you can continue to grow by sharing what you have learned. Reflect on the text you explored independently, and write notes about its connection to the unit. In your notes, consider why this text belongs in this unit.

EVIDENCE LOG

Go to your Evidence Log and record what you learned from the text you read.

Learn From Your Classmates

Discuss It Share your ideas about the text you explored on your own. As you talk with your classmates, jot down ideas that you learn from them.

Reflect

Review your notes, and underline the most important insight you gained from these writing and discussion activities. Explain how this idea adds to your understanding of the topic of the world's end.

STANDARDS

Speaking and Listening
Initiate and participate effectively in a range of collaborative discussions with diverse partners on *grades 9–10 topics, texts, and issues*, building on others' ideas and expressing their own clearly and persuasively.

Review Notes for a Narrative

At the beginning of this unit, you took a position on the following question:

Which matters more—the present or the future?

EVIDENCE LOG

Review your Evidence Log and your QuickWrite from the beginning of the unit. Has your position changed?

☐ YES	☐ NO
Identify at least three pieces of evidence that convinced you to change your mind.	Identify at least three pieces of evidence that reinforced your initial position.
1.	**1.**
2.	**2.**
3.	**3.**

State your position now: ______________________________

____

Use that position to write a theme for your narrative: ______________________________

____

Use the evidence in your chart to develop important details about the setting, plot, or characters in a narrative that develops this theme: ______________________________

____

Evaluate Your Ideas Do you have enough ideas to write a narrative that develops your theme? If not, make a plan.

- ☐ Do more research
- ☐ Reread a selection
- ☐ Talk with my classmates
- ☐ Ask an expert
- ☐ Other: ______________________________

SOURCES

- WHOLE-CLASS SELECTIONS
- SMALL-GROUP SELECTIONS
- INDEPENDENT LEARNING

PART 1

Writing to Sources: Narrative

In this unit, you read fictional accounts of the world's demise. You also read about responses to catastrophic disasters—real and fictional. Each story teaches us something new about the world and about ourselves.

Assignment

Write a **short story** in which you develop a theme related to the following question:

Which matters more—the present or the future?

First, introduce a main character and a situation or problem, and establish the narrator's point of view. Then, create a sequence of events in which you show how the characters address the situation or problem in an innovative way. Be sure that your conclusion provides a logical and meaningful resolution to the conflict. As you write your narrative, use a variety of techniques and descriptive language to depict the setting, events, and characters. Incorporate ideas from the texts in this unit to help develop details in your story.

Reread the Assignment Review the assignment to be sure you fully understand it. The task may reference some of the academic words presented at the beginning of the unit. Be sure you understand each of the words here in order to complete the assignment correctly.

Academic Vocabulary

innovate	depiction	conjecture
technique	introspective	

Review the Elements of Effective Narrative Before you begin writing, read the Narrative Rubric. Once you have completed your first draft, check it against the rubric. If one or more of the elements is missing or not as strong as it could be, revise your narrative to add or strengthen that component.

WORD NETWORK

As your write and revise your narrative, use your Word Network to help vary your word choices.

STANDARDS

Writing

- Write narratives to develop real or imagined experiences or events using effective technique, well-chosen details, and well-structured event sequences.
- Write routinely over extended time frames and shorter time frames for a range of tasks, purposes, and audiences.

Narrative Rubric

	Focus and Organization	Development of Ideas/Elaboration	Conventions
4	The introduction establishes a clear situation and establishes the narrator's point of view. Events are presented in a logical sequence, and the progression from one event to another is smooth. The conclusion resolves the situation or problem and clearly conveys the significance of the events in the story.	Narrative techniques such as dialogue, pacing, and description are used effectively to develop characters and events. Descriptive details, sensory language, and precise words and phrases are used effectively to engage the reader.	The narrative intentionally uses standard English conventions of usage and mechanics, except where language is manipulated for effect.
3	The introduction establishes the situation and point of view but leaves some details unclear. Events are presented logically, but the progression from one event to another is sometimes unclear. The conclusion resolves the situation or problem but does not clearly convey the significance of the events in the story.	Narrative techniques such as dialogue, pacing, and description are used occasionally. Descriptive details, sensory language, and precise words and phrases are used occasionally.	The narrative consistently uses standard English conventions of usage and mechanics.
2	The introduction provides little description of the situation or the point of view. The event sequence is evident, but the progression from one event to another is unclear. The conclusion comes abruptly and provides little or no reflection on the experiences related in the narrative.	Narrative techniques such as dialogue, pacing, and description are used sparingly, or the narrative relies too heavily on one technique. The story contains few examples of descriptive details, precise words and phrases, and sensory language.	The narrative contains some errors in standard English conventions of usage and mechanics.
1	The introduction does not introduce the situation and does not establish the narrator's point of view. The sequence of events is unclear and hard to follow. The narrative does not have a conclusion.	The narrative is not developed with dialogue, pacing, and description. The narrative lacks descriptive details and sensory language.	The narrative contains many errors in standard English conventions of usage and mechanics.

PART 2

Speaking and Listening: Dramatic Reading

Assignment

After completing the final draft of your narrative, record a **dramatic reading** of your narrative to present to the class.

Instead of simply reading your narrative, take the following steps to make your dramatic reading engaging:

- Use music and sound effects to enhance the narrative.
- Use effective pacing as you build your story to the climax. Vary your speed and tone to build suspense and drama.

STANDARDS

Speaking and Listening
Make strategic use of digital media in presentations to enhance understanding of findings, reasoning, and evidence and to add interest.

Review the Rubric The criteria by which your dramatic reading will be evaluated appear in the rubric below. Review these criteria before presenting or recording your narrative to ensure that you are prepared.

	Content	Organization	Presentation Technique
3	The introduction establishes a clear situation and establishes the narrator's point of view. Events are presented in an understandable sequence, and the progression from one event to another is smooth. The conclusion conveys the significance of the events in the story.	Audio is very effective in communicating ideas from the narrative. The use of audio is consistent.	The speaker uses tone and pace effectively. The narration and dialogue are clear throughout the entire presentation or recording.
2	The introduction establishes some setting. Point of view is established, though not detailed. The event sequence is logical, but the progression from one event to another may be unclear. The conclusion is logical, but does not conveys the significance of the events in the story clearly.	Audio is somewhat effective in communicating ideas from the narrative. The use of audio is somewhat consistent.	The speaker uses tone and pace somewhat effectively. The narration and dialogue are clear throughout most of the presentation or recording.
1	The introduction does not establish the situation, and the narrator's point of view is unclear. The sequence of events is hard to follow. The conclusion is abrupt and does not convey the significance of the events in the story.	Audio is ineffective in communicating ideas from the narrative. The use of audio is inconsistent.	The speaker does not use tone and pace effectively. The narration and dialogue are unclear in the presentation or recording.

Reflect on the Unit

Now that you've completed the unit, take a few moments to reflect on your learning. Use the questions below to think about where you succeeded, what skills and strategies helped you, and where you can continue to grow in the future.

Reflect on the Unit Goals

Look back at the goals at the beginning of the unit. Use a different colored pen to rate yourself again. Think about readings and activities that contributed the most to the growth of your understanding. Record your thoughts.

Reflect on the Learning Strategies

Discuss It Write a reflection on whether you were able to improve your learning based on your Action Plans. Think about what worked, what didn't, and what you might do to keep working on these strategies. Record your ideas before a class discussion.

Reflect on the Text

Choose a selection that you found challenging, and explain what made it difficult.

Explain something that surprised you about a text in the unit.

Which activity taught you the most about visions of the world's end? What did you learn?

RESOURCES

CONTENTS

Marking the Text: Strategies and Tips for Annotation

When you close read a text, you read for comprehension and then reread to unlock layers of meaning and to analyze a writer's style and techniques. Marking a text as you read it enables you to participate more fully in the close-reading process.

Following are some strategies for text mark-ups, along with samples of how the strategies can be applied. These mark-ups are suggestions; you and your teacher may want to use other mark-up strategies.

*	Key Idea
!	I love it!
?	I have questions
◯	Unfamiliar or important word
----	Context Clues

Suggested Mark-Up Notations

WHAT I NOTICE	HOW TO MARK UP	QUESTIONS TO ASK
Key Ideas and Details	• Highlight key ideas or claims. • Underline supporting details or evidence.	• What does the text say? What does it leave unsaid? • What inferences do you need to make? • What details lead you to make your inferences?
Word Choice	• Circle unfamiliar words. • Put a dotted line under context clues, if any exist. • Put an exclamation point beside especially rich or poetic passages.	• What inferences about word meaning can you make? • What tone and mood are created by word choice? • What alternate word choices might the author have made?
Text Structure	• Highlight passages that show key details supporting the main idea. • Use arrows to indicate how sentences and paragraphs work together to build ideas. • Use a right-facing arrow to indicate foreshadowing. • Use a left-facing arrow to indicate flashback.	• Is the text logically structured? • What emotional impact do the structural choices create?
Author's Craft	• Circle or highlight instances of repetition, either of words, phrases, consonants, or vowel sounds. • Mark rhythmic beats in poetry using checkmarks and slashes. • Underline instances of symbolism or figurative language.	• Does the author's style enrich or detract from the reading experience? • What levels of meaning are created by the author's techniques?

CLOSE READING

In a first read, work to get a sense of the main idea of a text. Look for key details and ideas that help you understand what the author conveys to you. Mark passages that prompt a strong response from you.

Here is how one reader marked up this text.

* Key Idea
! I love it!
? I have questions
◯ Unfamiliar or important word
---- Context Clues

NOTES

MODEL

INFORMATIONAL TEXT

from Classifying the Stars

Cecilia H. Payne

1 Sunlight and starlight are composed of waves of various lengths, which the eye, even aided by a telescope, is unable to separate. We must use more than a telescope. In order to sort out the component colors, the light must be dispersed by a prism, or split up by some other means. For instance, sunbeams passing through rain drops, are transformed into the myriad-tinted rainbow. The familiar rainbow spanning the sky is Nature's most glorious demonstration that light is composed of many colors.

2 The very beginning of our knowledge of the nature of a star dates back to 1672, when Isaac Newton gave to the world the results of his experiments on passing sunlight through a prism. To describe the beautiful band of rainbow tints, produced when sunlight was dispersed by his three-cornered piece of glass, he took from the Latin the word *spectrum*, meaning an appearance. The rainbow is the spectrum of the Sun. . . .

3 In 1814, more than a century after Newton, the spectrum of the Sun was obtained in such purity that an amazing detail was seen and studied by the German optician, Fraunhofer. He saw that the multiple spectral tints, ranging from delicate violet to deep red, were crossed by hundreds of fine dark lines. In other words, there were narrow gaps in the spectrum where certain shades were wholly blotted out. We must remember that the word spectrum is applied not only to sunlight, but also to the light of any glowing substance when its rays are sorted out by a prism or a grating.

MODEL

First-Read Guide

You may want to use a guide like this to organize your thoughts after you read. Here is how a reader completed a First-Read Guide.

Use this page to record your first-read ideas.

Selection Title: Classifying the Stars

NOTICE

NOTICE new information or ideas you learned about the unit topic as you first read this text.

Light = different waves of colors. (Spectrum)

Newton - the first person to observe these waves using a prism.

Faunhofer saw gaps in the spectrum.

ANNOTATE

ANNOTATE by marking vocabulary and key passages you want to revisit.

Vocabulary
- myriad
- grating
- component colors

Different light types = different lengths

Isaac Newton also worked theories of gravity.

Multiple spectral tints? "colors of various appearance"

Key Passage:
Paragraph 3 shows that Fraunhofer discovered more about the nature of light spectrums: he saw the spaces in between the tints.

NOTICE ANNOTATE First Read CONNECT RESPOND

CONNECT ideas within the selection to other knowledge and the selections you have read.

I remember learning about prisms in science class.

Double rainbows! My favorite. How are they made?

CONNECT

RESPOND by writing a brief summary of the selection.

Science allows us to see things not visible to the naked eye. What we see as sunlight is really a spectrum of colors. By using tools, such as prisms, we can see the components of sunlight and other light. They appear as single colors or as multiple colors separated by gaps of no color. White light contains a rainbow of colors.

CLOSE READING

* Key Idea
! I love it!
? I have questions
◯ Unfamiliar or important word
---- Context Clues

In a close read, go back into the text to study it in greater detail. Take the time to analyze not only the author's ideas but the way that those ideas are conveyed. Consider the genre of the text, the author's word choice, the writer's unique style, and the message of the text.

Here is how one reader close read this text.

MODEL

INFORMATIONAL TEXT

from Classifying the Stars

Cecilia H. Payne

NOTES

- explanation of sunlight and starlight
- What is light and where do the colors come from?
- This paragraph is about Newton and the prism.
- What discoveries helped us understand light?
- Fraunhofer and gaps in spectrum

1 Sunlight and starlight are composed of waves of various lengths, which the eye, even aided by a telescope, is unable to separate. We must use more than a telescope. In order to sort out the component colors, the light must be dispersed by a prism, or split up by some other means. For instance, sunbeams passing through rain drops, are transformed into the myriad-tinted rainbow. The familiar rainbow spanning the sky is Nature's most glorious demonstration that light is composed of many colors.

2 The very beginning of our knowledge of the nature of a star dates back to 1672, when Isaac Newton gave to the world the results of his experiments on passing sunlight through a prism. To describe the beautiful band of rainbow tints, produced when sunlight was dispersed by his three-cornered piece of glass, he took from the Latin the word *spectrum*, meaning an appearance. The rainbow is the spectrum of the Sun. . . .

3 In 1814, more than a century after Newton, the spectrum of the Sun was obtained in such purity that an amazing detail was seen and studied by the German optician, Fraunhofer. He saw that the multiple spectral tints, ranging from delicate violet to deep red, were crossed by hundreds of fine dark lines. In other words, there were narrow gaps in the spectrum where certain shades were wholly blotted out. We must remember that the word spectrum is applied not only to sunlight, but also to the light of any glowing substance when its rays are sorted out by a prism or a grating.

MODEL

Close-Read Guide

You can use the Close-Read Guide to help you dig deeper into the text. Here is how a reader completed a Close-Read Guide.

Use this page to record your close-read ideas.

Selection Title: Classifying the Stars

Close Read the Text

Revisit sections of the text you marked during your first read. Read these sections closely and **annotate** what you notice. Ask yourself **questions** about the text. What can you **conclude?** Write down your ideas.

ANNOTATE QUESTION Close Read CONCLUDE

Paragraph 3: Light is composed of waves of various lengths. Prisms let us see different colors in light. This is called the spectrum. Fraunhofer proved that there are gaps in the spectrum, where certain shades are blotted out.

More than one researcher studied this and each built off the ideas that were already discovered.

Analyze the Text

Think about the author's choices of patterns, structure, techniques, and ideas included in the text. Select one, and record your thoughts about what this choice conveys.

The author showed the development of human knowledge of the spectrum chronologically. Helped me see how ideas were built upon earlier understandings. Used dates and "more than a century after Newton" to show time.

QuickWrite

Pick a paragraph from the text that grabbed your interest. Explain the power of this passage.

The first paragraph grabbed my attention, specifically the sentence "The familiar rainbow spanning the sky is Nature's most glorious demonstration that light is composed of many colors." The paragraph began as a straightforward scientific explanation. When I read the word "glorious," I had to stop and deeply consider what was being said. It is a word loaded with personal feelings. With that one word, the author let the reader know what was important to her.

Argument

When you think of the word *argument*, you might think of a disagreement between two people, but an argument is more than that. An argument is a logical way of presenting a belief, conclusion, or stance. A good argument is supported with reasoning and evidence.

Argument writing can be used for many purposes, such as to change a reader's point of view or opinion or to bring about an action or a response from a reader.

Elements of an Argumentative Text

An **argument** is a logical way of presenting a viewpoint, belief, or stand on an issue. A well-written argument may convince the reader, change the reader's mind, or motivate the reader to take a certain action.

An effective argument contains these elements:

- a precise claim
- consideration of counterclaims, or opposing positions, and a discussion of their strengths and weaknesses
- logical organization that makes clear connections among claim, counterclaim, reasons, and evidence
- valid reasoning and evidence
- a concluding statement or section that logically completes the argument
- formal and objective language and tone
- error-free grammar, including accurate use of transitions

MODEL

ARGUMENT: SCORE 1

Selfies, Photoshop, and You: Superficial Image Culture is Hurtful for Teens

Selfies are kind of cool, also kind of annoying, and some say they might be bad for you if you take too many. Selfies of celebrities and ordinary people are everywhere. People always try to smile and look good, and they take a lot of selfies when they are somewhere special, like at the zoo or at a fair. Some people spend so much time taking selfies they forget to just go ahead and have fun.

The writer does not clearly state the claim in the introduction.

TV and other media are full of beautiful people. Looking at all those model's and celebrities can make kids feel bad about their one bodies, even when they are actually totally normal and fine and beautiful they way they are. Kids start to think they should look like the folks on TV which is mostly impossible. It's also a cheat because lots of the photos we see of celebrities and model's have been edited so they look even better.

The argument contains mistakes in standard English conventions of usage and mechanics.

Selfies make people feel even worse about the way they look. They're always comparing themselves and feeling that maybe they aren't as good as they should be. Selfies can make teens feel bad about their faces and bodies, and the stuff they are doing every day.

Regular people edit and change things before they post their pictures. That means, the pictures are kind of fake and it's impossible to compete with something that is fake. It's sad to think that teens can start to hate themselves and feel depressed just because they don't and can't look like a faked photo of a movie star.

The tone of the argument is informal, and the vocabulary is limited or ineffective.

Kids and teens post selfies to hear what others think about them, to show off, and to see how they compare with others. It can be kind of full of pressure always having to look great and smile. Even if you get positive comments about a selfie that you post, and everyone says you look beautiful, that feeling only lasts for a few minutes. After all, what you look like is just something on the outside. What's more important is what you are on the inside and what you do.

It's great for those few minutes, but then what? If you keep posting, people will not want to keep writing nice comments. Kids and teens should take a break from posting selfies all the time. It's better to go out and have fun rather than always keeping on posting selfies.

The writer does not address counterclaims.

The conclusion does not restate any information that is important.

MODEL

ARGUMENT: SCORE 2

Selfies and You: Superficial Image Culture is Hurtful for Teens

Selfies are bad for teens and everyone else. Selfies of celebrities and ordinary people are everywhere. It seems like taking and posting selfies is not such a big deal and not harmful, but that's not really true. Actually, taking too many selfies can be really bad.

The introduction establishes the writer's claim.

TV and other media are full of beautiful people. Looking at all those models and celebrities can make kids feel bad about their own bodies. Kids start to think they should look like the folks on TV which is mostly impossible. It's also a cheat because lots of the photos we see of celebrities and model's have been edited so they look even better.

The tone of the argument is occasionally formal and objective.

Regular people use image editing software as well. They edit and change things before they post their pictures. That means, the pictures are kind of fake and it's impossible to compete with something that is fake.

Selfies make people feel even worse about the way they look. They're always comparing themselves and feeling that maybe they aren't as good as they should be. Selfies can make teens feel bad about their faces and bodies.

But maybe selfies are just a fun way to stay in touch, but that's not really how people use selfies, I don't think. Kids and teens post selfies show off. It can be full of pressure always having to look great and smile.

The writer briefly acknowledges one counterclaim.

Sometimes posting a selfie can make you feel good if it gets lots of 'likes' and positive comments. But you can never tell. Someone also might say something mean. Also, even if you get positive comments and everyone says you look beautiful, that feeling only lasts for a few minutes. It's great for those few minutes, but then what? If you keep posting and posting, people will not want to keep writing nice comments.

The selfie culture today is just too much. Kids and teens can't be happy when they are always comparing themselves and worrying about what they look like. It's better to go out and have fun rather than always keeping on posting selfies.

The conclusion offers some insight into the claim and restates information.

MODEL

ARGUMENT: SCORE 3

Selfies and You: Superficial Image Culture is Hurtful for Teens

Selfies are everywhere. Check out any social media site and you'll see an endless parade of perfect smiles on both celebrities and ordinary people. It may seem as if this flood of seflies is harmless, but sadly that is not true. Selfies promote a superficial image culture that is harmful and dangerous for teens.

The argument's claim is clearly stated.

The problem starts with the unrealistic: idealized images teens are exposed to in the media. Most models and celebrities are impossibly beautiful and thin. Even young children can feel that there is something wrong with they way they look. According to one research group, more than half of girls and one third of boys ages 6-8 feel their ideal body is thinner than their current body weight. Negative body image can result in serious physical and mental health problems.

The tone of the argument is mostly formal and objective.

The writer includes reasons and evidence that address and support claims.

When teens look at selfies they automatically make comparisons with the idealized images they have in their minds. This can make them feel inadequate and sad about themselves, their bodies, and their lives. And with social media sites accessible 24/7, it's difficult to get a break from the constant comparisons, competition, and judgment.

Image editing software plays a role too. A recent study carried out by the Renfrew Center Foundation said that about 50% of people edit pictures of themselves before posting. They take away blemishes, change skin tone, maybe even make themselves look thinner. And why not? Even the photos of models and celebrities are heavily edited. Teens can start to hate themselves and feel depressed just because they don't and can't look like a faked photo of a movie star.

Some say that posting a selfie is like sending a postcard to your friends and family, but that's not how selfies are used: teens post selfies to get feedback, to compare themselves with others, and to present a false image to the world. There is a lot of pressure to look great and appear happy.

It's true that sometimes a selfie posted on social media gets 'likes' and positive comments that can make a person feel pretty. However, the boost you get from feeling pretty for five minutes doesn't last.

The ideas progress logically, and the writer includes sentence transitions that connect the reader to the argument.

A million selfies are posted every day—and that's way too many. Selfies promote a superficial image culture that is harmful to teens. In the end, the selfie life is not a healthy way to have fun. Let's hope the fad will fade.

The conclusion restates important information.

WRITING

MODEL

ARGUMENT: SCORE 4

Selfies and You: Superficial Image Culture Is Hurtful for Teens

Smile, Snap, Edit, Post—Repeat! That's the selfie life, and it's everywhere. A million selfies are posted every day. But this **tsunami** of self-portraits is not as harmless as it appears. Selfies promote a superficial image culture that is hurtful and dangerous for teens.

The introduction is engaging, and the writer's claim is clearly stated at the end of the paragraph.

It all starts with the unrealistic: When teens look at selfies they automatically make comparisons with the idealized images they have in their minds. This can cause them to feel inadequate and sad about themselves, their bodies, and their lives. According to Common Sense Media, more than half of girls and one third of boys ages 6-8 feel their ideal body is thinner than their current body weight. Negative body image can result in serious physical and mental health problems such as anorexia and other eating disorders.

To make matter worse, many or even most selfies have been edited. A recent study carried out by the Renfrew Center Foundation concluded that about 50% of people edit their own images before posting. They use image-editing software to take away blemishes, change skin tone, maybe even make themselves look thinner. And why not? Even the photos of models and celebrities are heavily edited.

The writer has included a variety of sentence transitions such as "To make matters worse…" "Some say…" "Another claim…" "It is true that…"

The sources of evidence are specific and contain relevant information.

Some say that selfies are a harmless and enjoyable way to communicate: posting a selfie is like sending a postcard to your friends and family, inviting them to share in your fun. But that is not how selfies are used: teens post selfies to get feedback, to compare themselves with others, and to present an (often false) image to the world.

The writer clearly acknowledges counterclaims.

It's true that posting a selfie on social media can generate 'likes' and positive comments that can make a person feel good.

However, the boost one gets from feeling pretty for five minutes is like junk food: it tastes good but it is not nourishing.

The selfie culture that is the norm today is out of control. The superficial image culture promoted by selfies is probably behind the recent 20 percent increase in plastic surgery—something with its own dangers and drawbacks. Let's hope the fad will fade, and look forward to a future where people are too busy enjoying life to spend so much time taking, editing, and posting pictures of themselves.

The conclusion offers fresh insights into the claim.

Argument Rubric

	Focus and Organization	Evidence and Elaboration	Conventions
4	The introduction engages the reader and establishes a claim in a compelling way. The argument includes valid reasons and evidence that address and support the claim while clearly acknowledging counterclaims. The ideas progress logically, and transitions make connections among ideas clear. The conclusion offers fresh insight into the claim.	The sources of evidence are comprehensive and specific and contain relevant information. The tone of the argument is always formal and objective. The vocabulary is always appropriate for the audience and purpose.	The argument intentionally uses standard English conventions of usage and mechanics.
3	The introduction engages the reader and establishes the claim. The argument includes reasons and evidence that address and support my claim while acknowledging counterclaims. The ideas progress logically, and some transitions are used to help make connections among ideas clear. The conclusion restates the claim and important information.	The sources of evidence contain relevant information. The tone of the argument is mostly formal and objective. The vocabulary is generally appropriate for the audience and purpose.	The argument demonstrates general accuracy in standard English conventions of usage and mechanics.
2	The introduction establishes a claim. The argument includes some reasons and evidence that address and support the claim while briefly acknowledging counterclaims. The ideas progress somewhat logically. A few sentence transitions are used that connect readers to the argument. The conclusion offers some insight into the claim and restates information.	The sources of evidence contain some relevant information. The tone of the argument is occasionally formal and objective. The vocabulary is somewhat appropriate for the audience and purpose.	The argument demonstrates some accuracy in standard English conventions of usage and mechanics.
1	The introduction does not clearly state the claim. The argument does not include reasons or evidence for the claim. No counterclaims are acknowledged. The ideas do not progress logically. Transitions are not included to connect ideas. The conclusion does not restate any information that is important.	Reliable and relevant evidence is not included. The vocabulary used is limited or ineffective. The tone of the argument is not objective or formal.	The argument contains mistakes in standard English conventions of usage and mechanics.

Informative/Explanatory Texts

Informative and explanatory writing should rely on facts to inform or explain. Informative writing can serve several purposes: to increase readers' knowledge of a subject, to help readers better understand a procedure or process, or to provide readers with an enhanced comprehension of a concept. It should also feature a clear introduction, body, and conclusion.

Elements of Informative/Explanatory Texts

Informative/explanatory texts present facts, details, data, and other kinds of evidence to give information about a topic. Readers turn to informational and explanatory texts when they wish to learn about a specific idea, concept, or subject area, or if they want to learn how to do something.

An effective informative/explanatory text contains these elements:

- a topic sentence or thesis statement that introduces the concept or subject
- relevant facts, examples, and details that expand upon a topic
- definitions, quotations, and/or graphics that support the information given
- headings (if desired) to separate sections of the essay
- a structure that presents information in a direct, clear manner
- clear transitions that link sections of the essay
- precise words and technical vocabulary where appropriate
- formal and object language and tone
- a conclusion that supports the information given and provides fresh insights

MODEL

INFORMATIVE/EXPLANATORY: SCORE 1

Moai: The Giant Statues of Easter Island

Easter Island is a tiny Island. It's far out in the middle of the pacific ocean, 2200 miles off the coast. The closest country is Chile, in south america. The nearest island where people live is called Pitcairn, and that's about 1,300 miles away, and only about 60 people live so their most of the time. Easter island is much bigger than Pitcairn, and lots more people live there now—about 5,000-6,000. Although in the past there were times when only about 111 people lived there.

The essay does not include a thesis statement.

The writer includes many details that are not relevant to the topic of the essay.

Even if you don't really know what it is, you've probably seen pictures of the easter island Statues. You'd recognize one if you saw it, with big heads and no smiles. Their lots of them on the island. Almost 900 of them. But some were never finished They're called *moai*. They are all different sizes. All the sizes together average out to about 13 feet tall and 14 tons of heavy.

The essay has many errors in grammar, spelling, capitalization, punctuation. The errors detract from the fluency and effectiveness of the essay.

Scientists know that Polynesians settled Easter Island (it's also called Rapa Nui, and the people are called the Rapanui people). Polynesians were very good at boats. And they went big distances across the Pacific. When these Polynesians arrived was probably 300, but it was probably 900 or 1200.

The island was covered with forests. They can tell by looking at pollin in lakes. The Rapanui people cut trees, to build houses. They didn't know that they wood run out of wood). They also carved *moai*.

The *moai* were made for important chiefs. They were made with only stone tools. They have large heads and narrow bodies. No 2 are the same. Although they look the same as far as their faces are concerned. They are very big and impressive and special.

The sentences are often not purposeful, varied, or well controlled.

Over the years, many of the statues were tipped over and broken. But some years ago scientists began to fix some of them and stand them up again. They look more better like that. The ones that have been fixed up are probably the ones you remember seeing in photographs.

The essay ends abruptly and lacks a conclusion.

MODEL

INFORMATIVE/EXPLANATORY: SCORE 2

Moai: The Giant Statues of Easter Island

Easter Island is a tiny Island. It's far out in the middle of the pacific ocean, 2200 miles off the coast. The closest South American country is Chile. The nearest island where people live is called Pitcairn, and that's almost 1,300 miles away. Even if don't know much about it, you've probably seen pictures of the Easter Island statues. You'd recognize one if you saw it. They're almost 900 of them. They're called *moai*. The average one is about 13 feet high (that's tall) and weighs a lot—almost 14 tons.

The writer does not include a thesis statement.

Scientists know that Polynesians settled Easter Island (it's also called Rapa Nui, and the people are called the Rapanui). Polynesians were very good sailers. And they traveled big distances across the Pacific. Even so, nobody really can say exactly *when* these Polynesians arrived and settled on the Island. Some say 300 A.D., while others say maybe as late as 900 or even 1200 A.D.

Some of the ideas are reasonably well developed.

Scientists can tell that when the settlers first arrived, the island was covered with forests of palm and hardwood. They can tell by looking at pollin deposits in lakes on the island. The Rapanui people cut trees, built houses, planted crops, and a thriving culture. They didn't know that cutting so many trees would cause problems later on (like running out of wood). They also began to carve *moai*.

The essay has many errors in grammar, spelling, capitalization, punctuation. The errors decrease the effectiveness of the essay.

The *moai* were built to honor important Rapanui ancestors or chiefs. The statutes all have large heads and narrow bodies, but no too are exactly the same. There faces are all similar. Some have places where eyes could be inserted.

Why did the Rapanui stopped making *moai*? Part of it might have been because there were no more trees and no more of the wood needed to transport them. Part of it was maybe because the people were busy fighting each other because food and other necessary things were running out. In any case, they stopped making moai and started tipping over and breaking the ones that were there already. Later on, archeologists began to try to restore some of the statues and set them up again. But even now that some have been set up again, we still don't know a lot about them. I guess some things just have to remain a mystery!

The writer's word choice shows that he is not fully aware of the essay's purpose and tone.

The writer does not include a clear conclusion.

MODEL

INFORMATIVE/EXPLANATORY: SCORE 3

Moai: The Giant Statues of Easter Island

Easter Island is a tiny place, far out in the middle of the Pacific Ocean, 2200 miles off the coast of South America. Another name for the island is Rapa Nui. Even if you don't know much about it, you would probably recognize the colossal head-and-torso carvings known as *moai*. Even after years of research by scientists, many questions about these extraordinary statues remain unanswered.

The thesis statement is clearly stated.

Scientists now agree that it was Polynesians who settled Easter Island. Earlier some argued South American voyagers were the first. But the Polynesians were expert sailors and navigators known to have traveled huge distances across the Pacific Ocean. However, scientists do not agree about *when* the settlers arrived. Some say A.D. 300, while others suggest as late as between A.D. 900 and 1200.

Scientists say that when the settlers first arrived on Rapa Nui, the island was covered with forests of palm and hardwood. They can tell by looking at the layers of pollen deposited over the years in the lakes on the island. The Rapa Nui began to carve *moai*. They developed a unique artistic and architectural tradition all of their own.

The essay has many interesting details, but some do not relate directly to the topic.

Archeologists agree that the *moai* were created to honor ancestor's or chief's. Most *moai* are made from a soft rock called *tuff* that's formed from hardened volcanic ash. The statues all have large heads on top of narrow bodies, but no two are exactly the same. Some have indented eye sockets where eyes could be inserted.

There are very few errors in grammar, usage, and punctuation. These errors do not interrupt the fluency and effectiveness of the essay.

At some point, the Rapanui stopped making *moai*. Why? Was it because there were no more trees and no longer enough wood needed to transport them? Was it because the people were too busy fighting each other over resources which had begun to run out? No one can say for sure. Rival groups began toppling their enemys' *moai* and breaking them. By the 19th century, most of the statues were tipped over, and many were destroyed. It wasn't until many years later that archeologists began to restore some of the statues.

The *moai* of Easter Island are one of the most awe-inspiring human achievements ever. Thanks to scientific studies, we know much more about the *moai, ahu,* and Rapanui people than we ever did in the past. But some questions remain unanswered. At least for now, the *moai* are keeping their mouths shut, doing a good job of guarding their secrets.

The writer's conclusion sums up the main points of the essay and supports the thesis statement.

MODEL

INFORMATIVE/EXPLANATORY: SCORE 4

Moai: The Giant Statues of Easter Island

Easter Island, 2200 miles off the coast of South America, is "the most remote inhabited island on the planet." Few have visited this speck in the middle of the vast Pacific Ocean, but we all recognize the colossal statues that bring this tiny island its fame: the head-and-torso carvings known as *moai*. Yet even after years of research by scientists, many questions about the *moai* remain unanswered.

The thesis statement of is clearly stated in an engaging manner.

Scientists now agree that it was Polynesians, not South Americans, who settled Easter Island (also known as Rapa Nui). Polynesians were expert sailors and navigators known to have traveled huge distances across the Pacific Ocean. Even so, there is little agreement about *when* the settlers arrived. Some say A.D. 300, while others suggest as late as between A.D. 900 and 1200.

The ideas in the essay relate to the thesis statement and focus on the topic.

Most archeologists agree that the *moai* were created to honor ancestors, chiefs, or other important people. Most *moai* are made from a soft rock called *tuff* that's formed from hardened volcanic ash. The statues have large heads atop narrow torsos, with eyes wide open and lips tightly closed. While the moai share these basic characteristics, no two are exactly the same: while all are huge, some are bigger than others. Some are decorated with carvings. Some have indented eye sockets where white coral eyes could be inserted. It's possible that the eyes were only put in for special occasions.

The writer includes many specific and well-chosen details that add substance to the essay.

In the late 1600s, the Rapanui stopped carving *moai*. Was it because the forests had been depleted and there was no longer enough wood needed to transport them? Was it because they were too busy fighting each other over dwindling resources? No one can say for sure. What is known is that rival groups began toppling their enemies' *moai* and breaking them. By the 19th century, most of the statues were tipped over, and many were destroyed. It wasn't until many years later that archeologists began restoration efforts.

The *moai* of Easter Island are one of humanity's most awe-inspiring cultural and artistic achievements. Part of Rapa Nui was designated as a World Heritage Site in 1995 to recognize and protect these extraordinary creations. Thanks to scientific studies, we know much more about the *moai* than we ever did in the past. But some questions remain unanswered, some mysteries unsolved. Don't bother asking the *moai*: their lips are sealed.

The fluency of the writing and effectiveness of the essay are unaffected by errors.

The conclusion relates to the thesis statement and is creative and memorable.

Informative/Explanatory Rubric

	Focus and Organization	Evidence and Elaboration	Conventions
4	The introduction engages the reader and states a thesis in a compelling way. The essay includes a clear introduction, body, and conclusion. The conclusion summarizes ideas and offers fresh insight into the thesis.	The essay includes specific reasons, details, facts, and quotations from selections and outside resources to support the thesis. The tone of the essay is always formal and objective. The language is always precise and appropriate for the audience and purpose.	The essay uses standard English conventions of usage and mechanics. The essay contains no spelling errors.
3	The introduction engages the reader and sets forth the thesis. The essay includes an introduction, body, and conclusion. The conclusion summarizes ideas and supports the thesis.	The essay includes some specific reasons, details, facts, and quotations from selections and outside resources to support the thesis. The tone of the essay is mostly formal and objective. The language is generally precise and appropriate for the audience and purpose.	The essay demonstrates general accuracy in standard English conventions of usage and mechanics. The essay contains few spelling errors.
2	The introduction sets forth the thesis. The essay includes an introduction, body, and conclusion, but one or more parts are weak. The conclusion partially summarizes ideas but may not provide strong support of the thesis.	The essay includes a few reasons, details, facts, and quotations from selections and outside resources to support the thesis. The tone of the essay is occasionally formal and objective. The language is somewhat precise and appropriate for the audience and purpose.	The essay demonstrates some accuracy in standard English conventions of usage and mechanics. The essay contains some spelling errors.
1	The introduction does not state the thesis clearly. The essay does not include an introduction, body, and conclusion. The conclusion does not summarize ideas and may not relate to the thesis.	Reliable and relevant evidence is not included. The tone of the essay is not objective or formal. The language used is imprecise and not appropriate for the audience and purpose.	The essay contains mistakes in standard English conventions of usage and mechanics. The essay contains many spelling errors.

Narration

Narrative writing conveys experience, either real or imaginary, and uses time to provide structure. It can be used to inform, instruct, persuade, or entertain. Whenever writers tell a story, they are using narrative writing. Most types of narrative writing share certain elements, such as characters, setting, a sequence of events, and, often, a theme.

Elements of a Narrative Text

A **narrative** is any type of writing that tells a story, whether it is fiction, nonfiction, poetry, or drama.

An effective nonfiction narrative usually contains these elements:

- an engaging beginning in which characters and setting are established
- characters who participate in the story events
- a well-structured, logical sequence of events
- details that show time and place
- effective story elements such as dialogue, description, and reflection
- the narrator's thoughts, feelings, or views about the significance of events
- use of language that brings the characters and setting to life

An effective fictional narrative usually contains these elements:

- an engaging beginning in which characters, setting, or a main conflict is introduced
- a main character and supporting characters who participate in the story events
- a narrator who relates the events of the plot from a particular point of view
- details that show time and place
- conflict that is resolved in the course of the narrative
- narrative techniques such as dialogue, description, and suspense
- use of language that vividly brings to life characters and events

MODEL

NARRATIVE: SCORE 1

The Remark-a-Ball

Eddie decided to invent a Remark-a-Ball. Eddie thought Barnaby should be able to speak to him.

That's when he invited the Remark-a-Ball.

Barnaby had a rubber ball. It could make a bunchs of sounds that made Barnaby bark. It had always seemed that Barnaby was using his squeaky toy to talk, almost.

This was before Barnaby got hit by a car and died. This was a big deal. He took his chemistry set and worked real hard to created a thing that would make the toy ball talk for Barnaby, his dog.

Eddie made a Remark-a-Ball that worked a little too well, tho. Barnaby could say anything he wanted too. And now he said complaints—his bed didn't feel good, he wanted to be walks, he wanted to eat food.

Barnaby became bossy to Eddy to take him on walks or wake up. It was like he became his boss. Like my dad's boss. Eddy didn't like having a mean boss for a dog.

Eddy wished he hadn't invented the Remark-a-Ball.

The story's beginning is choppy and vague.

The sequence of events is unclear and hard to follow.

The narrative lacks descriptive details and sensory language.

The narrative contains many errors in standard English conventions of usage and mechanics.

The conclusion is abrupt and unsatisfying.

MODEL

NARRATIVE: SCORE 2

The Remark-a-Ball

Eddie couldn't understand what his dog was barking about, so he decided to invent a Remark-a-Ball. Eddie thought Barnaby should be able to speak to him.

That's when he invented the Remark-a-Ball.

Barnaby had a rubber ball the size of an orange. It could make a bunch of sounds that made Barnaby bark. It had always seemed to Eddie that Barnaby was almost talking with his squeaky toy.

This was a big deal. Eddy would be the first human ever to talk to a dog, which was a big deal! He took his chemistry set and worked real hard to created a thing that would make the toy ball talk for Barnaby, his dog.

Eddie made a Remark-a-Ball that worked a little too well, tho. Barnaby could say anything he wanted now. And now he mostly said complaints—his bed didn't feel good, he wanted to be walked all the time, he wanted to eat people food.

Barnaby became bossy to Eddy to take him on walks or wake him up. It was like he became his boss. His really mean boss, like my dad's boss. Eddy didn't like having a mean boss for a dog.

Eddy started to ignore his best friend, which used to be his dog named Barnaby. He started tot think maybe dogs shouldn't be able to talk.

Things were much better when Barnaby went back to barking

The story's beginning provides few details to establish the situation.

Narrative techniques such as dialogue, pacing, and description are used sparingly.

The narrative contains some errors in standard English conventions of usage and mechanics.

The conclusion comes abruptly and provides little insight about the story's meaning.

MODEL

NARRATIVE: SCORE 3

The Remark-a-Ball

Any bark could mean anything: *I'm hungry*, *Take me outside*, or *There's that dog again*. Eddie thought Barnaby should be able to speak to him.

And that's how the Remark-a-Ball was born.

Barnaby had a rubber ball the size of an orange. It could make a wide range of sounds that made Barnaby howl. It had always seemed to Eddie that Barnaby was almost communicating with his squeaky toy.

This was big. This was epic. He would be the first human ever to bridge the communication gap between species! He dusted off his old chemistry set and, through trial and error, created a liquid bath that would greatly increase the toy's flexibility, resilience, and mouth-feel.

Eddie had a prototype that worked—perhaps too well. Barnaby was ready to speak his mind. This unleashed a torrent of complaints—his bed was lumpy, he couldn't *possibly* exist on just three walks a day, he wanted table food like the poodle next door.

Barnaby made increasingly specific demands to Eddie to take him on walks or wake him up. This kind of conversation did not bring them closer, as Eddie had thought, but instead it drove them apart.

Eddie started to avoid his former best friend, and he came to the realization that there is a good reason different species don't have a common language.

So Eddie quit letting Barnaby use the toy.

"Hey, Barn, want to go outside?" Eddie would say, and the dog, as if a switch was turned on, would shake, wag, pant, run in circles, and bark—just like he used to.

The story's beginning establishes the situation and the narrator's point of view but leaves some details unclear.

The narrative consistently uses standard English conventions of usage and mechanics.

Narrative techniques such as dialogue and description are used occasionally.

The conclusion resolves the situation or problem, but does not clearly convey the significance of the events in the story.

MODEL

NARRATIVE: SCORE 4

The Remark-a-Ball

Barnaby, for no apparent reason, leapt up and began to bark like a maniac. "Why are you barking?" asked Eddie, holding the leash tight. But Barnaby, being a dog, couldn't say. It could have been anything—a dead bird, a half-eaten sandwich, the Taj Mahal.

The story's beginning is engaging, sets up a point of view, and establishes characters and tone.

This was one of those times Eddie wished that Barnaby could talk. Any bark could mean anything: *I'm hungry, Take me outside,* or *There's that dog again.* Eddie thought, as buddies, they should be able to understand each other.

And that's how the Remark-a-Ball was born.

The narrative uses standard English conventions of usage and mechanics, except where language is manipulated for effect.

Barnaby had a squeaky toy—a rubber ball the size of an orange. It could emit a wide range of sounds. It made Barnaby howl even as he was squeaking it. And it had always seemed to Eddie that through this process Barnaby was almost communicating.

This was big. This was epic. He, Edward C. Reyes III, would be the first human ever to bridge the communication gap between species! He dusted off his old chemistry set and, through trial and error, created a liquid bath that would greatly increase the toy's flexibility, resilience, and mouth-feel.

By the end of the week Eddie had a prototype that worked—perhaps too well. Barnaby was ready to speak his mind. This unleashed a torrent of complaints—his bed was lumpy, he couldn't *possibly* exist on just three walks a day, he wanted table food like the poodle next door.

Events are presented in a logical sequence, and the progression from one even to another is smooth.

Barnaby made increasingly specific demands, such as "Wake me in ten minutes," and "I want filtered water." This kind of conversation did not bring them closer, as Eddie had thought, but instead it drove them apart.

Narrative techniques are used effectively to develop characters and events.

Eddie started to avoid his former best friend, and he came to the realization that there is a good reason different species don't have a common language. It didn't take long for the invention to be relegated to the very bottom of Barnaby's toy chest, too far down for him to get.

There followed a period of transition, after which Eddie and Barnaby returned to their former mode of communication, which worked out just fine.

"Hey, Barn, want to go outside?" Eddie would say, and the dog, as if a switch was turned on, would shake, wag, pant, run in circles, and bark—just like he used to.

"You're a good boy, Barnaby," Eddie would say, scratching him behind the ears.

The conclusion resolves the situation or problem and clearly conveys the significance of the events in the story.

Narrative Rubric

	Focus and Organization	Development of Ideas/ Elaboration	Conventions
4	The introduction establishes a clear context and point of view. Events are presented in a clear sequence, building to a climax, then moving toward the conclusion. The conclusion follows from and reflects on the events and experiences in the narrative.	Narrative techniques such as dialogue, pacing, and description are used effectively to develop characters, events, and setting. Descriptive details, sensory language, and precise words and phrases are used to convey the experiences in the narrative and to help the reader imagine the characters and setting. Voice is established through word choice, sentence structure, and tone.	The narrative uses standard English conventions of usage and mechanics. Deviations from standard English are intentional and serve the purpose of the narrative. Rules of spelling and punctuation are followed.
3	The introduction gives the reader some context and sets the point of view. Events are presented logically, though there are some jumps in time. The conclusion logically ends the story, but provides only some reflection on the experiences related in the story.	Narrative techniques such as dialogue, pacing, and description are used occasionally. Descriptive details, sensory language, and precise words and phrases are used occasionally. Voice is established through word choice, sentence structure, and tone occasionally, though not evenly.	The narrative mostly uses standard English conventions of usage and mechanics, though there are some errors. There are few errors in spelling and punctuation.
2	The introduction provides some description of a place. The point of view can be unclear at times. Transitions between events are occasionally unclear. The conclusion comes abruptly and provides only a small amount of reflection on the experiences related in the narrative.	Narrative techniques such as dialogue, pacing, and description are used sparingly. The story contains few examples of descriptive details and sensory language. Voice is not established for characters, so that it becomes difficult to determine who is speaking.	The narrative contains some errors in standard English conventions of usage and mechanics. There are many errors in spelling and punctuation.
1	The introduction fails to set a scene or is omitted altogether. The point of view is not always clear. The events are not in a clear sequence, and events that would clarify the narrative may not appear. The conclusion does not follow from the narrative or is omitted altogether.	Narrative techniques such as dialogue, pacing, and description are not used. Descriptive details are vague or missing. No sensory language is included. Voice has not been developed.	The text contains mistakes in standard English conventions of usage and mechanics. Rules of spelling and punctuation have not been followed.

RESEARCH

Conducting Research

We are lucky to live in an age when information is accessible and plentiful. However, not all information is equally useful, or even accurate. Strong research skills will help you locate and evaluate information.

Narrowing or Broadening a Topic

The first step of any research project is determining your topic. Consider the scope of your project and choose a topic that is narrow enough to address completely and effectively. If you can name your topic in just one or two words, it is probably too broad. Topics such as Shakespeare, jazz, or science fiction are too broad to cover in a single report. Narrow a broad topic into smaller subcategories.

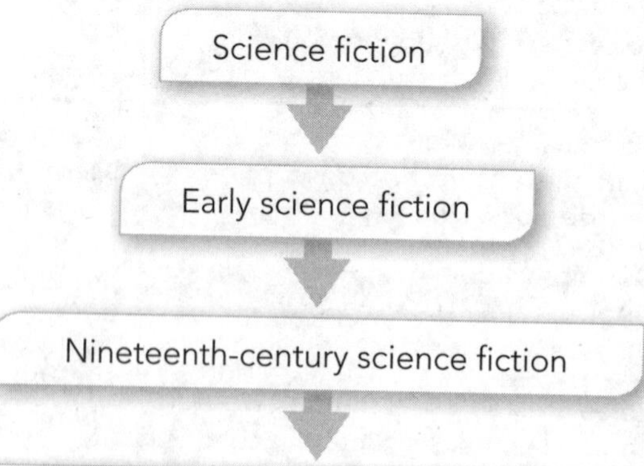

When you begin to research a topic, pay attention to the amount of information available. If you feel overwhelmed by the number of relevant sources, you may need to narrow your topic further.

If there isn't enough information available as your research, you might need to broaden your topic. A topic is too narrow when it can be thoroughly presented in less space than the required size of your assignment. It might also be too narrow if you can find little or no information in library and media sources, so consider broadening your topic to include other related ideas.

Generating Research Questions

Use research questions to focus your research. Specific questions can help you avoid time-wasting digressions. For example, instead of simply hunting for information about Mark Twain, you might ask, "What jobs did Mark Twain have, other than being a writer?" or "Which of Twain's books was most popular during his lifetime?"

In a research report, your research question often becomes your thesis statement, or may lead up to it. The question will also help you focus your research into a comprehensive but flexible search plan, as well as prevent you from gathering unnecessary details. As your research teaches you more about your topic, you may find it necessary to refocus your original question.

Consulting Print and Digital Sources

Effective research combines information from several sources, and does not rely too heavily on a single source. The creativity and originality of your research depends on how you combine ideas from multiple sources. Plan to consult a variety of resources, such as the following:

- **Primary and Secondary Sources:** To get a thorough view of your topic, use primary sources (firsthand or original accounts, such as interview transcripts, eyewitness reports, and newspaper articles) and secondary sources (accounts, created after an event occurred, such as encyclopedia entries).
- **Print and Digital Resources:** The Internet allows fast access to data, but print resources are often edited more carefully. Use both print and digital resources in order to guarantee the accuracy of your findings.
- **Media Resources:** You can find valuable information in media resources such as documentaries, television programs, podcasts, and museum exhibitions. Consider attending public lectures given by experts to gain an even more in-depth view of your topic.
- **Original Research:** Depending on your topic, you may wish to conduct original research to include among your sources. For example, you might interview experts or eyewitnesses, or conduct a survey of people in your community.

Using Online Encyclopedias

Online encyclopedias are often written by anonymous contributors who are not required to fact-check information. These sites can be very useful as a launching point for research, but should not be considered accurate. Look for footnotes, endnotes, or hyperlinks that support facts with reliable sources that have been carefully checked by editors.

Evaluating Sources It is important to evaluate the credibility, validity, and accuracy of any information you find, as well as its appropriateness for your purpose and audience. You may find the information you need to answer your research question in specialized and authoritative sources, such as almanacs (for social, cultural, and natural statistics), government publications (for law, government programs, and subjects such as agriculture), and information services. Also, consider consumer, workplace, and public documents.

Ask yourself questions such as these to evaluate these additional sources:

- **Authority:** Is the author well known? What are the author's credentials? Does the source include references to other reliable sources? Does the author's tone win your confidence? Why or why not?
- **Bias:** Does the author have any obvious biases? What is the author's purpose for writing? Who is the target audience?
- **Currency:** When was the work created? Has it been revised? Is there more current information available?

Using Search Terms

Finding information on the Internet can be both easy and challenging. Type a word or phrase into a general search engine and you will probably get hundreds—or thousands—of results. However, those results are not guaranteed to be relevant or accurate.

These strategies can help you find information from the Internet:

- Create a list of keywords that apply to your topic before you begin using a search engine. Consult a thesaurus to expand your list.
- Enter six to eight keywords.
- Choose precise nouns. Most search engines ignore articles and prepositions. Verbs may be used in multiple contexts, leading to sources that are not relevant. Use modifiers, such as adjectives, when necessary to specify a category.
- Use quotation marks to focus a search. Place a phrase in quotation marks to find pages that include exactly that phrase. Add several phrases in quotation marks to narrow your results.
- Spell carefully. Many search engines autocorrect spelling, but they cannot produce accurate results for all spelling errors.
- Scan search results before you click them. The first result isn't always the most relevant. Read the text and consider the domain before make a choice.
- Utilize more than one search engine.

Evaluating Internet Domains

Not everything you read on the Internet is true, so you have to evaluate sources carefully. The last three letters of an Internet URL identify the Website's domain, which can help you evaluate the information of the site.

- **.gov**—Government sites are sponsored by a branch of the United States federal government, such as the Census Bureau, Supreme Court, or Congress. These sites are considered reliable.
- **.edu**—Education domains include schools from kindergartens to universities. Information from an educational research center or department is likely to be carefully checked. However, education domains can also include student pages that are not edited or monitored.
- **.org**—Organizations are nonprofit groups and usually maintain a high level of credibility. Keep in mind that some organizations may express strong biases.
- **.com** and **.net**—Commercial sites exist to make a profit. Information may be biased to show a product or service in a good light. The company may be providing information to encourage sales or promote a positive image.

Taking Notes

Take notes as you locate and connect useful information from multiple sources, and keep a reference list of every source you use. This will help you make distinctions between the relative value and significance of specific data, facts, and ideas.

For long-term research projects, create source cards and notecards to keep track of information gathered from multiple resources.

Source Cards
Create a card that identifies each source.

- For print materials, list the author, title, publisher, date of publication, and relevant page numbers.
- For Internet sources, record the name and Web address of the site, and the date you accessed the information.
- For media sources, list the title, person, or group credited with creating the media, and the year of production.

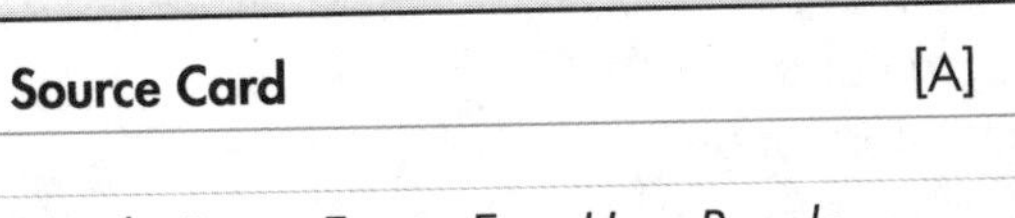

Source Card [A]

Marsh, Peter. *Eye to Eye: How People Interact.* Salem House Publishers, 1988.

Notecards
Create a separate notecard for each item of information.

- Include the fact or idea, the letter of the related source card, and the specific page(s) on which the fact or idea appears.
- Use quotation marks around words and phrases taken directly from print or media resources.
- Mark particularly useful or relevant details using your own annotation method, such as stars, underlining, or colored highlighting.

Notecard

Gestures vary from culture to culture. The American "OK" symbol (thumb and forefinger) is considered insulting in Greece and Turkey.

Source Card: A, p. 54.

Quote Accurately Responsible research begins with the first note you take. Be sure to quote and paraphrase your sources accurately so you can identify these sources later. In your notes, circle all quotations and paraphrases to distinguish them from your own comments. When photocopying from a source, include the copyright information. When printing out information from an online source, include the Web address.

Reviewing Research Findings

While conducting research, you will need to review your findings, checking that you have collected enough accurate and appropriate information.

Considering Audience and Purpose

Always keep your audience in mind as you gather information, since different audiences may have very different needs. For example, if you are writing an in-depth analysis of a text that your entire class has read together and you are writing for your audience, you will not need to gather background information that has been thoroughly discussed in class. However, if you are writing the same analysis for a national student magazine, you cannot assume that all of your readers have the same background information. You will need to provide facts from reliable sources to help orient these readers to your subject. When considering whether or not your research will satisfy your audience, ask yourself:

- Who are my readers? For whom am I writing?
- Have I collected enough information to explain my topic to this audience?
- Are there details in my research that I can omit because they are already familiar to my audience?

Your purpose for writing will also influence your review of research. If you are researching a question to satisfy your own curiosity, you can stop researching when you feel you understand the answer completely. If you are writing a research report that will be graded, you need to consider the criteria of the assignment. When considering whether or not you have enough information, ask yourself:

- What is my purpose for writing?
- Will the information I have gathered be enough to achieve my purpose?
- If I need more information, where might I find it?

Synthesizing Sources

Effective research writing does not merely present facts and details; it synthesizes—gathers, orders, and interprets—them. These strategies will help you synthesize information effectively:

- Review your notes and look for connections and patterns among the details you have collected.
- Arrange notes or notecards in different ways to help you decide how to best combine related details and present them in a logical way.
- Pay close attention to details that support one other, emphasizing the same main idea.
- Also look for details that challenge each other, highlighting ideas about which there is no single, or consensus, opinion. You might decide to conduct additional research to help you decide which side of the issue has more support.

Types of Evidence

When reviewing your research, also consider the kinds of evidence you have collected. The strongest writing contains a variety of evidence effectively. This chart describes three of the most common types of evidence: statistical, testimonial, and anecdotal.

TYPE OF EVIDENCE	DESCRIPTION	EXAMPLE
Statistical evidence includes facts and other numerical data used to support a claim or explain a topic.	Examples of statistical evidence include historical dates and information, quantitative analyses, poll results, and quantitative descriptions.	"Although it went on to become a hugely popular novel, the first edition of William Goldman's book sold fewer than 3,000 copies."
Testimonial evidence includes any ideas or opinions presented by others, especially experts in a field.	Firsthand testimonies present ideas from eyewitnesses to events or subjects being discussed.	"The ground rose and fell like an ocean at ebb tide." —Fred J. Hewitt, eyewitness to the 1906 San Francisco earthquake
	Secondary testimonies include commentaries on events by people who were not involved. You might quote a well-known literary critic when discussing a writer's most famous novel, or a prominent historian when discussing the effects of an important event	Gladys Hansen insists that "there was plenty of water in hydrants throughout [San Francisco] . . . The problem was this fire got away."
Anecdotal evidence presents one person's view of the world, often by describing specific events or incidents.	Compelling research should not rely solely on this form of evidence, but it can be very useful for adding personal insights and refuting inaccurate generalizations. An individual's experience can be used with other forms of evidence to present complete and persuasive support.	Although many critics claim the novel is universally beloved, at least one reader "threw the book against a wall because it made me so angry."

Incorporating Research Into Writing

Avoiding Plagiarism

Plagiarism is the unethical presentation of someone else's ideas as your own. You must cite sources for direct quotations, paraphrased information, or facts that are specific to a single source. When you are drafting and revising, circle any words or ideas that are not your own. Follow the instructions on pages R32 and R33 to correctly cite those passages.

Review for Plagiarism Always take time to review your writing for unintentional plagiarism. Read what you have written and take note of any phrases or sentences that do not have your personal writing voice. Compare those passages with your resource materials. You might have copied them without remembering the exact source. Add a correct citation to give credit to the original author. If you cannot find the questionable phrase in your notes, revise it to ensure that your final report reflects your own thinking and not someone else's work.

Quoting and Paraphrasing

When including ideas from research into your writing, you will decide to quote directly or paraphrase.

Direct Quotation Use the author's exact words when they are interesting or persuasive. You might decide to include direct quotations for these reasons:

- to share an especially clear and relevant statement
- to reference a historically significant passage
- to show that an expert agrees with your position
- to present an argument that you will counter in your writing.

Include complete quotations, without deleting or changing words. If you need to omit words for space or clarity, use ellipsis points to indicate the omission. Enclose direct quotations in quotation marks and indicate the author's name.

Paraphrase A paraphrase restates an author's ideas in your own words. Be careful to paraphrase accurately. Beware of making sweeping generalizations in a paraphrase that were not made by the original author. You may use some words from the original source, but a legitimate paraphrase does more than simply rearrange an author's phrases, or replace a few words with synonyms.

Original Text	"*The Tempest* was written as a farewell to art and the artist's life, just before the completion of his forty-ninth year, and everything in the play bespeaks the touch of autumn." Brandes, Georg. "Analogies Between *The Tempest* and *A Midsummer Night's Dream*." *The Tempest*, by William Shakespeare, William Heinemann, 1904, p. 668.
Patchwork Plagiarism phrases from the original are rearranged, but too closely follows the original text.	A farewell to art, Shakespeare's play, *The Tempest*, was finished just before the completion of his forty-ninth year. The artist's life was to end within three years. The touch of autumn is apparent in nearly everything in the play.
Good Paraphrase	Images of autumn occur throughout *The Tempest*, which Shakespeare wrote as a way of saying goodbye to both his craft and his own life.

Maintaining the Flow of Ideas

Effective research writing is much more that just a list of facts. Be sure to maintain the flow of ideas by connecting research information to your own ideas. Instead of simply stating a piece of evidence, use transition words and phrases to explain the connection between information you found from outside resources and your own ideas and purpose for writing. The following transitions can be used to introduce, compare, contrast, and clarify.

Useful Transitions

When providing examples:

for example | for instance | to illustrate | in [name of resource], [author]

When comparing and contrasting ideas or information:

in the same way | similarly | however | on the other hand

When clarifying ideas or opinions:

in other words | that is | to explain | to put it another way

Choosing an effective organizational structure for your writing will help you create a logical flow of ideas. Once you have established a clear organizational structure, insert facts and details from your research in appropriate places to provide evidence and support for your writing.

ORGANIZATIONAL STRUCTURE	USES
Chronological order presents information in the sequence in which it happens.	historical topics; science experiments; analysis of narratives
Part-to-whole order examines how several categories affect a larger subject.	analysis of social issues; historical topics
Order of importance presents information in order of increasing or decreasing importance.	persuasive arguments; supporting a bold or challenging thesis
Comparison-and-contrast organization outlines the similarities and differences of a given topic.	addressing two or more subjects

Formats for Citing Sources

In research writing, cite your sources. In the body of your paper, provide a footnote, an endnote, or a parenthetical citation, identifying the sources of facts, opinions, or quotations. At the end of your paper, provide a bibliography or a Works Cited list, a list of all the sources referred to in your research. Follow an established format, such as Modern Language Association (MLA) style.

Parenthetical Citations (MLA Style) A parenthetical citation briefly identifies the source from which you have taken a specific quotation, factual claim, or opinion. It refers readers to one of the entries on your Works Cited list. A parenthetical citation has the following features:

- It appears in parentheses.
- It identifies the source by the last name of the author, editor, or translator, or by the title (for a lengthy title, list the first word only).
- It provides a page reference, the page(s) of the source on which the information cited can be found.

A parenthetical citation generally falls outside a closing quotation mark but within the final punctuation of a clause or sentence. For a long quotation set off from the rest of your text, place the citation at the end of the excerpt without any punctuation following.

Sample Parenthetical Citations

It makes sense that baleen whales such as the blue whale, the bowhead whale, the humpback whale, and the sei whale (to name just a few) grow to immense sizes (Carwardine et al. 19–21). The blue whale has grooves running from under its chin to partway along the length of its underbelly. As in some other whales, these grooves expand and allow even more food and water to be taken in (Ellis 18–21).

Authors' last names

Page numbers where information can be found

Works Cited List (MLA Style) A Works Cited list must contain accurate information to enable a reader to locate each source you cite. The basic components of an entry are as follows:

- name of the author, editor, translator, and/or group responsible for the work
- title of the work
- publisher
- date of publication

For print materials, the information for a citation generally appears on the copyright and title pages. For the format of a Works Cited list, consult the examples on this page and in the MLA Style for Listing Sources chart.

Sample Works Cited List (MLA 8th Edition)

Carwardine, Mark, et al. *The Nature Company Guides: Whales, Dolphins, and Porpoises.* Time-Life, 1998.

"Discovering Whales." *Whales on the Net.* Whales in Danger, 1998, www.whales.org.au/discover/index.html. Accessed 11 Apr. 2017.

Neruda, Pablo. "Ode to Spring." *Odes to Opposites,* translated by Ken Krabbenhoft, edited and illustrated by Ferris Cook, Little, 1995, p. 16.

The Saga of the Volsungs. Translated by Jesse L. Byock, Penguin, 1990.

List an anonymous work by title.

List both the title of the work and the collection in which it is found.

Works Cited List or Bibliography?

A Works Cited list includes only those sources you paraphrased or quoted directly in your research paper. By contrast, a bibliography lists all the sources you consulted during research—even those you did not cite.

MLA (8th Edition) Style for Listing Sources

Book with one author	Pyles, Thomas. *The Origins and Development of the English Language.* 2nd ed., Harcourt Brace Jovanovich, 1971. [Indicate the edition or version number when relevant.]
Book with two authors	Pyles, Thomas, and John Algeo. *The Origins and Development of the English Language.* 5th ed., Cengage Learning, 2004.
Book with three or more authors	Donald, Robert B., et al. *Writing Clear Essays.* Prentice Hall, 1983.
Book with an editor	Truth, Sojourner. *Narrative of Sojourner Truth.* Edited by Margaret Washington, Vintage Books, 1993.
Introduction to a work in a published edition	Washington, Margaret. Introduction. *Narrative of Sojourner Truth,* by Sojourner Truth, edited by Washington, Vintage Books, 1993, pp. v–xi.
Single work in an anthology	Hawthorne, Nathaniel. "Young Goodman Brown." *Literature: An Introduction to Reading and Writing,* edited by Edgar V. Roberts and Henry E. Jacobs, 5th ed., Prentice Hall, 1998, pp. 376–385. [Indicate pages for the entire selection.]
Signed article from an encyclopedia	Askeland, Donald R. "Welding." *World Book Encyclopedia,* vol. 21, World Book, 1991, p. 58.
Signed article in a weekly magazine	Wallace, Charles. "A Vodacious Deal." *Time,* 14 Feb. 2000, p. 63.
Signed article in a monthly magazine	Gustaitis, Joseph. "The Sticky History of Chewing Gum." *American History,* Oct. 1998, pp. 30–38.
Newspaper article	Thurow, Roger. "South Africans Who Fought for Sanctions Now Scrap for Investors." *Wall Street Journal,* 11 Feb. 2000, pp. A1+. [For a multipage article that does not appear on consecutive pages, write only the first page number on which it appears, followed by the plus sign.]
Unsigned editorial or story	"Selective Silence." Editorial. *Wall Street Journal,* 11 Feb. 2000, p. A14. [If the editorial or story is signed, begin with the author's name.]
Signed pamphlet or brochure	[Treat the pamphlet as though it were a book.]
Work from a library subscription service	Ertman, Earl L. "Nefertiti's Eyes." *Archaeology,* Mar.–Apr. 2008, pp. 28–32. *Kids Search,* EBSCO, New York Public Library. Accessed 7 Jan. 2017. [Indicating the date you accessed the information is optional but recommended.]
Filmstrips, slide programs, videocassettes, DVDs, and other audiovisual media	*The Diary of Anne Frank.* 1959. Directed by George Stevens, performances by Millie Perkins, Shelley Winters, Joseph Schildkraut, Lou Jacobi, and Richard Beymer, Twentieth Century Fox, 2004. [Indicating the original release date after the title is optional but recommended.]
CD-ROM (with multiple publishers)	Simms, James, editor. *Romeo and Juliet.* By William Shakespeare, Attica Cybernetics / BBC Education / Harper, 1995.
Radio or television program transcript	"Washington's Crossing of the Delaware." *Weekend Edition Sunday,* National Public Radio, 23 Dec. 2013. Transcript.
Web page	"Fun Facts About Gum." ICGA, 2005–2017, www.gumassociation.org/index.cfm/facts-figures/fun-facts-about-gum. Accessed 19 Feb. 2017. [Indicating the date you accessed the information is optional but recommended.]
Personal interview	Smith, Jane. Personal interview, 10 Feb. 2017.

All examples follow the style given in the MLA Handbook, 8th edition, published in 2016.

MODEL

Evidence Log

Unit Title: Discovery

Perfomance-Based Assessment Prompt:
Do all discoveries benefit humanity?

My initial thoughts:
Yes - all knowledge moves us forward.

As you read multiple texts about a topic, your thinking may change. Use an Evidence Log like this one to record your thoughts, to track details you might use in later writing or discussion, and to make further connections.

Here is a sample to show how one reader's ideas deepened as she read two texts.

Title of Text: Classifying the Stars Date: Sept. 17

CONNECTION TO THE PROMPT	TEXT EVIDENCE/DETAILS	ADDITIONAL NOTES/IDEAS
Newton shared his discoveries and then other scientists built on his discoveries.	Paragraph 2: "Isaac Newton gave to the world the results of his experiments on passing sunlight through a prism." Paragraph 3: "In 1814 . . . the German optician, Fraunhofer . . . saw that the multiple spectral tints . . . were crossed by hundreds of fine dark lines."	It's not always clear how a discovery might benefit humanity in the future.

How does this text change or add to my thinking? This confirms what I think. Date: Sept. 20

Title of Text: Cell Phone Mania Date: Sept. 21

CONNECTION TO THE PROMPT	TEXT EVIDENCE/DETAILS	ADDITIONAL NOTES/IDEAS
Cell phones have made some forms of communication easier, but people don't talk to each other as much as they did in the past.	Paragraph 7: "Over 80% of young adults state that texting is their primary method of communicating with friends. This contrasts with older adults who state that they prefer a phone call."	Is it good that we don't talk to each other as much? Look for article about social media to learn more about this question.

How does this text change or add to my thinking? Date: Sept. 25
Maybe there are some downsides to discoveries. I still think that knowledge moves us forward, but there are sometimes unintended negative effects.

MODEL

Word Network

A word network is a collection of words related to a topic. As you read the selections in a unit, identify interesting theme-related words and build your vocabulary by adding them to your Word Network.

Use your Word Network as a resource for your discussions and writings. Here is an example:

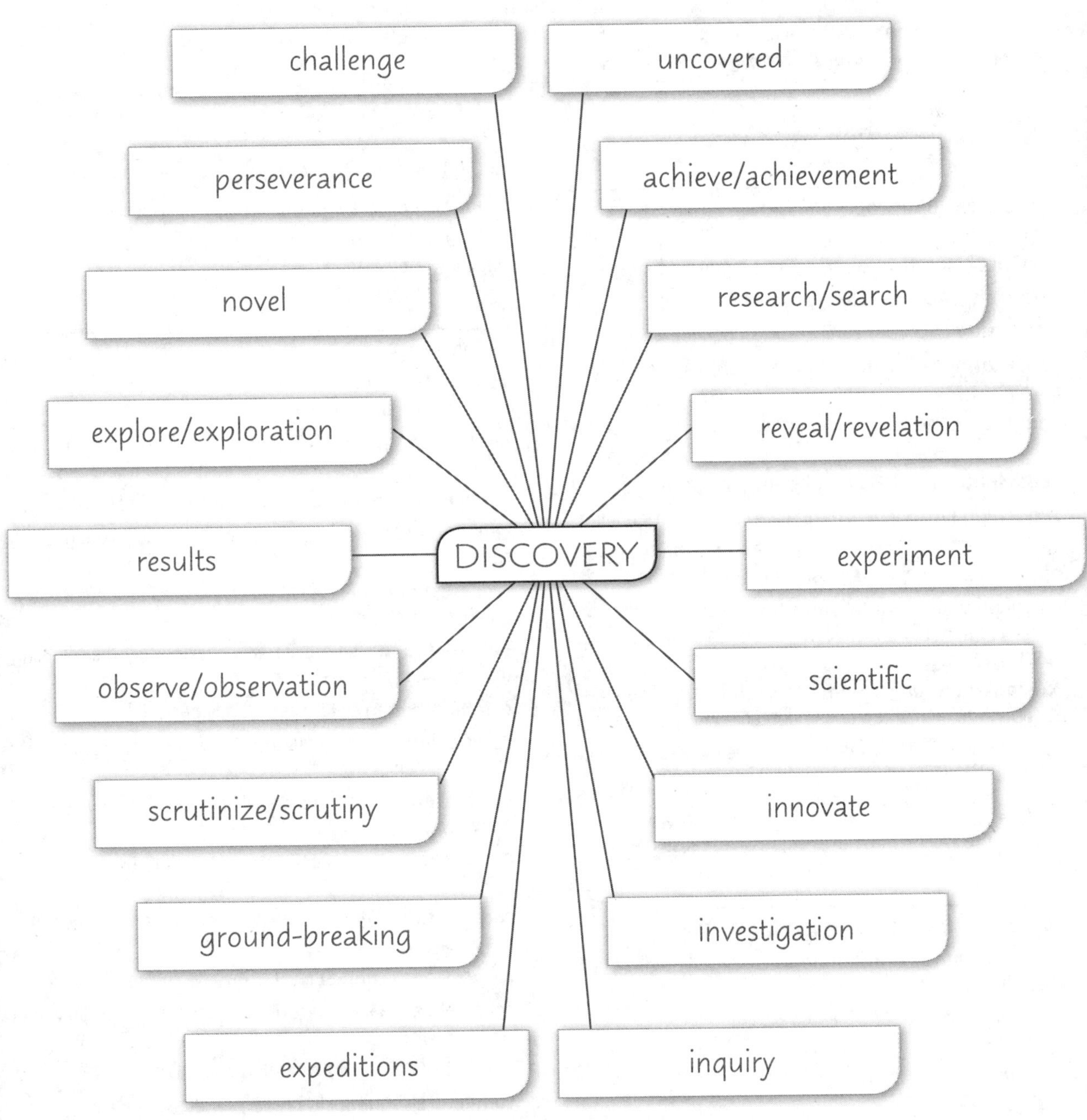

ACADEMIC / CONCEPT VOCABULARY

Academic vocabulary appears in **blue type**.

Pronunciation Key

Symbol	Sample Words	Symbol	Sample Words
a	***at, catapult, Alabama***	oo	***boot, soup, crucial***
ah	***father, charms, argue***	ow	***now, stout, flounder***
ai	***care, various, hair***	oy	***boy, toil, oyster***
aw	***law, maraud, caution***	s	***say, nice, press***
awr	***pour, organism, forewarn***	sh	***she, abolition, motion***
ay	***ape, sails, implication***	u	***full, put, book***
ee	***even, teeth, really***	uh	***ago, focus, contemplation***
eh	***ten, repel, elephant***	ur	***bird, urgent. perforation***
ehr	***merry, verify, terribly***	y	***by, delight, identify***
ih	***it, pin, hymn***	yoo	***music, confuse, few***
o	***shot, hopscotch, condo***	zh	***pleasure, treasure, vision***
oh	***own, parole, rowboat***		

A

absolute (AB suh loot) *adj.* certain; positive; perfectly whole

activist (AK tuh vihst) *n.* active supporter of a cause

adamant (AD uh muhnt) *adj.* not giving in; stubborn

adversary (AD vuhr sehr ee) *n.* opponent; enemy

advocating (AD vuh kayt ihng) *v.* speaking or writing in favor of a cause or person

aggregate (AG ruh giht) *n.* collection; sum of many parts

anticipated (an TIHS uh payt ihd) *v.* eagerly expected

apocryphal (uh POK ruh fuhl) *adj.* fake; not genuine

applicant information (AP luh kuhnt) (ihn fuhr MAY shuhn) *n.* data about a person applying for a job

archival audio (ahr KY vuhl) (AW dee oh) *n.* sound recorded from radio broadcasts, television shows, or films of past decades

assimilation (uh sihm uh LAY shuhn) *n.* process of adapting to the culture of an adopted country

attending (uh TEHND ihng) *adj.* being present; taking care of things

avenge (uh VEHNJ) *v.* get revenge for

awesome (AW suhm) *adj.* impressive; causing awe

B

bade (bayd) *v.* past tense of *bid;* requested

banishment (BAN ihsh muhnt) *n.* state of having been banished, or exiled

banter (BAN tuhr) *n.* friendly exchange between speakers

bemusing (bih MYOOZ ihng) *adj.* confusing; bewildering

besieged (bih SEEJD) *adj.* under military attack

bewildered (bih WIHL duhrd) *adj.* confused completely

blundering (BLUHN duhr ihng) *adj.* clumsy

burden (BUR duhn) *n.* something that is carried with difficulty or obligation

C

cadence (KAY duhns) *n.* rhythm and flow of language

caption (KAP shuhn) *n.* words in a separate box in a graphic novel or comic strip

check box (chehk) (boks) *n.* place on a form to indicate "yes," signifying that a certain statement is true

chimed (chymd) *v.* rang; made the sound of a bell

chirruped (CHIHR uhpt) *v.* made bird-like chirping sounds

coalescing (koh uh LEHS ihng) *n.* coming together in one body or place

coherent (koh HIHR ihnt) *adj.* sticking together; holding together; logically consistent

compact (kuhm PAKT) *adj.* firmly packed

compelling (kuhm PEHL ihng) *adj.* interesting and attractive; persuasive

complacency (kuhm PLAY suhn see) *n.* state of unthinking or satisfied acceptance

composed (kuhm POHZD) *n.* created music or literary work

composition (kom puh ZIHSH uhn) *n.* arrangement of the parts of a picture

concessions (kuhn SEHSH uhnz) *n.* special allowances

confidence (KON fuh duhns) *n.* meeting, especially one held in secret

conflict (KON flihkt) *n.* struggle; problem; fight

conjecture (kuhn JEHK chuhr) *n.* guess; *v.* guess

conscience (KON shuhns) *n.* inner sense of what is morally right or wrong in one's actions

correspondents (kawr uh SPON duhnts) *n.* reporters who send news from far away or on a special subject

counterfeit (KOWN tuhr fiht) *n.* something made to deceive

craft (kraft) *n.* activity that requires skill

credible (KREHD uh buhl) *adj.* believable; convincing

credulity (kruh DYOO luh tee) *n.* readiness to believe

culpability (kuhl puh BIHL uh tee) *n.* guilt or blame that is deserved; blameworthiness

cunning (KUHN ihng) *n.* skill in deception

customs (KUHS tuhmz) *n.* traditions; actions that are commonly done by a group of people

D

deceived (dih SEEVD) *v.* lied to; tricked

deftly (DEHFT lee) *adv.* in a way that is skillfull and quick

delicately (DEHL uh kiht lee) *adv.* carefully; with grace and gentleness

delivery (dih LIHV uhr ee) *n.* manner in which a speaker gives a speech

dependency (dih PEHN duhn see) *n.* act of leaning on another for support or help

depiction (dih PIHK shuhn) *n.* picture, description, or explanation

descendants (dih SEHN duhnts) *n.* people who are the offspring of an ancestor

description (dih SKRIHP shuhn) *n.* writing or speech that tells about something

desperate (DEHS puhr iht) *adj.* involving extreme danger or disaster; driven to action by a loss of hope

destined (DEHS tihnd) *adj.* caused by fate; meant to do; meant for

devoted (dih VOHT ihd) *adj.* loving, loyal, and concerned with another's well-being

dialogue (DY uh log) *n.* conversation between characters in writing, film, or drama

discordant (dihs KAWR duhnt) *adj.* unrelated; out of place

disparate (DIHS puhr iht) *adj.* essentially different in kind

dispatched (dihs PACHT) *v.* finished something quickly

disrupt (dihs RUHPT) *v.* break up; upset; interrupt

dissemble (dih SEHM buhl) *v.* put on an appearance or disguise

distressed (dihs TREHST) *adj.* full of anxiety and suffering

diversity (duh VUR suh tee) *n.* variety of different ethnic or cultural groups

E

eerily (EER uh lee) *adv.* strangely; weirdly

elation (ih LAY shuhn) *n.* great happiness and excitement

elucidate (ih LOO suh dayt) *v.* explain; make clear

empathic (ehm PATH ihk) *adj.* characterized by empathy, the ability to identify with the feelings or thoughts of others

endure (ehn DUR) *v.* last; continue; put up with

enthralled (ehn THRAWLD) *v.* captivated

entranced (ehn TRANST) *adj.* in a state of wonder or amazement

entrusted (ehn TRUHST ihd) *v.* given the responsibility of doing something or caring for someone or something

establishing shot (ehs TAB lihsh ihng) (shot) *n.* shot that shows the context of a scene in a film or video

eternal (ih TUR nuhl) *adj.* timeless; everlasting

evidence (EHV uh duhns) *n.* facts or details that support a position or claim

exalted (ehg ZAWL tihd) *adj.* elevated

exile (EHG zyl) *v.* punish someone by forcing that person to leave a place permanently

expedite (EHKS puh dyt) *v.* make easy and quick; do quickly

expert commentary (EHKS purht) (KOM ehn tair ee) *n.* information delivered by a person who has special knowledge of the subject

exposition (ehks spuh ZIH shuhn) *n.* writing or speech that explains or shows

express (ehks PREHS) *v.* say; convey; reveal

eyewitness (Y wiht nihs) *n.* someone who has firsthand experience of an event

F

factions (FAK shuhnz) *n.* groups of people inside a political party, club, government, etc., working against another group

faithless (FAYTH lihs) *adj.* without faith; unbelieving

fasting (FAS tihng) *v.* intentionally not eating, often for religious or spiritual reasons

fluttered (FLUH tuhrd) *v.* waved gently

forbidden (fuhr BIHD uhn) *adj.* prevented or prohibited

formulate (FAWR myuh layt) *v.* build; state definitely; develop

fugitives (FYOO juh tihvz) *n.* group of persons who have run away from danger

G

gesture (JEHS chuhr) *n.* movement of the hands or body that conveys meaning

guise (gyz) *n.* outward appearance

gutter (GUHT uhr) *n.* space between panels in a graphic novel

H

hallowed (HAL ohd) *adj.* holy; sacred

hallucination (huh loo suh NAY shuhn) *n.* something perceived that has no reality

heretics (HEHR uh tihks) *n.* people who hold a different belief from the official belief of their church

human interest story (HYOO muhn) (IHN trihst) (STAWR ee) *n.* story that focuses on the personal issues of people

I

idly (YD lee) *adv.* lazily; without taking action

impulse (IHM puhls) *n.* sudden urge to act or do something

incredulity (ihn kruh DYOO luh tee) *n.* doubt

indignation (ihn dihg NAY shuhn) *n.* righteous anger; hostility

inevitable (ihn EHV uh tuh buhl) *adj.* certain to occur; unavoidable

infantile (IHN fuhn tyl) *adj.* babyish; childish

infatuated (ihn FACH oo ayt ihd) *adj.* briefly but intensely in love

innovate (IHN uh vayt) *v.* make changes; introduce something new

inscribed (ihn SKRYBD) *adj.* written or engraved upon

interpreter (ihn TUR pruh tuhr) *n.* person who changes the words of one language into another for the benefit of listeners

intervened (ihn tuhr VEEND) *v.* came between groups

interwoven (ihn tuhr WOH vuhn) *adj.* intermingled; combined

intrigued (ihn TREEGD) *v.* interested and curious

introduction (ihn truh DUHK shuhn) *n.* context and background information about the topic of a radio broadcast, provided at its beginning

introspective (ihn truh SPEHK tihv) *adj.* having the habit of examining one's own thoughts and feelings

iridescent (ihr uh DEHS uhnt) *adj.* changing in color when seen from different angles

irresolvable (ihr ih ZOL vuh buhl) *adj.* impossible to resolve or settle

L

lamentable (luh MEHN tuh buhl) *adj.* grievous; mournful; sorrowful

languished (LANG gwihsht) *v.* grown weak; lived under distressing conditions

lighting and color (LY tihng) (KUHL uhr) *n.* use of light, shadow, and color in a picture

logical (LOJ uh kuhl) *adj.* based on reason or sound judgment

luminous (LOO muh nuhs) *adj.* shining; radiating light

M

macabre (muh KAH bruh) *adj.* grim and horrible

manipulated (muh NIHP yuh layt ihd) *v.* managed or controlled through clever moves

meager (MEE guhr) *adj.* extremely thin

meditative (MEHD uh tay tihv) *adj.* given to extended thought

melancholy (MEHL uhn kol ee) *adj.* sad and depressed

memento (muh MEHN toh) *n.* souvenir; keepsake

minority (muh NAWR uh tee) *n.* group of people that differs in some way from the larger population

misery (MIHZ uhr ee) *n.* condition of great wretchedness

montage (mon TOZH) *n.* group of images shown quickly, one after another, to create a single impression

mortality (mawr TAL uh tee) *n.* condition of being sure to die sometime

mutiny (MYOO tuh nee) *n.* open rebellion against lawful authority, especially by sailors or soldiers against their officers

N

naturalization (nach uhr uh luh ZAY shuhn) *n.* process of becoming a citizen

notation (noh TAY shuhn) *n.* brief note added to a text to explain, elaborate, remind, etc.

O

oppression (uh PREHSH uhn) *n.* cruel or unjust treatment

oratory (AWR uh tawr ee) *n.* formal public speaking

P

panel (PAN uhl) *n.* one of the drawings on a page, usually framed by a border

pardon (PAHR duhn) *n.* forgiveness for a crime

pathos (PAY thos) *n.* quality that creates a feeling of sadness or pity

penury (PEHN yuhr ee) *n.* destitution or poverty

perspective or angle (puhr SPEHK tihv) (ANG guhl) *n.* vantage point from which a photo is taken

physiology (fihz ee OL uh jee) *n.* all functions and activites of living things and their parts

pipes (pyps) *v.* says in a loud, clear, or shrill voice

pitched (pihcht) *v.* moved up and down

plotted (PLOT ihd) *v.* planned a strategy or activity

plundered (PLUHN duhrd) *v.* took something by force

pluralistic (pluhr uh LIHS tihk) *adj.* having multiple parts or aspects

point of view (poynt) (uhv) (vyoo) *n.* perspective from which the creators of a media piece approach a topic

postpone (pohst POHN) *v.* delay

prayerful (PRAIR fuhl) *adj.* appearing as if praying

predatory (PREHD uh tawr ee) *adj.* living by capturing and feeding on other animals

premonition (prehm uh NIHSH uhn) *n.* feeling that something bad will happen

primary source (PRY mehr ee) (sawrs) *n.* document, recording, image, or other source that was created at the same time as the events it describes or shows

privacy statement (PRY vuh see) (STAYT muhnt) *n.* statement from an institution that guarantees personal information will not be given out

procedure (pruh SEE juhr) *n.* steps to complete an action

profound (pruh FOWND) *adj.* intense; deep

prophet (PROF iht) *n.* person who predicts the future

propose (pruh POHZ) *v.* suggest

prosperity (pros PEHR uh tee) *n.* good fortune; success

proximity (prok SIHM uh tee) *n.* quality of being near or close to

psyche (SY kee) *n.* human mind or spirit

purified (PYUR uh fyd) *v.* cleaned by removing harmful or unwanted materials or qualities

R

radical (RAD uh kuhl) *adj.* extreme; fundamental

recurrent (rih KUR uhnt) *adj.* repeating

redemptive (rih DEHMP tihv) *adj.* serving to deliver from sorrow, make amends, or pay back

reeling (REE lihng) *adj.* going around and around in a whirling motion

reincarnation (ree ihn kahr NAY shuhn) *n.* belief that the soul reappears after death in another bodily form

relented (rih LEHNT ihd) *v.* agreed to do something after resisting it before

remorse (rih MAWRS) *n.* deep sense of regret for having done wrong

reporter stand-ups (rih POHR tuhr) (STAND uhps) *n.* shots that show a reporter looking into the camera and delivering information about a story

retaliating (rih TAL ee ayt ihng) *v.* paying back for injury; returning evil for evil

S

salient (SAY lee uhnt) *adj.* noticeable; prominent

secondary source (SEHK uhn dehr ee) (sawrs) *n.* document, recording, image, or other source that is written or created after an event by someone who did not witness it firsthand

sensationalized (sehn SAY shuh nuh lyzd) *v.* exaggerated for effect

sequence (SEE kwuhns) *n.* order, as a linear order of steps or events

serpentine (SUR puhn teen) *adj.* twisting; winding; like a serpent

sheer (sheer) *adj.* absolute; complete; utter

specter (SPEHK tuhr) *n.* ghost

speech bubble (speech) (BUHB uhl) *n.* rounded shape containing a character's words

splash (splash) *n.* large, full-page illustration

sprawling (SPRAWL ihng) *adj.* spread out

stagnation (stag NAY shuhn) *n.* state of being inactive and not moving or changing

steal (steel) *v.* move in a way that is secret or quiet

stern (sturn) *adj.* strict; severe

stock (stok) *n.* descendants of a particular individual or ethnic group; family or lineage

subsequent (SUHB suh kwuhnt) *adj.* coming after; following

summoned (SUHM uhnd) *v.* ordered someone or something to come to a place

surrounding (suh ROWN dihng) *adj.* enclosing on all sides

T

tactics (TAK tihks) *n.* military procedures

teased (teezd) *v.* made an affectionate, good-humored personal joke

technique (tehk NEEK) *n.* special method or skill

tier (tihr) *n.* row of panels in a graphic novel

tone (tohn) *n.* attitude a speaker takes toward a subject

transgression (tranz GREHSH uhn) *n.* act of breaking a law or command, or of committing a sin

treasure (TREHZH uhr) *v.* value greatly; cherish

trembling (TREHM blihng) *v.* shaking because of fear, excitement, or weakness, etc.

tremulous (TREHM yuh luhs) *adj.* trembling; quivering; timid; fearful

tribulations (trihb yuh LAY shuhnz) *n.* great trouble or misery

tryst (trihst) *n.* secret romantic meeting

U

understatement (UHN duhr stayt muhnt) *n.* downplaying a topic to make it seem less important

upheaval (uhp HEE vuhl) *n.* a lifting up

V

valid (VAL ihd) *adj.* well-founded; sound; effective

ventured (VEHN chuhrd) *v.* tried something dangerous

voluntary (VOL uhn tehr ee) *adj.* done freely

Y

yearning (YUR nihng) *n.* strong desire; longing

VOCABULARIO ACADÉMICO/ VOCABULARIO DE CONCEPTOS

A

absolute / absoluto *adj.* innegable; definitivo; completo

activist / activista *s.* partidario o defensor activo de una causa

adamant / inflexible *adj.* firme; terco

adversary / adversario *s.* oponente; enemigo

advocating / abogar *v.* hablar o escribir en favor de una causa o persona

aggregate / total *s.* conjunto; suma de varias partes

anticipated / esperado *adj.* deseado con ansias

apocryphal / apócrifo *adj.* falso; no legítimo

applicant information / información sobre el solicitante *s.* datos de una persona que está solicitando un trabajo

archival audio / grabación de archivo *s.* sonido grabado de programas de radio, televisión o películas de décadas pasadas

assimilation / asimilación *s.* proceso de adaptación a la cultura del país de adopción

attending / asistir *v.* estar presente; ocuparse de atender a alguien o algo

avenge / vengar *v.* tomar revancha; vengarse

awesome / impresionante *adj.* imponente; que causa asombro

B

bade / demandó *v.* pasado de *demandar*; pidió; requirió

banishment / destierro *s.* el estado de encontrarse desterrado o exiliado

banter / cotorreo *s.* intercambio amistoso entre dos interlocutores

bemusing / desconcertante *adj.* que confunde mucho; que deja perplejo

besieged / sitiado *adj.* bajo ataque militar

bewildered / perplejo *adj.* profundamente confundido

blundering / torpe *adj.* desmañado, inhábil

burden / carga *s.* algo que se hace o se lleva con dificultad o por obligación

C

cadence / cadencia *s.* el ritmo y la fluidez del lenguaje

caption / cartela *s.* texto que está en un recuadro aparte en las novelas gráficas o en los cómics

check box / casillero de verificación *s.* espacio en un formulario para indicar "sí", y que señala que un enunciado es verdadero

chimed / repicó *v.* sonó del modo en que suena una campana

chirruped / gorjeó *v.* hizo un sonido similar al gorjeo de un pájaro

coalescing / fusión *s.* acto de fundirse o juntarse en un solo cuerpo o lugar

coherent / cohesivo *adj.* que produce adherencia; que junta o pega

compact / compacto *adj.* denso, abarrotado

compelling / cautivador *adj.* interesante y atractivo; convincente

complacency / complacencia *s.* estado de aceptación despreocupada o irreflexiva

composed / compuesta *adj* escrita, creada, especialmente cuando se refiere a una obra musical o literaria

composition/ composición *s.* distribución o arreglo de las partes de un cuadro

concessions / concesiones *s.* permisos o prestaciones especiales

confidence / confianza *s.* reunión, especialmente la que se lleva a cabo en secreto

conflict / conflicto *s.* lucha; problema; pelea

conjecture / conjetura *s.* suposición; *v.* adivinar

conscience / conciencia *s.* sentido interior de lo que es moralmente correcto o incorrecto en nuestras acciones

correspondents / corresponsales *s.* reporteros que envían noticias sobre un determinado tema desde lugares lejanos

counterfeit / falsificación *s.* algo hecho para engañar

craft / oficio *s.* actividad que requiere ciertas destrezas

credible / creíble *adj.* verosímil; convincente

credulity / credulidad *s.* diposición a creer

culpability / culpabilidad *s.* culpa o responsabilidad en algún hecho censurable; reprobabilidad

cunning / astucia *s.* habilidad para mentir o engañar

customs / costumbres *s.* tradiciones; las acciones que por lo general realizan un grupo de personas

D

deceived / engañar *v.* mentir; burlarse de

deftly / hábilmente *adv.* de manera diestra y rápida

delicately / delicadamente *adv.* cuidadosamente; con gracia y suavidad

delivery / presentación oral *s.* la manera en que un orador pronuncia su discurso

dependency / dependencia *s.* condición de necesitar el apoyo o ayuda de otra persona

depiction / representación *s.* retrato, descripción o explicación de algo

descendants / descendientes *s.* las personas que son sucesoras de un ancentro

description / descripción *s.* texto o discurso que informa acerca de algo

desperate / desesperado *adj.* que implica algún desastre o peligro extremo ; que toma acción al perder la esperanza

destined / destinado *adj.* causado por el destino; llamado a hacer; nacido para realizar algo

devoted / dedicado *adj.* cariñoso, leal y preocupado por el bienestar de otra persona

dialogue / diálogo *s.* conversación entre los personajes de un texto, película u obra de teatro

discordant / discordante *adj.* no relacionado; fuera de lugar

disparate / dispar *adj.* de un tipo esencialmente distinto

dispatched / despachar *v.* terminar algo rápidamente

disrupt / irrumpir *v.* interrumpir; perturbar

dissemble / disimular *v.* simular, pretender

distressed / angustiado *adj.* lleno de ansiedad y preocupación

diversity / diversidad *s.* una variedad de distintos grupos étnicos o culturales

E

eerily / misteriosamente *adv.* extrañamente; inquietantemente o siniestramente

elation / euforia *s.* gran felicidad y entusiasmo

elucidate / elucidar *v.* explicar, aclarar

empathic / empático *adj.* que se caracteriza por la empatía, es decir, por la habilidad de identificarse con los sentimientos o pensamientos de otras personas

endure / perdurar *v.* durar, continuar; aguantar o tolerar algo

enthralled / embelesado *adj.* cautivado o fascinado

entranced / extasiado *adj.* maravillado o asombrado

entrusted / encargado *adj.* que se le ha asignado la responsabilidad de hacer algo o de cuidar de alguien o de algo

establishing shot / plano de situación *s.* plano que muestra el contexto de una escena en una película o video

eternal / eterno *adj.* sin final; perpetuo

evidence / evidencia *s.* datos o detalles que respaldan una posición o reclamo

exalted / exaltado *adj.* elevado

exile / exiliar *v.* castigar a una persona forzándola a abandonar un lugar de manera permanente

expedite / acelerar *v.* facilitar algo; hacer algo rápidamente

expert commentary / comentario experto *s.* información ofrecida por una persona con conocimiento especial sobre un tema

exposition / presentación *s.* texto o discurso que explica o muestra algo

express / expresar *v.* decir; transmitir; revelar

eyewitness / testigo presencial *s.* persona que ha presenciado un evento directamenete

F

factions / facciones *s.* grupos de personas que pertenecen a un partido político, club, gobierno, etc. y que se oponen a las posturas de otros grupos

faithless / ateo *adj.* que no profesa una fe religiosa; no creyente

fasting / ayunar *v.* privarse voluntariamente de la comida, generalmente por razones religiosas o espirituales

fluttered / aleteó *v.* ondeó suavemente

forbidden / prohibido *adj.* que se impide o se veta

formulate / formular *v.* construir; enunciar de forma precisa; desarrollar

framework script / borrador de guión *s.* se usa para bosquejar escenas de una película o video

fugitives / fugitivos *s.* personas que escaparon de un peligro

G

gesture / gesto *s.* movimiento de las manos o de otras partes del cuerpo que comunica algo

guise / aspecto *s.* apariencia exterior

gutter / canaleta *s.* en una novela gráfica, el espacio entre dos viñetas

H

hallowed / santificado *adj.* sagrado

hallucination / alucinación *s.* algo que se percibe pero que no tiene una existencia real

heretics / herejes *s.* personas que tienen creencias distintas de las aceptadas por su religión

human interest story / relato de interés humano *s.* una historia que se centra en los problemas personales de la gente

I

idly / descuidadamente *adv.* perezosamente; sin tomar acción

impulse / impulso *s.* súbita urgencia de actuar o de hacer algo

incredulity / incredulidad *s.* duda

indignation / indignación *s.* ira justificada; hostilidad

inevitable / inevitable *adj.* que ocurrirá; que no puede evitarse

infantile / infantil *adj.* ingenuo; propio de un niño pequeño

infatuated / prendado *adj.* estar breve pero intensamente enamorado

innovate / innovar *v.* hacer cambios; introducir algo nuevo

inscribed / inscripto *adj.* escrito o grabado

interpreter / intérprete *s.* persona que traduce de una lengua a otra de forma oral

intervened / intervino *v.* que terció entre dos grupos para ayudar a resolver diferencias

interwoven / entretejido *adj.* entrelazado; combinado

intrigued / intrigado *adj.* interesado, curioso

introduction / presentación *s.* contexto e información sobre el tema al inicio de un programa de radio

introspective / introspectivo *adj.* que tiene por costumbre analizar sus propios pensamientos y sentimientos

iridescent / iridiscente *adj.* que cambia de color cuando se lo mira desde distintos ángulos

irresolvable / irresoluble *adj.* que no se puede resolver o solucionar

L

lamentable / lamentable *adj.* penoso; doloroso; lastimoso

languished / languideció *v.* se debilitó poco a poco bajo condiciones angustiosas

lighting and color / luz y color *s.* uso de la luz, la sombra y el color en un cuadro

logical / lógico *adj.* que se basa en la razón o en un juicio sensato

luminous / luminoso *adj.* brillante, que irradia luz

M

macabre / macabro *adj.* lúgubre y horroroso

manipulated / manipulado *adj.* manejado o controlado por medio de movimientos atinados

meager / raquítico *adj.* sumamente delgado

meditative / meditativo *adj.* que tiende a pensar prolongadamente

melancholy / melancólico *adj.* triste y deprimido

memento / recuerdo *s.* souvenir; objeto que se da como recuerdo

minority / minoría *s.* grupo de personas que se distingue de alguna manera de la mayor parte de la población

misery / miseria *s.* estado de gran infortunio o desgracia

montage / montaje *s.* grupo de imágenes que se muestran rápidamente, una tras otra, para dar la impresión de que es una sola imagen

mortality / mortalidad *s.* seguridad de que en algún momento se va a morir

mutiny / motín *s.* rebelión o revuelta contra la autoridad legítima, especialmente la llevada a cabo por los marineros o los soldados contra los oficiales

N

naturalization / naturalización *s.* proceso de hacerse ciudadano de un país que no es el de su nacimiento

notation / anotación *s.* apunte; información que se pone por escrito

O

oppression / opresión *s.* tratamiento cruel o injusto

oratory / oratoria *s.* arte formal de hablar en público

P

panel / viñeta *s.* cada dibujo de una página, por lo general enmarcado por un borde

pardon / perdón *s.* indulto de un delito

pathos / patetismo *s.* cualidad que produce un sentimiento de tristeza o de compasión

penury / penuria *s.* indigencia o pobreza

perspective or angle / ángulo o perspectiva *s.* punto desde el cual se toma una foto

physiology / fisiología *s.* conjunto de funciones y actividades de los seres vivos y sus partes

pipes / chillar *v.* hablar en voz alta, clara o muy aguda

pitched / cabeceó *v.* se movió hacia arriba y hacia abajo

plotted / tramó *v.* planificó una estrategia o actividad

plundered / saqueó *v.* tomó algo por la fuerza

pluralistic / pluralista *adj.* que tiene múltiples partes o aspectos

point of view / punto de vista *s.* perspectiva desde la cual se observa lo que se narra

postpone / posponer *v.* retrasar

prayerful / piadoso *adj.* que parece que estuviera rezando

predatory / predatorio *adj.* que se alimenta de los animales que captura

premonition / premonición *s.* sensación de que algo malo va a pasar

primary source / fuente primaria *s.* documento, grabación, imagen u otra fuente original creada al mismo tiempo que los eventos que describe o muestra

privacy statement / aviso de privacidad *s.* garantía de una institución de que no se compartirá información personal

procedure / procedimiento *s.* conjunto de pasos para realizar una acción

profound / profundo *adj.* intenso; hondo

prophet / profeta *s.* persona que predice el futuro

propose / proponer *v.* sugerir

prosperity / prosperidad *s.* buena suerte; éxito

proximity / proximidad *s.* cualidad de estar cerca o próximo a algo

psyche / psiquis *s.* espíritu o mente humana

purified / purificado *adj.* limpio de todo atributo o materia dañina o no deseada

R

radical / radical *adj.* muy cambiado

recurrent / recurrente *adj.* que se repite

redemptive / redentor *adj.* que sirve para librar del dolor, para reparar o compensar

reeling / girar *v.* dar vueltas y más vueltas en un movimiento circular

reincarnation / reencarnación *s.* creencia de que, después de la muerte, el alma reaparece en otro cuerpo o forma material

relented / cedió *v.* accedió a hacer algo a lo que se había negado en el pasado

remorse / remordimiento *s.* un profundo sentido de arrepentimiento por haber hecho algo malo

reporter stand-ups / reportero *in situ* *s.* toma que muestra al reportero mirando a la cámara e informando sobre el evento que está cubriendo

retaliating / tomar represalias *v.* vengarse por un daño recibido; devolver un perjuicio con otro

S

salient / sobresaliente *adj.* notable, prominente

secondary source / fuente secundaria *s.* documento, grabación, imagen u otra fuente escrita o creada después de un evento por alguien que no lo presenció

sensationalized / hacer sensacionalismo *v.* exagerar una situación para provocar un efecto sensacionalista o tremendista

sequence / secuencia *s.* serie u orden lineal de pasos o sucesos

serpentine / serpentino *adj.* sinuoso; serpenteante, como el movimiento de una serpiente

sheer / transparente *adj.* muy fino; cuerpo a través del cual se puede ver

specter / espectro *s.* fantasma

speech bubble / globo (historieta) *s.* forma circular que contiene las palabras de los personajes

splash / *splash page* *s.* en una novela gráfica o cómic un dibujo de toda una página

sprawling / expandido *adj.* extendido

stagnation / estancamiento *s.* estado de inactividad, de no moverse ni cambiar

steal / escabullirse *v.* moverse en secreto o silenciosamente

stern / estricto *adj.* rígido; severo

stock / linaje *s.* línea de descendencia de un determinado individuo o grupo étnico; familia o antepasados

subsequent / subsecuente *adj.* que viene después; siguiente

summoned / convocó *v.* le ordenó a alguien o algo que fuera a un lugar determinado

surrounding / rodear *adj.* encerrando por todos lados

T

tactics / tácticas *s.* métodos militares

teased / bromeó *v.* hizo un chiste afectuoso, con buen humor

technique / técnica *s.* destreza o método especial

tier / hilera *s.* cada fila de viñetas de una novela gráfica

tone / tono *s.* la actitud que toma el hablante hacia su tema

transgression / transgresión *s.* la acción de violar una ley o un mandato, o de cometer un pecado

treasure / atesorar *v.* valorar enormemente; estimar mucho

trembling / tembloroso *adj.* que se agita o tirita por temor, entusiasmo, debilidad, etc.

tremulous / trémulo *adj.* tembloroso; estremecido; tímido; temeroso

tribulations / tribulaciones *s.* conjunto de adversidades o penurias

tryst / cita *s.* encuentro amoroso secreto

U

understatement / subestimación *s.* la acción de minimizar un tema para que parezca menos importante

upheaval / revuelta *s.* levantamiento

valid / válido *adj.* bien fundamentado; sensato; efectivo

ventured / arriesgó *v.* intentó algo peligroso

voluntary / voluntario *adj.* hecho libremente

Y

yearning / anhelo *s.* deseo profundo; añoranza

LITERARY TERMS HANDBOOK

ADAPTATION An ***adaptation*** is a work of art that uses the characters and tells the story originally presented in another work of art. Often, the adaptation is in a different form. A novel or play becomes a film, for example, or a poem becomes a story.

ALLITERATION ***Alliteration*** is the repetition of initial consonant sounds. Writers use alliteration to give emphasis to words, to imitate sounds, and to create musical effects.

ALLUSION An ***allusion*** is a reference to a well-known person, place, event, literary work, or work of art.

ANALOGY An ***analogy*** makes a comparison between two or more things that are similar in some ways but otherwise unalike.

ANECDOTE An ***anecdote*** is a brief story about an interesting, amusing, or strange event told to entertain or to make a point.

ANTAGONIST An ***antagonist*** is a character or force in conflict with a main character, or protagonist.

ANTITHESIS ***Antithesis*** is a form of parallelism that emphasizes strong contrasts.

ARCHETYPE An ***archetype*** is is a type of character, detail, image, or situation that appears in literature throughout history. Some critics believe that archetypes reveal deep truths about human experience.

ARGUMENT An ***argument*** is writing or speech that attempts to convince the reader to adopt a particular opinion or course of action. An argument is a logical way of presenting a belief, conclusion, or stance. A good argument is supported with reasoning and evidence.

ASIDE An ***aside*** is a short speech delivered by a character in a play in order to express his or her true thoughts and feelings. Traditionally, the aside is directed to the audience and is presumed to be inaudible to the other actors.

ASSONANCE ***Assonance*** is the repetition of vowel sounds followed by different consonants in two or more stressed syllables.

AUTHOR'S PURPOSE An ***author's purpose*** is his or her reason for writing. The four general purposes for writing are to inform, to persuade, to entertain, and to reflect.

AUTOBIOGRAPHICAL WRITING ***Autobiographical writing*** is any type of nonfiction in which an author tells his or her own story.

AUTOBIOGRAPHY An ***autobiography*** is a form of nonfiction in which a writer tells his or her own life story. An autobiography may tell about the person's whole life or only a part of it.

BIBLIOGRAPHY A ***bibliography*** or "works cited" lists all research sources used for an informative essay in an approved style.

BIOGRAPHY A ***biography*** is a form of nonfiction in which a writer tells the life story of another person. Biographies have been written about many famous people, historical and contemporary, but they can also be written about "ordinary" people.

BLANK VERSE ***Blank verse*** is poetry written in unrhymed iambic pentameter lines. This verse form was widely used by William Shakespeare.

CAUSE-AND-EFFECT CHAIN A single cause, which results in an effect, which leads to a second effect, which causes a third effect, and so on, is a ***cause-and-effect chain.***

CAUSE-AND-EFFECT RELATIONSHIP A cause-and-effect relationship shows how one event or situation leads to another.

CENTRAL IDEA The ***central idea*** is the main idea the author wants the audience to understand and remember

CHARACTER A ***character*** is a person or an animal that takes part in the action of a literary work. The main character, or protagonist, is the most important character in a story. This character often changes in some important way as a result of the story's events.

Characters are sometimes classified as round or flat, dynamic or static. A complex, or *round character*, shows many different traits—faults as well as virtues. A *flat character* shows only one trait. A *dynamic character* develops and grows during the course of the story; a *static character* does not change.

CHARACTERIZATION ***Characterization*** is the act of creating and developing a character. In ***direct characterization,*** the author directly states a character's traits.

In ***indirect characterization,*** an author provides clues about a character by describing what a character looks like, does, and says, as well as how other characters react to him or her. It is up to the reader to draw conclusions about the character based on this indirect information.

The most effective indirect characterizations usually result from showing characters acting or speaking.

CHARGED LANGUAGE Words or phrases that evoke strong positive or negative reactions are referred to as ***charged language.***

CLAIM The ***claim*** of a text is the key message that the writer wants to communicate about a topic.

CLARIFICATION A ***clarification*** focuses on a specific part of a response, sometimes simplifying the original idea and other times providing more detail.

COMIC RELIEF ***Comic relief*** is a technique that is used to interrupt a serious part of a literary work by introducing a humorous character or situation.

CONFLICT A ***conflict*** is a struggle between opposing forces. Characters in conflict form the basis of stories, novels, and plays.

There are two kinds of conflict: external and internal. In an ***external conflict,*** the main character struggles against an outside force.

An ***internal conflict*** involves a character in conflict with himself or herself.

CONNOTATION The ***connotation*** of a word is the set of ideas associated with it in addition to its explicit meaning.

CONSONANCE ***Consonance*** is the repetition of final consonant sounds in stressed syllables with different vowel sounds, as in *hat* and *sit*.

COUPLET A ***couplet*** is a pair of rhyming lines, usually of the same length and meter. Couplets are often found in poems and in plays written in verse.

CRITICISM ***Criticism*** is a form of argumentative writing in which an author expresses an opinion about a created work, such as a book, a film, or a performance.

DENOTATION The ***denotation*** of a word is its dictionary meaning, independent of other associations that the word may have.

DESCRIPTION A ***description*** is a portrait in words of a person, a place, or an object. Descriptive writing uses sensory details, those that appeal to the senses: sight, hearing, taste, smell, and touch. Description can be found in all types of writing. Rudolfo Anaya's essay "A Celebration of Grandfathers" contains descriptive passages.

DIALOGUE A ***dialogue*** is a conversation between characters that may reveal their traits and advance the action of a narrative. In fiction or nonfiction, quotation marks indicate a speaker's exact words, and a new paragraph usually indicates a change of speaker.

DICTION ***Diction*** refers to an author's choice of words, especially with regard to range of vocabulary, use of slang and colloquial language, and level of formality.

DRAMA A ***drama*** is a story written to be performed by actors. The script of a drama is made up of ***dialogue***—the words the actors say—and ***stage directions,*** which are comments on how and where action happens.

The drama's ***setting*** is the time and place in which the action occurs. It is indicated by one or more sets, including furniture and backdrops, that suggest interior or exterior scenes. *Props* are objects, such as a sword or a cup of tea, that are used onstage.

At the beginning of most plays, a brief ***exposition*** gives the audience some background information about the characters and the situation. Just as in a story or novel, the plot of a drama is built around characters in conflict.

Dramas are divided into large units called ***acts,*** which are divided into smaller units called ***scenes***. A long play may include many sets that change with the scenes, or it may indicate a change of scene with lighting.

DRAMATIC IRONY ***Dramatic irony*** is a contradiction between what a character thinks and what the audience knows to be true. For example: If a character tries desperately to crack a safe when the audience already knows the safe is empty, dramatic irony is created, causing humor or tension.

ELLIPSES ***Ellipses*** are used to show omitted words or sentences in quoted texts.

END-STOPPED LINE An ***end-stopped line*** is one in which both the grammatical structure and sense are complete at the end of the line.

EPIC An ***epic*** is a long narrative poem about the deeds of gods or heroes.

An epic is elevated in style and usually follows certain patterns. The poet begins by announcing the subject and asking a Muse—one of the nine goddesses of the arts, literature, and sciences—to help. An *epic hero* is the larger-than-life central character in an epic. Through behavior and deeds, the epic hero displays qualities that are valued by the society in which the epic originated.

See also ***Epic Simile*** and ***Narrative Poem***.

EPIC SIMILE An ***epic simile,*** also called ***Homeric simile,*** is an elaborate comparison of unlike subjects.

ESSAY An ***essay*** is a short nonfiction work about a particular subject. While classification is difficult, four types of essays are sometimes identified.

A *descriptive essay* seeks to convey an impression about a person, place, or object.

A *narrative essay* tells a true story.

An *expository essay* gives information, discusses ideas, or explains a process.

An *explanatory* essay describes and summarizes information gathered from a number of sources on a concept.

A *persuasive essay* tries to convince readers to do something or to accept the writer's point of view.

EXPOSITION ***Exposition*** is writing or speech that explains a process or presents information. In the plot of a story or drama, the exposition is the part of the work that introduces the characters, the setting, and the basic situation.

EXTENDED METAPHOR In an ***extended metaphor,*** as in regular metaphor, a writer speaks or writes of a subject as though it were something else. An extended metaphor sustains the comparison for several lines or for an entire poem.

FATE ***Fate*** is a destiny over which a hero has little or no control.

FEATURE ARTICLES ***Feature articles*** are a type of journalism that focuses on a specific event or situation.

FICTION ***Fiction*** is prose writing that tells about imaginary characters and events. The term is usually used for novels and short stories, but it also applies to dramas and narrative poetry. Some writers rely on their imaginations alone to create their works of fiction. Others base their fiction on actual events and people, to which they add invented characters, dialogue, and plot situations.

FIGURATIVE LANGUAGE ***Figurative language*** is writing or speech not meant to be interpreted literally. It is often used to create vivid impressions by setting up comparisons between dissimilar things.

Some frequently used figures of speech are ***metaphors, similes,*** and ***personifications.***

FLASHBACK A ***flashback*** is a means by which authors present material that occurred earlier than the present tense of the narrative. Authors may include this material in a character's memories, dreams, or accounts of past events.

FOIL A ***foil*** is a character who provides a contrast to another character. In *Romeo and Juliet*, the fiery temper of Tybalt serves as a foil to the good nature of Benvolio.

FOLLOW-UP QUESTION A ***follow-up question*** builds on the interview subject's response, clarifying and deepening answers.

FORESHADOWING ***Foreshadowing*** is the use in a literary work of clues that suggest events that have yet to occur. This technique helps create suspense, keeping readers wondering about what will happen next.

FRAME STORY A ***frame story*** is a story that brackets—or frames—another story or group of stories. This device creates a story-within-a-story narrative structure.

FREE VERSE ***Free verse*** is poetry not written in a regular pattern of meter or rhyme.

GENRE A ***genre*** is a category or type of literature. Literature is commonly divided into three major genres: poetry, prose, and drama. Each major genre is in turn divided into smaller genres, as follows:

1. **Poetry:** Lyric Poetry, Concrete Poetry, Dramatic Poetry, Narrative Poetry, and Epic Poetry
2. **Prose:** Fiction (Novels and Short Stories) and Nonfiction (Biography, Autobiography, Letters, Essays, and Reports)
3. **Drama:** Serious Drama and Tragedy, Comic Drama, Melodrama, and Farce

HYPERBOLE A ***hyperbole*** is a deliberate exaggeration or overstatement.

IAMB An ***iamb*** is an unstressed syllable followed by a stressed syllable.

IAMBIC PENTAMETER Blank verse written in ***iambic pentameter*** has five iambs, called "feet," in each line.

IN MEDIA RES In media res means "in the middle of things."

IDIOM An ***idiom*** is an expression that is characteristic of a language, region, community, or class of people. *Idiomatic expressions* often arise from figures of speech and therefore cannot be understood literally.

INTERVIEW An ***interview*** is an exchange of ideas between an interviewer and an expert or someone who has had a unique experience. The basic structure of an interview is the Q&A (question and answer) format.

IMAGE An ***image*** is a word or phrase that appeals to one or more of the five senses—sight, hearing, touch, taste, or smell. Writers use images to re-create sensory experiences in words.

IMAGERY ***Imagery*** is the descriptive or figurative language used in literature to create word pictures for the reader. These pictures, or images, are created by details of sight, sound, taste, touch, smell, or movement.

INTERNAL MONOLOGUE To show a character's thoughts with more dimension, an author uses ***internal monologue,*** a kind of "conversation" a character has with himself or herself.

INTERVIEW An ***interview*** is an exchange of ideas between an interviewer and an expert or someone who has had a unique experience.

IRONY ***Irony*** is the general term for literary techniques that portray differences between appearance and reality, or expectation and result. In ***verbal irony,*** words are used to suggest the opposite of what is meant. In ***dramatic irony,*** there is a contradiction between what a character thinks and what the reader or audience knows to be true. In ***situational irony,*** an event occurs that directly contradicts the expectations of the characters, the reader, or the audience.

JOURNALISM ***Journalism*** is a type of nonfiction writing that focuses on current events and nonfiction subjects of general interest to the public.

LYRIC POEM A ***lyric poem*** is a highly musical verse that expresses the thoughts, observations, and feelings of a single speaker.

MEMOIR A ***memoir*** is a limited kind of autobiographical writing that focuses on one period or aspect of the writer's life.

METAPHOR A ***metaphor*** is a figure of speech in which one thing is spoken of as though it were something else. Unlike a simile, which compares two things using *like* or *as*, a metaphor implies a comparison between them.

MONOLOGUE A ***monologue*** in a play is a speech by one character that, unlike a ***soliloquy,*** is addressed to another character or characters.

MOOD ***Mood,*** or ***atmosphere,*** is the feeling created in the reader by a literary work or passage. The mood is often suggested by descriptive details. Often the mood can be described in a single word, such as lighthearted, frightening, or despairing.

MOTIVE A ***motive*** is a reason for an action.

NARRATION ***Narration*** is writing that tells a story. The act of telling a story in speech is also called narration. Novels and short stories are fictional narratives. Nonfiction works—such as news stories, biographies, and autobiographies—are also narratives. A narrative poem tells a story in verse.

NARRATIVE A ***narrative*** is a story told in fiction, nonfiction, poetry, or drama.

NARRATIVE NONFICTION Writing that tells a real-life story is called ***narrative nonfiction.***

NARRATIVE POINT OF VIEW A ***narrative point of view*** is the vantage point from which a fiction writer chooses to tell a story.

NARRATOR A ***narrator*** is a speaker or character who tells a story. The writer's choice of narrator determines the story's ***point of view***, which directs the type and amount of information the writer reveals.

When a character in the story tells the story, that character is a *first-person narrator*. This narrator may be a major character, a minor character, or just a witness. Readers see only what this character sees, hear only what he or she hears, and so on. The first-person narrator may or may not be reliable.

When a voice outside the story narrates, the story has a third-person narrator. An omniscient, or all-knowing, third-person narrator can tell readers what any character thinks and feels. A limited third-person narrator sees the world through one character's eyes and reveals only that character's thoughts.

NONFICTION ***Nonfiction*** is prose writing that presents and explains ideas or that tells about real people, places, ideas, or events. To be classified as nonfiction, a work must be true. "Single Room, Earth View" is a nonfictional account of the view of Earth from space.

NOVEL A ***novel*** is a long work of fiction. It has a plot that explores characters in conflict. A novel may also have one or more subplots, or minor stories, and several themes.

ONOMATOPOEIA ***Onomatopoeia*** is the use of words that imitate sounds. *Whirr, thud,* and *hiss* are examples.

ORAL TRADITION The ***oral tradition*** is the passing of songs, stories, and poems from generation to generation by word of mouth. Many folk songs, ballads, fairy tales, legends, and myths originated in the oral tradition.

See also *Myth.*

OXYMORON An ***oxymoron*** is a combination of words, or parts of words, that contradict each other. Examples are "deafening silence," "honest thief," "wise fool," and "bittersweet."

PANTOUM A ***pantoum*** is an old, formal poetic structure consisting of a series of quatrains, or four-line stanzas.

PARADOX A ***paradox*** is a statement that seems contradictory but may actually be true. Because a paradox is surprising, it catches the reader's attention.

PARALLELISM ***Parallelism*** is the repetition of a grammatical structure in order to create a rhythm and make words more memorable.

PARAPHRASE A ***paraphrase*** is a restatement of a passage from an original text

PERSONIFICATION ***Personification*** is a type of figurative language in which a nonhuman subject is given human characteristics.

PERSUASION ***Persuasion*** is writing or speech that attempts to convince the reader to adopt a particular opinion or course of action. An ***argument*** is a logical way of presenting a belief, conclusion, or stance. A good argument is supported with reasoning and evidence.

PERSUASIVE APPEALS ***Persuasive appeals*** are methods of informing or convincing readers to see something in a new way.

PERSUASIVE ESSAY A ***persuasive essay*** is a short nonfiction work in which a writer seeks to convince the reader to think or act in a certain way.

PERSUASIVE SPEECH In a ***persuasive speech,*** the speaker uses rhetoric, logic, and oral-presentation techniques to convince listeners to think or act in a certain way.

PLOT ***Plot*** is the sequence of events in a literary work. In most novels, dramas, short stories, and narrative poems, the plot involves both characters and a central conflict. The plot usually begins with an ***exposition*** that introduces the setting, the characters, and the basic situation. This is followed by the ***inciting incident***, which introduces the central conflict. The conflict then increases during the ***development*** until it reaches a high point of interest or suspense, the ***climax***. All the events leading up to the climax make up the ***rising action***. The climax is followed by the ***falling action***, which leads to the ***denouement***, or ***resolution***, in which a general insight or change is conveyed.

POETIC STRUCTURE The basic structures of poetry are lines and stanzas. A ***line*** is a group of words arranged in a row. A line of poetry may break, or end, in different ways. An ***end-stopped line*** is one in which both the grammatical structure and sense are complete at the end of the line. A ***run-on,*** or ***enjambed, line*** is one in which both the grammatical structure and sense continue past the end of the line.

POETRY ***Poetry*** is one of the three major types of literature, the others being prose and drama. Most poems make use of highly concise, musical, and emotionally charged language. Many also make use of imagery, figurative language, and special devices of sound such as rhyme. Poems are often divided into lines and stanzas and often employ regular rhythmical patterns, or meters. However, some poems are written out just like prose, while others are written in free verse.

POINT OF VIEW An author's ***point of view*** is the perspective from which events are told or described.

PRIMARY SOURCE A ***primary source*** is raw material or first-hand information about what is being studied.

PROSE ***Prose*** is the ordinary form of written language. Most writing that is not poetry, drama, or song is considered prose. Prose is one of the major genres of literature and occurs in two forms: fiction and nonfiction.

PUN A ***pun*** is a play on words involving a word with two or more different meanings or two words that sound alike but have different meanings. In *Romeo and Juliet*, the dying Mercutio makes a pun involving two meanings of the word *grave*, "serious" and "burial site": "Ask for me tomorrow, and you shall find me a grave man" (Act III, Scene i, lines 92–93).

QUATRAIN A ***quatrain*** is a stanza or poem made up of four lines, usually with a definite rhythm and rhyme scheme.

QUOTATION A speaker's exact words are a ***direct quotation*** and are shown using quotation marks.

REPETITION ***Repetition*** is the use of any element of language—a sound, a word, a phrase, a clause, or a sentence—more than once.

Poets use many kinds of repetition. Alliteration, assonance, rhyme, and rhythm are repetitions of certain sounds and sound patterns. A refrain is a repeated line or group of lines. In both prose and poetry, repetition is used for musical effects and for emphasis.

RESTATEMENT ***Restatements,*** or paraphrases, help an interviewer make sure the audience understands the main point the interviewee is communicating.

RHETORIC ***Rhetoric*** refers to language devices, especially the art of speaking or writing effectively.

RHETORICAL DEVICES ***Rhetorical devices*** are special patterns of words and ideas that create emphasis and stir emotion, especially in speeches or other oral presentations. ***Parallelism,*** for example, is the repetition of a grammatical structure in order to create a rhythm and make words more memorable.

Other common rhetorical devices include: ***analogy***, drawing comparisions between two unlike things; ***charged language***, words that appeal to the emotions; ***restatement***, expressing the same idea in different words; and ***rhetorical questions***, questions with obvious answers.

RUN-ON, OR ENJAMBED, LINE A ***run-on, or enjambed, line*** is one in which both the grammatical structure and sense continue past the end of the line.

See also ***Meter***.

SCIENCE FICTION ***Science fiction*** is writing that tells about imaginary events involving science or technology. Many science-fiction stories are set in the future.

SENSORY LANGUAGE ***Sensory language*** is writing or speech that uses details to appeal to one or more of the senses.

SETTING The ***setting*** of a literary work is the time and lace of the action. Time can include not only the historical period—past, present, or future—but also a specific year, season, or time of day. Place may involve not only the geographical place—a region, country, state, or town—but also the social, economic, or cultural environment.

In some stories, setting serves merely as a backdrop for action, a context in which the characters move and speak. In others, however, setting is a crucial element.

SHORT STORY A ***short story*** is a brief work of fiction. In most short stories, one main character faces a conflict that is resolved in the plot of the story. Great craftsmanship must go into the writing of a good story, for it has to accomplish its purpose in relatively few words.

SIMILE A ***simile*** is a figure of speech in which the words *like* or *as* are used to compare two apparently dissimilar items. The comparison, however, surprises the reader into a fresh perception by finding an unexpected likeness.

SITUATIONAL IRONY ***Situational irony*** occurs when events in a story go directly against the expectations of the main characters or the readers.

SOCIAL AND HISTORICAL CONTEXT The circumstances of the time and place in which a story occurs are referred to as ***social and historical context.***

SOLILOQUY A ***soliloquy*** is a long speech expressing the thoughts of a character alone on stage.

SOUND DEVICES A ***sound device*** is a technique used by a poets and writers to emphasize the sound relationships among words in order to create musical and emotional effects and emphasize a poem's meaning. These devices include ***alliteration, consonance, assonance, onomatopoeia,*** and ***rhyme.***

SPEAKER The ***speaker*** is the imaginary voice assumed by the writer of a poem. In many poems, the speaker is not identified by name, and may be may be a person, an animal, a thing, or an abstraction.

SPECIFIC DETAILS ***Specific details*** are used by both fiction and nonfiction writers to support and develop a central idea or theme.

STAGE DIRECTIONS ***Stage directions*** are notes included in a drama to describe how the work is to be performed or staged. These instructions are printed in italics and are not spoken aloud. They are used to describe sets, lighting, sound effects, and the appearance, personalities, and movements of characters.

STANZA A ***stanza*** is a repeated grouping of two or more lines in a poem that often share a pattern of rhythm and rhyme. Stanzas are sometimes named according to the number of lines they have—for example, a ***couplet,*** two lines; a ***quatrain,*** four lines; a ***sestet,*** six lines; and an ***octave***, eight lines.

STYLE ***Style*** refers to an author's unique way of writing. Elements determining style include diction; tone; characteristic use of figurative language, dialect, or rhythmic devices; and syntax.

SUMMARY A ***summary*** is a concise, complete, and accurate overview of a text.

SUPPORTING DETAILS Pieces of information that illustrate, expand on, or prove an author's ideas are called ***supporting details.*** Supporting details can validate an argument, provide information, or add interest.

SYMBOL A ***symbol*** is anything that stands for something else. In addition to having its own meaning and reality, a symbol also represents abstract ideas. For example, a flag is a piece of cloth, but it also represents the idea of a country.

THEME A ***theme*** is a central message or insight into life revealed through a literary work. The theme of a literary work may be stated directly or implied. When the theme of a work is implied, readers think about what the work suggests about people or life.

Archetypal themes are those that occur in folklore and literature across the world and throughout history.

TONE The ***tone*** of a literary work is the writer's attitude toward his or her audience and subject.

TRAGEDY A ***tragedy*** is a work of literature, especially a play, that results in a catastrophe or great misfortune for the main character, or *tragic hero*. In ancient Greek drama, the main character was always a significant person—a king or a hero—and the cause of the tragedy was a *tragic flaw*, or weakness, in his or her character. In modern drama, the main character can be an ordinary person, and the cause of the tragedy can be some evil in society itself.

TRAGIC FLAW A ***tragic flaw*** is a personality defect that contributes to a hero's choice, and thus, to his or her tragic downfall.

TRAVEL JOURNALISM ***Travel journalism*** is a type of literary nonfiction in which a writer describes the experience of visiting a particular place.

VISUAL ESSAY A ***visual essay*** is an exploration of a topic that conveys its ideas through visual elements as well as language. Like a standard essay, a visual essay presents an author's views of a single topic. Unlike other essays, however, much of the meaning in a visual essay is conveyed through illustrations or photographs.

VIVID LANGUAGE ***Vivid language*** is strong, precise words that bring ideas to life.

VOICE ***Voice*** is a writer's distinctive "sound" or way of "speaking" on the page. It is related to such elements as word choice, sentence structure, and tone. It is similar to an individual's speech style and can be described in the same way—fast, slow, blunt, meandering, breathless, and so on.

Voice resembles ***style,*** an author's typical way of writing, but style usually refers to a quality that can be found throughout an author's body of work, while an author's voice may sometimes vary from work to work.

MANUAL DE TÉRMINOS LITERARIOS

ADAPTACIÓN Una ***adaptación*** es una obra de arte que incluye los personajes y cuenta la misma historia que se presentó originalmente en otra obra de arte. A menudo, la adaptación adopta una forma diferente. Una novela u obra de teatro puede transformarse en una película, por ejemplo, o un poema puede transformarse en un cuento.

ALITERACIÓN La ***aliteración*** es la repetición de los sonidos consonantes iniciales. Los escritores usan la aliteración para dar énfasis a las palabras, para imitar sonidos y para crear efectos de musicalida.

ALUSIÓN Una ***alusión*** es una referencia a una persona, lugar, hecho, obra literaria u obra de arte muy conocida.

ANALOGÍA Una ***analogía*** establece una comparación entre dos o más cosas que son parecidas en algunos aspectos pero se diferencian en otros.

ANÉCDOTA Una ***anécdota*** es un relato breve sobre un hecho interesante, divertido o extraño, que se narra con el fin de entretener o decir algo importante.

ANTAGONISTA Un ***antagonista*** es un personaje o fuerza en conflicto con el personaje principal o protagonista.

ANTÍTESIS Una ***antítesis*** es una forma de paralelismo que enfatiza los contrastes más importantes.

ARQUETIPO Un ***arquetipo*** es un tipo de personaje, detalle, imagen o situación que reaparece en la literatura a través de la historia. Algunos críticos piensan que los arquetipos revelan verdades profundas sobre la experiencia humana.

ARGUMENTO Un ***argumento*** es un escrito o discurso que trata de convencer al lector para que siga una acción o adopte una opinión en particular. Un argumento es una manera lógica de presentar una creencia, una conclusión o una postura. Un buen argumento se respalda con razonamientos y pruebas.

APARTE Un ***aparte*** es un parlamente breve en boca de un personaje en una obra de teatro, en el que expresa sus verdaderos pensamientos y sentimientos. Tradicionalmente, los apartes se dirigen a la audiencia y se suponen inaudibles a los otros personajes.

ASONANCIA La ***asonancia*** es la repetición de los sonidos vocálicos seguidos de distintas consonantes en dos o más sílabas acentuadas.

PROPÓSITO DEL AUTOR El ***propósito del autor*** es su razón para escribir. Los cuatro propósitos generales del autor son: informar, persuadir, entretener y reflexionar.

ESCRITURA AUTOBIOGRÁFICA La ***escritura autobiográfica*** es cualquier forma de no-ficción en la que el autor narra la historia de su vida

AUTOBIOGRAFÍA Una ***autobiografía*** es una forma de no-ficción en la que el escritor cuenta su propia vida. Una autobiografía puede contar toda la vida de una persona o solo una parte de ella.

BIBLIOGRAFÍA Una ***bibliografía*** o lista de "obras citadas" enumera todas las fuentes de investigación usadas para escribir un ensayo informativo en un estilo aprobado.

BIOGRAFÍA Una ***biografía*** es una forma de no-ficción en la que un escritor cuenta la vida de otra persona. Se han escrito biografías de muchas personas famosas de la historia o del mundo contemporáneo, pero también pueden escribirse biografías de personas comunes.

VERSO BLANCO El ***verso blanco*** es poesía escrita en líneas de pentámetros yámbicos sin rima. Esta forma de verso fue muy utilizada por William Shakespeare.

CADENA DE CAUSA Y CONSECUENCIA Una causa única, que tiene como resultado una consecuencia, la cual lleva a una segunda consecuencia, que a su vez causa una tercera consecuencia, etcétera, constituye una ***cadena de causa y consecuencia.***

RELACIÓN DE CAUSA Y CONSECUENCIA Una ***relación de causa y consecuencia*** muestra como un suceso o situación lleva a otro.

IDEA CENTRAL La ***idea central*** es la idea principal que el autor quiere que la audiencia comprenda y recuerde.

PERSONAJE Un ***personaje*** es una persona o animal que participa de la acción en una obra literaria. El personaje principal, o protagonista, es el personaje más importante del relato. Este personaje a menudo cambia de una manera importante como resultado de los eventos que se suceden en el cuento.

Los personajes a veces son clasificados como complejos o chatos, dinámicos o estáticos. Un *personaje complejo* muestra muchos rasgos diferentes—tanto faltas como virtudes. Un *personaje chato* muestra solo un rasgo. Un *personaje dinámico* se desarrolla y crece en el curso del relato; mientras que un *personaje estático* no cambia.

CARACTERIZACIÓN La ***caracterización*** es el acto de crear y desarrollar un personaje. En una ***caracterización directa,*** el autor expresa explícitamente los rasgos de un personaje. En una ***caracterización indirecta,*** el autor proporciona claves sobre el personaje, describiendo el aspecto del personaje, qué hace, qué dice, así como la manera en que otros personajes lo ven y reaccionan a él. Al lector le corresponde sacar conclusiones sobre los personajes basándose en información indirecta.

La caracterización indirecta más efectiva resulta por lo general de mostrar cómo hablan y actúan los personajes.

LENGUAJE EMOCIONALMENTE CARGADO Se conoce como ***lenguaje emocionalmente cargado*** a las palabras o frases que evocan reacciones intensas, ya sean positivas o negativas.

AFIRMACIÓN La ***afirmación*** de un texto es el mensaje clave que el escritor quiere comunicar acerca de un tema.

ACLARACIÓN La ***aclaración*** se centra en una parte determinada de la respuesta, simplificando la idea original o aportando más detalles.

ALIVIO CÓMICO El ***alivio cómico*** es una técnica que se usa para interrumpir una parte seria de una obra literaria introduciendo personajes o situaciones jocosas.

CONFLICTO Un ***conflicto*** es una lucha entre fuerzas opuestas. Los personajes en conflicto forman la base de cuentos, novelas y obras de teatro.

Hay dos tipos de conflicto: externos e internos. En un ***conflicto externo***, el personaje principal lucha contra una fuerza externa.

Un ***conflicto interno*** atañe a un personaje que entra en conflicto consigo mismo.

CONNOTACIÓN La ***connotación*** de una palabra es el conjunto de ideas que se asocian a ella, además de su significado explícito.

CONSONANCIA La ***consonancia*** es la repetición de los sonidos consonantes finales de sílabas acentuadas con distintos sonidos vocálicos, como en *hat* and *sit*.

PAREADO Un ***dístico*** o ***pareado*** es un par de versos rimados, por lo general de la misma extensión y metro. Por lo general, los pareados se usan en poemas y en obras de teatro escritas en verso.

CRÍTICA La ***crítica*** es un texto argumentativo en el que un autor expresa su opinión acerca de una obra como, por ejemplo, un libro, una película o una actuación.

DENOTACIÓN La ***denotación*** de una palabra es su significado en un diccionario, independientemente de otras asociaciones que la palabra suscita.

DESCRIPCIÓN Una ***descripción*** es un retrato en palabras de una persona, un lugar o un objeto. La escritura descriptiva utiliza detalles sensoriales, es decir, aquellos que apelan a los sentidos: la vista, el oído, el gusto, el olfato y el tacto. La descripción puede encontrarse en todo tipo de escritors. El ensayo de Rudolfo Anaya, "Una celebración de los abuelos" incluye pasajes descriptivos.

DIÁLOGO Un ***diálogo*** es una conversación entre personajes que puede revelar sus rasgos y hacer progresar la acción de un relato. Ya sea en un género de ficción o de no ficción —en inglés— las comillas reproducen las palabras exactas de un personaje, y un nuevo párrafo indica un cambio de personaje.

DICCIÓN La ***dicción*** comprende la elección de palabras que hace el autor, especialmente en relación a un abanico de posibilidades, al uso de un lenguaje coloquial o jerga, y al nivel de formalidad que utilizan tanto el narrador como los personajes.

DRAMA Un ***drama*** es una historia escrita para ser representada por actores. El guión de un drama está constituido por ***diálogo*** —las palabras que dicen los actores— y por ***direcciones escénicas***, que son los comentarios acerca de cómo y dónde se sitúa la acción.

La ***ambientación*** es la época y el lugar donde sucedes la acción. Se indica a través de una o varias escenografías, que incluyen el mobiliario y el fondo, o telón de fondo, que sugieren si las escenas son interiores o exteriores. La *tramoya o utilería* son los objetos, tales como una espada o una taza de té, que se usan en escena.

Al principio de la mayoría de los dramas, una breve ***exposición*** le da a la audiencia cierta información de contexto sobre los personajes y la situación. Al igual que en un cuento o una novela, el argumento o trama de una obra dramática se construye a partir de personajes en conflicto.

Los dramas se dividen a grandes unidades llamadas ***actos***, que a su vez se dividen en unidades más breves llamadas ***escenas***. Un drama de cierta extensión puede incluir muchas escenografías que cambian con las escenas, o pueden indicar un cambio de escena por medio de la iluminación.

IRONÍA DRAMÁTICA La ***ironía dramática*** es una contradicción entre lo que el personaje cree y lo que la audiencia sabe. Por ejemplo: se produce ironía dramática que provoca humor o tensión si el personaje intenta desesperadamente forzar una caja fuerte cuando la audiencia ya sabe que la caja está vacía.

PUNTOS SUSPENSIVOS Los ***puntos suspensivos*** se usan para indicar que se han omitido palabras u oraciones de un texto que se cita.

VERSO NO ENCABALGADO Un ***verso no encabalgado*** es aquel en el que tanto la estructura gramatical como el sentido se completan al final del renglón.

ÉPICA Un ***poema épico*** es un poema narrativo extenso sobre las hazañas de dioses o héroes.

Los poemas épicos son de estilo elevado y por lo general siguen ciertos patrones. El poeta comienza por anunciar el tema y le pide ayuda a la Musa—una de las nueve diosas de las artes, la literatura y las ciencias. Un *héroe épico* es el personaje principal de un poema épico y suele tener características sobrehumanas. A través de su conducta y sus hazañas, el héroe épico demuestra tener cualidades muy valoradas por la sociedad en la que se originó el poema.

Ver también ***Comparativo épico* y *Poema narrativo***

COMPARATIVO ÉPICO El ***comparativo épico***, también llamado ***comparativo homérico***, es una comparación muy elaborada de dos objetos disímiles.

ENSAYO Un ***ensayo*** es una obra breve de no-ficción sobre un tema en particular. Si bien es difícil llegar a una clasificación, suelen diferenciarse cinco tipos de ensayos.

El *ensayo descriptivo* se propone transmitir una impresión acerca de una persona, un lugar o un objeto.

El *ensayo narrativo* narra una historia real.

El *ensayo expositivo* proporciona información, discute ideas o explica un proceso.

El *ensayo explicativo* describe y resume información sobre un determinado concepto recogida de cierto número de fuentes.

El *ensayo persuasivo* intenta convencer a los lectores de que hagan algo o que acepten el punto de vista del escritor.

EXPOSICIÓN Una ***exposición*** es un escrito o un discurso que explica un proceso o presenta información. En un cuento o un drama, la exposición es la parte donde se presenta a los personajes, la ambientación y la situación básica.

METÁFORA EXTENDIDA En una ***metáfora extendida***, al igual que en una metáfora habitual, el escritor escribe o habla de algo como si fuera otra cosa. Una metáfora extendida prolonga la comparación a lo largo de varios versos o de un poema entero.

DESTINO El ***destino*** es la suerte del héroe, algo sobre lo que no tiene control.

ARTÍCULOS DESTACADOS Los ***artículos destacados*** son una forma de periodismo que se centra en una situación o suceso específico.

FICCIÓN Una obra de ***ficción*** es un escrito en prosa que cuenta algo sobre personajes y hechos imaginarios. El término se usa por lo general para referirse a novelas y cuentos, pero también se aplica a dramas y poemas narrativos. Algunos escritores se basan solamente en su imaginación para crear sus obras de ficción. Otros basan su ficción en hechos y personas reales, a las que agregan personajes, diálogos y situationes de su propia invención.

LENGUAJE FIGURADO El ***lenguaje figurado*** es un escrito o discurso que no se debe interpretar literalmente. A menudo se usa para crear impresiones vívidas, estableciendo comparaciones entre cosas disímiles.

Algunas de las formas más usadas del lenguaje figurado son las ***metáforas***, los ***símiles*** y las ***personificaciones***.

FLASHBACK Un ***flashback*** o ***escena retrospectiva*** es una de las maneras a través de las que los autores presentan materiales de algo que ocurrió antes del tiempo presente del relato. Los autores pueden incluir estos materiales en los recuerdos o sueños de un personaje, o como relatos de hechos pasados

PERSONAJE COMPLEMENTARIO Un ***personaje complementario*** es un personaje que se presenta como la contraposición de otro. En *Romeo y Julieta*, el mal carácter de Teobaldo sirve de complementario a la buena disposición de Benvolio.

PREGUNTA COMPLEMENTARIA En las entrevistas, una ***pregunta complementaria*** clarifica y profundiza en las respuestas del entrevistado.

PREFIGURACIÓN La ***prefiguración*** es el uso, en una obra literaria, de claves que sugieren hechos que van a suceder. Esta técnica ayuda a crear suspenso, manteniendo a los lectores interesados preguntándose qué sucederá.

CUENTO DE ENMARQUE Un ***cuento de enmarque*** es un relato dentro del cual se incluyen otros relatos. Este recurso permite crear una estructura narrativa del tipo "cuento dentro del cuento".

VERSO LIBRE El ***verso libre*** es una forma poética en la que no se sigue un patrón regular de metro ni de rima.

GÉNERO Un ***género*** es una categoría o tipo de literatura. La literatura se divide por lo general en tres géneros principales: poesía, prosa y drama. Cada uno de estos géneros principales se dividen a su vez en géneros más pequeños. Por ejemplo:

1. **Poesía:** Poesía lírica, Poesía concreta, Poesía dramática, Poesía narrativa y Poesía épica.
2. **Prosa:** Ficción (Novelas y Cuentos) y No-ficción (Biografía, Autobiografía, Cartas, Ensayos, Artículos).
3. **Drama:** Drama serio y Tragedia, Comedia dramática, Melodrama y Farsa.

HIPÉRBOLE Una ***hipérbole*** es una exageración o magnificación deliberada.

YAMBO Una sílaba átona seguida por una tónica constituyen un ***yambo.***

PENTÁMETRO YÁMBICO El verso libre escrito en ***pentámetro yámbico*** tiene cinco yambos, llamados "pies", en cada verso.

EXPRESIÓN IDIOMÁTICA Una ***expresión idiomática*** es una expresión propia de una lengua, región, comunidad, o clase de personas. Las *expresiones idiomáticas* surgen a menudo a partir de expresiones del lenguaje figurado y por lo tanto no pueden entenderse literalmente.

IN MEDIA RES La frase ***in media res*** significa "en el medio de las cosas".

ENTREVISTA Una ***entrevista*** es un intercambio de ideas entre un entrevistador y un experto o alguien que ha tenido una experiencia inusual. La estructura básica de una entrevista es una sucesión de preguntas y respuestas.

IMAGEN Una ***imagen*** es una palabra o frase que apela a uno o más de los cinco sentidos: la vista, el oído, el tacto, el gusto y el olfato. Los escritores usan imágenes para recrear en palabras las experiencias sensoriales.

IMÁGENES Las ***imágenes*** son el lenguaje figurado o descriptivo que se usa en la literatura para crear una descripción verbal para los lectores. Estas descripciones verbales, o imágenes, se crean incluyendo detalles visuales, auditivos, gustativos, táctiles, olfativos o de movimiento.

MONÓLOGO INTERIOR Para mostrar los pensamientos de un personaje con mayor profundidad, los autores usan ***monólogo interior,*** una especie de "conversación" que el personaje tiene consigo mismo.

ENTREVISTA Una ***entrevista*** es un intercambio de ideas entre el entrevistador y un experto o alguien que haya tenido una experiencia singular.

IRONÍA ***Ironía*** es un término general para distintas técnicas literarias que subrayan las diferencias entre apariencia y realidad, o entre expectativas y resultado. En una ***ironía verbal***, las palabras se usan para sugerir lo opuesto a los que se dice. En la ***ironía dramática*** hay una contradicción entre los que el personaje piensa y lo que el lector o la audiencia sabe que es verdad. En una ***ironía situacional,*** ocurre un suceso que contradice directamente las expectativas de los personajes, y del lector o la audiencia.

PERIODISMO El ***periodismo*** es un fipo de escritura de no-ficción que se centra en hechos presentes y en temas de no-ficción de interés general.

POEMA LÍRICO Un ***poema lírico*** es una sucesión de versos de mucha musicalidad que expresan los pensamientos, observaciones y sentimientos de un único hablante.

MEMORIAS Un libro de ***memorias*** es un tipo limitado de escrito autobiográfico que se centra en un período o aspecto de la vida del autor.

METÁFORA Una ***metáfora*** es una figura retórica en la que el escritor se refiere a algo como si fuera otra cosa. Al contrario del símil, que compara dos cosas con las palabras *como* o *tal como*, la metáfora insinúa la comparación.

MONÓLOGO Un ***monólogo*** en una obra de teatro es un parlamento por parte de un personaje que, a diferencia del ***soliloquio***, se dirige a otro u otros personajes.

TONO El ***tono*** o la ***atmósfera*** es la sensación que un pasaje u obra literaria crea en el lector. Por lo general, el tono se crea a partir de detalles descriptivos. A menudo puede ser descrito con una sola palabra, tal como desenfadado, aterrador o desesperante.

MOTIVO El ***motivo*** es la razón de una acción.

NARRACIÓN Una ***narración*** es un escrito que cuenta una historia. El acto de contar una historia de forma oral también se llama narración. Las novelas y los cuentos son obras narrativas de ficción. Las obras de no-ficción, como las noticias, las biografías y las autobiografías, también son narraciones. Un poema narrativo cuenta una historia en verso.

RELATO Se llama ***relato*** a la historia que se narra, en una obra de ficción, de no-ficción, en un poema o en un drama.

RELATO DE NO-FICCIÓN Se le llama ***relato de no-ficción*** al escrito que cuenta una historia de la vida real.

PUNTO DE VISTA NARRATIVO El ***punto de vista narrativo*** es la perspectiva desde la que el escritor de ficción cuenta la historia.

NARRADOR Un ***narrador*** es el hablante o el personaje que cuenta una historia. La elección del narrador por parte del autor determina el ***punto de vista*** desde el que se va a narrar la historia, lo que determina el tipo y la cantidad de información que se revelará.

Cuando el que cuenta la historia es uno de los personajes, a ese personaje se lo llama *narrador en primera persona*. Este narrador puede ser uno de los personajes principales, un personaje menor, o solo un testigo. Los lectores ven solo lo que este personaje ve, oyen solo lo que este personaje oye, etc. El narrador en primera persona puede ser confiable o no.

Cuando la que cuenta la historia es una voz exterior a la historia, hablamos de un *narrador en tercera persona*. Un narrador en tercera persona, omnisciente —es decir, que todo lo sabe— puede decirles a los lectores lo que cualquier personaje piensa o siente. Un narrador en tercera persona limitado ve el mundo a través de los ojos de un solo personaje y revela solo los pensamientos de ese personaje.

NO-FICCIÓN La ***no-ficción*** es un escrito en prosa que presenta y explica ideas o cuenta algo acerca de personas, lugares, ideas o hechos reales. Para ser clasificado como no-ficción un escrito debe ser verdadero. "Single Room, Earth View" es un relato no ficcional acerca de cómo se ve la Tierra desde el espacio.

NOVELA Una ***novela*** es una obra extensa de ficción. Tiene una trama que explora los personajes en conflicto. Una novela también puede tener una o más tramas secundarias —es decir, historias de menor importancia—, así como tocar varios temas.

ONOMATOPEYA La ***onomatopeya*** es el uso de palabras que imitan sonidos, tales como *pío-pío, tic-tac* o susurro.

TRADICIÓN ORAL La ***tradición oral*** es la transmisión de canciones, cuentos y poemas de una generación a otra, de boca a boca. Muchas canciones folklóricas, baladas, cuentos de hadas, leyendas y mitos se originaron en la tradición oral.

OXÍMORON Un ***oxímoron*** es una combinación de palabras, o partes de palabras, que se contradicen mutuamente. Por ejemplo, "un silencio ensordecedor", "un ladrón honesto", "la música callada".

CUARTETAS ENCADENADAS Las ***cuartetas encadenadas*** son una antigua estructura poética que consiste en un serie de cuartetas, o estrofas de cuatro versos.

PARADOJA Una ***paradoja*** es un enunciado que parece contradictorio, pero que sin embargo puede ser verdadero. Por ser siempre sorpresiva, la paradoja suele captar la atención de los lectores.

PARALELISMO El ***paralelismo*** es la repetición de una estructura gramatical con el fin de crear un ritmo y que las palabras resulten más memorables.

PARÁFRASIS La ***paráfrasis*** es reescribir o volver a contar una historia con nuestras propias palabras.

PERSONIFICACIÓN La ***personificación*** es un tipo de figura retórica en la que se dota a una instancia no humana de rasgos y actitudes humanas.

PERSUASIÓN La ***persuasión*** es un recurso escrito u oral por el que se intenta convencer al lector de que adopte una opinión o actúe de determinada manera. Un ***argumento*** es una manera lógica de presentar una creencia, una conclusión o una postura. Un buen argumento se respalda con razones y evidencias.

APELACIONES PERSUASIVAS Las ***apelaciones persuasivas*** son métodos que se utilizan para informar o convencer a los lectores de que vean algo desde una nueva perspectiva.

ENSAYO PERSUASIVO Un ***ensayo persuasivo*** es una obra corta de no-ficción en la que el escritor tiene como objetivo convencer al lector para que piense o actúe de una manera determinada.

DISCURSO PERSUASIVO En un ***discurso persuasivo*** el hablante utiliza técnicas de la retórica, la lógica y las presentaciones orales para convencer a los oyentes de que piensen o actúen de una manera determinada.

TRAMA o ARGUMENTO La ***trama*** o ***argumento*** es la secuencia de los eventos que suceden en una obra literaria. En la mayoría de las novelas, dramas, cuentos y poemas narrativos, la trama implica tanto a los personajes como al conflicto central. La trama por lo general empieza con una ***exposición*** que introduce la ambientación, los personajes y la situación básica. A ello le sigue el ***suceso desencadenante***, que introduce el conflicto central. Este conflicto aumenta durante el ***desarrollo*** hasta que alcanza el punto más alto de interés o suspenso, llamado ***clímax***. Todos los sucesos que conducen al clímax contribuyen a la ***acción dramática creciente***. Al clímax le sigue la ***acción dramática decreciente*** que conduce al ***desenlace***, o ***resolución***, en el que se produce un cambio significativo.

ESTRUCTURA POÉTICA Las ***estructuras poéticas*** básicas son los versos y las estrofas. Un verso es un grupo de palabras ordenadas en una misma hilera. Un verso puede terminar, o cortarse, de distintas maneras. En un ***verso no encabalgado*** la estructura gramatical y el sentido se completan al final de esa línea. En un verso encabalgado tanto la estructura gramatical como el sentido de una línea continúa en el verso que sigue.

POESÍA La ***poesía*** es uno de los tres géneros literarios más importantes. Los otros dos son la prosa y el drama. La mayoría de los poemas están escritos en un lenguaje altamente conciso, musical y emocionalmente rico. Muchos también hacen uso de imágenes, de figuras retóricas y de recursos especiales de sonido, tales como la rima. Los poemas a menudo se dividen en versos y estrofas y emplean patrones rítmicos regulares, llamados metros. Sin embargo, algunos poemas están escritos en un lenguaje similar al de la prosa, mientras que otros están escritos en verso libre.

PUNTO DE VISTA El ***punto de vista*** es la perspectiva desde la cual se narran o describen los hechos.

FUENTE PRIMARIA Una ***fuente primaria*** es el material o la información de primera mano acerca de lo que se estudia.

PROSA La ***prosa*** es la forma común del lenguaje escrito. La mayoría de los escritos que no son poesía, ni drama, ni canciones, se consideran prosa. La prosa es uno de los géneros literarios más importantes y puede ser de dos formas: de ficción y de no-ficción.

JUEGO DE PALABRAS Un ***juego de palabras*** es una frase que comprende una palabra con dos o más significados distintos, o dos palabras que suenan igual pero tienen distinto significado. En *Romeo y Julieta*, Mercurio, moribundo, hace un juego de palabras a partir de los dos sentidos que tiene en inglés la palabra "grave" (serio y tumba): "Pregunta por mí mañana, y me encontrarás serio/ enterrado". (Acto 3, Escena i, versos 92–93).

CUARTETA Una ***cuarteta*** es una estrofa o poema de cuatro versos, por lo general con un esquema de ritmo y rima determinados.

CITA Las palabras exactas que pronuncia un hablante constituyen una ***cita directa*** y se indican encerrándolas entre comillas.

REPETICIÓN La ***repetición*** es el uso de cualquier elemento del lenguaje —un sonido, una palabra, una frase, una cláusula o una oración— más de una vez.

Los poetas usan muchos tipos de repeticiones. La aliteración, la asonancia, la rima y el ritmo son repeticiones de ciertos sonidos o patrones sonoros. Un estribillo es un verso o grupo de versos que se repiten. Tanto en prosa como en poesía, la repetición se usa tanto para lograr efectos de musicalidad como para dar énfasis.

REAFIRMACIÓN Las ***reafirmaciones*** o paráfrasis le ayudan al entrevistador a asegurarse de que la audiencia entienda el mensaje del entrevistado.

RETÓRICA La ***retórica*** se refiere a recursos lingüísticos, en especial el arte de hablar o escribir eficazmente.

FIGURAS RETÓRICAS Las ***figuras retóricas*** son patrones especiales de palabras e ideas que dan énfasis y producen emoción, especialmente en discursos y otras presentaciones orales. El ***paralelismo***, por ejemplo, es la repetición de una estructura gramatical con el propósito de crear un ritmo y hacer que las palabras resulten más memorables.

Otras figuras retóricas muy frecuentes son: la ***analogía***, que establece una comparación entre dos cosas diferentes; el ***lenguaje emocionalmente cargado***, en el que las palabras apelan a las emociones; la ***reafirmación***, en la que se expresa la misma idea con distintas palabras y las ***preguntas retóricas***, que son preguntas cuyas respuestas son obvias.

VERSO ENCABALGADO Un ***verso encabalgado*** es aquel en el que tanto la estructura gramatical como el sentido no se completan al final del verso, sino que continúan en el verso siguiente.

CIENCIA FICCIÓN La ***ciencia ficción*** es un escrito que narra hechos imaginarios relacionados con la ciencia o la tecnología. Muchos relatos de ciencia ficción están ambientados en el futuro.

LENGUAJE SENSORIAL El ***lenguaje sensorial*** es un escrito o discurso que incluye detalles que apelan a uno o más de los sentidos.

AMBIENTACIÓN La ***ambientación*** de una obra literaria es la época y el lugar en el que se desarrolla la acción. La época incluye no solo el período histórico —pasado, presente o futuro—, sino también el año específico, la estación, la hora del día. El lugar puede incluir no solo el espacio geográfico —una región, un país, un estado, un pueblo— sino también el entorno social, económico o cultural.

En algunos cuentos, la ambientación sirve solo como un telón de fondo para la acción, un contexto en el que los personajes se mueven y hablan. En otros casos, en cambio, la ambientación es un elemento crucial.

CUENTO Un ***cuento*** es una obra breve de ficción. En la mayoría de los cuentos, un personaje principal se enfrenta a un conflicto que se resuelve a lo largo de la trama. Para escribir un buen cuento se necesita mucho dominio técnico, porque el cuento debe cumplir su cometido en relativamente pocas palabras.

SÍMIL Un ***símil*** es una figura retórica en la que se usa la palabra *como* para establecer una comparación entre dos cosas aparentemente disímiles. La comparación sorprende al lector permitiéndole una nueva percepción que se deriva de descubrir una semejanza inesperada.

IRONÍA SITUACIONAL La ***ironía situacional*** tiene lugar cuando los eventos de una historia suceden de manera opuesta a lo esperado por los personajes principales o los lectores.

CONTEXTO SOCIAL E HISTÓRICO Se conoce como ***contexto social e histórico*** a las circunstancias de tiempo y lugar en las que se desarrolla la historia.

SOLILOQUIO Un ***soliloquio*** es un largo parlamento en el que un personaje, solo en escena, expresa sus sentimientos.

RECURSOS SONOROS Un ***recurso sonoro*** es una técnica usada por poetas y prosistas para enfatizar la relación sonora entre las palabras con el fin de crear efectos musicales y emotivos, y de subrayar el significado del texto. Estos recursos incluyen la ***aliteración***, la ***consonancia***, la ***asonancia***, la ***onomatopeya*** y la ***rima***.

HABLANTE El ***hablante*** es la voz imaginaria que asume el escritor en un poema. En muchos poemas, el hablante no se identifica con un nombre. Al leer un poema, recuerda que el hablante que habla en el poema puede ser una persona, un animal, un objeto, o una abstracción.

DETALLES ESPECÍFICOS Tanto los escritores de ficción como los de no-ficción utilizan ***detalles específicos*** para respaldar una idea central o un tema.

DIRECCIONES ESCÉNICAS Las ***direcciones escénicas*** son notas que se incluyen en una obra de teatro para describir cómo debe ser actuada o puesta en escena. Estas instrucciones aparecen en itálicas y no se pronuncian durante la representación. Se usan para describir decorados, la iluminación, los efectos sonoros y el aspecto, la personalidad y los movimientos de los personajes.

ESTROFA Una ***estrofa*** es un grupo de dos o más versos cuya estructura se repite. Las distintas estrofas de un poema suelen seguir un mismo patrón de ritmo y de rima. Las estrofas a menudo reciben su nombre del número de versos que las componen. Por ejemplo, un ***dístico*** o ***pareado*** (dos versos), una ***cuarteta*** (cuatro versos), una ***sextina*** (seis versos), una ***octava real*** (ocho versos endecasílabos).

ESTILO El ***estilo*** es la manera particular en que escribe un autor. Los elementos que determinan el estilo son: la dicción, el tono; el uso característico de ciertas figuras retóricas, del dialecto, o de los recursos rítmicos; y la sintaxis, es decir, los patrones y estructuras gramaticales que usa con más fecuencia.

RESUMEN Un ***resumen*** es una síntesis concisa, completa y precisa de un texto.

DETALLES DE APOYO Se conoce como ***detalles de apoyo*** a la información que explica, amplía o demuestra las ideas del autor. Los detalles de apoyo validan un argumento, informan o añaden interés al texto.

SÍMBOLO Un ***símbolo*** es algo que representa otra cosa. Además de tener su propio significado y realidad, un símbolo también representa ideas abstractas. Por ejemplo, una bandera es un trozo de tela, pero también representa la idea de un país. Los escritores a veces usan símbolos convencionales como las banderas. Con frecuencia, sin embargo, crean sus propios símbolos, a veces a través del énfasis o la repetición.

TEMA Un ***tema*** es el mensaje central o la concepción de la vida que revela una obra literaria.

El tema de una obra literaria puede estar implícito o bien puede expresarse directamente. Cuando el tema de una obra está implícito, los lectores piensan qué sugiere la obra acerca de la vida o la gente.

Los ***temas arquetípicos*** son aquellos temas que aparecen en el folklore y en la literatura de todo el mundo, y a lo largo de toda la historia.

TONO El ***tono*** de una obra literaria es la actitud del escritor hacia su tema y su audiencia.

TRAGEDIA Una ***tragedia*** es una obra literaria, por lo general una obra de teatro, que termina en una catástrofe, un desastre o un gran infortunio para el personaje principal, también llamado *héroe trágico*. En el drama de la antigua Grecia, el personaje principal siempre era una persona importante —un rey o un héroe— y la causa de la tragedia era un *error trágico,* una debilidad de su carácter. En el drama moderno, el personaje principal puede ser una persona común, y la causa de la tragedia puede ser algún problema o falla de la sociedad misma. La tragedia no solo despierta miedo y piedad en la audiencia, sino también, en algunos casos, transmite un sentido de la majestuosidad y la nobleza del espíritu humano.

ERROR TRÁGICO Un ***error trágico*** es un defecto de la personalidad que contribuye a las decisiones del héroe y, por lo tanto, a su ruina.

PERIODISMO DE VIAJES El ***periodismo de viajes*** es un tipo de literatura de no-ficción en la que el escritor describe la experiencia de visitar un lugar determinado.

ENSAYO VISUAL Un ***ensayo visual*** es una exploración de un tema que transmite sus ideas tanto con el lenguaje como con los elementos visuales. Al igual que un ensayo estándar, un ensayo visual presenta las opiniones del autor acerca de un tema en particular. A diferencia de otros tipos de ensayos, sin embargo, gran parte del sentido del ensayo visual se expresa en las ilustraciones o fotografías.

LENGUAJE VÍVIDO Las palabras convincentes y precisas que dan vida a las ideas y las comunican de manera contundente constituyen ***lenguaje vívido.***

VOZ La ***voz*** es el "sonido" distintivo de un escritor, o la manera en que "habla" en la página. Se relaciona a elementos tales como la elección del vocabulario, la estructura de las oraciones y el tono. Es similar al estilo en que habla un individuo y puede describirse de la misma manera: rápida, lenta, directa, dispersa, entrecortadamente, etc.

La voz se parece al ***estilo***, es decir, a la manera típica en que escribe un autor, pero el estilo por lo general se refiere a una cualidad que puede encontrarse a lo largo de toda la obra de un autor, mientras que la voz de un autor puede variar de una obra a otra.

PARTS OF SPEECH

Every English word, depending on its meaning and its use in a sentence, can be identified as one of the eight parts of speech. These are nouns, pronouns, verbs, adjectives, adverbs, prepositions, conjunctions, and interjections. Understanding the parts of speech will help you learn the rules of English grammar and usage.

Nouns A **noun** names a person, place, or thing. A **common noun** names any one of a class of persons, places, or things. A **proper noun** names a specific person, place, or thing.

Common Noun	**Proper Noun**
writer, country, novel	Charles Dickens, Great Britain, *Hard Times*

Pronouns A **pronoun** is a word that stands for one or more nouns. The word to which a pronoun refers (whose place it takes) is the **antecedent** of the pronoun.

A **personal pronoun** refers to the person speaking (first person); the person spoken to (second person); or the person, place, or thing spoken about (third person).

	Singular	**Plural**
First Person	I, me, my, mine	we, us, our, ours
Second Person	you, your, yours	you, your, yours
Third Person	he, him, his, she, her, hers, it, its	they, them, their, theirs

A **reflexive pronoun** reflects the action of a verb back on its subject. It indicates that the person or thing performing the action also is receiving the action.

I keep *myself* fit by taking a walk every day.

An **intensive pronoun** adds emphasis to a noun or pronoun.

It took the work of the president *himself* to pass the law.

A **demonstrative** pronoun points out a specific person(s), place(s), or thing(s).

this, that, these, those

A **relative pronoun** begins a subordinate clause and connects it to another idea in the sentence.

that, which, who, whom, whose

An **interrogative pronoun** begins a question.

what, which, who, whom, whose

An **indefinite pronoun** refers to a person, place, or thing that may or may not be specifically named.

all, another, any, both, each, everyone, few, most, none, no one, somebody

Verbs A **verb** expresses action or the existence of a state or condition.

An **action verb** tells what action someone or something is performing.

gather, read, work, jump, imagine, analyze, conclude

A **linking verb** connects the subject with another word that identifies or describes the subject. The most common linking verb is *be*.

appear, be, become, feel, look, remain, seem, smell, sound, stay, taste

A **helping verb,** or **auxiliary verb,** is added to a main verb to make a verb phrase.

be, do, have, should, can, could, may, might, must, will, would

Adjectives An **adjective** modifies a noun or pronoun by describing it or giving it a more specific meaning. An adjective answers the questions:

What kind?	*purple* hat, *happy* face, *loud* sound
Which one?	*this* bowl
How many?	*three* cars
How much?	*enough* food

The articles *the, a,* and *an* are adjectives.

A **proper adjective** is an adjective derived from a proper noun.

French, Shakespearean

Adverbs An **adverb** modifies a verb, an adjective, or another adverb by telling *where, when, how,* or *to what extent.*

will answer *soon, extremely* sad, calls *more* often

Prepositions A **preposition** relates a noun or pronoun that appears with it to another word in the sentence.

Dad made a meal *for* us. We talked *till* dusk. Bo missed school *because of* his illness.

Conjunctions A **conjunction** connects words or groups of words. A **coordinating conjunction** joins words or groups of words of equal rank.

bread *and* cheese, brief *but* powerful

Correlative conjunctions are used in pairs to connect words or groups of words of equal importance.

both Luis *and* Rosa, *neither* you *nor* I

Subordinating conjunctions indicate the connection between two ideas by placing one below the other in rank or importance. A subordinating conjunction introduces a subordinate, or dependent, clause.

We will miss her *if* she leaves. Hank shrieked *when* he slipped on the ice.

Interjections An **interjection** expresses feeling or emotion. It is not related to other words in the sentence.

ah, hey, ouch, well, yippee

PHRASES AND CLAUSES

Phrases A **phrase** is a group of words that does not have both a subject and a verb and that functions as one part of speech. A phrase expresses an idea but cannot stand alone.

Prepositional Phrases A **prepositional phrase** is a group of words that begins with a preposition and ends with a noun or pronoun that is the **object of the preposition.**

before dawn   as a result of the rain

An **adjective phrase** is a prepositional phrase that modifies a noun or pronoun.

Eliza appreciates the beauty **of a well-crafted poem.**

An **adverb phrase** is a prepositional phrase that modifies a verb, an adjective, or an adverb.

She reads Spenser's sonnets **with great pleasure.**

Appositive Phrases An **appositive** is a noun or pronoun placed next to another noun or pronoun to add information about it. An **appositive phrase** consists of an appositive and its modifiers.

Mr. Roth, **my music teacher**, is sick.

Verbal Phrases A **verbal** is a verb form that functions as a different part of speech (not as a verb) in a sentence. **Participles, gerunds,** and **infinitives** are verbals.

A **verbal phrase** includes a verbal and any modifiers or complements it may have. Verbal phrases may function as nouns, as adjectives, or as adverbs.

A **participle** is a verb form that can act as an adjective. Present participles end in *-ing;* past participles of regular verbs end in *-ed.*

A **participial phrase** consists of a participle and its modifiers or complements. The entire phrase acts as an adjective.

Jenna's backpack, **loaded with equipment,** was heavy.

Barking incessantly, the dogs chased the squirrels out of sight.

A **gerund** is a verb form that ends in *-ing* and is used as a noun.

A **gerund phrase** consists of a gerund with any modifiers or complements, all acting together as a noun.

Taking photographs of wildlife is her main hobby. [acts as subject]

We always enjoy **listening to live music.** [acts as object]

An **infinitive** is a verb form, usually preceded by *to,* that can act as a noun, an adjective, or an adverb.

An **infinitive phrase** consists of an infinitive and its modifiers or complements, and sometimes its subject, all acting together as a single part of speech.

She tries **to get out into the wilderness often.** [acts as a noun; direct object of *tries*]

The Tigers are the team **to beat.** [acts as an adjective; describes *team*]

I drove twenty miles **to witness the event.** [acts as an adverb; tells why I drove]

Clauses A **clause** is a group of words with its own subject and verb.

Independent Clauses An independent clause can stand by itself as a complete sentence.

George Orwell wrote with extraordinary insight.

Subordinate Clauses A subordinate clause, also called a dependent clause, cannot stand by itself as a complete sentence. Subordinate clauses always appear connected in some way with one or more independent clauses.

George Orwell, **who wrote with extraordinary insight,** produced many politically relevant works.

An **adjective clause** is a subordinate clause that acts as an adjective. It modifies a noun or a pronoun by telling *what kind* or *which one.* Also called relative clauses, adjective clauses usually begin with a **relative pronoun:** *who, which, that, whom, or whose.*

"The Lamb" is the poem **that I memorized for class.**

An **adverb clause** is a subordinate clause that, like an adverb, modifies a verb, an adjective, or an adverb. An adverb clause tells *where, when, in what way, to what extent, under what condition,* or *why.*

The students will read another poetry collection **if their schedule allows.**

When I recited the poem, Mr. Lopez was impressed.

A **noun clause** is a subordinate clause that acts as a noun.

William Blake survived on **whatever he made as an engraver.**

SENTENCE STRUCTURE

Subject and Predicate A **sentence** is a group of words that expresses a complete thought. A sentence has two main parts: a *subject* and a *predicate*.

A **fragment** is a group of words that does not express a complete thought. It lacks an independent clause.

The **subject** tells *whom* or *what* the sentence is about. The **predicate** tells what the subject of the sentence does or is.

A subject or a predicate can consist of a single word or of many words. All the words in the subject make up the **complete subject.** All the words in the predicate make up the **complete predicate.**

Complete Subject **Complete Predicate**
Both of those girls | have already read *Macbeth*.

The **simple subject** is the essential noun, pronoun, or group of words acting as a noun that cannot be left out of the complete subject. The **simple predicate** is the essential verb or verb phrase that cannot be left out of the complete predicate.

Both of those girls | **have** already **read** *Macbeth*.
[Simple subject: *Both;* simple predicate: *have read*]

A **compound subject** is two or more subjects that have the same verb and are joined by a conjunction.

Neither the horse nor the driver looked tired.

A **compound predicate** is two or more verbs that have the same subject and are joined by a conjunction.

She **sneezed and coughed** throughout the trip.

Complements A **complement** is a word or word group that completes the meaning of the subject or verb in a sentence. There are four kinds of complements: *direct objects, indirect objects, objective complements,* and *subject complements.*

A **direct object** is a noun, a pronoun, or a group of words acting as a noun that receives the action of a transitive verb.

We watched the **liftoff**.
She drove **Zach** to the launch site.

An **indirect object** is a noun or pronoun that appears with a direct object and names the person or thing to which or for which something is done.

He sold the **family** a mirror. [The direct object is *mirror.*]

An **objective complement** is an adjective or noun that appears with a direct object and describes or renames it.

The decision made her **unhappy**.
[The direct object is *her.*]
Many consider Shakespeare the greatest **playwright.** [The direct object is *Shakespeare.*]

A **subject complement** follows a linking verb and tells something about the subject. There are two kinds: *predicate nominatives* and *predicate adjectives.*

A **predicate nominative** is a noun or pronoun that follows a linking verb and identifies or renames the subject.

"A Modest Proposal" is a **pamphlet.**

A **predicate adjective** is an adjective that follows a linking verb and describes the subject of the sentence.

"A Modest Proposal" is **satirical.**

Classifying Sentences by Structure

Sentences can be classified according to the kind and number of clauses they contain. The four basic sentence structures are *simple, compound, complex,* and *compound-complex.*

A **simple sentence** consists of one independent clause.

Terrence enjoys modern British literature.

A **compound sentence** consists of two or more independent clauses. The clauses are joined by a conjunction or a semicolon.

Terrence enjoys modern British literature, but his brother prefers the classics.

A **complex sentence** consists of one independent clause and one or more subordinate clauses.

Terrence, who reads voraciously, enjoys modern British literature.

A **compound-complex sentence** consists of two or more independent clauses and one or more subordinate clauses.

Terrence, who reads voraciously, enjoys modern British literature, but his brother prefers the classics.

Classifying Sentences by Function

Sentences can be classified according to their function or purpose. The four types are *declarative, interrogative, imperative,* and *exclamatory.*

A **declarative sentence** states an idea and ends with a period.

An **interrogative sentence** asks a question and ends with a question mark.

An **imperative sentence** gives an order or a direction and ends with either a period or an exclamation mark.

An **exclamatory sentence** conveys a strong emotion and ends with an exclamation mark.

PARAGRAPH STRUCTURE

An effective paragraph is organized around one **main idea,** which is often stated in a **topic sentence.** The other sentences support the main idea. To give the paragraph **unity,** make sure the connection between each sentence and the main idea is clear.

Unnecessary Shift in Person

Do not change needlessly from one grammatical person to another. Keep the person consistent in your sentences.

Max went to the bakery, but **you** can't buy mints there. [shift from third person to second person]

Max went to the bakery, but **he** can't buy mints there. [consistent]

Unnecessary Shift in Voice

Do not change needlessly from active voice to passive voice in your use of verbs.

Elena and I **searched** the trail for evidence, but no clues **were found.** [shift from active voice to passive voice]

Elena and I **searched** the trail for evidence, but we **found** no clues. [consistent]

AGREEMENT

Subject and Verb Agreement

A singular subject must have a singular verb. A plural subject must have a plural verb.

Dr. Boone uses a telescope to view the night sky.

The **students use** a telescope to view the night sky.

A verb always agrees with its subject, not its object.

Incorrect: The best part of the show were the jugglers.

Correct: The best part of the show was the jugglers.

A phrase or clause that comes between a subject and verb does not affect subject-verb agreement.

His **theory**, as well as his claims, **lacks** support.

Two subjects joined by *and* usually take a plural verb.

The **dog** and the **cat are** healthy.

Two singular subjects joined by *or* or *nor* take a singular verb.

The **dog** or the **cat is** hiding.

Two plural subjects joined by *or* or *nor* take a plural verb.

The **dogs** or the **cats are** coming home with us.

When a singular and a plural subject are joined by *or* or *nor,* the verb agrees with the closer subject.

Either the **dogs** or the **cat is** behind the door.

Either the **cat** or the **dogs are** behind the door.

Pronoun and Antecedent Agreement

Pronouns must agree with their antecedents in number and gender. Use singular pronouns with singular antecedents and plural pronouns with plural antecedents.

Doris Lessing uses **her** writing to challenge ideas about women's roles.

Writers often use **their** skills to promote social change.

Use a singular pronoun when the antecedent is a singular indefinite pronoun such as *anybody, each, either, everybody, neither, no one, one, or someone.*

Judge **each** of the articles on **its** merits.

Use a plural pronoun when the antecedent is a plural indefinite pronoun such as *both, few, many,* or *several.*

Both of the articles have **their** flaws.

The indefinite pronouns *all, any, more, most, none,* and *some* can be singular or plural depending on the number of the word to which they refer.

Most of the *books* are in **their** proper places.

Most of the *book* has been torn from **its** binding.

USING VERBS

Principal Parts of Regular and Irregular Verbs

A verb has four principal parts:

Present	Present Participle	Past	Past Participle
learn	learning	learned	learned
discuss	discussing	discussed	discussed
stand	standing	stood	stood
begin	beginning	began	begun

Regular verbs such as *learn* and *discuss* form the past and past participle by adding *-ed* to the present form. **Irregular verbs** such as *stand* and *begin* form the past and past participle in other ways. If you are in doubt about the principal parts of an irregular verb, check a dictionary.

The Tenses of Verbs

The different tenses of verbs indicate the time an action or condition occurs.

The **present tense** expresses an action that happens regularly or states a current condition or general truth.

Tourists **flock** to the site yearly.

Daily exercise **is** good for your heallth.

The **past tense** expresses a completed action or a condition that is no longer true.

The squirrel **dropped** the nut and **ran** up the tree.

I **was** very tired last night by 9:00.

The **future tense** indicates an action that will happen in the future or a condition that will be true.

The Glazers **will visit** us tomorrow.

They **will be** glad to arrive from their long journey.

The **present perfect tense** expresses an action that happened at an indefinite time in the past or an action that began in the past and continues into the present.

Someone **has cleaned** the trash from the park.

The puppy **has been** under the bed all day.

The **past perfect tense** shows an action that was completed before another action in the past.

Gerard **had revised** his essay before he turned it in.

The **future perfect tense** indicates an action that will have been completed before another action takes place.

Mimi **will have painted** the kitchen by the time we finish the shutters.

USING MODIFIERS

Degrees of Comparison

Adjectives and adverbs take different forms to show the three degrees of comparison: the *positive*, the *comparative*, and the *superlative*.

Positive	Comparative	Superlative
fast	faster	fastest
crafty	craftier	craftiest
abruptly	more abruptly	most abruptly
badly	worse	worst

Using Comparative and Superlative Adjectives and Adverbs

Use comparative adjectives and adverbs to compare two things. Use superlative adjectives and adverbs to compare three or more things.

This season's weather was **drier** than last year's.

This season has been one of the **driest** on record.

Jake practices **more often** than Jamal.

Of everyone in the band, Jake practices **most often.**

USING PRONOUNS

Pronoun Case

The **case** of a pronoun is the form it takes to show its function in a sentence. There are three pronoun cases: *nominative*, *objective*, and *possessive*.

Nominative	Objective	Possessive
I, you, he, she, it, we, you, they	me, you, him, her, it, us, you, them	my, your, yours, his, her, hers, its, our, ours, their, theirs

Use the **nominative case** when a pronoun functions as a *subject* or as a *predicate nominative.*

They are going to the movies. [subject]

The biggest movie fan is **she.** [predicate nominative]

Use the **objective case** for a pronoun acting as a *direct object*, an *indirect object*, or the *object of a preposition.*

The ending of the play surprised **me**. [direct object]

Mary gave **us** two tickets to the play. [indirect object]

The audience cheered for **him.** [object of preposition]

Use the **possessive case** to show ownership.

The red suitcase is **hers.**

Diction The words you choose contribute to the overall effectiveness of your writing. **Diction** refers to word choice and to the clearness and correctness of those words. You can improve one aspect of your diction by choosing carefully between commonly confused words, such as the pairs listed below.

accept, except

Accept is a verb that means "to receive" or "to agree to." *Except* is a preposition that means "other than" or "leaving out."

Please **accept** my offer to buy you lunch this weekend.

He is busy every day **except** the weekends.

affect, effect

Affect is normally a verb meaning "to influence" or "to bring about a change in." *Effect* is usually a noun meaning "result."

The distractions outside **affect** Steven's ability to concentrate.

The teacher's remedies had a positive **effect** on Steven's ability to concentrate.

among, between

Among is usually used with three or more items, and it emphasizes collective relationships or indicates distribution. *Between* is generally used with only two items, but it can be used with more than two if the emphasis is on individual (one-to-one) relationships within the group.

I had to choose a snack **among** the various vegetables.

He handed out the booklets **among** the conference participants.

Our school is **between** a park and an old barn.

The tournament included matches **between** France, Spain, Mexico, and the United States.

amount, number

Amount refers to overall quantity and is mainly used with mass nouns (those that can't be counted). *Number* refers to individual items that can be counted.

The **amount** of attention that great writers have paid to Shakespeare is remarkable.

A **number** of important English writers have been fascinated by the legend of King Arthur.

assure, ensure, insure

Assure means "to convince [someone of something]; to guarantee." *Ensure* means "to make certain [that something happens]." *Insure* means "to arrange for payment in case of loss."

The attorney **assured** us we'd win the case.

The rules **ensure** that no one gets treated unfairly.

Many professional musicians **insure** their valuable instruments.

bad, badly

Use the adjective *bad* before a noun or after linking verbs such as *feel, look,* and *seem*. Use *badly* whenever an adverb is required.

The situation may seem **bad**, but it will improve over time.

Though our team played **badly** today, we will focus on practicing for the next match.

beside, besides

Beside means "at the side of" or "close to." *Besides* means "in addition to."

The stapler sits **beside** the pencil sharpener in our classroom.

Besides being very clean, the classroom is also very organized.

can, may

The helping verb *can* generally refers to the ability to do something. The helping verb *may* generally refers to permission to do something.

I **can** run one mile in six minutes.

May we have a race during recess?

complement, compliment

The verb *complement* means "to enhance"; the verb *compliment* means "to praise."

Online exercises **complement** the textbook lessons.

Ms. Lewis **complimented** our team on our excellent debate.

compose, comprise

Compose means "to make up; constitute." *Comprise* means "to include or contain." Remember that the whole comprises its parts or is composed of its parts, and the parts compose the whole.

The assignment **comprises** three different tasks.

The assignment is **composed** of three different tasks.

Three different tasks **compose** the assignment.

different from, different than

Different from is generally preferred over *different than,* but *different than* can be used before a clause. Always use *different from* before a noun or pronoun.

Your point of view is so **different from** mine.

His idea was so **different from** [or **different than**] what we had expected.

farther, further

Use *farther* to refer to distance. Use *further* to mean "to a greater degree or extent" or "additional."

Chiang has traveled **farther** than anybody else in the class.

If I want **further** details about his travels, I can read his blog.

fewer, less

Use *fewer* for things that can be counted. Use *less* for amounts or quantities that cannot be counted. *Fewer* must be followed by a plural noun.

Fewer students drive to school since the weather improved.

There is **less** noise outside in the mornings.

good, well

Use the adjective *good* before a noun or after a linking verb. Use *well* whenever an adverb is required, such as when modifying a verb.

I feel **good** after sleeping for eight hours.

I did **well** on my test, and my soccer team played **well** in that afternoon's game. It was a **good** day!

its, it's

The word *its* with no apostrophe is a possessive pronoun. The word *it's* is a contraction of "it is."

Angelica will try to fix the computer and **its** keyboard.

It's a difficult job, but she can do it.

lay, lie

Lay is a transitive verb meaning "to set or put something down." Its principal parts are *lay, laying, laid, laid. Lie* is an intransitive verb meaning "to recline" or "to exist in a certain place." Its principal parts are *lie, lying, lay, lain.*

Please **lay** that box down and help me with the sofa.

When we are done moving, I am going to **lie** down.

My hometown **lies** sixty miles north of here.

like, as

Like is a preposition that usually means "similar to" and precedes a noun or pronoun. The conjunction *as* means "in the way that" and usually precedes a clause.

Like the other students, I was prepared for a quiz.

As I said yesterday, we expect to finish before noon.

Use **such as,** not **like,** before a series of examples.

Foods **such as** apples, nuts, and pretzels make good snacks.

of, have

Do not use *of* in place of *have* after auxiliary verbs such as *would, could, should, may, might,* or *must.* The contraction of *have* is formed by adding *-ve* after these verbs.

I **would have** stayed after school today, but I had to help cook at home.

Mom **must've** called while I was still in the gym.

principal, principle

Principal can be an adjective meaning "main; most important." It can also be a noun meaning "chief officer of a school." *Principle* is a noun meaning "moral rule" or "fundamental truth."

His strange behavior was the **principal** reason for our concern.

Democratic **principles** form the basis of our country's laws.

raise, rise

Raise is a transitive verb that usually takes a direct object. *Rise* is intransitive and never takes a direct object.

Iliana and Josef **raise** the flag every morning.

They **rise** from their seats and volunteer immediately whenever help is needed.

than, then

The conjunction *than* is used to connect the two parts of a comparison. The adverb *then* usually refers to time.

My backpack is heavier **than** hers.

I will finish my homework and **then** meet my friends at the park.

that, which, who

Use the relative pronoun *that* to refer to things or people. Use *which* only for things and *who* only for people.

That introduces a restrictive phrase or clause, that is, one that is essential to the meaning of the sentence. *Which* introduces a nonrestrictive phrase or clause—one that adds information but could be deleted from the sentence—and is preceded by a comma.

Ben ran to the park **that** just reopened.

The park, **which** just reopened, has many attractions.

The man **who** built the park loves to see people smiling.

when, where, why

Do not use *when, where,* or *why* directly after a linking verb, such as *is*. Reword the sentence.

Incorrect: The morning is when he left for the beach.

Correct: He left for the beach in the morning.

who, whom

In formal writing, use *who* only as a subject in clauses and sentences. Use *whom* only as the object of a verb or of a preposition.

Who paid for the tickets?

Whom should I pay for the tickets?

I can't recall to **whom** I gave the money for the tickets.

your, you're

Your is a possessive pronoun expressing ownership. *You're* is the contraction of "you are."

Have you finished writing **your** informative essay?

You're supposed to turn it in tomorrow. If **you're** late, **your** grade will be affected.

Capitalization

First Words

Capitalize the first word of a sentence.

Stories about knights and their deeds interest me.

Capitalize the first word of direct speech.

Sharon asked, "**D**o you like stories about knights?"

Capitalize the first word of a quotation that is a complete sentence.

Einstein said, "**A**nyone who has never made a mistake has never tried anything new."

Proper Nouns and Proper Adjectives

Capitalize all proper nouns, including geographical names, historical events and periods, and names of organizations.

Thames **R**iver　**J**ohn **K**eats　the **R**enaissance
United **N**ations　**W**orld **W**ar II　**S**ierra **N**evada

Capitalize all proper adjectives.

Shakespearean play　**B**ritish invaision
American citizen　**L**atin **A**merican literature

Academic Course Names

Capitalize course names only if they are language courses, are followed by a number, or are preceded by a proper noun or adjective.

Spanish　**H**onors **C**hemistry　**H**istory 101
geology　**al**gebra　**s**ocial **s**tudies

Titles

Capitalize personal titles when followed by the person's name.

Ms. Hughes　**D**r. Perez　**K**ing George

Capitalize titles showing family relationships when they are followed by a specific person's name, unless they are preceded by a possessive noun or pronoun.

Uncle Oscar　Mangan's **s**ister　his **a**unt Tessa

Capitalize the first word and all other key words in the titles of books, stories, songs, and other works of art.

Frankenstein　"**S**hooting an **E**lephant"

Punctuation

End Marks

Use a **period** to end a declarative sentence or an imperative sentence.

We are studying the structure of sonnets.

Read the biography of Mary Shelley.

Use periods with initials and abbreviations.

D. H. Lawrence　Mrs. Browning
Mt. Everest　Maple St.

Use a **question mark** to end an interrogative sentence.

What is Macbeth's fatal flaw?

Use an **exclamation mark** after an exclamatory sentence or a forceful imperative sentence.

That's a beautiful painting!　Let me go now!

Commas

Use a **comma** before a coordinating conjunction to separate two independent clauses in a compound sentence.

The game was very close, but we were victorious.

Use commas to separate three or more words, phrases, or clauses in a series.

William Blake was a writer, artist, and printer.

Use commas to separate coordinate adjectives.

It was a witty, amusing novel.

Use a comma after an introductory word, phrase, or clause.

When the novelist finished his book, he celebrated with his family.

Use commas to set off nonessential expressions.

Old English, of course, requires translation.

Use commas with places and dates.

Coventry, England　September 1, 1939

Semicolons

Use a **semicolon** to join closely related independent clauses that are not already joined by a conjunction.

Tanya likes to write poetry; Heather prefers prose.

Use semicolons to avoid confusion when items in a series contain commas.

They traveled to London, England; Madrid, Spain; and Rome, Italy.

Colons

Use a **colon** before a list of items following an independent clause.

Notable Victorian poets include the following: Tennyson, Arnold, Housman, and Hopkins.

Use a colon to introduce information that summarizes or explains the independent clause before it.

She just wanted to do one thing: rest.

Malcolm loves volunteering: He reads to sick children every Saturday afternoon.

Quotation Marks

Use **quotation marks** to enclose a direct quotation.

"Short stories," Ms. Hildebrand said, "should have rich, well-developed characters."

An **indirect quotation** does not require quotation marks.

Ms. Hildebrand said that short stories should have well-developed characters.

Use quotation marks around the titles of short written works, episodes in a series, songs, and works mentioned as parts of collections.

"The Lagoon"　"Boswell Meets Johnson"

Italics

Italicize the titles of long written works, movies, television and radio shows, lengthy works of music, paintings, and sculptures.

Howards End *60 Minutes* *Guernica*

For handwritten material, you can use underlining instead of italics.

The Princess Bride Mona Lisa

Dashes

Use **dashes** to indicate an abrupt change of thought, a dramatic interrupting idea, or a summary statement.

I read the entire first act of *Macbeth*—you won't believe what happens next.

The director—what's her name again?—attended the movie premiere.

Hyphens

Use a **hyphen** with certain numbers, after certain prefixes, with two or more words used as one word, and with a compound modifier that comes before a noun.

seventy-two
self-esteem
president-elect
five-year contract

Parentheses

Use **parentheses** to set off asides and explanations when the material is not essential or when it consists of one or more sentences. When the sentence in parentheses interrupts the larger sentence, it does not have a capital letter or a period.

He listened intently (it was too dark to see who was speaking) to try to identify the voices.

When a sentence in parentheses falls between two other complete sentences, it should start with a capital letter and end with a period.

The quarterback threw three touchdown passes. (We knew he could do it.) Our team won the game by two points.

Apostrophes

Add an **apostrophe** and an *s* to show the possessive case of most singular nouns and of plural nouns that do not end in *-s* or *-es*.

Blake's poems the mice's whiskers

Names ending in *s* form their possessives in the same way, except for classical and biblical names, which add only an apostrophe to form the possessive.

Dickens's Hercules'

Add an apostrophe to show the possessive case of plural nouns ending in *-s* and *-es*.

the girls' songs the Ortizes' car

Use an apostrophe in a contraction to indicate the position of the missing letter or letters.

She's never read a Coleridge poem she didn't like.

Brackets

Use **brackets** to enclose clarifying information inserted within a quotation.

Columbus's journal entry from October 21, 1492, begins as follows: "At 10 o'clock, we arrived at a cape of the island [San Salvador], and anchored, the other vessels in company."

Ellipses

Use three ellipsis points, also known as an **ellipsis,** to indicate where you have omitted words from quoted material.

Wollestonecraft wrote, "The education of women has of late been more attended to than formerly; yet they are still . . . ridiculed or pitied. . . ."

In the example above, the four dots at the end of the sentence are the three ellipsis points plus the period from the original sentence.

Use an ellipsis to indicate a pause or interruption in speech.

"When he told me the news," said the coach, "I was . . . I was shocked . . . completely shocked."

Spelling

Spelling Rules

Learning the rules of English spelling will help you make **generalizations** about how to spell words.

Word Parts

The three word parts that can combine to form a word are roots, prefixes, and suffixes. Many of these word parts come from the Greek, Latin, and Anglo-Saxon languages.

The **root word** carries a word's basic meaning.

Root and Origin	Meaning	Examples
-leg- (-log-) [Gr.]	to say, speak	*legal, logic*
-pon- (-pos-) [L.]	to put, place	*postpone, deposit*

A **prefix** is one or more syllables added to the beginning of a word that alter the meaning of the root.

Prefix and Origin	Meaning	Example
anti- [Gr.]	against	*antipathy*
inter- [L.]	between	*international*
mis- [A.S.]	wrong	*misplace*

A **suffix** is a letter or group of letters added to the end of a root word that changes the word's meaning or part of speech.

Suffix and Origin	Meaning and Example	Part of Speech
-ful [A.S.]	full of: *scornful*	adjective
-ity [L.]	state of being: *adversity*	noun
-ize (-ise) [Gr.]	to make: *idolize*	verb
-ly [A.S.]	in a manner: *calmly*	adverb

Rules for Adding Suffixes to Root Words

When adding a suffix to a root word ending in *y* preceded by a consonant, change *y* to *i* unless the suffix begins with *i*.

ply + -able = pliable happy + -ness = happiness
defy + -ing = defying cry + -ing = crying

For a root word ending in *e*, drop the *e* when adding a suffix beginning with a vowel.

drive + -ing = driving move + -able = movable
SOME EXCEPTIONS: traceable, seeing, dyeing

For root words ending with a consonant + vowel + consonant in a stressed syllable, double the final consonant when adding a suffix that begins with a vowel.

mud + -y = muddy submit + -ed = submitted
SOME EXCEPTIONS: mixing, fixed

Rules for Adding Prefixes to Root Words

When a prefix is added to a root word, the spelling of the root remains the same.

un- + certain = uncertain mis- + spell = misspell

With some prefixes, the spelling of the prefix changes when joined to the root to make the pronunciation easier.

in- + mortal = immortal ad- + vert = avert

Orthographic Patterns

Certain letter combinations in English make certain sounds. For instance, *ph* sounds like *f*, *eigh* usually makes a long *a* sound, and the *k* before an *n* is often silent.

pharmacy **neigh**bor **k**nowledge

Understanding **orthographic patterns** such as these can help you improve your spelling.

Forming Plurals

The plural form of most nouns is formed by adding *-s* to the singular.

computers gadgets Washingtons

For words ending in *s, ss, x, z, sh,* or *ch,* add *-es.*

circus**es** tax**es** wish**es** bench**es**

For words ending in *y* or *o* preceded by a vowel, add *-s.*

key**s** patio**s**

For words ending in *y* preceded by a consonant, change the *y* to an *i* and add *-es.*

cit**ies** enem**ies** troph**ies**

For most words ending in *o* preceded by a consonant, add *-es.*

echo**es** tomato**es**

Some words form the plural in irregular ways.

women oxen children teeth deer

Foreign Words Used in English

Some words used in English are actually foreign words that have been adopted. Learning to spell these words requires memorization. When in doubt, check a dictionary.

sushi enchilada au pair fiancé
laissez faire croissant

INDEX OF SKILLS

INDEX OF SKILLS

Boldface numbers indicate pages where terms are defined.

Analyzing Text

Assessment

Language Conventions

Research

Speaking and Listening

Vocabulary

INDEX OF SKILLS

Writing

INDEX OF AUTHORS AND TITLES

The following authors and titles appear in the print and online versions of *my*Perspectives.

T

V

W

ADDITIONAL SELECTIONS: AUTHOR AND TITLE INDEX

The following authors and titles appear in the Online Literature Library.

ACKNOWLEDGMENTS AND CREDITS

Acknowledgments

The following selections appear in this grade level (Grade 9) of *my*Perspectives. Some selections appear online only.

ABC News - Permissions Dept. "Amazing Stories of Rescues and Survival in Nepal" ©ABC News; "Misty Copeland's Hard-Fought Journey to Ballet Stardom" ©ABC News; "Doomsday Plane Ready for Nuclear Attack" ©ABC News.

Abner Stein. "Rules of the Game" by Amy Tan, from *The Joy Luck Club.* Used with permission of Abner Stein.

Alfred A. Knopf. "The Seventh Man" by Haruki Murakami, translated by Jay Rubin; from *Blind Willow Sleeping Woman* by Haruki Murakami and translated by Philip Gabriel and Jay Rubin, copyright © 2006 by Haruki Murakami. Used by permission of Alfred A. Knopf, an imprint of the Knopf Doubleday Publishing Group, a division of Penguin Random House LLC. All rights reserved. Any third party use of this material, outside of this publication, is prohibited. Interested parties must apply directly to Penguin Random House LLC for permission; "The Voyage of the James Caird" from *The Endurance: Shackleton's Legendary Antarctic Expedition* by Caroline Alexander, copyright © 1998 by Caroline Alexander. Used by permission of Alfred A. Knopf, an imprint of the Knopf Doubleday Publishing Group, a division of Penguin Random House LLC. All rights reserved. Any third party use of this material, outside of this publication, is prohibited. Interested parties must apply directly to Penguin Random House LLC for permission.

Apostrophe S Productions, Inc. "The Hero's Adventure" from *The Power of Myth* by Joseph Campbell. Used with permission of Apostrophe S Productions.

Arte Publico Press. "Legal Alien" is reprinted with permission from the publisher of *Chants* by Pat Mora ©1994 Arte Publico Press - University of Houston).

BBC Worldwide Americas, Inc. "Grace Abbott and the Fight for Immigrant Rights in America" ©BBC Worldwide Learning; "Civil Rights Movement and the MLK Assassination" ©BBC Worldwide Learning; "Fannie Lou Hamer" ©BBC Worldwide Learning; "A Modern Take on Romeo and Juliet" ©BBC Worldwide Learning.

BOA Editions, Ltd. Lucille Clifton, excerpt from "mulberry fields" from *The Collected Poems of LucilleClifton*. Copyright © 2004 by Lucille Clifton. Reprinted with the permission of The Permissions Company, Inc. on behalf of BOA Editions Ltd.; Lucille Clifton, "the beginning of the end of the world" from *The Collected Poems of Lucille Clifton*. Copyright ©1991 by Lucille Clifton. Reprinted with the permission of The Permissions Company, Inc. on behalf of BOA Editions Ltd.

Brandt & Hochman Literary Agents Inc. "The Most Dangerous Game" by Richard Connell. Copyright ©1924 by Richard Connell. Copyright renewed © 1952 by Louise Fox Connell. Used by permission of Brandt & Hochman Literary Agents, Inc. Any copying or distribution of this text is expressly forbidden. All rights reserved.; "By the Waters of Babylon" by Stephen Vincent Benet. Copyright ©1937 by Stephen Vincent Benet Copyright renewed ©1965 by Thomas C. Benet, Stephanie Mahin and Rachel B. Lewis. Used by permission of Brandt & Hochman Literary Agents, Inc. Any copying or distribution of this text is expressly forbidden. All rights reserved.

Candlewick Press. *The Odyssey.* Copyright © 2010 by Gareth Hinds. Reproduced by permission of the publisher, Candlewick Press, Somerville, MA.

Canongate Books Limited. *From The Life of Pi.* Used with permission of Canongate Books Ltd.; Used with permission of Canongate Books Ltd.

Carnegie Mellon University Press. Gregory Djanikian, "Immigrant Picnic" from *So I Will Till the Ground.* Originally published in Poetry (July 1999). Copyright ©1999, 2007 by Gregory Djanikian. Reprinted with the permission of The Permissions Company, Inc., on behalf of Carnegie Mellon University Press.

CBS News. "A Visit to the Doomsday Vault," CBS, 60 Minutes. Used with permission of CBS News.

CBS Rights & Permissions. "A Visit to the Doomsday Vault," CBS, 60 Minutes, Copyright ©2008.

Center for Disease Control. "Preparedness 101: Zombie Apocalypse" by Ali S. Khan (CDC, 2011).

Cesar Chavez Foundation. "Lessons of Dr. Martin Luther King, Jr." TM/©2015 The Cesar Chavez Foundation.

CNN ImageSource. CNN newscast of "Tragic Romeo and Juliet Offers Bosnia Hope" ©CNN.

Copyright Clearance Center. "Ithaka" republished with permission of Princeton University Press, from *Collected Poems* by C.P. Cavafy, translated by Keeyley & Sherrard, 1992; permission conveyed through Copyright Clearance Center, Inc.

Define American. "Define American." Hiep Le, Culver City, CA ©Define American.

Don Congdon Associates. "There Will Come Soft Rains." Reprinted by permission of Don Congdon Associates, Inc. Copyright ©1950 by the Crowell Collier Publishing Company, renewed 1977 by Ray Bradbury.

Dunbar, Paul Laurence. "We Wear the Mask" by Paul Laurence Dunbar.

Dungy, Camille. "The Writing on the Wall." First published on Harriet, the blog for the Poetry Foundation. Reprinted with permission of the author.

Farrar, Straus and Giroux. "Traveling" from *Just as I Thought* by Grace Paley. Copyright ©1998 by Grace Paley. Reprinted by permission Farrar, Straus and Giroux, LLC. CAUTION: Users are warned that this work is protected under copyright laws and downloading is strictly prohibited. The right to reproduce or transfer the work via any medium must be secured with Farrar, Straus and Giroux, LLC.; Excerpts from *The Odyssey* by Homer, translated by Robert Fitzgerald. Copyright ©1961, 1963 by Robert Fitzgerald. Copyright renewed 1989 by Benedict R.C. Fitzgerald, on behalf of the Fitzgerald children. Reprinted by permission of Farrar, Straus and Giroux, LLC. CAUTION: Users are warned that this work is protected under copyright laws and downloading is strictly prohibited. The right to reproduce or transfer the work via any medium must be secured with Farrar, Straus and Giroux, LLC.

Farrell, Joanna. "Popocatepetl and Ixtlaccihuatl" by permission of Mrs. J.S.E. Farrell.

Fitzgerald, Benedict. From *The Odyssey* translated by Robert Fitzgerald. Reprinted with permission of Benedict R.C. Fitzgerald.

Frost, Robert. "Fire and Ice" by Robert Frost (1920).

Hanging Loose Press. "The Powwow at the End of the World." Reprinted from *The Summer of Black Widows* ©1996 by Sherman Alexie, by permission of Hanging Loose Press.

HarperCollins Publishers. Chapter 5: "The Immigrant Contribution" [pp. 32–5: 1500 words] from *A Nation of Immigrants* by John F. Kennedy. Copyright ©1964, 2008 by Anti-Defamation League of B'nai B'rith. Reprinted by permission of HarperCollins Publishers; "A Song on the End of the World" from *New and Collected Poems: 1931–2001* by Czeslaw Milosz. Copyright ©1988, 1991, 1995, 2001 by Czeslaw Milosz Royalties, Inc. Reprinted by permission of HarperCollins Publishers.

HarperCollins Publishers Ltd. From *Unbroken.* Reprinted by permission of HarperCollins Publishers Ltd. ©Laura Hillenbrand.

Hill Nadell Literary Agency. "With a Little Help From My Friends." Copyright ©2003 Firouzeh Dumas. Used by permission of the author.

Hinds, Gareth. *The Odyssey.* Copyright ©2010 by Gareth Hinds. Reproduced by permission of the publisher, Candlewick Press, Somerville, MA.

Holy Cow! Press. Roberta Hill Whiteman "Morning Talk" from *Philadelphia Flowers.* Copyright ©1996 by Roberta Hill Whiteman. Reprinted with the permission of The Permissions Company, Inc., on behalf of Holy Cow! Press, www.holycowpress.org.

Houghton Mifflin Harcourt Publishing Co. Excerpts from *Life of Pi:* A Novel by Yann Martel. Copyright ©2001 by Yann Martel. Reprinted by permission of Houghton Mifflin Publishing Company. All rights reserved; "The Writer" from *The Mind-Reader* by Richard WIlbur. Copyright ©1971, and renewed 1999 by Richard Wilbur. Reprinted by permission of Houghton Mifflin Harcourt Publishing Company. All rights reserved; "Incident" from *Native Guard: Poems* by Natasha Trethewey. Copyright ©2006 by Natasha Trethewey. Reprinted by permission of Houghton Mifflin Company. All rights reserved; "Courage" from *The Awful Rowing Toward God* by Anne Sexton. Copyright ©1975 by Loring Conant, Jr., Executor of the Estate of Anne Sexton. Reprinted by permission of Houghton Mifflin Harcourt Publishing Company. All rights reserved.

ICM. "A Quilt of a Country" ©[2001] by Anna Quindlen. Used by Permission. All rights reserved; "The Seventh Man" ©2006 by Haruki Murakami. Used by Permission. All rights reserved.

Knopf Doubleday Publishing Group (Alfred A. Knopf). "The Hero's Adventure." Excerpt(s) from *The Power of Myth* by Joseph Campbell, copyright ©1988 by Apostrophe S Productions, Inc., and Bill Moyers and Alfred Van der Marck Editions, Inc., for itself and the estate of Joseph Campbell. Used by permission of Doubleday, an imprint of the Knopf Doubleday Publishing Group, a division of Penguin Random House LLC. All rights reserved. Any third party use of this material, outside of this publication, is prohibited. Interested parties must apply directly to Penguin Random House LLC for permission.

LA Theatre Works. LA Theatre Works' *Romeo and Juliet* by William Shakespeare ©LA Theatre Works.

Little, Brown and Co. (New York). "Pyramus and Thisbe" from *Mythology* by Edith Hamilton. Copyright 1940, 1942 by Edith Hamilton, renewed ©1969 by Doris Fielding Reid, Executrix of the will of Edith Hamilton. Reprinted with the permission of Little, Brown and Company. All rights reserved.

London, Jack. London, Jack. "To Build a Fire."

MacNeil/Lehrer Productions. "Remembering Civil Rights History: When Words Meant Everything" ©2014 NewsHour Productions LLC.

Mekko Productions. "Perhaps the World Ends Here," from *The Woman Who Fell From the Sky* by Joy Harjo. Copyright ©1994 by Joe Harjo. Used by permission of W.W. Norton & Company, Inc. and by the author.

Moorland-Spingarn Research Centers. "Your World" by Georgia Douglas Johnson. Used with permission of Moorland-Spingam Research Center, Howard University.

National Archives. Robert F. Kennedy's remarks on the assassination of Martin Luther ©National Archives.

National Geographic Society. "The Nuclear Tourist," *National Geographic,* October 2014. ©Johnson, George L./National Geographic Creative.

National Park Service. "Survival Is Your Own Responsibility: Thoughts from a Retired Mountaineering Ranger" by Daryl R. Miller.

New Directions Publishing Corp. "I Am Offering This Poem" by Jimmy Santiago Baca, from *Immigrants in Our Own Land,* Copyright ©1979 by Jimmy Santiago Baca. Reprinted by permission of New Directions Publishing Corp.

New York Public Radio. Podcast of "War of the Worlds" from Radiolab ©New York Public Radio.

New York Times. "The Moral Logic of Survival Guilt" from *The New York Times,* July 16, 2008 ©2008 The New York Times. All rights reserved. Used by permission and protected by the Copyright Laws of the United States. The printing, copying, redistribution, or retransmission of this Content without express written permission is prohibited.

NPR. "The Secret Bunker Congress Never Used" ©2011 National Public Radio, Inc. News report titled "The Secret Bunker Congress Never Used" by NPR Staff was originally published on NPR.org on March 26, 2011, and is used with the permission of NPR. Any unauthorized duplication is strictly prohibited.

NPR (National Public Radio). "The Key To Disaster Survival? Friends And Neighbors" ©2011 National Public Radio, Inc. News report titled "The Key To Disaster Survival? Friends And Neighbors" was originally broadcast on NPR's All Things Considered on July 4, 2011, and is used with the permission of NPR. Any unauthorized duplication is strictly prohibited.

Outside Magazine. "The Value of a Sherpa Life" by Grayson Schaffer, from *Outside,* April 18, 2014. Used with permission of Outside Magazine.

PARS International Corporation. "In New York with Six Weeks to Adapt to America" from *New York Times,* August 26, 2012 ©2012 The New York Times. All rights reserved. Used by permission and protected by the Copyright Laws of the United States. The printing, copying, redistribution, or retransmission of this Content without express written permission is prohibited."; "How the Children of Birmingham Changed the Civil-Rights Movement" from *The Daily Beast,* May 2, 2013 ©2013 The Daily Beast Company LLC. All rights reserved. Used by permission and protected by the Copyright Laws of the United States. The printing, copying, redistribution, or retransmission of this Content without express written permission is prohibited; "The Myth of the *War of the Worlds* Panic" from *Slate*, October 28, 2013 ©2013 The Slate Group. All rights reserved. Used by permission and protected by the Copyright Laws of the United States. The printing, copying, redistribution, or retransmission of this Content without express written permission is prohibited; "Romeo and Juliet is a Terrible Play, and David Leveaux Can't Change That" from *Slate*, April 2, 2013 ©2013 The Slate Group. All rights reserved.

Used by permission and protected by the Copyright Laws of the United States. The printing, copying, redistribution, or retransmission of this Content without express written permission is prohibited; "13 Epic Animal Migrations That Prove Just How Cool Mother Nature Is" from *The Huffington Post*, April 2, 2014 ©2014 AOL Inc. All rights reserved. Used by permission and protected by the Copyright Laws of the United States. The printing, copying, redistribution, or retransmission of this Content without express written permission is prohibited.

Penguin Books, Ltd. (UK). "A Song on the End of the World" taken from *New and Collected Poems: 1931–2001* by Czeslaw Milosz (Penguin Classics 2005) Copyright ©Czeslaw Milosz Royalties Inc., 1988, 1991, 1995, 2001. Reproduced by permission of Penguin Books Ltd.

Penguin Publishing Group. "Rules of the Game," from *The Joy Luck Club* by Amy Tan, copyright ©1989 by Amy Tan. Used by permission of G. P. Putnam's Sons, an imprint of Penguin Publishing Group, a division of Penguin Random House LLC.

Penguin Random House Canada Limited (McClelland & Stewart). From *Life of Pi* excerpted from *Life of Pi: A Novel* by Yann Martel. Copyright (C)2001 by Yann Martel. Reprinted by permission of Alfred A. Knopf Canada, a division of Penguin Random House Canada Limited.

Perseus Books Group (direct). From *When I Was Puerto Rican* by Esmeralda Santiago, copyright ©1993. Reprinted by permission of Da Capo Press, a member of The Perseus Books Group.

Postmedia Network, Inc. "If Romeo and Juliet Had Cell Phones" by Misty Harris, from Canada.com, January 30, 2013. Material reprinted with the express permission of: Postmedia News, a division of Postmedia Network Inc.

Random House Group Ltd., Permissions Department. "Ithaka" from *Collected Poems* by C. P. Cavafy (translated by Edmund Keeley and Philip Sherrard). Published by The Hogarth Press. Reprinted by permission of The Random House Group Limited.

Random House, Inc. "With a Little Help from My Friends" from *Funny in Farsi: A Memoir of Growing Up Iranian in America* by Firoozeh Dumas, copyright ©2003 by Firoozeh Dumas. Used by permission of Villard Books, an imprint of Random House, a division of Penguin Random House LLC. All rights reserved. Any third party use of this material, outside of this publication, is prohibited. Interested parties must apply directly to Penguin Random House LLC for permission; "Chapter Fifteen: Sharks and Bullets," and "Chapter Sixteen: Singing in the Clouds" from *Unbroken: A World War II Story of Survival, Resilience, and Redemption* by Laura Hillenbrand, copyright ©2010 by Laura Hillenbrand. Used by permission of Random House, an imprint and division of Penguin Random House LLC. All rights reserved. Any third party use of this material, outside of this publication, is prohibited. Interested parties must apply directly to Penguin Random House LLC for permission; Excerpt(s) from *Wild: From Lost to Found on the Pacific Crest Trail* by Cheryl Strayed, copyright ©2012 by Cheryl Strayed. Used by permission of Alfred A. Knopf, an imprint of the Knopf Doubleday Publishing Group, a division of Penguin Random House LLC. All rights reserved. Any third party use of this material, outside of this publication, is prohibited. Interested parties must apply directly to Penguin Random House LLC for permission.

RFE/RL. "Twenty Years On—The Unfinished Lives of Bosnia's Romeo and Juliet" Copyright ©2015. RFE/RL, Inc. Reprinted with the permission of Radio Free Europe/Radio Liberty, 1201 Connecticut Ave NW, Ste 400, Washington DC 20036.

Rogers, Coleridge and White Ltd. "Ithaka" from *Collected Poems* by C. P. Cavafy. Published by Princeton University Press, 1990. Copyright ©C. P. Cavafy. Reproduced by permission of the Estate of C. P. Cavafy c/o Rogers, Coleridge & White., 20 Powis Mews, London W11 1JN.

Sheil Land Associates Ltd. "The Voyage of the James Caird." Extract from *Endurance* by F. A. Worsley. ©The Estate of F. A. Worsle, 1931. Reproduced by permission of Sheil Land Associates Ltd.

Shihab Nye, Naomi. "Hugging the Jukebox" by permission of the author, Naomi Shihab Nye, 2015.

Smithsonian Enterprises. "The End of the World May Look Like This" by Megan Gambino, from *Smithsonian*, July 18, 2013. Copyright 2013 Smithsonian Institution. Reprinted with permission from Smithsonian Enterprises. All rights reserved. Reproduction in any medium is strictly prohibited without permission from Smithsonian Institution.

Stanford University Press. "Narrow Road of the Interior" by Matsuo Basho. From *Classical Japanese Prose: An Anthology*, compiled and edited by Helen Craig McCullough. Copyright ©1990 by the Board of Trustees of the Leland Stanford Jr., University. All rights reserved. With the permission of Stanford University Press.

Sterling Lord Literistic, Inc. "Courage" from *The Awful Rowing Toward God* by Anne Sexton. Copyright ©1975 by Loring Conant, Jr., Executor of the Estate of Anne Sexton. Reprinted by permission of SLL/Sterling Lord Literistic, Inc.

Time Magazine. "Titanic vs. Lusitania: How People Behave in a Disaster" ©2010 Time Inc. All rights reserved. Reprinted/Translated from TIME and published with permission of Time Inc. Reproduction in any manner in any language in whole or in part without written permission is prohibited. TIME and the TIME logo are registered trademarks of Time Inc. used under license.

Tribune Content Agency, LLC. "In Defense of Romeo and Juliet" ©2013 The Atlantic Media Co., as first published in *The Atlantic Magazine*. All rights reserved. Distributed by Tribune Content Agency, LLC.

Tsai, Diane. "Finding a Voice: A Taiwanese Family Adapts to America" from Immigrant Connect. Used with permission of Diane Tsai.

Union Literary. "Traveling" from *Just As I Thought* by Grace Paley. Used with permission of Union Literary.

United States Department of Homeland Security. Application for a Mariner's License (U.S. Department of Homeland Security).

University of Alabama Press. Excerpt, pp 95–106, from *Selma, Lord, Selma: Girlhood Memories of the Civil-Rights Days* by Sheyann Webb and Rachel West Nelson, as told to Frank Sikora. ©1980, The University of Alabama Press. Reprinted with permission.

University of Georgia Press. "American History" from *The Latin Deli* by Judith Ortiz Cofer. Copyright ©1992 by Judith Ortiz Cofer. Reprinted by permission of University of Georgia Press; "For My People" by Margaret Walker from *This is My Century: New and Collected Poems.* Copyright ©1989. Used with permission of University of Georgia Press.

University of Washington Press. "The Writing on the Wall." Lai, Him Mark, Genny Lim, and Judy Yung, eds. *Island: Poetry and History of Chinese Immigrants on Angel Island, 1910–1940* ©1991. Reprinted with permission of the University of Washington Press.

W. W. Norton & Co. "The Voyage of the James Caird" from *Endurance: An Epic of Polar Adventure* by F. A. Worsley. Copyright ©1931 by the Estate of F. A. Worsley. Used by permission of W.W. Norton & Company, Inc.; "Perhaps the World Ends Here," from *The Woman Who Fell From the Sky* by Joy Harjo. Copyright ©1994 by Joe Harjo. Used by permission of W.W. Norton & Company, Inc.

Watkins/Loomis Agency. "The Return" from *Secret Lives* by Ngugi wa Thiong'o. Reprinted by Permission of Ngugi wa' Thiong'o and the Watkins Loomis Agency.

Westwood Creative Artists. From *Life of Pi* by Yann Martel (Harcourt, 2001). Copyright ©2001 Yann Martel. With permission of the author.

Writers House LLC. "I Have a Dream" / "Letter From a Birmingham City Jail"—Reprinted by arrangement with The Heirs to the Estate of Martin Luther King Jr., c/o Writers House as agent for the proprietor New York, NY; Reprinted by arrangement with the Heirs to the Estate of Martin Luther King Jr., c/o Writers House as agent for the proprietor New York, NY. Copyright ©1963 Dr. Martin Luther King, Jr. Copyright renewed 1991 Coretta Scott King; Reprinted by arrangement with The Heirs to the Estate of Martin Luther King Jr., c/o Writers House as agent for the proprietor New York, NY. Copyright ©1963 Dr. Martin Luther King, Jr. Copyright renewed 1991 Coretta Scott King.

WUNC. "Franklin McCain Dies—Helped Start Sit-In Movement At Greensboro Lunch Counter" ©National Public Radio, Inc.

Wylie Agency. "A Song on the End of the World" by Czeslaw Milosz, collected in *New and Collected Poems: 1931–2001*. Copyright ©1988, 1991, 1995, 2001 by Czeslaw Milosz Royalties, Inc., used by permission of The Wylie Agency LLC.

Yale University Press. "The Many Lives of Hazel Bryan" from *Elizabeth & Hazel: Two Women of Little Rock* by David Margolick. Copyright ©2011. Used with permission of the publisher, Yale University Press.

YGS Group. "Seven Steps to Surviving a Disaster" used with permission of Bloomberg L.P. Copyright ©2015. All rights reserved.

Zachary Shuster Harmsworth Literary Agency. From *Wild* by Cheryl Strayed; copyright ©2012 by Cheryl Strayed. Used by permission of Zachary Shuster Harmsworth Literary Agency.

Credits

Photo locators denoted as follows: Top (T), Center (C), Bottom (B), Left (L), Right (R), Background (Bkgd)

vi P_Wei/Getty Images; **viii** All Canada Photos/Alamy: **x** William James Warren/Getty Images; **xii** Archivart/Alamy; **xiv** Soft_light/Shutterstock; **2** P_Wei/Getty Images; **3** (BC) Gary Carter/Corbis, (BL) Roni Ben Ishay/ Shutterstock, (B) Don Mason/Blend Images/Corbis, (CL) Everett Historical/ Shutterstock, (CT) Brant Ward/San Francisco Chronicle/Corbis, (T) Juanmonino/Getty Images, (C) Zerophoto/Fotolia, (TL) Blvdone/ Shutterstock; 6 Juanmonino/Getty Images; **11**(B) Roni Ben Ishay/ Shutterstock, (C) Everett Historical/Shutterstock, (T) Blvdone/ Shutterstock; **12** (CL) Dpa picture alliance/Alamy, (TL) Blvdone/ Shutterstock, (TR) Everett Historical/Shutterstock; **13, 18, 20** Blvdone/ Shutterstock; **22** (CL) National Archives/Handout/Hulton Archive/Getty Images, (TL) Blvdone/Shutterstock, (TR) Everett Historical/Shutterstock; **23** Everett Historical/Shutterstock; **25** Everett Historical/Shutterstock; **30, 32, 34** Everett Historical/Shutterstock; **36** Photo by Tanya Cofer; 37 Roni Ben Ishay/Shutterstock; **41** Peopleimages/Getty Images; **46, 48, 50** Roni Ben Ishay/Shutterstock; **59** (B) Gary Carter/Corbis, (CB) Don Mason/ Blend Images/Corbis, (CT) Brant Ward/San Francisco Chronicle/Corbis, (T) Zerophoto/Fotolia; **62** J.J. GUILLEN/EPA/Newscom; **63** Zerophoto/Fotolia; **69** Peter Dazeley/Getty Images; **74** Zerophoto/Fotolia; **76** Zerophoto/ Fotolia; **78** Frazer Harrison/Getty Images; **79** Brant Ward/San Francisco Chronicle/Corbis; **81** Camille Dungy; **82** Kurt Rogers/San Francisco Chronicle/Corbis; **84, 86** Brant Ward/San Francisco Chronicle/Corbis; **88** Lynn Goldsmith/Corbis; **89, 96** Don Mason/Blend Images/Corbis; **98** Gary Carter/Corbis; **99** (C) Alysa Bennett, (T) Chris Felver/Getty Images; **100** Gary Carter/Corbis; **102** Lauri Patterson/Getty Images;**122** All Canada Photos/Alamy, (BCL) Wonderlust/Photonica/Getty Images, (C) AF archive/ Alamy, (L) Guylain Doyle/AGE fotostock; (BL) FUKUSHIMA MINPO/AFP/ Getty Images, (T) Scazza/Fotolia, (TC) Dmytro Pylypenko/Shutterstock, (TCL) Deposit Photos/Glow Images, (TL) Water Rights/SuperStock; **131** (B) FUKUSHIMA MINPO/AFP/Getty Images, **131** (C) Deposit Photos/Glow Images, (T) Water Rights/SuperStock; **132** Jeremy sutton hibbert/Alamy; **133** Water Rights/SuperStock; **137** Olga Ptashko/Shutterstock; **142** Vetryanaya/o/Shutterstock; **146, 148, 150** Water Rights/SuperStock; **152** Patrick McMullan Co/McMullan/Sipa USA/Newscom; **153, 158, 160, 162** Deposit Photos/Glow Images; **165** FUKUSHIMA MINPO/AFP/Getty Images; **168** Scazza/Fotolia; **175** (B) Wonderlust/Photonica/Getty Images, (BC) Guylain Doyle/AGE footstock, (C) AF archive/Alamy; (T) Dmytro Pylypenko/Shutterstock; **178** (CL) Janette Beckman/Getty Images, (TL) Dmytro Pylypenko/Shutterstock, (TR) Library of Congress Prints and Photographs Division [LC 3a11347u]; **183** Nejron/123RF; **187** Maksimilian/Shutterstock; **191, 194** Dmytro Pylypenko/Shutterstock; **194** (CL) Hulton Deutsch Collection/Corbis, (TR) Library of Congress Prints and Photographs Division [LC 3a11347u]; **195** Library of Congress Prints and Photographs Division [LC 3a11347u]; **196** (B) Library of Congress Prints and Photographs Division [LC 3a12748u], (T) Library of Congress Prints and Photographs Division [LC 3a19377u]; **197** (B) Library of Congress Prints and Photographs Division [LC 3a11986u], (T) Hulton Archive/Getty Images; **198** Library of Congress Prints and Photographs Division [LC 3a12746u]; **199** Library of Congress Prints and Photographs Division [LC 3a11347u]; **200** (B) Library of Congress Prints and Photographs Division [LC 3a11347u], (TL) Dmytro Pylypenko/ Shutterstock; **202** Rachel Torres/Alamy; **207** Alistair Hobbs/Shutterstock; **210** Danté Fenolio/Science Source; **212, 214** AF archive/Alamy; **217** Guylain Doyle/AGE fotostock; **220** Guylain Doyle/AGE fotostock; **222** Guylain Doyle/AGE fotostock; **224** Wonderlust/Photonica/Getty Images; **225** (BL) Handout/KRT/Newscom, (CL) Oscar White/Corbis, (TL) Christopher Felver/Corbis; **226** Wonderlust/Photonica/Getty Images; **228** Yulkapopkova/Vetta/Getty Images; **230** Icetray/123RF; **251**(BC) Jack Delano/PhotoQuest/Getty Images, (B) Bettmann/Corbis; (CL) Everett Collection Inc/Alamy, (CT) Everett Collection Historical/Alamy, (T) Charles Moore/Black Star/Alamy, (TL) Photoshot; **254** Charles Moore/Black Star/ Alamy; **259** (B) National Archives, (C) Everett Collection Inc/Alamy; (T) Photoshot; **260** Stephen F. Somerstein/Getty Images; **260** (TL) Photoshot; **266** Photoshot; **268** Photoshot; **270** Stephen F. Somerstein/Getty Image; **275** Bettmann/Corbis; **280** Bob Adelman/Corbis; **288** Everett Collection Inc/Alamy; **290** Everett Collection Inc/Alamy; **292** Everett Collection Inc/ Alamy; **294** PhotoQuest/Getty Images; **295** National Archives; **297** National Archives; **305** (B) Jack Delano/PhotoQuest/Getty Images, (BC) Bettmann/Corbis, (CT) Everett Collection Historical/Alamy; **308** Andrea Jacobson, The Observatory. MacNeil/Lehrer Productions; **312** Everett Collection Historical/Alamy; **313** (B) Everett Collection Historical/Alamy, (T) Bill O'Leary/The Washington Post/Getty Images; **314** Everett Collection Historical/Alamy; **316** Thall/iStock/Getty Images; **318** Everett Collection Historical/Alamy; **320** Everett Collection Historical/Alamy; **322** ZUMA Press, Inc./Alamy; **323** Bettmann/Corbis; **327** Viramontes, Xavier (1947) ©Copyright Smithsonian American Art Museum, Washington, DC/Art Resource, NY; **327** Xavier Viramontes; **330** Bettmann/Corbis; **332** Bettmann/Corbis; **334** Chris Felver/Getty Images; **335** Jack Delano/ PhotoQuest/Getty Images; **337** AP Images; **340** Jack Delano/PhotoQuest/ Getty Images; **342** Jack Delano/PhotoQuest/Getty Images; **365** Sotheby's/ akg images/Newscom; **374** GL Archive/Alamy; **356** Kichigin/Shutterstock; **357** (BL) Sotheby's/akg images/Newscom, (C) Reuters, (CL) Relativity Media/courtesy Everett Collection, (T) Leo Mason/Leo Mason/Corbis, (TC) Ben Welsh/age fotostock/Alamy, (TL) GL Archive/Alamy; **360** Leo Mason/ Leo Mason/Corbis; **365** (BL) Relativity Media/courtesy Everett Collection, **365** (CBL) Relativity Media/courtesy Everett Collection; **365** (CL) Relativity Media/courtesy Everett Collection, (TR) Georgios Kollidas/Shutterstock, (R) GL Archive/Alamy; **367** The Print Collector/Corbis; **368** Peter Phipp/ Britain On View/Getty Images; **369** Hugo Philpott/Epa/Newscom; **370** GL Archive/Alamy; **375** Sergii Figurnyi/Fotolia; **376** Relativity Media/courtesy Everett Collection; **400** GL Archive/Alamy; **401** Relativity Media/courtesy Everett Collection; **450** GL Archive/Alamy; **457** BHE FILMS/DINO DE LAURENTIIS CINEMATOGRAFICA/VERONA PROD/Ronald Grant Archive/ Mary Evans; **466** GL Archive/Alamy; **479** Cantonatty/Shutterstock; **480** Relativity Media/courtesy Everett Collection; **486** (B) ZU_09/Getty Images, (L) Relativity Media/courtesy Everett Collection, (R) Sotheby''s/ akg images/Newscom; **501**(B) Courtesy CNN, (C) Reuters, (T) Ben Welsh/ age fotostock/Alamy; **504** Ben Welsh/age fotostock/Alamy; **505** Frederick M. Brown/Getty Images; **506** Ben Welsh/age fotostock/Alamy; **508** Ben Welsh/age fotostock/Alamy; **516**(L) Reuters,(R) Courtesy CNN; **517** Reuters; **518** Snvv/Shutterstock; **521** Reuters; **522** Reuters; **524**(B) Nicolas Khayat/KRT/Newscom, (L) Reuters, (R) Courtesy CNN; **528** Courtesy CNN; **529**(B) Courtesy CNN, (T) Reuters; Dinka Jurkovic, Radio Free Europe/Radio Liberty; **542** Soft_light/Shutterstock; **543**(BL) Oleksandr Kalinichenko/Shutterstock, (C) FWStudio/Shutterstock, (BC) A.G.A/Shutterstock, (CL) De Agostini Picture Lib./A. Dagli Orti/akg images, (CTL) Archivart/Alamy, (T)cunaplus/Shutterstock, (TC) Galyna Andrushko/Shutterstock, (TL) Beerkoff/Fotolia; **546** cunaplus/ Shutterstock; **551**(B) Oleksandr Kalinichenko/Shutterstock, (CT) De Agostini Picture Lib./A. Dagli Orti/akg images, (T) Beerkoff/Fotolia Kichigin/Shutterstock; **552** Beerkoff/Fotolia; **554** Roman replica of the Athena Farnese (marble), Phidias (c.500 c.432 BC) Museo Archeologico Nazionale, Naples, Italy/Bridgeman Images; **555** Statue of Zeus at Oympia, English School, (20th century)/Private Collection / © Look and Learn/Bridgeman Images; **556** GeoM/Fotolia; **558** Hulton Archive/ Handout/Getty Images; **559** The Siege of Troy (oil on canvas), French School, (17th century)/Musee des Beaux Arts, Blois, France/Bridgeman Art Images; **559** The Siege of Troy (oil on canvas), French School, (17th century)/Musee des Beaux Arts, Blois, France/Bridgeman Images; **567** Ivy Close Images/Alamy; **560** Archivart/Alamy; **572** Mary Evans Picture Library/Alamy; **580 581** JOHN WILLIAM/akg images; **584** Scylla attacking Olysseus's ship, Payne, Roger (b.1934)/Private Collection/Look and Learn/ Bridgeman Art Images; **584** Scylla attacking Olysseus's ship, Payne, Roger (b.1934)/Private Collection/Look and Learn/Bridgeman Images; **591** Archivart/Alamy; **592** Archivart/Alamy; **594** Hulton Archive/Handout/ Getty Images; **595** De Agostini Picture Lib./A. Dagli Orti/akg images; **602** Penelope and the Suitors, 1900 (oil on canvas), Robertson, Victor John (fl.1892 1903)/Private Collection/Photo © Peter Nahum at The Leicester Galleries, London/Bridgeman Art Images; **609** Odysseus punishes the suitors (colour litho), Robinson, Thomas Heath (1869 1954)/Private Collection/The Stapleton Collection/Bridgeman Art Images; **614** North Wind Picture Archives/Alamy; **618** De Agostini Picture Lib./ A. Dagli Orti/akg images; **620** De Agostini Picture Lib./A. Dagli Orti/akg images; **622** De Agostini Picture Lib./A. Dagli Orti/akg images;

624 (B) Photo by Scott LaPierre, (T) Archivart/Alamy; **632** Archivart/ Alamy; **635** Oleksandr Kalinichenko/Shutterstock; **636** USCG; **639** Oleksandr Kalinichenko/Shutterstock; **647** Galyna Andrushko/ Shutterstock; **650** Colin McPherson/Corbis; **651** Galyna Andrushko/ Shutterstock; **656** Galyna Andrushko/Shutterstock; **658** Galyna Andrushko/Shutterstock; **660**(R) Marc Bryan Brown/Wirelmage/Getty Images, (TL) Matthew Naythons/The LIFE Images Collection/Getty images; **666** FWStudio/Shutterstock; **668** A.G.A/Shutterstock; **661** FWStudio/Shutterstock; **669**(B) Tony Mcnicol/Alamy, (C) P Anastasselis/ REX/Newscom; (T) Everett Collection Historical/Alamy; **670** A.G.A/ Shutterstock; **672** Kovalenko Inna/Fotolia; **674** Shukaylova Zinaida/ Shutterstock; **694** Angela Harburn/fotolia; **695** (BC) Everett Collection/ Shutterstock, (C) World History Archive/Alamy,(TC) B Christopher/Alamy, (T)djgis/Shutterstock, (TCL) Liukov/Shutterstock, (TL) Falcon Eyes/ Shutterstock; **703** Falcon Eyes/Shutterstock; **704** Pirie MacDonald/Corbis; Eyes/Shutterstock; **711** Dezi/Shutterstock; **722** Everett Collection Inc/ Alamy; **743**(B) Everett Collection/Shutterstock, (BC)World History Archive/Alamy, (T) Liukov/Shutterstock, (TR) B Christopher/Alamy; **746** Photo by Kerry Sherck; **747** Liukov/Shutterstock; **751** Iryna Rasko/ Shutterstock; **754** Liukov/Shutterstock; **759**(B) Louis Monier/Gamma Rapho/Getty Images, (T) Mark Lennihan/AP Images; **760** (B) Christopher/ Alamy; **762** Cultura RM/Art Wolfe Stock/Cultura/Getty Images; **764** Inkwelldodo/Fotolia; **770**(B) Sam Simmonds/Polaris/Newscom; (TL) World History Archive/Alamy, (TR) Everett Collection/Shutterstock; **771** World History Archive/Alamy; **773** World History Archive/Alamy; **774**(B) Michael Tran/Contributor/FilmMagic/Getty Images, (TL) World History Archive/ Alamy, (TR) Everett Collection/Shutterstock; **784** World History Archive/ Alamy; Courtesy of University of Maine.

Credits for Images in Interactive Student Edition Only

Unit 1

BBC Worldwide Americas, Inc.; BBC Worldwide Learning; Bettmann/ Corbis; Charles Eshelman/Getty Images; lithian/Shutterstock; Pat Mora

Unit 2

Amos Chapple/Lonely Planet Images/Getty Images; Antonio Busiello/ Moment Open/Getty Images; B.Stefanov/Fotolia; Daryl Miller; Dean Lambert/Alamy; Fotosearch/Getty Images; James A. Parcell/The Washington Post/Getty Images; Oriontrail/iStockphoto/Getty Images; Richard A McMillin/Shutterstock; Saez Pascal/SIPA/Newscom; Saul Loeb/ AFP/Getty Images; Serezniy/123RF; Stephen Frink/Corbis; Ullstein bild/ Getty Images; AS400 DB/Corbis

Unit 3

John G. Moebes/Corbis; Bettmann/Corbis; David Margolick; Hulton Archive/Getty Images; Mark Bennington; Sheyann Webb Christburg; WUNC

Unit 4

DeAgostini/Getty Images; Elizabeth I, Armada Portrait, c.1588 (oil on panel), Gower, George (1540 96) (attr. to)/Woburn Abbey, Bedfordshire, UK/Bridgeman Art Library; Elizabeth I, Armada Portrait, c.1588 (oil on panel), Gower, George (1540 96) (attr. to)/Woburn Abbey, Bedfordshire, UK/Bridgeman Images; Misty Harris;

Unit 5

Courtesy National Park Service; David Nunuk/All Canada Photos/Getty Images; Doug Allan/Oxford Scientific/Getty Images; Epa european pressphoto agency b.v./Alamy; Frans Lanting/Mint Images/Getty Images; James R.D. Scott/Moment/Getty Images; Owen Newman/Oxford Scientific/Getty Images; Paul Popper/Popperfoto/Getty Images; Perrine Doug/Perspectives/Getty Images; readyimage/Shutterstock; Richard Ellis/ Getty Images; Rodney Ungwiluk, Jr./Getty Images; Schomburg Center, NYPL/Art Resource, NY; Sue Flood/Photodisc/Getty Images; Wayne Lynch/ All Canada Photos/Getty Images

Unit 6

Solarseven/Shutterstock; Chris Felver/Archive Photos/Getty Images; Dennis Van Tine/ABACAUSA.COM/Newscom; Eric Francis/Getty Images; Eric Schaal/The LIFE Picture Collection/Getty Images; Ron Miller; S_Photo/ Shutterstock; Smithsonian Magazine